W9-BCF-544

WITHDRAWN

Salem Academy and College
FRIENDS of the LIBRARY

Gift of

The Friends of
the Library

Gramley Library
Salem Academy and College
Winston-Salem, N.C. 27108

H. L. MENCKEN

H. L. MENCKEN

PREJUDICES:
FIRST, SECOND, AND THIRD SERIES

THE LIBRARY OF AMERICA

Gramley Library
Salem Academy and College
Winston-Salem, N.C. 27108

Volume compilation, notes, and chronology copyright © 2010 by
Literary Classics of the United States, Inc., New York, N.Y.
All rights reserved.
No part of this book may be reproduced commercially
by offset-lithographic or equivalent copying devices without
the permission of the publisher.

Prejudices: First Series, Second Series, and Third Series copyright © 1919,
1920, 1922 by Alfred A. Knopf, Inc., renewed 1947, 1948, 1950 by
H. L. Mencken. Reprinted by arrangement with Alfred A.
Knopf, an imprint of The Knopf Doubleday Publishing
Group, a division of Random House, Inc.

My Life as Author and Editor copyright ©
1992 by Enoch Pratt Free Library.

Permission to quote H. L. Mencken has been granted by
the Enoch Pratt Free Library, Baltimore, in accordance
with the terms of the bequest of H. L. Mencken.

The paper used in this publication meets the
minimum requirements of the American National Standard for
Information Sciences—Permanence of Paper for Printed
Library Materials, ANSI Z39.48—1984.

Distributed to the trade in the United States
by Penguin Group (USA) Inc.
and in Canada by Penguin Books Canada Ltd.

Library of Congress Control Number: 2010924448
ISBN 978-1-59853-074-2

First Printing
The Library of America—206

Manufactured in the United States of America

MARION ELIZABETH RODGERS
WROTE THE CHRONOLOGY AND NOTES FOR THIS VOLUME

H. L. Mencken's
Prejudices
is published with a gift in honor of

JAY CARL PENSKE

on his 30th birthday
from his parents,

Kathryn & Roger Penske

.

Contents

PREJUDICES:
FIRST SERIES

I.

Criticism of Criticism of Criticism

E VERY now and then, a sense of the futility of their daily endeavors falling suddenly upon them, the critics of Christendom turn to a somewhat sour and depressing consideration
of the nature and objects of their own craft. That is to say, they
turn to criticizing criticism. What is it in plain words? What is
its aim, exactly stated in legal terms? How far can it go? What
good can it do? What is its normal effect upon the artist and
the work of art?

Such a spell of self-searching has been in progress for several
years past, and the critics of various countries have contributed
theories of more or less lucidity and plausibility to the discussion. Their views of their own art, it appears, are quite as divergent as their views of the arts they more commonly deal
with. One group argues, partly by direct statement and partly
by attacking all other groups, that the one defensible purpose
of the critic is to encourage the virtuous and oppose the sinful
—in brief, to police the fine arts and so hold them in tune with
the moral order of the world. Another group, repudiating this
constabulary function, argues hotly that the arts have nothing
to do with morality whatsoever—that their concern is solely
with pure beauty. A third group holds that the chief aspect of a
work of art, particularly in the field of literature, is its aspect as
psychological document—that if it doesn't help men to know
themselves it is nothing. A fourth group reduces the thing to
an exact science, and sets up standards that resemble algebraic
formulæ—this is the group of metrists, of contrapuntists and
of those who gabble of light-waves. And so, in order, follow
groups five, six, seven, eight, nine, ten, each with its theory
and its proofs.

Against the whole corps, moral and æsthetic, psychological
and algebraic, stands Major J. E. Spingarn, U.S.A. Major Spingarn lately served formal notice upon me that he had abandoned the life of the academic grove for that of the armed
array, and so I give him his military title, but at the time he

3

wrote his "Creative Criticism" he was a professor in Columbia University, and I still find myself thinking of him, not as a soldier extraordinarily literate, but as a professor in rebellion. For his notions, whatever one may say in opposition to them, are at least magnificently unprofessorial—they fly violently in the face of the principles that distinguish the largest and most influential group of campus critics. As witness: "To say that poetry is moral or immoral is as meaningless as to say that an equilateral triangle is moral and an isosceles triangle immoral." Or, worse: "It is only conceivable in a world in which dinner-table conversation runs after this fashion: 'This cauliflower would be good if it had only been prepared in accordance with international law.'" One imagines, on hearing such atheism flying about, the amazed indignation of Prof. Dr. William Lyon Phelps, with his discovery that Joseph Conrad preaches "the axiom of the moral law"; the "Hey, what's that!" of Prof. Dr. W. C. Brownell, the Amherst Aristotle, with his eloquent plea for standards as iron-clad as the Westminster Confession; the loud, patriotic alarm of the gifted Prof. Dr. Stuart P. Sherman, of Iowa, with his maxim that Puritanism is the official philosophy of America, and that all who dispute it are enemy aliens and should be deported. Major Spingarn, in truth, here performs a treason most horrible upon the reverend order he once adorned, and having achieved it, he straightway performs another and then another. That is to say, he tackles all the antagonistic groups of orthodox critics seriatim, and knocks them about unanimously—first the aforesaid agents of the sweet and pious; then the advocates of unities, meters, all rigid formulæ; then the experts in imaginary psychology; then the historical comparers, pigeonholers and makers of categories; finally, the professors of pure esthetic. One and all, they take their places upon his operating table, and one and all they are stripped and anatomized.

But what is the anarchistic ex-professor's own theory?—for a professor must have a theory, as a dog must have fleas. In brief, what he offers is a doctrine borrowed from the Italian, Benedetto Croce, and by Croce filched from Goethe—a doctrine anything but new in the world, even in Goethe's time, but nevertheless long buried in forgetfulness—to wit, the doctrine that it is the critic's first and only duty, as Carlyle once put it, to find out "what the poet's aim really and truly was, how the task he had to do stood before his eye, and how far, with such materials as were afforded him, he has fulfilled it." For poet, read artist, or, if literature is in question, substitute the Germanic word *Dichter*—that is, the artist in words, the creator of beautiful letters, whether in verse or in prose. Ibsen always called himself a *Digter*, not a *Dramatiker* or *Skuespiller*. So, I daresay, did Shakespeare. . . . Well, what is this generalized poet trying to do? asks Major Spingarn, and how has he done it? That, and no more, is the critic's quest. The morality of the work does not concern him. It is not his business to determine whether it heeds Aristotle or flouts Aristotle. He passes no judgment on its rhyme scheme, its length and breadth, its iambics, its politics, its patriotism, its piety, its psychological exactness, its good taste. He may note these things, but he may not protest about them—he may not complain if the thing criticized fails to fit into a pigeon-hole. Every sonnet, every drama, every novel is *sui generis*; it must stand on its own bottom; it must be judged by its own inherent intentions. "Poets," says Major Spingarn, "do not really write epics, pastorals, lyrics, however much they may be deceived by these false abstractions; they express *themselves, and this expression is their only form*. There are not, therefore, only three or ten or a hundred literary kinds; there are as many kinds as there are individual poets." Nor is there any valid appeal *ad hominem*. The character and background of the poet are beside the mark; the poem itself is the thing. Oscar Wilde, weak and swine-like, yet wrote beautiful prose. To reject that prose on the ground that Wilde had filthy habits is as absurd as to reject "What Is Man?" on the ground that its theology is beyond the intelligence of the editor of the New York *Times*.

This Spingarn-Croce-Carlyle-Goethe theory, of course, throws a heavy burden upon the critic. It presupposes that he is a civilized and tolerant man, hospitable to all intelligible ideas and capable of reading them as he runs. This is a demand that at once rules out nine-tenths of the grown-up sophomores who carry on the business of criticism in America. Their trouble is simply that they lack the intellectual resilience necessary for taking in ideas, and particularly new ideas. The only way they can ingest one is by transforming it into the nearest related formula—usually a harsh and devastating operation. This fact accounts for their chronic inability to understand all that is most personal and original and hence most forceful and significant in the emerging literature of the country. They can get down what has been digested and re-digested, and so brought into forms that they know, and carefully labeled by predecessors of their own sort—but they exhibit alarm immediately they come into the presence of the extraordinary. Here we have an explanation of Brownell's loud appeal for a tightening of standards—*i.e.*, a larger respect for precedents, patterns, rubber-stamps—and here we have an explanation of Phelps's inability to comprehend the colossal phenomenon of Dreiser, and of Boynton's childish nonsense about realism, and of Sherman's effort to apply the Espionage Act to the arts, and of More's querulous enmity to romanticism, and of all the fatuous pigeon-holing that passes for criticism in the more solemn literary periodicals.

As practiced by all such learned and diligent but essentially ignorant and unimaginative men, criticism is little more than a branch of homiletics. They judge a work of art, not by its clarity and sincerity, not by the force and charm of its ideas, not by the technical virtuosity of the artist, not by his originality and artistic courage, but simply and solely by his orthodoxy. If he is what is called a "right thinker," if he devotes himself to advocating the transient platitudes in a sonorous manner, then he is worthy of respect. But if he lets fall the slightest hint that he is in doubt about any of them, or, worse still, that he is indifferent, then he is a scoundrel, and hence, by their theory, a bad artist. Such pious piffle is horribly familiar among us. I do not exaggerate its terms. You will find it running through the critical writings of practically all the dull fellows who combine criticism with tutoring; in the words of many of them it is stated in the plainest way and defended with much heat, theological and pedagogical. In its baldest form it shows itself in the doctrine that it is scandalous for an artist—say a dramatist or a novelist—to depict vice as attractive. The fact that vice, more often than not, undoubtedly *is* attractive—else why should it ever gobble any of us?—is disposed of with a lofty gesture. What of it? say these birchmen. The artist is not a reporter, but a Great Teacher. It is not his business to depict the world as it is, but as it ought to be.

Against this notion American criticism makes but feeble headway. We are, in fact, a nation of evangelists; every third American devotes himself to improving and lifting up his fellow-citizens, usually by force; the messianic delusion is our national disease. Thus the moral *Privatdozenten* have the crowd on their side, and it is difficult to shake their authority; even the vicious are still in favor of crying vice down. "Here is a novel," says the artist. "Why didn't you write a tract?" roars the professor—and down the chute go novel and novelist. "This girl is pretty," says the painter. "But she has left off her undershirt," protests the head-master—and off goes the poor dauber's head. At its mildest, this balderdash takes the form of the late Hamilton Wright Mabie's "White List of Books"; at its worst, it is comstockery, an idiotic and abominable thing. Genuine criticism is as impossible to such inordinately narrow and cocksure men as music is to a man who is tone-deaf. The critic, to interpret his artist, even to understand his artist, must be able to get into the mind of his artist; he must feel and comprehend the vast pressure of the creative passion; as Major Spingarn says, "æsthetic judgment and artistic creation are instinct with the same vital life." This is why all the best criticism of the world has been written by men who have had within them, not only the reflective and analytical faculty of critics, but also the gusto of artists—Goethe, Carlyle, Lessing, Schlegel, Saint-Beuve, and, to drop a story or two, Hazlitt, Hermann Bahr, Georg Brandes and James Huneker. Huneker, tackling "Also sprach Zarathustra," revealed its content in illuminating flashes. But tackled by Paul Elmer More, it became no more than a dull student's exercise, ill-naturedly corrected. . . .

So much for the theory of Major J. E. Spingarn, U.S.A., late professor of modern languages and literatures in Columbia University. Obviously, it is a far sounder and more stimulating theory than any of those cherished by the other professors. It demands that the critic be a man of intelligence, of toleration, of wide information, of genuine hospitality to ideas, whereas the others only demand that he have learning, and accept anything as learning that has been said before. But once he has stated his doctrine, the ingenious ex-professor, professor-like, immediately begins to corrupt it by claiming too much for it. Having laid and hatched, so to speak, his somewhat stale but still highly nourishing egg, he begins to argue fatuously that the resultant flamingo is the whole mustering of the critical *Aves*. But the fact is, of course, that criticism, as humanly practiced, must needs fall a good deal short of this intuitive recreation of beauty, and what is more, it must go a good deal further. For one thing, it must be interpretation in terms that are not only exact but are also comprehensible to the reader, else it will leave the original mystery as dark as before—and once interpretation comes in, paraphrase and transliteration come in. What is recondite must be made plainer; the transcendental, to some extent at least, must be done into common modes of thinking. Well, what are morality, trochaics, hexameters, movements, historical principles, psychological maxims, the dramatic unities—what are all these save common modes of thinking, short cuts, rubber stamps, words of one syllable? Moreover, beauty as we know it in this world is by no means the apparition *in vacuo* that Dr. Spingarn seems to see. It has its social, its political, even its moral implications. The finale of Beethoven's C minor symphony is not only colossal as music; it is also colossal as revolt; it says something against something. Yet more, the springs of beauty are not within itself alone, nor even in genius alone, but often in things without. Brahms wrote his Deutsches Requiem, not only because he was a great artist, but also because he was a good German. And in Nietzsche there are times when the divine afflatus takes a back seat, and the *spirochaetae* have the floor.

Major Spingarn himself seems to harbor some sense of this limitation on his doctrine. He gives warning that "the poet's intention must be judged at the moment of the creative act"—which opens the door enough for many an ancient to creep in. But limited or not, he at least clears off a lot of moldy rubbish, and gets further toward the truth than any of his former colleagues. They waste themselves upon theories that only conceal the poet's achievement the more, the more diligently they are applied; he, at all events, grounds himself upon the sound notion that there should be free speech in art, and no protective tariffs, and no *a priori* assumptions, and no testing of ideas by mere words. The safe ground probably lies between the contestants, but nearer Spingarn. The critic who really illuminates starts off much as he starts off, but with a due regard for the prejudices and imbecilities of the world. I think the best feasible practice is to be found in certain chapters of Huneker, a critic of vastly more solid influence and of infinitely more value to the arts than all the prating pedagogues since Rufus Griswold. Here, as in the case of Poe, a sensitive and intelligent artist recreates the work of other artists, but there also comes to the ceremony a man of the world, and the things he has to say are apposite and instructive too. To denounce moralizing out of hand is to pronounce a moral judgment. To dispute the categories is to set up a new anti-categorical category. And to admire the work of Shakespeare is to be interested in his handling of blank verse, his social aspirations, his shot-gun marriage and his frequent concessions to the bombastic frenzy of his actors, and to have some curiosity about Mr. W. H. The really competent critic must be an empiricist. He must conduct his exploration with whatever means lie within the bounds of his personal limitation. He must produce his effects with whatever tools will work. If pills fail, he gets out his saw. If the saw won't cut, he seizes a club. . . .

Perhaps, after all, the chief burden that lies upon Major Spingarn's theory is to be found in its label. The word "creative" is a bit too flamboyant; it says what he wants to say, but it probably says a good deal more. In this emergency, I propose getting rid of the misleading label by pasting another over it. That is, I propose the substitution of "catalytic" for "creative," despite the fact that "catalytic" is an unfamiliar word, and suggests the dog-Latin of the seminaries. I borrow it from chemistry, and its meaning is really quite simple. A catalyzer, in chemistry, is a substance that helps two other substances to react. For example, consider the case of ordinary cane sugar and water. Dissolve the sugar in the water and nothing happens. But add a few drops of acid and the sugar changes into glucose and fructose. Meanwhile, the acid itself is absolutely unchanged. All it does is to stir up the reaction between the water and the sugar. The process is called catalysis. The acid is a catalyzer.

Well, this is almost exactly the function of a genuine critic of the arts. It is his business to provoke the reaction between the work of art and the spectator. The spectator, untutored, stands unmoved; he sees the work of art, but it fails to make any intelligible impression on him; if he were spontaneously sensitive to it, there would be no need for criticism. But now comes the critic with his catalysis. He makes the work of art live for the spectator; he makes the spectator live for the work of art. Out of the process comes understanding, appreciation, intelligent enjoyment—and that is precisely what the artist tried to produce.

II.

The Late Mr. Wells

THE man as artist, I fear, is extinct—not by some sudden and romantic catastrophe, like his own Richard Remington, but after a process of gradual and obscure decay. In his day he was easily the most brilliant, if not always the most profound, of contemporary English novelists. There were in him all of the requisites for the business and most of them very abundantly. He had a lively and charming imagination, he wrote with the utmost fluency and address, he had humor and eloquence, he had a sharp eye for the odd and intriguing in human character, and, most of all, he was full of feeling and could transmit it to the reader. That high day of his lasted, say, from 1908 to 1912. It began with "Tono-Bungay" and ended amid the last scenes of "Marriage," as the well-made play of Scribe gave up the ghost in the last act of "A Doll's House." There, in "Marriage," were the first faint signs of something wrong. Invention succumbed to theories that somehow failed to hang together, and the story, after vast heavings, incontinently went to pieces. One had begun with an acute and highly diverting study of monogamy in modern London; one found one's self, toward the close, gaping over an unconvincing fable of marriage in the Stone Age. Coming directly after so vivid a personage as Remington, Dr. Richard Godwin Trafford simply refused to go down. And his Marjorie, following his example, stuck in the gullet of the imagination. One ceased to believe in them when they set out for Labrador, and after that it was impossible to revive interest in them. The more they were explained and vivisected and drenched with theories, the more unreal they became.

Since then the decline of Wells has been as steady as his rise was rapid. Call the roll of his books, and you will discern a progressive and unmistakable falling off. Into "The Passionate Friends" there crept the first downright dullness. By this time his readers had become familiar with his machinery and his materials—his elbowing suffragettes, his tea-swilling London

Gramley Library
Salem Academy and College
Winston-Salem, N.C. 27108

uplifters, his smattering of quasi-science, his intellectualized adulteries, his Thackerayan asides, his text-book paragraphs, his journalistic raciness—and all these things had thus begun to lose the blush of their first charm. To help them out he heaved in larger and larger doses of theory—often diverting enough, and sometimes even persuasive, but in the long run a poor substitute for the proper ingredients of character, situation and human passion. Next came "The Wife of Sir Isaac Harman," an attempt to rewrite "A Doll's House" (with a fourth act) in terms of ante-bellum 1914. The result was 500-odd pages of bosh, a flabby and tedious piece of work, Wells for the first time in the rôle of unmistakable bore. And then "Bealby," with its Palais Royal jocosity, its running in and out of doors, its humor of physical collision, its reminiscences of "A Trip to Chinatown" and "Peck's Bad Boy." And then "Boon," a heavy-witted satire, often incomprehensible, always incommoded by its disguise as a novel. And then "The Research Magnificent": a poor soup from the dry bones of Nietzsche. And then "Mr. Britling Sees It Through" . . .

Here, for a happy moment, there seemed to be something better—almost, in fact, a recrudescence of the Wells of 1910. But that seeming was only seeming. What confused the judgment was the enormous popular success of the book. Because it presented a fifth-rate Englishman in an heroic aspect, because it sentimentalized the whole reaction of the English proletariat to the war, it offered a subtle sort of flattery to other fifth-rate Englishmen, and, *per corollary*, to Americans of corresponding degree, to wit, the second. Thus it made a great pother, and was hymned as a masterpiece in such gazettes as the New York *Times*, as Blasco Ibáñez's "The Four Horsemen of the Apocalypse" was destined to be hymned three years later. But there was in the book, in point of fact, a great hollowness, and that hollowness presently begat an implosion that disposed of the shell. I daresay many a novel-reader returns, now and then, to "Tono-Bungay," and even to "Ann Veronica." But surely only a reader with absolutely nothing else to read would return to "Mr. Britling Sees It Through." There followed—what? "The Soul of a Bishop," perhaps the worst novel ever written by a serious novelist since novel-writing began. And then—or perhaps a bit before, or simultaneously

—an idiotic religious tract—a tract so utterly feeble and preposterous that even the Scotchman, William Archer, could not
stomach it. And then, to make an end, came "Joan and Peter"
—and the collapse of Wells was revealed at last in its true
proportions.

This "Joan and Peter" I confess, lingers in my memory as
unpleasantly as a summer cold, and so, in retrospect, I may
perhaps exaggerate its intrinsic badness. I would not look into
it again for gold and frankincense. I was at the job of reading it
for days and days, endlessly daunted and halted by its laborious
dullness, its flatulent fatuity, its almost fabulous inconsequen-
tiality. It was, and is, nearly impossible to believe that the Wells
of "Tono-Bungay" and "The History of Mr. Polly" wrote it,
or that he was in the full possession of his faculties when he allowed it to be printed under his name. For in it there is the
fault that the Wells of those days, almost beyond any other fictioneer of the time, was incapable of—the fault of dismalness,
of tediousness—the witless and contagious coma of the evangelist. Here, for nearly six hundred pages of fine type, he rolls
on in an intellectual cloud, boring one abominably with uninteresting people, pointless situations, revelations that reveal
nothing, arguments that have no appositeness, expositions that
expose naught save an insatiable and torturing garrulity.
Where is the old fine address of the man? Where is his sharp
eye for the salient and significant in character? Where is his instinct for form, his skill at putting a story together, his hand
for making it unwind itself? These things are so far gone that it
becomes hard to believe that they ever existed. There is not
the slightest sign of them in "Joan and Peter." The book is a
botch from end to end, and in that botch there is not even the
palliation of an arduous enterprise gallantly attempted. No inherent difficulty is visible. The story is anything but complex,
and surely anything but subtle. Its badness lies wholly in the
fact that the author made a mess of the writing, that his quon-
dam cunning, once so exhilarating, was gone when he began it.

Reviewing it at the time of its publication, I inclined mo-
mentarily to the notion that the war was to blame. No one
could overestimate the cost of that struggle to the English, not
only in men and money, but also and more importantly in the
things of the spirit. It developed national traits that were

greatly at odds with the old ideal of Anglo-Saxon character—
an extravagant hysteria, a tendency to whimper under blows,
political radicalism and credulity. It overthrew the old ruling
caste of the land and gave over the control of things to upstarts
from the lowest classes—shady Jews, snuffling Methodists,
prehensile commercial gents, disgusting demagogues, all sorts
of self-seeking adventurers. Worst of all, the strain seemed to
work havoc with the customary dignity and reticence, and
even with the plain commonsense of many Englishmen on a
higher level, and in particular many English writers. The astounding bawling of Kipling and the no less astounding bombast of G. K. Chesterton were anything but isolated; there
were, in fact, scores of other eminent authors in the same state
of eruption, and a study of the resultant literature of objurga-
tion will make a fascinating job for some sweating *Privatdozent* of to-morrow, say out of Göttingen or Jena. It occurred
to me, as I say, that Wells might have become afflicted by this
same demoralization, but reflection disposed of the notion.
On the one hand, there was the plain fact that his actual writings on the war, while marked by the bitterness of the time,
were anything but insane, and on the other hand there was the
equally plain fact that his decay had been in progress a long
while before the Germans made their fateful thrust at Liège.

The precise thing that ailed him I found at last on page 272
et seq. of the American edition of his book. There it was plainly
described, albeit unwittingly, but if you will go back to the
other novels since "Marriage" you will find traces of it in all of
them, and even more vivid indications in the books of exposition and philosophizing that have accompanied them. What
has slowly crippled him and perhaps disposed of him is his
gradual acceptance of the theory, corrupting to the artist and
scarcely less so to the man, that he is one of the Great Thinkers
of his era, charged with a pregnant Message to the Younger
Generation—that his ideas, rammed into enough skulls, will
Save the Empire, not only from the satanic Nietzscheism of the
Hindenburgs and post-Hindenburgs, but also from all those
inner Weaknesses that taint and flabbergast its vitals, as the
tapeworm with nineteen heads devoured Atharippus of Mace-
don. In brief, he suffers from a messianic delusion—and once
a man begins to suffer from a messianic delusion his days as a

serious artist are ended. He may yet serve the state with laudable devotion; he may yet enchant his millions; he may yet
posture and gyrate before the world as a man of mark. But not
in the character of artist. Not as a creator of sound books. Not in
the separate place of one who observes the eternal tragedy of
man with full sympathy and understanding, and yet with a
touch of god-like remoteness. Not as Homer saw it, smiting
the while his blooming lyre.

I point, as I say, to page 272 of "Joan and Peter," whereon,
imperfectly concealed by jocosity, you will find Wells' private
view of Wells—a view at once too flattering and libelous. What
it shows is the absorption of the artist in the tin-pot reformer
and professional wise man. A descent, indeed! The man im-
pinged upon us and made his first solid success, not as a merchant of banal pedagogics, not as a hawker of sociological
liver-pills, but as a master of brilliant and life-like representation, an evoker of unaccustomed but none the less deep-seated
emotions, a dramatist of fine imagination and highly resourceful execution. It was the stupendous drama and spectacle of
modern life, and not its dubious and unintelligible lessons,
that drew him from his test-tubes and guinea-pigs and made
an artist of him, and to the business of that artist, once he had
served his apprenticeship, he brought a vision so keen, a point
of view so fresh and sane and a talent for exhibition so lively
and original that he straightway conquered all of us. Nothing
could exceed the sheer radiance of "Tono-Bungay." It is a
work that glows with reality. It projects a whole epoch with
unforgettable effect. It is a moving-picture conceived and
arranged, not by the usual ex-bartender or chorus man, but by
an extremely civilized and sophisticated observer, alert to
every detail of the surface and yet acutely aware of the internal
play of forces, the essential springs, the larger, deeper lines of
it. In brief, it is a work of art of the soundest merit, for it both
represents accurately and interprets convincingly, and under
everything is a current of feeling that co-ordinates and informs
the whole.

But in the success of the book and of the two or three following it there was a temptation, and in the temptation a peril.
The audience was there, high in expectation, eagerly demanding more. And in the ego of the man—a true proletarian, and

hence born with morals, faiths, certainties, vasty gaseous hopes
—there was an urge. That urge, it seems to me, began to torture him when he set about "The Passionate Friends." In the
presence of it, he was dissuaded from the business of an
artist,—made discontented with the business of an artist. It
was not enough to display the life of his time with accuracy
and understanding; it was not even enough to criticize it with
a penetrating humor and sagacity. From the depths of his
being, like some foul miasma, there arose the old, fatuous
yearning to change it, to improve it, to set it right where it was
wrong, to make it over according to some pattern superior to
the one followed by the Lord God Jehovah. With this sinister
impulse, as aberrant in an artist as a taste for legs in an archbishop, the instinct that had created "Tono-Bungay" and
"The New Machiavelli" gave battle, and for a while the issue
was in doubt. But with "Marriage," its trend began to be
apparent—and before long the evangelist was triumphant, and
his bray battered the ear, and in the end there was a quite different Wells before us, and a Wells worth infinitely less than
the one driven off. To-day one must put him where he has
begun to put himself—not among the literary artists of English, but among the brummagem prophets of England. His
old rival was Arnold Bennett. His new rival is the Fabian Society, or maybe Lord Northcliffe, or the surviving Chesterton,
or the later Hillaire Belloc.

The prophesying business is like writing fugues; it is fatal to
every one save the man of absolute genius. The lesser fellow—
and Wells, for all his cleverness, is surely one of the lesser
fellows—is bound to come to grief at it, and one of the first
signs of his coming to grief is the drying up of his sense of
humor. Compare "The Soul of a Bishop" or "Joan and Peter"
to "Ann Veronica" or "The History of Mr. Polly." One notices
instantly the disappearance of the comic spirit, the old searching irony—in brief, of the precise thing that keeps the breath
of life in Arnold Bennett. It was in "Boon," I believe, that this
irony showed its last flare. There is a passage in that book
which somehow lingers in the memory: a portrait of the
United States as it arose in the mind of an Englishman reading
the *Nation* of yesteryear: "a vain, garrulous and prosperous female of uncertain age, and still more uncertain temper, with

unfounded pretensions to intellectuality and an idea of refinement of the most negative description . . . the Aunt Errant
of Christendom." A capital whimsy—but blooming almost
alone. A sense of humor, had it been able to survive the theology, would certainly have saved us from Lady Sunderbund, in
"The Soul of a Bishop," and from Lady Charlotte Sydenham
in "Joan and Peter." But it did not and could not survive. It
always withers in the presence of the messianic delusion, like
justice and the truth in front of patriotic passion. What takes
its place is the oafish, witless buffoonishness of the chautauquas and the floor of Congress—for example, the sort of
thing that makes an intolerable bore of "Bealby."

Nor are Wells' ideas, as he has so laboriously expounded
them, worth the sacrifice of his old lively charm. They are, in
fact, second-hand, and he often muddles them in the telling.
In "First and Last Things" he preaches a flabby Socialism, and
then, toward the end, admits frankly that it doesn't work. In
"Boon" he erects a whole book upon an eighth-rate platitude,
to wit, the platitude that English literature, in these latter times,
is platitudinous—a three-cornered banality, indeed, for his own
argument is a case in point, and so helps to prove what was
already obvious. In "The Research Magnificent" he smouches
an idea from Nietzsche, and then mauls it so badly that one
begins to wonder whether he is in favor of it or against it. In
"The Undying Fire" he first states the obvious, and then flees
from it in alarm. In his war books he borrows right and left—
from Dr. Wilson, from the British Socialists, from Romain
Rolland, even from such profound thinkers as James M. Beck,
Lloyd-George and the editor of the New York *Tribune*—and
everything that he borrows is flat. In "Joan and Peter" he first
argues that England is going to pot because English education
is too formal and archaic, and then that Germany is going to
pot because German education is too realistic and opportunist.
He seems to respond to all the varying crazes and fallacies of
the day; he swallows them without digesting them; he tries to
substitute mere timeliness for reflection and feeling. And
under all the rumble-bumble of bad ideas is the imbecile assumption of the jitney messiah at all times and everywhere:
that human beings may be made over by changing the rules
under which they live, that progress is a matter of intent and

foresight, that an act of Parliament can cure the blunders and check the practical joking of God.

Such notions are surely no baggage for a serious novelist. A novelist, of course, must have a point of view, but it must be a point of view untroubled by the crazes of the moment, it must regard the internal workings and meanings of existence and not merely its superficial appearances. A novelist must view life from some secure rock, drawing it into a definite perspective, interpreting it upon an ordered plan. Even if he hold (as Conrad does, and Dreiser, and Hardy, and Anatole France) that it is essentially meaningless, he must at least display that meaninglessness with reasonable clarity and consistency. Wells shows no such solid and intelligible attitude. He is too facile, too enthusiastic, too eager to teach to-day what he learned yesterday. Van Wyck Brooks once tried to reduce the whole body of his doctrine to a succinct statement. The result was a little volume a great deal more plausible than any that Wells himself has ever written—but also one that probably surprised him now and then as he read it. In it all his contradictions were reconciled, all his gaps bridged, all his shifts ameliorated. Brooks did for him, in brief, what William Bayard Hale did for Dr. Wilson in "The New Freedom," and has lived to regret it, I daresay, or at all events the vain labor of it, in the same manner. . . .

What remains of Wells? There remains a little shelf of very excellent books, beginning with "Tono-Bungay" and ending with "Marriage." It is a shelf flanked on the one side by a long row of extravagant romances in the manner of Jules Verne, and on the other side by an even longer row of puerile tracts. But let us not underestimate it because it is in such uninviting company. There is on it some of the liveliest, most original, most amusing, and withal most respectable fiction that England has produced in our time. In that fiction there is a sufficient memorial to a man who, between two debauches of claptrap, had his day as an artist.

III.
Arnold Bennett

O F Bennett it is quite easy to conjure up a recognizable
picture by imaging everything that Wells is not—that is,
everything interior, everything having to do with attitudes and
ideas, everything beyond the mere craft of arranging words in
ingratiating sequences. As stylists, of course, they have many
points of contact. Each writes a journalese that is extraordinarily fluent and tuneful; each is apt to be carried away by the rush
of his own smartness. But in their matter they stand at opposite poles. Wells has a believing mind, and cannot resist the lascivious beckonings and eye-winkings of meretricious novelty;
Bennett carries skepticism so far that it often takes on the appearance of a mere peasant-like suspicion of ideas, bellicose
and unintelligent. Wells is astonishingly intimate and confidential; and more than one of his novels reeks with a shameless
sort of autobiography; Bennett, even when he makes use of personal experience, contrives to get impersonality into it. Wells,
finally, is a sentimentalist, and cannot conceal his feelings; Bennett, of all the English novelists of the day, is the most steadily
aloof and ironical.

This habit of irony, in truth, is the thing that gives Bennett
all his characteristic color, and is at the bottom of both his peculiar merit and his peculiar limitation. On the one hand it sets
him free from the besetting sin of the contemporary novelist:
he never preaches, he has no messianic delusion, he is above
the puerile theories that have engulfed such romantic men as
Wells, Winston Churchill and the late Jack London, and even,
at times, such sentimental agnostics as Dreiser. But on the
other hand it leaves him empty of the passion that is, when all
is said and done, the chief mark of the true novelist. The trouble with him is that he cannot feel with his characters, that he
never involves himself emotionally in their struggles against
destiny, that the drama of their lives never thrills or dismays
him—and the result is that he is unable to arouse in the reader
that penetrating sense of kinship, that profound and instinctive

sympathy, which in its net effect is almost indistinguishable
from the understanding born of experiences actually endured
and emotions actually shared. Joseph Conrad, in a memorable
piece of criticism, once put the thing clearly. "My task," he
said, "is, by the power of the written word, to make you hear,
to make you feel—it is, above all, to make you *see*." Here seeing, it must be obvious, is no more than feeling put into physical terms; it is not the outward aspect that is to be seen, but
the inner truth—and the end to be sought by that apprehension of inner truth is responsive recognition, the sympathy of
poor mortal for poor mortal, the tidal uprush of feeling that
makes us all one. Bennett, it seems to me, cannot evoke it. His
characters, as they pass, have a deceptive brilliance of outline,
but they soon fade; one never finds them haunting the memory as Lord Jim haunts it, or Carrie Meeber, or Huck Finn, or
Tom Jones. The reason is not far to seek. It lies in the plain fact
that they appear to their creator, not as men and women
whose hopes and agonies are of poignant concern, not as
tragic comedians in isolated and concentrated dramas, but as
mean figures in an infinitely dispersed and unintelligible farce,
as helpless nobodies in an epic struggle that transcends both
their volition and their comprehension. Thus viewing them,
he fails to humanize them completely, and so he fails to make
their emotions contagious. They are, in their way, often vividly
real; they are thoroughly accounted for; what there is of them
is unfailingly life-like; they move and breathe in an environment
that pulses and glows. But the attitude of the author toward
them remains, in the end, the attitude of a biologist toward his
laboratory animals. He does not *feel* with them—and neither
does his reader.

   Bennett's chief business, in fact, is not with individuals at all,
even though he occasionally brings them up almost to life-size.
What concerns him principally is the common life of large
groups, the action and reaction of castes and classes, the struggle among societies. In particular, he is engrossed by the colossal and disorderly functioning of the English middle class—a
division of mankind inordinately mixed in race, confused in
ideals and illogical in ideas. It is a group that has had inter-
preters aplenty, past and present; a full half of the literature of
the Victorian era was devoted to it. But never, I believe, has it

had an interpreter more resolutely detached and relentless—never has it had one less shaken by emotional involvement. Here the very lack that detracts so much from Bennett's stature as a novelist in the conventional sense is converted into a valuable possession. Better than any other man of his time he has got upon paper the social anatomy and physiology of the masses of average, everyday, unimaginative Englishmen. One leaves the long series of Five Towns books with a sense of having looked down the tube of a microscope upon a huge swarm of infinitely little but incessantly struggling organisms —creatures engaged furiously in the pursuit of grotesque and unintelligible ends—helpless participants in and victims of a struggle that takes on, to their eyes, a thousand lofty purposes, all of them puerile to the observer above its turmoil. Here, he seems to say, is the middle, the average, the typical Englishman. Here is the fellow as he appears to himself—virtuous, laborious, important, intelligent, made in God's image. And here he is in fact—swinish, ineffective, inconsequential, stupid, a feeble parody upon his maker. It is irony that penetrates and devastates, and it is unrelieved by any show of the pity that gets into the irony of Conrad, or of the tolerant claim of kinship that mitigates that of Fielding and Thackeray. It is harsh and cocksure. It has, at its moments, some flavor of actual bounderism: one instinctively shrinks from so smart-alecky a pulling off of underclothes and unveiling of warts.

It is easy to discern in it, indeed, a note of distinct hostility, and even of disgust. The long exile of the author is not without its significance. He not only got in France something of the Frenchman's aloof and disdainful view of the English; he must have taken a certain distaste for the national scene with him in the first place, else he would not have gone at all. The same attitude shows itself in W. L. George, another Englishman smeared with Gallic foreignness. Both men, it will be recalled, reacted to the tremendous emotional assault of the war, not by yielding to it ecstatically in the manner of the unpolluted islanders, but by shrinking from it into a reserve that was naturally misunderstood. George has put his sniffs into "Blind Alley"; Bennett has got his into "The Pretty Lady." I do not say that either book is positively French; what I do say is that both mirror an attitude that has been somehow emptied of mere nationalism. An Italian adventure, I daresay, would have produced the same effect, or a Spanish, or Russian, or German. But it happened to be French. What the Bennett story attempts to do is what every serious Bennett story attempts to do: to exhibit dramatically the great gap separating the substance from the appearance in the English character. It seems to me that its prudent and self-centered G. J. Hoape is a vastly more real Englishman of his class, and, what is more, an Englishman vastly more useful and creditable to England, than any of the gaudy Bayards and Cids of conventional war fiction. Here, indeed, the irony somehow fails. The man we are obviously expected to disdain converts himself, toward the end, into a man not without his touches of the admirable. He is no hero, God knows, and there is no more brilliance in him than you will find in an average country squire or Parliament man, but he has the rare virtue of common sense, and that is probably the virtue that has served the English better than all others. Curiously enough, the English reading public recognized the irony but failed to observe its confutation, and so the book got Bennett into bad odor at home, and into worse odor among the sedulous apes of English ideas and emotions on this side of the water. But it is a sound work nevertheless— a sound work with a large and unescapable defect.

That defect is visible in a good many of the other things that Bennett has done. It is the product of his emotional detachment and it commonly reveals itself as an inability to take his own story seriously. Sometimes he pokes open fun at it, as in "The Roll-Call"; more often he simply abandons it before it is done, as if weary of a too tedious foolery. This last process is plainly visible in "The Pretty Lady." The thing that gives form and direction to that story is a simple enough problem in psychology, to wit: what will happen when a man of sound education and decent instincts, of sober age and prudent habit, of common sense and even of certain mild cleverness—what will happen, logically and naturally, when such a normal, respectable, cautious fellow finds himself disquietingly in love with a lady of no position at all—in brief, with a lady but lately of the town? Bennett sets the problem, and for a couple of hundred pages investigates it with the utmost ingenuity and address, exposing and discussing its sub-problems, tracing the gradual shifting of its terms, prodding with sharp insight into the psychological material entering into it. And then, as if suddenly tired of it—worse, as if suddenly convinced that the thing has gone on long enough, that he has given the public enough of a book for its money—he forthwith evades the solution altogether, and brings down his curtain upon a palpably artificial dénouement. The device murders the book. One is arrested at the start by a fascinating statement of the problem, one follows a discussion of it that shows Bennett at his brilliant best, fertile in detail, alert to every twist of motive, incisively ironical at every step—and then, at the end, one is incontinently turned out of the booth. The effect is that of being assaulted with an ice-pick by a hitherto amiable bartender, almost that of being bitten by a pretty girl in the midst of an amicable buss.

That effect, unluckily, is no stranger to the reader of Bennett novels. One encounters it in many of them. There is a tremendous marshaling of meticulous and illuminating observation, the background throbs with color, the sardonic humor is never failing, it is a capital show—but always one goes away from it with a sense of having missed the conclusion, always there is a final begging of the question. It is not hard to perceive the attitude of mind underlying this chronic evasion of issues. It is, in essence, agnosticism carried to the last place of decimals. Life itself is meaningless; therefore, the discussion of life is meaningless; therefore, why try futilely to get a meaning into it? The reasoning, unluckily, has holes in it. It may be sound logically, but it is psychologically unworkable. One goes to novels, not for the bald scientific fact, but for a romantic amelioration of it. When they carry that amelioration to the point of uncritical certainty, when they are full of "ideas" that click and whirl like machines, then the mind revolts against the childish naïveté of the thing. But when there is no organization of the spectacle at all, when it is presented as a mere formless panorama, when to the sense of its unintelligibility is added the suggestion of its inherent chaos, then the mind revolts no less. Art can never be simple representation. It cannot deal solely with precisely what is. It must, at the least, present the real in the light of some recognizable ideal; it must give to the eternal farce, if not some moral, then at all events some direction. For without that formulation there can be no clear-cut

separation of the individual will from the general stew and turmoil of things, and without that separation there can be no
coherent drama, and without that drama there can be no evocation of emotion, and without that emotion art is unimaginable. The field of the novel is very wide. There is room, on the
one side, for a brilliant play of ideas and theories, provided
only they do not stiffen the struggle of man with man, or of
man with destiny, into a mere struggle of abstractions. There is
room, on the other side, for the most complete agnosticism,
provided only it be tempered by feeling. Joseph Conrad is
quite as unshakable an agnostic as Bennett; he is a ten times
more implacable ironist. But there is yet a place in his scheme
for a sardonic sort of pity, and pity, however sardonic, is perhaps as good an emotion as another. The trouble with Bennett
is that he essays to sneer, not only at the futile aspiration of
man, but also at the agony that goes with it. The result is an air
of affectation, of superficiality, almost of stupidity. The manner, on the one hand, is that of a highly skillful and profoundly
original artist, but on the other hand it is that of a sophomore
just made aware of Haeckel, Bradlaugh and Nietzsche.

Bennett's unmitigated skepticism explains two things that
have constantly puzzled the reviewers, and that have been the
cause of a great deal of idiotic writing about him—for him as
well as against him. One of these things is his utter lack of anything properly describable as artistic conscience—his extreme
readiness to play the star houri in the seraglio of the publishers;
the other is his habit of translating platitudes into racy journalese and gravely offering them to the suburban trade as
"pocket philosophies." Both crimes, it seems to me, have their
rise in his congenital incapacity for taking ideas seriously, even
including his own. "If this," he appears to say, "is the tosh you
want, then here is another dose of it. Personally, I have little
interest in that sort of thing. Even good novels—the best I can
do—are no more than compromises with a silly convention. I
am not interested in stories; I am interested in the anatomy of
human melancholy; I am a descriptive sociologist, with overtones of malice. But if you want stories, and can pay for them,
I am willing to give them to you. And if you prefer bad stories,
then here is a bad one. Don't assume you can shame me by
deploring my willingness. Think of what your doctors do every

day, and your lawyers, and your men of God, and your stock-brokers, and your traders and politicians. I am surely no worse than the average. In fact, I am probably a good deal superior to the average, for I am at least not deceived by my own mountebankery—I at least know my sound goods from my shoddy." Such, I daresay, is the process of thought behind such hollow trade-goods as "Buried Alive" and "The Lion's Share." One does not need the man's own amazing confidences to hear his snickers at his audience, at his work and at himself.

The books of boiled-mutton "philosophy" in the manner of Dr. Orison Swett Marden and Dr. Frank Crane and the occasional pot-boilers for the newspapers and magazines probably have much the same origin. What appears in them is not a weakness for ideas that are stale and obvious, but a distrust of all ideas whatsoever. The public, with its mob yearning to be instructed, edified and pulled by the nose, demands certainties; it must be told definitely and a bit raucously that this is true and that is false. But there *are* no certainties. *Ergo*, one notion is as good as another, and if it happens to be utter flub-dub, so much the better—for it is precisely flubdub that penetrates the popular skull with the greatest facility. The way is already made: the hole already gapes. An effort to approach the hidden and baffling truth would simply burden the enterprise with difficulty. Moreover, the effort is intrinsically laborious and ungrateful. Moreover, there is probably no hidden truth to be uncovered. Thus, by the route of skepticism, Bennett apparently arrives at his sooth-saying. That he actually believes in his own theorizing is inconceivable. He is far too intelligent a man to hold that any truths within the comprehension of the popular audience are sound enough to be worth preaching, or that it would do any good to preach them if they were. No doubt he is considerably amused *in petto* by the gravity with which his bedizened platitudes have been received by persons accustomed to that sort of fare, particularly in America. It would be interesting to hear his private view of the corn-fed critics who hymn him as a profound and impassioned moralist, with a mission to rescue the plain people from the heresies of such fellows as Dreiser.

So much for two of the salient symptoms of his underlying

skepticism. Another is to be found in his incapacity to be, in the ordinary sense, ingratiating; it is simply beyond him to say the pleasant thing with any show of sincerity. Of all his books, probably the worst are his book on the war and his book on the United States. The latter was obviously undertaken with some notion of paying off a debt. Bennett had been to the United States; the newspapers had hailed him in their side-show way; the women's clubs had pawed over him; he had, no doubt, come home a good deal richer. What he essayed to do was to write a volume on the republic that should be at once colorably accurate and discreetly agreeable. The enterprise was quite beyond him. The book not only failed to please Americans; it offended them in a thousand subtle ways, and from its appearance dates the decline of the author's vogue among us. He is not, of course, completely forgotten, but it must be plain that Wells now stands a good deal above him in the popular estimation—even the later Wells of bad novel after bad novel. His war book missed fire in much the same way. It was work-manlike, it was deliberately urbane, it was undoubtedly truthful —but it fell flat in England and it fell flat in America. There is no little significance in the fact that the British government, in looking about for English authors to uphold the British cause in America and labor for American participation in the war, found no usefulness in Bennett. Practically every other novel-ist with an American audience was drafted for service, but not Bennett. He was *non est* during the heat of the fray, and when at length he came forward with "The Pretty Lady" the pained manner with which it was received quite justified the judgment of those who had passed him over.

What all this amounts to may be very briefly put: in one of the requisite qualities of the first-rate novelist Bennett is almost completely lacking, and so it would be no juggling with para-dox to argue that, at bottom, he is scarcely a novelist at all. His books, indeed,—that is, his serious books, the books of his better canon—often fail utterly to achieve the effect that one associates with the true novel. One carries away from them, not the impression of a definite transaction, not the memory of an outstanding and appealing personality, not the after-taste of a profound emotion, but merely the sense of having wit-nessed a gorgeous but incomprehensible parade, coming out of nowhere and going to God knows where. They are magnificent as representation, they bristle with charming detail, they radiate the humors of an acute and extraordinary man, they are entertainment of the best sort—but there is seldom anything in them of that clear, well-aimed and solid effect which one associates with the novel as work of art. Most of these books, indeed, are no more than collections of essays defectively dramatized. What is salient in them is not their people, but their backgrounds—and their people are forever fading into their backgrounds. Is there a character in any of these books that shows any sign of living as Pendennis lives, and Barry Lyndon, and Emma Bovary, and David Copperfield, and the George Moore who is always his own hero? Who remembers much about Sophia Baines, save that she lived in the Five Towns, or even about Clayhanger? Young George Cannon, in "The Roll-Call," is no more than an anatomical chart in a lecture on modern marriage. Hilda Lessways-Cannon-Clayhanger is not only inscrutable; she is also dim. The man and woman of "Whom God Hath Joined," perhaps the best of all the Bennett novels, I have so far forgotten that I cannot remember their names. Even Denry the Audacious grows misty. One remembers that he was the center of the farce, but now he is long gone and the farce remains.

This constant remainder, whether he be actually novelist or no novelist, is sufficient to save Bennett, it seems to me, from the swift oblivion that so often overtakes the popular fictioneer. He may not play the game according to the rules, but the game that he plays is nevertheless extraordinarily diverting and calls for an incessant display of the finest sort of skill. No writer of his time has looked into the life of his time with sharper eyes, or set forth his findings with a greater charm and plausibility. Within his deliberately narrow limits he had done precisely the thing that Balzac undertook to do, and Zola after him: he has painted a full-length portrait of a whole society, accurately, brilliantly and, in certain areas, almost exhaustively. The middle Englishman—not the individual, but the type—is there displayed more vividly than he is displayed anywhere else that I know of. The thing is rigidly held to its aim; there is no episodic descent or ascent to other fields. But within that one field every resource of observation, of invention and of imagination has been brought to bear upon the business—every one save that deep feeling for man in his bitter tragedy which is the most important of them all. Bennett, whatever his failing in this capital function of the artist, is certainly of the very highest consideration as craftsman. Scattered through his books, even his bad books, there are fragments of writing that are quite unsurpassed in our day—the shoe-shining episode in "The Pretty Lady," the adulterous interlude in "Whom God Hath Joined," the dinner party in "Paris Nights," the whole discussion of the Cannon-Ingram marriage in "The Roll-Call," the studio party in "The Lion's Share." Such writing is rare and exhilarating. It is to be respected. And the man who did it is not to be dismissed.

IV.

The Dean

AMERICANS, obsessed by the problem of conduct, usually judge their authors, not as artists, but as citizens, Christians, men. Edgar Allan Poe, I daresay, will never live down the fact that he was a periodical drunkard, and died in an alcoholic ward. Mark Twain, the incomparable artist, will probably never shake off Mark Twain, the after-dinner comedian, the flaunter of white dress clothes, the public character, the national wag. As for William Dean Howells, he gains rather than loses by this confusion of values, for, like the late Joseph H. Choate, he is almost the national ideal: an urbane and highly respectable old gentleman, a sitter on committees, an intimate of professors and the prophets of movements, a worthy vouched for by both the *Atlantic Monthly* and Alexander Harvey, a placid conformist. The result is his general acceptance as a member of the literary peerage, and of the rank of earl at least. For twenty years past his successive books have not been criticized, nor even adequately reviewed; they have been merely fawned over; the lady critics of the newspapers would no more question them than they would question Lincoln's Gettysburg speech, or Paul Elmer More, or their own virginity. The dean of American letters in point of years, and in point of published quantity, and in point of public prominence and influence, he has been gradually enveloped in a web of superstitious reverence, and it grates harshly to hear his actual achievement discussed in cold blood.

Nevertheless, all this merited respect for an industrious and inoffensive man is bound, soon or late, to yield to a critical examination of the artist within, and that examination, I fear, will have its bitter moments for those who naïvely accept the Howells legend. It will show, without doubt, a first-rate journeyman, a contriver of pretty things, a clever stylist—but it will also show a long row of uninspired and hollow books, with no more ideas in them than so many volumes of the *Ladies' Home Journal*, and no more deep and contagious feeling than so many reports of autopsies, and no more glow and gusto than so many tables of bond prices. The profound dread and agony of life, the surge of passion and aspiration, the grand crash and glitter of things, the tragedy that runs eternally under the surface—all this the critic of the future will seek in vain in Dr. Howells' elegant and shallow volumes. And seeking it in vain, he will probably dismiss all of them together with fewer words than he gives to "Huckleberry Finn." . . .

Already, indeed, the Howells legend tends to become a mere legend, and empty of all genuine significance. Who actually reads the Howells novels? Who even remembers their names? "The Minister's Charge," "An Imperative Duty," "The Unexpected Guests," "Out of the Question," "No Love Lost"—these titles are already as meaningless as a roll of Sumerian kings. Perhaps "The Rise of Silas Lapham" survives —but go read it if you would tumble downstairs. The truth about Howells is that he really has nothing to say, for all the charm he gets into saying it. His psychology is superficial, amateurish, often nonsensical; his irony is scarcely more than a polite facetiousness; his characters simply refuse to live. No figure even remotely comparable to Norris' McTeague or Dreiser's Frank Cowperwood is to be encountered in his novels. He is quite unequal to any such evocation of the race-spirit, of the essential conflict of forces among us, of the peculiar drift and color of American life. The world he moves in is suburban, caged, flabby. He could no more have written the last chapters of "Lord Jim" than he could have written the Book of Mark.

The vacuity of his method is well revealed by one of the books of his old age, "The Leatherwood God." Its composition, we are told, spread over many years; its genesis was in the days of his full maturity. An examination of it shows nothing but a suave piling up of words, a vast accumulation of nothings. The central character, one Dylks, is a backwoods evangelist who acquires a belief in his own buncombe, and ends by announcing that he is God. The job before the author was obviously that of tracing the psychological steps whereby this mountebank proceeds to that conclusion; the fact, indeed, is recognized in the canned review, which says that the book is "a study of American religious psychology." But an inspection of the text shows that no such study is really in it. Dr. Howells does not *show* how Dylks came to believe himself God; he merely *says* that he did so. The whole discussion of the process, indeed, is confined to two pages—172 and 173—and is quite infantile in its inadequacy. Nor do we get anything approaching a revealing look into the heads of the other converts—the saleratus-sodden, hell-crazy, half-witted Methodists and Baptists of a remote Ohio settlement of seventy or eighty years ago. All we have is the casual statement that they are converted, and begin to offer Dylks their howls of devotion. And when, in the end, they go back to their original bosh, dethroning Dylks overnight and restoring the gaseous vertebrate of Calvin and Wesley—when this contrary process is recorded, it is accompanied by no more illumination. In brief, the story is not a "study" at all, whether psychological or otherwise, but simply an anecdote, and without either point or interest. Its virtues are all negative ones: it is short, it keeps on the track, it deals with a religious maniac and yet contrives to offer no offense to other religious maniacs. But on the positive side it merely skims the skin.

So in all of the other Howells novels that I know. Somehow, he seems blissfully ignorant that life is a serious business, and full of mystery; it is a sort of college town *Weltanschauung* that one finds in him; he is an Agnes Repplier in pantaloons. In one of the later stories, "New Leaf Mills," he makes a faltering gesture of recognition. Here, so to speak, one gets at least a sniff of the universal mystery; Howells seems about to grow profound at last. But the sniff is only a sniff. The tragedy, at the end, peters out. Compare the story to E. W. Howe's "The Story of a Country Town," which Howells himself has intelligently praised, and you will get some measure of his own failure. Howe sets much the same stage and deals with much the same people. His story is full of technical defects—for one thing, it is overladen with melodrama and sentimentality. But nevertheless it achieves the prime purpose of a work of the imagination: it grips and stirs the emotions, it implants a sense of something experienced. Such a book leaves scars; one is not quite the same after reading it. But it would be difficult to point to a Howells book that produces any such effect. If he actually tries, like Conrad, "to make you hear, to make you feel—before all, to make you *see*," then he fails almost completely. One often suspects, indeed, that he doesn't really feel or see himself. . . .

As a critic he belongs to a higher level, if only because of his eager curiosity, his gusto in novelty. His praise of Howe I have mentioned. He dealt valiant licks for other débutantes: Frank Norris, Edith Wharton and William Vaughn Moody among them. He brought forward the Russians diligently and persuasively, albeit they left no mark upon his own manner. In his ingratiating way, back in the seventies and eighties, he made war upon the prevailing sentimentalities. But his history as a critic is full of errors and omissions. One finds him loosing a fanfare for W. B. Trites, the Philadelphia Zola, and praising Frank A. Munsey—and one finds him leaving the discovery of all the Shaws, George Moores, Dreisers, Synges, Galsworthys, Phillipses and George Ades to the Pollards, Meltzers and Hunekers. Busy in the sideshows, he didn't see the elephants go by. . . . Here temperamental defects handicapped him. Turn to his "My Mark Twain" and you will see what I mean. The Mark that is exhibited in this book is a Mark whose Himalayan outlines are discerned but hazily through a pink fog of Howells. There is a moral note in the tale—an obvious effort to palliate, to touch up, to excuse. The poor fellow, of course, was charming, and there was talent in him, but what a weakness he had for thinking aloud—and such shocking thoughts! What oaths in his speech! What awful cigars he smoked! How barbarous his contempt for the strict sonata form! It seems incredible, indeed, that two men so unlike should have found common denominators for a friendship lasting forty-four years. The one derived from Rabelais, Chaucer, the Elizabethans and Benvenuto—buccaneers of the literary high seas, loud laughers, law-breakers, giants of a lordlier day; the other came down from Jane Austen, Washington Irving and Hannah More. The one wrote English as Michelangelo hacked marble, broadly, brutally, magnificently; the other was a maker of pretty waxen groups. The one was utterly unconscious of the way he achieved his staggering effects; the other was the most toilsome, fastidious and self-conscious of craftsmen. . . .

What remains of Howells is his style. He invented a new harmony of "the old, old words." He destroyed the stately pe-

riods of the Poe tradition, and erected upon the ruins a complex and savory carelessness, full of naïvetés that were sophisticated to the last degree. He loosened the tightness of English,
and let a blast of Elizabethan air into it. He achieved, for all his
triviality, for all his narrowness of vision, a pungent and admirable style.

V.

Professor Veblen

TEN or twelve years ago, being engaged in a bombastic discussion with what was then known as an intellectual Socialist (like the rest of the *intelligentsia*, he succumbed to the first fife-corps of the war, pulled down the red flag, damned Marx as a German spy, and began whooping for Elihu Root, Otto Kahn and Abraham Lincoln), I was greatly belabored and incommoded by his long quotations from a certain Prof. Dr. Thorstein Veblen, then quite unknown to me. My antagonist manifestly attached a great deal of importance to these borrowed sagacities, for he often heaved them at me in lengths of a column or two, and urged me to read every word of them. I tried hard enough, but found it impossible going. The more I read them, in fact, the less I could make of them, and so in the end, growing impatient and impolite, I denounced this Prof. Veblen as a geyser of pishposh, refused to waste any more time upon his incomprehensible syllogisms, and applied myself to the other Socialist witnesses in the case, seeking to set fire to their shirts.

That old debate, which took place by mail (for the Socialist lived like a munitions patriot on his country estate and I was a wage-slave attached to a city newspaper), was afterward embalmed in a dull book, and made the mild pother of a day. The book, by name, "Men vs. the Man," is now as completely forgotten as Baxter's "Saint's Rest" or the Constitution of the United States. I myself, perhaps the only man who remembers it at all, have not looked into it for six or eight years, and all I can recall of my opponent's argument (beyond the fact that it not only failed to convert me to the nascent Bolshevism of the time, but left me a bitter and incurable scoffer at democracy in all its forms) is his curious respect for the aforesaid Prof. Dr. Thorstein Veblen, and his delight in the learned gentleman's long, tortuous and (to me, at least) intolerably flapdoodlish phrases.

There was, indeed, a time when I forgot even this—when

my mind was empty of the professor's very name. That was, say, from 1909 or thereabout to the middle of 1917. During those years, having lost all my old superior interest in Socialism, even as an amateur psychiatrist, I ceased to read its literature, and thus lost track of its Great Thinkers. The periodicals that I then gave an eye to, setting aside newspapers, were chiefly the familiar American imitations of the English weeklies of opinion, and in these the dominant Great Thinker was, first, the late Prof. Dr. William James, and, after his decease, Prof. Dr. John Dewey. The reign of James, as the illuminated will recall, was long and glorious. For three or four years running he was mentioned in every one of those American *Spectators* and *Saturday Reviews* at least once a week, and often a dozen times. Among the less somber gazettes of the republic, to be sure, there were other heroes: Maeterlinck, Rabindranath Tagore, Judge Ben B. Lindsey, the late Major-General Roosevelt, Tom Lawson and so on. Still further down the literary and intellectual scale there were yet others: Hall Caine, Brieux and Jack Johnson among them, with paper-bag cookery and the twilight sleep to dispute their popularity. But on the majestic level of the old *Nation*, among the white and lavender peaks of professorial ratiocination, there was scarcely a serious rival to James. Now and then, perhaps, Jane Addams had a month of vogue, and during one winter there was a rage for Bergson, and for a short space the unspeakable Bernstorff tried to set up Eucken (now damned with Wagner, Nietzsche and Ludendorff), but taking one day with another James held his own against the field. His ideas, immediately they were stated, became the ideas of every pedagogue from Harvard to Leland Stanford, and the pedagogues, laboring furiously at space rates, rammed them into the skulls of the lesser *cerebelli*. To have called James an ass, during the year 1909, would have been as fatal as to have written a sentence like this one without having used so many *haves*. He died a bit later, but his ghost went marching on: it took three or four years to interpret and pigeon-hole his philosophical remains and to take down and redact his messages (via Sir Oliver Lodge, Little Brighteyes, Wah-Wah the Indian Chief, and other gifted psychics) from the spirit world. But then, gradually, he achieved the ultimate, stupendous and irrevocable act of death, and there was a vacancy. To it Prof. Dr. Dewey was elected by the acclamation of all right-thinking and forward-looking men. He was an expert in pedagogics, metaphysics, psychology, ethics, logic, politics, pedagogical metaphysics, metaphysical psychology, psychological ethics, ethical logic, logical politics and political pedagogics. He was *Artium Magister*, *Philosophiæ Doctor* and twice *Legum Doctor*. He had written a book called "How to Think." He sat in a professor's chair and caned sophomores for blowing spit-balls. *Ergo*, he was the ideal candidate, and so he was nominated, elected and inaugurated, and for three years, more or less, he enjoyed a peaceful reign in the groves of sapience, and the inferior *umbilicarii* venerated him as they had once venerated James.

I myself greatly enjoyed and profited by the discourses of this Prof. Dewey and was in hopes that he would last. Born so recently as 1859 and a man of the highest bearable sobriety, he seemed likely to peg along until 1935 or 1940, a gentle and charming volcano of correct thought. But it was not, alas, to be. Under cover of pragmatism, that serpent's metaphysic, there was unrest beneath the surface. Young professors in remote and obscure universities, apparently as harmless as so many convicts in the death-house, were secretly flirting with new and red-hot ideas. Whole regiments and brigades of them yielded in stealthy privacy to rebellious and often incomprehensible yearnings. Now and then, as if to reveal what was brewing, a hell fire blazed and a Prof. Dr. Scott Nearing went sky-hooting through its smoke. One heard whispers of strange heresies—economic, sociological, even political. Gossip had it that pedagogy was hatching vipers, nay, was already brought to bed. But not much of this got into the home-made *Saturday Reviews* and Yankee *Athenæums*—a hint or two maybe, but no more. In the main they kept to their old resolute demands for a pure civil-service, the budget system in Congress, the abolition of hazing at the Naval Academy, an honest primary and justice to the Filipinos, with extermination of the Prussian serpent added after August, 1914. And Dr. Dewey, on his remote Socratic Alp, pursued the calm reënforcement of the philosophical principles underlying these and all other lofty and indignant causes. . . .

Then, of a sudden, Siss! Boom! Ah! Then, overnight, the

upspringing of the intellectual soviets, the headlong assault upon all the old axioms of pedagogical speculation, the nihilistic dethronement of Prof. Dewey—and rah, rah, rah for Prof. Dr. Thorstein Veblen! Veblen? Could it be—? Aye, it was! My old acquaintance! The *Doctor obscurus* of my half-forgotten bout with the so-called intellectual Socialist! The Great Thinker *redivivus*! Here, indeed, he was again, and in a few months—almost it seemed a few days—he was all over the *Nation*, the *Dial*, the *New Republic* and the rest of them, and his books and pamphlets began to pour from the presses, and the newspapers reported his every wink and whisper, and everybody who was anybody began gabbling about him. The spectacle, I do not hesitate to say, somewhat disconcerted me and even distressed me. On the one hand, I was sorry to see so learned and interesting a man as Dr. Dewey sent back to the insufferable dungeons of Columbia, there to lecture in imperfect Yiddish to classes of Grand Street Platos. And on the other hand, I shrunk supinely from the appalling job, newly rearing itself before me, of re-reading the whole canon of the singularly laborious and muggy, the incomparably tangled and unintelligible works of Prof. Dr. Thorstein Veblen. . . .

But if a sense of duty tortures a man, it also enables him to achieve prodigies, and so I managed to get through the whole infernal job. I read "The Theory of the Leisure Class," I read "The Theory of Business Enterprise," and then I read "The Instinct of Workmanship." An hiatus followed; I was racked by a severe neuralgia, with delusions of persecution. On recovering I tackled "Imperial Germany and the Industrial Revolution." Malaria for a month, and then "The Nature of Peace and the Terms of Its Perpetuation." What ensued was never diagnosed; probably it was some low infection of the mesentery or spleen. When it passed off, leaving only an asthmatic cough, I read "The Higher Learning in America," and then went to Mt. Clemens to drink the Glauber's salts. Eureka! the business was done! It had strained me, but now it was over. Alas, a good part of the agony had been needless. What I found myself aware of, coming to the end, was that practically the whole system of Prof. Dr. Veblen was in his first book and his last—that is, in "The Theory of the Leisure Class," and "The Higher Learning in America." I pass on the good news.

Read these two, and you won't have to read the others. And if even two daunt you, then read the first. Once through it, though you will have missed many a pearl and many a pain, you will have a fairly good general acquaintance with the gifted metaphysician's ideas.

For those ideas, in the main, are quite simple, and often anything but revolutionary in essence. What is genuinely remarkable about them is not their novelty, or their complexity, nor even the fact that a professor should harbor them; it is the astoundingly grandiose and rococo manner of their statement, the almost unbelievable tediousness and flatulence of the gifted headmaster's prose, his unprecedented talent for saying nothing in an august and heroic manner. There are tales of an actress of the last generation, probably Sarah Bernhardt, who could put pathos and even terror into a recitation of the multiplication table. The late Louis James did something of the sort; he introduced limericks into "Peer Gynt" and still held the yokelry agape. The same talent, raised to a high power, is in this Prof. Dr. Veblen. Tunnel under his great moraines and stalagmites of words, dig down into his vast kitchen-midden of discordant and raucous polysyllables, blow up the hard, thick shell of his almost theological manner, and what you will find in his discourse is chiefly a mass of platitudes—the self-evident made horrifying, the obvious in terms of the staggering. Marx, I daresay, said a good deal of it, and what Marx overlooked has been said over and over again by his heirs and assigns. But Marx, at this business, labored under a technical handicap: he wrote in German, a language he actually understood. Prof. Dr. Veblen submits himself to no such disadvantage. Though born, I believe, in These States, and resident here all his life, he achieves the effect, perhaps without employing the means, of thinking in some unearthly foreign language—say Swahili, Sumerian or Old Bulgarian—and then painfully clawing his thoughts into a copious but uncertain and book-learned English. The result is a style that affects the higher cerebral centers like a constant roll of subway expresses. The second result is a sort of bewildered numbness of the senses, as before some fabulous and unearthly marvel. And the third result, if I make no mistake, is the celebrity of the professor as a Great Thinker. In brief, he states his hollow nothings in such high, astounding terms that they must inevitably arrest and blister the right-thinking mind. He makes them mysterious. He makes them shocking. He makes them portentous. And so, flinging them at naïve and believing minds, he makes them stick and burn.

No doubt you think that I exaggerate—perhaps even that I lie. If so, then consider this specimen—the first paragraph of Chapter XIII of "The Theory of the Leisure Class":

> In an increasing proportion as time goes on, the anthropomorphic cult, with its code of devout observances, suffers a progressive disintegration through the stress of economic exigencies and the decay of the system of status. As this disintegration proceeds, there come to be associated and blended with the devout attitude certain other motives and impulses that are not always of an anthropomorphic origin, nor traceable to the habit of personal subservience. Not all of these subsidiary impulses that blend with the bait of devoutness in the later devotional life are altogether congruous with the devout attitude or with the anthropomorphic apprehension of sequence of phenomena. Their origin being not the same, their action upon the scheme of devout life is also not in the same direction. In many ways they traverse the underlying norm of subservience or vicarious life to which the code of devout observances and the ecclesiastical and sacerdotal institutions are to be traced as their substantial basis. Through the presence of these alien motives the social and industrial régime of status gradually disintegrates, and the canon of personal subservience loses the support derived from an unbroken tradition. Extraneous habits and proclivities encroach upon the field of action occupied by this canon, and it presently comes about that the ecclesiastical and sacerdotal structures are partially converted to other uses, in some measure alien to the purposes of the scheme of devout life as it stood in the days of the most vigorous and characteristic development of the priesthood.

Well, what have we here? What does this appalling salvo of rhetorical artillery signify? What is the sweating professor trying to say? What is his Message now? Simply that in the course of time, the worship of God is commonly corrupted by other enterprises, and that the church, ceasing to be a mere temple of adoration, becomes the headquarters of these other enterprises. More simply still, that men sometimes vary serving God by serving other men, which means, of course, serving themselves. This bald platitude, which must be obvious to any child who has ever been to a church bazaar or a parish house, is here tortured, worried and run through rollers until it is spread out to 241 words, of which fully 200 are unnecessary. The next paragraph is even worse. In it the master undertakes to explain in his peculiar dialect the meaning of "that non-reverent sense of æsthetic congruity with the environment which is left as a residue of the latter-day act of worship after elimination of its anthropomorphic content." Just what does he mean by this "non-reverent sense of æsthetic congruity"? I have studied the whole paragraph for three days, halting only for prayer and sleep, and I have come to certain conclusions. I may be wrong, but nevertheless it is the best that I can do. What I conclude is this: he is trying to say that many people go to church, not because they are afraid of the devil but because they enjoy the music, and like to look at the stained glass, the potted lilies and the rev. pastor. To get this profound and highly original obser-vation upon paper, he wastes, not merely 241, but more than 300 words! To say what might be said on a postage stamp he takes more than a page in his book! . . .

And so it goes, alas, alas, in all his other volumes—a cent's worth of information wrapped in a bale of polysyllables. In "The Higher Learning in America" the thing perhaps reaches its damndest and worst. It is as if the practice of that incredibly obscure and malodorous style were a relentless disease, a sort of progressive intellectual diabetes, a leprosy of the horse sense. Words are flung upon words until all recollection that there must be a meaning in them, a ground and excuse for them, is lost. One wanders in a labyrinth of nouns, adjectives, verbs, pronouns, adverbs, prepositions, conjunctions and par-ticiples, most of them swollen and nearly all of them unable to walk. It is difficult to imagine worse English, within the limits of intelligible grammar. It is clumsy, affected, opaque, bom-bastic, windy, empty. It is without grace or distinction and it is often without the most elementary order. The learned profes-sor gets himself enmeshed in his gnarled sentences like a bull trapped by barbed wire, and his efforts to extricate himself are quite as furious and quite as spectacular. He heaves, he leaps, he writhes; at times he seems to be at the point of yelling for the police. It is a picture to bemuse the vulgar and to give the judicious grief.

Worse, there is nothing at the bottom of all this strident

wind-music—the ideas it is designed to set forth are, in the overwhelming main, poor ideas, and often they are ideas that are almost idiotic. One never gets the thrill of sharp and original thinking, dexterously put into phrases. The concepts underlying, say, "The Theory of the Leisure Class" are simply Socialism and water; the concepts underlying "The Higher Learning in America" are so childishly obvious that even the poor drudges who write editorials for newspapers have often voiced them. When, now and then, the professor tires of this emission of stale bosh and attempts flights of a more original character, he straightway comes tumbling down into absurdity. What the reader then has to struggle with is not only intolerably bad writing, but also loose, flabby, cocksure and preposterous thinking. . . . Again I take refuge in an example. It is from Chapter IV of "The Theory of the Leisure Class." The problem before the author here has to do with the social convention which frowns upon the consumption of alcohol by women—at least to the extent to which men may consume it decorously. Well, then, what is his explanation of this convention? Here, in brief, is his process of reasoning:

1. The leisure class, which is the predatory class of feudal times, reserves all luxuries for itself, and disapproves their use by members of the lower classes, for this use takes away their charm by taking away their exclusive possession.

2. Women are chattels in the possession of the leisure class, and hence subject to the rules made for inferiors. "The patriarchal tradition . . . says that the woman, being a chattel, should consume only what is necessary to her sustenance, except so far as her further consumption contributes to the comfort or the good repute of her master."

3. The consumption of alcohol contributes nothing to the comfort or good repute of the woman's master, but "detracts sensibly from the comfort or pleasure" of her master. *Ergo*, she is forbidden to drink.

This, I believe, is a fair specimen of the Veblenian ratiocination. Observe it well, for it is typical. That is to say, it starts off with a gratuitous and highly dubious assumption, proceeds to an equally dubious deduction, and then ends with a platitude which begs the whole question. What sound reason is there for believing that exclusive possession is the hall-mark of luxury?

There is none that I can see. It may be true of a few luxuries, but it is certainly not true of the most familiar ones. Do I enjoy a decent bath because I know that John Smith cannot afford one—or because I delight in being clean? Do I admire Beethoven's Fifth Symphony because it is incomprehensible to Congressmen and Methodists—or because I genuinely love music? Do I prefer terrapin à la Maryland to fried liver because plowhands must put up with the liver—or because the terrapin is intrinsically a more charming dose? Do I prefer kissing a pretty girl to kissing a charwoman because even a janitor may kiss a charwoman—or because the pretty girl looks better, smells better and kisses better? Now and then, to be sure, the idea of exclusive possession enters into the concept of luxury. I may, if I am a bibliophile, esteem a book because it is a unique first edition. I may, if I am fond, esteem a woman because she smiles on no one else. But even here, save in a very small minority of cases, other attractions plainly enter into the matter. It pleases me to have a unique first edition, but I wouldn't care anything for a unique first edition of Robert W. Chambers or Elinor Glyn; the author must have my respect, the book must be intrinsically valuable, there must be much more to it than its mere uniqueness. And if, being fond, I glory in the exclusive smiles of a certain Miss —— or Mrs. ——, then surely my satisfaction depends chiefly upon the lady herself, and not upon my mere monopoly. Would I delight in the fidelity of the charwoman? Would it give me any joy to learn that, through a sense of duty to me, she had ceased to kiss the janitor?

Confronted by such considerations, it seems to me that there is little truth left in Prof. Dr. Veblen's theory of conspicuous consumption and conspicuous waste—that what remains of it, after it is practically applied a few times, is no more than a wraith of balderdash. In so far as it is true it is obvious. All the professor accomplishes with it is to take what every one knows and pump it up to such proportions that every one begins to doubt it. What could be plainer than his failure in the case just cited? He starts off with a platitude, and ends in absurdity. No one denies, I take it, that in a clearly limited sense, women occupy a place in the world—or, more accurately, aspire to a place in the world—that is a good deal like that of a chattel. Marriage, the goal of their only honest and permanent hopes, invades their individuality; a married woman becomes the function of another individuality. Thus the appearance she presents to the world is often the mirror of her husband's egoism. A rich man hangs his wife with expensive clothes and jewels for the same reason, among others, that he adorns his own head with a plug hat: to notify everybody that he can afford it—in brief, to excite the envy of Socialists. But he also does it, let us hope, for another and far better and more powerful reason, to wit, that she intrigues him, that he delights in her, that he loves her—and so wants to make her gaudy and happy. This reason may not appeal to Socialist sociologists. In Russia, according to an old scandal (officially endorsed by the British bureau for pulling Yankee noses) the Bolsheviki actually repudiated it as insane. Nevertheless, it continues to appeal very forcibly to the majority of normal husbands in the nations of the West, and I am convinced that it is a hundred times as potent as any other reason. The American husband, in particular, dresses his wife like a circus horse, not primarily because he wants to display his wealth upon her person, but because he is a soft and moony fellow and ever ready to yield to her desires, however preposterous. If any conception of her as a chattel were actively in him, even unconsciously, he would be a good deal less her slave. As it is, her vicarious practice of conspicuous waste commonly reaches such a development that her master himself is forced into renunciations—which brings Prof. Dr. Veblen's theory to self-destruction.

His final conclusion is as unsound as his premises. All it comes to is a plain begging of the question. Why does a man forbid his wife to drink all the alcohol she can hold? Because, he says, it "detracts sensibly from his comfort or pleasure." In other words, it detracts from his comfort and pleasure because it detracts from his comfort and pleasure. Meanwhile, the real answer is so plain that even a professor should know it. A man forbids his wife to drink too much because, deep in his secret archives, he has records of the behavior of other women who drank too much, and is eager to safeguard his wife's self-respect and his own dignity against what he knows to be certain invasion. In brief, it is a commonplace of observation, familiar to all males beyond the age of twenty-one, that once a woman is drunk the rest is a mere matter of time and place: the girl is already there. A husband, viewing this prospect, perhaps shrinks from having his chattel damaged. But let us be soft enough to think that he may also shrink from seeing humiliation, ridicule and bitter regret inflicted upon one who is under his protection, and one whose dignity and happiness are precious to him, and one whom he regards with deep and (I surely hope) lasting affection. A man's grandfather is surely not his chattel, even by the terms of the Veblen theory, and yet I am sure that no sane man would let the old gentleman go beyond a discreet cocktail or two if a bout of genuine bibbing were certain to be followed by the complete destruction of his dignity, his chastity and (if a Presbyterian) his immortal soul. . . .

One more example of the Veblenian logic and I must pass on: I have other fish to fry. On page 135 of "The Theory of the Leisure Class" he turns his garish and buzzing search-light upon another problem of the domestic hearth, this time a double one. First, why do we have lawns around our country houses? Secondly, why don't we employ cows to keep them clipped, instead of importing Italians, Croatians and blackamoors? The first question is answered by an appeal to ethnology: we delight in lawns because we are the descendants of "a pastoral people inhabiting a region with a humid climate." True enough, there is in a well-kept lawn "an element of sensuous beauty," but that is secondary: the main thing is that our dolicho-blond ancestors had flocks, and thus took a keen professional interest in grass. (The Marx *motif*! The economic interpretation of history in E flat.) But why don't *we* keep flocks? Why do we renounce cows and hire Jugo-Slavs? Because "to the average popular apprehension a herd of cattle so pointedly suggests thrift and usefulness that their presence . . . would be intolerably cheap." With the highest veneration, Bosh! Plowing through a bad book from end to end, I can find nothing sillier than this. Here, indeed, the whole "theory of conspicuous waste" is exposed for precisely what it is: one per cent. platitude and ninety-nine per cent. nonsense. Has the genial professor, pondering his great problems, ever taken a walk in the country? And has he, in the course of that walk, ever crossed a pasture inhabited by a cow (*Bos taurus*)? And has he, making that crossing, ever passed astern of the cow herself? And has he, thus passing astern, ever stepped carelessly, and—

But this is not a medical work, and so I had better haul up. The cow, to me, symbolizes the whole speculation of this laborious and humorless pedagogue. From end to end you will find the same tedious torturing of plain facts, the same relentless piling up of thin and over-labored theory, the same flatulent bombast, the same intellectual strabismus. And always with an air of vast importance, always in vexed and formidable sentences, always in the longest words possible, always in the most cacophonous English that even a professor ever wrote. One visualizes him with his head thrown back, searching for cryptic answers in the firmament and not seeing the overt and disconcerting cow, not watching his step. One sees him as the pundit *par excellence*, infinitely earnest and diligent, infinitely honest and patient, but also infinitely humorless, futile and hollow. . . .

So much, at least for the present, for this Prof. Dr. Thorstein Veblen, head Great Thinker to the parlor radicals, Socrates of the intellectual Greenwich Village, chief star (at least transiently) of the American *Athanæums*. I am tempted to crowd in mention of some of his other astounding theories—for example, the theory that the presence of pupils, the labor of teaching, a concern with pedagogy, is necessary to the highest functioning of a scientific investigator—a notion magnificently supported by the examples of Flexner, Ehrlich, Metchnikoff, Loeb and Carrel! I am tempted, too, to devote a thirdly to the astounding materialism, almost the downright hoggishness, of his whole system—its absolute exclusion of everything approaching an æsthetic motive. But I must leave all these fallacies and absurdities to your own inquiry. More important than any of them, more important as a phenomenon than the professor himself and all his works, is the gravity with which his muddled and highly dubious ideas have been received. At the moment, I daresay, he is in decline; such Great Thinkers have a way of going out as quickly as they come in. But a year or so ago he dominated the American scene. All the reviews were full of his ideas. A hundred lesser sages reflected them. Every one of intellectual pretentions read his books. Veblenism was shining in full brilliance. There were Veblenists, Veblen clubs, Veblen remedies for all the sorrows of the world. There were even, in Chicago, Veblen Girls—perhaps Gibson girls grown middle-aged and despairing.

The spectacle, unluckily, was not novel. Go back through the history of America since the early nineties, and you will find a long succession of just such violent and uncritical enthusiasms. James had his day; Dewey had his day; Ibsen had his day; Maeterlinck had his day. Almost every year sees another intellectual Munyon arise, with his infallible peruna for all the current malaises. Sometimes this Great Thinker is imported. Once he was Pastor Wagner; once he was Bergson; once he was Eucken; once he was Tolstoi; once he was a lady, by name Ellen Key; again he was another lady, Signorina Montessori. But more often he is of native growth, and full of the pervasive cocksureness and superficiality of the land. I do not rank Dr. Veblen among the worst of these haruspices, save perhaps as a stylist; I am actually convinced that he belongs among the best of them. But that best is surely depressing enough. What lies behind it is the besetting intellectual sin of the United States— the habit of turning intellectual concepts into emotional concepts, the vice of orgiastic and inflammatory thinking. There is, in America, no orderly and thorough working out of the fundamental problems of our society; there is only, as one Englishman has said, an eternal combat of crazes. The things of capital importance are habitually discussed, not by men soberly trying to get at the truth about them, but by brummagem Great Thinkers trying only to get *kudos* out of them. We are beset endlessly by quacks—and they are not the less quacks when they happen to be quite honest. In all fields, from politics to pedagogics and from theology to public hygiene, there is a constant emotional obscuration of the true issues, a violent combat of credulities, an inane debasement of scientific curiosity to the level of mob gaping.

The thing to blame, of course, is our lack of an intellectual aristocracy—sound in its information, skeptical in its habit of mind, and, above all, secure in its position and authority. Every other civilized country has such an aristocracy. It is the natural corrective of enthusiasms from below. It is hospitable to ideas, but as adamant against crazes. It stands against the pollution of logic by emotion, the sophistication of evidence to the glory of God. But in America there is nothing of the sort. On the one hand there is the populace—perhaps more powerful here, more capable of putting its idiotic ideas into execution, than anywhere else—and surely more eager to follow platitudinous messiahs. On the other hand there is the ruling plutocracy—ignorant, hostile to inquiry, tyrannical in the exercise of its power, suspicious of ideas of whatever sort. In the middle ground there is little save an indistinct herd of intellectual eunuchs, chiefly professors—often quite as stupid as the plutocracy and always in great fear of it. When it produces a stray rebel he goes over to the mob; there is no place for him within his own order. This feeble and vacillating class, unorganized and without authority, is responsible for what passes as the well-informed opinion of the country—for the sort of opinion that one encounters in the serious periodicals—for what later on leaks down, much diluted, into the few newspapers that are not frankly imbecile. Dr. Veblen has himself described it in "The Higher Learning in America"; he is one of its characteristic products, and he proves that he is thoroughly of it by the timorousness he shows in that book. It is, in the main, only half-educated. It lacks experience of the world, assurance, the consciousness of class solidarity and security. Of no definite position in our national life, exposed alike to the clamors of the mob and the discipline of the plutocracy, it gets no public respect and is deficient in self-respect. Thus the better sort of men are not tempted to enter it. It recruits only men of feeble courage, men of small originality. Its sublimest flower is the American college president, well described by Dr. Veblen—a perambulating sycophant and platitudinarian, a gaudy mendicant and bounder, engaged all his life, not in the battle of ideas, the pursuit and dissemination of knowledge, but in the courting of rich donkeys and the entertainment of mobs. . . .

Nay, Veblen is not the worst. Veblen is almost the best. The worst is—but I begin to grow indignant, and indignation, as old Friedrich used to say, is foreign to my nature.

VI.

The New Poetry Movement

THE current pother about poetry, now gradually subsiding, seems to have begun about seven years ago—say in 1912. It was during that year that Harriet Monroe established *Poetry: A Magazine of Verse*, in Chicago, and ever since then she has been the mother superior of the movement. Other leaders have occasionally disputed her command—the bombastic Braithwaite, with his annual anthology of magazine verse; Amy Lowell, with her solemn pronunciamentos in the manner of a Harvard professor; Vachel Lindsay, with his nebulous vaporings and chautauqua posturings; even such cheap jacks as Alfred Kreymborg, out of Greenwich Village. But the importance of Miss Monroe grows more manifest as year chases year. She was, to begin with, clearly the pioneer. *Poetry* was on the stands nearly two years before the first Braithwaite anthology, and long before Miss Lowell had been lured from her earlier finishing-school doggerels by the Franco-British Imagists. It antedated, too, all the other salient documents of the movement —Master's "Spoon River Anthology," Frost's "North of Boston," Lindsay's "General William Booth Enters Heaven," the historic bulls of the Imagists, the frantic balderdash of the "Others" group. Moreover, Miss Monroe has always managed to keep on good terms with all wings of the heaven-kissed host, and has thus managed to exert a ponderable influence both to starboard and to port. This, I daresay, is because she is a very intelligent woman, which fact is alone sufficient to give her an austere eminence in a movement so beset by mountebanks and their dupes. I have read *Poetry* since the first number, and find it constantly entertaining. It has printed a great deal of extravagant stuff, and not a little downright nonsensical stuff, but in the main it has steered a safe and intelligible course, with no salient blunders. No other poetry magazine— and there have been dozens of them—has even remotely approached it in interest, or, for that matter, in genuine hospitality to ideas. Practically all of the others have been operated by passionate enthusiasts, often extremely ignorant and always narrow and humorless. But Miss Monroe has managed to retain a certain judicial calm in the midst of all the whooping and clapper-clawing, and so she has avoided running amuck, and her magazine has printed the very best of the new poetry and avoided much of the worst.

As I say, the movement shows signs of having spent its strength. The mere bulk of the verse that it produces is a great deal less than it was three or four years ago, or even one or two years ago, and there is a noticeable tendency toward the conservatism once so loftily disdained. I daresay the Knish-Morgan burlesque of Witter Bynner and Arthur Davison Ficke was a hard blow to the more fantastic radicals. At all events, they subsided after it was perpetrated, and for a couple of years nothing has been heard from them. These radicals, chiefly collected in what was called the "Others" group, rattled the slapstick in a sort of side-show to the main exhibition. They attracted, of course, all the more credulous and uninformed partisans of the movement, and not a few advanced professors out of one-building universities began to lecture upon them before bucolic women's clubs. They committed hari-kari in the end by beginning to believe in their own buncombe. When their leaders took to the chautauquas and sought to convince the peasantry that James Whitcomb Riley was a fraud the time was ripe for the lethal buffoonery of MM. Bynner and Ficke. That buffoonery was enormously successful—perhaps the best hoax in American literary history. It was swallowed, indeed, by so many magnificoes that it made criticism very timorous thereafter, and so did damage to not a few quite honest bards. To-day a new poet, if he departs ever so little from the path already beaten, is kept in a sort of literary delousing pen until it is established that he is genuinely sincere, and not merely another Bynner in hempen whiskers and a cloak to go invisible.

Well, what is the net produce of the whole uproar? How much actual poetry have all these truculent rebels against Stedman's Anthology and McGuffey's Sixth Reader manufactured? I suppose I have read nearly all of it—a great deal of it, as a magazine editor, in manuscript—and yet, as I look back, my memory is lighted up by very few flashes of any lasting

brilliance. The best of all the lutists of the new school, I am inclined to think, are Carl Sandburg and James Oppenheim, and
particularly Sandburg. He shows a great deal of raucous cru-
dity, he is often a bit uncertain and wobbly, and sometimes he
is downright banal—but, taking one bard with another, he is
probably the soundest and most intriguing of the lot. Compare, for example, his war poems—simple, eloquent and extraordinarily moving—to the humorless balderdash of Amy
Lowell, or, to go outside the movement, to the childish gush
of Joyce Kilmer, Hermann Hagedorn and Charles Hanson
Towne. Often he gets memorable effects by astonishingly austere means, as in his famous "Chicago" rhapsody and his
"Cool Tombs." And always he is thoroughly individual, a true
original, his own man. Oppenheim, equally eloquent, is more
conventional. He stands, as to one leg, on the shoulders of
Walt Whitman, and, as to the other, on a stack of Old Testaments. The stuff he writes, despite his belief to the contrary, is
not American at all; it is absolutely Jewish, Levantine, almost
Asiatic. But here is something criticism too often forgets: the
Jew, intrinsically, is the greatest of poets. Beside his gorgeous
rhapsodies the highest flights of any western bard seem feeble
and cerebral. Oppenheim, inhabiting a brick house in New
York, manages to get that sonorous Eastern note into his
dithyrambs. They are often inchoate and feverish, but at their
best they have the gigantic gusto of Solomon's Song.

Miss Lowell is the schoolmarm of the movement, and vastly
more the pedagogue than the artist. She has written perhaps
half a dozen excellent pieces in imitation of Richard Aldington
and John Gould Fletcher, and a great deal of highfalutin
bathos. Her "A Dome of Many-Colored Glass" is full of infantile poppycock, and though it is true that it was first printed in
1912, before she joined the Imagists, it is not to be forgotten
that it was reprinted with her consent in 1915, after she had definitely set up shop as a foe of the *cliché*. Her celebrity, I fancy,
is largely extra-poetical; if she were Miss Tilly Jones, of Fort
Smith, Ark., there would be a great deal less rowing about her,
and her successive masterpieces would be received less gravely.
A literary craftsman in America, as I have already said once or
twice, is never judged by his work alone. Miss Lowell has been
helped very much by her excellent social position. The major-

ity, and perhaps fully nine-tenths of the revolutionary poets are of no social position at all—newspaper reporters, Jews, foreigners of vague nationality, school teachers, lawyers, advertisement writers, itinerant lecturers, Greenwich Village posturers, and so on. I have a suspicion that it has subtly flattered such denizens of the *demi-monde* to find the sister of a president of Harvard in their midst, and that their delight has materially corrupted their faculties. Miss Lowell's book of exposition, "Tendencies in Modern American Poetry," is commonplace to the last degree. Louis Untermeyer's "The New Era in American Poetry" is very much better. And so is Prof. Dr. John Livingston Lowes' "Convention and Revolt in Poetry."

As for Edgar Lee Masters, for a short season the undisputed Homer of the movement, I believe that he is already extinct. What made the fame of "The Spoon River Anthology" was not chiefly any great show of novelty in it, nor any extraordinary poignancy, nor any grim truthfulness unparalleled, but simply the public notion that it was improper. It fell upon the country at the height of the last sex wave—a wave eternally ebbing and flowing, now high, now low. It was read, not as work of art, but as document; its large circulation was undoubtedly mainly among persons to whom poetry *qua* poetry was as sour a dose as symphonic music. To such persons, of course, it seemed something new under the sun. They were unacquainted with the verse of George Crabbe; they were quite innocent of E. A. Robinson and Robert Frost; they knew nothing of the *Ubi sunt* formula; they had never heard of the Greek Anthology. The roar of his popular success won Masters' case with the critics. His undoubted merits in detail—his half-wistful cynicism, his capacity for evoking simple emotions, his deft skill at managing the puny difficulties of *vers libre*—were thereupon pumped up to such an extent that his defects were lost sight of. Those defects, however, shine blindingly in his later books. Without the advantage of content that went with the anthology, they reveal themselves as volumes of empty doggerel, with now and then a brief moment of illumination. It would be difficult, indeed, to find poetry that is, in essence, less poetical. Most of the pieces are actually tracts, and many of them are very bad tracts.

Lindsay? Alas, he has done his own burlesque. What was

new in him, at the start, was an echo of the barbaric rhythms of the Jubilee Songs. But very soon the thing ceased to be a marvel, and of late his elephantine college yells have ceased to be amusing. His retirement to the chautauquas is self-criticism of uncommon penetration. Frost? A standard New England poet, with a few changes in phraseology, and the substitution of sour resignationism for sweet resignationism. Whittier without the whiskers. Robinson? Ditto, but with a politer bow. He has written sound poetry, but not much of it. The late Major-General Roosevelt ruined him by praising him, as he ruined Henry Bordeaux, Pastor Wagner, Francis Warrington Dawson and many another. Giovannitti? A forth-rate Sandburg. Ezra Pound? The American in headlong flight from America—to England, to Italy, to the Middle Ages, to ancient Greece, to Cathay and points East. Pound, it seems to me, is the most picturesque man in the whole movement—a professor turned fantee, Abelard in grand opera. His knowledge is abysmal; he has it readily on tap; moreover, he has a fine ear, and has written many an excellent verse. But now all the glow and gusto of the bard have been transformed into the rage of the pamphleteer: he drops the lute for the bayonet. One sympathizes with him in his choler. The stupidity he combats is actually almost unbearable. Every normal man must be tempted, at times, to spit on his hands, hoist the black flag, and begin slitting throats. But this business, alas, is fatal to the placid moods and fine other-worldliness of the poet. Pound gives a thrilling show, but—. . . . The remaining stars of the liberation need not detain us. They are the street-boys following the calliope. They have labored with diligence, but they have produced no poetry. . . .

Miss Monroe, if she would write a book about it, would be the most competent historian of the movement, and perhaps also its keenest critic. She has seen it from the inside. She knows precisely what it is about. She is able, finally, to detach herself from its extravagances, and to estimate its opponents without bile. Her failure to do a volume about it leaves Untermeyer's "The New Era in American Poetry" the best in the field. Prof. Dr. Lowes' treatise is very much more thorough, but it has the defect of stopping with the fundamentals—it has too little to say about specific poets. Untermeyer discusses all of them, and then throws in a dozen or two orthodox bards, wholly untouched by Bolshevism, for good measure. His criticism is often trenchant and always very clear. He thinks he knows what he thinks he knows, and he states it with the utmost address—sometimes, indeed, as in the case of Pound, with a good deal more address than its essential accuracy deserves. But the messianic note that gets into the bulls and ukases of Pound himself, the profound solemnity of Miss Lowell, the windy chautauqua-like nothings of Lindsay, the contradictions of the Imagists, the puerilities of Kreymborg *et al*—all these things are happily absent. And so it is possible to follow him amiably even when he is palpably wrong.

That is not seldom. At the very start, for example, he permits himself a lot of highly dubious rumble-bumble about the "inherent Americanism" and soaring democracy of the movement. "Once," he says, "the most exclusive and aristocratic of the arts, appreciated and fostered only by little *salons* and erudite groups, poetry has suddenly swung away from its self-imposed strictures and is expressing itself once more in terms of democracy." Pondering excessively, I can think of nothing that would be more untrue than this. The fact is that the new poetry is neither American nor democratic. Despite its remote grounding on Whitman, it started, not in the United States at all, but in France, and its exotic color is still its most salient characteristic. Practically every one of its practitioners is palpably under some strong foreign influence, and most of them are no more Anglo-Saxon than a samovar or a toccata. The deliberate strangeness of Pound, his almost fanatical anti-Americanism, is a mere accentuation of what is in every other member of the fraternity. Many of them, like Frost, Fletcher, H. D. and Pound, have exiled themselves from the republic. Others, such as Oppenheim, Sandburg, Giovannitti, Benét and Untermeyer himself, are palpably Continental Europeans, often with Levantine traces. Yet others, such as Miss Lowell and Masters, are little more, at their best, than translators and adapters—from the French, from the Japanese, from the Greek. Even Lindsay, superficially the most national of them all, has also his exotic smear, as I have shown. Let Miss Lowell herself be a witness. "We shall see them," she says at the opening of her essay on E. A. Robinson, "ceding more and more to the influence of other, alien, peoples. . . ." A glance is sufficient to show the correctness of this observation. There is no more "inherent Americanism" in the new poetry than there is in the new American painting and music. It lies, in fact, quite outside the main stream of American culture.

Nor is it democratic, in any intelligible sense. The poetry of Whittier and Longfellow was democratic. It voiced the elemental emotions of the masses of the people; it was full of their simple, rubber-stamp ideas; they comprehended it and cherished it. And so with the poetry of James Whitcomb Riley, and with that of Walt Mason and Ella Wheeler Wilcox. But the new poetry, grounded firmly upon novelty of form and boldness of idea, is quite beyond their understanding. It seems to them to be idiotic, just as the poetry of Whitman seemed to them to be idiotic, and if they could summon up enough interest in it to examine it at length they would undoubtedly clamor for laws making the confection of it a felony. The mistake of Untermeyer, and of others who talk to the same effect, lies in confusing the beliefs of poets and the subject matter of their verse with its position in the national consciousness. Oppenheim, Sandburg and Lindsay are democrats, just as Whitman was a democrat, but their poetry is no more a democratic phenomenon than his was, or than, to go to music, Beethoven's Eroica Symphony was. Many of the new poets, in truth, are ardent enemies of democracy, for example, Pound. Only one of them has ever actually sought to take his strophes to the vulgar. That one is Lindsay—and there is not the slightest doubt that the yokels welcomed him, not because they were interested in his poetry, but because it struck them as an amazing, and perhaps even a fascinatingly obscene thing, for a sane man to go about the country on any such bizarre and undemocratic business.

No sound art, in fact, could possibly be democratic. Tolstoi wrote a whole book to prove the contrary, and only succeeded in making his case absurd. The only art that is capable of reaching the *Homo Boobus* is art that is already debased and polluted—band music, official sculpture, Pears' Soap painting, the popular novel. What is honest and worthy of praise in the new poetry is Greek to the general. And, despite much nonsense, it seems to me that there is no little in it that is honest and worthy of praise. It has, for one thing, made an effective war upon the *cliché*, and so purged the verse of the nation of much of its old banality in subject and phrase. The elegant album pieces of Richard Henry Stoddard and Edmund Clarence Stedman are no longer in fashion—save, perhaps, among the democrats that Untermeyer mentions. And in the second place, it has substituted for this ancient conventionality an eager curiosity in life as men and women are actually living it—a spirit of daring experimentation that has made poetry vivid and full of human interest, as it was in the days of Elizabeth. The thing often passes into the grotesque, it is shot through and through with *héliogabalisme*, but at its high points it has achieved invaluable pioneering. A new poet, emerging out of the Baptist night of Peoria or Little Rock to-day, comes into an atmosphere charged with subtle electricities. There is a stimulating restlessness; ideas have a welcome; the art he aspires to is no longer a merely formal exercise, like practicing Czerny. When a Henry Van Dyke arises at some college banquet and begins to discharge an old-fashioned ode to *alma mater* there is a definite snicker; it is almost as if he were to appear in Congress gaiters or a beaver hat. An audience for such things, of course, still exists. It is, no doubt, an enormously large audience. But it has changed a good deal qualitatively, if not quantitatively. The relatively civilized reader has been educated to something better. He has heard a music that has spoiled his ear for the old wheezing of the melodeon. He weeps no more over what wrung him yesteryear.

Unluckily, the new movement, in America even more than in England, France and Germany, suffers from a very crippling lack, and that is the lack of a genuinely first-rate poet. It has produced many talents, but it has yet to produce any genius, or even the shadow of genius. There has been a general lifting of the plain, but no vasty and melodramatic throwing up of new peaks. Worse still, it has had to face hard competition from without—that is, from poets who, while also emerged from platitude, have yet stood outside it, and perhaps in some doubt of it. Untermeyer discusses a number of such poets in his book. There is one of them, Lizette Woodworth Reese, who has written more sound poetry, more genuinely eloquent and beautiful poetry, than all the new poets put together—more than a whole posse of Masterses and Lindsays, more than a hundred Amy Lowells. And there are others, Neihardt and John McClure among them—particularly McClure. Untermeyer, usually anything but an ass, once committed the unforgettable asininity of sneering at McClure. The blunder, I daresay, is already lamented; it is not embalmed in his book. But it will haunt him on Tyburn Hill. For this McClure, attempting the simplest thing in the simplest way, has done it almost superbly. He seems to be entirely without theories. There is no pedagogical passion in him. He is no reformer. But more than any of the reformers now or lately in the arena, he is a poet.

VII.
The Heir of Mark Twain

NOTHING could be stranger than the current celebrity of Irvin S. Cobb, an author of whom almost as much is heard as if he were a new Thackeray or Molière. One is solemnly told by various extravagant partisans, some of them not otherwise insane, that he is at once the successor to Mark Twain and the heir of Edgar Allan Poe. One hears of public dinners given in devotion to his genius, of public presentations, of learned degrees conferred upon him by universities, of other extraordinary adulations, few of them shared by such relatively puny fellows as Howells and Dreiser. His talents and sagacity pass into popular anecdotes; he has sedulous Boswells; he begins to take on the august importance of an actor-manager. Behind the scenes, of course, a highly dexterous publisher pulls the strings, but much of it is undoubtedly more or less sincere; men pledge their sacred honor to the doctrine that his existence honors the national literature. Moreover, he seems to take the thing somewhat seriously himself. He gives his *imprimatur* to various other authors, including Joseph Conrad; he engages himself to lift the literary tone of moving-pictures; he lends his name to movements; he exposes himself in the chautauquas; he takes on the responsibilities of a patriot and a public man. . . . Altogether, a curious, and, in some of its aspects, a caressingly ironical spectacle. One wonders what the graduate sophomores of to-morrow, composing their dull tomes upon American letters, will make of it. . . .

In the actual books of the man I can find nothing that seems to justify so much enthusiasm, nor even the hundredth part of it. His serious fiction shows a certain undoubted facility, but there are at least forty other Americans who do the thing quite as well. His public bulls and ukases are no more than clever journalism—superficial and inconsequential, first saying one thing and then quite another thing. And in his humor, which his admirers apparently put first among his products, I can discover, at best, nothing save a somewhat familiar aptitude for grotesque anecdote, and, at worst, only the laborious laugh-squeezing of Bill Nye. In the volume called "Those Times and These" there is an excellent comic story, to wit, "Hark, From the Tomb!" But it would surely be an imbecility to call it a masterpiece; too many other authors have done things quite as good; more than a few (I need cite only George Ade, Owen Johnson and Ring W. Lardner) have done things very much better. Worse, it lies in the book like a slice of Smithfield ham between two slabs of stale store-bread. On both sides of it are very stupid artificialities—stories without point, stories in which rustic characters try to talk like Wilson Mizner, stories altogether machine-made and depressing. Turn, now, to another book, vastly praised in its year—by name, "Cobb's Anatomy." One laughs occasionally—but precisely as one laughs over a comic supplement or the jokes in *Ayer's Almanac*. For example:

There never was a hansom cab made that would hold a fat man comfortably unless he left the doors open, and that makes him feel undressed.

Again:

Your hair gives you bother so long as you have it and more bother when it starts to go. You are always doing something for it and it is always showing deep-dyed ingratitude in return; or else the dye isn't deep enough, which is even worse.

Exactly; it is even worse. And then this:

Once there was a manicure lady who wouldn't take a tip, but she is now no more. Her indignant sisters stabbed her to death with hatpins and nail-files.

I do not think I quote unfairly; I have tried to select honest specimens of the author's fancy. . . . Perhaps it may be well to glance at another book. I choose, at random, "Speaking of Operations—," a work described by the publisher as "the funniest yet written by Cobb" and "the funniest book we know of." In this judgment many other persons seem to have concurred. The thing was an undoubted success when it appeared as an article in the *Saturday Evening Post* and it sold thousands of copies between covers. Well, what is in it? In it, after a dili-

gent reading, I find half a dozen mildly clever observations—
and sixty odd pages of ancient and infantile wheezes, as flat to
the taste as so many crystals of hyposulphite of soda. For example, the wheeze to the effect that in the days of the author's
nonage "germs had not been invented yet." For example, the
wheeze to the effect that doctors bury their mistakes. For example, the wheeze to the effect that the old-time doctor
always prescribed medicines of abominably evil flavor. . . .
But let us go into the volume more in detail, and so unearth all
its gems.

On page 1, in the very first paragraph, there is the doddering
old joke about the steepness of doctors' bills. In the second
paragraph there is the somewhat newer but still fully adult joke
about the extreme willingness of persons who have been
butchered by surgeons to talk about it afterward. These two
witticisms are all that I can find on page 1. For the rest, it consists almost entirely of a reference to MM. Bryan and Roosevelt
—a reference well known by all newspaper paragraphists and
vaudeville monologists to be as provocative of laughter as a
mention of bunions, mothers-in-law or Pottstown, Pa. On
page 2 Bryan and Roosevelt are succeeded by certain heavy
stuff in the Petroleum V. Nasby manner upon the condition of
obstetrics, pediatrics and the allied sciences among whales.
Page 3 starts off with the old jocosity to the effect that people
talk too much about the weather. It progresses or resolves, as
the musicians say, into the wheeze to the effect that people like
to dispute over what is the best thing to eat for breakfast. On
page 4 we come to what musicians would call the formal statement of the main theme—that is, of the how-I-like-to-talk-of-
my-operation motif. We have thus covered four pages.

Page 5 starts out with an enharmonic change: to wit, from
the idea that ex-patients like to talk of their operations to the
idea that patients in being like to swap symptoms. Following
this there is a repetition of the gold theme—that is, the theme
of the doctor's bill. On page 6 there are two chuckles. One
springs out of a reference to "light housekeeping," a phrase
which invariably strikes an American vaudeville audience as
salaciously whimsical. The other is grounded upon the well-
known desire of baseball fans to cut the umpire's throat. On
page 6 there enters for the first time what may be called the

second theme of the book. This is the whiskers motif. The whole of this page, with the exception of a sentence embodying the old wheeze about the happy times before germs were invented, is given over to variations of the whiskers joke. Page 8 continues this development section. Whiskers of various fantastic varieties are mentioned—trellis whiskers, bosky whiskers, ambush whiskers, loose, luxuriant whiskers, landscaped whiskers, whiskers that are winter quarters for pathogenic organisms. Some hard, hard squeezing, and the humor in whiskers is temporarily exhausted. Page 8 closes with the old joke about the cruel thumping which doctors perform upon their patients' clavicles.

Now for page 9. It opens with a third statement of the gold motif—"He then took my temperature and $15." Following comes the dentist's office motif—that is, the motif of reluctance, of oozing courage, of flight. At the bottom of the page the gold motif is repeated in the key of E minor. Pages 10 and 11 are devoted to simple description, with very little effort at humor. On page 12 there is a second statement, for the full brass choir, of the dentist's office motif. On page 13 there are more echoes from Petroleum V. Nasby, the subject this time being a man "who got his spleen back from the doctor's and now keeps it in a bottle of alcohol." On page 14 one finds the innocent bystander joke; on page 15 the joke about the terrifying effects of reading a patent medicine almanac. Also, at the bottom of the page, there is a third statement of the dentist's office joke. On page 16 it gives way to a restatement of the whiskers theme, in augmentation, which in turn yields to the third or fifth restatement of the gold theme.

Let us now jump a few pages. On page 19 we come to the old joke about the talkative barber; on page 22 to the joke about the book agent; on the same page to the joke about the fashionableness of appendicitis; on page 23 to the joke about the clumsy carver who projects the turkey's gizzard into the visiting pastor's eye; on page 28 to a restatement of the barber joke; on page 31 to another statement—is it the fifth or sixth? —of the dentist's office joke; on page 37 to the katzenjammer joke; on page 39 to the old joke about doctors burying their mistakes. . . . And so on. And so on and so on. And so on and so on and so on. On pages 48 and 49 there is a perfect riot of old jokes, including the nth variation of the whiskers joke and a fearful and wonderful pun about Belgian hares and heirs. . . .

On second thoughts I go no further. . . . This, remember, is the book that Cobb's publishers, apparently with his own *Nihil Obstat*, choose at his best. This is the official masterpiece of the "new Mark Twain." Nevertheless, even so laboriously flabby a farceur has his moments. I turn to Frank J. Wilstach's Dictionary of Similes and find this credited to him: "No more privacy than a goldfish." Here, at last, is something genuinely humorous. Here, moreover, is something apparently new.

VIII.
Hermann Sudermann

T HE fact that Sudermann is the author of the most successful play that has come out of Germany since the collapse
of the romantic movement is the most eloquent of all proofs,
perhaps, of his lack of force and originality as a dramatist.
"Heimat," Englished, Frenched and Italianized as "Magda,"
gave a new and gaudy leading rôle to all the middle-aged
chewers of scenery; they fell upon it as upon a new Marguerite
Gautier, and with it they coaxed the tears of all nations. That
was in the middle nineties. To-day the piece seems almost as
old-fashioned as "The Princess Bonnie," and even in Germany
it has gone under the counter. If it is brought out at all, it is to
adorn the death agonies of some doddering star of the last
generation.

Sudermann was one of the first deer flushed by Arno Holz
and Johannes Schlaf, the founders of German naturalism. He
had written a couple of successful novels, "Frau Sorge" and
"Der Katzensteg," before the *Uberbrettl'* got on its legs, and
so he was a recruit worth snaring. The initial fruit of his enlist-
ment was "Die Ehre," a *reductio ad absurdum* of Prussian notions of honor, as incomprehensible outside of Germany as
Franz Adam Beyerlein's "Zapfenstreich" or Carl Bleibtreu's
"Die Edelsten der Nation." Then followed "Sodoms Ende,"
and after it, "Heimat." Already the emptiness of naturalism
was beginning to oppress Sudermann, as it was also oppressing
Hauptmann. The latter, in 1892, rebounded from it to the un-
blushing romanticism of "Hanneles Himmelfahrt." As for Sudermann, he chose to temper the rigors of the Schlaf-Holz
formula (by Ibsen out of Zola) with sardoodledum. The result
was this "Heimat," in which naturalism was wedded to a mellow sentimentality, caressing to audiences bred upon the
drama of perfumed adultery. The whole last scene of the play,
indeed, was no more than an echo of Augier's "Le Mariage
d'Olympe." It is no wonder that even Sarah Bernhardt pronounced it a great work.

Since then Sudermann has wobbled, and in the novel as well as in the drama. Lacking the uncanny versatility of Hauptmann, he has been unable to conquer the two fields of romance and reality. Instead he has lost himself between them, a rat without a tail. "Das hohe Lied," his most successful novel since "Frau Sorge," is anything but a first-rate work. Its opening chapter is a superlatively fine piece of writing, but after that he grows uncertain of his way, and toward the end one begins to wonder what it is all about. No coherent idea is in it; it is simply a sentimentalization of the unpleasant; if it were not for the naughtiness of some of the scenes no one would read it. An American dramatist has made a play of it—a shocker for the same clowns who were entranced by Brieux's "Les Avariés."

The trouble with Sudermann, here and elsewhere, is that he has no sound underpinnings, and is a bit uncertain about his characters and his story. He starts off furiously, let us say, as a Zola, and then dilutes Zolaism with romance, and then pulls himself up and begins to imitate Ibsen, and then trips and falls headlong into the sugar bowl of sentimentality. Lily Czepanek, in "Das hohe Lied," swoons at critical moments, like the heroine of a tale for chambermaids. It is almost as if Lord Jim should get converted at a gospel mission, or Nora Helmer let down her hair. . . . But these are defects in Sudermann the novelist and dramatist, and in that Sudermann only. In the short story they conceal themselves; he is done before he begins to vacillate. In this field, indeed, all his virtues—of brisk, incisive writing, of flashing observation, of dexterous stage management, of emotional fire and address—have a chance to show themselves, and without any wearing thin. The book translated as "The Indian Lily" contains some of the best short stories that German—or any other language, for that matter— can offer. They are mordant, succinct and extraordinarily vivid character studies, each full of penetrating irony and sardonic pity, each with the chill wind of disillusion blowing through it, each preaching that life is a hideous farce, that good and bad are almost meaningless words, that truth is only the lie that is easiest to believe. . . .

It is hard to choose between stories so high in merit, but surely "The Purpose" is one of the best. Of all the latter-day Germans, only Ludwig Thoma, in "Ein bayrischer Soldat," has

ever got a more brilliant reality into a crowded space. Here, in
less than fifteen thousand words, Sudermann rehearses the
tragedy of a whole life, and so great is the art of the thing that
one gets a sense of perfect completeness, almost of exhaustive-
ness. . . . Antonie Wiesner, the daughter of a country inn-
keeper, falls in love with Robert Messerschmidt, a medical
student, and they sin the scarlet sin. To Robert, perhaps, the
thing is a mere interlude of midsummer, but to Toni it is all
life's meaning and glory. Robert is poor and his degree is still
two years ahead; it is out of the question for him to marry.
Very well, Toni will find a father for her child; she is her lover's
property, and that property must be protected. And she will
wait willingly, careless of the years, for the distant day of triumph and redemption. All other ideas and ideals drop out of
her mind; she becomes an automaton moved by the one impulse, the one yearning. She marries one Wiegand, a decayed
innkeeper; he, poor fool, accepts the parentage of her child.
Her father, rich and unsuspicious, buys them a likely inn; they
begin to make money. And then begins the second chapter
of Toni's sacrifice. She robs her husband systematically and
steadily; she takes commissions on all his goods; she becomes
the houri of his bar, that trade may grow and pickings increase.
Mark by mark, the money goes to Robert. It sees him through
the university; it gives him his year or two in the hospitals; it
buys him a practice; it feeds and clothes him, and his mother
with him. The months and years pass endlessly—a young doctor's progress is slow. But finally the great day approaches.
Soon Robert will be ready for his wife. But Wiegand—what of
him? Toni thinks of half a dozen plans. The notion of poison-
ing him gradually formulates itself. Not a touch of horror stays
her. She is, by this time, beyond all the common moralities—a
monomaniac with no thought for anything save her great purpose. But an accident saves Wiegand. Toni, too elaborate in
her plans, poisons herself by mischance, and comes near dying.
Very well, if not poison, then some more subtle craft. She puts
a barmaid into Wiegand's path; she manages the whole affair;
before long she sees her victim safely enmeshed. A divorce follows; the inn is sold; her father's death makes her suddenly
rich—at last she is off to greet her lord!

   That meeting! . . . Toni waits in the little flat that she has rented in the city—she and her child, the child of Robert. Robert is to come at noon; as the slow moments pass the burden of her happiness seems too great to bear. And then suddenly the ecstatic climax—the ring at the door. . . . "A gentleman entered. A strange gentleman. Wholly strange. Had she met him on the street she would not have known him. He had grown old—forty, fifty, a hundred years. Yet his real age could not be over twenty-eight! . . . He had grown fat. He carried a little paunch around with him, round and comfortable. And the honorable scars gleamed in round, red cheeks. His eyes seemed small and receding. . . . And when he said: 'Here I am at last,' it was no longer the old voice, clear and a little resonant, which had echoed and reëchoed in her spiritual ear. He gurgled as though he had swallowed dumplings." An oaf without and an oaf within! Toni is for splendors, triumphs, the life; Robert has "settled down." His remote village, hard by the Russian border, is to his liking; he has made comfortable friends there; he is building up a practice. He is, of course, a man of honor. He will marry Toni—willingly and with gratitude, even with genuine affection. Going further, he will pay back to her every cent that ever came from Wiegand's till. He has kept a strict account. Here it is, in a little blue notebook— seven years of entries. As he reads them aloud the events of those seven years unroll themselves before Toni and every mark brings up its picture—stolen cash and trinkets, savings in railroad fares and food, commissions upon furniture and wines, profits of champagne debauches with the county councilor, sharp trading in milk and eggs, "suspense and longing, an inextricable web of falsification and trickery, of terror and lying without end. The memory of no guilt is spared her." Robert is an honest, an honorable man. He has kept a strict account; the money is waiting in bank. What is more, he will make all necessary confessions. He has not, perhaps, kept to the letter of fidelity. There was a waitress in Berlin; there was a nurse at the surgical clinic; there is even now a Lithuanian servant girl at his bachelor quarters. The last named, of course, will be sent away forthwith. Robert is a man of honor, a man sensitive to every requirement of the punctilio, a gentleman. He will order the announcement cards, consult a clergyman— and not forget to get rid of the Lithuanian and air the

house. . . . Poor Toni stares at him as he departs. "Will he
come back soon?" asks the child. "I scarcely think so," she answers. . . . "That night she broke the purpose of her life, the
purpose that had become interwoven with a thousand others,
and when the morning came she wrote a letter of farewell to
the beloved of her youth."

A short story of rare and excellent quality. A short story—
oh, miracle!—worth reading twice. It is not so much that its
motive is new—that motive, indeed, has appeared in fiction
many times, though usually with the man as the protagonist—
as that its workmanship is superb. Sudermann here shows that,
for all his failings elsewhere, he knows superlatively how to
write. His act divisions are exactly right; his *scènes à faire* are
magnificently managed; he has got into the thing that rhyth-
mic ebb and flow of emotion which makes for great drama.
And in most of the other stories in this book you will find
much the same skill. No other, perhaps, is quite so good as
"The Purpose," but at least one of them, "The Song of
Death," is not far behind. Here we have the tragedy of a
woman brought up rigorously, puritanically, stupidly, who discovers, just as it is too late, that love may be a wild dance, an
ecstasy, an orgy. I can imagine no more grotesquely pathetic
scene than that which shows this drab preacher's wife watching by her husband's death-bed—while through the door
comes the sound of amorous delirium from the next room.
And then there is a strangely moving Christmas story, "Merry
Folk"—pathos with the hard iron in it. And there are "Autumn" and "The Indian Lily," elegies to lost youth—the first
of them almost a fit complement to Joseph Conrad's great
paean to youth triumphant. Altogether, a collection of short
stories of the very first rank. Write off "Das hohe Lied," "Frau
Sorge" and all the plays: a Sudermann remains who must be
put in a high and honorable place, and will be remembered.

IX.

George Ade

W HEN, after the Japs and their vassals conquer us and put us to the sword, and the republic descends into hell, some literary don of Oxford or Mittel-Europa proceeds to the predestined autopsy upon our Complete Works, one of the things he will surely notice, reviewing our literary history, is the curious persistence with which the dons native to the land have overlooked its emerging men of letters. I mean, of course, its genuine men of letters, its salient and truly original men, its men of intrinsic and unmistakable distinction. The fourth-raters have fared well enough, God knows. Go back to any standard literature book of ten, or twenty, or thirty, or fifty years ago, and you will be amazed by its praise of shoddy mediocrities, long since fly-blown and forgotten. George William Curtis, now seldom heard of at all, save perhaps in the reminiscences of senile publishers, was treated in his day with all the deference due to a prince of the blood. Artemus Ward, Petroleum V. Nasby and half a dozen other such hollow buffoons were ranked with Mark Twain, and even above him. Frank R. Stockton, for thirty years, was the delight of all right-thinking reviewers. Richard Henry Stoddard and Edmund Clarence Stedman were eminent personages, both as critics and as poets. And Donald G. Mitchell, to make an end of dull names, bulked so grandly in the academic eye that he was snatched from his tear-jugs and his tea-pots to become a charter member of the National Institute of Arts and Letters, and actually died a member of the American Academy!

Meanwhile, three of the five indubitably first-rate artists that America has produced went quite without orthodox recognition at home until either foreign enthusiasm or domestic clamor from below forced them into a belated and grudging sort of notice. I need not say that I allude to Poe, Whitman and Mark Twain. If it ever occurred to any American critic of position, during Poe's lifetime, that he was a greater man than either Cooper or Irving, then I have been unable to find any trace of the fact in the critical literature of the time. The truth is that he was looked upon as a facile and somewhat dubious journalist, too cocksure by half, and not a man to be encouraged. Lowell praised him in 1845 and at the same time denounced the current over-praise of lesser men, but later on this encomium was diluted with very important reservations, and there the matter stood until Baudelaire discovered the poet and his belated fame came winging home. Whitman, as every one knows, fared even worse. Emerson first hailed him and then turned tail upon him, eager to avoid any share in his ill-repute among blockheads. No other critic of any influence gave him help. He was carried through his dark days of poverty and persecution by a few private enthusiasts, none of them with the ear of the public, and in the end it was Frenchmen and Englishmen who lifted him into the light. Imagine a Harvard professor lecturing upon him in 1865! As for Mark Twain, the story of his first fifteen years has been admirably told by Prof. Dr. William Lyon Phelps, of Yale. The dons were unanimously against him. Some sneered at him as a feeble mountebank; others refused to discuss him at all; not one harbored the slightest suspicion that he was a man of genius, or even one leg of a man of genius. Phelps makes merry over this academic attempt to dispose of Mark by putting him into Coventry—and himself joins the sanctimonious brethren who essay the same enterprise against Dreiser. . . .

I come by this route to George Ade—who perhaps fails to fit into the argument doubly, for on the one hand he is certainly not a literary artist of the first rank, and on the other hand he has long enjoyed a meed of appreciation and even of honor, for the National Institute of Arts and Letters elevated him to its gilt-edged purple in its first days, and he is still on its roll of men of "notable achievement in art, music or literature," along with Robert W. Chambers, Henry Sydnor Harrison, Oliver Herford, E. S. Martin and E. W. Townsend, author of "Chimmie Fadden." Nevertheless, he does not fall too far outside, after all, for if he is not of the first rank then he surely deserves a respectable place in the second rank, and if the National Institute broke the spell by admitting him then it was probably on the theory that he was a second Chambers or Herford, or maybe even a second Martin or Townsend. As for the text-book dons, they hold resolutely to the doctrine that he scarcely exists, and is not worth noticing at all. For example, there is Prof. Fred Lewis Pattee, author of "A History of American Literature Since 1870." Prof. Pattee notices Chambers, Marion Harland, Herford, Townsend, Amélie Rives, R. K. Munkittrick and many other such ornaments of the national letters, and even has polite bows for Gelett Burgess, Carolyn Wells and John Kendrick Bangs, but the name of Ade is missing from his index, as is that of Dreiser. So with the other pedagogues. They are unanimously shy of Ade in their horn-books for sophomores, and they are gingery in their praise of him in their innumerable review articles. He is commended, when at all, much as the late Joseph Jefferson used to be commended—that is, to the accompaniment of reminders that even a clown is one of God's creatures, and may have the heart of a Christian under his motley. The most laudatory thing ever said of him by any critic of the apostolic succession, so far as I can discover, is that he is clean—that he does not import the lewd buffooneries of the barroom, the smoking-car and the wedding reception into his books. . . .

But what are the facts? The facts are that Ade is one of the few genuinely original literary craftsmen now in practice among us; that he comes nearer to making literature, when he has full steam up, than any save a scant half-dozen of our current novelists, and that the whole body of his work, both in books and for the stage, is as thoroughly American, in cut and color, in tang and savor, in structure and point of view, as the work of Howells, E. W. Howe or Mark Twain. No single American novel that I can think of shows half the sense of nationality, the keen feeling for national prejudice and peculiarity, the sharp and pervasive Americanism of such Adean fables as "The Good Fairy of the Eighth Ward and the Dollar Excursion of the Steam-Fitters," "The Mandolin Players and the Willing Performer," and "The Adult Girl Who Got Busy Before They Could Ring the Bell on Her." Here, amid a humor so grotesque that it almost tortures the midriff, there is a startlingly vivid and accurate evocation of the American scene. Here, under all the labored extravagance, there are brilliant flashlight pictures of the American people, and American ways of thinking, and the whole of American *Kultur*. Here the veritable Americano stands forth, lacking not a waggery, a superstition, a snuffle or a wen.

Ade himself, for all his story-teller's pretense of remoteness, is as absolutely American as any of his prairie-town traders and pushers, Shylocks and Dogberries, beaux and belles. No other writer of our generation, save perhaps Howe, is more unescapably national in his every gesture and trick of mind. He is as American as buckwheat cakes, or the Knights of Pythias, or the chautauqua, or Billy Sunday, or a bull by Dr. Wilson. He fairly reeks of the national Philistinism, the national respect for respectability, the national distrust of ideas. He is a marcher, one fancies, in parades; he joins movements, and movements against movements; he knows no language save his own; he regards a Roosevelt quite seriously and a Mozart or an Ibsen as a joke; one would not be surprised to hear that, until he went off to his fresh-water college, he slept in his underwear and read the *Epworth Herald*. But, like Dreiser, he is a peasant touched by the divine fire; somehow, a great instinctive artist got himself born out there on that lush Indiana farm. He has the rare faculty of seeing accurately, even when the thing seen is directly under his nose, and he has the still rarer faculty of recording vividly, of making the thing seen move with life. One often doubts a character in a novel, even in a good novel, but who ever doubted Gus in "The Two Mandolin Players," or Mae in "Sister Mae," or, to pass from the fables, Payson in "Mr. Payson's Satirical Christmas"? Here, with strokes so crude and obvious that they seem to be laid on with a broom, Ade achieves what O. Henry, with all his ingenuity, always failed to achieve: he fills his bizarre tales with human beings. There is never any artfulness on the surface. The tale itself is never novel, or complex; it never surprises; often it is downright banal. But underneath there is an artfulness infinitely well wrought, and that is the artfulness of a story-teller who dredges his story out of his people, swiftly and skillfully, and does not squeeze his people into his story, laboriously and unconvincingly.

Needless to say, a moralist stands behind the comedian. He would teach; he even grows indignant. Roaring like a yokel at a burlesque show over such wild and light-hearted jocosities as "Paducah's Favorite Comedians" and "Why 'Gondola' Was

Put Away," one turns with something of a start to such things as "Little Lutie," "The Honest Money Maker" and "The Corporation Director and the Mislaid Ambition." Up to a certain point it is all laughter, but after that there is a flash of the knife, a show of teeth. Here a national limitation often closes in upon the satirist. He cannot quite separate the unaccustomed from the abominable; he is unable to avoid rattling his Philistine trappings a bit proudly; he must prove that he, too, is a right-thinking American, a solid citizen and a patriot, unshaken in his lofty rectitude by such poisons as aristocracy, adultery, *hors d'œuvres* and the sonata form. But in other directions this thorough-going nationalism helps him rather than hinders him. It enables him, for one thing, to see into sentimentality, and to comprehend it and project it accurately. I know of no book which displays the mooniness of youth with more feeling and sympathy than "Artie," save it be Frank Norris' forgotten "Blix." In such fields Ade achieves a success that is rare and indubitable. He makes the thing charming and he makes it plain.

But all these fables and other compositions of his are mere sketches, inconsiderable trifles, impromptus in bad English, easy to write and of no importance! Are they, indeed? Do not believe it for a moment. Fifteen or twenty years ago, when Ade was at the height of his celebrity as a newspaper Sganarelle, scores of hack comedians tried to imitate him—and all failed. I myself was of the number. I operated a so-called funny column in a daily newspaper, and like my colleagues near and far, I essayed to manufacture fables in slang. What miserable botches they were! How easy it was to imitate Ade's manner—and how impossible to imitate his matter! No; please don't get the notion that it is a simple thing to write such a fable as that of "The All-Night Seance and the Limit That Ceased to Be," or that of "The Preacher Who Flew His Kite, But Not Because He Wished to Do So," or that of "The Roystering Blades." Far from it! On the contrary, the only way you will ever accomplish the feat will be by first getting Ade's firm grasp upon American character, and his ability to think out a straightforward, simple, amusing story, and his alert feeling for contrast and climax, and his extraordinary talent for devising novel, vivid and unforgettable phrases. Those phrases of his sometimes wear the external vestments of a passing slang, but they are no more commonplace and vulgar at bottom than Gray's "mute, inglorious Milton" or the "somewheres East of Suez" of Kipling. They reduce an idea to a few pregnant syllables. They give the attention a fillip and light up a whole scene in a flash. They are the running evidences of an eye that sees clearly and of a mind that thinks shrewdly. They give distinction to the work of a man who has so well concealed a highly complex and efficient artistry that few have ever noticed it.

X.

The Butte Bashkirtseff

O F all the pseudo-rebels who have raised a tarletan black flag in These States, surely Mary MacLane is one of the most pathetic. When, at nineteen, she fluttered Vassar with "The Story of Mary MacLane," the truth about her was still left somewhat obscure; the charm of her flapperhood, so to speak, distracted attention from it, and so concealed it. But when, at thirty-five, she achieved "I, Mary MacLane," it emerged crystal-clear; she had learned to describe her malady accurately, though she still wondered, a bit wistfully, just what it was. And that malady? That truth? Simply that a Scotch Presbyterian with a soaring soul is as cruelly beset as a wolf with fleas, a zebra with the botts. Let a spark of the divine fire spring to life in that arid corpse, and it must fight its way to flame through a drum fire of wet sponges. A humming bird immersed in *Kartoffelsuppe*. Walter Pater writing for the London *Daily Mail*. Lucullus traveling steerage. . . . A Puritan wooed and tortured by the leers of beauty, Mary MacLane in a moral republic, in a Presbyterian diocese, in Butte. . . .

I hope my figures of speech are not too abstruse. What I mean to say is simply this: that the secret of Mary MacLane is simply this: that the origin of all her inchoate naughtiness is simply this: that she is a Puritan who has heard the call of joy and is struggling against it damnably. Remember so much, and the whole of her wistful heresy becomes intelligible. On the one hand the loveliness of the world enchants her; on the other hand the fires of hell warn her. This tortuous conflict accounts for her whole bag of tricks; her timorous flirtations with the devil, her occasional outbreaks of finishing-school rebellion, her hurried protestations of virginity, above all her incurable Philistinism. One need not be told that she admires the late Major General Roosevelt and Mrs. Atherton, that she wallows in the poetry of Keats. One knows quite as well that her phonograph plays the "Peer Gynt" suite, and that she is charmed by the syllogisms of G. K. Chesterton. She is, in brief, an absolutely typical American of the transition stage between Christian Endeavor and civilization. There is in her a definite poison of ideas, an æsthetic impulse that will not down—but every time she yields to it she is halted and plucked back by qualms and doubts, by the dominant superstitions of her race and time, by the dead hand of her kirk-crazy Scotch forebears.

It is precisely this grisly touch upon her shoulder that stimulates her to those naïve explosions of scandalous confidence which make her what she is. If there were no sepulchral voice in her ear, warning her that it is the mark of a hussy to be kissed by a man with "iron-gray hair, a brow like Apollo and a jowl like Bill Sykes," she would not confess it and boast of it, as she does on page 121 of "I, Mary MacLane." If it were not a Presbyterian axiom that a lady who says "damn" is fit only to join the white slaves, she would not pen a defiant Damniad, as she does on pages 108, 109 and 110. And if it were not held universally in Butte that sex passion is the exclusive infirmity of the male, she would not blab out in meeting that—but here I get into forbidden waters and had better refer you to page 209. It is not the godless voluptuary who patronizes leg-shows and the cabaret; it is the Methodist deacon with unaccustomed vine-leaves in his hair. It is not genuine artists, serving beauty reverently and proudly, who herd in Greenwich Village and bawl for art; it is precisely a mob of Middle Western Baptists to whom the very idea of art is still novel, and intoxicating, and more than a little bawdy. And to make an end, it is not co-cottes who read the highly-spiced magazines which burden all the book-stalls; it is sedentary married women who, while faithful to their depressing husbands in the flesh, yet allow their imaginations to play furtively upon the charms of theo-retical intrigues with such pretty fellows as Francis X. Bushman, Enrico Caruso and Vincent Astor.

An understanding of this plain fact not only explains the MacLane and her gingery carnalities of the *chair*; it also explains a good part of latter-day American literature. That literature is the self-expression of a people who have got only half way up the ladder leading from moral slavery to intellectual freedom. At every step there is a warning tug, a protest from below. Sometimes the climber docilely drops back; sometimes he emits a petulant defiance and reaches boldly for the next round. It is this occasional defiance which accounts for the periodical efflorescence of mere school-boy naughtiness in the midst of our oleaginous virtue—for the shouldering out of the *Ladies' Home Journal* by magazines of adultery all compact—for the provocative baring of calf and scapula by women who regard it as immoral to take Benedictine with their coffee—for the peopling of Greenwich Village by oafs who think it a devilish adventure to victual in cellars, and read Krafft-Ebing, and stare at the corset-scarred nakedness of decadent cloak-models.

I have said that the climber is but half way up the ladder. I wish I could add that he is moving ahead, but the truth is that he is probably quite stationary. We have our spasms of revolt, our flarings up of peekaboo waists, free love and "art," but a mighty backwash of piety fetches each and every one of them soon or late. A mongrel and inferior people, incapable of any spiritual aspiration above that of second-rate English colonials, we seek refuge inevitably in the one sort of superiority that the lower castes of men can authentically boast, to wit, superiority in docility, in credulity, in resignation, in morals. We are the most moral race in the world; there is not another that we do not look down upon in that department; our confessed aim and destiny as a nation is to inoculate them all with our incomparable rectitude. In the last analysis, all ideas are judged among us by moral standards; moral values are our only permanent tests of worth, whether in the arts, in politics, in philosophy or in life itself. Even the instincts of man, so intrinsically immoral, so innocent, are fitted with moral false-faces. That bedevilment by sex ideas which punishes continence, so abhorrent to nature, is converted into a moral frenzy, pathological in the end. The impulse to cavort and kick up one's legs, so healthy, so universal, is hedged in by incomprehensible taboos; it becomes stealthy, dirty, degrading. The desire to create and linger over beauty, the sign and touchstone of man's rise above the brute, is held down by doubts and hesitations; when it breaks through it must do so by orgy and explosion, half ludicrous and half pathetic. Our function, we choose to believe, is to teach and inspire the world. We are wrong. Our function is to amuse the world. We are the Bryan, the Henry Ford, the Billy Sunday among the nations. . . .

XI.

Six Members of the Institute

I

The Boudoir Balzac

THE late Percival Pollard was, in my nonage, one of my enthusiasms, and, later on, one of my friends. How, as a youngster, I used to lie in wait for the *Criterion* every week, and devour Pollard, Huneker, Meltzer and Vance Thompson! That was in the glorious middle nineties and savory pots were brewing. Scarcely a week went by without a new magazine of some unearthly *Tendenz* or other appearing on the stands; scarcely a month failed to bring forth its new genius. Pollard was up to his hips in the movement. He had a hand for every débutante. He knew everything that was going on. Polyglot, catholic, generous, alert, persuasive, forever oscillating between New York and Paris, London and Berlin, he probably covered a greater territory in the one art of letters than Huneker covered in all seven. He worked so hard as introducer of intellectual ambassadors, in fact, that he never had time to write his own books. One very brilliant volume, "Masks and Minstrels of New Germany," adequately represents him. The rest of his criticism, clumsily dragged from the files of the *Criterion* and *Town Topics*, is thrown together ineptly in "Their Day in Court." Death sneaked upon him from behind; he was gone before he could get his affairs in order. I shall never forget his funeral—no doubt a fit finish for a critic. Not one of the authors he had whooped and battled for was present—not one, that is, save old Ambrose Bierce. Bierce came in an elegant plug-hat and told me some curious anecdotes on the way to the crematory, chiefly of morgues, dissecting-rooms and lonely church-yards: he was the most gruesome of men. A week later, on a dark, sleety Christmas morning, I returned to the crematory, got the ashes, and shipped them West. Pollard awaits the Second Coming of his Redeemer in Iowa, hard by the birthplace of Prof. Dr. Stuart P. Sherman. Well, let us not repine. Huneker lives in Flatbush and was born in Philadelphia.

Cabell is a citizen of Richmond, Va. Willa Sibert Cather was once one of the editors of *McClure's Magazine*. Dreiser, before his annunciation, edited dime novels for Street & Smith, and will be attended by a Methodist friar, I daresay, on the gallows. . . .

Pollard, as I say, was a man I respected. He knew a great deal. Half English, half German and wholly cosmopolitan, he brought valuable knowledges and enthusiasms to the developing American literature of his time. Moreover, I had affection for him as well as respect, for he was a capital companion at the *Biertisch* and was never too busy to waste a lecture on my lone ear—say on Otto Julius Bierbaum (one of his friends), or Anatole France, or the technic of the novel, or the scoundrelism of publishers. It thus pains me to violate his tomb—but let his shade forgive me as it hopes to be forgiven! For it was Pollard, I believe, who set going the doctrine that Robert W. Chambers is a man of talent—a bit too commercial, perhaps, but still fundamentally a man of talent. You will find it argued at length in "Their Day in Court." There Pollard called the roll of the "promising young men" of the time, *circa* 1908. They were Winston Churchill, David Graham Phillips—and Chambers! Alas, for all prophets and their prognostications! Phillips, with occasional reversions to honest work, devoted most of his later days to sensational serials for the train-boy magazines, and when he died his desk turned out to be full of them, and they kept dribbling along for three or four years. Churchill, seduced by the uplift, has become an evangelist and a bore—a worse case, even, than that of H. G. Wells. And Chambers? Let the New York *Times* answer. Here, in all sobriety, is its description of the heroine of "The Moonlit Way," one of his latest pieces:

She is a lovely and fascinating dancer who, before the war, held the attention of all Europe and incited a great many men who had nothing better to do to fall in love with her. She bursts upon the astonished gaze of several of the important characters of the story when she dashes into the ballroom of the German Embassy *standing upon a bridled ostrich*, which she compels to dance and go through its paces at her command. She is dressed, Mr. Chambers assures us, *in nothing but the skin of her virtuous youth, modified slightly by a yashmak and a zone of blue jewels about her hips and waist.*

The italics are mine. I wonder what poor Pollard would think of it. He saw the shoddiness in Chambers, the leaning toward "profitable pot-boiling," but he saw, too, a fundamental earnestness and a high degree of skill. What has become of these things? Are they visible, even as ghosts, in the preposterous serials that engaud the magazines of Mr. Hearst, and then load the department-stores as books? Were they, in fact, ever there at all? Did Pollard observe them, or did he merely imagine them? I am inclined to think that he merely imagined them —that his delight in what he described as "many admirable tricks" led him into a fatuity that he now has an eternity to regret. Chambers grows sillier and sillier, emptier and emptier, worse and worse. But was he ever more than a fifth-rater? I doubt it. Let us go back half a dozen years, to the days before the war forced the pot-boiler down into utter imbecility. I choose, at random, "The Gay Rebellion." Here is a specimen of the dialogue:

"It startled me. How did I know what it might have been? It might have been a bear—or a cow."

"You talk," said Sayre angrily, "like William Dean Howells! Haven't you *any* romance in you?"

"Not what *you* call romance. Pass the flapjacks." Sayre passed them.

"My attention," he said, "instantly became riveted upon the bushes. I strove to pierce them with a piercing glance. Suddenly—"

"Sure! 'Suddenly' always comes next."

"Suddenly . . . the leaves were stealthily parted, and—"

"A naked savage in full war paint—"

"Naked nothing! a young girl in—a perfectly fitting gown stepped noiselessly out."

"Out of what, you gink?"

"The bushes, dammit! . . . She looked at me; I gazed at her. Somehow—"

"In plainer terms, she gave you the eye. What?"

"That's a peculiarly coarse observation."

"Then tell it in your own way."

"I will. The sunlight fell softly upon the trees of the ancient wood."

"*Woodn't* that bark you!"

And so on, and so on, for page after page. Can you imagine more idiotic stuff—"pierce and piercing," "you gink," "she gave you the eye," "*woodn't* that bark you?" One is reminded of horrible things—the repartees of gas-house comedians in vaudeville, the whimsical editorials in *Life*, the forbidding ghouleries of Irvin Cobb among jokes pale and clammy in death. . . . But let us, you may say, go back a bit further— back to the days of the *Chap-Book*. There was then, perhaps, a far different Chambers—a fellow of sound talent and artistic self-respect, well deserving the confidence and encouragement of Pollard. Was there, indeed? If you think so, go read "The King in Yellow," *circa* 1895—if you can. I myself, full of hope, have tried it. In it I have found drivel almost as dull as that, say, in "Ailsa Page."

2

A Stranger on Parnassus

The case of Hamlin Garland belongs to pathos in the grand manner, as you will discover on reading his autobiography, "A Son of the Middle Border." What ails him is a vision of beauty, a seductive strain of bawdy music over the hills. He is a sort of male Mary MacLane, but without either Mary's capacity for picturesque blasphemy or her skill at plain English. The vision, in his youth, tore him from his prairie plow and set him to clawing the anthills at the foot of Parnassus. He became an elocutionist—what, in modern times, would be called a chautauquan. He aspired to write for the *Atlantic Monthly*. He fell under the spell of the Boston *aluminados* of 1885, which is as if one were to take fire from a June-bug. Finally, after embracing the Single Tax, he achieved a couple of depressing storybooks, earnest, honest and full of indignation.

American criticism, which always mistakes a poignant document for æsthetic form and organization, greeted these moral volumes as works of art, and so Garland found himself an accepted artist and has made shift to be an artist ever since. No more grotesque miscasting of a diligent and worthy man is recorded in profane history. He has no more feeling for the intrinsic dignity of beauty, no more comprehension of it as a thing in itself, than a policeman. He is, and always has been, a moralist endeavoring ineptly to translate his messianic passion into æsthetic terms, and always failing. "A Son of the Middle Border," undoubtedly the best of all his books, projects his failure brilliantly. It is, in substance, a document of considerable value—a naïve and often highly illuminating contribution to the history of the American peasantry. It is, in form, a thoroughly third-rate piece of writing—amateurish, flat, banal, repellent. Garland gets facts into it; he gets the relentless sincerity of the rustic Puritan; he gets a sort of evangelical passion. But he doesn't get any charm. He doesn't get any beauty.

In such a career, as in such a book, there is something profoundly pathetic. One follows the progress of the man with a constant sense that he is steering by faulty compasses, that fate is leading him into paths too steep and rocky—nay, too dark and lovely—for him. An awareness of beauty is there, and a wistful desire to embrace it, but the confident gusto of the artist is always lacking. What one encounters in its place is the enthusiasm of the pedagogue, the desire to yank the world up to the soaring Methodist level, the hot yearning to displace old ideas with new ideas, and usually much worse ideas, for example, the Single Tax and spook-chasing. The natural goal of the man was the evangelical stump. He was led astray when those Boston Brahmins of the last generation, enchanted by his sophomoric platitudes about Shakespeare, set him up as a critic of the arts, and then as an imaginative artist. He should have gone back to the saleratus belt, taken to the chautauquas, preached his foreordained perunas, got himself into Congress, and so helped to save the republic from the demons that beset it. What a gladiator he would have made against the Plunderbund, the White Slave Traffic, the Rum Demon, the Kaiser! What a rival to the Hon. Claude Kitchin, the Rev. Dr. Newell Dwight Hillis!

His worst work, I daresay, is in some of his fiction—for example, in "The Forester's Daughter." But my own favorite among his books is "The Shadow World," a record of his communings with the gaseous precipitates of the departed. He takes great pains at the start to assure us that he is a man of alert intelligence and without prejudices or superstitions. He has no patience, it appears, with those idiots who swallow the buffooneries of spiritualist mediums too greedily. For him the scientific method—the method which examines all evidence cynically and keeps on doubting until the accumulated proof, piled mountain-high, sweeps down in an overwhelming avalanche. . . . Thus he proceeds to the haunted chamber and begins his dalliance with the banshees. They touch him with clammy, spectral hands; they wring music for him out of locked pianos; they throw heavy tables about the room; they give him messages from the golden shore and make him the butt of their coarse, transcendental humor. Through it all he sits tightly and solemnly, his mind open and his verdict up his sleeve. He is belligerently agnostic, and calls attention to it proudly. . . . Then, in the end, he gives himself away. One of his fellow "scientists," more frankly credulous, expresses the belief that real scientists will soon prove the existence of spooks. "I hope they will," says the agnostic Mr. Garland. . . .

Well, let us not laugh. The believing mind is a curious thing. It must absorb its endless rations of balderdash, or perish. . . . "A Son of the Middle Border" is less amusing, but a good deal more respectable. It is an honest book. There is some bragging in it, of course, but not too much. It tells an interesting story. It radiates hard effort and earnest purpose. . . . But what a devastating exposure of a member of the American Academy of Arts and Letters!

3
A Merchant of Mush

Henry Sydnor Harrison is thoroughly American to this extent: that his work is a bad imitation of something English. Find me a second-rate American in any of the arts and I'll find you his master and prototype among third, fourth or fifth-rate Englishmen. In the present case the model is obviously W. J. Locke. But between master and disciple there is a great gap. Locke, at his high points, is a man of very palpable merit. He has humor. He has ingenuity. He has a keen eye for the pathos that so often lies in the absurd. I can discover no sign of any of these things in Harrison's 100,000 word Christmas cards. They are simply sentimental bosh—huge gum-drops for fat women to snuffle over. Locke's grotesque and often extremely amusing characters are missing; in place of them there are the heroic cripples, silent lovers, maudlin war veterans and angelic grandams of the old-time Sunday-school books. The people of "V. V.'s Eyes" are preposterous and the thesis is too silly to be stated in plain words. No sane person would believe it if it were put into an affidavit. "Queed" is simply Locke diluted with vast drafts from "Laddie" and "Pollyanna." Queed, himself, long before the end, becomes a marionette without a toe on the ground; his Charlotte is incredible from the start. "Angela's Business" touches the bottom of the tear-jug; it would be impossible to imagine a more vapid story. Harrison, in fact, grows more mawkish book by book. He is touched, I should say, by the delusion that he has a mission to make life sweeter, to preach the Finer Things, to radiate Gladness. What! More Gladness? Another volt or two, and all civilized adults will join the Italians and Jugo-Slavs in their headlong hegira. A few more amperes, and the land will be abandoned to the Jews, the ex-Confederates and the Bolsheviki.

4

The Last of the Victorians

If William Allen White lives as long as Tennyson, and does not reform, our grandchildren will see the Victorian era gasping out its last breath in 1951. And eighty-three is no great age in Kansas, where sin is unknown. It may be, in fact, 1960, or even 1970, before the world hears the last of Honest Poverty, Chaste Affection and Manly Tears. For so long as White holds a pen these ancient sweets will be on sale at the department-store book-counters, and they will grow sweeter and sweeter, I daresay, as he works them over and over. In his very first book of fiction there was a flavor of chewing-gum and marshmallows. In "A Certain Rich Man" the intelligent palate detected saccharine. In "In the Heart of a Fool," his latest, the thing is carried a step further. If you are a forward-looker and a right-thinker, if you believe that God is in His heaven and all is for the best, if you yearn to uplift and like to sob, then the volume will probably affect you, in the incomparable phrase of Clayton Hamilton, like "the music of a million Easter-lilies leaping from the grave and laughing with a silver singing." But if you are a carnal fellow, as I am, with a stomach ruined by alcohol, it will gag you.

When I say that White is a Victorian I do not allude, of course, to the Victorianism of Thackeray and Tennyson, but to that of Felicia Hemens, of Samuel Smiles and of Dickens at his most maudlin. Perhaps an even closer relative is to be found in "The Duchess." White, like "The Duchess" is absolutely humorless, and, when he begins laying on the mayonnaise, absolutely shameless. I daresay the same sort of reader admires both: the high-school girl first seized by amorous tremors, the obese multipara in her greasy kimono, the remote and weepful farm-wife. But here a doubt intrudes itself: is it possible to imagine a woman sentimental enough to survive "In the Heart of a Fool"? I am constrained to question it. In women, once they get beyond adolescence, there is always a saving touch of irony; the life they lead infallibly makes cynics of them, though sometimes they don't know it. Observe the books they write—chiefly sardonic stuff, with heroes who are fools. Even their "glad" books, enormously successful among other women, stop far short of the sentimentality put between covers by men—for example, the aforesaid Harrison, Harold Bell Wright and the present White. Nay, it is the male sex that snuffles most and is easiest touched, particularly in America. The American man is forever falling a victim to his tender feelings. It was by that route that the collectors for the Y.M.C.A. reached him; it is thus that he is bagged incessantly by political tear-squeezers; it is precisely his softness that makes him the slave of his women-folk. What White gives him is exactly the sort of mush that is on tap in the chautauquas. "In the Heart of a Fool," like "A Certain Rich Man" is aimed deliberately and with the utmost accuracy at the delicate gizzard of the small-town yokel, the small-town yokel *male*, the horrible end-product of fifty years of Christian Endeavor, the little red school-house and the direct primary.

The White formula is simple to the verge of austerity. It is, in essence, no more than a dramatization of all the current political and sociological rumble-bumble, by Roosevelt out of Coxey's Army, with music by the choir of the First Methodist Church. On the one side are the Hell Hounds of Plutocracy, the Money Demons, the Plunderbund, and their attendant Bosses, Strike Breakers, Seducers, Nietzscheans, Free Lovers, Atheists and Corrupt Journalists. On the other side are the great masses of the plain people, and their attendant Uplifters, Good Samaritans, Honest Workingmen, Faithful Husbands,

Inspired Dreamers and tin-horn Messiahs. These two armies join battle, the Bad against the Good, and for five hundred pages or more the Good get all the worst of it. Their jobs are taken away from them, their votes are bartered, their mortgages are foreclosed, their women are debauched, their savings are looted, their poor orphans are turned out to starve. A sad business, surely. One wallows in almost unendurable emotions. The tears gush. It is as affecting as a movie. Even the prose rises to a sort of gospel-tent chant, like that of a Baptist Savonarola, with every second sentence beginning with *and*, *but* or *for*. . . . But we are already near the end, and no escape is in sight. Can it be that White is stumped, like Mark Twain in his mediæval romance—that Virtue will succumb to the Interests? Do not fear! In the third from the last chapter Hen Jackson, the stage-hand, returns from the Dutchman's at the corner and throws on a rose spot-light, and then an amber, and then a violet, and then a blue. One by one the rays of Hope begin to shoot across the stage, Dr. Hamilton's Easter-lilies leap from their tomb, the *dramatis personæ* (all save the local J. Pierpont Morgan!) begin "laughing with a silver singing," and as the curtain falls the whole scene is bathed in luminiferous ether, and the professor breaks into "Onward, Christian Soldiers!" on the cabinet-organ, and there is a happy, comfortable sobbing, and an upward rolling of eyes, and a vast blowing of noses. In brief, the finish of a chautauqua lecture on "The Grand Future of America, or, The Glory of Service." In brief, slobber. . . .

It would be difficult to imagine more saccharine writing or a more mawkish and preposterous point of view. Life, as White sees it, is a purely moral phenomenon, like living pictures by the Epworth League. The virtuous are the downtrodden; the up and doing are all scoundrels. It pays to be poor and pious. Ambition is a serpent. One honest Knight of Pythias is worth ten thousand Rockefellers. The pastor is always right. So is the *Ladies' Home Journal.* The impulse that leads a young yokel of, say, twenty-two to seek marriage with a poor working-girl of, say, eighteen, is the most elevating, noble, honorable and godlike impulse native to the human consciousness. . . . Not the slightest sign of an apprehension of life as the gaudiest and most gorgeous of spectacles—not a trace of healthy delight in the eternal struggle for existence—not the faintest suggestion of Dreiser's great gusto or of Conrad's penetrating irony! Not even in the massive fact of death itself—and, like all the other Victorians, this one from the Kansas steppes is given to whole-sale massacres—does he see anything mysterious, staggering, awful, inexplicable, but only an excuse for a sentimental orgy.

Alas, what would you? It is ghastly drivel, to be sure, but isn't it, after all, thoroughly American? I have an uneasy suspicion that it is—that "In the Heart of a Fool" is, at bottom, a vastly more American book than anything that James Branch Cabell has done, or Vincent O'Sullivan, or Edith Wharton, or even Howells. It springs from the heart of the land. It is the æsthetic echo of thousands of movements, of hundreds of thousands of sentimental crusades, of millions of ecstatic gospel-meetings. This is what the authentic American public, unpolluted by intelligence, wants. And this is one of the reasons why the English sniff whenever they look our way. . . .

But has White no merit? He has. He is an honest and a re-spectable man. He is a patriot. He trusts God. He venerates what is left of the Constitution. He once wrote a capital editorial, "What's the Matter With Kansas?" He has the knack, when his tears are turned off, of writing a clear and graceful English. . . .

5
A Bad Novelist

As I have said, it is not the artistic merit and dignity of a novel, but often simply its content as document, that makes for its success in the United States. The criterion of truth applied to it is not the criterion of an artist, but that of a newspaper editorial writer; the question is not, Is it in accord with the profoundest impulses and motives of humanity? but Is it in accord with the current pishposh? This accounts for the huge popularity of such confections as Upton Sinclair's "The Jungle" and Blasco Ibáñez's "The Four Horsemen of the Apocalypse." Neither had much value as a work of art—at all events, neither was perceptibly superior to many contemporary novels that made no stir at all—but each had the advantage of reënforcing an emotion already aroused, of falling into step with the procession of the moment. Had there been no fever of muck-raking and trust busting in 1906, "The Jungle" would have died the death in the columns of the *Appeal to Reason*, un-heard of by the populace in general. And had the United States been engaged against France instead of for France in 1918, there would have been no argument in the literary week-lies that Blasco was a novelist of the first rank and his story a masterpiece comparable to "Germinal."

Sinclair was made by "The Jungle" and has been trying his hardest to unmake himself ever since. Another of the same sort is Ernest Poole, author of "The Harbor." "The Harbor," judged by any intelligible æsthetic standard, was a bad novel. Its transactions were forced and unconvincing; its central char-acter was shadowy and often incomprehensible; the manner of its writing was quite without distinction. But it happened to be printed at a time when the chief ideas in it had a great deal of popularity—when its vague grappling with insoluble sociolog-ical problems was the sport of all the weeklies and of half the more sober newspapers—when a nebulous, highfalutin Bol-shevism was in the air—and so it excited interest and took on an aspect of profundity. That its discussion of those problems was superficial, that it said nothing new and got nowhere—all this was not an influence against its success, but an influence in favor of its success, for the sort of mind that fed upon the neb-ulous, professor-made politics and sociology of 1915 was the sort of mind that is chronically avid of half-truths and as chronically suspicious of forthright thinking. This has been demonstrated since that time by its easy *volte face* in the pres-ence of emotion. The very ideas that Poole's vapid hero toyed with in 1915, to the delight of the novel-reading *intelligentsia*, would have damned the book as a pamphlet for the I.W.W., or even, perhaps, as German propaganda, three years later. But meanwhile, it had been forgotten, as novels are always forgot-ten, and all that remained of it was a general impression that Poole, in some way or other, was a superior fellow and to be treated with respect.

His subsequent books have tried that theory severely. "The Family" was grounded upon one of the elemental tragedies which serve a novelist most safely—the dismay of an aging man as his children drift away from him. Here was a subject full of poignant drama, and what is more, drama simple enough to develop itself without making any great demand upon the invention. Poole burdened it with too much background, and then killed it altogether by making his characters wooden. It began with a high air; it creaked and wobbled at the close; the catastrophe was quite without effect. "His Second Wife" dropped several stories lower. It turned out, on inspection, to be no more than a moral tale, feeble, wishy-washy and irritating. Everything in it—about the corrupting effects of money-lust and display, about the swinishness of cabaret "society" in New York, about the American male's absurd slavery to his women—had been said before by such gifted Balzacs as Robert W. Chambers and Owen Johnson, and, what is more, far better said. The writing, in fact, exactly matched the theme. It was labored, artificial, dull. In the whole volume there was not a single original phrase. Once it was put down, not a scene remained in the memory, or a character. It was a cheap, a hollow and, in places, almost an idiotic book. . . .

At the time I write, this is the whole product of Poole as novelist: three novels, bad, worse, worst.

6
A Broadway Brandes

I have hitherto, in discussing White de Kansas, presented a fragile dahlia from the rhetorical garden of Clayton Hamilton, M.A. (Columbia). I now print the whole passage:

Whenever in a world-historic war the side of righteousness has triumphed, a great overflowing of art has followed soon upon the fact of victory. The noblest instincts of mankind—aroused in perilous moments fraught with intimations of mortality—have surged and soared, beneath the sunshine of a subsequent and dear-bought peace, into an immeasurable empyrean of heroic eloquence. Whenever right has circumvented might, Art has sprung alive into the world, with the music of a million Easter-lilies leaping from the grave and laughing with a silver singing.

With the highest respect for a *Magister Artium*, a pedagogue of Columbia University, a lecturer in Miss Spence's School and the Classical School for Girls, and a vice-president of the National Institute of Arts and Letters—Booh!

XII.

The Genealogy of Etiquette

BARRING sociology (which is yet, of course, scarcely a science at all, but rather a monkey-shine which happens to pay, like play-acting or theology), psychology is the youngest of the sciences, and hence chiefly guesswork, empiricism, hocus-pocus, poppycock. On the one hand, there are still enormous gaps in its data, so that the determination of its simplest principles remains difficult, not to say impossible; and, on the other hand, the very hollowness and nebulosity of it, particularly around its edges, encourages a horde of quacks to invade it, sophisticate it and make nonsense of it. Worse, this state of affairs tends to such confusion of effort and direction that the quack and the honest inquirer are often found in the same man. It is, indeed, a commonplace to encounter a professor who spends his days in the laborious accumulation of psychological statistics, sticking pins into babies and platting upon a chart the ebb and flow of their yells, and his nights chasing poltergeists and other such celestial fauna over the hurdles of a spiritualist's atelier, or gazing into a crystal in the privacy of his own chamber. The Binét test and the buncombe of mesmerism are alike the children of what we roughly denominate psychology, and perhaps of equal legitimacy. Even so ingenious and competent an investigator as Prof. Dr. Sigmund Freud, who has told us a lot that is of the first importance about the materials and machinery of thought, has also told us a lot that is trivial and dubious. The essential doctrines of Freudism, no doubt, come close to the truth, but many of Freud's remoter deductions are far more scandalous than sound, and many of the professed Freudians, both American and European, have grease-paint on their noses and bladders in their hands and are otherwise quite indistinguishable from evangelists and circus clowns.

In this condition of the science it is no wonder that we find it wasting its chief force upon problems that are petty and idle when they are not downright and palpably insoluble, and passing over problems that are of immediate concern to all of us, and that might be quite readily solved, or, at any rate, considerably illuminated, by an intelligent study of the data already available. After all, not many of us care a hoot whether Sir Oliver Lodge and the Indian chief Wok-a-wok-a-mok are happy in heaven, for not many of us have any hope or desire to meet them there. Nor are we greatly excited by the discovery that, of twenty-five freshmen who are hit with clubs, $17\frac{3}{4}$ will say "Ouch!" and $22\frac{1}{5}$ will say "Damn!"; nor by a table showing that 38.2 per centum of all men accused of homicide confess when locked up with the carcasses of their victims, including 23.4 per centum who are innocent; nor by plans and specifications, by Cagliostro out of Lucrezia Borgia, for teaching poor, God-forsaken school children to write before they can read and to multiply before they can add; nor by endless disputes between half-witted pundits as to the precise difference between perception and cognition; nor by even longer feuds, between pundits even crazier, over free will, the subconscious, the endoneurium, the functions of the corpora quadrigemina, and the meaning of dreams in which one is pursued by hyenas, process-servers or grass-widows.

Nay; we do not bubble with rejoicing when such fruits of psychological deep-down-diving and much-mud-upbringing researches are laid before us, for after all they do not offer us any nourishment, there is nothing in them to engage our teeth, they fail to make life more comprehensible, and hence more bearable. What we yearn to know something about is the process whereby the ideas of everyday are engendered in the skulls of those about us, to the end that we may pursue a straighter and a safer course through the muddle that is life. Why do the great majority of Presbyterians (and, for that matter, of Baptists, Episcopalians, and Swedenborgians as well) regard it as unlucky to meet a black cat and lucky to find a pin? What are the logical steps behind the theory that it is indecent to eat peas with a knife? By what process does an otherwise sane man arrive at the conclusion that he will go to hell unless he is baptized by total immersion in water? What causes men to be faithful to their wives: habit, fear, poverty, lack of imagination, lack of enterprise, stupidity, religion? What is the psychological basis of commercial morality? What is the true nature of the vague pooling of desires that Rousseau called the social contract? Why does an American regard it as scandalous to wear dress clothes at a funeral, and a Frenchman regard it as equally scandalous *not* to wear them? Why is it that men trust one another so readily, and women trust one another so seldom? Why are we all so greatly affected by statements that we know are not true?—e.g. in Lincoln's Gettysburg speech, the Declaration of Independence and the CIII Psalm. What is the origin of the so-called double standard of morality? Why are women forbidden to take off their hats in church? What is happiness? Intelligence? Sin? Courage? Virtue? Beauty?

All these are questions of interest and importance to all of us, for their solution would materially improve the accuracy of our outlook upon the world, and with it our mastery of our environment, but the psychologists, busily engaged in chasing their tails, leave them unanswered, and, in most cases, even unasked. The late William James, more acute than the general, saw how precious little was known about the psychological inwardness of religion, and to the illumination of this darkness he addressed himself in his book, "The Varieties of Religious Experience." But life being short and science long, he got little beyond the statement of the problem and the marshaling of the grosser evidence—and even at this business he allowed himself to be constantly interrupted by spooks, hobgoblins, seventh sons of seventh sons and other such characteristic pets of psychologists. In the same way one Gustav le Bon, a Frenchman, undertook a psychological study of the crowd mind— and then blew up. Add the investigations of Freud and his school, chiefly into abnormal states of mind, and those of Lombroso and his school, chiefly quackish and for the yellow journals, and the idle romancing of such inquirers as Prof. Dr. Thorstein Veblen, and you have exhausted the list of contributions to what may be called practical and everyday psychology. The rev. professors, I daresay, have been doing some useful plowing and planting. All of their meticulous pin-sticking and measuring and chart-making, in the course of time, will enable their successors to approach the real problems of mind with more assurance than is now possible, and perhaps help to their solution. But in the meantime the public and social utility of psychology remains very small, for it is still unable to differentiate accurately between the true and the false, or to give us any effective protection against the fallacies, superstitions, crazes and hysterias which rage in the world.

In this emergency it is not only permissible but even laudable for the amateur to sniff inquiringly through the psychological pasture, essaying modestly to uproot things that the myopic (or, perhaps more accurately, hypermetropic) professionals have overlooked. The late Friedrich Wilhelm Nietzsche did it often, and the usufructs were many curious and daring guesses, some of them probably close to accuracy, as to the genesis of this, that or the other common delusion of man— *i.e.*, the delusion that the law of the survival of the fittest may be repealed by an act of Congress. Into the same field several very interesting expeditions have been made by Dr. Elsie Clews Parsons, a lady once celebrated by Park Row for her invention of trial marriage—an invention, by the way, in which the Nietzsche aforesaid preceded her by at least a dozen years. The records of her researches are to be found in a brief series of books: "The Family," "The Old-Fashioned Woman" and "Fear and Conventionality." Apparently they have wrung relatively little esteem from the learned, for I seldom encounter a reference to them, and Dr. Parsons herself is denied the very modest reward of mention in "Who's Who in America." Nevertheless, they are extremely instructive books, particularly "Fear and Conventionality." I know of no other work, indeed, which offers a better array of observations upon that powerful complex of assumptions, prejudices, instinctive reactions, racial emotions and unbreakable vices of mind which enters so massively into the daily thinking of all of us. The author does not concern herself, as so many psychologists fall into the habit of doing, with thinking as a purely laboratory phenomenon, a process in vacuo. What she deals with is thinking as it is done by men and women in the real world—thinking that is only half intellectual, the other half being as automatic and unintelligent as swallowing, blinking the eye or falling in love.

The power of the complex that I have mentioned is usually very much underestimated, not only by psychologists, but also by all other persons who pretend to culture. We take pride in the fact that we are thinking animals, and like to believe that our thoughts are free, but the truth is that nine-tenths of them are rigidly conditioned by the babbling that goes on around us from birth, and that the business of considering this babbling objectively, separating the true in it from the false, is an intellectual feat of such stupendous difficulty that very few men are ever able to achieve it. The amazing slanging which went on between the English professors and the German professors in the early days of the late war showed how little even cold and academic men are really moved by the bald truth and how much by hot and unintelligible likes and dislikes. The patriotic hysteria of the war simply allowed these eminent pedagogues to say of one another openly and to loud applause what they would have been ashamed to say in times of greater amenity, and what most of them would have denied stoutly that they believed. Nevertheless, it is probably a fact that before there was a sign of war the average English professor, deep down in his heart, thought that any man who ate sauerkraut, and went to the opera in a sackcoat, and intrigued for the appellation of *Geheimrat*, and preferred German music to English poetry, and venerated Bismarck, and called his wife "Mutter," was a scoundrel. He did not say so aloud, and no doubt it would have offended him had you accused him of believing it, but he believed it all the same, and his belief in it gave a muddy, bilious color to his view of German metaphysics, German electrochemistry and the German chronology of Babylonian kings. And by the same token the average German professor, far down in the ghostly recesses of his hulk, held that any man who read the London *Times*, and ate salt fish at first breakfast, and drank tea of an afternoon, and spoke of Oxford as a university was a *Schafskopf*, a *Schuft* and possibly even a *Schweinehund*.

Nay, not one of us is a free agent. Not one of us actually thinks for himself, or in any orderly and scientific manner. The pressure of environment, of mass ideas, of the socialized intelligence, improperly so called, is too enormous to be withstood. No American, no matter how sharp his critical sense, can ever get away from the notion that democracy is, in some subtle and mysterious way, more conducive to human progress and more pleasing to a just God than any of the systems of government which stand opposed to it. In the privacy of his study he may observe very clearly that it exalts the facile and specious man above the really competent man, and from this observation he may draw the conclusion that its abandonment would be desirable, but once he emerges from his academic seclusion and resumes the rubbing of noses with his fellow-men, he will begin to be tortured by a sneaking feeling that such ideas are heretical and unmanly, and the next time the band begins to play he will thrill with the best of them—or the worst. The actual phenomenon, in truth, was copiously on display during the war. Having myself the character among my acquaintances of one holding the democratic theory in some doubt, I was often approached by gentlemen who told me, in great confidence, that they had been seized by the same tremors. Among them were journalists employed daily in demanding that democracy be forced upon the whole world, and army officers engaged, at least theoretically, in forcing it. All these men, in reflective moments, struggled with ifs and buts. But every one of them, in his public capacity as a good citizen, quickly went back to *thinking* as a good citizen was then expected to think, and even to a certain inflammatory ranting for what, behind the door, he gravely questioned. . . .

It is the business of Dr. Parsons, in "Fear and Conventionality," to prod into certain of the ideas which thus pour into every man's mind from the circumambient air, sweeping away, like some huge cataract, the feeble resistance that his own powers of ratiocination can offer. In particular, she devotes herself to an examination of those general ideas which condition the thought and action of man as a social being—those general ideas which govern his everyday attitude toward his fellow-men and his prevailing view of himself. In one direction they lay upon us the bonds of what we call etiquette, *i.e.*, the duty of considering the habits and feelings of those around us—and in another direction they throttle us with what we call morality—*i.e.*, the rules which protect the life and property of those around us. But, as Dr. Parsons shows, the boundary between etiquette and morality is very dimly drawn, and it is often impossible to say of a given action whether it is downright immoral or merely a breach of the punctilio. Even when the moral law is plainly running, considerations of mere amenity and politeness may still make themselves felt. Thus, as Dr. Parsons points out, there is even an etiquette of adultery.

"The *ami de la famille* vows not to kiss his mistress in her husband's house"—not in fear, but "as an expression of conjugal consideration," as a sign that he has not forgotten the thoughtfulness expected of a gentleman. And in this delicate field, as might be expected, the differences in racial attitudes are almost diametrical. The Englishman, surprising his wife with a lover, sues the rogue for damages and has public opinion behind him, but for an American to do it would be for him to lose caste at once and forever. The plain and only duty of the American is to open upon the fellow with artillery, hitting him if the scene is south of the Potomac and missing him if it is above.

I confess to an endless interest in such puzzling niceties, and to much curiosity as to their origins and meaning. Why do we Americans take off our hats when we meet a flapper on the street, and yet stand covered before a male of the highest eminence? A Continental would regard this last as boorish to the last degree; in greeting any equal or superior, male or female, actual or merely conventional, he lifts his head-piece. Why does it strike us as ludicrous to see a man in dress clothes before 6 P.M.? The Continental puts them on whenever he has a solemn visit to make, whether the hour be six or noon. Why do we regard it as indecent to tuck the napkin between the waistcoat buttons—or into the neck!—at meals? The Frenchman does it without thought of crime. So does the Italian. So does the German. All three are punctilious men—far more so, indeed, than we are. Why do we snicker at the man who wears a wedding ring? Most Continentals would stare askance at the husband who didn't. Why is it bad manners in Europe and America to ask a stranger his or her age, and a friendly attention in China? Why do we regard it as absurd to distinguish a woman by her husband's title—*e.g.*, Mrs. Judge Jones, Mrs. Professor Smith? In Teutonic and Scandinavian Europe the omission of the title would be looked upon as an affront.

Such fine distinctions, so ardently supported, raise many interesting questions, but the attempt to answer them quickly gets one bogged. Several years ago I ventured to lift a sad voice against a custom common in America: that of married men, in speaking of their wives, employing the full panoply of "Mrs. Brown." It was my contention—supported, I thought, by logical considerations of the loftiest order—that a husband, in speaking of his wife to his equals, should say "my wife"— that the more formal mode of designation should be reserved for inferiors and for strangers of undetermined position. This contention, somewhat to my surprise, was vigorously combated by various volunteer experts. At first they rested their case upon the mere authority of custom, forgetting that this custom was by no means universal. But finally one of them came forward with a more analytical and cogent defense—the defense, to wit, that "my wife" connoted proprietorship and was thus offensive to a wife's *amour propre*. But what of "my sister" and "my mother"? Surely it is nowhere the custom for a man, addressing an equal, to speak of his sister as "Miss Smith." . . . The discussion, however, came to nothing. It was impossible to carry it on logically. The essence of all such inquiries lies in the discovery that there is a force within the liver and lights of man that is infinitely more potent than logic. His reflections, perhaps, may take on intellectually recognizable forms, but they seldom lead to intellectually recognizable conclusions.

Nevertheless, Dr. Parsons offers something in her book that may conceivably help to a better understanding of them, and that is the doctrine that the strange persistence of these rubber-stamp ideas, often unintelligible and sometimes plainly absurd, is due to fear, and that this fear is the product of a very real danger. The safety of human society lies in the assumption that every individual composing it, in a given situation, will act in a manner hitherto approved as seemly. That is to say, he is expected to react to his environment according to a fixed pattern, not necessarily because that pattern is the best imaginable, but simply because it is determined and understood. If he fails to do so, if he reacts in a novel manner—conducive, perhaps, to his better advantage or to what he thinks is his better advantage—then he disappoints the expectation of those around him, and forces them to meet the new situation he has created by the exercise of independent thought. Such independent thought, to a good many men, is quite impossible, and to the overwhelming majority of men, extremely painful. "To all of us," says Dr. Parsons, "to the animal, to the savage and to the civilized being, few demands are as uncomfortable, . . .

disquieting or fearful, as the call to innovate. . . . Adaptations we all of us dislike or hate. We dodge or shirk them as best we may." And the man who compels us to make them against our wills we punish by withdrawing from him that understanding and friendliness which he, in turn, looks for and counts upon. In other words, we set him apart as one who is anti-social and not to be dealt with, and according as his rebellion has been small or great, we call him a boor or a criminal.

This distrust of the unknown, this fear of doing something unusual, is probably at the bottom of many ideas and institutions that are commonly credited to other motives. For example, monogamy. The orthodox explanation of monogamy is that it is a manifestation of the desire to have and to hold property—that the husband defends his solitary right to his wife, even at the cost of his own freedom, because she is the pearl among his chattels. But Dr. Parsons argues, and with a good deal of plausibility, that the real moving force, both in the husband and the wife, may be merely the force of habit, the antipathy to experiment and innovation. It is easier and safer to stick to the one wife than to risk adventures with another wife—and the immense social pressure that I have just described is all on the side of sticking. Moreover, the indulgence of a habit automatically strengthens its bonds. What we have done once or thought once, we are more apt than we were before to do and think again. Or, as the late Prof. William James put it, "the selection of a particular hole to live in, of a particular mate, . . . a particular anything, in short, out of a possible multitude . . . carries with it an insensibility to *other* opportunities and occasions—an insensibility which can only be described physiologically as an inhibition of new impulses by the habit of old ones already formed. The possession of homes and wives of our own makes us strangely insensible to the charms of other people. . . . The original impulse which got us homes, wives, . . . seems to exhaust itself in its first achievements and to leave no surplus energy for reacting on new cases." Thus the benedict looks no more on women (at least for a while), and the post-honeymoon bride, as the late David Graham Phillips once told us, neglects the bedizenments which got her a man.

In view of the popular or general character of most of the

taboos which put a brake upon personal liberty in thought and action—that is to say, in view of their enforcement by people in the mass, and not by definite specialists in conduct—it is quite natural to find that they are of extra force in democratic societies, for it is the distinguishing mark of democratic societies that they exalt the powers of the majority almost infinitely, and tend to deny the minority any rights whatever. Under a society dominated by a small caste the revolutionist in custom, despite the axiom to the contrary, has a relatively easy time of it, for the persons whose approval he seeks for his innovation are relatively few in number, and most of them are already habituated to more or less intelligible and independent thinking. But under a democracy he is opposed by a horde so vast that it is a practical impossibility for him, without complex and expensive machinery, to reach and convince all of its members, and even if he could reach them he would find most of them quite incapable of rising out of their accustomed grooves. They cannot understand innovations that are genuinely novel and they don't want to understand them; their one desire is to put them down. Even at this late day, with enlightenment raging through the republic like a pestilence, it would cost the average Southern or Middle Western Congressman his seat if he appeared among his constituents in spats, or wearing a wrist-watch. And if a Justice of the Supreme Court of the United States, however gigantic his learning and his juridic rectitude, were taken in crim. con. with the wife of a Senator, he would be destroyed instanter. And if, suddenly revolting against the democratic idea, he were to propose, however gingerly, its abandonment, he would be destroyed with the same dispatch.

But how, then, explain the fact that the populace is constantly ravished and set aflame by fresh brigades of moral, political and sociological revolutionists—that it is forever playing the eager victim to new mountebanks? The explanation lies in the simple circumstance that these performers upon the public midriff are always careful to ladle out nothing actually new, and hence nothing incomprehensible, alarming and accursed. What they offer is always the same old panacea with an extra-gaudy label—the tried, tasted and much-loved dose, the colic cure that mother used to make. Superficially, the United States seems to suffer from an endless and astounding neophilism; actually all its thinking is done within the boundaries of a very small group of political, economic and religious ideas, most of them unsound. For example, there is the fundamental idea of democracy—the idea that all political power should remain in the hands of the populace, that its exercise by superior men is intrinsically immoral. Out of this idea spring innumerable notions and crazes that are no more, at bottom, than restatements of it in sentimental terms: rotation in office, direct elections, the initiative and referendum, the recall, the popular primary, and so on. Again, there is the primary doctrine that the possession of great wealth is a crime—a doctrine half a religious heritage and half the product of mere mob envy. Out of it have come free silver, trust-busting, government ownership, muck-raking, Populism, Bleaseism, Progressivism, the milder forms of Socialism, the whole gasconade of "reform" politics. Yet again, there is the ineradicable peasant suspicion of the man who is having a better time in the world—a suspicion grounded, like the foregoing, partly upon undisguised envy and partly upon archaic and barbaric religious taboos. Out of it have come all the glittering pearls of the uplift, from Abolition to Prohibition, and from the crusade against horse-racing to the Mann Act. The whole political history of the United States is a history of these three ideas. There has never been an issue before the people that could not be translated into one or another of them. What is more, they have also colored the fundamental philosophical (and particularly epistemological) doctrines of the American people, and their moral theory, and even their foreign relations. The late war, very unpopular at the start, was "sold" to them, as the advertising phrase has it, by representing it as a campaign for the salvation of democracy, half religious and wholly altruistic. So represented to them, they embraced it; represented as the highly obscure and complex thing it actually was, it would have been beyond their comprehension, and hence abhorrent to them.

Outside this circle of their elemental convictions they are quite incapable of rational thought. One is not surprised to hear of Bismarck, a thorough royalist, discussing democracy with calm and fairness, but it would be unimaginable for the

American people, or for any other democratic people, to discuss royalism in the same manner: it would take a cataclysm to bring them to any such violation of their mental habits. When such a cataclysm occurs, they embrace the new ideas that are its fruits with the same adamantine firmness. One year before the French Revolution, disobedience to the king was unthinkable to the average Frenchman; only a few daringly immoral men cherished the notion. But one year *after* the fall of the Bastille, obedience to the king was equally unthinkable. The Russian Bolsheviki, whose doings have furnished a great deal of immensely interesting material to the student of popular psychology, put the principle into plain words. Once they were in the saddle, they decreed the abolition of the old imperial censorship and announced that speech would be free henceforth —but only so long as it kept within the bounds of the Bolshevist revelation! In other words, any citizen was free to think and speak whatever he pleased—but only so long as it did not violate certain fundamental ideas. This is precisely the sort of freedom that has prevailed in the United States since the first days. It is the only sort of freedom comprehensible to the average man. It accurately reveals his constitutional inability to shake himself free from the illogical and often quite unintelligible prejudices, instincts and mental vices that condition ninety per cent. of all his thinking. . . .

But here I wander into political speculation and no doubt stand in contumacy of some statute of Congress. Dr. Parsons avoids politics in her very interesting book. She confines herself to the purely social relations, *e.g.*, between man and woman, parent and child, host and guest, master and servant. The facts she offers are vastly interesting, and their discovery and coördination reveal a tremendous industry, but of even greater interest are the facts that lie over the margin of her inquiry. Here is a golden opportunity for other investigators: I often wonder that the field is so little explored. Perhaps the Freudians, once they get rid of their sexual obsession, will enter it and chart it. No doubt the inferiority complex described by Prof. Dr. Alfred Adler will one day provide an intelligible explanation of many of the puzzling phenomena of mob thinking. In the work of Prof. Dr. Freud himself there is, perhaps, a clew to the origin and anatomy of Puritanism, that worst of intellectual nephritises. I live in hope that the Freudians will fall upon the business without much further delay. Why do otherwise sane men believe in spirits? What is the genesis of the American axiom that the fine arts are unmanly? What is the precise machinery of the process called falling in love? Why do people believe newspapers? . . . Let there be light!

XIII.

The American Magazine

I T is astonishing, considering the enormous influence of the
popular magazine upon American literature, such as it is,
that there is but one book in type upon magazine history in
the republic. That lone volume is "The Magazine in America,"
by Prof. Dr. Algernon Tassin, a learned birchman of the great
university of Columbia, and it is so badly written that the interest of its matter is almost concealed—almost, but fortunately not quite. The professor, in fact, puts English to paper
with all the traditional dullness of his flatulent order, and, as
usual, he is most horribly dull when he is trying most kitten-
ishly to be lively. I spare you examples of his writing; if you
know the lady essayists of the United States, and their academic imitators in pantaloons, you know the sort of arch and
whimsical jocosity he ladles out. But, as I have hinted, there is
something worth attending to in his story, for all the defects of
its presentation, and so his book is not to be sniffed at. He has,
at all events, brought together a great mass of scattered and
concealed facts, and arranged them conveniently for whoever
deals with them next. The job was plainly a long and laborious
one, and rasping to the higher cerebral centers. The historian
had to make his mole-like way through the endless files of old
and stupid magazines; he had to read the insipid biographies
and autobiographies of dead and forgotten editors, many of
them college professors, preachers out of work, pre-historic
uplifters and bad poets; he had to sort out the facts from the
fancies of such incurable liars as Griswold; he had to hack and
blast a path across a virgin wilderness. The thing was worth
doing, and, as I say, it has been done with commendable
pertinacity.

Considering the noisiness of the American magazines of to-
day, it is rather instructive to glance back at the timorous and
bloodless quality of their progenitors. All of the early ones,
when they were not simply monthly newspapers or almanacs,
were depressingly "literary" in tone, and dealt chiefly in stupid

poetry, silly essays and artificial fiction. The one great fear of
their editors seems to have been that of offending some one;
all of the pioneer prospectuses were full of assurances that
nothing would be printed which even "the most fastidious"
could object to. Literature, in those days,—say from 1830 to
1860—was almost completely cut off from contemporary life.
It mirrored, not the struggle for existence, so fierce and dramatic in the new nation, but the pallid reflections of poet-
asters, self-advertising clergymen, sissified "gentlemen of taste,"
and other such donkeys. Poe waded into these *literati* and
shook them up a bit, but even after the Civil War the majority
of them continued to spin pretty cobwebs. Edmund Clarence
Stedman and Donald G. Mitchell were excellent specimens
of the clan; its last survivor was the lachrymose William Winter. The "literature" manufactured by these tear-squeezers,
though often enough produced in beer cellars, was frankly
aimed at the Young Person. Its main purpose was to avoid giving offense; it breathed a heavy and oleaginous piety, a snug
niceness, a sickening sweetness. It is as dead to-day as Baalam's
ass.

The *Atlantic Monthly* was set up by men in revolt against
this reign of mush, as *Putnam's* had been a few years before,
but the business of reform proved to be difficult and hazardous, and it was a long while before a healthier breed of authors
could be developed, and a public for them found. "There is
not much in the *Atlantic*," wrote Charles Eliot Norton to
Lowell in 1874, "that is likely to be read twice save by its
writers, and this is what the great public likes. . . . You
should hear Godkin express himself in private on this topic."
Harper's Magazine, in those days, was made up almost wholly
of cribbings from England; the *North American Review* had
sunk into stodginess and imbecility; *Putnam's* was dead, or dying; the *Atlantic* had yet to discover Mark Twain; it was the
era of *Godey's Lady's Book*. The new note, so long awaited, was
struck at last by *Scribner's*, now the *Century* (and not to be
confused with the *Scribner's* of to-day). It not only threw all
the old traditions overboard; it established new traditions
almost at once. For the first time a great magazine began to
take notice of the daily life of the American people. It started
off with a truly remarkable series of articles on the Civil War; it

plunged into contemporary politics; it eagerly sought out and encouraged new writers; it began printing decent pictures instead of the old chromos; it forced itself, by the sheer originality and enterprise of its editing, upon the public attention. American literature owes more to the *Century* than to any other magazine, and perhaps American thinking owes almost as much. It was the first "literary" periodical to arrest and interest the really first-class men of the country. It beat the *Atlantic* because it wasn't burdened with the *Atlantic's* decaying cargo of Boston Brahmins. It beat all the others because it was infinitely and obviously better. Almost everything that is good in the American magazine of to-day, almost everything that sets it above the English magazine or the Continental magazine, stems from the *Century.*

At the moment, of course, it holds no such clear field; perhaps it has served its function and is ready for a placid old age. The thing that displaced it was the yellow magazine of the *McClure's* type—a variety of magazine which surpassed it in the race for circulation by exaggerating and vulgarizing all its merits. Dr. Tassin seems to think, with William Archer, that S. S. McClure was the inventor of this type, but the truth is that its real father was the unknown originator of the Sunday supplement. What McClure—a shrewd literary bagman—did was to apply the sensational methods of the cheap newspaper to a new and cheap magazine. Yellow journalism was rising and he went in on the tide. The satanic Hearst was getting on his legs at the same time, and I daresay that the muck-raking magazines, even in their palmy days, followed him a good deal more than they led him. McClure and the imitators of McClure borrowed his adept thumping of the tom-tom; Munsey and the imitators of Munsey borrowed his mush. *McClure's* and *Everybody's*, even when they had the whole nation by the ears, did little save repeat in solemn, awful tones what Hearst had said before. As for *Munsey's*, at the height of its circulation, it was little more than a Sunday "magazine section" on smooth paper, and with somewhat clearer half-tones than Hearst could print. Nearly all the genuinely original ideas of these Yankee Harmsworths of yesterday turned out badly. John Brisben Walker, with the *Cosmopolitan,* tried to make his magazine a sort of national university, and it went to pot. Ridgway, of

Everybody's, planned a weekly to be published in a dozen cities simultaneously, and lost a fortune trying to establish it. McClure, facing a situation to be described presently, couldn't manage it, and his magazine got away from him. As for Munsey, there are many wrecks behind him; he is forever experimenting boldly and failing gloriously. Even his claim to have invented the all-fiction magazine is open to caveat; there were probably plenty of such things, in substance if not in name, before the *Argosy*. Hearst, the teacher of them all, now openly holds the place that belongs to him He has galvanized the corpse of the old *Cosmopolitan* into a great success, he has distanced all rivals with *Hearst's*, he has beaten the English on their own ground with *Nash's*, and he has rehabilitated various lesser magazines. More, he has forced the other magazine publishers to imitate him. A glance at *McClure's* to-day offers all the proof that is needed of his influence upon his inferiors.

Dr. Tassin, apparently in fear of making his book too nearly good, halts his chronicle at its most interesting point, for he says nothing of what has gone on since 1900—and very much, indeed, has gone on since 1900. For one thing, the *Saturday Evening Post* has made its unparalleled success, created its new type of American literature for department store buyers and shoe drummers, and bred its school of brisk, business-like, high-speed authors. For another thing, the *Ladies' Home Journal*, once supreme in its field, has seen the rise of a swarm of imitators, some of them very prosperous. For a third thing, the all-fiction magazine of Munsey, Robert Bonner and Street & Smith has degenerated into so dubious a hussy that Munsey, a very moral man, must blush every time he thinks of it. For a fourth thing, the moving-picture craze has created an entirely new type of magazine, and it has elbowed many other types from the stands. And for a fifth thing, to make an end, the muck-raking magazine has blown up and is no more.

Why this last? Have all the possible candidates for the rake been raked? Is there no longer any taste for scandal in the popular breast? I have heard endless discussion of these questions and many ingenious answers, but all of them fail to answer. In this emergency I offer one of my own. It is this: that the muck-raking magazine came to grief, not because the public tired of muck-raking, but because the muck-raking that it began with succeeded. That is to say, the villains so long belabored by the Steffenses, the Tarbells and the Phillipses were either driven from the national scene or forced (at least temporarily) into rectitude. Worse, their places in public life were largely taken by nominees whose chemical purity was guaranteed by these same magazines, and so the latter found their occupation gone and their following with it. The great masses of the plain people, eager to swallow denunciation in horse-doctor doses, gagged at the first spoonful of praise. They chortled and read on when Aldrich, Boss Cox, Gas Addicks, John D. Rockefeller and the other bugaboos of the time were belabored every month, but they promptly sickened and went elsewhere when Judge Ben B. Lindsey, Francis J. Heney, Governor Folk and the rest of the bogus saints began to be hymned.

The same phenomenon is constantly witnessed upon the lower level of daily journalism. Let a vociferous "reform" news-paper overthrow the old gang and elect its own candidates, and at once it is in a perilous condition. Its stock in trade is gone. It can no longer give a good show—within the popular meaning of a good show. For what the public wants eternally —at least the American public—is rough work. It delights in vituperation. It revels in scandal. It is always on the side of the man or journal making the charges, no matter how slight the probability that the accused is guilty. The late Roosevelt, per-haps one of the greatest rabble-rousers the world has ever seen, was privy to this fact, and made it the corner-stone of his singularly cynical and effective politics. He was forever call-ing names, making accusations, unearthing and denouncing demons. Dr. Wilson, a performer of scarcely less talent, has sought to pursue the same plan, with varying fidelity and suc-cess. He was a popular hero so long as he confined himself to reviling men and things—the Hell Hounds of Plutocracy, the Socialists, the Kaiser, the Irish, the Senate minority. But the moment he found himself on the side of the defense, he began to wobble, just as Roosevelt before him had begun to wobble when he found himself burdened with the intricate construc-tive program of the Progressives. Roosevelt shook himself free by deserting the Progressives, but Wilson found it impossible to get rid of his League of Nations, and so, for awhile at least, he presented a quite typical picture of a muck-raker ham-strung by blows from the wrong end of the rake.

That the old appetite for bloody shows is not dead but only sleepeth is well exhibited by the recent revival of the weekly of opinion. Ten years ago the weekly seemed to be absolutely ex-tinct; even the *Nation* survived only as a half-forgotten ap-pendage of the *Evening Post*. Then, of a sudden, the alliance was broken, the *Evening Post* succumbed to Wall Street, the *Nation* started on an independent course—and straightway made a great success. And why? Simply because it began breaking heads—not the old heads of the *McClure's* era, of course, but nevertheless heads salient enough to make excel-lent targets. For years it had been moribund; no one read it save a dwindling company of old men; its influence gradually approached *nil*. But by the elementary device of switching from mild expostulation to violent and effective denunciation it made a new public almost over-night, and is now very widely read, extensively quoted and increasingly heeded. . . . I often wonder that so few publishers of periodicals seem aware of the psychological principle here exposed. It is known to every newspaper publisher of the slightest professional intelligence; all successful newspapers are ceaselessly querulous and belli-cose. They never defend any one or anything if they can help it; if the job is forced upon them, they tackle it by denouncing some one or something else. The plan never fails. Turn to the moving-picture trade magazines: the most prosperous of them is given over, in the main, to bitter attacks upon new films. Come back to daily journalism. The New York *Tribune*, a de-caying paper, well nigh rehabilitated itself by attacking Hearst, the cleverest muck-raker of them all. For a moment, appar-ently dismayed, he attempted a defense of himself—and came near falling into actual disaster. Then, recovering his old form, he began a whole series of counter attacks and cover attacks, and in six months he was safe and sound again. . . .

XIV.

The Ulster Polonius

A GOOD half of the humor of the late Mark Twain consisted of admitting frankly the possession of vices and weaknesses that all of us have and few of us care to acknowledge. Practically all of the sagacity of George Bernard Shaw consists of bellowing vociferously what every one knows. I think I am as well acquainted with his works, both hortatory and dramatic, as the next man. I wrote the first book ever devoted to a discussion of them, and I read them pretty steadily, even today, and with endless enjoyment. Yet, so far as I know, I have never found an original idea in them—never a single statement of fact or opinion that was not anteriorly familiar, and almost commonplace. Put the thesis of any of his plays into a plain proposition, and I doubt that you could find a literate man in Christendom who had not heard it before, or who would seriously dispute it. The roots of each one of them are in platitude; the roots of *every* effective stage-play are in platitude; that a dramatist is inevitably a platitudinarian is itself a platitude double damned. But Shaw clings to the obvious even when he is not hampered by the suffocating conventions of the stage. His Fabian tracts and his pamphlets on the war are veritable compendiums of the undeniable; what is seriously stated in them is quite beyond logical dispute. They have excited a great deal of ire, they have brought down upon him a great deal of amusing abuse, but I have yet to hear of any one actually controverting them. As well try to controvert the Copernican astronomy. They are as bullet-proof in essence as the multiplication table, and vastly more bullet-proof than the Ten Commandments or the Constitution of the United States.

Well, then, why does the Ulsterman kick up such a pother? Why is he regarded as an arch-heretic, almost comparable to Galileo, Nietzsche or Simon Magnus? For the simplest of reasons. Because he practices with great zest and skill the fine art of exhibiting the obvious in unexpected and terrifying lights—because he is a master of the logical trick of so matching two apparently safe premises that they yield an incongruous and inconvenient conclusion—above all, because he is a fellow of the utmost charm and address, quick-witted, bold, limber-tongued, persuasive, humorous, iconoclastic, ingratiating—in brief, a true Kelt, and so the exact antithesis of the solemn Sassenachs who ordinarily instruct and exhort us. Turn to his "Man and Superman," and you will see the whole Shaw machine at work. What he starts out with is the self-evident fact, disputed by no one not idiotic, that a woman has vastly more to gain by marriage, under Christian monogamy, than a man. That fact is as old as monogamy itself; it was, I dare say, the admitted basis of the palace revolution which brought monogamy into the world. But now comes Shaw with an implication that the sentimentality of the world chooses to conceal—with a deduction plainly resident in the original proposition, but kept in safe silence there by a preposterous and hypocritical taboo—to wit, the deduction that women are well aware of the profit that marriage yields for them, and that they are thus much more eager to marry than men are, and ever alert to take the lead in the business. This second fact, to any man who has passed through the terrible years between twenty-five and forty, is as plain as the first, but by a sort of general consent it is not openly stated. Violate that general consent and you are guilty of *scandalum magnatum*. Shaw is simply one who is guilty of *scandalum magnatum* habitually, a professional criminal in that department. It is his life work to announce the obvious in terms of the scandalous.

What lies under the horror of such blabbing is the deepest and most widespread of human weaknesses, which is to say, intellectual cowardice, the craven appetite for mental ease and security, the fear of thinking things out. All men are afflicted by it more or less; not even the most courageous and frank of men likes to admit, in specific terms, that his wife is fat, or that she seduced him to the altar by a transparent trick, or that their joint progeny resemble her brother or father, and are thus cads. A few extraordinary heroes of logic and evidence may do it occasionally, but only occasionally. The average man never does it at all. He is eternally in fear of what he knows in his heart; his whole life is made up of efforts to dodge it and conceal it; he is always running away from what passes for his intelligence and taking refuge in what pass for his higher feelings, *i.e.*, his stupidities, his delusions, his sentimentalities. Shaw is devoted to the art of hauling this recreant fellow up. He is one who, for purposes of sensation, often for the mere joy of outraging the tender-minded, resolutely and mercilessly thinks things out—sometimes with the utmost ingenuity and humor, but often, it must be said, in the same muddled way that the average right-thinker would do it if he ever got up the courage. Remember this formula, and all of the fellow's alleged originality becomes no more than a sort of bad-boy audacity, usually in bad taste. He drags skeletons from their closet and makes them dance obscenely—but every one, of course, knew that they were there all the while. He would produce an excitement of exactly the same kind (though perhaps superior in intensity) if he should walk down the Strand bared to the waist, and so remind the shocked Londoners of the unquestioned fact (though conventionally concealed and forgotten) that he is a mammal, and has an umbilicus.

Turn to a typical play-and-preface of his later canon, say "Androcles and the Lion." Here the complete Shaw formula is exposed. On the one hand there is a mass of platitudes; on the other hand there is the air of a peep-show. On the one hand he rehearses facts so stale that even Methodist clergymen have probably heard of them; on the other hand he states them so scandalously that the pious get all of the thrills out of the business that would accompany a view of the rector in liquor in the pulpit. Here, for example, are some of his contentions:

(a) That the social and economic doctrines preached by Jesus were indistinguishable from what is now called Socialism.

(b) That the Pauline transcendentalism visible in the Acts and the Epistles differs enormously from the simple humanitarianism set forth in the Four Gospels.

(c) That the Christianity on tap to-day would be almost as abhorrent to Jesus, supposing Him returned to earth, as the theories of Nietzsche, Hindenburg or Clemenceau, and vastly more abhorrent than those of Emma Goldman.

(d) That the rejection of the Biblical miracles, and even of the historical credibility of the Gospels, by no means disposes of Christ Himself.

(e) That the early Christians were persecuted, not because their

theology was regarded as unsound, but because their public conduct
constituted a nuisance.

It is unnecessary to go on. Could any one imagine a more
abject surrender to the undeniable? Would it be possible to
reduce the German exegesis of a century and a half to a more
depressing series of platitudes? But his discussion of the incon-
sistencies between the Four Gospels is even worse; you will
find all of its points set forth in any elemental treatise upon
New Testament criticism—even in so childish a tract as Ramsden Balmforth's. He actually dishes up, with a heavy air of
profundity, the news that there is a glaring conflict between
the genealogy of Jesus in Matthew i, 1–17, and the direct claim
of divine paternity in Matthew i, 18. More, he breaks out with
the astounding discovery that Jesus was a good Jew, and that
Paul's repudiation of circumcision (now a cardinal article of
the so-called Christian faith) would have surprised Him and
perhaps greatly shocked Him. The whole preface, running to
114 pages, is made up of just such shop-worn stuff. Searching it
from end to end with eagle eye, I have failed to find a single
fact or argument that was not previously familiar to me, despite the circumstance that I ordinarily give little attention to
the sacred sciences and thus might have been expected to be
surprised by their veriest commonplaces.

Nevertheless, this preface makes bouncing reading—and
therein lies the secret of the continued vogue of Shaw. He has
a large and extremely uncommon capacity for provocative utterance; he knows how to get a touch of bellicosity into the
most banal of doctrines; he is forever on tiptoe, forever challenging, forever *sforzando*. His matter may be from the public
store, even from the public junk-shop, but his manner is
always all his own. The tune is old, but the words are new. Consider, for example, his discussion of the personality of Jesus.
The idea is simple and obvious: Jesus was not a long-faced
prophet of evil, like John the Baptist, nor was He an ascetic, or
a mystic. But here is the Shaw way of saying it: "He was . . .
what we call an artist and a Bohemian in His manner of life."
The fact remains unchanged, but in the extravagant statement
of it there is a shock for those who have been confusing the
sour donkey they hear of a Sunday with the tolerant, likable

Man they profess to worship—and perhaps there is even a genial snicker in it for their betters. So with his treatment of the Atonement. His objections to it are time-worn, but suddenly he gets the effect of novelty by pointing out the quite manifest fact that acceptance of it is apt to make for weakness, that the man who rejects it is thrown back upon his own courage and circumspection, and is hence stimulated to augment them. The first argument—that Jesus was of free and easy habits—is so commonplace that I have heard it voiced by a bishop. The second suggests itself so naturally that I myself once employed it against a chance Christian encountered in a Pullman smoking-room. This Christian was at first shocked as he might have been by reading Shaw, but in half an hour he was confessing that he had long ago thought of the objection himself, and put it away as immoral. I well remember his fascinated interest as I showed him how my inability to accept the doctrine put a heavy burden of moral responsibility upon me, and forced me to be more watchful of my conduct than the elect of God, and so robbed me of many pleasant advantages in finance, the dialectic and amour. . . .

A double jest conceals itself in the Shaw legend. The first half of it I have already disclosed. The second half has to do with the fact that Shaw is not at all the wholesale agnostic his fascinated victims see him, but an orthodox Scotch Presbyterian of the most cock-sure and bilious sort—in fact, almost the archetype of the blue-nose. In the theory that he is Irish I take little stock. His very name is as Scotch as haggis, and the part of Ireland from which he springs is peopled almost exclusively by Scots. The true Irishman is a romantic. He senses life as a mystery, a thing of wonder, an experience of passion and beauty. In politics he is not logical, but emotional. In religion his interest centers, not in the commandments, but in the sacraments. The Scot, on the contrary, is almost devoid of romanticism. He is a materialist, a logician, a utilitarian. Life to him is not a poem, but a series of police regulations. God is not an indulgent father, but a hanging judge. There are no saints, but only devils. Beauty is a lewdness, redeemable only in the service of morality. It is more important to get on in the world than to be brushed by angels' wings. Here Shaw runs exactly true to type. Read his critical writings from end to end, and you will not find the slightest hint that objects of art were passing before him as he wrote. He founded, in England, the superstition that Ibsen was no more than a tin-pot evangelist —a sort of brother to General Booth, Mrs. Pankhurst and the syndics of the Sex Hygiene Society. He turned Shakespeare into a bird of evil, croaking dismally in a rain-barrel. He even injected a moral content (by dint of herculean straining) into the music dramas of Richard Wagner—surely the most colossal sacrifices of moral ideas ever made on the altar of beauty! Always the ethical obsession, the hall-mark of the Scotch Puritan, is visible in him. His politics is mere moral indignation. His æsthetic theory is cannibalism upon æsthetics. And in his general writing he is forever discovering an atrocity in what was hitherto passed as no more than a human weakness; he is forever inventing new sins, and demanding their punishment; he always sees his opponent, not only as wrong, but also as a scoundrel. I have called him a Presbyterian. Need I add that he flirts with predestination under the quasi-scientific *nom de guerre* of determinism—that he seems to be convinced that, while men may not be responsible for their virtues, they are undoubtedly responsible for their offendings, and deserve to be clubbed therefor? . . .

And this is Shaw the revolutionist, the heretic! Next, perhaps, we shall be hearing of Benedict XV, the atheist. . . .

XV.
An Unheeded Law-Giver

O NE discerns, in all right-thinking American criticism, the doctrine that Ralph Waldo Emerson was a great man, but the specifications supporting that doctrine are seldom displayed with any clarity. Despite the vast mass of writing about him, he remains to be worked out critically; practically all the existing criticism of him is marked by his own mellifluous obscurity. Perhaps a good deal of this obscurity is due to contradictions inherent in the man's character. He was dualism ambulant. What he actually *was* was seldom identical with what he represented himself to be or what his admirers thought him to be. Universally greeted, in his own day, as a revolutionary, he was, in point of fact, imitative and cautious—an importer of stale German elixirs, sometimes direct and sometimes through the Carlylean branch house, who took good care to dilute them with buttermilk before merchanting them. The theoretical spokesman, all his life long, of bold and forthright thinking, of the unafraid statement of ideas, he stated his own so warily and so muggily that they were ratified on the one hand by Nietzsche and on the other hand by the messiahs of the New Thought, that lavender buncombe.

What one notices about him chiefly is his lack of influence upon the main stream of American thought, such as it is. He had admirers and even worshipers, but no apprentices. Nietzscheism and the New Thought are alike tremendous violations of orthodox American doctrine. The one makes a headlong attack upon egalitarianism, the corner-stone of American politics; the other substitutes mysticism, which is the notion that the true realities are all concealed, for the prevailing American notion that the only true realities lie upon the surface, and are easily discerned by Congressmen, newspaper editorial writers and members of the Junior Order of United American Mechanics. The Emerson cult, in America, has been an affectation from the start. Not many of the chautauqua orators, literary professors, vassarized old maids and other such bogus *intelligentsia*

who devote themselves to it have any intelligible understanding of the Transcendentalism at the heart of it, and not
one of them, so far as I can make out, has ever executed Emerson's command to "defer never to the popular cry." On the
contrary, it is precisely within the circle of Emersonian adula-
tion that one finds the greatest tendency to test all ideas by
their respectability, to combat free thought as something intrinsically vicious, and to yield placidly to "some great decorum, some fetish of a government, some ephemeral trade, or
war, or man." It is surely not unworthy of notice that the
country of this prophet of Man Thinking is precisely the country in which every sort of dissent from the current pishposh is
combated most ferociously, and in which there is the most vigorous existing tendency to suppress free speech altogether.

Thus Emerson, on the side of ideas, has left but faint tracks
behind him. His quest was for "facts amidst appearances," and
his whole metaphysic revolved around a doctrine of transcendental first causes, a conception of interior and immutable
realities, distinct from and superior to mere transient phenomena. But the philosophy that actually prevails among his
countrymen—a philosophy put into caressing terms by William
James—teaches an almost exactly contrary doctrine: its central
idea is that whatever satisfies the immediate need is substantially true, that appearance is the only form of fact worthy the
consideration of a man with money in the bank, and the old
flag floating over him, and hair on his chest. Nor has Emerson
had any ponderable influence as a literary artist in the technical
sense, or as the prophet of a culture—that is, at home. Despite
the feeble imitations of campus critics, his manner has vanished with his matter. There is, in the true sense, no Emersonian school of American writers. Current American writing,
with its cocksureness, its somewhat hard competence, its air of
selling goods, is utterly at war with his loose, impressionistic
method, his often mystifying groping for ideas, his relentless
pursuit of phrases. In the same way, one searches the country
in vain for any general reaction to the cultural ideal that he set
up. When one casts about for salient men whom he moved
profoundly, men who got light from his torch, one thinks first
and last, not of Americans, but of such men as Nietzsche and
Hermann Grimm, the Germans, and Tyndall and Matthew

Arnold, the Englishmen. What remains of him at home, as I have said, is no more than, on the one hand, a somewhat absurd affectation of intellectual fastidiousness, now almost extinct even in New England, and, on the other hand, a debased Transcendentalism rolled into pills for fat women with vague pains and inattentive husbands—in brief, the New Thought—in brief, imbecility. This New Thought, a decadent end-product of American superficiality, now almost monopolizes him. One hears of him in its preposterous literature and one hears of him in text-books for the young, but not often elsewhere. Allowing everything, it would surely be absurd to hold that he has colored and conditioned the main stream of American thought as Goethe colored and conditioned the thought of Germany, or Pushkin that of Russia, or Voltaire that of France. . . .

XVI.

The Blushful Mystery

Sex Hygiene

THE literature of sex hygiene, once so scanty and so timorous, now piles mountain high. There are at least a dozen formidable series of books of instruction for inquirers of all ages, beginning with "What Every Child of Ten Should Know" and ending with "What a Woman of Forty-five Should Know," and they all sell amazingly. Scores of diligent authors, some medical, some clerical and some merely shrewdly chautauqual, grow rich at the industry of composing them. One of these amateur Havelock Ellises had the honor, during the last century, of instructing me in the elements of the sacred sciences. He was then the pastor of a fourth-rate church in a decaying neighborhood and I was sent to his Sunday-school in response to some obscure notion that the agony of it would improve me. Presently he disappeared, and for a long while I heard nothing about him. Then he came into sudden prominence as the author of such a series of handbooks and as the chief stockholder, it would seem, in the publishing house printing them. By the time he died, a few years ago, he had been so well rewarded by a just God that he was able to leave funds to establish a missionary college in some remote and heathen land.

This holy man, I believe, was honest, and took his platitudinous compositions quite seriously. Regarding other contributors to the literature it may be said without malice that their altruism is obviously corrupted by a good deal of hocus-pocus. Some of them lecture in the chautauquas, peddling their books before and after charming the yokels. Others, being members of the faculty, seem to carry on medical practice on the side. Yet others are kept in profitable jobs by the salacious old men who finance vice crusades. It is hard to draw the line between the mere thrifty enthusiast and the downright fraud. So, too, with the actual vice crusaders. The books of the latter, like the sex hygiene books, are often sold, not as wisdom, but as pornography. True enough, they are always displayed in the show-window of the small-town Methodist Book Concern— but you will also find them in the back-rooms of dubious second-hand book-stores, side by side with the familiar scarlet-backed editions of Rabelais, Margaret of Navarre and Balzac's "Droll Tales." Some time ago, in a book advertisement headed "Snappy Fiction," I found announcements of "My Battles With Vice," by Virginia Brooks—and "Life of My Heart," by Victoria Cross. The former was described by the publisher as a record of "personal experiences in the fight against the gray wolves and love pirates of modern society." The book was offered to all comers by mail. One may easily imagine the effects of such an offer.

But even the most serious and honest of the sex hygiene volumes are probably futile, for they are all founded upon a pedagogical error. That is to say, they are all founded upon an attempt to explain a romantic mystery in terms of an exact science. Nothing could be more absurd: as well attempt to interpret Beethoven in terms of mathematical physics—as many a fatuous contrapuntist, indeed, has tried to do. The mystery of sex presents itself to the young, not as a scientific problem to be solved, but as a romantic emotion to be accounted for. The only result of the current endeavor to explain its phenomena by seeking parallels in botany is to make botany obscene. . . .

2

Art and Sex

One of the favorite notions of the Puritan mullahs who specialize in this moral pornography is that the sex instinct, if suitably repressed, may be "sublimated" into the higher sorts of idealism, and especially into aesthetic idealism. That notion is to be found in all their books; upon it they ground the theory that the enforcement of chastity by a huge force of spies, stool pigeons and police would convert the republic into a nation of incomparable uplifters, forward-lookers and artists. All this, of course, is simply pious fudge. If the notion were actually sound, then all the great artists of the world would come from the ranks of the hermetically repressed, *i.e.*, from the ranks of

Puritan old maids, male and female. But the truth is, as every one knows, that the great artists of the world are never Puritans, and seldom even ordinarily respectable. No virtuous man —that is, virtuous in the Y.M.C.A. sense—has ever painted a picture worth looking at, or written a symphony worth hearing, or a book worth reading, and it is highly improbable that the thing has ever been done by a virtuous woman. The actual effect of repression, lamentable though it may be, is to destroy idealism altogether. The Puritan, for all his pretensions, is the worst of materialists. Passed through his sordid and unimaginative mind, even the stupendous romance of sex is reduced to a disgusting transaction in physiology. As artist he is thus hopeless; as well expect an auctioneer to qualify for the Sistine Chapel choir. All he ever achieves, taking pen or brush in hand, is a feeble burlesque of his betters, all of whom, by his hog's theology, are doomed to hell.

3
A Loss to Romance

Perhaps the worst thing that this sex hygiene nonsense has accomplished is the thing mourned by Agnes Repplier in "The Repeal of Reticence." In America, at least, innocence has been killed, and romance has been sadly wounded by the same discharge of smutty artillery. The flapper is no longer naïve and charming; she goes to the altar of God with a learned and even cynical glitter in her eye. The veriest school-girl of to-day, fed upon Forel, Sylvanus Stall, Reginald Wright Kauffman and the Freud books, knows as much as the midwife of 1885, and spends a good deal more time discharging and disseminating her information. All this, of course, is highly embarrassing to the more romantic and ingenuous sort of men, of whom I have the honor to be one. We are constantly in the position of General Mitchener in Shaw's one-acter, "Press Cuttings," when he begs Mrs. Farrell, the talkative charwoman, to reserve her confidences for her medical adviser. One often wonders, indeed, what women now talk of to doctors. . . .

Please do not misunderstand me here. I do not object to this New Freedom on moral grounds, but on æsthetic grounds. In the relations between the sexes all beauty is founded upon romance, all romance is founded upon mystery, and all mystery is founded upon ignorance, or, failing that, upon the deliberate denial of the known truth. To be in love is merely to be in a state of perceptual anæsthesia—to mistake an ordinary young man for a Greek god or an ordinary young woman for a goddess. But how can this condition of mind survive the deadly matter-of-factness which sex hygiene and the new science of eugenics impose? How can a woman continue to believe in the honor, courage and loving tenderness of a man after she has learned, perhaps by affidavit, that his hæmoglobin count is 117%, that he is free from sugar and albumen, that his blood pressure is 112/79 and that his Wassermann reaction is negative? . . . Moreover, all this new-fangled "frankness" tends to dam up, at least for civilized adults, one of the principal well-springs of art, to wit, impropriety. What is neither hidden nor forbidden is seldom very charming. If women, continuing their present tendency to its logical goal, end by going stark naked, there will be no more poets and painters, but only dermatologists and photographers. . . .

4
Sex on the Stage

The effort to convert the theater into a forum of solemn sex discussion is another abhorrent by-product of the sex hygiene rumble-bumble. Fortunately, it seems to be failing. A few years ago, crowds flocked to see Brieux's "Les Avariés," but to-day it is forgotten, and its successors are all obscure. The movement originated in Germany with the production of Frank Wedekind's "Frühlings Erwachen." The Germans gaped and twisted in their seats for a season or two, and then abandoned sex as a horror and went back to sex as a comedy. This last is what it actually should be, at least in the theater. The theater is no place for painful speculation; it is a place for diverting representation. Its best and truest sex plays are not such overstrained shockers as "Le Mariage d'Olympe" and "Damaged Goods," but such penetrating and excellent comedies as "Much Ado About Nothing" and "The Taming of the Shrew." In "Much Ado" we have an accurate and unforgettable picture of the way in which the normal male of the human species is

brought to the altar—that is, by the way of appealing to his
hollow vanity, the way of capitalizing his native and ineradicable asininity. And in "The Taming of the Shrew" we have a
picture of the way in which the average woman, having so
snared him, is purged of her resultant vainglory and bombast,
and thus reduced to decent discipline and decorum, that the
marriage may go on in solid tranquillity.

The whole drama of sex, in real life, as well as on the stage,
revolves around these two enterprises. One-half of it consists
of pitting the native intelligence of women against the native
sentimentality of men, and the other half consists of bringing
women into a reasonable order, that their superiority may not
be too horribly obvious. To the first division belong the dramas of courtship, and a good many of those of marital conflict.
In each case the essential drama is not a tragedy but a comedy
—nay, a farce. In each case the conflict is not between imper-
ishable verities but between mere vanities and pretensions.
This is the essence of the comic: the unmasking of fraud, its
destruction by worse fraud. Marriage, as we know it in Christendom, though its utility is obvious and its necessity is at least
arguable, is just such a series of frauds. It begins with the fraud
that the impulse to it is lofty, unearthly and disinterested. It
proceeds to the fraud that both parties are equally eager for it
and equally benefited by it—which actually happens only when
two Mondays come together. And it rests thereafter upon the
fraud that what is once agreeable (or tolerable) remains agreeable ever thereafter—that I shall be exactly the same man in 1938
that I am to-day, and that my wife will be the same woman,
and intrigued by the merits of the same man. This last assumption is so outrageous that, on purely evidential and logical
grounds, not even the most sentimental person would support
it. It thus becomes necessary to reënforce it by attaching to it
the concept of honor. That is to say, it is held up, not on the
ground that it is actually true, but on the ground that a recognition of its truth is part of the bargain made at the altar, and
that a repudiation of this bargain would be dishonorable. Here
we have honor, which is based upon a sense of the deepest and
most inviolable truth, brought in to support something admittedly not true. Here, in other words, we have a situation in
comedy, almost exactly parallel to that in which a colored

bishop whoops "Onward, Christian Soldiers!" like a calliope in order to drown out the crowing of the rooster concealed beneath his chasuble.

In all plays of the sort that are regarded as "strong" and "significant" in Greenwich Village, in the finishing schools and by the newspaper critics, connubial infidelity is the chief theme. Smith, having a wife, Mrs. Smith, betrays her love and trust by running off with Miss Rabinowitz, his stenographer. Or Mrs. Brown, detecting her husband, Mr. Brown, in lamentable proceedings with a neighbor, the grass widow Kraus, forgives him and continues to be true to him in consideration of her children, Fred, Pansy and Little Fern. Both situations produce a great deal of eye-rolling and snuffling among the softies aforesaid. Yet neither contains the slightest touch of tragedy, and neither at bottom is even honest. Both, on the contrary, are based upon an assumption that is unsound and ridiculous —the assumption, to wit, that the position of the injured wife is grounded upon the highest idealism—that the injury she suffers is directed at her lofty and impeccable spirit—that it leaves her standing in an heroic attitude. All this, soberly examined, is found to be untrue. The fact is that her moving impulse is simply a desire to cut a good figure before her world— in brief, that plain vanity is what animates her.

This public expectation that she will endure and renounce is itself hollow and sentimental, and so much so that it can seldom stand much strain. If, for example, her heroism goes beyond a certain modest point—if she carries it to the extent of complete abnegation and self-sacrifice—her reward is not that she is thought heroic, but that she is thought weak and foolish. And if, by any chance, the external pressure upon her is removed and she is left to go on with her alleged idealism alone—if, say, her recreant husband dies and some new suitor enters to dispute the theory of her deathless fidelity—then it is regarded as down-right insane for her to continue playing her artificial part.

In frank comedy we see the situation more accurately dealt with and hence more honestly and more instructively. Instead of depicting one party as revolting against the assumption of eternal fidelity melodramatically and the other as facing the revolt heroically and tragically, we have both criticizing it by a good-humored flouting of it—not necessarily by act, but by attitude. This attitude is normal and sensible. It rests upon genuine human traits and tendencies. It is sound, natural and honest. It gives the comedy of the stage a high validity that the bombastic fustian of the stage can never show, all the sophomores to the contrary notwithstanding.

When I speak of infidelity, of course, I do not mean only the gross infidelity of "strong" sex plays and the divorce courts, but that lighter infidelity which relieves and makes bearable the burdens of theoretical fidelity—in brief, the natural reaction of human nature against an artificial and preposterous assumption. The assumption is that a sexual choice, once made, is irrevocable—more, that all desire to revoke it, even transiently, disappears. The fact is that no human choice can ever be of that irrevocable character, and that the very existence of such an assumption is a constant provocation to challenge it and rebel against it.

What we have in marriage actually—or in any other such contract—is a constant war between the impulse to give that rebellion objective reality and a social pressure which puts a premium on submission. The rebel, if he strikes out, at once collides with a solid wall, the bricks of which are made up of the social assumption of his docility, and the mortar of which is the frozen sentimentality of his own lost yesterday—his fatuous assumption that what was once agreeable to him would be always agreeable to him. Here we have the very essence of comedy—a situation almost exactly parallel to that of the pompous old gentleman who kicks a plug hat lying on the sidewalk, and stumps his toe against the cobblestone within.

Under the whole of the conventional assumption reposes an assumption even more foolish, to wit, that sexual choice is regulated by some transcendental process, that a mysterious accuracy gets into it, that it is limited by impenetrable powers, that there is for every man one certain woman. This sentimentality not only underlies the theory of marriage, but is also the chief apology for divorce. Nothing could be more ridiculous. The truth is that marriages in Christendom are determined, not by elective affinities, but by the most trivial accidents, and that the issue of those accidents is relatively unimportant. That is to say, a normal man could be happy with any one of at least two dozen women of his acquaintance, and a man specially fitted to accept the false assumptions of marriage could be happy with almost any presentable woman of his race, class and age. He is married to Marie instead of to Gladys because Marie definitely decided to marry him, whereas Gladys vacillated between him and some other. And Marie decided to marry him instead of some other, not because the impulse was irresistibly stronger, but simply because the thing seemed more feasible. In such choices, at least among women, there is often not even any self-delusion. They see the facts clearly, and even if, later on, they are swathed in sentimental trappings, the revelation is not entirely obliterated.

Here we have comedy double distilled—a combat of pretensions, on the one side, perhaps, risen to self-hallucination, but on the other side more or less uneasily conscious and deliberate. This is the true soul of high farce. This is something not to snuffle over but to roar at.

XVII.
George Jean Nathan

ONE thinks of Gordon Craig, not as a jester, but as a very serious and even solemn fellow. For a dozen years past all the more sober dramatic critics of America have approached him with the utmost politeness, and to the gushing old maids and autointoxicated professors of the Drama League of America he has stood for the last word in theatrical æstheticism. Moreover, a good deal of this veneration has been deserved, for Craig has done excellent work in the theater, and is a man of much force and ingenuity and no little originality. Nevertheless, there must be some flavor of low, bar-room wit in him, some echo of Sir Toby Belch and the Captain of Köpenick, for a year or so ago he shook up his admirers with a joke most foul. Need I say that I refer to the notorious Nathan affair? Imagine the scene: the campus Archers and Walkleys in ponderous conclave, perhaps preparing their monthly cablegram of devotion to Maeterlinck. Arrives now a messenger with dreadful news. Gordon Craig, from his far-off Italian retreat, has issued a bull praising Nathan! Which Nathan? George Jean, of course. What! The *Smart Set* scaramouche, the ribald fellow, the raffish mocker, with his praise of Florenz Ziegfeld, his naughty enthusiasm for pretty legs, his contumacious scoffing at Brieux, Belasco, Augustus Thomas, Mrs. Fiske? Aye; even so. And what has Craig to say of him? . . . In brief, that he is the *only* American dramatic critic worth reading, that he knows far more about the theater than all the honorary pallbearers of criticism rolled together, that he is immeasurably the superior, in learning, in sense, in shrewdness, in candor, in plausibility, in skill at writing, of—

But names do not matter. Craig, in fact, did not bother to rehearse them. He simply made a clean sweep of the board, and then deftly placed the somewhat disconcerted Nathan in the center of the vacant space. It was a sad day for the honest donkeys who, for half a decade, had been laboriously establishing Craig's authority in America, but it was a glad day for

Knopf, the publisher. Knopf, at the moment, had just issued Nathan's "The Popular Theater." At once he rushed to a job printer in Eighth avenue, ordered 100,000 copies of the Craig encomium, and flooded the country with them. The result was amusing, and typical of the republic. Nathan's previous books, when praised at all, had been praised faintly and with reservations. The fellow, it appeared, was too spoofish; he lacked the sobriety and dignity necessary to a True Critic; he was entertaining but not to be taken seriously. But now, with foreign backing, and particularly English backing, he suddenly began to acquire merit and even a certain vague solemnity—and "The Popular Theater" was reviewed more lavishly and more favorably than I have ever seen any other theater book reviewed, before or since. The phenomenon, as I say, was typical. The childish mass of superstitions passing for civilized opinion in America was turned inside out over-night by one authoritative foreign voice. I have myself been a figure in the same familiar process. All of my books up to "The American Language" were, in the main, hostilely noticed. "A Book of Prefaces," in particular, was manhandled by the orthodox reviewers. Then, just before "The American Language" was issued, the *Mercure de France* printed an article commending "A Book of Prefaces" in high, astounding terms. The consequence was that "The American Language," a far inferior work, was suddenly discovered to be full of merit, and critics of the utmost respectability, who had ignored all my former books, printed extremely friendly reviews of it. . . .

But to return to Nathan. What deceived the Drama Leaguers and other such imposing popinjays for so long, causing them to mistake him for a mere sublimated Alan Dale, was his refusal to take imbecilities seriously, his easy casualness and avoidance of pedagogics, his frank delight in the theater as a show-shop—above all, his bellicose iconoclasm and devastating wit. What Craig, an intelligent man, discerned underneath was his extraordinary capacity for differentiating between sham and reality, his catholic freedom from formulæ and prejudice, his astonishing acquaintance with the literature of the practical theater, his firm grounding in rational æsthetic theory —above all, his capacity for making the thing he writes of interesting, his uncommon craftsmanship. This craftsmanship had already got him a large audience; he had been for half a dozen years, indeed, one of the most widely read of American dramatic critics. But the traditional delusion that sagacity and dullness are somehow identical had obscured the hard and accurate thinking that made the show. What was so amusing seemed necessarily superficial. It remained for Craig to show that this appearance of superficiality was only an appearance, that the Nathan criticism was well planned and soundly articulated, that at the heart of it there was a sound theory of the theater, and of the literature of the theater no less.

And what was that theory? You will find it nowhere put into a ready formula, but the outlines of it must surely be familiar to any one who has read "Another Book on the Theater," "The Popular Theater" and "Mr. George Jean Nathan Presents." In brief, it is the doctrine preached with so much ardor by Benedetto Croce and his disciple, Dr. J. E. Spingarn, and by them borrowed from Goethe and Carlyle—the doctrine, to wit, that every work of art is, at bottom, unique, and that it is the business of the critic, not to label it and pigeon-hole it, but to seek for its inner intent and content, and to value it according as that intent is carried out and that content is valid and worth while. This is the precise opposite of the academic critical attitude. The professor is nothing if not a maker of card-indexes; he must classify or be damned. His masterpiece is the dictum that "it is excellent, but it is not a play." Nathan has a far more intelligent and hospitable eye. His criterion, elastic and undefined, is inimical only to the hollow, the meretricious, the fraudulent. It bars out the play of flabby and artificial sentiment. It bars out the cheap melodrama, however gaudily set forth. It bars out the moony mush of the bad imitators of Ibsen and Maeterlinck. It bars out all mere clap-trap and sensation-monging. But it lets in every play, however conceived or designed, that contains an intelligible idea well worked out. It lets in every play by a dramatist who is ingenious, and original, and genuinely amusing. And it lets in every other sort of theatrical spectacle that has an honest aim, and achieves that aim passably, and is presented frankly for what it is.

Bear this theory in mind, and you have a clear explanation of Nathan's actual performances—first, his merciless lampooning of the trade-goods of Broadway and the pifflings of the Drama

League geniuses, and secondly, his ardent championing of such widely diverse men as Avery Hopwood, Florenz Ziegfeld, Ludwig Thoma, Lord Dunsany, Sasha Guitry, Lothar Schmidt, Ferenz Molnar, Roberto Bracco and Gerhart Hauptmann, all of whom have one thing in common: they are intelligent and full of ideas and know their trade. In Europe, of course, there are many more such men than in America, and some of the least of them are almost as good as our best. That is why Nathan is forever announcing them and advocating the presentation of their works—not because he favors foreignness for its own sake, but because it is so often accompanied by sound achievement and by stimulating example to our own artists. And that is why, when he tackles the maudlin flubdub of the Broadway dons, he does it with the weapons of comedy, and even of farce. Does an Augustus Thomas rise up with his corn-doctor magic and Sunday-school platitudes, proving heavily that love is mightier than the sword, that a pure heart will baffle the electric chair, that the eye is quicker than the hand? Then Nathan proceeds against him with a slapstick, and makes excellent practice upon his pantaloons. Does a Belasco, thumb on forelock, posture before the yeomanry as a Great Artist, the evidence being a large chromo of a Childs' restaurant, and a studio like a Madison avenue antique-shop? Then Nathan flings a laugh at him and puts him in his place. And does some fat rhinoceros of an actress, unearthing a smutty play by a corn-fed Racine, loose its banal obscenities upon the vulgar in the name of Sex Hygiene, presuming thus to teach a Great Lesson, and break the Conspiracy of Silence, and carry on the Noble Work of Brieux and company, and so save impatient flappers from the Moloch's Sacrifice of the Altar—does such a bumptious and preposterous baggage fill the newspapers with her pishposh and the largest theater in Manhattan with eager dunderheads? Then the ribald Jean has at her with a flour-sack filled with the pollen of the *Ambrosia artemisiaefolia*, driving her from the scene to the tune of her own unearthly sneezing.

Necessarily, he has to lay on with frequency. For one honest play, honestly produced and honestly played, Broadway sees two dozen that are simply so much green-goods. To devote serious exposition to the badness of such stuff would be to descend to the donkeyish futility of William Winter. Sometimes, indeed, even ridicule is not enough; there must be a briefer and more dramatic display of the essential banality. Well, then, why not recreate it in the manner of Croce—but touching up a line here, a color there? The result is burlesque, but burlesque that is the most searching and illuminating sort of criticism. Who will forget Nathan's demonstration that a platitudinous play by Thomas would be better if played backward? A superb bravura piece, enormously beyond the talents of any other American writer on the theater, it smashed the Thomas legend with one stroke. In the little volume called "Bottoms Up" you will find many other such annihilating waggeries. Nathan does not denounce melodrama with a black cap upon his head, painfully demonstrating its inferiority to the drama of Ibsen, Scribe and Euripides; he simply sits down and writes a little melodrama so extravagantly ludicrous that the whole genus collapses. And he does not prove in four columns of a Sunday paper that French plays done into American are spoiled; he simply shows the spoiling in six lines.

This method, of course, makes for broken heads; it outrages the feelings of tender theatrical mountebanks; it provokes reprisals more or less furtive and behind the door. The theater in America, as in most other countries, is operated chiefly by bounders. Men so constantly associated with actors tend to take on the qualities of the actor—his idiotic vanity, his herculean stupidity, his chronic underrating of his betters. The miasma spreads to dramatists and dramatic critics; the former drift into charlatanery and the latter into a cowardly and disgusting dishonesty. Amid such scenes a man of positive ideas, of civilized tastes and of unshakable integrity is a stranger, and he must face all the hostility that the lower orders of men display to strangers. There is, so far as I know, no tripe-seller in Broadway who has not tried, at one time or another, to dispose of Nathan by *attentat*. He has been exposed to all the measures ordinarily effective against rebellious reviewers, and, resisting them, he has been treated to special treatment with infernal machines of novel and startling design. No writer for the theater has been harder beset, and none has been less incommoded by the onslaught. What is more, he has never made the slightest effort to capitalize this drum-fire—the invariable device of lesser men. So far as I am aware, and I have been in close association with him for ten years, it has had not the slightest effect upon him whatsoever. A thoroughgoing skeptic, with no trace in him of the messianic delusion, he has avoided timorousness on the one hand and indignation on the other. No man could be less a public martyr of the Metcalfe type; it would probably amuse him vastly to hear it argued that his unbreakable independence (and often somewhat high and mighty sniffishness) has been of any public usefulness. I sometimes wonder what keeps such a man in the theater, breathing bad air nightly, gaping at prancing imbeciles, sitting cheek by jowl with cads. Perhaps there is, at bottom, a secret romanticism —a lingering residuum of a boyish delight in pasteboard and spangles, gaudy colors and soothing sounds, preposterous heroes and appetizing wenches. But more likely it is a sense of humor—the zest of a man to whom life is a spectacle that never grows dull—a show infinitely surprising, amusing, buffoonish, vulgar, obscene. The theater, when all is said and done, is not life in miniature, but life enormously magnified, life hideously exaggerated. Its emotions are ten times as powerful as those of reality, its ideas are twenty times as idiotic as those of real men, its lights and colors and sounds are forty times as blinding and deafening as those of nature, its people are grotesque burlesques of every one we know. Here is diversion for a cynic. And here, it may be, is the explanation of Nathan's fidelity.

Whatever the cause of his enchantment, it seems to be lasting. To a man so fertile in ideas and so facile in putting them into words there is a constant temptation to make experiments, to plunge into strange waters, to seek self-expression in ever-widening circles. And yet, at the brink of forty years, Nathan remains faithful to the theater; of his half dozen books, only one does not deal with it, and that one is a very small one. In four or five years he has scarcely written of aught else. I doubt that anything properly describable as enthusiasm is at the bottom of this assiduity; perhaps the right word is curiosity. He is interested mainly, not in the staple fare of the playhouse, but in what might be called its fancy goods—in its endless stream of new men, its restless innovations, the radical overhauling that it has been undergoing in our time. I do not recall, in any of his books or articles, a single paragraph appraising the classics

of the stage, or more than a brief note or two on their interpretation. His attention is always turned in a quite opposite direction. He is intensely interested in novelty of whatever sort,
if it be only free from sham. Such experimentalists as Max
Reinhardt, George Bernard Shaw, Sasha Guitry and the daring
nobodies of the Grand Guignol, such divergent originals as
Dunsany, Ziegfeld, George M. Cohan and Schnitzler, have enlisted his eager partisanship. He saw something new to our
theater in the farces of Hopwood before any one else saw it; he
was quick to welcome the novel points of view of Eleanor
Gates and Clare Kummer; he at once rescued what was sound
in the Little Theatre movement from what was mere attitudi-
nizing and pseudo-intellectuality. In the view of Broadway, an
exigent and even malignant fellow, wielding a pen dipped in
aqua fortis, he is actually amiable to the last degree, and constantly announces pearls in the fodder of the swine. Is the new
play in Forty-second Street a serious work of art, as the press-
agents and the newspaper reviewers say? Then so are your
grandmother's false teeth! Is Maeterlinck a Great Thinker?
Then so is Dr. Frank Crane! Is Belasco a profound artist? Then
so is the man who designs the ceilings of hotel dining rooms!
But let us not weep too soon. In the play around the corner
there is a clever scene. Next door, amid sickening dullness,
there are two buffoons who could be worse: one clouts the
other with a *Blutwurst* filled with mayonnaise. And a block
away there is a girl in the second row with a very charming
twist of the *vastus medialis*. Let us sniff the roses and forget
the thorns!

What this attitude chiefly wars with, even above cheapness,
meretriciousness and banality, is the fatuous effort to turn the
theater, a place of amusement, into a sort of outhouse to the
academic grove—the Maeterlinck-Brieux-Barker complex. No
critic in America, and none in England save perhaps Walkley,
has combated this movement more vigorously than Nathan.
He is under no illusion as to the functions and limitations of
the stage. He knows, with Victor Hugo, that the best it can
do, in the domain of ideas, is to "turn thoughts into food for
the crowd," and he knows that only the simplest and shakiest
ideas may undergo that transformation. Coming upon the
scene at the height of the Ibsen mania of half a generation ago,

he ranged himself against its windy pretenses from the start. He saw at once the high merit of Ibsen as a dramatic craftsman and welcomed him as a reformer of dramatic technique, but he also saw how platitudinous was the ideational content of his plays and announced the fact in terms highly offensive to the Ibsenites. . . . But the Ibsenites have vanished and Nathan remains. He has survived, too, the Brieux hubbub. He has lived to preach the funeral sermon of the Belasco legend. He has himself sworded Maeterlinck and Granville Barker. He has done frightful execution upon many a poor mime. And meanwhile, breasting the murky tide of professorial buncombe, of solemn pontificating, of Richard-Burtonism, Clayton-Hamiltonism and other such decaying forms of William-Winterism, he has rescued dramatic criticism among us from its exile with theology, embalming and obstetrics, and given it a place among what Nietzsche called the gay sciences, along with war, fiddle-playing and laparotomy. He has made it amusing, stimulating, challenging, even, at times, a bit startling. And to the business, artfully concealed, he has brought a sound and thorough acquaintance with the heavy work of the pioneers, Lessing, Schlegel, Hazlitt, Lewes *et al*—and an even wider acquaintance, lavishly displayed, with every nook and corner of the current theatrical scene across the water. And to discharge this extraordinarily copious mass of information he has hauled and battered the English language into new and often astounding forms, and when English has failed he has helped it out with French, German, Italian, American, Swedish, Russian, Turkish, Latin, Sanskrit and Old Church Slavic, and with algebraic symbols, chemical formulæ, musical notation and the signs of the Zodiac. . . .

This manner, of course, is not without its perils. A man so inordinately articulate is bound to succumb, now and then, to the seductions of mere virtuosity. The average writer, and particularly the average critic of the drama, does well if he gets a single new and racy phrase into an essay; Nathan does well if he dilutes his inventions with enough commonplaces to enable the average reader to understand his discourse at all. He carries the avoidance of the *cliché* to the length of an *idée fixe*. It would be difficult, in all his books, to find a dozen of the usual rubber stamps of criticism; I daresay it would kill him, or, at all events, bring him down with cholera morbus, to discover that he had called a play "convincing" or found "authority" in the snorting of an English actor-manager. At best, this incessant flight from the obvious makes for a piquant and arresting style, a procession of fantastic and often highly pungent neologisms —in brief, for Nathanism. At worst, it becomes artificiality, pedantry, obscurity. I cite an example from an essay on Eleanor Gates' "The Poor Little Rich Girl," prefaced to the printed play:

> As against the not unhollow symbolic strut and gasconade of such over-pæaned pieces as, let us for example say, "The Blue Bird" of Maeterlinck, so simple and unaffected a bit of stage writing as this— of school dramatic intrinsically the same—cajoles the more honest heart and satisfies more plausibly and fully those of us whose thumbs are ever being pulled professionally for a native stage less smeared with the snobberies of empty, albeit high-sounding, nomenclatures from overseas.

Fancy that, Hedda!—and in praise of a "simple and unaffected bit of stage writing"! I denounced it at the time, *circa* 1916, and perhaps with some effect. At all events, I seem to notice a gradual disentanglement of the parts of speech. The old florid invention is still there; one encounters startling coinages in even the most casual of reviews; the thing still flashes and glitters; the tune is yet upon the E string. But underneath I hear a more sober rhythm than of old. The fellow, in fact, takes on a sedater habit, both in style and in point of view. Without abandoning anything essential, without making the slightest concession to the orthodox opinion that he so magnificently disdains, he yet begins to yield to the middle years. The mere shocking of the stupid is no longer as charming as it used to be. What he now offers is rather more *gemütlich*, sometimes it even verges upon the instructive. . . . But I doubt that Nathan will ever become a professor, even if he enjoys the hideously prolonged senility of a William Winter. He will be full of surprises to the end. With his last gasp he will make a phrase to flabbergast a dolt.

XVIII.
Portrait of an Immortal Soul

O NE day in Spring, six or eight years ago, I received a letter
from a man somewhere beyond the Wabash announcing
that he had lately completed a very powerful novel and hinting
that my critical judgment upon it would give him great comfort. Such notifications, at that time, reached me far too often
to be agreeable, and so I sent him a form-response telling him
that I was ill with pleurisy, had just been forbidden by my
oculist to use my eyes, and was about to become a father. The
aim of this form-response was to shunt all that sort of trade off
to other reviewers, but for once it failed. That is to say, the unknown kept on writing to me, and finally offered to pay me an
honorarium for my labor. This offer was so unusual that it
quite demoralized me, and before I could recover I had received, cashed and dissipated a modest check, and was confronted by an accusing manuscript, perhaps four inches thick,
but growing thicker every time I glanced at it.

One night, tortured by conscience and by the inquiries and
reminders arriving from the author by every post, I took up
the sheets and settled down for a depressing hour or two of
it. . . . No, I did *not* read all night. No, it was *not* a masterpiece. No, it has *not* made the far-off stranger famous. Let me
tell the story quite honestly. I am, in fact, far too rapid a reader
to waste a whole night on a novel; I had got through this one
by midnight and was sound asleep at my usual time. And it was
by no means a masterpiece; on the contrary, it was inchoate,
clumsy, and, in part, artificial, insincere and preposterous. And
to this day the author remains obscure. . . . But underneath
all the amateurish writing, the striving for effects that failed to
come off, the absurd literary self-consciousness, the recurrent
falsity and banality—underneath all these stigmata of a neo-
phyte's book there was yet a capital story, unusual in content,
naïve in manner and enormously engrossing. What is more,
the faults that it showed in execution were, most of them, not
ineradicable. On page after page, as I read on, I saw chances to

improve it—to get rid of its intermittent bathos, to hasten its action, to eliminate its spells of fine writing, to purge it of its imitations of all the bad novels ever written—in brief, to tighten it, organize it, and, as the painters say, tease it up.

The result was that I spent the next morning writing the author a long letter of advice. It went to him with the manuscript, and for weeks I heard nothing from him. Then the manuscript returned, and I read it again. This time I had a genuine surprise. Not only had the unknown followed my suggestions with much intelligence; in addition, once set up on the right track, he had devised a great many excellent improvements of his own. In its new form, in fact, the thing was a very competent and even dexterous piece of writing, and after re-reading it from the first word to the last with even keener interest than before, I sent it to Mitchell Kennerley, then an active publisher, and asked him to look through it. Kennerley made an offer for it at once, and eight or nine months later it was published with his imprint. The author chose to conceal himself behind the *nom de plume* of Robert Steele; I myself gave the book the title of "One Man." It came from the press—and straightway died the death. The only favorable review it received was mine in the *Smart Set*. No other reviewer paid any heed to it. No one gabbled about it. No one, so far as I could make out, even read it. The sale was small from the start, and quickly stopped altogether. . . . To this day the fact fills me with wonder. To this day I marvel that so dramatic, so penetrating and so curiously moving a story should have failed so overwhelmingly. . . .

For I have never been able to convince myself that I was wrong about it. On the contrary, I am more certain than ever, re-reading it after half a dozen years, that I was right—that it was and is one of the most honest and absorbing human documents ever printed in America. I have called it, following the author, a novel. It is, in fact, nothing of the sort; it is autobiography. More, it is autobiography unadorned and shameless, autobiography almost unbelievably cruel and betraying, autobiography that is as devoid of artistic sophistication as an operation for gall-stones. This so-called Steele is simply too stupid, too ingenuous, too moral to lie. He is the very reverse of an artist; he is a born and incurable Puritan—and in his alleged novel he draws the most faithful and merciless picture of an American Puritan that has ever got upon paper. There is never the slightest effort at amelioration; he never evades the ghastly horror of it; he never tries to palm off himself as a good fellow, a hero. Instead, he simply takes his stand in the center of the platform, where all the spotlights meet, and there calmly strips off his raiment of reticence—first his Sunday plug-hat, then his long-tailed coat, then his boiled shirt, then his shoes and socks, and finally his very B.V.D.'s. The closing scene shows the authentic *Mensch-an-sich*, the eternal blue-nose in the nude, with every wart and pimple glittering and every warped bone and flabby muscle telling its abhorrent tale. There stands the Puritan stripped of every artifice and conceal-ment, like Thackeray's Louis XIV.

Searching my memory, I can drag up no recollection of an-other such self-opener of secret chambers and skeletonic clos-ets. Set beside this pious babbler, the late Giovanni Jacopo Casanova de Seingalt shrinks to the puny proportions of a mere barroom boaster, a smoking-car Don Juan, an Eigh-teenth Century stock company leading man or whiskey drum-mer. So, too, Benvenuto Cellini: a fellow vastly entertaining, true enough, but after all, not so much a psychological histo-rian as a liar, a yellow journalist. One always feels, in reading Benvenuto, that the man who is telling the story is quite dis-tinct from the man about whom it is being told. The fellow, indeed, was too noble an artist to do a mere portrait with fi-delity; he could not resist the temptation to repair a cauli-flower ear here, to paint out a tell-tale scar there, to shine up the eyes a bit, to straighten the legs down below. But this Steele—or whatever his name may be—never steps out of him-self. He is never describing the gaudy one he would *like* to be, but always the commonplace, the weak, the emotional, the ig-norant, the third-rate Christian male that he actually is. He de-plores himself, he distrusts himself, he plainly wishes heartily that he was not himself, but he never makes the slightest at-tempt to disguise and bedizen himself. Such as he is, cheap, mawkish, unæsthetic, conscience-stricken, he depicts himself with fierce and unrelenting honesty.

Superficially, the man that he sets before us seems to be a felonious fellow, for he confesses frankly to a long series of youthful larcenies, to a somewhat banal adventure in forgery (leading to a term in jail), to sundry petty deceits and breaches of trust, and to an almost endless chain of exploits in amour, most of them sordid and unrelieved by anything approaching romance. But the inner truth about him, of course, is that he is really a moralist of the moralists—that his one fundamental and all-embracing virtue is what he himself regards as his viciousness —that he is never genuinely human and likable save in those moments which lead swiftly to his most florid self-accusing. In brief, the history is that of a moral young man, the child of God-fearing parents, and its moral, if it has one, is that a strictly moral upbringing injects poisons into the system that even the most steadfast morality cannot resist. It is, in a way, the old story of the preacher's son turned sot and cutthroat.

Here we see an apparently sound and normal youngster converted into a sneak and rogue by the intolerable pressure of his father's abominable Puritanism. And once a rogue, we see him make himself into a scoundrel by the very force of his horror of his roguery. Every step downward is helped from above. It is not until he resigns himself frankly to the fact of his incurable degradation, and so ceases to struggle against it, that he ever steps out of it.

The external facts of the chronicle are simple enough. The son of a school teacher turned petty lawyer and politician, the hero is brought up under such barbaric rigors that he has already become a fluent and ingenious liar, in sheer self-protection, at the age of five or six. From lying he proceeds quite naturally to stealing: he lifts a few dollars from a neighbor, and then rifles a tin bank, and then takes to filching all sorts of small articles from the store-keepers of the vicinage. His harsh, stupid, Christian father, getting wind of these peccadilloes, has at him in the manner of a mad bull, beating him, screaming at him, half killing him. The boy, for all the indecent cruelty of it, is convinced of the justice of it. He sees himself as one lost; he accepts the fact that he is a disgrace to his family; in the end, he embraces the parental theory that there is something strange and sinister in his soul, that he couldn't be good if he tried. Finally, filled with some vague notion of taking his abhorrent self out of sight, he runs away from home. Brought back in the character of a felon, he runs away again. Soon he is a felon in fact. That is to say, he forges his father's name to a sheaf of checks, and his father allows him to go to prison.

This prison term gives the youngster a chance to think things out for himself, without the constant intrusion of his father's Presbyterian notions of right or wrong. The result is a measurably saner philosophy than that he absorbed at home, but there is still enough left of the old moral obsession to cripple him in all his thinking, and especially in his thinking about himself. His attitude toward women, for example, is constantly conditioned by puritanical misgivings and superstitions. He can never view them innocently, joyously, unmorally, as a young fellow of twenty or twenty-one should, but is always oppressed by Sunday-schoolish notions of his duty to them, and to society in general. On the one hand, he is appalled by his ready yielding to those hussies who have at him unofficially, and on the other hand he is filled with the idea that it would be immoral for him, an ex-convict, to go to the altar with a virgin. The result of these doubts is that he gives a good deal more earnest thought to the woman question than is good for him. The second result is that he proves an easy victim to the discarded mistress of his employer. This worthy working girl craftily snares him and marries him—and then breaks down on their wedding night, unwomaned, so to speak, by the pathetic innocence of the ass, and confesses to a choice roll of her past doings, ending with the news that she is suffering from what the vice crusaders mellifluously denominate a "social disease."

Naturally enough, the blow almost kills the poor boy—he is still, in fact, scarcely out of his nonage—and the problems that grow out of the confession engage him for the better part of the next two years. Always he approaches them and wrestles with them morally; always his search is for the way that the copybook maxims approve, not for the way that self-preservation demands. Even when a brilliant chance for revenge presents itself, and he is forced to embrace it by the sheer magnetic pull of it, he does so hesitatingly, doubtingly, ashamedly. His whole attitude to this affair, indeed, is that of an Early Christian Father. He hates himself for gathering rose-buds while he may; he hates the woman with a double hatred for strewing them so temptingly in his path. And in the end, like the moral and upright fellow that he is, he sells out the temptress for cash in hand, and salves his conscience by handing over the money to an orphan asylum. This after prayers for divine guidance. A fact! Don't miss the story of it in the book. You will go far before you get another such illuminating glimpse into a pure and righteous mind.

So in episode after episode. One observes a constant oscillation between a pharisaical piety and a hoggish carnality. The praying brother of yesterday is the night-hack roisterer of to-day; the roisterer of to-day is the snuffling penitent and pledge-taker of to-morrow. Finally, he is pulled both ways at once and suffers the greatest of all his tortures. Again, of course, a woman is at the center of it—this time a stenographer. He has no delusions about her virtue—she admits herself, in fact, that it is extinct—but all the same he falls head over heels in love with her, and is filled with an inordinate yearning to marry her and settle down with her. Why not, indeed? She is pretty and a nice girl; she seems to reciprocate his affection; she is naturally eager for the obliterating gold band; she will undoubtedly make him an excellent wife. But he has forgotten his conscience—and it rises up in revenge and floors him. What! Marry a girl with such a Past! Take a fancy woman to his bosom! Jealousy quickly comes to the aid of conscience. Will he be able to forget? Contemplating the damsel in the years to come, at breakfast, at dinner, across the domestic hearth, in the cold, blue dawn, will he ever rid his mind of those abhorrent images, those phantasms of men?

Here, at the very end, we come to the most engrossing chapter in this extraordinary book. The duelist of sex, thrust through the gizzard at last, goes off to a lonely hunting camp to wrestle with his intolerable problem. He describes his vacillations faithfully, elaborately, cruelly. On the one side he sets his honest yearning, his desire to have done with light loves, the girl herself. On the other hand he ranges his moral qualms, his sneaking distrusts, the sinister shadows of those nameless ones, his morganatic brothers-in-law. The struggle within his soul is gigantic. He suffers as Prometheus suffered on the rock; his very vitals are devoured; he emerges battered and exhausted. He decides, in the end, that he will marry the girl. She has wasted the shining dowry of her sex; she comes to him spotted and at second-hand; snickers will appear in the polyphony of the wedding music—but he will marry her nevertheless. It will be a marriage unblessed by Holy Writ; it will be a flying in the face of Moses; luck and the archangels will be against it—but he will marry her all the same, Moses or no Moses. And so, with his face made bright by his first genuine revolt against the archaic, barbaric morality that has dragged him down, and his heart pulsing to his first display of authentic, unpolluted charity, generosity and nobility, he takes his departure from us. May the fates favor him with their mercy! May the Lord God strain a point to lift him out of his purgatory at last! He has suffered all the agonies of belief. He has done abominable penance for the Westminster Catechism, and for the moral order of the world, and for all the despairing misery of back-street, black bombazine, Little Bethel goodness. He is Puritanism incarnate, and Puritanism become intolerable. . . .

I daresay any second-hand bookseller will be able to find a copy of the book for you: "One Man," by Robert Steele. There is some raciness in the detail of it. Perhaps, despite its public failure, it enjoys a measure of *pizzicato* esteem behind the door. The author, having achieved its colossal self-revelation, became intrigued by the notion that he was a literary man of sorts, and informed me that he was undertaking the story of the girl last-named—the spotted ex-virgin. But he apparently never finished it. No doubt he discovered, before he had gone very far, that the tale was intrinsically beyond him—that his fingers all turned into thumbs when he got beyond his own personal history. Such a writer, once he has told the one big story, is done for.

XIX.
Jack London

THE quasi-science of genealogy, as it is practiced in the United States, is directed almost exclusively toward establishing aristocratic descents for nobodies. That is to say, it records and glorifies decay. Its typical masterpiece is the discovery that the wife of some obscure county judge is the grandchild, infinitely removed, of Mary Queen of Scots, or that the blood of Geoffrey of Monmouth flows in the veins of a Philadelphia stockbroker. How much more profitably its professors might be employed in tracing the lineage of truly salient and distinguished men! For example, the late Jack London. Where did he get his hot artistic passion, his delicate feeling for form and color, his extraordinary skill with words? The man, in truth, was an instinctive artist of a high order, and if ignorance often corrupted his art, it only made the fact of his inborn mastery the more remarkable. No other popular writer of his time did any better writing than you will find in "The Call of the Wild," or in parts of "John Barleycorn," or in such short stories as "The Sea Farmer" and "Samuel." Here, indeed, are all the elements of sound fiction: clear thinking, a sense of character, the dramatic instinct, and, above all, the adept putting together of words—words charming and slyly significant, words arranged, in a French phrase, for the respiration and the ear. You will never convince me that this æsthetic sensitiveness, so rare, so precious, so distinctively aristocratic, burst into abiogenetic flower on a San Francisco sand-lot. There must have been some intrusion of an alien and superior strain, some *pianissimo* fillup from above; there was obviously a great deal more to the thing than a routine hatching in low life. Perhaps the explanation is to be sought in a Jewish smear. Jews were not few in the California of a generation ago, and one of them, at least, attained to a certain high, if transient, fame with the pen. Moreover, the name, London, has a Jewish smack; the Jews like to call themselves after great cities. I have, indeed, heard this possibility of an Old Testament descent put into an actual rumor. Stranger genealogies are not unknown in seaports. . . .

But London the artist did not live *a cappella*. There was also London the amateur Great Thinker, and the second often hamstrung the first. That great thinking of his, of course, took color from the sordid misery of his early life; it was, in the main, a jejune Socialism, wholly uncriticised by humor. Some of his propagandist and expository books are almost unbelievably nonsensical, and whenever he allowed any of his so-called ideas to sneak into an imaginative work the intrusion promptly spoiled it. Socialism, in truth, is quite incompatible with art; its cook-tent materialism is fundamentally at war with the first principle of the æsthetic gospel, which is that one daffodil is worth ten shares of Bethlehem Steel. It is not by accident that there has never been a book on Socialism which was also a work of art. Papa Marx's "Das Kapital" at once comes to mind. It is as wholly devoid of graces as "The Origin of Species" or "Science and Health"; one simply cannot conceive a reasonable man reading it without aversion; it is as revolting as a barrel organ. London, preaching Socialism, or quasi-Socialism, or whatever it was that he preached, took over this offensive dullness. The materialistic conception of history was too heavy a load for him to carry. When he would create beautiful books he had to throw it overboard as Wagner threw overboard democracy, the superman and free thought. A sort of temporary Christian created "Parsifal." A sort of temporary aristocrat created "The Call of the Wild."

Also in another way London's early absorption of social and economic nostrums damaged him as an artist. It led him into a socialistic exaltation of mere money; it put a touch of avarice into him. Hence his too deadly industry, his relentless thousand words a day, his steady emission of half-done books. The prophet of freedom, he yet sold himself into slavery to the publishers, and paid off with his soul for his ranch, his horses, his trappings of a wealthy cheese-monger. His volumes rolled out almost as fast as those of E. Phillips Oppenheim; he simply could not make them perfect at such a gait. There are books on his list—for example, "The Scarlet Plague" and "The Little Lady of the Big House"—that are little more than garrulous notes for books.

But even in the worst of them one comes upon sudden splashes of brilliant color, stray proofs of the adept penman, half-wistful reminders that London, at bottom, was no fraud. He left enough, I am convinced, to keep him in mind. There was in him a vast delicacy of perception, a high feeling, a sensitiveness to beauty. And there was in him, too, under all his blatancies, a poignant sense of the infinite romance and mystery of human life.

XX.

Among the Avatars

IT may be, as they say, that we Americanos lie in the gutter of civilization, but all the while our eyes steal cautious glances at the stars. In the midst of the prevailing materialism—the thin incense of mysticism. As a relief from money drives, politics and the struggle for existence—Rosicrucianism, the Knights of Pythias, passwords, grips, secret work, the 33rd degree. In flight from Peruna, Mandrake Pills and Fletcherism—Christian Science, the Emmanuel Movement, the New Thought. The tendency already has its poets: Edwin Markham and Ella Wheeler Wilcox. It has acquired its romancer: Will Levington Comfort. . . .

This Comfort wields an easy pen. He has done, indeed, some capital melodramas, and when his ardor heats him up he grows downright eloquent. But of late the whole force of his æsthetic engines has been thrown into propaganda, by the Bhagavad-Gītā out of Victorian sentimentalism. The nature of this propaganda is quickly discerned. What Comfort preaches is a sort of mellowed mariolatry, a humorless exaltation of woman, a flashy effort to turn the inter-attraction of the sexes, ordinarily a mere cause of scandal, into something transcendental and highly portentous. Woman, it appears, is the beyond-man, the trans-mammal, the nascent angel; she is the Upward Path, the Way to Consecration, the door to the Third Lustrous Dimension; all the mysteries of the cosmos are concentrated in Mystic Motherhood, whatever that may be. I capitalize in the Comfortian (and New Thought) manner. On one page of "Fate Knocks at the Door" I find Voices, Pits of Trade, Woman, the Great Light, the Big Deep and the Twentieth Century Lie. On another are the Rising Road of Man, the Transcendental Soul Essence, the Way Uphill, the Sempiternal Mother. Thus Andrew Bedient, the spouting hero of the tale:

> I believe in the natural greatness of Woman; that through the spirit of Woman are born sons of strength; that only through the potential greatness of Woman comes the militant greatness of man.

I believe Mothering is the loveliest of the Arts; that great mothers are handmaidens of the Spirit, to whom are intrusted God's avatars; that no prophet is greater than his mother.

I believe when humanity arises to Spiritual evolution (as it once evolved through Flesh, and is now evolving through Mind) Woman will assume the ethical guiding of the race.

I believe that the Holy Spirit of the Trinity is Mystic Motherhood, and the source of the divine principle is Woman; that the prophets are the union of this divine principle and the higher manhood; that they are beyond the attractions of women of flesh, because unto their manhood has been added Mystic Motherhood. . . .

I believe that the way to Godhood is the Rising Road of Man.

I believe that, as the human mother brings a child to her husband, the father—so Mystic Motherhood, the Holy Spirit, is bringing the world to God, the Father.

The capitals are Andrew's—or Comfort's. I merely transcribe and perspire. This Andrew, it appears, is a sea cook who has been mellowed and transfigured by exhaustive study of the Bhagavad Gītā, one of the sacred nonsense books of the Hindus. He doesn't know who his father was, and he remembers his mother only as one dying in a strange city. When she finally passed away he took to the high seas and mastered marine cookery. Thus for many years, up and down the world. Then he went ashore at Manila and became chef to an army packtrain. Then he proceeded to China, to Japan. Then to India, where he entered the forestry service and plodded the Himalayan heights, always with the Bhagavad Gītā under his arm. At some time or other, during his years of culinary seafaring, he saved the life of a Yankee ship captain, and that captain, later dying, left him untold millions in South America. But it is long after all this is past that we have chiefly to do with him. He is now a young Monte Cristo at large in New York, a Monte Cristo worshiped and gurgled over by a crowd of mushy old maids, a hero of Uneeda-biscuit parties in God-forsaken studios, the madness and despair of senescent virgins.

But it is not Andrew's wealth that inflames these old girls, nor even his manly beauty, but rather his revolutionary and astounding sapience, his great gift for solemn and incomprehensible utterance, his skill as a metaphysician. They hang upon his every word. His rhetoric makes their heads swim. Once he gets fully under way, they almost swoon. . . . And what girls they are! Alas, what pathetic neck-stretching toward tinsel stars! What eager hearing of the soulful, gassy stuff! One of them has red hair and "wine dark eyes, now cryptic black, now suffused with red glows like the night sky above a prairie fire." Another is "tall and lovely in a tragic, flower-like way" and performs upon the violoncello. A third is "a tanned woman rather variously weathered," who writes stupefying epigrams about Whitman and Nietzsche—making the latter's name Nietschze, of course! A fourth is "the Gray One"—O mystic appellation! A fifth—but enough! You get the picture. You can imagine how Andrew's sagacity staggers these poor dears. You can see them fighting for him, each against all, with sharp, psychical excaliburs.

Arm in arm with all this exaltation of Woman, of course, goes a great suspicion of mere woman. The combination is as old as Christian mysticism, and Havelock Ellis has discussed its origin and nature at great length. On the one hand is the *Übermensch*; on the other hand is the temptress, the Lorelei. The Madonna and Mother Eve, the celestial virgins and the succubi! The hero of "Fate Knocks at the Door," for all his flaming words, still distrusts his goddess. His colleague of "Down Among Men" is poisoned by the same suspicions. Woman has led him up to grace, she has shown him the Upward Path, she has illuminated him with her Mystic Motherhood—but the moment she lets go his hand he takes to his heels. What is worse, he sends a friend to her (I forget her name, and his) to explain in detail how unfavorably any further communion with her would corrupt his high mission, *i.e.*, to save the downtrodden by writing plays that fail and books that not even Americans will read. An intellectual milk-toast! A mixture of Dr. Frank Crane and Mother Tingley, of Edward Bok and the Archangel Eddy! . . .

So far, not much of this ineffable stuff has got among the best-sellers, but I believe that it is on its way. Despite materialism and pragmatism, mysticism is steadily growing in fashion. I hear of paunchy Freemasons holding sacramental meetings on Maundy Thursday, of Senators in Congress railing against *materia medica*, of Presidents invoking divine intercession at Cabinet meetings. The New Thoughters march on; they have at least a dozen prosperous magazines, and one of them has a circulation comparable to that of any 20-cent repository of lingerie fiction. Such things as Karma, the Ineffable Essence and the Zeitgeist become familiar fauna, chained up in the cage of every woman's club. Thousands of American women know far more about the Subconscious than they know about plain sewing. The pungency of myrrh and frankincense is mingled with *odeur de femme*. Physiology is formally repealed and repudiated; its laws are all lies. No doubt the fleshly best-seller of the last decade, with its blushing amorousness, its flashes of underwear, its obstetrics between chapters, will give place to a more delicate piece of trade-goods to-morrow. In this New Thought novel the hero and heroine will seek each other out, not to spoon obscenely behind the door, but for the purpose of uplifting the race. Kissing is already unsanitary; in a few years it may be downright sacrilegious, a crime against some obscure avatar or other, a business libidinous and accursed.

XXI.
Three American Immortals

I
Aristotelean Obsequies

I TAKE the following from the Boston *Herald* of May 1, 1882:

A beautiful floral book stood at the left of the pulpit, being spread
out on a stand. . . . Its last page was composed of white carnations,
white daisies and light-colored immortelles. On the leaf was displayed, in neat letters of purple immortelles, the word "Finis." This
device was about two feet square, and its border was composed of different colored tea-roses. The other portion of the book was composed of dark and light-colored flowers. . . . The front of the large
pulpit was covered with a mass of white pine boughs laid on loosely.
In the center of this mass of boughs appeared a large harp composed
of yellow jonquils. . . . Above this harp was a handsome bouquet of
dark pansies. On each side appeared large clusters of calla lilies.

Well, what have we here? The funeral of a Grand Exalted
Pishposh of the Odd Fellows, of an East Side Tammany leader,
of an aged and much respected brothel-keeper? Nay. What we
have here is the funeral of Ralph Waldo Emerson. It was thus
that New England lavished the loveliest fruits of the Puritan
æsthetic upon the bier of her greatest son. It was thus that Puritan *Kultur* mourned a philosopher.

2
Edgar Allan Poe

The myth that there is a monument to Edgar Allan Poe in
Baltimore is widely believed; there are even persons who, stopping off in Baltimore to eat oysters, go to look at it. As a
matter of fact, no such monument exists. All that the explorer
actually finds is a cheap and hideous tombstone in the corner
of a Presbyterian churchyard—a tombstone quite as bad as the
worst in Père La Chaise. For twenty-six years after Poe's death
there was not even this: the grave remained wholly unmarked.

Poe had surviving relatives in Baltimore, and they were well-to-do. One day one of them ordered a local stonecutter to put a plain stone over the grave. The stonecutter hacked it out and was preparing to haul it to the churchyard when a runaway freight-train smashed into his stoneyard and broke the stone to bits. Thereafter the Poes seem to have forgotten Cousin Edgar; at all events, nothing further was done.

The existing tombstone was erected by a committee of Baltimore schoolmarms, and cost about $1,000. It took the dear girls ten long years to raise the money. They started out with a "literary entertainment" which yielded $380. This was in 1865. Six years later the fund had made such slow progress that, with accumulated interest, it came to but $587.02. Three years more went by: it now reached $627.55. Then some anonymous Poeista came down with $100, two others gave $50 each, one of the devoted schoolmarms raised $52 in nickels and dimes, and George W. Childs agreed to pay any remaining deficit. During all this time not a single American author of position gave the project any aid. And when, finally, a stone was carved and set up and the time came for the unveiling, the only one who appeared at the ceremony was Walt Whitman. All the other persons present were Baltimore nobodies—chiefly school-teachers and preachers. There were three set speeches—one by the principal of a local high school, the second by a teacher in the same seminary, and the third by a man who was invited to give his "personal recollections" of Poe, but who announced in his third sentence that "I never saw Poe but once, and our interview did not last an hour."

This was the gaudiest Poe celebration ever held in America. The poet has never enjoyed such august posthumous attentions as those which lately flattered the shade of James Russell Lowell. At his actual burial, in 1849, exactly eight persons were present, of whom six were relatives. He was planted, as I have said, in a Presbyterian churchyard, among generations of honest believers in infant damnation, but the officiating clergyman was a Methodist. Two days after his death a Baptist gentleman of God, the illustrious Rufus W. Griswold, printed a defamatory article upon him in the New York *Tribune*, and for years it set the tone of native criticism of him. And so he rests: thrust among Presbyterians by a Methodist and formally damned by a Baptist.

3
Memorial Service

Let us summon from the shades the immortal soul of James Harlan, born in 1820, entered into rest in 1899. In the year 1865 this Harlan resigned from the United States Senate to enter the cabinet of Abraham Lincoln as Secretary of the Interior. One of the clerks in that department, at $600 a year, was Walt Whitman, lately emerged from three years of hard service as an army nurse during the Civil War. One day, discovering that Whitman was the author of a book called "Leaves of Grass," Harlan ordered him incontinently kicked out, and it was done forthwith. Let us remember this event and this man; he is too precious to die. Let us repair, once a year, to our accustomed houses of worship and there give thanks to God that one day in 1865 brought together the greatest poet that America has ever produced and the damndest ass.

PREJUDICES:
SECOND SERIES

I.

The National Letters

Prophets and Their Visions

I T is convenient to begin, like the gentlemen of God, with a glance at a text or two. The first, a short one, is from Ralph Waldo Emerson's celebrated oration, "The American Scholar," delivered before the Phi Beta Kappa Society at Cambridge on August 31st, 1837. Emerson was then thirty-four years old and almost unknown in his own country, though he had already published "Nature" and established his first contacts with Landor and Carlyle. But "The American Scholar" brought him into instant notice at home, partly as man of letters but more importantly as seer and prophet, and the fame thus founded has endured without much diminution, at all events in New England, to this day. Oliver Wendell Holmes, giving words to what was undoubtedly the common feeling, hailed the address as the intellectual declaration of independence of the American people, and that judgment, amiably passed on by three generations of pedagogues, still survives in the literature books. I quote from the first paragraph:

Our day of dependence, our long apprenticeship to the learning of other lands, draws to a close. . . . Events, actions arise, that must be sung, that will sing themselves. Who can doubt that poetry will revive and lead in a new age, as the star in the constellation Harp, which now flames in our zenith, astronomers announce, shall one day be the pole-star for a thousand years?

This, as I say, was in 1837. Thirty-three years later, in 1870, Walt Whitman echoed the prophecy in his even more famous "Democratic Vistas." What he saw in his vision and put into his gnarled and gasping prose was

a class of native authors, literatuses, far different, far higher in grade, than any yet known, sacerdotal, modern, fit to cope with our occasions, lands, permeating the whole mass of American morality, taste, belief, breathing into it a new breath of life, giving it decision, affecting politics far more than the popular superficial suffrage, with results inside and underneath the elections of Presidents or Congress—radiating, begetting appropriate teachers, schools, manners, and, as its grandest result, accomplishing, (what neither the schools nor the churches and their clergy have hitherto accomplished, and without which this nation will no more stand, permanently, soundly, than a house will stand without a substratum,) a religious and moral character beneath the political and productive and intellectual bases of the States.

And out of the vision straightway came the prognostication:

The promulgation and belief in such a class or order—a new and greater literatus order—its possibility, (nay, certainty,) underlies these entire speculations. . . . Above all previous lands, a great original literature is sure to become the justification and reliance, (in some respects the sole reliance,) of American democracy.

Thus Whitman in 1870, the time of the first draft of "Democratic Vistas." He was of the same mind, and said so, in 1888, four years before his death. I could bring up texts of like tenor in great number, from the years before 1837, from those after 1888, and from every decade between. The dream of Emerson, though the eloquence of its statement was new and arresting, embodied no novel projection of the fancy; it merely gave a sonorous *Waldhorn* tone to what had been dreamed and said before. You will find almost the same high hope, the same exuberant confidence in the essays of the elder Channing and in the "Lectures on American Literature" of Samuel Lorenzo Knapp, LL.D., the first native critic of beautiful letters—the primordial tadpole of all our later Mores, Brownells, Phelpses, Mabies, Brander Matthewses and other such grave and glittering fish. Knapp believed, like Whitman long after him, that the sheer physical grandeur of the New World would inflame a race of bards to unprecedented utterance. "What are the Tibers and Scamanders," he demanded, "measured by the Missouri and the Amazon? Or what the loveliness of Illysus or Avon by the Connecticut or the Potomack? Whenever a nation wills it, prodigies are born." That is to say, prodigies literary and ineffable as well as purely material—prodigies aimed, in his own words, at "the olympick crown" as well as at mere railroads,

ships, wheat-fields, droves of hogs, factories and money. Nor
were Channing and Knapp the first of the haruspices. Noah
Webster, the lexicographer, who "taught millions to spell but
not one to sin," had seen the early starlight of the same
Golden Age so early as 1789, as the curious will find by examining his "Dissertations on the English Language," a work
fallen long since into undeserved oblivion. Nor was Whitman,
taking sober second thought exactly a century later, the last of
them. Out of many brethren of our own day, extravagantly articulate in print and among the chautauquas, I choose one—
not because his hope is of purest water, but precisely because,
like Emerson, he dilutes it with various discreet whereases.
He is Van Wyck Brooks, a young man far more intelligent,
penetrating and hospitable to fact than any of the reigning
professors—a critic who is sharply differentiated from them,
indeed, by the simple circumstance that he has information
and sense. Yet this extraordinary Mr. Brooks, in his "Letters
and Leadership," published in 1918, rewrites "The American
Scholar" in terms borrowed almost bodily from "Democratic
Vistas"—that is to say, he prophesies with Emerson and exults
with Whitman. First there is the Emersonian doctrine of the
soaring individual made articulate by freedom and realizing
"the responsibility that lies upon us, each in the measure of
his own gift." And then there is Whitman's vision of a self-
interpretative democracy, forced into high literary adventures
by Joseph Conrad's "obscure inner necessity," and so achieving a "new synthesis adaptable to the unique conditions of our
life." And finally there is the specific prediction, the grandiose,
Adam Forepaugh mirage: "We shall become a luminous
people, dwelling in the light and sharing our light." . . .

As I say, the roll of such soothsayers might be almost endlessly lengthened. There is, in truth, scarcely a formal discourse upon the national letters (forgetting, perhaps, Barrett
Wendell's sour threnody upon the New England *Aufklärung*)
that is without some touch of this previsional exultation, this
confident hymning of glories to come, this fine assurance that
American literature, in some future always ready to dawn, will
burst into so grand a flowering that history will cherish its
loveliest blooms even above such salient American gifts to culture as the moving-picture, the phonograph, the New Thought

and the bichloride tablet. If there was ever a dissenter from the national optimism, in this as in other departments, it was surely Edgar Allan Poe—without question the bravest and most original, if perhaps also the least orderly and judicious, of all the critics that we have produced. And yet even Poe, despite his general habit of disgust and dismay, caught a flash or two of that engaging picture—even Poe, for an instant, in 1846, thought that he saw the beginnings of a solid and autonomous native literature, its roots deep in the soil of the republic—as you will discover by turning to his forgotten essay on J.G.C. Brainard, a thrice-forgotten doggereleer of Jackson's time. Poe, of course, was too cautious to let his imagination proceed to details; one feels that a certain doubt, a saving peradventure or two, played about the unaccustomed vision as he beheld it. But, nevertheless, he unquestionably beheld it. . . .

2
The Answering Fact

Now for the answering fact. How has the issue replied to these visionaries? It has replied in a way that is manifestly to the discomfiture of Emerson as a prophet, to the dismay of Poe as a pessimist disarmed by transient optimism, and to the utter collapse of Whitman. We have, as every one knows, produced no such "new and greater literatus order" as that announced by old Walt. We have given a gaping world no books that "radiate," and surely none intelligibly comparable to stars and constellations. We have achieved no prodigies of the first class, and very few of the second class, and not many of the third and fourth classes. Our literature, despite several false starts that promised much, is chiefly remarkable, now as always, for its respectable mediocrity. Its typical great man, in our own time, has been Howells, as its typical great man a generation ago was Lowell, and two generations ago, Irving. Viewed largely, its salient character appears as a sort of timorous flaccidity, an amiable hollowness. In bulk it grows more and more formidable, in ease and decorum it makes undoubted progress, and on the side of mere technic, of the bald capacity to write, it shows an ever-widening competence. But when one proceeds from such agencies and externals to the intrinsic substance, to the creative passion within, that substance quickly reveals itself as thin and watery, and that passion fades to something almost puerile. In all that mass of suave and often highly diverting writing there is no visible movement toward a distinguished and singular excellence, a signal national quality, a ripe and stimulating flavor, or, indeed, toward any other describable goal. What one sees is simply a general irresolution, a pervasive superficiality. There is no sober grappling with fundamentals, but only a shy sporting on the surface; there is not even any serious approach, such as Whitman dreamed of, to the special experiences and emergencies of the American people. When one turns to any other national literature—to Russian literature, say, or French, or German or Scandinavian—one is conscious immediately of a definite attitude toward the primary mysteries of existence, the unsolved and ever-fascinating problems at the bottom of human life, and of a definite preoccupation with some of them, and a definite way of translating their challenge into drama. These attitudes and preoccupations raise a literature above mere poetizing and tale-telling; they give it dignity and importance; above all, they give it national character. But it is precisely here that the literature of America, and especially the later literature, is most colorless and inconsequential. As if paralyzed by the national fear of ideas, the democratic distrust of whatever strikes beneath the prevailing platitudes, it evades all resolute and honest dealing with what, after all, must be every healthy literature's elementary materials. One is conscious of no brave and noble earnestness in it, of no generalized passion for intellectual and spiritual adventure, of no organized determination to think things out. What is there is a highly self-conscious and insipid correctness, a bloodless respectability, a submergence of matter in manner—in brief, what is there is the feeble, uninspiring quality of German painting and English music.

It was so in the great days and it is so to-day. There has always been hope and there has always been failure. Even the most optimistic prophets of future glories have been united, at all times, in their discontent with the here and now. "The mind of this country," said Emerson, speaking of what was currently visible in 1837, "is taught to aim at low objects. . . . There is no work for any but the decorous and the

complaisant. . . . Books are written . . . by men of talent
. . . who start wrong, who set out from accepted dogmas,
not from their own sight of principles." And then, turning to
the way out: "The office of the scholar (*i.e.*, of Whitman's 'literatus') is to cheer, to raise and to guide men by showing them
facts amid appearances." Whitman himself, a full generation
later, found that office still unfilled. "Our fundamental want
to-day in the United States," he said, "with closest, amplest
reference to present conditions, and to the future, is of a class,
and the clear idea of a class, of native authors, literatuses, far
different, far higher in grade, than any yet known"—and so
on, as I have already quoted him. And finally, to make an end
of the prophets, there is Brooks, with nine-tenths of his book
given over, not to his prophecy—it is crowded, indeed, into
the last few pages—but to a somewhat heavy mourning over
the actual scene before him. On the side of letters, the æsthetic
side, the side of ideas, we present to the world at large, he says,
"the spectacle of a vast, undifferentiated herd of good-
humored animals"—Knights of Pythias, Presbyterians, standard model Ph.D.'s, readers of the *Saturday Evening Post*, admirers of Richard Harding Davis and O. Henry, devotees of
Hamilton Wright Mabie's "white list" of books, members of
the Y.M.C.A. or the Drama League, weepers at chautauquas,
wearers of badges, 100 per cent. patriots, children of God. Poe
I pass over; I shall turn to him again later on. Nor shall I repeat
the parrotings of Emerson and Whitman in the jeremiads of
their innumerable heirs and assigns. What they all establish is
what is already obvious: that American thinking, when it concerns itself with beautiful letters as when it concerns itself with
religious dogma or political theory, is extraordinarily timid and
superficial—that it evades the genuinely serious problems of
life and art as if they were stringently taboo—that the outward
virtues it undoubtedly shows are always the virtues, not of profundity, not of courage, not of originality, but merely those of
an emasculated and often very trashy dilettantism.

3
The Ashes of New England

The current scene is surely depressing enough. What one observes is a literature in three layers, and each inordinately doughy and uninspiring—each almost without flavor or savor. It is hard to say, with much critical plausibility, which layer deserves to be called the upper, but for decorum's sake the choice may be fixed upon that which meets with the approval of the reigning Lessings. This is the layer of the novels of the late Howells, Judge Grant, Alice Brown and the rest of the dwindling survivors of New England *Kultur*, of the brittle, academic poetry of Woodberry and the elder Johnson, of the tea-party essays of Crothers, Miss Repplier and company, and of the solemn, highly judicial, coroner's inquest criticism of More, Brownell, Babbitt and their imitators. Here we have manner, undoubtedly. The thing is correctly done; it is never crude or gross; there is in it a faint perfume of college-town society. But when this highly refined and attenuated manner is allowed for what remains is next to nothing. One never remembers a character in the novels of these aloof and de-Americanized Americans; one never encounters an idea in their essays; one never carries away a line out of their poetry. It is literature as an academic exercise for talented grammarians, almost as a genteel recreation for ladies and gentlemen of fashion—the exact equivalent, in the field of letters, of eighteenth century painting and German *Augenmusik*.

What ails it, intrinsically, is a dearth of intellectual audacity and of æsthetic passion. Running through it, and characterizing the work of almost every man and woman producing it, there is an unescapable suggestion of the old Puritan suspicion of the fine arts as such—of the doctrine that they offer fit asylum for good citizens only when some ulterior and superior purpose is carried into them. This purpose, naturally enough, most commonly shows a moral tinge. The aim of poetry, it appears, is to fill the mind with lofty thoughts—not to give it joy, but to give it a grand and somewhat gaudy sense of virtue. The essay is a weapon against the degenerate tendencies of the age. The novel, properly conceived, is a means of uplifting the spirit; its aim is to inspire, not merely to satisfy the low curiosity of man in man. The Puritan, of course, is not entirely devoid of æsthetic feeling. He has a taste for good form; he responds to style; he is even capable of something approaching a purely æsthetic emotion. But he fears this æsthetic emotion as an insinuating distraction from his chief business in life: the sober consideration of the all-important problem of conduct. Art is a temptation, a seduction, a Lorelei, and the Good Man may safely have traffic with it only when it is broken to moral uses—in other words, when its innocence is pumped out of it, and it is purged of gusto. It is precisely this gusto that one misses in all the work of the New England school, and in all the work of the formal schools that derive from it. One observes in such a fellow as Dr. Henry Van Dyke an excellent specimen of the whole clan. He is, in his way, a genuine artist. He has a hand for pretty verses. He wields a facile rhetoric. He shows, in indiscreet moments, a touch of imagination. But all the while he remains a sound Presbyterian, with one eye on the devil. He is a Presbyterian first and an artist second, which is just as comfortable as trying to be a Presbyterian first and a chorus girl second. To such a man it must inevitably appear that a Molière, a Wagner, a Goethe or a Shakespeare was more than a little bawdy.

The criticism that supports this decaying caste of literary Brahmins is grounded almost entirely upon ethical criteria. You will spend a long while going through the works of such typical professors as More, Phelps, Boynton, Burton, Perry, Brownell and Babbitt before ever you encounter a purely æsthetic judgment upon an æsthetic question. It is almost as if a man estimating daffodils should do it in terms of artichokes. Phelps' whole body of "we churchgoers" criticism—the most catholic and tolerant, it may be said in passing, that the faculty can show—consists chiefly of a plea for correctness, and particularly for moral correctness; he never gets very far from "the axiom of the moral law." Brownell argues eloquently for standards that would bind an imaginative author as tightly as a Sunday-school superintendent is bound by the Ten Commandments and the Mann Act. Sherman tries to save Shakespeare for the right-thinking by proving that he was an Iowa Methodist—a member of his local Chamber of Commerce, a contemner of Reds, an advocate of democracy and the League

of Nations, a patriotic dollar-a-year-man during the Armada
scare. Elmer More devotes himself, year in and year out, to denouncing the Romantic movement, *i.e.*, the effort to emanci-
pate the artist from formulæ and categories, and so make him
free to dance with arms and legs. And Babbitt, to make an end,
gives over his days and his nights to deploring Rousseau's anarchistic abrogation of "the veto power" over the imagination,
leading to such "wrongness" in both art and life that it threatens "to wreck civilization." In brief, the alarms of schoolmasters. Not many of them deal specifically with the literature
that is in being. It is too near to be quite nice. To More or
Babbitt only death can atone for the primary offense of the
artist. But what they preach nevertheless has its echoes con-
temporaneously, and those echoes, in the main, are woefully
falsetto. I often wonder what sort of picture of These States is
conjured up by foreigners who read, say, Crothers, Van Dyke,
Babbitt, the later Winston Churchill, and the old maids of the
Freudian suppression school. How can such a foreigner, moving in those damp, asthmatic mists, imagine such phenomena
as Roosevelt, Billy Sunday, Bryan, the Becker case, the I.W.W.,
Newport, Palm Beach, the University of Chicago, Chicago
itself—the whole, gross, glittering, excessively dynamic, infinitely grotesque, incredibly stupendous drama of American
life?

As I have said, it is not often that the *ordentlichen Professoren* deign to notice contemporary writers, even of their own
austere kidney. In all the Shelburne Essays there is none on
Howells, or on Churchill, or on Mrs. Wharton; More seems to
think of American literature as expiring with Longfellow and
Donald G. Mitchell. He has himself hinted that in the department of criticism of criticism there enters into the matter
something beyond mere aloof ignorance. "I soon learned (as
editor of the pre-Bolshevik *Nation*)," he says, "that it was virtually impossible to get fair consideration for a book written by
a scholar not connected with a university from a reviewer so
connected." This class consciousness, however, should not apply to artists, who are admittedly inferior to professors, and it
surely does not show itself in such men as Phelps and Spingarn, who seem to be very eager to prove that they are not
professorial. Yet Phelps, in the course of a long work on the

novel, pointedly omits all mention of such men as Dreiser, and
Spingarn, as the aforesaid Brooks has said, "appears to be less
inclined even than the critics with whom he is theoretically at
war to play an active, public part in the secular conflict of darkness and light." When one comes to the *Privat-Dozenten* there
is less remoteness, but what takes the place of it is almost as
saddening. To Sherman and Percy Boynton the one aim of
criticism seems to be the enforcement of correctness—in
Emerson's phrase, the upholding of "some great decorum,
some fetish of a government, some ephemeral trade, or war, or
man"—*e.g.*, Puritanism, democracy, monogamy, the League of
Nations, the Wilsonian piffle. Even among the critics who escape the worst of this schoolmastering frenzy there is some
touch of the heavy "culture" of the provincial schoolma'm.
For example, consider Clayton Hamilton, M.A., vice-president
of the National Institute of Arts and Letters. Here are the tests
he proposes for dramatic critics, *i.e.*, for gentlemen chiefly employed in reviewing such characteristic American compositions
as the Ziegfeld Follies, "Up in Mabel's Room," "Ben-Hur"
and "The Witching Hour":

　　1. Have you ever stood bareheaded in the nave of Amiens?
　　2. Have you ever climbed to the Acropolis by moonlight?
　　3. Have you ever walked with whispers into the hushed presence of
the Frari Madonna of Bellini?

　　What could more brilliantly evoke an image of the eternal
Miss Birch, blue veil flying and Baedeker in hand, plodding
along faithfully through the interminable corridors and cata-
combs of the Louvre, the while bands are playing across the
river, and young bucks in three-gallon hats are sparking the
gals, and the Jews and harlots uphold the traditions of French
hig leef at Longchamps, and American deacons are frisked and
debauched up on martyrs' hill? The banality of it is really too
exquisite to be borne; the lack of humor is almost that of a
Fifth avenue divine. One seldom finds in the pronunciamentoes of these dogged professors, indeed, any trace of either At-
tic or Gallic salt. When they essay to be jocose, the result is
usually simply an elephantine whimsicality, by the chautauqua
out of the *Atlantic Monthly*. Their satire is mere ill-nature.
One finds it difficult to believe that they have ever read Lewes,

or Hazlitt, or, above all, Saintsbury. I often wonder, in fact, how Saintsbury would fare, an unknown man, at the hands of, say, Brownell or More. What of his iconoclastic gayety, his boyish weakness for tweaking noses and pulling whiskers, his obscene delight in slang? . . .

4

The Ferment Underground

So much for the top layer. The bottom layer is given over to the literature of Greenwich Village, and by Greenwich Village, of course, I mean the whole of the advanced wing in letters, whatever the scene of its solemn declarations of independence and forlorn hopes. Miss Amy Lowell is herself a fully-equipped and automobile Greenwich Village, domiciled in Boston amid the crumbling gravestones of the New England *intelligentsia*, but often in waspish joy-ride through the hinterland. Vachel Lindsay, with his pilgrim's staff, is another. There is a third in Chicago, with *Poetry: A Magazine of Verse* as its Exhibit A; it is, in fact, the senior of the Village fornenst Washington Square. Others you will find in far-flung factory towns, wherever there is a Little Theater, and a couple of local Synges and Chekovs to supply its stage. St. Louis, before Zoë Akins took flight, had the busiest of all these Greenwiches, and the most interesting. What lies under the whole movement is the natural revolt of youth against the pedagogical Prussianism of the professors. The oppression is extreme, and so the rebellion is extreme. Imagine a sentimental young man of the provinces, awaking one morning to the somewhat startling discovery that he is full of the divine afflatus, and nominated by the hierarchy of hell to enrich the literature of his fatherland. He seeks counsel and aid. He finds, on consulting the official treatises on that literature, that its greatest poet was Longfellow. He is warned, reading More and Babbitt, that the literatus who lets feeling get into his compositions is a psychic fornicator, and under German influences. He has formal notice from Sherman that Puritanism is the lawful philosophy of the country, and that any dissent from it is treason. He gets the news, plowing through the New York *Times Book Review*, the *Nation* (so far to the left in its politics, but hugging the right so desperately in letters!), the *Bookman*, the *Atlantic* and the rest, that the salient artists of the living generation are such masters as Robert Underwood Johnson, Owen Wister, James Lane Allen, George E. Woodberry, Hamlin Garland, William Roscoe Thayer and Augustus Thomas, with polite bows to Margaret Deland, Mary Johnston and Ellen Glasgow. It slowly dawns upon him that Robert W. Chambers is an academician and Theodore Dreiser isn't, that Brian Hooker is and George Sterling isn't, that Henry Sydnor Harrison is and James Branch Cabell isn't, that "Chimmie Fadden" Townsend is and Sherwood Anderson isn't.

Is it any wonder that such a young fellow, after one or two sniffs of that prep-school fog, swings so vastly backward that one finds him presently in corduroy trousers and a velvet jacket, hammering furiously upon a pine table in a Macdougal street cellar, his mind full of malicious animal magnetism against even so amiable an old maid as Howells, and his discourse full of insane hair-splittings about *vers libre*, futurism, spectrism, vorticism, *Expressionismus, héliogabalisme?* The thing, in truth, is in the course of nature. The Spaniards who were outraged by the Palmerism of Torquemada did not become members of the Church of England; they became atheists. The American colonists, in revolt against a bad king, did not set up a good king; they set up a democracy, and so gave every honest man a chance to become a rogue on his own account. Thus the young literatus, emerging from the vacuum of Ohio or Arkansas. An early success, as we shall see, tends to halt and moderate him. He finds that, after all, there is still a place for him, a sort of asylum for such as he, not over-populated or very warmly-heated, but nevertheless quite real. But if his sledding at the start is hard, if the corrective birch finds him while he is still tender, then he goes, as Andrew Jackson would say, the whole hog, and another voice is added to the raucous bellowing of the literary Reds.

I confess that the spectacle gives me some joy, despite the fact that the actual output of the Village is seldom worth noticing. What commonly engulfs and spoils the Villagers is their concern with mere technique. Among them, it goes without saying, are a great many frauds—poets whose yearning to write is unaccompanied by anything properly describable as capacity, dramatists whose dramas are simply Schnitzler and well-water, workers in prose fiction who gravitate swiftly and inevitably to the machine-made merchandise of the cheap magazines—in brief, American equivalents of the bogus painters of the Boul' Mich'. These pretenders, having no ideas, naturally try to make the most of forms. Half the wars in the Village are over form; content is taken for granted, or forgotten altogether. The extreme leftists, in fact, descend to a meaningless gibberish, both in prose and in verse; it is their last defiance to intellectualism. This childish concentration upon externals unfortunately tends to debauch the small minority that is of more or less genuine parts; the good are pulled in by the bad. As a result, the Village produces nothing that justifies all the noise it makes. I have yet to hear of a first-rate book coming out of it, or a short story of arresting quality, or even a poem of any solid distinction. As one of the editors of a magazine which specializes in the work of new authors I am in an exceptional position to report. Probably nine-tenths of the stuff written in the dark dens and alleys south of the arch comes to my desk soon or late, and I go through all of it faithfully. It is, in the overwhelming main, jejune and imitative. The prose is quite without distinction, either in matter or in manner. The verse seldom gets beyond a hollow audaciousness, not unlike that of cubist painting. It is not often, indeed, that even personality is in it; all of the Villagers seem to write alike. "Unless one is an expert in some detective method," said a recent writer in *Poetry*, "one is at a loss to assign correctly the ownership of much free verse—that is, if one plays fairly and refuses to look at the signature until one has ventured a guess. It is difficult, for instance, to know whether Miss Lowell is writing Mr. Bynner's verse, or whether he is writing hers." Moreover, this monotony keeps to a very low level. There is no poet in the movement who has produced anything even remotely approaching the fine lyrics of Miss Reese, Miss Teasdale and John McClure, and for all its war upon the *cliché* it can show nothing to equal the *cliché*-free beauty of Robert Loveman's "Rain Song." In the drama the Village has gone further. In Eugene O'Neill, Rita Wellman and Zoë Akins it offers dramatists who are obviously many cuts above the well-professored mechanicians who pour out of Prof. Dr. Baker's *Ibsenfabrik* at Cambridge. But here we must probably give the credit, not to any influence residing within the movement itself, but to mere acts of God. Such pieces as O'Neill's one-acters, Miss Wellman's "The Gentile Wife" and Miss Akins' extraordinary "Papa" lie quite outside the Village scheme of things. There is no sign of formal revolt in them. They are simply first-rate work, done miraculously in a third-rate land.

But if the rebellion is thus sterile of direct results, and, in more than one aspect, fraudulent and ridiculous, it is at all events an evidence of something not to be disregarded, and that something is the gradual formulation of a challenge to the accepted canons in letters and to the accepted canon lawyers. The first hoots come from a tatterdemalion horde of rogues and vagabonds without the gates, but soon or late, let us hope, they will be echoed in more decorous quarters, and with much greater effect. The Village, in brief, is an earnest that somewhere or other new seeds are germinating. Between the young tutor who launches into letters with imitations of his seminary chief's imitations of Agnes Repplier's imitations of Charles Lamb, and the young peasant who tries to get his honest exultations into free verse there can be no hesitant choice: the peasant is, by long odds, the sounder artist, and, what is more, the sounder American artist. Even the shy and somewhat stagey carnality that characterizes the Village has its high symbolism and its profound uses. It proves that, despite repressions unmatched in civilization in modern times, there is still a sturdy animality in American youth, and hence good health. The poet hugging his Sonia in a Washington square beanery, and so giving notice to all his world that he is a devil of a fellow, is at least a better man than the emasculated stripling in a Y.M.C.A. gospel-mill, pumped dry of all his natural appetites and the vacuum filled with double-entry book-keeping, business economics and autoerotism. In so foul a nest of imprisoned and fermenting sex as the United States, plain fornication becomes a mark of relative decency.

5
In the Literary Abattoir

But the theme is letters, not wickedness. The upper and lower layers have been surveyed. There remains the middle layer, the thickest and perhaps the most significant of the three. By the middle layer I mean the literature that fills the magazines and burdens the book-counters in the department-stores—the literature adorned by such artists as Richard Harding Davis, Rex Beach, Emerson Hough, O. Henry, James Whitcomb Riley, Augustus Thomas, Robert W. Chambers, Henry Sydnor Harrison, Owen Johnson, Cyrus Townsend Brady, Irvin Cobb and Mary Roberts Rinehart—in brief, the literature that pays like a bucket-shop or a soap-factory, and is thus thoroughly American. At the bottom this literature touches such depths of banality that it would be difficult to match it in any other country. The "inspirational" and patriotic essays of Dr. Frank Crane, Orison Swett Marden, Porter Emerson Browne, Gerald Stanley Lee, E. S. Martin, Ella Wheeler Wilcox and the Rev. Dr. Newell Dwight Hillis, the novels of Harold Bell Wright, Eleanor H. Porter and Gene Stratton-Porter, and the mechanical sentimentalities in prose and verse that fill the cheap fiction magazines—this stuff has a native quality that is as unmistakable as that of Mother's Day, Billy-Sundayism or the Junior Order of United American Mechanics. It is the natural outpouring of a naïve and yet half barbarous people, full of delight in a few childish and inaccurate ideas. But it would be a grave error to assume that the whole of the literature of the middle layer is of the same infantile quality. On the contrary, a great deal of it—for example, the work of Mrs. Rinehart, and that of Corra Harris, Gouverneur Morris, Harold MacGrath and the late O. Henry—shows an unmistakably technical excellence, and even a certain civilized sophistication in point of view. Moreover, this literature is constantly graduating adept professors into something finer, as witness Booth Tarkington, Zona Gale, Ring W. Lardner and Montague Glass. S. L. Clemens came out of it forty years ago. Nevertheless, its general tendency is distinctly in the other direction. It seduces by the power of money, and by the power of great acclaim no less. One constantly observes the collapse and surrender of writers who started out with aims far above that of the magazine nabob. I could draw up a long, long list of such victims: Henry Milner Rideout, Jack London, Owen Johnson, Chester Bailey Fernald, Hamlin Garland, Will Levington Comfort, Stephen French Whitman, James Hopper, Harry Leon Wilson, and so on. They had their forerunner, in the last generation, in Bret Harte. It is, indeed, a characteristic American phenomenon for a young writer to score a success with novel and meritorious work, and then to yield himself to the best-seller fever, and so disappear down the sewers. Even the man who struggles to emerge again is commonly hauled back. For example, Louis Joseph Vance, Rupert Hughes, George Bronson-Howard, and, to go back a few years, David Graham Phillips and Elbert Hubbard—all men flustered by high aspiration, and yet all pulled down by the temptations below. Even Frank Norris showed signs of yielding. The pull is genuinely powerful. Above lies not only isolation, but also a dogged and malignant sort of opposition. Below, as Morris has frankly admitted, there is the place at Aiken, the motor-car, babies, money in the bank, and the dignity of an important man.

It is a commonplace of the envious to put all the blame upon the *Saturday Evening Post*, for in its pages many of the Magdalens of letters are to be found, and out of its bulging coffers comes much of the lure. But this is simply blaming the bull for the sins of all the cows. The *Post*, as a matter of fact, is a good deal less guilty than such magazines as the *Cosmopolitan*, *Hearst's*, *McClure's* and the *Metropolitan*, not to mention the larger women's magazines. In the *Post* one often discerns an effort to rise above the level of shoe-drummer fiction. It is edited by a man who, almost alone among editors of the great periodicals of the country, is himself a writer of respectable skill. It has brought out (after lesser publications unearthed them) a member of authors of very solid talents, notably Glass, Lardner and E. W. Howe. It has been extremely hospitable to men not immediately comprehensible to the mob, for example, Dreiser and Hergesheimer. Most of all, it has avoided the Barnum-like exploitation of such native bosh-mongers as Crane, Hillis and Ella Wheeler Wilcox, and of such exotic mountebanks as D'Annunzio, Hall Caine and Maeterlinck. In brief, the *Post* is a great deal better than ever Greenwich Village and the Cambridge campus are disposed to admit. It is the largest of all the literary Hog Islands, but it is by no means the worst. Appealing primarily to the great masses of right-thinking and unintelligent Americans, it must necessarily print a great deal of preposterous tosh, but it flavors the mess with not a few things of a far higher quality, and at its worst it is seldom downright idiotic. In many of the other great magazines one finds stuff that it would be difficult to describe in any other words. It is gaudily romantic, furtively sexual, and full of rubber-stamp situations and personages—a sort of amalgam of the worst drivel of Marie Corelli, Elinor Glyn, E. Phillips Oppenheim, William Le Quex and Hall Caine. This is the literature of the middle layer—the product of the national Rockefellers and Duponts of letters. This is the sort of thing that the young author of facile pen is encouraged to manufacture. This is the material of the best sellers and the movies.

Of late it is the movies that have chiefly provoked its composition: the rewards they offer are even greater than those held out by the commercial book-publishers and the train-boy magazines. The point of view of an author responsive to such rewards was recently set forth very naïvely in the *Authors' League Bulletin*. This author undertook, in a short article, to refute the fallacies of an unknown who ventured to protest against the movies on the ground that they called only for bald plots, elementary and generally absurd, and that all the rest of a sound writer's equipment—"the artistry of his style, the felicity of his apt expression, his subtlety and thoroughness of observation and comprehension and sympathy, the illuminating quality of his analysis of motive and character, even the fundamental skillful development of the bare plot"—was disdained by the Selznicks, Goldfishes, Zukors and other such *entrepreneurs*, and by the overwhelming majority of their customers. I quote from the reply:

There are some conspicuous word merchants who deal in the English language, but the general public doesn't clamor for their wares. They write for the "thinking class." The élite, the discriminating. As a rule, they scorn the crass commercialism of the magazines and movies and such catchpenny devices. However, literary masterpieces live because they have been and will be read, not by the few, but by the many. That was true in the time of Homer, and even to-day the first move made by an editor when he receives a manuscript, or a gentle reader when he buys a book, or a T.B.M. when he sinks into an orchestra chair is to look around for John Henry Plot. If Mr. Plot is too long delayed in arriving or doesn't come at all, the editor usually sends regrets, the reader yawns and the tired business man falls asleep. It's a sad state of affairs and awful tough on art, but it can't be helped.

Observe the lofty scorn of mere literature—the superior irony at the expense of everything beyond the bumping of boobs. Note the sound judgment as to the function and fate of literary masterpieces, *e.g.*, "Endymion," "The Canterbury Tales," "Faust," "Typhoon." Give your eye to the chaste diction— "John Henry Plot," "T.B.M.," "awful tough," and so on. No doubt you will at once assume that this curious counterblast to literature was written by some former bartender now engaged in composing scenarios for Pearl White and Theda Bara. But it was not. It was written and signed by the president of the Authors' League of America.

Here we have, unconsciously revealed, the secret of the depressing badness of what may be called the staple fiction of the country—the sort of stuff that is done by the Richard Harding Davises, Rex Beaches, Houghs, McCutcheons, and their like, male and female. The worse of it is not that it is addressed primarily to shoe-drummers and shop-girls; the worst of it is that it is written by authors who *are*, to all intellectual intents and purposes, shoe-drummers and shop-girls. American literature, even on its higher levels, seldom comes out of the small and lonesome upper classes of the people. An American author with traditions behind him and an environment about him comparable to those, say, of George Moore, or Hugh Walpole, or E. F. Benson is and always has been relatively rare. On this side of the water the arts, like politics and religion, are chiefly in the keeping of persons of obscure origin, defective education and elemental tastes. Even some of the most violent upholders of the New England superstition are aliens to the actual New England heritage; one discovers, searching "Who's Who in America," that they are recent fugitives from the six-day sock and saleratus *Kultur* of the cow and hog States. The artistic merchandise produced by liberated yokels of that sort is bound to show its intellectual newness, which is to say, its deficiency in civilized culture and sophistication. It is, on the plane of letters, precisely what evangelical Christianity is on the plane of religion, to wit, the product of ill-informed, emotional and more or less pushing and oafish folk. Life, to such Harvardized peasants, is not a mystery; it is something absurdly simple, to be described with surety and in a few words. If they set up as critics their criticism is all a matter of facile labeling, chiefly ethical; find the pigeon-hole, and the rest is easy. If they presume to discuss the great problems of human society, they are equally ready with their answers: draw up and pass a harsh enough statute, and the corruptible will straightway put on incorruption. And if, fanned by the soft breath of beauty, they go into practice as creative artists, as poets, as dramatists, as novelists, then one learns from them that we inhabit a country that is the model and despair of other states, that its culture is coextensive with human culture and enlightenment, and that every failure to find happiness under that culture is the result of sin.

<h2 style="text-align:center">6</h2>

<h3 style="text-align:center">Underlying Causes</h3>

Here is one of the fundamental defects of American fiction —perhaps the one character that sets it off sharply from all other known kinds of contemporary fiction. It habitually exhibits, not a man of delicate organization in revolt against the inexplicable tragedy of existence, but a man of low sensibilities and elemental desires yielding himself gladly to his environment, and so achieving what, under a third-rate civilization, passes for success. To get on: this is the aim. To weigh and reflect, to doubt and rebel: this is the thing to be avoided. I describe the optimistic, the inspirational, the Authors' League, the popular magazine, the peculiarly American school. In character creation its masterpiece is the advertising agent who, by devising some new and super-imbecile boob-trap, puts his hook-and-eye factory "on the map," ruins all other factories, marries the daughter of his boss, and so ends as an eminent man. Obviously, the drama underlying such fiction—what Mr. Beach would call its John Henry Plot—is false drama, Sunday-school drama, puerile and disgusting drama. It is the sort of thing that awakens a response only in men who are essentially unimaginative, timorous and degraded—in brief, in democrats, bagmen, yahoos. The man of reflective habit cannot conceivably take any passionate interest in the conflicts it deals with. He doesn't want to marry the daughter of the owner of the hook-and-eye factory; he would probably burn down the factory itself if it ever came into his hands. What interests this man is the far more poignant and significant conflict between a salient individual and the harsh and meaningless fiats of destiny, the unintelligible mandates and vagaries of God. His hero is not one who yields and wins, but one who resists and fails.

Most of these conflicts, of course, are internal, and hence do not make themselves visible in the overt melodrama of the Beaches, Davises and Chamberses. A superior man's struggle in the world is not with exterior lions, trusts, margraves, policemen, rivals in love, German spies, radicals and tornadoes, but with the obscure, atavistic impulses within him—the impulses, weaknesses and limitations that war with his notion of what life should be. Nine times out of ten he succumbs. Nine times out of ten he must yield to the dead hand. Nine times out of ten his aspiration is almost infinitely above his achievement. The result is that we see him sliding downhill—his ideals breaking up, his hope petering out, his character in decay. Character in decay is thus the theme of the great bulk of superior fiction. One has it in Dostoievsky, in Balzac, in Hardy, in Conrad, in Flaubert, in Zola, in Turgenieff, in Goethe, in Sudermann, in Bennett, and, to come home, in Dreiser. In nearly all first-rate novels the hero is defeated. In perhaps a majority he is completely destroyed. The hero of the inferior—*i.e.*, the typically American—novel engages in no such doomed and fateful combat. His conflict is not with the inexplicable ukases of destiny, the limitations of his own strength, the dead hand upon him, but simply with the superficial desires of his elemental fellow men. He thus has a fair chance of winning—and in bad fiction that chance is always converted into a certainty. So he marries the daughter of the owner of the factory and eventually gobbles the factory itself. His success gives thrills to persons who can imagine no higher aspiration. He embodies their optimism, as the other hero embodies the pessimism of more introspective and idealistic men. He is the protagonist of that great majority which is so inferior that it is quite unconscious of its inferiority.

It is this superficiality of the inferior man, it seems to me, that is the chief hallmark of the American novel. Whenever one encounters a novel that rises superior to it the thing takes on a subtle but unmistakable air of foreignness—for example, Frank Norris' "Vandover and the Brute," Hergesheimer's "The Lay Anthony" and Miss Cather's "My Antonía," or, to drop to short stories, Stephen Crane's "The Blue Hotel" and Mrs. Wharton's "Ethan Frome." The short story is commonly regarded, at least by American critics, as a preëminently American form; there are even patriots who argue that Bret Harte invented it. It meets very accurately, in fact, certain characteristic demands of the American temperament: it is simple, economical and brilliantly effective. Yet the same hollowness that marks the American novel also marks the American short story. Its great masters, in late years, have been such cheese-mongers as Davis, with his servant-girl romanticism, and O. Henry, with his smoke-room and variety show smartness. In the whole canon of O. Henry's work you will not find a single recognizable human character; his people are unanimously marionettes; he makes Mexican brigands, Texas cowmen and New York cracksmen talk the same highly ornate Broadwayese. The successive volumes of Edward J. O'Brien's "Best Short-Story" series throw a vivid light upon the feeble estate of the art in the land. O'Brien, though his æsthetic judgments are ludicrous, at least selects stories that are thoroughly representative; his books are trade successes because the crowd is undoubtedly with him. He has yet to discover a single story that even the most naïve professor would venture to mention in the same breath with Joseph Conrad's "Heart of Darkness," or Andrieff's "Silence," or Sudermann's "Das Sterbelied," or the least considerable tale by Anatole France. In many of the current American makers of magazine short stories—for example, Gouverneur Morris—one observes, as I have said, a truly admirable technical skill. They have mastered the externals of the form. They know how to get their effects. But in content their

work is as hollow as a jug. Such stuff has no imaginable relation to life as men live it in the world. It is as artificial as the
heroic strut and romantic eyes of a moving-picture actor.

I have spoken of the air of foreignness that clings to certain
exceptional American compositions. In part it is based upon a
psychological trick—upon the surprise which must inevitably
seize upon any one who encounters a decent piece of writing
in so vast a desert of mere literacy. But in part it is grounded
soundly enough on the facts. The native author of any genuine
force and originality is almost invariably found to be under
strong foreign influences, either English or Continental. It was
so in the earliest days. Freneau, the poet of the Revolution,
was thoroughly French in blood and traditions. Irving, as
H. R. Haweis has said, "took to England as a duck takes to
water," and was in exile seventeen years. Cooper, with the
great success of "The Last of the Mohicans" behind him, left
the country in disgust and was gone for seven years. Emerson,
Bryant, Lowell, Hawthorne and even Longfellow kept their
eyes turned across the water; Emerson, in fact, was little more
than an importer and popularizer of German and French ideas.
Bancroft studied in Germany; Prescott, like Irving, was enchanted by Spain. Poe, unable to follow the fashion, invented
mythical travels to save his face—to France, to Germany, to the
Greek isles. The Civil War revived the national consciousness
enormously, but it did not halt the movement of *émigrés*.
Henry James, in the seventies, went to England, Bierce and
Bret Harte followed him, and even Mark Twain, absolutely
American though he was, was forever pulling up stakes and
setting out for Vienna, Florence or London. Only poverty tied
Whitman to the soil; his audience, for many years, was chiefly
beyond the water, and there, too, he often longed to be. This
distaste for the national scene is often based upon a genuine
alienness. The more, indeed, one investigates the ancestry of
Americans who have won distinction in the fine arts, the more
one discovers tempting game for the critical Know Nothings.
Whitman was half Dutch, Harte was half Jew, Poe was partly
German, James had an Irish grandfather, Howells was largely
Irish and German, Dreiser is German and Hergesheimer is
Pennsylvania Dutch. Fully a half of the painters discussed in
John C. van Dyke's "American Painting and Its Tradition"

were of mixed blood, with the Anglo-Saxon plainly recessive. And of the five poets singled out for encomium by Miss Lowell in "Tendencies in Modern American Poetry" one is a Swede, two are partly German, one was educated in the German language, and three of the five exiled themselves to England as soon as they got out of their nonage. The exiles are of all sorts: Frank Harris, Vincent O'Sullivan, Ezra Pound, Herman Scheffauer, T. S. Eliot, Henry B. Fuller, Stuart Merrill, Edith Wharton. They go to England, France, Germany, Italy—anywhere to escape. Even at home the literatus is perceptibly foreign in his mien. If he lies under the New England tradition he is furiously colonial—more English than the English. If he turns to revolt, he is apt to put on a French hat and a Russian red blouse. *The Little Review*, the organ of the extreme wing of *révoltés*, is so violently exotic that several years ago, during the plupatriotic days of the war, some of its readers protested. With characteristic lack of humor it replied with an American number—and two of the stars of that number bore the fine old Anglo-Saxon names of Ben Hecht and Elsa von Freytag-Loringhoven.

This tendency of American literature, the moment it begins to show enterprise, novelty and significance, to radiate an alien smell is not an isolated phenomenon. The same smell accompanies practically all other sorts of intellectual activity in the republic. Whenever one hears that a new political theory is in circulation, or a scientific heresy, or a movement toward rationalism in religion, it is always safe to guess that some discontented stranger or other has a hand in it. In the newspapers and on the floor of Congress a new heterodoxy is always denounced forthwith as a product of foreign plotting, and here public opinion undoubtedly supports both the press and the politicians, and with good reason. The native culture of the country—that is, the culture of the low caste Anglo-Saxons who preserve the national tradition—is almost completely incapable of producing ideas. It is a culture that roughly corresponds to what the culture of England would be if there were no universities over there, and no caste of intellectual individualists and no landed aristocracy—in other words, if the tone of the national thinking were set by the nonconformist industrials, the camorra of Welsh and Scotch political scoundrels, and the town and country mobs. As we shall see, the United States has not yet produced anything properly describable as an aristocracy, and so there is no impediment to the domination of the inferior orders. Worse, the Anglo-Saxon strain, second-rate at the start, has tended to degenerate steadily to lower levels—in New England, very markedly. The result is that there is not only a great dearth of ideas in the land, but also an active and relentless hostility to ideas. The chronic suspiciousness of the inferior man here has full play; never in modern history has there been another civilization showing so vast a body of prohibitions and repressions, in both conduct and thought. The second result is that intellectual experimentation is chiefly left to the immigrants of the later migrations, and to the small sections of the native population that have been enriched with their blood. For such a pure Anglo-Saxon as Cabell to disport himself in the field of ideas is a rarity in the United States—and no exception to the rule that I have just mentioned, for Cabell belongs to an aristocracy that is now almost extinct, and has no more in common with the general population than a Baltic baron has with the indigenous herd of Letts and Esthonians. All the arts in America are thoroughly exotic. Music is almost wholly German or Italian, painting is French, literature may be anything from English to Russian, architecture (save when it becomes a mere branch of engineering) is a maddening phantasmagoria of borrowings. Even so elemental an art as that of cookery shows no native development, and is greatly disesteemed by Americans of the Anglo-Saxon majority; any decent restaurant that one blunders upon in the land is likely to be French, and if not French, then Italian or German or Chinese. So with the sciences: they have scarcely any native development. Organized scientific research began in the country with the founding of the Johns Hopkins University, a bald imitation of the German universities, and long held suspect by native opinion. Even after its great success, indeed, there was rancorous hostility to its scheme of things on chauvinistic grounds, and some years ago efforts were begun to Americanize it, with the result that it is now sunk to the level of Princeton, Amherst and other such glorified high-schools, and is dominated by native savants who would be laughed at in any Continental university. Science, oppressed by such assaults from below, moves out of the academic grove into the freer air of the great foundations, where the pursuit of the shy fact is uncontaminated by football and social pushing. The greatest of these foundations is the Rockefeller Institute. Its salient men are such investigators as Flexner, Loeb and Carrel—all of them Continental Jews.

Thus the battle of ideas in the United States is largely carried on under strange flags, and even the stray natives on the side of free inquiry have to sacrifice some of their nationality when they enlist. The effects of this curious condition of affairs are both good and evil. The good ones are easily apparent. The racial division gives the struggle a certain desperate earnestness, and even bitterness, and so makes it the more inviting to lively minds. It was a benefit to the late D. C. Gilman rather than a disadvantage that national opinion opposed his traffic with Huxley and the German professors in the early days of the Johns Hopkins; the stupidity of the opposition stimulated him, and made him resolute, and his resolution, in the long run, was of inestimable cultural value. Scientific research in America, indeed, was thus set securely upon its legs precisely because the great majority of right-thinking Americans were violently opposed to it. In the same way it must be obvious that Dreiser got something valuable out of the grotesque war that was carried on against him during the greater war overseas because of his German name—a *jehad* fundamentally responsible for the suppression of "The 'Genius.'" The chief danger that he ran six or seven years ago was the danger that he might be accepted, explained away, and so seduced downward to the common level. The attack of professional patriots saved him from that calamity. More, it filled him with a keen sense of his isolation, and stirred up the vanity that was in him as it is in all of us, and so made him cling with new tenacity to the very peculiarities that differentiate him from his inferiors. Finally, it is not to be forgotten that, without this rebellion of immigrant iconoclasts, the whole body of the national literature would tend to sink to the 100% American level of such patriotic literary business men as the president of the Authors' League. In other words, we must put up with the æsthetic Bolshevism of the Europeans and Asiatics who rage in the land, for without them we might not have any literature at all.

But the evils of the situation are not to be gainsaid. One of them I have already alluded to: the tendency of the beginning literatus, once he becomes fully conscious of his foreign affiliations, to desert the republic forthwith, and thereafter view it from afar, and as an actual foreigner. More solid and various cultures lure him; he finds himself uncomfortable at home. Sometimes, as in the case of Henry James, he becomes a downright expatriate, and a more or less active agent of anti-American feeling; more often, he goes over to the outlanders without yielding up his theoretical citizenship, as in the cases of Irving, Harris, Pound and O'Sullivan. But all this, of course, works relatively light damage, for not many native authors are footloose enough to indulge in any such physical desertion of the soil. Of much more evil importance is the tendency of the cultural alienism that I have described to fortify the uncontaminated native in his bilious suspicion of all the arts, and particularly of all artists. The news that the latest poet to flutter the dovecotes is a Jew, or that the last novelist mauled by comstockery has a German or Scandinavian or Russian name, or that the critic newly taken in sacrilege is a partisan of Viennese farce or of the French moral code or of English literary theory—this news, among a people so ill-informed, so horribly well-trained in flight from bugaboos, and so savagely suspicious of the unfamiliar in ideas, has the inevitable effect of stirring up opposition that quickly ceases to be purely æsthetic objection, and so becomes increasingly difficult to combat. If Dreiser's name were Tompkins or Simpson, there is no doubt whatever that he would affright the professors a good deal less, and appear less of a hobgoblin to the *intelligentsia* of the women's clubs. If Oppenheim were less palpably levantine, he would come much nearer to the popularity of Edwin Markham and Walt Mason. And if Cabell kept to the patriotic business of a Southern gentleman, to wit, the praise of General Robert E. Lee, instead of prowling the strange and terrible fields of mediæval Provence, it is a safe wager that he would be sold openly over the counter instead of stealthily behind the door.

In a previous work I have discussed this tendency in America to estimate the artist in terms of his secular character. During the war, when all of the national defects in intelligence were enormously accentuated, it went to ludicrous lengths. There were then only authors who were vociferous patriots and thus geniuses, and authors who kept their dignity and were thus suspect and without virtue. By this gauge Chambers became the superior of Dreiser and Cabell, and Joyce Kilmer and Amy Lowell were set above Sandburg and Oppenheim. The test was even extended to foreigners: by it H. G. Wells took precedence of Shaw, and Blasco Ibáñez became a greater artist than Romain Rolland. But the thing is not peculiar to war times; when peace is densest it is to be observed. The man of letters, pure and simple, is a rarity in America. Almost always he is something else—and that something else commonly determines his public eminence. Mark Twain, with only his books to recommend him, would probably have passed into obscurity in middle age; it was in the character of a public entertainer, not unrelated to Coxey, Dr. Mary Walker and Citizen George Francis Train, that he wooed and won his country. The official criticism of the land denied him any solid literary virtue to the day of his death, and even to-day the campus critics and their journalistic valets stand aghast before "The Mysterious Stranger" and "What is Man?" Emerson passed through almost the same experience. It was not as a man of letters that he was chiefly thought of in his time, but as the prophet of a new cult, half religious, half philosophical, and wholly unintelligible to nine-tenths of those who discussed it. The first author of a handbook of American literature to sweep away the codfish Moses and expose the literary artist was the Polish Jew, Leon Kellner, of Czernowitz. So with Whitman and Poe—both hobgoblins far more than artists. So, even, with Howells: it was as the exponent of a dying culture that he was venerated, not as the practitioner of an art. Few actually read his books. His celebrity, of course, was real enough, but it somehow differed materially from that of a pure man of letters—say Shelley, Conrad, Hauptmann, Hardy or Synge. That he was himself keenly aware of the national tendency to judge an artist in terms of the citizen was made plain at the time of the Gorky scandal, when he joined Clemens in an ignominious desertion of Gorky, scared out of his wits by the danger of being manhandled for a violation of the national pecksniffery. Howells also refused to sign the Dreiser Protest.

The case of Frank Harris is one eloquently in point. Harris has written, among other books, perhaps the best biography ever done by an American. Yet his politics keep him in a sort of Coventry and the average American critic would no more think of praising him than of granting Treitschke any merit as an historian.

7
The Lonesome Artist

Thus falsely judged by standards that have no intelligible appositeness when applied to an artist, however accurately they may weigh a stockbroker or a Presbyterian elder, and forced to meet not only the hunkerous indifference of the dominant mob but also the bitter and disingenuous opposition of the classes to which he might look reasonably for understanding and support, the American author is forced into a sort of social and intellectual vacuum, and lives out his days, as Henry James said of Hawthorne, "an alien everywhere, an æsthetic solitary."

The wonder is that, in the face of so metallic and unyielding a front, any genuine artists in letters come to the front at all. But they constantly emerge; the first gestures are always on show; the prodigal and gorgeous life of the country simply forces a sensitive minority to make some attempt at representation and interpretation, and out of many trying there often appears one who can. The phenomenon of Dreiser is not unique. He had his forerunners in Fuller and Frank Norris and he has his *compagnons du voyage* in Anderson, Charles G. Norris and more than one other. But the fact only throws up his curious isolation in a stronger light. It would be difficult to imagine an artist of his sober purpose and high accomplishment, in any civilized country, standing so neglected. The prevailing criticism, when it cannot dispose of him by denying that he exists —in the two chief handbooks of latter-day literature by professors he is not even mentioned!—seeks to dispose of him by arraying the shoddy fury of the mob against him. When he was under attack by the Comstocks, more than one American critic gave covert aid to the common enemy, and it was with difficulty that the weight of the Authors' League was held upon his side. More help for him, in fact, came from England, and quite voluntarily, than could be drummed up for him at home. No public sense of the menace that the attack offered to free speech and free art was visible; it would have made a nine-days' sensation for any layman of public influence to have gone to his rescue, as would have certainly happened in France, England or Germany. As for the newspaper-reading mob, it probably went unaware of the business altogether. When Arnold Bennett, landing in New York some time previously, told the reporters that Dreiser was the American he most desired to meet, the news was quite unintelligible to perhaps nine readers out of ten: they had no more heard of Dreiser than their fathers had heard of Whitman in 1875.

So with all the rest. I have mentioned Harris. It would be difficult to imagine Rolland meeting such a fate in France or Shaw in England as he has met in the United States. O'Sullivan, during the war, came home with "A Good Girl" in his pocket. The book was republished here—and got vastly less notice than the latest piece of trade-goods by Kathleen Norris. Fuller, early in his career, gave it up as hopeless. Norris died vainly battling for the young Dreiser. An Abraham Cahan goes unnoticed. Miss Cather, with four sound books behind her, lingers in the twilight of an esoteric reputation. Cabell, comstocked, is apprehended by his country only as a novelist to be bought by stealth and read in private. When Hugh Walpole came to America a year or two ago he favored the newspapers, like Bennett before him, with a piece of critical news that must have puzzled all readers save a very small minority. Discussing the living American novelists worth heeding, he nominated three—and of them only one was familiar to the general run of novel-buyers, or had ever been mentioned by a native critic of the apostolic succession. Only the poets of the land seem to attract the notice of the professors, and no doubt this is largely because most of the more salient of them—notably Miss Lowell and Lindsay—are primarily press-agents. Even so, the attention that they get is seldom serious. The only professor that I know of who has discussed the matter in precise terms holds that Alfred Noyes is the superior of all of them. Moreover, the present extraordinary interest in poetry stops short with a few poets, and one of its conspicuous phenomena is its lack of concern with the poets outside the movement, some of them unquestionably superior to any within.

Nor is this isolation of the artist in America new. The contemporary view of Poe and Whitman was almost precisely like the current view of Dreiser and Cabell. Both were neglected by the Brahmins of their time, and both were regarded hostilely by the great body of right-thinking citizens. Poe, indeed, was the victim of a furious attack by Rufus W. Griswold, the Hamilton Wright Mabie of the time, and it set the tone of native criticism for years. Whitman, living, narrowly escaped going to jail as a public nuisance. One thinks of Hawthorne and Emerson as writers decently appreciated by their contemporaries, but it is not to be forgotten that the official criticism of the era saw no essential difference between Hawthorne and Cooper, and that Emerson's reputation, to the end of his life, was far more that of a theological prophet and ethical platitudinarian, comparable to Lyman Abbott or Frank Crane, than that of a literary artist, comparable to Tennyson or Matthew Arnold. Perhaps Carlyle understood him, but who in America understood him? To this day he is the victim of gross misrepresentation by enthusiasts who read into him all sorts of flatulent bombast, as Puritanism is read into the New Testament by Methodists. As for Hawthorne, his extraordinary physical isolation during his lifetime was but the symbol of a complete isolation of the spirit, still surviving. If his preference for the internal conflict as opposed to the external act were not sufficient to set him off from the main stream of American speculation, there would always be his profound ethical skepticism —a state of mind quite impossible to the normal American, at least of Anglo-Saxon blood. Hawthorne, so far as I know, has never had a single professed follower in his own country. Even his son, attempting to carry on his craft, yielded neither to his meticulous method nor to his detached point of view. In the third generation, with infinite irony, there is a grand-daughter who is a reviewer of books for the New York *Times*, which is almost as if Wagner should have a grand-daughter singing in the operas of Massenet.

Of the four indubitable masters thus named, Hawthorne, Emerson, Whitman and Poe, only the last two have been sufficiently taken into the consciousness of the country to have any effect upon its literature, and even here that influence has been exerted only at second-hand, and against very definite adverse pressure. It would certainly seem reasonable for a man of so forceful a habit of mind as Poe, and of such prodigal and arresting originality, to have founded a school, but a glance at the record shows that he did nothing of the sort. Immediately he was dead, the shadows of the Irving tradition closed around his tomb, and for nearly thirty years thereafter all of his chief ideas went disregarded in his own country. If, as the literature books argue, Poe was the father of the American short story, then it was a posthumous child, and had step-fathers who did their best to conceal its true parentage. When it actually entered upon the vigorous life that we know to-day Poe had been dead for a generation. Its father, at the time of its belated adolescence, seemed to be Bret Harte—and Harte's debt to Dickens was vastly more apparent, first and last, than his debt to Poe. What he got from Poe was essential; it was the inner structure of the modern short story, the fundamental devices whereby a mere glimpse at events could be made to yield brilliant and seemingly complete images. But he himself was probably largely unaware of this indebtedness. A man little given to critical analysis, and incompetent for it when his own work was under examination, he saw its externals much more clearly than he saw its intrinsic organization, and these externals bore the plain marks of Dickens. It remained for one of his successors, Ambrose Bierce, to bridge belatedly the space separating him from Poe, and so show the route that he had come. And it remained for foreign criticism, and particularly for French criticism, to lift Poe himself to the secure place that he now holds. It is true enough that he enjoyed, during his lifetime, a certain popular reputation, and that he was praised by such men as N. P. Willis and James Russell Lowell, but that reputation was considerably less than the fame of men who were much his inferiors, and that praise, especially in Lowell's case, was much corrupted by reservations. Not many native critics of respectable position, during the 50's and 60's, would have ranked him clearly above, say, Irving or Cooper, or even above Longfellow, his old enemy. A few partisans argued for him, but in the main, as Saintsbury has said, he was the victim of "extreme and almost incomprehensible injustice" at the hands of his countrymen. It is surely not without significance that it took ten years to raise money enough to put a cheap and hideous tombstone upon his neglected grave, that it was not actually set up until he had been dead twenty-six years, that no contemporary American writer took any part in furthering the project, and that the only one who attended the final ceremony was Whitman.

It was Baudelaire's French translation of the prose tales and Mallarmé's translation of the poems that brought Poe to Valhalla. The former, first printed in 1856, founded the Poe cult in France, and during the two decades following it flourished amazingly, and gradually extended to England and Germany. It was one of the well-springs, in fact, of the whole so-called decadent movement. If Baudelaire, the father of that movement, "cultivated hysteria with delight and terror," he was simply doing what Poe had done before him. Both, reacting against the false concept of beauty as a mere handmaiden of logical ideas, sought its springs in those deep feelings and inner experiences which lie beyond the range of ideas and are to be interpreted only as intuitions. Emerson started upon the same quest, but was turned off into mazes of contradiction and unintelligibility by his ethical obsession—the unescapable burden of his Puritan heritage. But Poe never wandered from the path. You will find in "The Poetic Principle" what is perhaps the clearest statement of this new and sounder concept of beauty that has ever been made—certainly it is clearer than any ever made by a Frenchman. But it was not until Frenchmen had watered the seed out of grotesque and vari-colored pots that it began to sprout. The tide of Poe's ideas, set in motion in France early in the second half of the century, did not wash England until the last decade, and in America, save for a few dashes of spray, it has yet to show itself. There is no American writer who displays the influence of this most potent and original of Americans so clearly as whole groups of Frenchmen display it, and whole groups of Germans, and even a good many Englishmen. What we have from Poe at first hand is simply a body of obvious yokel-shocking in the *Black Cat* manner, with the tales of Ambrose Bierce as its finest flower—in brief, an imitation of Poe's externals without any comprehension what-

ever of his underlying aims and notions. What we have from
him at second-hand is a somewhat childish Maeterlinckism, a
further dilution of Poe-and-water. This Maeterlinckism, some
time ago, got itself intermingled with the Whitmanic stream
flowing back to America through the channel of French Imag-
ism, with results destructive to the sanity of earnest critics and
fatal to the gravity of those less austere. It is significant that the
critical writing of Poe, in which there lies most that was best in
him, has not come back; no normal American ever thinks of
him as a critic, but only as a poet, as a raiser of goose-flesh, or
as an immoral fellow. The cause thereof is plain enough. The
French, instead of borrowing his critical theory directly, de-
duced it afresh from his applications of it; it became criticism
of him rather than *by* him. Thus his own speculations have
lacked the authority of foreign approval, and have conse-
quently made no impression. The weight of native opinion is
naturally against them, for they are at odds, not only with its
fundamental theories, but also with its practical doctrine that
no criticism can be profound and respectable which is not also
dull.

"Poe," says Arthur Ransome, in his capital study of the man
and the artist, "was like a wolf chained by the leg among a lot
of domestic dogs." The simile here is somewhat startling, and
Ransome, in a footnote, tries to ameliorate it: the "domestic
dogs" it refers to were magnificoes of no less bulk than Longfellow, Whittier, Holmes and Emerson. In the case of Whitman,
the wolf was not only chained, but also muzzled. Nothing, indeed, could be more amazing than the hostility that surrounded him at home until the very end of his long life. True
enough, it was broken by certain feeble mitigations. Emerson,
in 1855, praised him—though later very eager to forget it and
desert him, as Clemens and Howells, years afterward, deserted
Gorky. Alcott, Thoreau, Lowell and even Bryant, during his
brief Bohemian days, were polite to him. A group of miscellaneous enthusiasts gradually gathered about him, and out
of this group emerged at least one man of some distinction,
John Burroughs. Young adventurers of letters—for example,
Huneker—went to see him and hear him, half drawn by genuine admiration and half by mere deviltry. But the general
tone of the opinion that beat upon him, the attitude of

domestic criticism, was unbrokenly inimical; he was opposed by misrepresentation and neglect. "The prevailing range of criticism on my book," he wrote in "A Backward Glance on My Own Road" in 1884, "has been either mockery or denunciation—and . . . I have been the marked object of two or three (to me pretty serious) official buffetings." "After thirty years of trial," he wrote in "My Book and I," three years later, "public criticism on the book and myself as author of it shows marked anger and contempt more than anything else." That is, at home. Abroad he was making headway all the while, and long years afterward, by way of France and England, he began to force his way into the consciousness of his countrymen. What could have been more ironical than the solemn celebrations of Whitman's centenary that were carried off in various American universities in 1919? One can picture the old boy rolling with homeric mirth in hell. Imagine the fate of a university don of 1860, or 1870, or 1880, or even 1890 who had ventured to commend "Leaves of Grass" to the young gentlemen of his seminary! He would have come to grief as swiftly as that Detroit pedagogue of day before yesterday who brought down the Mothers' Legion upon him by commending "Jurgen."

8
The Cultural Background

So far, the disease. As to the cause, I have delivered a few hints. I now describe it particularly. It is, in brief, a defect in the general culture of the country—one reflected, not only in the national literature, but also in the national political theory, the national attitude toward religion and morals, the national habit in all departments of thinking. It is the lack of a civilized aristocracy, secure in its position, animated by an intelligent curiosity, skeptical of all facile generalizations, superior to the sentimentality of the mob, and delighting in the battle of ideas for its own sake.

The word I use, despite the qualifying adjective, has got itself meanings, of course, that I by no means intend to convey. Any mention of an aristocracy, to a public fed upon democratic fustian, is bound to bring up images of stockbrokers' wives lolling obscenely in opera boxes, or of haughty Englishmen slaughtering whole generations of grouse in an inordinate and incomprehensible manner, or of Junkers with tight waists elbowing American schoolmarms off the sidewalks of German beer towns, or of perfumed Italians coming over to work their abominable magic upon the daughters of breakfast-food and bathtub kings. Part of this misconception, I suppose, has its roots in the gaudy imbecilities of the yellow press, but there is also a part that belongs to the general American tradition, along with the oppression of minorities and the belief in political panaceas. Its depth and extent are constantly revealed by the naïve assumption that the so-called fashionable folk of the large cities—chiefly wealthy industrials in the interior-decorator and country-club stage of culture—constitute an aristocracy, and by the scarcely less remarkable assumption that the peerage of England is identical with the gentry—that is, that such men as Lord Northcliffe, Lord Iveagh and even Lord Reading are English gentlemen, and of the ancient line of the Percys.

Here, as always, the worshiper is the father of the gods, and no less when they are evil than when they are benign. The inferior man must find himself superiors, that he may marvel at his political equality with them, and in the absence of recognizable superiors *de facto* he creates superiors *de jure*. The sublime principle of one man, one vote must be translated into terms of dollars, diamonds, fashionable intelligence; the equality of all men before the law must have clear and dramatic proofs. Sometimes, perhaps, the thing goes further and is more subtle. The inferior man needs an aristocracy to demonstrate, not only his mere equality, but also his actual superiority. The society columns in the newspapers may have some such origin: they may visualize once more the accomplished journalist's understanding of the mob mind that he plays upon so skillfully, as upon some immense and cacophonous organ, always going *fortissimo*. What the inferior man and his wife see in the sinister revels of those amazing first families, I suspect, is often a massive witness to their own higher rectitude—to their relative innocence of cigarette-smoking, poodle-coddling, child-farming and the more abstruse branches of adultery—in brief, to their firmer grasp upon the immutable axioms of

Christian virtue, the one sound boast of the nether nine-tenths of humanity in every land under the cross.

But this bugaboo aristocracy, as I hint, is actually bogus, and the evidence of its bogusness lies in the fact that it is insecure. One gets into it only onerously, but out of it very easily. Entrance is effected by dint of a long and bitter struggle, and the chief incidents of that struggle are almost intolerable humiliations. The aspirant must school and steel himself to sniffs and sneers; he must see the door slammed upon him a hundred times before ever it is thrown open to him. To get in at all he must show a talent for abasement—and abasement makes him timorous. Worse, that timorousness is not cured when he succeeds at last. On the contrary, it is made even more tremulous, for what he faces within the gates is a scheme of things made up almost wholly of harsh and often unintelligible taboos, and the penalty for violating even the least of them is swift and disastrous. He must exhibit exactly the right social habits, appetites and prejudices, public and private. He must harbor exactly the right political enthusiasms and indignations. He must have a hearty taste for exactly the right sports. His attitude toward the fine arts must be properly tolerant and yet not a shade too eager. He must read and like exactly the right books, pamphlets and public journals. He must put up at the right hotels when he travels. His wife must patronize the right milliners. He himself must stick to the right haberdashery. He must live in the right neighborhood. He must even embrace the right doctrines of religion. It would ruin him, for all opera box and society column purposes, to set up a plea for justice to the Bolsheviki, or even for ordinary decency. It would ruin him equally to wear celluloid collars, or to move to Union Hill, N.J., or to serve ham and cabbage at his table. And it would ruin him, too, to drink coffee from his saucer, or to marry a chambermaid with a gold tooth, or to join the Seventh Day Adventists. Within the boundaries of his curious order he is worse fettered than a monk in a cell. Its obscure conception of propriety, its nebulous notion that this or that is honorable, hampers him in every direction, and very narrowly. What he resigns when he enters, even when he makes his first deprecating knock at the door, is every right to attack the ideas that happen to prevail within. Such as they are, he must accept

them without question. And as they shift and change in response to great instinctive movements (or perhaps, now and
then, to the punished but not to be forgotten revolts of extraordinary rebels) he must shift and change with them,
silently and quickly. To hang back, to challenge and dispute, to
preach reforms and revolutions—these are crimes against the
brummagen Holy Ghost of the order.

Obviously, that order cannot constitute a genuine aristocracy, in any rational sense. A genuine aristocracy is grounded
upon very much different principles. Its first and most salient
character is its interior security, and the chief visible evidence
of that security is the freedom that goes with it—not only freedom in act, the divine right of the aristocrat to do what he jolly
well pleases, so long as he does not violate the primary guarantees and obligations of his class, but also and more importantly
freedom in thought, the liberty to try and err, the right to be
his own man. It is the instinct of a true aristocracy, not to punish eccentricity by expulsion, but to throw a mantle of protection about it—to safeguard it from the suspicions and
resentments of the lower orders. Those lower orders are inert,
timid, inhospitable to ideas, hostile to changes, faithful to a
few maudlin superstitions. All progress goes on on the higher
levels. It is there that salient personalities, made secure by artificial immunities, may oscillate most widely from the normal
track. It is within that entrenched fold, out of reach of the immemorial certainties of the mob, that extraordinary men of the
lower orders may find their city of refuge, and breathe a clear
air. This, indeed, is at once the hall-mark and the justification
of an aristocracy—that it is beyond responsibility to the general masses of men, and hence superior to both their degraded
longings and their no less degraded aversions. It is nothing if it
is not autonomous, curious, venturesome, courageous, and
everything if it is. It is the custodian of the qualities that make
for change and experiment; it is the class that organizes danger
to the service of the race; it pays for its high prerogatives by
standing in the forefront of the fray.

No such aristocracy, it must be plain, is now on view in the
United States. The makings of one were visible in the Virginia
of the later eighteenth century, but with Jefferson and Washington the promise died. In New England, it seems to me, there

was never any aristocracy, either in being or in nascency: there was only a theocracy that degenerated very quickly into a plutocracy on the one hand and a caste of sterile *Gelehrten* on the other—the passion for God splitting into a lust for dollars and a weakness for mere words. Despite the common notion to the contrary—a notion generated by confusing literacy with intelligence—New England has never shown the slightest sign of a genuine enthusiasm for ideas. It began its history as a slaughter-house of ideas, and it is to-day not easily distinguishable from a cold-storage plant. Its celebrated adventures in mysticism, once apparently so bold and significant, are now seen to have been little more than an elaborate hocus-pocus— respectable Unitarians shocking the peasantry and scaring the horned cattle in the fields by masquerading in the robes of Roscicrucians. The ideas that it embraced in those austere and far-off days were stale, and when it had finished with them they were dead: to-day one hears of Jakob Böhme almost as rarely as one hears of Allen G. Thurman. So in politics. Its glory is Abolition—an English invention, long under the interdict of the native plutocracy. Since the Civil War its six states have produced fewer political ideas, as political ideas run in the Republic, than any average county in Kansas or Nebraska. Appomattox seemed to be a victory for New England idealism. It was actually a victory for the New England plutocracy, and that plutocracy has dominated thought above the Housatonic ever since. The sect of professional idealists has so far dwindled that it has ceased to be of any importance, even as an opposition. When the plutocracy is challenged now, it is challenged by the proletariat.

Well, what is on view in New England is on view in all other parts of the nation, sometimes with ameliorations, but usually with the colors merely exaggerated. What one beholds, sweeping the eye over the land, is a culture that, like the national literature, is in three layers—the plutocracy on top, a vast mass of undifferentiated human blanks at the bottom, and a forlorn *intelligentsia* gasping out a precarious life between. I need not set out at any length, I hope, the intellectual deficiencies of the plutocracy—its utter failure to show anything even remotely resembling the makings of an aristocracy. It is badly educated, it is stupid, it is full of low-caste superstitions and indignations, it is without decent traditions or informing vision; above all, it is extraordinarily lacking in the most elemental independence and courage. Out of this class comes the grotesque fashionable society of our big towns, already described. Imagine a horde of peasants incredibly enriched and with almost infinite power thrust into their hands, and you will have a fair picture of its habitual state of mind. It shows all the stigmata of inferiority—moral certainty, cruelty, suspicion of ideas, fear. Never did it function more revealingly than in the late *pogrom* against the so-called Reds, *i.e.*, against humorless idealists who, like Andrew Jackson, took the platitudes of democracy quite seriously. The machinery brought to bear upon these feeble and scattered fanatics would have almost sufficed to repel an invasion by the united powers of Europe. They were hunted out of their sweat-shops and coffee-houses as if they were so many Carranzas or Ludendorffs, dragged to jail to the tooting of horns, arraigned before quaking judges on unintelligible charges, condemned to deportation without the slightest chance to defend themselves, torn from their dependent families, herded into prison-ships, and then finally dumped in a snow waste, to be rescued and fed by the Bolsheviki. And what was the theory at the bottom of all these astounding proceedings? So far as it can be reduced to comprehensible terms it was much less a theory than a fear—a shivering, idiotic, discreditable fear of a mere banshee—an overpowering, paralyzing dread that some extra-eloquent Red, permitted to emit his balderdash unwhipped, might eventually convert a couple of courageous men, and that the courageous men, filled with indignation against the plutocracy, might take to the highroad, burn down a nail-factory or two, and slit the throat of some virtuous profiteer. In order to lay this fear, in order to ease the jangled nerves of the American successors to the Hapsburgs and Hohenzollerns, all the constitutional guarantees of the citizen were suspended, the statute-books were burdened with laws that surpass anything heard of in the Austria of Maria Theresa, the country was handed over to a frenzied mob of detectives, informers and *agents provocateurs*—and the Reds departed laughing loudly, and were hailed by the Bolsheviki as innocents escaped from an asylum for the criminally insane.

Obviously, it is out of reason to look for any hospitality to ideas in a class so extravagantly fearful of even the most palpably absurd of them. Its philosophy is firmly grounded upon the thesis that the existing order must stand forever free from attack, and not only from attack, but also from mere academic criticism, and its ethics are as firmly grounded upon the thesis that every attempt at any such criticism is a proof of moral turpitude. Within its own ranks, protected by what may be regarded as the privilege of the order, there is nothing to take the place of this criticism. A few feeble platitudes by Andrew Carnegie and a book of moderate merit by John D. Rockefeller's press-agent constitute almost the whole of the interior literature of ideas. In other countries the plutocracy has often produced men of reflective and analytical habit, eager to rationalize its instincts and to bring it into some sort of relationship to the main streams of human thought. The case of David Ricardo at once comes to mind. There have been many others: John Bright, Richard Cobden, George Grote, and, in our own time, Walther von Rathenau. But in the United States no such phenomenon has been visible. There was a day, not long ago, when certain young men of wealth gave signs of an unaccustomed interest in ideas on the political side, but the most they managed to achieve was a banal sort of Socialism, and even this was abandoned in sudden terror when the war came, and Socialism fell under suspicion of being genuinely international —in brief, of being honest under the skin. Nor has the plutocracy of the country ever fostered an inquiring spirit among its intellectual valets and footmen, which is to say, among the gentlemen who compose headlines and leading articles for its newspapers. What chiefly distinguishes the daily press of the United States from the press of all other countries pretending to culture is not its lack of truthfulness or even its lack of dignity and honor, for these deficiencies are common to the newspapers everywhere, but its incurable fear of ideas, its constant effort to evade the discussion of fundamentals by translating all issues into a few elemental fears, its incessant reduction of all reflection to mere emotion. It is, in the true sense, never well-informed. It is seldom intelligent, save in the arts of the mob-master. It is never courageously honest. Held harshly to a rigid correctness of opinion by the plutocracy that controls it with less and less attempt at disguise, and menaced on all sides by censorships that it dare not flout, it sinks rapidly into formalism and feebleness. Its yellow section is perhaps its most respectable section, for there the only vestige of the old free journalist survives. In the more conservative papers one finds only a timid and petulant animosity to all questioning of the existing order, however urbane and sincere—a pervasive and ill-concealed dread that the mob now heated up against the orthodox hobgoblins may suddenly begin to unearth hobgoblins of its own, and so run amok. For if is upon the emotions of the mob, of course, that the whole comedy is played. Theoretically the mob is the repository of all political wisdom and virtue; actually it is the ultimate source of all political power. Even the plutocracy cannot make war upon it openly, or forget the least of its weaknesses. The business of keeping it in order must be done discreetly, warily, with delicate technique. In the main that business consists of keeping alive its deep-seated fears—of strange faces, of unfamiliar ideas, of unhackneyed gestures, of untested liberties and responsibilities. The one permanent emotion of the inferior man, as of all the simpler mammals, is fear—fear of the unknown, the complex, the inexplicable. What he wants beyond everything else is safety. His instincts incline him toward a society so organized that it will protect him at all hazards, and not only against perils to his hide but also against assaults upon his mind—against the need to grapple with unaccustomed problems, to weigh ideas, to think things out for himself, to scrutinize the platitudes upon which his everyday thinking is based. Content under kaiserism so long as it functions efficiently, he turns, when kaiserism falls, to some other and perhaps worse form of paternalism, bringing to its benign tyranny only the docile tribute of his pathetic allegiance. In America it is the newspaper that is his boss. From it he gets support for his elemental illusions. In it he sees a visible embodiment of his own wisdom and consequence. Out of it he draws fuel for his simple moral passion, his congenital suspicion of heresy, his dread of the unknown. And behind the newspaper stands the plutocracy, ignorant, unimaginative and timorous.

Thus at the top and at the bottom. Obviously, there is no aristocracy here. One finds only one of the necessary elements, and that only in the plutocracy, to wit, a truculent egoism. But where is intelligence? Where are ease and surety of manner? Where are enterprise and curiosity? Where, above all, is courage, and in particular, moral courage—the capacity for independent thinking, for difficult problems, for what Nietzsche called the joys of the labyrinth? As well look for these things in a society of half-wits. Democracy, obliterating the old aristocracy, has left only a vacuum in its place; in a century and a half it has failed either to lift up the mob to intellectual autonomy and dignity or to purge the plutocracy of its inherent stupidity and swinishness. It is precisely here, the first and favorite scene of the Great Experiment, that the culture of the individual has been reduced to the most rigid and absurd regimentation. It is precisely here, of all civilized countries, that eccentricity in demeanor and opinion has come to bear the heaviest penalties. The whole drift of our law is toward the absolute prohibition of all ideas that diverge in the slightest from the accepted platitudes, and behind that drift of law there is a far more potent force of growing custom, and under that custom there is a national philosophy which erects conformity into the noblest of virtues and the free functioning of personality into a capital crime against society.

9
Under the Campus Pump

But there remain the *intelligentsia*, the free spirits in the middle ground, neither as anæsthetic to ideas as the plutocracy on the one hand nor as much the slaves of emotion as the proletariat on the other. Have I forgotten them? I have not. But what actually reveals itself when this small brotherhood of the superior is carefully examined? What reveals itself, it seems to me, is a gigantic disappointment. Superficially, there are all the marks of a caste of learned and sagacious men—a great book-knowledge, a laudable diligence, a certain fine reserve and sniffishness, a plain consciousness of intellectual superiority, not a few gestures that suggest the aristocratic. But under the surface one quickly discovers that the whole thing is little more than play-acting, and not always very skillful. Learning is there, but not curiosity. A heavy dignity is there, but not much genuine self-respect. Pretentiousness is there, but not a trace of courage. Squeezed between the plutocracy on one side and the mob on the other, the *intelligentsia* face the eternal national problem of maintaining their position, of guarding themselves against challenge and attack, of keeping down suspicion. They have all the attributes of knowledge save the sense of power. They have all the qualities of an aristocracy save the capital qualities that arise out of a feeling of security, of complete independence, of absolute immunity to onslaught from above and below. In brief, the old bogusness hangs about them, as about the fashionable aristocrats of the society columns. They are safe so long as they are good, which is to say, so long as they neither aggrieve the plutocracy nor startle the proletariat. Immediately they fall into either misdemeanor all their apparent dignity vanishes, and with it all of their influence, and they become simply somewhat ridiculous rebels against a social order that has no genuine need of them and is disposed to tolerate them only when they are not obtrusive.

For various reasons this shadowy caste is largely made up of men who have official stamps upon their learning—that is, of professors, of doctors of philosophy; outside of academic circles it tends to shade off very rapidly into a half-world of isolated anarchists. One of those reasons is plain enough: the old democratic veneration for mere schooling, inherited from the Puritans of New England, is still in being, and the mob, always eager for short cuts in thinking, is disposed to accept a schoolmaster without looking beyond his degree. Another reason lies in the fact that the higher education is still rather a novelty in the country, and there have yet to be developed any devices for utilizing learned men in any trade save teaching. Yet other reasons will suggest themselves. Whatever the ramification of causes, the fact is plain that the pedagogues have almost a monopoly of what passes for the higher thinking in the land. Not only do they reign unchallenged in their own chaste grove; they also penetrate to all other fields of ratiocination, to the almost complete exclusion of unshrived rivals. They dominate the weeklies of opinion; they are to the fore in every review; they write nine-tenths of the serious books of the country; they begin to invade the newspapers; they instruct and exhort the yokelry from the stump; they have even begun to penetrate into the government. One cannot turn in the United States without encountering a professor. There is one on every municipal commission. There is one in every bureau of the federal government. There is one at the head of every intellectual movement. There is one to explain every new mystery. Professors appraise all works of art, whether graphic, tonal or literary. Professors supply the brain power for agriculture, diplomacy, the control of dependencies and the distribution of commodities. A professor was until lately sovereign of the country, and pope of the state church.

So much for their opportunity. What, now, of their achievement? I answer as one who has had thrown upon him, by the impenetrable operations of fate, the rather thankless duties of a specialist in the ways of pedagogues, a sort of professor of professors. The job has got me enemies. I have been accused of carrying on a defamatory *jehad* against virtuous and laborious men; I have even been charged with doing it in the interest of the Wilhelmstrasse, the White Slave Trust and the ghost of Friedrich Wilhelm Nietzsche. Nothing could be more absurd. All my instincts are on the side of the professors. I esteem a man who devotes himself to a subject with hard diligence; I esteem even more a man who puts poverty and a shelf of books above profiteering and evenings of jazz; I am naturally monkish. Moreover, there are more Ph.D.'s on my family tree than even a Boston bluestocking can boast; there was a whole century when even the most ignorant of my house was at least *Juris utriusque Doctor.* But such predispositions should not be permitted to color sober researches. What I have found, after long and arduous labors, is a state of things that is surely not altogether flattering to the *Gelehrten* under examination. What I have found, in brief, is that pedagogy turned to general public uses is almost as timid and flatulent as journalism—that the professor, menaced by the timid dogmatism of the plutocracy above him and the incurable suspiciousness of the mob beneath him, is almost invariably inclined to seek his own security in a mellifluous inanity—that, far from being a courageous spokesman of ideas and an apostle of their free dissemination, in politics, in the fine arts, in practical ethics, he comes close to being the most prudent and skittish of all men concerned with them—in brief, that he yields to the prevailing correctness of thought in all departments, north, east, south and west, and is, in fact, the chief exponent among us of the democratic doctrine that heresy is not only a mistake, but also a crime.

A philosophy is not put to much of a test in ordinary times, for in ordinary times philosophies are permitted to lie like sleeping dogs. When it shows its inward metal is when the band begins to play. The turmoils of the late lamentable war, it seems to me, provided for such a trying out of fundamental ideas and attitudes upon a colossal scale. The whole thinking of the world was thrown into confusion; all the worst fears and prejudices of ignorant and emotional men came to the front; it was a time, beyond all others in modem history, when intellectual integrity was subjected to a cruel strain. How did the *intelligentsia* of These States bear up under that strain? What was the reaction of our learned men to the challenge of organized hysteria, mob fear, incitement to excess, downright insanity? How did they conduct themselves in that universal whirlwind? They conducted themselves, I fear, in a manner that must leave a brilliant question mark behind their claim to independence and courage, to true knowledge and dignity, to ordinary self-respect—in brief, to every quality that belongs to the authentic aristocrat. They constituted themselves, not a restraining influence upon the mob run wild, but the loudest spokesmen of its worst imbecilities. They fed it with bogus history, bogus philosophy, bogus idealism, bogus heroics. They manufactured blather for its entertainment. They showed themselves to be as naïve as so many Liberty Loan orators, as emotional, almost, as the spy hunters, and as disdainful of the ordinary intellectual decencies as the editorial writers. I accumulated, in those great days, for the instruction and horror of posterity, a very large collection of academic arguments, expositions and pronunciamentos; it fills a trunk, and got me heavily into debt to three clipping-bureaux. Its contents range from solemn hymns of hate in the learned (and even the theological) reviews and such official donkeyisms as the formal ratification of the so-called Sisson documents down to childish harangues to student-bodies, public demands that the study of the enemy language and literature be prohibited by law, violent denunciations of all enemy science as negligible and fraudulent, vitriolic attacks upon enemy magnificos, and elaborate proofs that the American Revolution was the result of a foul plot hatched in the Wilhelmstrasse of the time, to the wanton injury of two loving bands of brothers. I do not exaggerate in the slightest. The proceedings of Mr. Creel's amazing corps of "twenty-five hundred American historians" went further than anything I have described. And in every far-flung college town, in every one-building "university" on the prairie, even the worst efforts of those "historians" were vastly exceeded.

But I am forgetting the like phenomena on the other side of the bloody chasm? I am overlooking the darker crimes of the celebrated German professors? Not at all. Those crimes against all reason and dignity, had they been committed in fact, would not be evidence in favor of the Americans in the dock: the principle of law is too well accepted to need argument. But I venture to deny them, and out of a very special and singular knowledge, for I seem to be one of the few Americans who has ever actually read the proclamations of the German professors: all the most indignant critics of them appear to have accepted second-hand accounts of their contents. Having suffered the onerous labor of reading them, I now offer sworn witness to their relative mildness. Now and then one encounters in them a disconcerting bray. Now and then one weeps with sore heart. Now and then one is bogged in German made wholly unintelligible by emotion. But taking them as they stand, and putting them fairly beside the corresponding documents of American vintage, one is at once struck by their comparative suavity and decorum, their freedom from mere rhetoric and fustian— above all, by their effort to appeal to reason, such as it is, rather than to emotion. No German professor, from end to end of the war, put his hand to anything as transparently silly as the Sisson documents. No German professor essayed to prove that the Seven Years' War was caused by Downing Street. No German professor argued that the study of English would corrupt the soul. No German professor denounced Darwin as an ignoramus and Lister as a scoundrel. Nor was anything of the sort done, so far as I know, by any French professor. Nor even by any reputable English professor. All such honorable efforts on behalf of correct thought in wartime were monopolized by American professors. And if the fact is disputed, then I threaten upon some future day, when the stealthy yearning to forget has arisen, to print my proofs in parallel columns—the most esteemed extravagances of the German professors in one column and the corresponding masterpieces of the American professors in the other.

I do not overlook, of course, the self-respecting men who, in the midst of all the uproar, kept their counsel and their dignity. A small minority, hard beset and tested by the fire! Nor do I overlook the few sentimental fanatics who, in the face of devastating evidence to the contrary, proceeded upon the assumption that academic freedom was yet inviolable, and so got themselves cashiered, and began posturing in radical circles as martyrs, the most absurd of men. But I think I draw a fair picture of the general. I think I depict with reasonable accuracy the typical response of the only recognizable *intelligentsia* of the land to the first great challenge to their aristocratic aloofness —the first test in the grand manner of their freedom alike from the bellicose imbecility of the plutocracy and the intolerable fears and childish moral certainties of the mob. That test exposed them shamelessly. It revealed their fast allegiance to the one thing that is the antithesis of all free inquiry, of all honest hospitality to ideas, of all intellectual independence and integrity. They proved that they were correct—and in proving it they threw a brilliant light upon many mysteries of our national culture.

10

The Intolerable Burden

Among others, upon the mystery of our literature—its faltering feebleness, its lack of genuine gusto, its dearth of salient personalities, its general air of poverty and imitation. What ails the beautiful letters of the Republic, I repeat, is what ails the general culture of the Republic—the lack of a body of sophisticated and civilized public opinion, independent of plutocratic control and superior to the infantile philosophies of the mob—a body of opinion showing the eager curiosity, the educated skepticism and the hospitality to ideas of a true aristocracy. This lack is felt by the American author, imagining him to have anything new to say, every day of his life. He can hope for no support, in ordinary cases, from the mob: it is too suspicious of all ideas. He can hope for no support from the spokesmen of the plutocracy: they are too diligently devoted to maintaining the intellectual *status quo*. He turns, then, to the *intelligentsia*—and what he finds is correctness! In his two prime functions, to represent the life about him accurately and to criticize it honestly, he sees that correctness arrayed against him. His representation is indecorous, unlovely, too harsh to be borne. His criticism is in contumacy to the ideals upon which the whole structure rests. So he is either attacked vigorously as an anti-patriot whose babblings ought to be put down by law, or enshrouded in a silence which commonly disposes of him even more effectively.

Soon or late, of course, a man of genuine force and originality is bound to prevail against that sort of stupidity. He will unearth an adherent here and another there; in the long run they may become numerous enough to force some recognition of him, even from the most immovable exponents of correctness. But the business is slow, uncertain, heart-breaking. It puts a burden upon the artist that ought not to be put upon him. It strains beyond reason his diligence and passion. A man who devotes his life to creating works of the imagination, a man who gives over all his strength and energy to struggling with problems that are essentially delicate and baffling and pregnant with doubt—such a man does not ask for recognition as a mere reward for his industry; he asks for it as a necessary *help* to his industry; he needs it as he needs decent subsistence and peace of mind. It is a grave damage to the artist and a grave loss to the literature when such a man as Poe has to seek consolation among his inferiors, and such a man as the Mark Twain of "What Is Man?" is forced to conceal his most profound beliefs, and such men as Dreiser and Cabell are exposed to incessant attacks by malignant stupidity. The notion that artists flourish upon adversity and misunderstanding, that they are able to function to the utmost in an atmosphere of indifference or hostility—this notion is nine-tenths nonsense. If it were true, then one would never hear of painters going to France or of musicians going to Germany. What the artist actually needs is comprehension of his aims and ideals by men he respects—not necessarily approval of his products, but simply an intelligent sympathy for him in the great agony of creation.

And that sympathy must be more than the mere fellow-feeling of other craftsmen; it must come, in large part, out of a connoisseurship that is beyond the bald trade interest; it must have its roots in the intellectual curiosity of an aristocracy of taste. Billroth, I believe, was more valuable to Brahms than even Schumann. His eager interest gave music-making a solid dignity. His championship offered the musician a visible proof that his labors had got for him a secure place in a civilized and stable society, and that he would be judged by his peers, and safeguarded against the obtuse hostility of his inferiors.

No such security is thrown about an artist in America. It is not that the country lacks the standards that Dr. Brownell pleads for; it is that its standards are still those of a primitive and timorous society. The excesses of Comstockery are profoundly symbolical. What they show is the moral certainty of the mob in operation against something that is as incomprehensible to it as the theory of least squares, and what they show even more vividly is the distressing lack of any automatic corrective of that outrage—of any firm and secure body of educated opinion, eager to hear and test all intelligible ideas and sensitively jealous of the right to discuss them freely. When "The Genius" was attacked by the Comstocks, it fell to my lot to seek assistance for Dreiser among the *intelligentsia*. I found them almost unanimously disinclined to lend a hand. A small number permitted themselves to be induced, but the majority held back, and not a few, as I have said, actually offered more or less furtive aid to the Comstocks. I pressed the matter and began to unearth reasons. It was, it appeared, dangerous for a member of the *intelligentsia*, and particularly for a member of the academic *intelligentsia*, to array himself against the mob inflamed—against the moral indignation of the sort of folk who devour vice reports and are converted by the Rev. Billy Sunday! If he came forward, he would have to come forward alone. There was no organized support behind him. No instinctive urge of class, no prompting of a great tradition, moved him to speak out for artistic freedom . . . England supplied the lack. Over there they have a mob too, and something akin to Comstockery, and a cult of hollow correctness—but they also have a caste that stands above all that sort of thing, and out of that caste came aid for Dreiser.

England is always supplying the lack—England, or France, or Germany, or some other country, but chiefly England. "My market and my reputation," said Prescott in 1838, "rest principally with England." To Poe, a few years later, the United States was "a literary colony of Great Britain." And there has been little change to this day. The English leisure class, says Prof. Dr. Veblen, is "for purposes of reputable usage the upper leisure class of this country." Despite all the current highfalutin about melting pots and national destinies the United States remains almost as much an English colonial possession, intellectually and spiritually, as it was on July 3, 1776. The American social pusher keeps his eye on Mayfair; the American literatus dreams of recognition by the London weeklies; the American don is lifted to bliss by the imprimatur of Oxford or Cambridge; even the American statesman knows how to cringe to Downing Street. Most of the essential policies of Dr. Wilson between 1914 and 1920—when the realistic English, finding him no longer useful, incontinently dismissed him— were, to all intents and purposes, those of a British colonial premier. He went into the Peace Conference willing to yield everything to English interests, and he came home with a treaty that was so extravagantly English that it fell an easy prey to the anti-English minority, ever alert for the makings of a bugaboo to scare the plain people. What lies under all this subservience is simple enough. The American, for all his braggadocio, is quite conscious of his intrinsic inferiority to the Englishman, on all cultural counts. He may put himself first as a man of business, as an adventurer in practical affairs or as a pioneer in the applied arts and sciences, but in all things removed from the mere pursuit of money and physical ease he well understands that he belongs at the second table. Even his recurrent attacks of Anglophobia are no more than Freudian evidences of his inferiority complex. He howls in order to still his inner sense of inequality, as he howls against imaginary enemies in order to convince himself that he is brave and against fabulous despotisms in order to prove that he is free. The Englishman is never deceived by this hocus-pocus. He knows that it is always possible to fetch the rebel back into camp by playing upon his elemental fears and vanities. A few dark threats, a few patronizing speeches, a few Oxford degrees, and the thing is done. More, the English scarcely regard it as hunting in the grand manner; it is a business of subalterns. When, during the early stages of the war, they had occasion to woo the American *intelligentsia*, what agents did they choose? Did they nominate Thomas Hardy, Joseph Conrad, George Moore and company? Nay, they nominated Conan Doyle, Coningsby Dawson, Alfred Noyes, Ian Hay, Chesterton, Kipling, Zangwill and company. In the choice there was high sagacity and no little oblique humor—as there was a bit later in the appointment of Lord Reading and Sir Auckland Geddes to Washington. The valuation they set upon the *aluminados* of the Republic was exactly the valuation they were in the habit of setting, at home, upon MM. of the Free Church Federation. They saw the eternal green-grocer beneath the master's gown and mortarboard. Let us look closely and we shall see him, too.

The essence of a self-reliant and autonomous culture is an unshakable egoism. It must not only regard itself as the peer of any other culture; it must regard itself as the superior of any other. You will find this indomitable pride in the culture of any truly first-rate nation: France, Germany or England. But you will not find it in the so-called culture of America. Here the decadent Anglo-Saxon majority still looks obediently and a bit wistfully toward the motherland. No good American ever seriously questions an English judgment on an æsthetic question, or even on an ethical, philosophical or political question. There is, in fact, seldom any rational reason why he should: it is almost always more mature, more tolerant, more intelligent than any judgment hatched at home. Behind it lies a settled scheme of things, a stable point of view, the authority of a free intellectual aristocracy, the pride of tradition and of power. The English are sure-footed, well-informed, persuasive. It is beyond their imagination that any one should seriously challenge them. In this overgrown and oafish colony there is no such sureness. The American always secretly envies the Englishman, even when he professes to flout him. The Englishman never envies the American.

The extraordinary colonist, moved to give utterance to the ideas bubbling within him, is thus vastly handicapped, for he must submit them to the test of a culture that, in the last analysis, is never quite his own culture, despite its dominance.

Looking within himself, he finds that he is different, that he diverges from the English standard, that he is authentically American—and to be authentically American is to be officially inferior. He thus faces dismay at the very start: support is lacking when he needs it most. In the motherland—in any motherland, in any wholly autonomous nation—there is a class of men like himself, devoted to translating the higher manifestations of the national spirit into ideas—men differing enormously among themselves, but still united in common cause against the lethargy and credulity of the mass. But in a colony that class, if it exists at all, lacks coherence and certainty; its authority is not only disputed by the inertia and suspiciousness of the lower orders, but also by the superior authority overseas; it is timorous and fearful of challenge. Thus it affords no protection to an individual of assertive originality, and he is forced to go as a suppliant to a quarter in which nothing is his by right, but everything must go by favor—in brief to a quarter where his very application must needs be regarded as an admission of his inferiority. The burden of proof upon him is thus made double. Obviously, he must be a man of very strong personality to surmount such obstacles triumphantly. Such strong men, of course, sometimes appear in a colony, but they always stand alone; their worst opposition is at home. For a colonial of less vigorous soul the battle is almost hopeless. Either he submits to subordination and so wears docilely the inferior badge of a praiseworthy and tolerated colonist, or he deserts the minority for the far more hospitable and confident majority, and so becomes a mere mob-artist.

Examples readily suggest themselves. I give you Poe and Whitman as men strong enough to weather the adverse wind. The salient thing about each of these men was this: that his impulse to self-expression, the force of his "obscure, inner necessity," was so powerful that it carried him beyond all ordinary ambitions and prudences—in other words, that the ego functioned so heroically that it quite disregarded the temporal welfare of the individual. Neither Poe nor Whitman made the slightest concession to what was the predominant English taste, the prevailing English authority, of his time. And neither yielded in the slightest to the maudlin echoes of English notions that passed for ideas in the United States; in neither will you find any recognizable reflection of the things that Americans were saying and doing all about them. Even Whitman, preaching democracy, preached a democracy that not one actual democrat in a hundred thousand could so much as imagine. What happened? *Imprimis*, English authority, at the start, dismissed them loftily; they were, at best, simply rare freaks from the colonies. Secondly, American stupidity, falling into step, came near overlooking them altogether. The accident that maintained them was an accident of personality and environment. They happened to be men accustomed to social isolation and of the most meager wants, and it was thus difficult to deter them by neglect and punishment. So they stuck to their guns—and presently they were "discovered," as the phrase is, by men of a culture wholly foreign to them and perhaps incomprehensible to them, and thereafter, by slow stages, they began to win a slow and reluctant recognition in England (at first only from rebels and iconoclasts), and finally even in America. That either, without French prompting, would have come to his present estate I doubt very much. And in support of that doubt I cite again the fact that Poe's high talents as a critic, not having interested the French, have never got their deserts either in England or at home.

It is lesser men that we chiefly have to deal with in this world, and it is among lesser men that the lack of a confident intellectual viewpoint in America makes itself most evident. Examples are numerous and obvious. On the one hand, we have Fenimore Cooper first making a cringing bow for English favor, and then, on being kicked out, joining the mob against sense; he wrote books so bad that even the Americans of 1830 admired them. On the other hand, we have Henry James, a deserter made by despair; one so depressed by the tacky company at the American first table that he preferred to sit at the second table of the English. The impulse was, and is common; it was only the forthright act that distinguished him. And in the middle ground, showing both seductions plainly, there is Mark Twain—at one moment striving his hardest for the English *imprimatur*, and childishly delighted by every favorable gesture; at the next, returning to the native mob as its premier clown—monkey-shining at banquets, cavorting in the newspapers, shrinking poltroonishly from his own ideas, obscenely eager to give no offense. A much greater artist than either Poe or Whitman, so I devoutly believe, but a good deal lower as a man. The ultimate passion was not there; the decent house-holder always pulled the ear of the dreamer. His fate has irony in it. In England they patronize him: he is, for an American, not so bad. In America, appalled by his occasional ascents to honesty, his stray impulses to be wholly himself, the dunder-heads return him to arm's length, his old place, and one of the most eminent of them, writing in the New York *Times*, argues piously that it is impossible to imagine him actually believing the commonplace heresies he put into "What Is Man?"

II
Epilogue

I have described the disease. Let me say at once that I have no remedy to offer. I simply set down a few ideas, throw out a few hints, attempt a few modest inquiries into causes. Perhaps my argument often turns upon itself: the field is weed-grown and paths are hard to follow. It may be that insurmountable natural obstacles stand in the way of the development of a dis-tinctively American culture, grounded upon a truly egoistic na-tionalism and supported by a native aristocracy. After all, there is no categorical imperative that ordains it. In such matters, when the conditions are right, nature often arranges a division of labor. A nation shut in by racial and linguistic isolation—a Sweden, a Holland or a France—is forced into autonomy by sheer necessity; if it is to have any intellectual life at all it must develop its own. But that is not our case. There is England to hold up the torch for us, as France holds it up for Belgium, and Spain for Latin America, and Germany for Switzerland. It is our function, as the younger and less confident partner, to do the simpler, rougher parts of the joint labor—to develop the virtues of the more elemental orders of men: industry, piety, docility, endurance, assiduity and ingenuity in practical affairs —the wood-hewing and water-drawing of the race. It seems to me that we do all this very well; in these things we are better than the English. But when it comes to those larger and more difficult activities which concern only the superior minority, and are, in essence, no more than products of its efforts to *demonstrate* its superiority—when it comes to the higher varieties of speculation and self-expression, to the fine arts and the game of ideas—then we fall into a bad second place. Where we stand, intellectually, is where the English non-conformists stand; like them, we are marked by a fear of ideas as disturbing and corrupting. Our art is imitative and timorous. Our political theory is hopelessly sophomoric and superficial; even English Toryism and Russian Bolshevism are infinitely more profound and penetrating. And of the two philosophical systems that we have produced, one is so banal that it is now imbedded in the New Thought, and the other is so shallow that there is nothing in it either to puzzle or to outrage a school-marm.

Nevertheless, hope will not down, and now and then it is supported by something rather more real than mere desire. One observes an under-current of revolt, small but vigorous, and sometimes it exerts its force, not only against the superficial banality but also against the fundamental, flabbiness, the intrinsic childishness of the Puritan *Anschauung*. The remedy for that childishness is skepticism, and already skepticism shows itself: in the iconoclastic political realism of Harold Stearns, Waldo Frank and company, in the grouping questions of Dreiser, Cabell and Anderson, in the operatic rebellions of the Village. True imagination, I often think, is no more than a function of this skepticism. It is the dull man who is always sure, and the sure man who is always dull. The more a man dreams, the less he believes. A great literature is thus chiefly the product of doubting and inquiring minds in revolt against the immovable certainties of the nation. Shakespeare, at a time of rising democratic feeling in England, flung the whole force of his genius against democracy. Cervantes, at a time when all Spain was romantic, made a headlong attack upon romance. Goethe, with Germany groping toward nationalism, threw his influences on the side of internationalism. The central trouble with America is conformity, timorousness, lack of enterprise and audacity. A nation of third-rate men, a land offering hospitality only to fourth-rate artists. In Elizabethan England they would have bawled for democracy, in the Spain of Cervantes they would have yelled for chivalry, and in the Germany of Goethe they would have wept and beat their breasts for the Fatherland. To-day, as in the day of Emerson, they set the tune. . . . But into the singing there occasionally enters a discordant note. On some dim to-morrow, perhaps, per-chance, peradventure, they may be challenged.

II.

Roosevelt: An Autopsy

ONE thinks of Dr. Woodrow Wilson's biography of George Washington as of one of the strangest of all the world's books. Washington: the first, and perhaps also the last American gentleman. Wilson: the self-bamboozled Presbyterian, the right-thinker, the great moral statesman, the perfect model of the Christian cad. It is as if the Rev. Dr. Billy Sunday should do a biography of Charles Darwin—almost as if Dr. Wilson himself should dedicate his senility to a life of the Chevalier Bayard, or the Cid, or Christ. . . . But such phenomena, of course, are not actually rare in the republic; here everything happens that is forbidden by the probabilities and the decencies. The chief native critic of beautiful letters, for a whole generation, was a Baptist clergyman; he was succeeded by a literary Wall Street man, who gave way, in turn, to a soviet of ninth-rate pedagogues; this very curious apostolic succession I have already discussed. The dean of the music critics, even today, is a translator of grand opera libretti, and probably one of the worst that ever lived. Return, now, to political biography. Who can think of anything in American literature comparable to Morley's life of Gladstone, or Trevelyan's life of Macaulay, or Carlyle's Frederick, or even Winston Churchill's life of his father? I dredge my memory hopelessly; only William Graham Sumner's study of Andrew Jackson emerges—an extraordinarily astute and careful piece of work by one of the two most underestimated Americans of his generation, the other being Daniel Coit Gilman. But where is the first-rate biography of Washington—sound, fair, penetrating, honest, done by a man capable of comprehending the English gentry of the eighteenth century? And how long must we wait for adequate treatises upon Jefferson, Hamilton, Sam Adams, Aaron Burr, Henry Clay, Calhoun, Webster, Sumner, Grant, Sherman, Lee?

Even Lincoln is yet to be got vividly between the covers of a book. The Nicolay-Hay work is quite impossible; it is not a biography, but simply a huge storehouse of biographical raw materials; whoever can read it can also read the official Records of the Rebellion. All the other standard lives of old Abe—for instance, those of Lamon, Herndon and Weik, Stoddard, Morse and Miss Tarbell—fail still worse; when they are not grossly preachy and disingenuous they are trivial. So far as I can make out, no genuinely scientific study of the man has ever been attempted. The amazing conflict of testimony about him remains a conflict; the most elemental facts are yet to be established; he grows vaguer and more fabulous as year follows year. One would think that, by this time, the question of his religious views (to take one example) ought to be settled, but apparently it is not, for no longer than a year ago there came a reverend author, Dr. William E. Barton, with a whole volume upon the subject, and I was as much in the dark after reading it as I had been before I opened it. All previous biographers, it appeared by this author's evidence, had either dodged the problem, or lied. The official doctrine, in this as in other departments, is obviously quite unsound. One hears in the Sunday-schools that Abe was an austere and pious fellow, constantly taking the name of God in whispers, just as one reads in the school history-books that he was a shining idealist, holding all his vast powers by the magic of an inner and ineffable virtue. Imagine a man getting on in American politics, interesting and enchanting the boobery, sawing off the horns of other politicians, elbowing his way through primaries and conventions, by the magic of virtue! As well talk of fetching the mob by hawking exact and arctic justice! Abe, in fact, must have been a fellow highly skilled at the great democratic art of gum-shoeing. I like to think of him as one who defeated such politicians as Stanton, Douglas and Sumner with their own weapons—deftly leading them into ambuscades, boldly pulling their noses, magnificently ham-stringing and horn-swoggling them—in brief, as a politician of extraordinary talents, who loved the game for its own sake, and had the measure of the crowd. His official portraits, both in prose and in daguerreotype, show him wearing the mien of a man about to be hanged; one never sees him smiling. Nevertheless, one hears that, until he emerged from Illinois, they always put the women, children and clergy to bed when he got a few gourds of corn aboard, and it is a matter of unescapable record that his career in the State Legislature was indistinguishable from that of a Tammany Nietzsche.

But, as I say, it is hopeless to look for the real man in the biographies of him: they are all full of distortion, chiefly pious and sentimental. The defect runs through the whole of American political biography, and even through the whole of American history. Nearly all our professional historians are poor men holding college posts, and they are ten times more cruelly beset by the ruling politico-plutocratic-social oligarchy than ever the Prussian professors were by the Hohenzollerns. Let them diverge in the slightest from what is the current official doctrine, and they are turned out of their chairs with a ceremony suitable for the expulsion of a drunken valet. During the recent war a herd of two thousand and five hundred such miserable slaves was organized by Dr. Creel to lie for their country, and they at once fell upon the congenial task of rewriting American history to make it accord with the ideas of H. P. Davison, Admiral Sims, Nicholas Murray Butler, the Astors, Barney Baruch and Lord Northcliffe. It was a committee of this herd that solemnly pledged the honor of American scholarship to the authenticity of the celebrated Sisson documents. . . .

In the face of such acute miliary imbecility it is not surprising to discover that all of the existing biographies of the late Colonel Roosevelt—and they have been rolling off the presses at a dizzy rate since his death—are feeble, inaccurate, ignorant and preposterous. I have read, I suppose, at least ten of these tomes during the past year or so, and in all of them I have found vastly more gush than sense. Lawrence Abbott's "Impressions of Theodore Roosevelt" and William Roscoe Thayer's "Theodore Roosevelt" may well serve as specimens. Abbott's book is the composition, not of an unbiased student of the man, but of a sort of groom of the hero. He is so extremely eager to prove that Roosevelt was the perfect right-thinker, according to the transient definitions of right-thinking, that he manages to get a flavor of dubiousness into his whole chronicle. I find myself doubting him even when I know that he is honest and suspect that he is right. As for Thayer, all he offers is a hasty and hollow pot-boiler—such a work as might have been well within the talents of, say, the late Murat Halstead or the editor of the New York *Times*. This Thayer has been heavily praised of late as the Leading American Biographer, and one constantly hears that some new university has made him *Legum Doctor*, or that he has been awarded a medal by this or that learned society, or that the post has brought him a new ribbon from some literary potentate in foreign parts. If, in fact, he is actually the cock of the walk in biography, then all I have said against American biographers is too mild and mellow. What one finds in his book is simply the third-rate correctness of a Boston colonial. Consider, for example, his frequent discussions of the war—a necessity in any work on Roosevelt. In England there is the mob's view of the war, and there is the view of civilized and intelligent men, *e.g.*, Lansdowne, Loreburn, Austin Harrison, Morel, Keynes, Haldane, Hirst, Balfour, Robert Cecil. In New England, it would appear, the two views coalesce, with the first outside. There is scarcely a line on the subject in Thayer's book that might not have been written by Horatio Bottomley. . . .

Obviously, Roosevelt's reaction to the war must occupy a large part of any adequate biography of him, for that reaction was probably more comprehensively typical of the man than any other business of his life. It displayed not only his whole stock of political principles, but also his whole stock of political tricks. It plumbed, on the one hand, the depths of his sagacity, and on the other hand the depths of his insincerity. Fundamentally, I am convinced, he was quite out of sympathy with, and even quite unable to comprehend the body of doctrine upon which the Allies, and later the United States, based their case. To him it must have seemed insane when it was not hypocritical, and hypocritical when it was not insane. His instincts were profoundly against a new loosing of democratic fustian upon the world; he believed in strongly centralized states, founded upon power and devoted to enterprises far transcending mere internal government; he was an imperialist of the type of Cecil Rhodes, Treitschke and Delcassé. But the fortunes of domestic politics jockeyed him into the position of standing as the spokesman of an almost exactly contrary philosophy. The visible enemy before him was Wilson. What he wanted as a politician was something that he could get only by wresting it from Wilson, and Wilson was too cunning to yield it without making a tremendous fight, chiefly by chicane— whooping for peace while preparing for war, playing mob fear against mob fear, concealing all his genuine motives and de- sires beneath clouds of chautauqual rhetoric, leading a mad dance whose tune changed at every swing. Here was an oppo- nent that more than once puzzled Roosevelt, and in the end flatly dismayed him. Here was a mob-master with a technique infinitely more subtle and effective than his own. So lured into an unequal combat, the Rough Rider got bogged in absurdi- ties so immense that only the democratic anæsthesia to absurd- ity saved him. To make any progress at all he was forced into fighting against his own side. He passed from the scene bawl- ing piteously for a cause that, at bottom, it is impossible to imagine him believing in, and in terms of a philosophy that was as foreign to his true faith as it was to the faith of Wilson. In the whole affair there was a colossal irony. Both contestants were intrinsically frauds.

The fraudulence of Wilson is now admitted by all save a few survivors of the old corps of official press-agents, most of them devoid of both honesty and intelligence. No unbiased man, in the presence of the revelations of Bullitt, Keynes and a hun- dred other witnesses, and of the Russian and Shantung perfor- mances, and of innumerable salient domestic phenomena, can now believe that the *Doctor dulcifluus* was ever actually in favor of any of the brummagem ideals he once wept for, to the edification of a moral universe. They were, at best, no more than ingenious *ruses de guerre*, and even in the day of their widest credit it was the Espionage Act and the Solicitor- General to the Postoffice, rather than any plausibility in their substance, that got them their credit. In Roosevelt's case the imposture is less patent; he died before it was fully unmasked. What is more, his death put an end to whatever investigation of it was under way, for American sentimentality holds that it is indecent to inquire into the weaknesses of the dead, at least until all the flowers have withered on their tombs. When, a year ago, I ventured in a magazine article to call attention to Roosevelt's philosophical kinship to the Kaiser I received letters of denunciation from all parts of the United States, and not a few forthright demands that I recant on penalty of lynch law. Prudence demanded that I heed these demands. We live in a curious and often unsafe country. Haled before a Roosevelt judge for speeding my automobile, or spitting on the sidewalk, or carrying a jug, I might have been railroaded for ten years under some constructive corollary of the Espionage Act. But there were two things that supported me in my contumacy to the departed. One was a profound reverence for and fidelity to the truth, sometimes almost amounting to fanaticism. The other was the support of my venerable brother in epistemology, the eminent Iowa right-thinker and patriot, Prof. Dr. S. P. Sherman. Writing in the *Nation*, where he survives from more seemly days than these, Prof. Dr. Sherman put the thing in plain terms. "With the essentials in the religion of the militarists of Germany," he said, "Roosevelt was utterly in sympathy."

Utterly? Perhaps the adverb is a bit too strong. There was in the man a certain instinctive antipathy to the concrete aristocrat and in particular to the aristocrat's private code—the product, no doubt, of his essentially *bourgeois* origin and training. But if he could not go with the Junkers all the way, he could at least go the whole length of their distrust of the third order—the undifferentiated masses of men below. Here, I daresay, he owed a lot to Nietzsche. He was always reading German books, and among them, no doubt, were "Also sprach Zarathustra" and "Jenseits von Gut und Böse." In fact, the echoes were constantly sounding in his own harangues. Years ago, as an intellectual exercise while confined to hospital, I devised and printed a give-away of the Rooseveltian philosophy in parallel columns—in one column, extracts from "The Strenuous Life"; in the other, extracts from Nietzsche. The borrowings were numerous and unescapable. Theodore had swallowed Friedrich as a peasant swallows Peruna—bottle, cork, label and testimonials. Worse, the draft whetted his appetite, and soon he was swallowing the Kaiser of the *Garde-Kavallerie*-mess and battleship-launching speeches—another somewhat defective Junker. In his palmy days it was often impossible to distinguish his politico-theological bulls from those of Wilhelm; during the war, indeed, I suspect that some of them were boldly lifted by the British press bureau, and palmed off as felonious imprudences out of Potsdam. Wilhelm was his model in *Weltpolitik*, and in sociology, exegetics, administration, law, sport and connubial polity no less. Both roared for doughty armies, eternally prepared—for the theory that the way to prevent war is to make all conceivable enemies think twice, thrice, ten times. Both dreamed of gigantic navies, with battleships as long as Brooklyn Bridge. Both preached incessantly the duty of the citizen to the state, with the soft pedal upon the duty of the state to the citizen. Both praised the habitually gravid wife. Both delighted in the armed pursuit of the lower fauna. Both heavily patronized the fine arts. Both were intimates of God, and announced His desires with authority. Both believed that all men who stood opposed to them were prompted by the devil and would suffer for it in hell.

If, in fact, there was any difference between them, it was all in favor of Wilhelm. For one thing, he made very much fewer speeches; it took some colossal event, such as the launching of a dreadnaught or the birthday of a colonel-general, to get him upon his legs; the Reichstag was not constantly deluged with his advice and upbraiding. For another thing, he was a milder and more modest man—one more accustomed, let us say, to circumstance and authority, and hence less intoxicated by the greatness of his state. Finally, he had been trained to think, not only of his own immediate fortunes, but also of the remote interests of a family that, in his most expansive days, promised to hold the throne for many years, and so he cultivated a certain prudence, and even a certain ingratiating suavity. He could, on occasion, be extremely polite to an opponent. But Roosevelt was never polite to an opponent; perhaps a gentleman, by American standards, he was surely never a gentle man. In a political career of nearly forty years he was never even fair to an opponent. All of his gabble about the square deal was merely so much protective coloration, easily explicable on elementary Freudian grounds. No man, facing Roosevelt in the heat of controversy, ever actually got a square deal. He took extravagant advantages; he played to the worst idiocies of the mob; he hit below the belt almost habitually. One never thinks of him as a duelist, say of the school of Disraeli, Palmerston and, to drop a bit, Blaine. One always thinks of him as a glorified longshoreman engaged eternally in cleaning out bar-rooms—and not too proud to gouge when the inspiration came to him, or to bite in the clinches, or to oppose the relatively fragile brass knuckles of the code with chair-legs, bung-starters, cuspidors, demijohns, and ice-picks.

Abbott and Thayer, in their books, make elaborate efforts to depict their hero as one born with a deep loathing of the whole Prussian scheme of things, and particularly of the Prussian technique in combat. Abbott even goes so far as to hint that the attentions of the Kaiser, during Roosevelt's historic tour of Europe on his return from Africa, were subtly revolting to him. Nothing could be more absurd. Prof. Dr. Sherman, in the article I have mentioned, blows up that nonsense by quoting from a speech made by the tourist in Berlin—a speech arguing for the most extreme sort of militarism in a manner that must have made even some of the Junkers blow their noses dubiously. The disproof need not be piled up; the America that Roosevelt dreamed of was always a sort of swollen Prussia, truculent without and regimented within. There was always a clank of the saber in his discourse; he could not discuss the tamest matter without swaggering in the best dragoon fashion. Abbott gets into yet deeper waters when he sets up the doctrine that the invasion of Belgium threw his darling into an instantaneous and tremendous fit of moral indignation, and that the curious delay in the public exhibition thereof, so much discussed since, was due to his (Abbott's) fatuous interference—a *faux pas* later regretted with much bitterness. Unluckily, the evidence he offers leaves me full of doubts. What the doctrine demands that one believe is simply this: that the man who, for mere commercial advantage and (in Frederick's famous phrase) "to make himself talked of in the world," tore up the treaty of 1848 between the United States and Colombia (*geb.* New Granada), whereby the United States forever guaranteed the "sovereignty and ownership" of the Colombians in the isthmus of Panama—that this same man, thirteen years later, was horrified into a fever when Germany, facing powerful foes on two fronts, tore up the treaty of 1832, guaranteeing, not the sovereignty, but the bald neutrality of Belgium—a neutrality already destroyed, according to the evidence before the Germans, by Belgium's own acts.

It is hard, without an inordinate strain upon the credulity, to believe any such thing, particularly in view of the fact that this instantaneous indignation of the most impulsive and vocal of men was diligently concealed for at least six weeks, with reporters camped upon his doorstep day and night, begging him to say the very thing that he left so darkly unsaid. Can one imagine Roosevelt, with red-fire raging within him and sky-rockets bursting in his veins, holding his peace for a month and a half? I have no doubt whatever that Abbott, as he says, desired to avoid embarrassing Dr. Wilson—but think of Roosevelt showing any such delicacy! For one, I am not equal to the feat. All that unprecedented reticence, in fact, is far more readily explicable on other and less lofty grounds. What really happened I presume to guess. My guess is that Roosevelt, like the great majority of other Americans, was *not* instantly and automatically outraged by the invasion of Belgium. On the contrary, he probably viewed it as a regrettable, but not unexpected or unparalleled device of war—if anything, as something rather thrillingly gaudy and effective—a fine piece of virtuosity, pleasing to a military connoisseur. But then came the deluge of Belgian atrocity stories, and the organized campaign to enlist American sympathies. It succeeded very quickly. By the middle of August the British press bureau was in full swing; by the beginning of September the country was flooded with inflammatory stuff; six weeks after the war opened it was already hazardous for a German in America to state his country's case. Meanwhile, the Wilson administration had declared for neutrality, and was still making a more or less sincere effort to practice it, at least on the surface. Here was Roosevelt's opportunity, and he leaped to it with sure instinct. On the one side was the adminstration that he detested, and that all his self-interest (*e.g.*, his yearning to get back his old leadership and to become President again in 1917) prompted him to deal a mortal blow, and on the other side was a ready-made issue, full of emotional possibilities, stupendously pumped up by extremely clever propaganda, and so far unembraced by any other rabble-rouser of the first magnitude. Is it any wonder that he gave a whoop, jumped upon his cayuse, and began screaming for war? In war lay the greatest chance of his life. In war lay the confusion and destruction of Wilson, and the melodramatic renaissance of the Rough Rider, the professional hero, the national Barbarossa.

In all this, of course, I strip the process of its plumes and spangles, and expose a chain of causes and effects that Roosevelt himself, if he were alive, would denounce as grossly contumelious to his native purity of spirit—and perhaps in all honesty. It is not necessary to raise any doubts as to that honesty. No one who has given any study to the development and propagation of political doctrine in the United States can have failed to notice how the belief in issues among politicians tends to run in exact ratio to the popularity of those issues. Let the populace begin suddenly to swallow a new panacea or to take fright at a new bugaboo, and almost instantly nine-tenths of the master-minds of politics begin to believe that the panacea is a sure cure for all the malaises of the republic, and the bugaboo an immediate and unbearable menace to all law, order and domestic tranquillity. At the bottom of this singular intellectual resilience, of course, there is a good deal of hard calculation; a man must keep up with the procession of crazes, or his day is swiftly done. But in it there are also considerations a good deal more subtle, and maybe less discreditable. For one thing, a man devoted professionally to patriotism and the wisdom of the fathers is very apt to come to a resigned sort of acquiescence in all the doctrinaire rubbish that lies beneath the national scheme of things—to believe, let us say, if not that the plain people are gifted with an infallible sagacity, then at least that they have an inalienable right to see their follies executed. Poll-parroting nonsense as a matter of daily routine, the politician ends by assuming that it is sense, even though he doesn't believe it. For another thing, there is the contagion of mob enthusiasm—a much underestimated murrain. We all saw what it could do during the war—college professors taking their tune from the yellow journals, the rev. clergy performing in the pulpit like so many Liberty Loan orators in five-cent moving-picture houses, hysteria grown epidemic like the influenza. No man is so remote and arctic that he is wholly safe from that contamination; it explains many extravagant phenomena of a democratic society; in particular, it explains why the mob leader is so often a victim to his mob.

Roosevelt, a perfectly typical politician, devoted to the trade, not primarily because he was gnawed by ideals, but because he frankly enjoyed its rough-and-tumble encounters and its gaudy rewards, was probably moved in both ways—and also by the hard calculation that I have mentioned. If, by any ineptness of the British press-agents, tear-squeezers and orphan-exhibitors, indignation over the invasion of Belgium had failed to materialize—if, worse still, some gross infringement of American rights by the English had caused it to be forgotten completely—if, finally, Dr. Wilson had been whooping for war with the populace firmly against him—in such event it goes without saying that the moral horror of Dr. Roosevelt would have stopped short at a very low amperage, and that he would have refrained from making it the center of his polity. But with things as they were, lying neatly to his hand, he permitted it to take on an extraordinary virulence, and before long all his old delight in German militarism had been converted into a lofty detestation of German militarism, and its chief spokesman on this side of the Atlantic became its chief opponent. Getting rid of that old delight, of course, was not easily achieved. The concrete enthusiasm could be throttled, but the habit of mind remained. Thus one beheld the curious spectacle of militarism belabored in terms of militarism—of the Kaiser arraigned in unmistakably *kaiserliche* tones.

Such violent swallowings and regurgitations were no novelties to the man. His whole political career was marked, in fact, by performances of the same sort. The issues that won him most votes were issues that, at bottom, he didn't believe in; there was always a mental reservation in his rhetoric. He got into politics, not as a tribune of the plain people, but as an amateur reformer of the snobbish type common in the eighties, by the *Nation* out of the Social Register. He was a young Harvard man scandalized by the discovery that his town was run by men with such names as Michael O'Shaunnessy and Terence Googan—that his social inferiors were his political superiors. His sympathies were essentially anti-democratic. He had a high view of his private position as a young fellow of wealth and education. He believed in strong centralization—the concentration of power in a few hands, the strict regimentation of the nether herd, the abandonment of democratic platitudes. His heroes were such Federalists as Morris and Hamilton; he made his first splash in the world by writing about them and praising them. Worse, his daily associations were with the old

Union League crowd of high-tariff Republicans—men almost apoplectically opposed to every movement from below—safe and sane men, highly conservative and suspicious men—the profiteers of peace, as they afterward became the profiteers of war. His early adventures in politics were not very fortunate, nor did they reveal any capacity for leadership. The bosses of the day took him in rather humorously, played him for what they could get out of him, and then turned him loose. In a few years he became disgusted and went West. Returning after a bit, he encountered catastrophe: as a candidate for Mayor of New York he was drubbed unmercifully. He went back to the West. He was, up to this time, a comic figure—an anti-politician victimized by politicians, a pseudo-aristocrat made ridiculous by the mob-masters he detested.

But meanwhile something was happening that changed the whole color of the political scene, and was destined, eventually, to give Roosevelt his chance. That something was a shifting in what might be called the foundations of reform. Up to now it had been an essentially aristocratic movement—superior, sniffish and anti-democratic. But hereafter it took on a strongly democratic color and began to adopt democratic methods. More, the change gave it new life. What Harvard, the Union League Club and the *Nation* had failed to accomplish, the plain people now undertook to accomplish. This invasion of the old citadel of virtue was first observed in the West, and its manifestations out there must have given Roosevelt a good deal more disquiet than satisfaction. It is impossible to imagine him finding anything to his taste in the outlandish doings of the Populists, the wild schemes of the pre-Bryan dervishes. His instincts were against all that sort of thing. But as the movement spread toward the East it took on a certain urbanity, and by the time it reached the seaboard it had begun to be quite civilized. With this new brand of reform Roosevelt now made terms. It was full of principles that outraged all his pruderies, but it at least promised to work. His entire political history thereafter, down to the day of his death, was a history of compromises with the new forces—of a gradual yielding, for strategic purposes, to ideas that were intrinsically at odds with his congenital prejudices. When, after a generation of that sort of compromising, the so-called Progressive party was organized and he seized the leadership of it from the Westerners who had founded it, he performed a feat of wholesale englutination that must forever hold a high place upon the roll of political prodigies. That is to say, he swallowed at one gigantic gulp, and out of the same herculean jug, the most amazing mixture of social, political and economic perunas ever got down by one hero, however valiant, however athirst—a cocktail made up of all the elixirs hawked among the boobery in his time, from woman suffrage to the direct primary, and from the initiative and referendum to the short ballot, and from prohibition to public ownership, and from trust-busting to the recall of judges.

This homeric achievement made him the head of the most tatterdemalion party ever seen in American politics—a party composed of such incompatible ingredients and hung together so loosely that it began to disintegrate the moment it was born. In part it was made up of mere disordered enthusiasts —believers in anything and everything, pathetic victims of the credulity complex, habitual followers of jitney messiahs, incurable hopers and snufflers. But in part it was also made up of rice converts like Roosevelt himself—men eager for office, disappointed by the old parties, and now quite willing to accept any aid that half-idiot doctrinaires could give them. I have no doubt that Roosevelt himself, carried away by the emotional storms of the moment and especially by the quasi-religious monkey-shines that marked the first Progressive convention, gradually convinced himself that at least some of the doctrinaires, in the midst of all their imbecility, yet preached a few ideas that were workable, and perhaps even sound. But at bottom he was against them, and not only in the matter of their specific sure cures, but also in the larger matter of their childish faith in the wisdom and virtue of the plain people. Roosevelt, for all his fluent mastery of democratic counter-words, democratic gestures and all the rest of the armamentarium of the mob-master, had no such faith in his heart of hearts. He didn't believe in democracy; he believed simply in government. His remedy for all the great pangs and longings of existence was not a dispersion of authority, but a hard concentration of authority. He was not in favor of unlimited experiment; he was in favor of a rigid control from above, a despotism of inspired prophets and policemen. He was not for democracy as his followers understood democracy, and as it actually is and must be; he was for a paternalism of the true Bismarckian pattern, almost of the Napoleonic or Ludendorffian pattern—a paternalism concerning itself with all things, from the regulation of coal-mining and meat-packing to the regulation of spelling and marital rights. His instincts were always those of the property-owning Tory, not those of the romantic Liberal. All the fundamental objects of Liberalism—free speech, unhampered enterprise, the least possible governmental interference—were abhorrent to him. Even when, for campaign purposes, he came to terms with the Liberals his thoughts always ranged far afield. When he tackled the trusts the thing that he had in his mind's eye was not the restoration of competition but the subordination of all private trusts to one great national trust, with himself at its head. And when he attacked the courts it was not because they put their own prejudice before the law but because they refused to put *his* prejudices before the law.

In all his career no one ever heard him make an argument for the rights of the citizen; his eloquence was always expended in expounding the duties of the citizen. I have before me a speech in which he pleaded for "a spirit of kindly justice toward every man and woman," but that seems to be as far as he ever got in that direction—and it was the gratuitous justice of the absolute monarch that he apparently had in mind, not the autonomous and inalienable justice of a free society. The duties of the citizen, as he understood them, related not only to acts, but also to thoughts. There was, to his mind, a simple body of primary doctrine, and dissent from it was the foulest of crimes. No man could have been more bitter against opponents, or more unfair to them, or more ungenerous. In this department, indeed, even so gifted a specialist in dishonorable controversy as Dr. Wilson has seldom surpassed him. He never stood up to a frank and chivalrous debate. He dragged herrings across the trail. He made seductive faces at the gallery. He capitalized his enormous talents as an entertainer, his rank as a national hero, his public influence and consequence. The two great law-suits in which he was engaged were screaming burlesques upon justice. He tried them in the newspapers before ever they were called; he befogged them with irrelevant issues; his appearances in court were not the appearances of a witness standing on a level with other witnesses, but those of a comedian sure of his crowd. He was, in his dealings with concrete men as in his dealings with men in the mass, a charlatan of the very highest skill—and there was in him, it goes without saying, the persuasive charm of the charlatan as well as the daring deviousness, the humanness of naïveté as well as the humanness of chicane. He knew how to woo—and not only boobs. He was, for all his ruses and ambuscades, a jolly fellow.

It seems to be forgotten that the current American theory that political heresy should be put down by force, that a man who disputes whatever is official has no rights in law or equity, that he is lucky if he fares no worse than to lose his constitutional benefits of free speech, free assemblage and the use of the mails—it seems to be forgotten that this theory was invented, not by Dr. Wilson, but by Roosevelt. Most Liberals, I suppose, would credit it, if asked, to Wilson. He has carried it to extravagant lengths; he is the father superior of all the present advocates of it; he will probably go down into American history as its greatest prophet. But it was first clearly stated, not in any Wilsonian bull to the right-thinkers of all lands, but in Roosevelt's proceedings against the so-called Paterson anarchists. You will find it set forth at length in an opinion prepared for him by his Attorney-General, Charles J. Bonaparte, another curious and almost fabulous character, also an absolutist wearing the false whiskers of a democrat. Bonaparte furnished the law, and Roosevelt furnished the blood and iron. It was an almost ideal combination; Bonaparte had precisely the touch of Italian finesse that the Rough Rider always lacked. Roosevelt believed in the Paterson doctrine—in brief, that the Constitution does not throw its cloak around heretics —to the end of his days. In the face of what he conceived to be contumacy to revelation his fury took on a sort of lyrical grandeur. There was nothing too awful for the culprit in the dock. Upon his head were poured denunciations as violent as the wildest interdicts of a mediæval pope.

The appearance of such men, of course, is inevitable under a democracy. Consummate showmen, they arrest the wonder of the mob, and so put its suspicions to sleep. What they actually believe is of secondary consequence; the main thing is what they say; even more, the way they say it. Obviously, their activity does a great deal of damage to the democratic theory, for they are standing refutations of the primary doctrine that the common folk choose their leaders wisely. They damage it again in another and more subtle way. That is to say, their ineradicable contempt for the minds they must heat up and bamboozle leads them into a fatalism that shows itself in a cynical and opportunistic politics, a deliberate avoidance of fundamentals. The policy of a democracy thus becomes an eternal improvisation, changing with the private ambitions of its leaders and the transient and often unintelligible emotions of its rank and file. Roosevelt, incurably undemocratic in his habits of mind, often found it difficult to gauge those emotional oscillations. The fact explains his frequent loss of mob support, his periodical journeys into Coventry. There were times when his magnificent talents as a public comedian brought the proletariat to an almost unanimous groveling at his feet, but there were also times when he puzzled and dismayed it, and so awakened its hostility. When he assaulted Wilson on the neutrality issue, early in 1915, he made a quite typical mistake. That mistake consisted in assuming that public indignation over the wrongs of the Belgians would maintain itself at a high temperature—that it would develop rapidly into a demand for intervention. Roosevelt made himself the spokesman of that demand, and then found to his consternation that it was waning—that the great masses of the plain people, prospering under the Wilsonian neutrality, were inclined to preserve it, at no matter what cost to the Belgians. In 1915, after the *Lusitania* affair, things seemed to swing his way again, and he got vigorous support from the British press bureau. But in a few months he found himself once more attempting to lead a mob that was fast slipping away. Wilson, a very much shrewder politician, with little of Roosevelt's weakness for succumbing to his own rhetoric, discerned the truth much more quickly and clearly. In 1916 he made his campaign for reëlection on a flatly anti-Roosevelt peace issue, and not only got himself reëlected, but also drove Roosevelt out of the ring.

What happened thereafter deserves a great deal more careful study than it will ever get from the timorous eunuchs who posture as American historians. At the moment, it is the official doctrine in England, where the thing is more freely discussed than at home, that Wilson was forced into the war by an irresistible movement from below—that the plain people compelled him to abandon neutrality and move reluctantly upon the Germans. Nothing could be more untrue. The plain people, at the end of 1916, were in favor of peace, and they believed that Wilson was in favor of peace. How they were gradually worked up to complaisance and then to enthusiasm and then to hysteria and then to acute mania—this is a tale to be told in more leisurely days and by historians without boards of trustees on their necks. For the present purpose it is sufficient to note that the whole thing was achieved so quickly and so neatly that its success left Roosevelt surprised and helpless. His issue had been stolen from directly under his nose. He was left standing daunted and alone, a boy upon a burning deck. It took him months to collect his scattered wits, and even then his attack upon the administration was feeble and ineffective. To the plain people it seemed a mere ill-natured snapping at a successful rival, which in fact it was, and so they paid no heed to it, and Roosevelt found himself isolated once more. Thus he passed from the scene in the shadows, a broken politician and a disappointed man.

I have a notion that he died too soon. His best days were probably not behind him, but ahead of him. Had he lived ten years longer, he might have enjoyed a great rehabilitation and exchanged his old false leadership of the inflammatory and fickle mob for a sound and true leadership of the civilized minority. For the more one studies his mountebankeries as mobmaster, the more one is convinced that there was a shrewd man beneath the motley, and that his actual beliefs were anything but nonsensical. The truth of them, indeed, emerges more clearly day by day. The old theory of a federation of free and autonomous states has broken down by its own weight, and we are moved toward centralization by forces that have long been powerful and are now quite irresistible. So with the old theory of national isolation: it, too, has fallen to pieces. The United States can no longer hope to lead a separate life in the world, undisturbed by the pressure of foreign aspirations. We came out of the war to find ourselves hemmed in by hostilities that no longer troubled to conceal themselves, and if they are not as close and menacing today as those that have hemmed in Germany for centuries they are none the less plainly there and plainly growing. Roosevelt, by whatever route of reflection or intuition, arrived at a sense of these facts at a time when it was still somewhat scandalous to state them, and it was the capital effort of his life to reconcile them, in some dark way or other, to the prevailing platitudes, and so get them heeded. To-day no one seriously maintains, as all Americans once maintained, that the states can go on existing together as independent commonwealths, each with its own laws, its own legal theory and its own view of the common constitutional bond. And to-day no one seriously maintains, as all Americans once maintained, that the nation may safely potter on without adequate means of defense. However unpleasant it may be to contemplate, the fact is plain that the American people, during the next century, will have to fight to maintain their place in the sun.

Roosevelt lived just long enough to see his notions in these directions take on life, but not long enough to see them openly adopted. To the extent of his prevision he was a genuine leader of the nation, and perhaps in the years to come, when his actual ideas are disentangled from the demagogic fustian in which he had to wrap them, his more honest pronunciamentoes will be given canonical honors, and he will be ranked among the prophets. He saw clearly more than one other thing that was by no means obvious to his age—for example, the inevitability of frequent wars under the new world-system of extreme nationalism; again, the urgent necessity, for primary police ends, of organizing the backward nations into groups of vassals, each under the hoof of some first-rate power; yet again, the probability of the breakdown of the old system of free competition; once more, the high social utility of the Spartan virtues and the grave dangers of sloth and ease; finally, the incompatibility of free speech and democracy. I do not say that he was always quite honest, even when he was most indubitably right. But in so far as it was possible for him to be honest and exist at all politically, he inclined toward the straightforward thought and the candid word. That is to say, his instinct prompted him to tell the truth, just as the instinct of Dr. Wilson prompts him to shift and dissimulate. What ailed him was the fact that his lust for glory, when it came to a struggle, was always vastly more powerful than his lust for the eternal verities. Tempted sufficiently, he would sacrifice anything and everything to get applause. Thus the statesman was debauched by the politician, and the philosopher was elbowed out of sight by the popinjay.

Where he failed most miserably was in his remedies. A remarkably penetrating diagnostician, well-read, unprejudiced and with a touch of genuine scientific passion, he always stooped to quackery when he prescribed a course of treatment. For all his sensational attacks upon the trusts, he never managed to devise a scheme to curb them—and even when he sought to apply the schemes of other men he invariably corrupted the business with timorousness and insincerity. So with his campaign for national preparedness. He displayed the disease magnificently, but the course of medication that he proposed was vague and unconvincing; it was not, indeed, without justification that the plain people mistook his advocacy of an adequate army for a mere secret yearning to prance upon a charger at the head of huge hordes. So, again, with his eloquent plea for national solidarity and an end of hyphenism. The dangers that he pointed out were very real and very menacing, but his plan for abating them only made them worse. His objurgations against the Germans surely accomplished nothing; the hyphenate of 1915 is still a hyphenate in his heart —with bitter and unforgettable grievances to support him. Roosevelt, very characteristically, swung too far. In denouncing German hyphenism so extravagantly he contrived to give an enormous impetus to English hyphenism, a far older and more perilous malady. It has already gone so far that a large and influential party endeavors almost openly to convert the United States into a mere vassal state of England's. Instead of national solidarity following the war, we have only a revival of Know-Nothingism; one faction of hyphenates tries to exterminate another faction. Roosevelt's error here was one that he was always making. Carried away by the ease with which he could heat up the mob, he tried to accomplish instantly and by *force majeure* what could only be accomplished by a long and complex process, with more good will on both sides than ever so opinionated and melodramatic a pseudo-Junker was capable of. But though he thus made a mess of the cure, he was undoubtedly right about the disease.

The talented Sherman, in the monograph that I have praised, argues that the chief contribution of the dead gladiator to American life was the example of his gigantic gusto, his delight in toil and struggle, his superb aliveness. The fact is plain. What he stood most clearly in opposition to was the superior pessimism of the three Adams brothers—the notion that the public problems of a democracy are unworthy the thought and effort of a civilized and self-respecting man—the sad error that lies in wait for all of us who hold ourselves above the general. Against this suicidal aloofness Roosevelt always hurled himself with brave effect. Enormously sensitive and resilient, almost pathological in his appetite for activity, he made it plain to every one that the most stimulating sort of sport imaginable was to be obtained in fighting, not for mere money, but for ideas. There was no aristocratic reserve about him. He was not, in fact, an aristocrat at all, but a quite typical member of the upper *bourgeoisie*; his people were not *patroons* in New Amsterdam, but simple traders; he was himself a social pusher, and eternally tickled by the thought that he had had a Bonaparte in his cabinet. The marks of the thoroughbred were simply not there. The man was blatant, crude, overly confidential, devious, tyrannical, vainglorious, sometimes quite childish. One often observed in him a certain pathetic wistfulness, a reaching out for a grand manner that was utterly beyond him. But the sweet went with the bitter. He had all the virtues of the fat and complacent burgher. His disdain of affectation and prudery was magnificent. He hated all pretension save his own pretension. He had a sound respect for hard effort, for loyalty, for thrift, for honest achievement.

His worst defects, it seems to me, were the defects of his race and time. Aspiring to be the leader of a nation of third-rate men, he had to stoop to the common level. When he struck out for realms above that level he always came to grief: this was the "unsafe" Roosevelt, the Roosevelt who was laughed at, the Roosevelt retired suddenly to cold storage. This was the Roosevelt who, in happier times and a better place, might have been. Well, one does what one can.

III.

The Sahara of the Bozart

Alas, for the South! Her books have grown fewer—
She never was much given to literature.

I N the lamented J. Gordon Coogler, author of these elegaic
lines, there was the insight of a true poet. He was the last
bard of Dixie, at least in the legitimate line. Down there a poet
is now almost as rare as an oboe-player, a dry-point etcher or a
metaphysician. It is, indeed, amazing to contemplate so vast a
vacuity. One thinks of the interstellar spaces, of the colossal
reaches of the now mythical ether. Nearly the whole of Europe
could be lost in that stupendous region of fat farms, shoddy
cities and paralyzed cerebrums: one could throw in France,
Germany and Italy, and still have room for the British Isles.
And yet, for all its size and all its wealth and all the "progress"
it babbles of, it is almost as sterile, artistically, intellectually,
culturally, as the Sahara Desert. There are single acres in Europe that house more first-rate men than all the states south of
the Potomac; there are probably single square miles in America. If the whole of the late Confederacy were to be engulfed
by a tidal wave to-morrow, the effect upon the civilized minority of men in the world would be but little greater than that of
a flood on the Yang-tse-kiang. It would be impossible in all
history to match so complete a drying-up of a civilization.

I say a civilization because that is what, in the old days, the
South had, despite the Baptist and Methodist barbarism that
reigns down there now. More, it was a civilization of manifold
excellences—perhaps the best that the Western Hemisphere
has ever seen—undoubtedly the best that These States have
ever seen. Down to the middle of the last century, and even
beyond, the main hatchery of ideas on this side of the water
was across the Potomac bridges. The New England shop-
keepers and theologians never really developed a civilization;
all they ever developed was a government. They were, at their
best, tawdry and tacky fellows, oafish in manner and devoid of

imagination; one searches the books in vain for mention of a salient Yankee gentleman; as well look for a Welsh gentleman. But in the south there were men of delicate fancy, urbane instinct and aristocratic manner—in brief, superior men—in brief, gentry. To politics, their chief diversion, they brought active and original minds. It was there that nearly all the political theories we still cherish and suffer under came to birth. It was there that the crude dogmatism of New England was refined and humanized. It was there, above all, that some attention was given to the art of living—that life got beyond and above the state of a mere infliction and became an exhilarating experience. A certain noble spaciousness was in the ancient southern scheme of things. The *Ur*-Confederate had leisure. He liked to toy with ideas. He was hospitable and tolerant. He had the vague thing that we call culture.

But consider the condition of his late empire today. The picture gives one the creeps. It is as if the Civil War stamped out every last bearer of the torch, and left only a mob of peasants on the field. One thinks of Asia Minor, resigned to Armenians, Greeks and wild swine, of Poland abandoned to the Poles. In all that gargantuan paradise of the fourth-rate there is not a single picture gallery worth going into, or a single orchestra capable of playing the nine symphonies of Beethoven, or a single opera-house, or a single theater devoted to decent plays, or a single public monument (built since the war) that is worth looking at, or a single workshop devoted to the making of beautiful things. Once you have counted Robert Loveman (an Ohioan by birth) and John McClure (an Oklahoman) you will not find a single southern poet above the rank of a neighborhood rhymester. Once you have counted James Branch Cabell (a lingering survivor of the *ancien régime*: a scarlet dragonfly imbedded in opaque amber) you will not find a single southern prose writer who can actually write. And once you have—but when you come to critics, musical composers, painters, sculptors, architects and the like, you will have to give it up, for there is not even a bad one between the Potomac mud-flats and the Gulf. Nor an historian. Nor a sociologist. Nor a philosopher. Nor a theologian. Nor a scientist. In all these fields the south is an awe-inspiring blank—a brother to Portugal, Serbia and Esthonia.

Consider, for example, the present estate and dignity of Virginia—in the great days indubitably the premier American state, the mother of Presidents and statesmen, the home of the first American university worthy of the name, the *arbiter elegantiarum* of the western world. Well, observe Virginia to-day. It is years since a first-rate man, save only Cabell, has come out of it; it is years since an idea has come out of it. The old aristocracy went down the red gullet of war; the poor white trash are now in the saddle. Politics in Virginia are cheap, ignorant, parochial, idiotic; there is scarcely a man in office above the rank of a professional job-seeker; the political doctrine that prevails is made up of hand-me-downs from the bumpkinry of the Middle West—Bryanism, Prohibition, vice crusading, all that sort of filthy claptrap; the administration of the law is turned over to professors of Puritanism and espionage; a Washington or a Jefferson, dumped there by some act of God, would be denounced as a scoundrel and jailed overnight. Elegance, *esprit*, culture? Virginia has no art, no literature, no philosophy, no mind or aspiration of her own. Her education has sunk to the Baptist seminary level; not a single contribution to human knowledge has come out of her colleges in twenty-five years; she spends less than half upon her common schools, *per capita*, than any northern state spends. In brief, an intellectual Gobi or Lapland. Urbanity, *politesse*, chivalry? Go to! It was in Virginia that they invented the device of searching for contraband whiskey in women's underwear. . . . There remains, at the top, a ghost of the old aristocracy, a bit wistful and infinitely charming. But it has lost all its old leadership to fabulous monsters from the lower depths; it is submerged in an industrial plutocracy that is ignorant and ignominious. The mind of the state, as it is revealed to the nation, is pathetically naïve and inconsequential. It no longer reacts with energy and elasticity to great problems. It has fallen to the bombastic trivialities of the camp-meeting and the chautauqua. Its foremost exponent—if so flabby a thing may be said to have an exponent—is a stateman whose name is synonymous with empty words, broken pledges and false pretenses. One could no more imagine a Lee or a Washington in the Virginia of to-day than one could imagine a Huxley in Nicaragua.

I choose the Old Dominion, not because I disdain it, but precisely because I esteem it. It is, by long odds, the most civilized of the southern states, now as always. It has sent a host of creditable sons northward; the stream kept running into our own time. Virginians, even the worst of them, show the effects of a great tradition. They hold themselves above other southerners, and with sound pretension. If one turns to such a commonwealth as Georgia the picture becomes far darker. There the liberated lower orders of whites have borrowed the worst commercial bounderism of the Yankee and superimposed it upon a culture that, at bottom, is but little removed from savagery. Georgia is at once the home of the cotton-mill sweater and of the most noisy and vapid sort of chamber of commerce, of the Methodist parson turned Savonarola and of the lynching bee. A self-respecting European, going there to live, would not only find intellectual stimulation utterly lacking; he would actually feel a certain insecurity, as if the scene were the Balkans or the China Coast. The Leo Frank affair was no isolated phenomenon. It fitted into its frame very snugly. It was a natural expression of Georgian notions of truth and justice. There is a state with more than half the area of Italy and more population than either Denmark or Norway, and yet in thirty years it has not produced a single idea. Once upon a time a Georgian printed a couple of books that attracted notice, but immediately it turned out that he was little more than an amanuensis for the local blacks—that his works were really the products, not of white Georgia, but of black Georgia. Writing afterward *as* a white man, he swiftly subsided into the fifth rank. And he is not only the glory of the literature of Georgia; he is, almost literally, the whole of the literature of Georgia—nay, of the entire art of Georgia.

Virginia is the best of the south to-day, and Georgia is perhaps the worst. The one is simply senile; the other is crass, gross, vulgar and obnoxious. Between lies a vast plain of mediocrity, stupidity, lethargy, almost of dead silence. In the north, of course, there is also grossness, crassness, vulgarity. The north, in its way, is also stupid and obnoxious. But nowhere in the north is there such complete sterility, so depressing a lack of all civilized gesture and aspiration. One would find it difficult to unearth a second-rate city between the Ohio and the

Pacific that isn't struggling to establish an orchestra, or setting up a little theater, or going in for an art gallery, or making some other effort to get into touch with civilization. These efforts often fail, and sometimes they succeed rather absurdly, but under them there is at least an impulse that deserves respect, and that is the impulse to seek beauty and to experiment with ideas, and so to give the life of every day a certain dignity and purpose. You will find no such impulse in the south. There are no committees down there cadging subscriptions for orchestras; if a string quartet is ever heard there, the news of it has never come out; an opera troupe, when it roves the land, is a nine days' wonder. The little theater movement has swept the whole country, enormously augmenting the public interest in sound plays, giving new dramatists their chance, forcing reforms upon the commercial theater. Everywhere else the wave rolls high—but along the line of the Potomac it breaks upon a rock-bound shore. There is no little theater beyond. There is no gallery of pictures. No artist ever gives exhibitions. No one talks of such things. No one seems to be interested in such things.

As for the cause of this unanimous torpor and doltishness, this curious and almost pathological estrangement from everything that makes for a civilized culture, I have hinted at it already, and now state it again. The south has simply been drained of all its best blood. The vast blood-letting of the Civil War half exterminated and wholly paralyzed the old aristocracy, and so left the land to the harsh mercies of the poor white trash, now its masters. The war, of course, was not a complete massacre. It spared a decent number of first-rate southerners—perhaps even some of the very best. Moreover, other countries, notably France and Germany, have survived far more staggering butcheries, and even showed marked progress thereafter. But the war not only cost a great many valuable lives; it also brought bankruptcy, demoralization and despair in its train—and so the majority of the first-rate southerners that were left, broken in spirit and unable to live under the new dispensation, cleared out. A few went to South America, to Egypt, to the Far East. Most came north. They were fecund; their progeny is widely dispersed, to the great benefit of the north. A southerner of good blood almost always does well in the north. He finds, even in the big cities, surroundings fit for a man of condition. His peculiar qualities have a high social value, and are esteemed. He is welcomed by the codfish aristocracy as one palpably superior. But in the south he throws up his hands. It is impossible for him to stoop to the common level. He cannot brawl in politics with the grandsons of his grandfather's tenants. He is unable to share their fierce jealousy of the emerging black—the cornerstone of all their public thinking. He is anæsthetic to their theological and political enthusiasms. He finds himself an alien at their feasts of soul. And so he withdraws into his tower, and is heard of no more. Cabell is almost a perfect example. His eyes, for years, were turned toward the past; he became a professor of the grotesque genealogizing that decaying aristocracies affect; it was only by a sort of accident that he discovered himself to be an artist. The south is unaware of the fact to this day; it regards Woodrow Wilson and Col. John Temple Graves as much finer stylists, and Frank L. Stanton as an infinitely greater poet. If it has heard, which I doubt, that Cabell has been hoofed by the Comstocks, it unquestionably views that assault as a deserved rebuke to a fellow who indulges a lewd passion for fancy writing, and is a covert enemy to the Only True Christianity.

What is needed down there, before the vexatious public problems of the region may be intelligently approached, is a survey of the population by competent ethnologists and anthropologists. The immigrants of the north have been studied at great length, and any one who is interested may now apply to the Bureau of Ethnology for elaborate data as to their racial strains, their stature and cranial indices, their relative capacity for education, and the changes that they undergo under American *Kultur*. But the older stocks of the south, and particularly the emancipated and dominant poor white trash, have never been investigated scientifically, and most of the current generalizations about them are probably wrong. For example, the generalization that they are purely Anglo-Saxon in blood. This I doubt very seriously. The chief strain down there, I believe, is Celtic rather than Saxon, particularly in the hill country. French blood, too, shows itself here and there, and so does Spanish, and so does German. The last-named entered from the northward, by way of the limestone belt just east of the

Alleghenies. Again, it is very likely that in some parts of the south a good many of the plebeian whites have more than a trace of negro blood. Interbreeding under concubinage produced some very light half-breeds at an early day, and no doubt appreciable numbers of them went over into the white race by the simple process of changing their abode. Not long ago I read a curious article by an intelligent negro, in which he stated that it is easy for a very light negro to pass as white in the south on account of the fact that large numbers of southerners accepted as white have distinctly negroid features. Thus it becomes a delicate and dangerous matter for a train conductor or a hotel-keeper to challenge a suspect. But the Celtic strain is far more obvious than any of these others. It not only makes itself visible in physical stigmata—*e.g.*, leanness and dark coloring—but also in mental traits. For example, the religious thought of the south is almost precisely identical with the religious thought of Wales. There is the same naïve belief in an anthropomorphic Creator but little removed, in manner and desire, from an evangelical bishop; there is the same submission to an ignorant and impudent sacerdotal tyranny, and there is the same sharp contrast between doctrinal orthodoxy and private ethics. Read Caradoc Evans' ironical picture of the Welsh Wesleyans in his preface to "My Neighbors," and you will be instantly reminded of the Georgia and Carolina Methodists. The most booming sort of piety, in the south, is not incompatible with the theory that lynching is a benign institution. Two generations ago it was not incompatible with an ardent belief in slavery.

It is highly probable that some of the worst blood of western Europe flows in the veins of the southern poor whites, now poor no longer. The original strains, according to every honest historian, were extremely corrupt. Philip Alexander Bruce (a Virginian of the old gentry) says in his "Industrial History of Virginia in the Seventeenth Century" that the first native-born generation was largely illegitimate. "One of the most common offenses against morality committed in the lower ranks of life in Virginia during the seventeenth century," he says, "was bastardy." The mothers of these bastards, he continues, were chiefly indentured servants, and "had belonged to the lowest class in their native country." Fanny Kemble Butler, writing of the Georgia poor whites of a century later, described them as "the most degraded race of human beings claiming an Anglo-Saxon origin that can be found on the face of the earth—filthy, lazy, ignorant, brutal, proud, penniless savages." The Sunday-school and the chautauqua, of course, have appreciably mellowed the descendants of these "savages," and their economic progress and rise to political power have done perhaps even more, but the marks of their origin are still unpleasantly plentiful. Every now and then they produce a political leader who puts their secret notions of the true, the good and the beautiful into plain words, to the amazement and scandal of the rest of the country. That amazement is turned into downright incredulity when news comes that his platform has got him high office, and that he is trying to execute it.

In the great days of the south the line between the gentry and the poor whites was very sharply drawn. There was absolutely no intermarriage. So far as I know there is not a single instance in history of a southerner of the upper class marrying one of the bondwomen described by Mr. Bruce. In other societies characterized by class distinctions of that sort it is common for the lower class to be improved by extra-legal crosses. That is to say, the men of the upper class take women of the lower class as mistresses, and out of such unions spring the extraordinary plebeians who rise sharply from the common level, and so propagate the delusion that all other plebeians would do the same thing if they had the chance—in brief, the delusion that class distinctions are merely economic and conventional, and not congenital and genuine. But in the south the men of the upper classes sought their mistresses among the blacks, and after a few generations there was so much white blood in the black women that they were considerably more attractive than the unhealthy and bedraggled women of the poor whites. This preference continued into our own time. A southerner of good family once told me in all seriousness that he had reached his majority before it ever occurred to him that a white woman might make quite as agreeable a mistress as the octaroons of his jejune fancy. If the thing has changed of late, it is not the fault of the southern white man, but of the southern mulatto women. The more sightly yellow girls of the region, with improving economic opportunities, have gained self-respect, and so they are no longer as willing to enter into concubinage as their grand-dams were.

As a result of this preference of the southern gentry for mulatto mistresses there was created a series of mixed strains containing the best white blood of the south, and perhaps of the whole country. As another result the poor whites went unfertilized from above, and so missed the improvement that so constantly shows itself in the peasant stocks of other countries. It is a commonplace that nearly all negroes who rise above the general are of mixed blood, usually with the white predominating. I know a great many negroes, and it would be hard for me to think of an exception. What is too often forgotten is that this white blood is not the blood of the poor whites but that of the old gentry. The mulatto girls of the early days despised the poor whites as creatures distinctly inferior to negroes, and it was thus almost unheard of for such a girl to enter into relations with a man of that submerged class. This aversion was based upon a sound instinct. The southern mulatto of to-day is a proof of it. Like all other half-breeds he is an unhappy man, with disquieting tendencies toward anti-social habits of thought, but he is intrinsically a better animal than the pure-blooded descendant of the old poor whites, and he not infrequently demonstrates it. It is not by accident that the negroes of the south are making faster progress, economically and culturally, than the masses of the whites. It is not by accident that the only visible æsthetic activity in the south is wholly in their hands. No southern composer has ever written music so good as that of half a dozen white-black composers who might be named. Even in politics, the negro reveals a curious superiority. Despite the fact that the race question has been the main political concern of the southern whites for two generations, to the practical exclusion of everything else, they have contributed nothing to its discussion that has impressed the rest of the world so deeply and so favorably as three or four books by southern negroes.

Entering upon such themes, of course, one must resign one's self to a vast misunderstanding and abuse. The south has not only lost its old capacity for producing ideas; it has also taken on the worst intolerance of ignorance and stupidity. Its prevailing mental attitude for several decades past has been that of its own hedge ecclesiastics. All who dissent from its orthodox doctrines are scoundrels. All who presume to discuss its ways realistically are damned. I have had, in my day, several experiences in point. Once, after I had published an article on some phase of the eternal race question, a leading southern newspaper replied by printing a column of denunciation of my father, then dead nearly twenty years—a philippic placarding him as an ignorant foreigner of dubious origin, inhabiting "the Baltimore ghetto" and speaking a dialect recalling that of Weber & Fields—two thousand words of incandescent nonsense, utterly false and beside the point, but exactly meeting the latter-day southern notion of effective controversy. Another time, I published a short discourse on lynching, arguing that the sport was popular in the south because the backward culture of the region denied the populace more seemly recreations. Among such recreations I mentioned those afforded by brass bands, symphony orchestras, boxing matches, amateur athletic contests, shoot-the-chutes, roof gardens, horse races, and so on. In reply another great southern journal denounced me as a man "of wineshop temperament, brass-jewelry tastes and pornographic predilections." In other words, brass bands, in the south, are classed with brass jewelry, and both are snares of the devil! To advocate setting up symphony orchestras is pornography! . . . Alas, when the touchy southerner attempts a greater urbanity, the result is often even worse. Some time ago a colleague of mine printed an article deploring the arrested cultural development of Georgia. In reply he received a number of protests from patriotic Georgians, and all of them solemnly listed the glories of the state. I indulge in a few specimens:

Who has not heard of Asa G. Candler, whose name is synonymous with Coca-Cola, a Georgia product?

The first Sunday-school in the world was opened in Savannah.

Who does not recall with pleasure the writings of . . . Frank L. Stanton, Georgia's brilliant poet?

Georgia was the first state to organize a Boys' Corn Club in the South—Newton county, 1904.

The first to suggest a common United Daughters of the Confederacy badge was Mrs. Raynes, of Georgia.

The first to suggest a state historian of the United Daughters of the Confederacy was Mrs. C. Helen Plane (Macon convention, 1896).

The first to suggest putting to music Heber's "From Greenland's Icy Mountains" was Mrs. F. R. Goulding, of Savannah.

And so on, and so on. These proud boasts came, remember, not from obscure private persons, but from "Leading Georgians"—in one case, the state historian. Curious side-lights upon the ex-Confederate mind! Another comes from a stray copy of a negro paper. It describes an ordinance lately passed by the city council of Douglas, Ga., forbidding any trousers presser, on penalty of forfeiting a $500 bond, to engage in "pressing for both white and colored." This in a town, says the negro paper, where practically all of the white inhabitants have "their food prepared by colored hands," "their babies cared for by colored hands," and "the clothes which they wear right next to their skins washed in houses where negroes live"—houses in which the said clothes "remain for as long as a week at a time." But if you marvel at the absurdity, keep it dark! A casual word, and the united press of the south will be upon your trail, denouncing you bitterly as a scoundrelly Yankee, a Bolshevik Jew, an agent of the Wilhelmstrasse. . . .

Obviously, it is impossible for intelligence to flourish in such an atmosphere. Free inquiry is blocked by the idiotic certainties of ignorant men. The arts, save in the lower reaches of the gospel hymn, the phonograph and the chautauqua harangue, are all held in suspicion. The tone of public opinion is set by an upstart class but lately emerged from industrial slavery into commercial enterprise—the class of "hustling" business men, of "live wires," of commercial club luminaries, of "drive" managers, of forward-lookers and right-thinkers—in brief, of third-rate southerners inoculated with all the worst traits of the Yankee sharper. One observes the curious effects of an old tradition of truculence upon a population now merely pushful and impudent, of an old tradition of chivalry upon a population now quite without imagination. The old repose is gone. The old romanticism is gone. The philistinism of the new type of town-boomer southerner is not only indifferent to the ideals of the old south; it is positively antagonistic to them. That philistinism regards human life, not as an agreeable adventure, but as a mere trial of rectitude and efficiency. It is overwhelmingly utilitarian and moral. It is inconceivably hollow and obnoxious. What remains of the ancient tradition is simply a certain charming civility in private intercourse—often broken down, alas, by the hot rages of Puritanism, but still generally visible. The southerner, at his worst, is never quite the surly cad that the Yankee is. His sensitiveness may betray him into occasional bad manners, but in the main he is a pleasant fellow—hospitable, polite, good-humored, even jovial. . . . But a bit absurd. . . . A bit pathetic.

IV.

The Divine Afflatus

THE suave and œdematous Chesterton, in a late effort to earn the honorarium of a Chicago newspaper, composed a thousand words of labored counterblast to what is called inspiration in the arts. The thing itself, he argued, has little if any actual existence; we hear so much about it because its alleged coyness and fortuitousness offer a convenient apology for third-rate work. The man taken in such third-rate work excuses himself on the ground that he is a helpless slave of some power that stands outside him, and is quite beyond his control. On days when it favors him he teems with ideas and creates masterpieces, but on days when it neglects him he is crippled and impotent—a fiddle without a bow, an engine without steam, a tire without air. All this, according to Chesterton, is nonsense. A man who can really write at all, or paint at all, or compose at all should be able to do it at almost any time, provided only "he is not drunk or asleep."

So far Chesterton. The formula of the argument is simple and familiar: to dispose of a problem all that is necessary is to deny that it exists. But there are plenty of men, I believe, who find themselves unable to resolve the difficulty in any such cavalier manner—men whose chief burden and distinction, in fact, is that they do not employ formulæ in their thinking, but are thrown constantly upon industry, ingenuity and the favor of God. Among such men there remains a good deal more belief in what is vaguely called inspiration. They know by hard experience that there are days when their ideas flow freely and clearly, and days when they are dammed up damnably. Say a man of that sort has a good day. For some reason quite incomprehensible to him all his mental processes take on an amazing ease and slickness. Almost without conscious effort he solves technical problems that have badgered him for weeks. He is full of novel expedients, extraordinary efficiencies, strange cunnings. He has a feeling that he has suddenly and unaccountably broken through a wall, dispersed a fog, got himself out of the dark. So he does a double or triple stint of the best work that he is capable of—maybe of far better work than he has ever been capable of before—and goes to bed impatient for the morrow. And on the morrow he discovers to his consternation that he has become almost idiotic, and quite incapable of any work at all.

I challenge any man who trades in ideas to deny that he has this experience. The truth is that he has it constantly. It overtakes poets and contrapuntists, critics and dramatists, philosophers and journalists; it may even be shared, so far as I know, by advertisement writers, chautauqua orators and the rev. clergy. The characters that all anatomists of melancholy mark in it are the irregular ebb and flow of the tides, and the impossibility of getting them under any sort of rational control. The brain, as it were, stands to one side and watches itself pitching and tossing, full of agony but essentially helpless. Here the man of creative imagination pays a ghastly price for all his superiorities and immunities; nature takes revenge upon him for dreaming of improvements in the scheme of things. Sitting there in his lonely room, gnawing the handle of his pen, racked by his infernal quest, horribly bedevilled by incessant flashes of itching, toothache, eye-strain and evil conscience—thus tortured, he makes atonement for his crime of being intelligent. The normal man, the healthy and honest man, the good citizen and householder—this man, I daresay, knows nothing of all that travail. It is reserved especially for artists and metaphysicians. It is the particular penalty of those who pursue strange butterflies into dark forests, and go fishing in enchanted and forbidden streams.

Let us, then, assume that the fact is proved: the nearest poet is a witness to it. But what of the underlying mystery? How are we to account for that puckish and inexplicable rise and fall of inspiration? My questions, of course, are purely rhetorical. Explanations exist; they have existed for all time; there is always a well-known solution to every human problem—neat, plausible, and wrong. The ancients, in the case at bar, laid the blame upon the gods: sometimes they were remote and surly, and sometimes they were kind. In the Middle Ages lesser powers took a hand in the matter, and so one reads of works of art inspired by Our Lady, by the Blessed Saints, by the souls of the departed, and even by the devil. In our own day there are explanations less supernatural but no less fanciful—to wit, the explanation that the whole thing is a matter of pure chance, and not to be resolved into any orderly process—to wit, the explanation that the controlling factor is external circumstance, that the artist happily married to a dutiful wife is thereby inspired—finally, to make an end, the explanation that it is all a question of Freudian complexes, themselves lurking in impenetrable shadows. But all of these explanations fail to satisfy the mind that is not to be put off with mere words. Some of them are palpably absurd; others beg the question. The problem of the how remains, even when the problem of the why is disposed of. What is the precise machinery whereby the cerebrum is bestirred to such abnormal activity on one day that it sparkles and splutters like an arclight, and reduced to such feebleness on another day that it smokes and gutters like a tallow dip?

In this emergency, having regard for the ages-long and unrelieved sufferings of artists great and small, I offer a new, simple, and at all events not ghostly solution. It is supported by the observed facts, by logical analogies and by the soundest known principles of psychology, and so I present it without apologies. It may be couched, for convenience, in the following brief terms: that inspiration, so-called, is a function of metabolism, and that it is chiefly conditioned by the state of the intestinal flora—in larger words, that a man's flow of ideas is controlled and determined, both quantitatively and qualitatively, not by the whims of the gods, nor by the terms of his armistice with his wife, nor by the combinations of some transcendental set of dice, but by the chemical content of the blood that lifts itself from his liver to his brain, and that this chemical content is established in his digestive tract, particularly south of the pylorus. A man may write great poetry when he is drunk, when he is cold and miserable, when he is bankrupt, when he has a black eye, when his wife glowers at him across the table, when his children lie dying of smallpox; he may even write it during an earthquake, or while crossing the English channel, or in the midst of a Methodist revival, or in New York. But I am so far gone in materialism that I am disposed to deny flatly and finally, and herewith do deny flatly and finally, that there has lived a poet in the whole history of the world, ancient or modern, near or far, who ever managed to write great poetry, or even passably fair and decent poetry, at a time when he was suffering from stenosis at any point along the thirty-foot *via dolorosa* running from the pylorus to the sigmoid flexure. In other words, when he was—

But perhaps I had better leave your medical adviser to explain. After all, it is not necessary to go any further in this direction; the whole thing may be argued in terms of the blood stream—and the blood stream is respectable, as the duodenum is an outcast. It is the blood and the blood only, in fact, that the cerebrum is aware of; of what goes on elsewhere it can learn only by hearsay. If all is well below, then the blood that enters the brain through the internal carotid is full of the elements necessary to bestir the brain-cells to their highest activity; if, on the contrary, anabolism and katabolism are going on ineptly, if the blood is not getting the supplies that it needs and not getting rid of the wastes that burden it, then the brain-cells will be both starved and poisoned, and not all the king's horses and all the king's men can make them do their work with any show of ease and efficiency. In the first case the man whose psyche dwells in the cells will have a moment of inspiration—that is, he will find it a strangely simple and facile matter to write his poem, or iron out his syllogism, or make his bold modulation from F sharp minor to C major, or get his flesh-tone, or maybe only perfect his swindle. But in the second case he will be stumped and helpless. The more he tries, the more vividly he will be conscious of his impotence. Sweat will stand out in beads upon his brow, he will fish patiently for the elusive thought, he will try coaxing and subterfuge, he will retire to his ivory tower, he will tempt the invisible powers with black coffee, tea, alcohol and the alkaloids, he may even curse God and invite death—but he will not write his poem, or iron out his syllogism, or find his way into C major, or get his flesh-tone, or perfect his swindle.

Fix your eye upon this hypothesis of metabolic inspiration, and at once you will find the key to many a correlative mystery. For one thing, it quickly explains the observed hopelessness of trying to pump up inspiration by mere hard industry—the essential imbecility of the 1,000 words a day formula. Let there be stenosis below, and not all the industry of a Hercules will suffice to awaken the lethargic brain. Here, indeed, the harder the striving, the worse the stagnation—as every artist knows only too well. And why not? Striving in the face of such an interior obstacle is the most cruel of enterprises—a business more nerve-wracking and exhausting than reading a newspaper or watching a bad play. The pain thus produced, the emotions thus engendered, react upon the liver in a manner scientifically displayed by Dr. George W. Crile in his "Man: An Adaptive Mechanism," and the result is a steady increase in the intestinal demoralization, and a like increase in the pollution of the blood. In the end the poor victim comes to a familiar pass; beset on the one hand by impotence and on the other hand by an impatience grown pathological, he gets into a state indistinguishable from the frantic. It is at such times that creative artists suffer most atrociously. It is then that they writhe upon the sharp spears and red-hot hooks of a jealous and unjust Creator for their invasion of His monopoly. It is then that they pay a grisly supertax upon their superiority to the great herd of law-abiding and undistinguished men. The men of this herd never undergo any comparable torture; the agony of the artist is quite beyond their experience and even beyond their imagination. No catastrophe that could conceivably overtake a lime and cement dealer, a curb broker, a lawyer, a plumber or a Presbyterian is to be mentioned in the same breath with the torments that, to the most minor of poets, are familiar incidents of his professional life, and, to such a man as Poe, or Beethoven, or Brahms, are the commonplaces of every day. Beethoven suffered more during the composition of the Fifth symphony than all the judges on the supreme benches of the world have suffered jointly since the time of the Gerousia.

Again, my hypothesis explains the fact that inspiration, save under extraordinary circumstances, is never continuous for more than a relatively short period. A banker, a barber or a manufacturer of patent medicines does his work day after day without any noticeable rise or fall of efficiency; save when he is drunk, jailed or ill in bed the curve of his achievement is flattened out until it becomes almost a straight line. But the curve of an artist, even of the greatest of artists, is frightfully zigzagged. There are moments when it sinks below the bottom of

the chart, and immediately following there may be moments
when it threatens to run off the top. Some of the noblest passages written by Shakespeare are in his worst plays, cheek by
jowl with padding and banality; some of the worst music of
Wagner is in his finest music dramas. There is, indeed, no such
thing as a flawless masterpiece. Long labored, it may be gradually enriched with purple passages—the high inspirations of
widely separated times crowded together—, but even so it will
remain spotty, for those purple passages will be clumsily
joined, and their joints will remain as apparent as so many false
teeth. Only the most elementary knowledge of psychology is
needed to show the cause of the zig-zagging that I have mentioned. It lies in the elemental fact that the chemical constitution of the blood changes every hour, almost every minute.
What it is at the beginning of digestion is not what it is at the
end of digestion, and in both cases it is enormously affected by
the nature of the substances digested. No man, within twenty-
four hours after eating a meal in a Pennsylvania Railroad
dining-car, could conceivably write anything worth reading. A
tough beefsteak, I daresay, has ditched many a promising sonnet, and bad beer, as every one knows, has spoiled hundreds
of sonatas. Thus inspiration rises and falls, and even when it
rises twice to the same height it usually shows some qualitative
difference—there is the inspiration, say, of Spring vegetables
and there is the inspiration of Autumn fruits. In a long work
the products of greatly differing inspirations, of greatly differing streams of blood, are hideously intermingled, and the result is the inevitable spottiness that I have mentioned. No one
but a maniac argues that "Die Meistersinger" is *all* good. One
detects in it days when Wagner felt, as the saying goes, like a
fighting cock, but one also detects days when he arose in the
morning full of acidosis and despair—days when he turned
heavily from the Pierian spring to castor oil.

Moreover, it must be obvious that the very conditions
under which works of art are produced tend to cause great
aberrations in metabolism. The artist is forced by his calling to
be a sedentary man. Even a poet, perhaps the freest of artists,
must spend a good deal of time bending over a desk. He may
conceive his poems in the open air, as Beethoven conceived his
music, but the work of reducing them to actual words requires

diligent effort in camera. Here it is a sheer impossibility for him to enjoy the ideal hygienic conditions which surround the farmhand, the curb-broker and the sailor. His viscera are congested; his eyes are astrain; his muscles are without necessary exercise. Furthermore, he probably breathes bad air and goes without needed sleep. The result is inevitably some disturbance of metabolism, with a vitiated blood supply and a starved cerebrum. One is always surprised to encounter a poet who is ruddy and stout; the standard model is a pale and flabby stenotic, kept alive by patent medicines. So with the painter, the musical composer, the sculptor, the artist in prose. There is no more confining work known to man than instrumentation. The composer who has spent a day at it is invariably nervous and ill. For hours his body is bent over his music-paper, the while his pen engrosses little dots upon thin lines. I have known composers, after a week or so of such labor, to come down with auto-intoxication in its most virulent forms. Perhaps the notorious ill health of Beethoven, and the mental break-downs of Schumann, Tschaikowsky and Hugo Wolf had their origin in this direction. It is difficult, going through the history of music, to find a single composer in the grand manner who was physically and mentally up to par.

I do not advance it as a formal corollary, but no doubt this stenosis hypothesis also throws some light upon two other immemorial mysteries, the first being the relative æsthetic sterility of women, and the other being the low æsthetic development of certain whole classes, and even races, of men, *e.g.*, the Puritans, the Welsh and the Confederate Americans. That women suffer from stenosis far more than men is a commonplace of internal medicine; the weakness is chiefly to blame, rather than the functional peculiarities that they accuse, for their liability to headache. A good many of them, in fact, are habitually in the state of health which, in the artist, is accompanied by an utter inability to work. This state of health, as I have said, does not inhibit *all* mental activity. It leaves the powers of observation but little impaired; it does not corrupt common sense; it is not incompatible with an intelligent discharge of the ordinary duties of life. Thus a lime and cement dealer, in the midst of it, may function almost as well as when his metabolic processes are perfectly normal, and by the same token a woman chronically a victim to it may yet show all the sharp mental competence which characterizes her sex. But here the thing stops. To go beyond—to enter the realm of constructive thinking, to abandon the mere application of old ideas and essay to invent new ideas, to precipitate novel and intellectual concepts out of the chaos of memory and perception—this is quite impossible to the stenotic. *Ergo*, it is unheard of among classes and races of men who feed grossly and neglect personal hygiene; the pill-swallower is the only artist in such groups. One may thus argue that the elder Beecham saved poetry in England, as the younger Beecham saved music. . . . But, as I say, I do not stand behind the hypothesis in this department, save, perhaps, in the matter of women. I could amass enormous evidences in favor of it, but against them there would always loom the disconcerting contrary evidence of the Bulgarians. Among them, I suppose, stenosis must be unknown—but so are all the fine arts.

"La force et la foiblesse de l'esprit," said Rochefoucauld, "sont mal nommées; elles ne sont, en effect, que la bonne ou la mauvaise des organes du corps." Science wastes itself hunting in the other direction. We are flooded with evidences of the effects of the mind on the body, and so our attention is diverted from the enormously greater effects of the body on the mind. It is rather astonishing that the Wassermann reaction has not caused the latter to be investigated more thoroughly. The first result of the general employment of that great diagnostic device was the discovery that thousands of cases of so-called mental disease were really purely physical in origin—that thousands of patients long supposed to have been crazed by seeing ghosts, by love, by grief, or by reverses in the stock-market were actually victims of the small but extremely enterprising *spirochaete pallida*. The news heaved a bomb into psychiatry, but it has so far failed to provoke a study of the effects of other such physical agents. Even the effects of this one agent remain to be inquired into at length. One now knows that it may cause insanity, but what of the lesser mental aberrations that it produces? Some of these aberrations may be actually beneficial. That is to say, the mild toxemia accompanying the less virulent forms of infection may stimulate the brain to its highest functioning, and so give birth to what is called genius—a state of mind long recognized, by popular empiricism, as a sort of half-way station on the road to insanity. Beethoven, Nietzsche and Schopenhauer suffered from such mild toxemias, and there is not the slightest doubt that their extraordinary mental activity was at least partly due to the fact. That tuberculosis, in its early stages, is capable of the same stimulation is a commonplace of observation. The consumptive may be weak physically, but he is usually very alert mentally. The history of the arts, in fact, shows the names of hundreds of inspired consumptives.

Here a physical infirmity produces a result that is beneficial, just as another physical infirmity, the stenosis aforesaid, produces a result that is baleful. The artist often oscillates horribly between the two effects; he is normally anything but a healthy animal. Perfect health, indeed, is a boon that very few men above the rank of clodhoppers ever enjoy. What health means is a degree of adaptation to the organism's environment so nearly complete that there is no irritation. Such a state, it must be obvious, is not often to be observed in organisms of the highest complexity. It is common, perhaps, in the earthworm. This elemental beast makes few demands upon its environment, and is thus subject to few diseases. It seldom gets out of order until the sands of its life are run, and then it suffers one grand illness and dies forthwith. But man is forever getting out of order, for he is enormously complicated—and the higher he rises in complexity, the more numerous and the more serious are his derangements. There are whole categories of diseases, *e.g.*, neurasthenia and hay-fever, that afflict chiefly the more civilized and delicate ranks of men, leaving the inferior orders unscathed. Good health in man, indeed, is almost invariably a function of inferiority. A professionally healthy man, *e.g.*, an acrobat, an osteopath or an ice-wagon driver, is always stupid. In the Greece of the great days the athletes we hear so much about were mainly slaves. Not one of the eminent philosophers, poets or statesmen of Greece was a good high-jumper. Nearly all of them, in fact, suffered from the same malaises which afflict their successors of to-day, as you will quickly discern by examining their compositions. The æsthetic impulse, like the thirst for truth, might almost be called a disease. It seldom if ever appears in a perfectly healthy man.

But we must take the aloes with the honey. The artist suffers damnably, but there is compensation in his dreams. Some of his characteristic diseases cripple him and make his whole life a misery, but there are others that seem to help him. Of the latter, the two that I have mentioned carry with them concepts of extreme obnoxiousness. Both are infections, and one is associated in the popular mind with notions of gross immorality. But these concepts of obnoxiousness should not blind us to the benefits that apparently go with the maladies. There are, in fact, maladies much more obnoxious, and they carry no compensating benefits. Cancer is an example. Perhaps the time will come when the precise effects of these diseases will be worked out accurately, and it will be possible to gauge in advance their probable influence upon this or that individual. If that time ever comes the manufacture of artists will become a feasible procedure, like the present manufacture of soldiers, capons, right-thinkers and doctors of philosophy. In those days the promising young men of the race, instead of being protected from such diseases at all hazards, will be deliberately infected with them, as soils are now inoculated with nitrogen-liberating bacteria. . . . At the same time, let us hope, some progress will be made against stenosis. It is, after all, simply a question of technique, like the artificial propagation of the race by the device of Dr. Jacques Loeb. The poet of the future, come upon a period of doldrums, will not tear his hair in futile agony. Instead, he will go to the nearest clinic, and there get his rasher of Bulgarian bacilli, or an injection of some complex organic compound out of a ductless gland, or an order on a masseur, or a diet list, or perchance a barrel of Russian oil.

V.

Scientific Examination of a Popular Virtue

An old *Corpsbruder*, assaulting my ear lately with an abstruse tale of his sister's husband's brother's ingratitude, ended by driving me quite out of his house, firmly resolved to be his acquaintance no longer. The exact offense I heard inattentively, and have already partly forgotten—an obscure tort arising out of a lawsuit. My ex-friend, it appears, was appealed to for help in a bad case by his grapevine relative, and so went on the stand for him and swore gallantly to some complex and unintelligible lie. Later on, essaying to cash in on the perjury, he asked the fellow to aid him in some domestic unpleasantness, and was refused on grounds of morals. Hence his indignation—and my spoiled evening. . . .

What is one to think of a man so asinine that he looks for gratitude in this world, or so puerilely egotistical that he enjoys it when found? The truth is that the sentiment itself is not human but doggish, and that the man who demands it in payment for his doings is precisely the sort of man who feels noble and distinguished when a dog licks his hand. What a man says when he expresses gratitude is simply this: "You did something for me that I could not have done myself. *Ergo*, you are my superior. Hail, *Durchlaucht!*" Such a confession, whether true or not, is degrading to the confessor, and so it is very hard to make, at all events for a man of self-respect. That is why such a man always makes it clumsily and with many blushes and hesitations. It is hard for him to put so embarrassing a doctrine into plain words. And that is why the business is equally uncomfortable to the party of the other part. It distresses him to see a human being of decent instincts standing before him in so ignominious a position. He is as flustered as if the fellow came in handcuffs, or in rags, or wearing the stripes of a felon. Moreover, his confusion is helped out by his inward knowledge—very clear if he is introspective, and plain enough even if he is not—that he really deserves no such tribute to his high mightiness; that the altruism for which he is being praised was really bogus; that he did the thing behind the gratitude which now assails him, not for any grand and lofty reason, but for a purely selfish and inferior reason, to wit, for the reason that it pleases all of us to show what we can do when an appreciative audience is present; that we delight to exercise our will to power when it is safe and profitable. This is the primary cause of the benefits which inspire gratitude, real and pretended. This is the fact at the bottom of altruism. Find me a man who is always doing favors for people and I will show you a man of petty vanity, forever trying to get fuel for it in the cheapest way. And find me a man who is notoriously grateful in habit and I'll show you a man who is essentially third rate and who is conscious of it at the bottom of his heart. The man of genuine self-respect—which means the man who is more or less accurately aware, not only of his own value, but also and more importantly, of his own limitations—tries to avoid entering either class. He hesitates to demonstrate his superiority by such banal means, and he shrinks from confessing an inferiority that he doesn't believe in.

Nevertheless, the popular morality of the world, which is the creation, not of its superior men but of its botches and half-men—in brief, of its majorities—puts a high value on gratitude and denounces the withholding of it as an offense against the proprieties. To be noticeably ungrateful for benefits—that is, for the by-products of the egotism of others—is to be disliked. To tell a tale of ingratitude is to take on the aspect of a martyr to the defects of others, to get sympathy in an affliction. All of us are responsive to such ideas, however much we may resent them logically. One may no more live in the world without picking up the moral prejudices of the world than one will be able to go to hell without perspiring. . . .

Let me recall a case within my own recent experience. One day I received a letter from a young woman I had never heard of before, asking me to read the manuscripts of two novels that she had written. She represented that she had venerated my critical parts for a long while, and that her whole future career in letters would be determined by my decision as to her talents. The daughter of a man apparently of some consequence in some sordid business or other, she asked me to meet her at her father's office, and there to impart to her, under socially aseptic conditions, my advice. Having a standing rule against meeting women authors, even in their fathers' banks and soap factories, I pleaded various imaginary engagements, but finally agreed, after a telephone debate, to read her manuscripts. They arrived promptly and I found them to be wholly without merit—in fact, the veriest twaddle. Nevertheless I plowed through them diligently, wasted half an hour at the job, wrote a polite letter of counsel and returned the manuscripts to her house, paying a blackamoor 50 cents to haul them.

By all ordinary standards, an altruistic service and well deserving some show of gratitude. Had she knitted me a pair of pulse-warmers it would have seemed meet and proper. Even a copy of the poems of Alfred Noyes would not have been too much. At the very least I expected a note of thanks. Well, not a word has ever reached me. For all my laborious politeness and disagreeable labor my reward is exactly nil. The lady is improved by my counsel—and I am shocked by her gross ingratitude. . . . That is, conventionally, superficially, as a member of society in good standing. But when on sour afternoons I roll the affair in my mind, examining, not the mere surface of it but the inner workings and anatomy of it, my sense of outrage gradually melts and fades away—the inevitable recompense of skepticism. What I see clearly is that I was an ass to succumb to the blandishments of this discourteous miss, and that she was quite right in estimating my service trivially, and out of that clear seeing comes consolation, and amusement, and, in the end, even satisfaction. I got exactly what I deserved. And she, whether consciously or merely instinctively, measured out the dose with excellent accuracy.

Let us go back. Why did I waste two hours, or maybe three, reading those idiotic manuscripts? Why, in the first place, did I answer her opening request—the request, so inherently absurd, that I meet her in her father's office? For a very plain reason: she accompanied it with flattery. What she said, in effect, was that she regarded me as a critic of the highest talents, and this ludicrous cajolery—sound, I dare say, in substance, but reduced to naught by her obvious obscurity and stupidity—was quite enough to fetch me. In brief, she assumed that, being a man, I was vain to the point of imbecility, and this assumption was correct, as it always is. To help out, there was the concept of romantic adventure vaguely floating in my mind. Her voice, as I heard it by telephone, was agreeable; her appearance, since she seemed eager to show herself, I probably judged (subconsciously) to be at least not revolting. Thus curiosity got on its legs, and vanity in another form. Am I fat and half decrepit, a man seldom noticed by cuties? Then so much the more reason why I should respond. The novelty of an apparently comely and respectable woman desiring to witness me finished what the primary (and very crude) appeal to my vanity had begun. I was, in brief, not only the literary popinjay but also the eternal male—and hard at the immemorial folly of the order.

Now turn to the gal and her ingratitude. The more I inspect it the more I became convinced that it is not discreditable to her, but highly creditable—that she demonstrates a certain human dignity, despite her imbecile writings, by exhibiting it. Would a show of gratitude put her in a better light? I doubt it. That gratitude, considering the unfavorable report I made on her manuscripts, would be doubly invasive of her *amour propre*. On the one hand it would involve a confession that my opinion of her literary gifts was better than her own, and that I was thus her superior. And on the other hand it would involve a confession that my own actual writings (being got into print without aid) were better than hers, and that I was thus her superior again. Each confession would bring her into an attitude of abasement, and the two together would make her position intolerable. Moreover, both would be dishonest: she would privately believe in neither doctrine. As for my opinion, its hostility to her aspiration is obviously enough to make her ego dismiss it as false, for no organism acquiesces in its own destruction. And as for my relative worth as a literary artist, she must inevitably put it very low, for it depends, in the last analysis, upon my dignity and sagacity as a man, and she has proved by experiment, and quite easily, that I am almost as susceptible to flattery as a moving picture actor, and hence surely no great shakes.

Thus there is not the slightest reason in the world why the fair creature should knit me a pair of pulse-warmers or send me the poems of Noyes, or even write me a polite note. If she did any of these things, she would feel herself a hypocrite and hence stand embarrassed before the mirror of her own thoughts.

Confronted by a choice between this sort of shame and the incomparably less uncomfortable shame of violating a social convention and an article of popular morals, secretly and without danger of exposure, she very sensibly chooses the more innocuous of the two. At the very start, indeed, she set up barriers against gratitude, for her decision to ask a favor of me was, in a subtle sense, a judgment of my inferiority. One does not ask favors, if it can be avoided, of persons one genuinely respects; one puts such burdens upon the naïve and colorless, upon what are called the good natured; in brief, upon one's inferiors. When that girl first thought of me as a possible aid to her literary aspiration she thought of me (perhaps vaguely, but none the less certainly) as an inferior fortuitously outfitted with a body of puerile technical information and competence, of probable use to her. This unfavorable view was immediately reënforced by her discovery of my vanity.

In brief, she showed and still shows the great instinctive sapience of her sex. She is female, and hence far above the nonsensical delusions, vanities, conventions and moralities of men.

VI.

Exeunt Omnes

O NE of the hardest jobs that faces an American magazine editor in this, the one-hundred-and-forty-fifth year of the Republic, is that of keeping the minnesingers of the land from filling his magazine with lugubrious dithyrambs to, on and against somatic death. Of spiritual death, of course, not many of them ever sing. Most of them, in fact, deny its existence in plain terms; they are all sure of the immortality of the soul, and in particular they are absolutely sure of the immortality of their own souls, and of those of their best girls. In this department the most they ever allow to the materialism of the herds that lie bogged in prose is such a benefit of the half doubt as one finds in Christina Rossetti's "When I am Dead." But when it comes to somatic death, the plain brutal death of coroners' inquests and vital statistics, their optimism vanishes, and, try as they may, they can't get around the harsh fact that on such and such a day, often appallingly near, each and every one of us will heave a last sigh, roll his eyes despairingly, turn his face to the wall and then suddenly change from a proud and highly complex mammal, made in the image of God, to a mere inert aggregate of disintegrating colloids, made in the image of a stale cabbage.

The inevitability of it seems to fascinate them. They write about it more than they write about anything else save love. Every day my editorial desk is burdened with their manuscripts —poems in which the poet serves notice that, when his time comes, he will die bravely and even a bit insolently; poems in which he warns his mistress that he will wait for her on the roof of the cosmos and keep his harp in tune; poems in which he asks her grandly to forget him, and, above all, to avoid torturing herself by vain repining at his grave; poems in which he directs his heirs and assigns to bury him in some lonely, romantic spot, where the whippoorwills sing; poems in which he hints that he will not rest easily if Philistines are permitted to begaud his last anchorage with *couronnes des perles*; poems in which he speaks jauntily of making a rendezvous with death, as if death were a wench; poems in which—

But there is no need to rehearse the varieties. If you read the strophes that are strung along the bottoms of magazine pages you are familiar with all of them; even in the great moral periodical that I help to edit, despite my own excessive watchfulness and Dr. Nathan's general theory that both death and poetry are nuisances and in bad taste, they have appeared multitudinously, no doubt to the disgust of the *intelligentsia*. As I say, it is almost impossible to keep the minnesingers off the subject. When my negro flops the morning bale of poetry manuscripts upon my desk and I pull up my chair to have at them, I always make a bet with myself that, of the first dozen, at least seven will deal with death—and it is so long since I lost that I don't remember it. Periodically I send out a circular to all the recognized poets of the land, begging them in the name of God to be less mortuary, but it never does any good. More, I doubt that it ever will—or any other sort of appeal. Take away death and love and you would rob poets of both their liver and their lights; what would remain would be little more than a feeble gurgle in an illimitable void. For the business of poetry, remember, is to set up a sweet denial of the harsh facts that confront all of us—to soothe us in our agonies with emollient words—in brief, to lie sonorously and reassuringly. Well, what is the worst curse of life? Answer: the abominable magnetism that draws unlikes and incompatibles into delirious and intolerable conjunction—the kinetic over-stimulation called love. And what is the next worst? Answer: the fear of death. No wonder the poets give so much attention to both! No other foe of human peace and happiness is one-half so potent, and hence none other offers such opportunities to poetry, and, in fact, to all art. A sonnet designed to ease the dread of bankruptcy, even if done by a great master, would be banal, for that dread is itself banal, and so is bankruptcy. The same may be said of the old fear of hell, now no more. There was a day when this latter raged in the breast of nearly every man—and in that day the poets produced antidotes that were very fine poems. But to-day only the elect and anointed of God fear hell, and so there is no more production of sound poetry in that department.

As I have hinted, I tire of reading so much necrotic verse in manuscript, and wish heartily that the poets would cease to assault me with it. In prose, curiously enough, one observes a corresponding shortage. True enough, the short story of commerce shows a good many murders and suicides, and not less than eight times a day I am made privy to the agonies of a widower or widow who, on searching the papers of his wife or her husband immediately after her or his death, discovers that she or he had a lover or a mistress. But I speak of serious prose: not of trade balderdash. Go to any public library and look under "Death: Human" in the card index, and you will be surprised to find how few books there are on the subject. Worse, nearly all the few are by psychical researchers who regard death as a mere removal from one world to another or by New Thoughters who appear to believe that it is little more than a sort of illusion. Once, seeking to find out what death was physiologically—that is, to find out just what happened when a man died—I put in a solid week without result. There seemed to be nothing whatever on the subject even in the medical libraries. Finally, after much weariness, I found what I was looking for in Dr. George W. Crile's "Man: An Adaptive Mechanism" —incidentally, a very solid and original work, much less heard of than it ought to be. Crile said that death was acidosis—that it was caused by the failure of the organism to maintain the alkalinity necessary to its normal functioning—and in the absence of any proofs or even arguments to the contrary I accepted his notion forthwith and have held to it ever since. I thus think of death as a sort of deleterious fermentation, like that which goes on in a bottle of Château Margaux when it becomes corked. Life is a struggle, not against sin, not against the Money Power, not against malicious animal magnetism, but against hydrogen ions. The healthy man is one in whom those ions, as they are dissociated by cellular activity, are immediately fixed by alkaline bases. The sick man is one in whom the process has begun to lag, with the hydrogen ions getting ahead. The dying man is one in whom it is all over save the charges of fraud.

But here I get into chemical physics, and not only run afoul of revelation but also reveal, perhaps, a degree of ignorance verging upon intellectual coma. The thing I started out to do was to call attention to the only full-length and first-rate treatise on death that I have ever encountered or heard of, to wit, "Aspects of Death and Correlated Aspects of Life," by Dr. F. Parkes Weber, a fat, hefty and extremely interesting tome, the fruit of truly stupendous erudition. What Dr. Weber has attempted is to bring together in one volume all that has been said or thought about death since the time of the first human records, not only by poets, priests and philosophers, but also by painters, engravers, soldiers, monarchs and the populace generally. The author, I take it, is primarily a numismatist, and he apparently began his work with a collection of inscriptions on coins and medals. But as it stands it covers a vastly wider area. One traces, in chapter after chapter, the ebb and flow of human ideas upon the subject, of the human attitude to the last and greatest mystery of them all—the notion of it as a mere transition to a higher plane of life, the notion of it as a benign panacea for all human suffering, the notion of it as an incentive to this or that way of living, the notion of it as an impenetrable enigma, inevitable and inexplicable. Few of us quite realize how much the contemplation of death has colored human thought throughout the ages. There have been times when it almost shut out all other concerns; there has never been a time when it has not bulked enormously in the racial consciousness. Well, what Dr. Weber does in his book is to detach and set forth the salient ideas that have emerged from all that consideration and discussion—to isolate the chief theories of death, ancient and modern, pagan and Christian, scientific and mystical, sound and absurd.

The material thus digested is appallingly copious. If the learned author had confined himself to printed books alone, he would have faced a labor fit for a new Hercules. But in addition to books he has given his attention to prints, to medals, to paintings, to engraved gems and to monumental inscriptions. His authorities range from St. John on what is to happen at the Day of Judgment to Sir William Osler on what happens upon the normal human death-bed, and from Socrates on the relation of death to philosophy to Havelock Ellis on the effects of Christian ideas of death upon the mediæval temperament. The one field that Dr. Weber has overlooked is that of music, a somewhat serious omission. It is hard to think of a great composer who never wrote a funeral march, or a requiem, or at least a sad song to some departed love. Even old Papa Haydn had moments when he ceased to be merry, and let his thought turn stealthily upon the doom ahead. To me, at all events, the slow movement of the Military Symphony is the saddest of music—an elegy, I take it, on some young fellow who went out in the incomprehensible wars of those times and got himself horribly killed in a far place. The trumpet blasts towards the end fling themselves over his hasty grave in a remote cabbage field; one hears, before and after them, the honest weeping of his comrades into their wine-pots. In truth, the shadow of death hangs over all the music of Haydn, despite its lightheartedness. Life was gay in those last days of the Holy Roman Empire, but it was also precarious. If the Turks were not at the gate, then there was a peasant rising somewhere in the hinterland, or a pestilence swept the land. Beethoven, a generation later, growled at death surlily, but Haydn faced it like a gentleman. The romantic movement brought a sentimentalization of the tragedy; it became a sort of orgy. Whenever Wagner dealt with death he treated it as if it were some sort of gaudy tournament—a thing less dreadful than ecstatic. Consider, for example, the *Char-Freitag* music in "Parsifal"— death music for the most memorable death in the history of the world. Surely no one hearing it for the first time, without previous warning, would guess that it had to do with anything so gruesome as a crucifixion. On the contrary, I have a notion that the average auditor would guess that it was a musical setting for some lamentable fornication between a Bayreuth baritone seven feet in height and a German soprano weighing at least three hundred pounds.

But if Dr. Weber thus neglects music, he at least gives full measure in all other departments. His book, in fact, is encyclopædic; he almost exhausts the subject. One idea, however, I do not find in it: the conception of death as the last and worst of all the practical jokes played upon poor mortals by the gods. That idea apparently never occurred to the Greeks, who thought of almost everything, but nevertheless it has an ingratiating plausibility. The hardest thing about death is not that men die tragically, but that most of them die ridiculously. If it were possible for all of us to make our exits at great moments, swiftly, cleanly, decorously, and in fine attitudes, then the experience would be something to face heroically and with high and beautiful words. But we commonly go off in no such gorgeous, poetical way. Instead, we die in raucous prose—of arterio-sclerosis, of diabetes, of toxemia, of a noisome perforation in the ileo-cæcal region, of carcinoma of the liver. The abominable acidosis of Dr. Crile sneaks upon us, gradually paralyzing the adrenals, flabbergasting the thyroid, crippling the poor old liver, and throwing its fog upon the brain. Thus the ontogenetic process is recapitulated in reverse order, and we pass into the mental obscurity of infancy, and then into the blank unconsciousness of the prenatal state, and finally into the condition of undifferentiated protoplasm. A man does not die quickly and brilliantly, like a lightning stroke; he passes out by inches, hesitatingly and, one may almost add, gingerly. It is hard to say just when he is fully dead. Long after his heart has ceased to beat and his lungs have ceased to swell him up with the vanity of his species, there are remote and obscure parts of him that still live on, quite unconcerned about the central catastrophe. Dr. Alexis Carrel has cut them out and kept them alive for months. The hair keeps on growing for a long while. Every time another one of the corpses of Barbarossa or King James I is examined it is found that the hair is longer than it was the last time. No doubt there are many parts of the body, and perhaps even whole organs, which wonder what it is all about when they find that they are on the way to the crematory. Burn a man's mortal remains, and you inevitably burn a good portion of him alive, and no doubt that portion sends alarmed messages to the unconscious brain, like dissected tissue under anæsthesia, and the resultant shock brings the deceased before the hierarchy of heaven in a state of collapse, with his face white, sweat bespangling his forehead and a great thirst upon him. It would not be pulling the nose of reason to argue that many a cremated Sunday-school superintendent thus confronting the ultimate tribunal in the aspect of a man taken with the goods, has been put down as suffering from an uneasy conscience when what actually ailed him was simply surgical shock. The cosmic process is not only incurably idiotic; it is also indecently unjust.

But here I become medico-legal. What I had in mind when

I began was this: that the human tendency to make death dramatic and heroic has little excuse in the facts. No doubt you remember the scene in the last act of "Hedda Gabler," in which Dr. Brack comes in with the news of Lövborg's suicide. Hedda immediately thinks of him putting the pistol to his temple and dying instantly and magnificently. The picture fills her with romantic delight. When Brack tells her that the shot was actually through the breast she is disappointed, but soon begins to romanticise even *that*. "The breast," she says, "is also a good place. . . . There is something beautiful in this!" A bit later she recurs to the charming theme, "In the breast— ah!" Then Brack tells her the plain truth—in the original, thus: *"Nej,—det traf ham i underlivet!"* . . . Edmund Gosse, in his first English translation of the play, made the sentence: "No— it struck him in the abdomen." In the last edition William Archer makes it "No—in the bowels!" Abdomen is nearer to *underlivet* than bowels, but belly would probably render the meaning better than either. What Brack wants to convey to Hedda is the news that Lövborg's death was not romantic in the least—that he went to a brothel, shot himself, not through the cerebrum or the heart, but through the duodenum or perhaps the jejunum, and is at the moment of report awaiting autopsy at the Christiania *Allgemeine-krankenhaus*. The shock floors her, but it is a shock that all of us must learn to bear. Men upon whom we lavish our veneration reduce it to an absurdity at the end by dying of chronic cystitis, or by choking upon marshmallows or dill pickles, or as the result of getting cut by dirty barbers. Women whom we place upon pedestals worthy of the holy saints come down at last with mastoid abscesses or die obscenely of hiccoughs. And we ourselves? Let us not have too much hope. The chances are that, if we go to war, eager to leap superbly at the cannon's mouth, we'll be finished on the way by an ingrowing toenail or by being run over by an army truck driven by a former Greek bus-boy and loaded with imitation Swiss cheeses made in Oneida, N.Y. And that if we die in our beds, it will be of measles or albuminuria.

The aforesaid Crile, in one of his smaller books, "A Mechanistic View of War and Peace," has a good deal to say about death in war, and in particular, about the disparity between the glorious and inspiring passing imagined by the young soldier and the messy finish that is normally in store for him. He shows two pictures of war, the one ideal and the other real. The former is the familiar print, "The Spirit of '76," with the three patriots springing grandly to the attack, one of them with a neat and romantic bandage around his head—apparently, to judge by his liveliness, to cover a wound no worse than an average bee-sting. The latter picture is what the movie folks call a close-up of a French soldier who was struck just below the mouth by a German one-pounder shell—a soldier suddenly converted into the hideous simulacrum of a cruller. What one notices especially is the curious expression upon what remains of his face—an expression of the utmost surprise and indignation. No doubt he marched off to the front firmly convinced that, if he died at all, it would be at the climax of some heroic charge, up to his knees in blood and with his bayonet run clear through a Bavarian at least four feet in diameter. He imagined the clean bullet through the heart, the stately last gesture, the final words: "Thérèse! Sophie! Olympe! Marie! Suzette! Odette! Dénise! Julie! . . . France!" Go to the book and see what he got. . . . Dr. Crile, whose experience of war has soured him against it, argues that the best way to abolish it would be to prohibit such romantic prints as "The Spirit of '76" and substitute therefor a series of actual photographs of dead and wounded men. The plan is plainly of merit. But it would be expensive. Imagine a war getting on its legs before the conversion of the populace had become complete. Think of the huge herds of spy-chasers, letter-openers, pacifist-hounds, burlesons and other such operators that it would take to track down and confiscate all those pictures! . . .

Even so, the vulgar horror of death would remain, for, as Ellen La Motte well says in her little book, "The Backwash of War," the finish of a civilian in a luxurious hospital, with trained nurses fluttering over him and his pastor whooping and heaving for him at the foot of his bed, is often quite as terrible as any form of exitus witnessed in war. It is, in fact, always an unpleasant business. Let the poets disguise it all they may and the theologians obscure the issue with promises of post-mortem felicity, the plain truth remains that it gives one pause to reflect that, on some day not far away, one must yield supinely to acidosis, sink into the mental darkness of an idiot, and so suffer a withdrawal from these engaging scenes. "No. 8," says the nurse in faded pink, tripping down the corridor with a hooch of rye for the diabetic in No. 2, "has just passed out." "Which is No. 8?" asks the new nurse. "The one whose wife wore that awful hat this afternoon?" . . . But all the authorities, it is pleasant to know, report that the final scene is placid enough. Dr. Weber quotes many of them. The dying man doesn't struggle much and he isn't much afraid. As his alkalies give out he succumbs to a blest stupidity. His mind fogs. His will power vanishes. He submits decently. He scarcely gives a damn.

VII.
The Allied Arts

I
On Music-Lovers

OF all forms of the uplift, perhaps the most futile is that which addresses itself to educating the proletariat in music. The theory behind it is that a taste for music is an elevating passion, and that if the great masses of the plain people could be inoculated with it they would cease to herd into the moving-picture theaters, or to listen to Socialists, or to beat their wives and children. The defect in this theory lies in the fact that such a taste, granting it to be elevating, simply cannot be implanted. Either it is born in a man or it is not born in him. If it is, then he will get gratification for it at whatever cost—he will hear music if hell freezes over. But if it isn't, then no amount of education will ever change him—he will remain stone deaf until the last sad scene on the gallows.

No child who has this congenital taste ever has to be urged or tempted or taught to love music. It takes to tone inevitably and irresistibly; nothing can restrain it. What is more, it always tries to *make* music, for the delight in sounds is invariably accompanied by a great desire to make them. I have never encountered an exception to this rule. All genuine music-lovers try to make music. They may do it badly, and even absurdly, but nevertheless they do it. Any man who pretends to a delight in the tone-art and yet has never learned the scale of C major —any and every such man is a fraud. The opera-houses of the world are crowded with such liars. You will even find hundreds of them in the concert-halls, though here the suffering they have to undergo to keep up their pretense is almost too much for them to bear. Many of them, true enough, deceive themselves. They are honest in the sense that they credit their own buncombe. But it is buncombe none the less.

Music, of course, has room for philanthropy. The cost of giving an orchestral concert is so great that ordinary music-lovers could not often pay for it. Here the way is open for rich backers, most of whom have no more ear for music than so many Chinamen. Nearly all the opera of the world is so supported. A few rich cads pay the bills, their wives posture obscenely in the boxes, and the genuine music-lovers upstairs and down enjoy the more or less harmonious flow of sound. But this business doesn't *make* music-lovers. It merely gives pleasure to music-lovers who already exist. In twenty-five years, I am sure, the Metropolitan Opera Company hasn't converted a single music-lover. On the contrary, it has probably disgusted and alienated many thousands of faint-hearted quasi-music-lovers, *i.e.*, persons with no more than the most nebulous taste for music—so nebulous that one or two evenings of tremendous gargling by fat tenors was enough to kill it altogether.

In the United States the number of genuine music-lovers is probably very low. There are whole states, *e.g.*, Alabama, Arkansas and Idaho, in which it would be difficult to muster a hundred. In New York, I venture, not more than one person in every thousand of the population deserves to be counted. The rest are, to all intents and purposes, tone-deaf. They can not only sit through the infernal din made by the current jazz-bands; they actually like it. This is precisely as if they preferred the works of The Duchess to those of Thomas Hardy, or the paintings of the men who make covers for popular novels to those of El Greco. Such persons inhabit the sewers of the bozart. No conceivable education could rid them of their native ignobility of soul. They are born unspeakable and incurable.

2

Opera

Opera, to a person genuinely fond of aural beauty, must inevitably appear tawdry and obnoxious, if only because it presents aural beauty in a frame of purely visual gaudiness, with overtones of the grossest sexual provocation. The most successful opera singers of the female sex, at least in America, are not those whom the majority of auditors admire most as singers but those whom the majority of male spectators desire most as mistresses. Opera is chiefly supported in all countries by the same sort of wealthy sensualists who also support

musical comedy. One finds in the directors' room the traditional stock company of the stage-door alley. Such vermin, of
course, pose in the newspapers as devout and almost fanatical
partisans of art; they exhibit themselves at every performance;
one hears of their grand doings, through their press agents,
almost every day. But one has merely to observe the sort of
opera they think is good to get the measure of their actual
artistic discrimination.

The genuine music-lover may accept the carnal husk of
opera to get at the kernel of actual music within, but that is
no sign that he approves the carnal husk or enjoys gnawing
through it. Most musicians, indeed, prefer to hear operatic
music outside the opera house; that is why one so often hears
such things as "The Ride of the Valkyrie" in the concert hall.
"The Ride of the Valkyrie" has a certain intrinsic value as pure
music; played by a competent orchestra it may give civilized
pleasure. But as it is commonly performed in an opera house,
with a posse of flat beldames throwing themselves about the
stage, it can only produce the effect of a dose of ipecacuanha.
The sort of person who actually delights in such spectacles is the
sort of person who delights in plush furniture. Such half-wits
are in a majority in every opera house west of the Rhine. They
go to the opera, not to hear music, not even to hear bad
music, but merely to see a more or less obscene circus. A few,
perhaps, have a further purpose; they desire to assist in that circus, to show themselves in the capacity of fashionables, to enchant the yokelry with their splendor. But the majority must
be content with the more lowly aim. What they get for the
outrageous prices they pay for seats is a chance to feast their
eyes upon glittering members of the superior *demi-monde*, and
to abase their groveling souls before magnificoes on their own
side of the footlights. They esteem a performance, not in proportion as true music is on tap, but in proportion as the display of notorious characters on the stage is copious, and the
exhibition of wealth in the boxes is lavish. A soprano who can
gargle her way up to G sharp in alto is more to such simple
souls than a whole drove of Johann Sebastian Bachs; her one
real rival, in the entire domain of art, is the contralto who has
a pension from a grand duke and is reported to be *enceinte* by
several profiteers. Heaven visualizes itself as an opera house with

forty-eight Carusos, each with forty-eight press agents. . . . On the Continent, where frankness is unashamed, the opera audience often reveals its passion for tone very naïvely. That is to say, it arises on its hind legs, turns its back upon the stage and gapes at the boxes in charming innocence.

The music that such ignobles applaud is usually quite as shoddy as they are themselves. To write a successful opera a knowledge of harmony and counterpoint is not enough; one must also be a sort of Barnum. All the first-rate musicians who have triumphed in the opera house have been skillful mounte-banks as well. I need cite only Richard Wagner and Richard Strauss. The business, indeed, has almost nothing to do with music. All the actual music one finds in many a popular opera —for example, "Thaïs"—mounts up to less than one may find in a pair of Gung'l waltzes. It is not this mild flavor of tone that fetches the crowd; it is the tinpot show that goes with it. An opera may have plenty of good music in it and fail, but if it has a good enough show it will succeed.

Such a composer as Wagner, of course, could not write even an opera without getting some music into it. In nearly all of his works, even including "Parsifal," there are magnificent pas-sages, and some of them are very long. Here his natural genius overcame him, and he forgot temporarily what he was about. But these magnificent passages pass unnoticed by the average opera audience. What it esteems in his music dramas is pre-cisely what is cheapest and most mountebankish—for example, the more lascivious parts of "Tristan und Isolde." The sound music it dismisses as tedious. The Wagner it venerates is not the musician, but the showman. That he had a king for a backer and was seduced by Liszt's daughter—these facts, and not the fact of his stupendous talent, are the foundation stones of his fame in the opera house.

Greater men, lacking his touch of the quack, have failed where he succeeded—Beethoven, Schubert, Schumann, Brahms, Bach, Haydn, Haendel. Not one of them produced a genuinely successful opera; most of them didn't even try. Imagine Brahms writing for the diamond horseshoe! Or Bach! Or Haydn! Beethoven attempted it, but made a mess of it; "Fidelio" survives to-day chiefly as a set of concert overtures.

Schubert wrote more actual music every morning between 10 o'clock and lunch time than the average opera composer produces in 250 years, and yet he always came a cropper in the opera house.

3
The Music of To-morrow

Viewing the current musical scene, Carl Van Vechten finds it full of sadness. Even Debussy bores him; he heard nothing interesting from that quarter for a long while before the final scene. As for Germany, he finds it a desert, with Arnold Schoenberg behind the bar of its only inviting *Gasthaus.* Richard Strauss? Pooh! Strauss is an exploded torpedo, a Zeppelin brought to earth; "he has nothing more to say." (Even the opening of the Alpine symphony, it would appear, is mere stick-candy.) England? Go to! Italy? Back to the barrel-organ! Where, then, is the tone poetry of to-morrow to come from? According to Van Vechten, from Russia. It is the steppes that will produce it—or, more specifically, Prof. Igor Strawinsky, author of "The Nightingale" and of various revolutionary ballets. In the scores of Strawinsky, says Van Vechten, music takes a vast leap forward. Here, at last, we are definitely set free from melody and harmony; the thing becomes an ineffable complex of rhythms; "all rhythms are beaten into the ears."

New? Of the future? I have not heard all of the powerful shiverings and tremblings of M. Strawinsky, but I presume to doubt it none the less. "The ancient Greeks," says Van Vechten, "accorded rhythm a higher place than either melody or harmony." Well, what of it? So did the ancient Goths and Huns. So do the modern Zulus and New Yorkers. The simple truth is that the accentuation of mere rhythm is a proof, not of progress in music, but of a reversion to barbarism. Rhythm is the earliest, the underlying element. The African savage, beating his tom-tom, is content to go no further; the American composer of fox trots is with him. But music had scarcely any existence as an art-form until melody came to rhythm's aid, and its fruits were little save dullness until harmony began to support melody. To argue that mere rhythm, unsupported by anything save tone-color, may now take their place is to argue something so absurd that its mere statement is a sufficient answer to it.

The rise of harmony, true enough, laid open a dangerous field. Its exploration attracted meticulous minds; it was rigidly mapped in hard, geometrical forms; in the end, it became almost unnavigable to the man of ideas. But no melodramatic rejection of all harmony is needed to work a reform. The business, indeed, is already gloriously under way. The dullest conservatory pupil has learned how to pull the noses of the old-time schoolmasters. No one cares a hoot any more about the ancient laws of preparation and resolution. (The rules grow so loose, indeed, that I may soon be tempted to write a tone-poem myself). But out of this chaos new laws will inevitably arise, and though they will not be as rigid as the old ones, they will still be coherent and logical and intelligible. Already, in fact, gentlemen of professorial mind are mapping them out; one needs but a glance at such a book as René Lenormand's to see that there is a certain order hidden in even the wildest vagaries of the moment. And when the boiling in the pot dies down, the truly great musicians will be found to be, not those who have been most daring, but those who have been most discreet and intelligent—those who have most skillfully engrafted what is good in the new upon what was sound in the old. Such a discreet fellow is Richard Strauss. His music is modern enough—but not too much. One is thrilled by its experiments and novelties, but at the same time one can enjoy the thing as music.

Haydn, Mozart, Beethoven and Wagner belonged to the same lodge. They were by no means the wildest revolutionaries of their days, but they were the best musicians. They didn't try to improve music by purging it of any of the elements that made it music; they tried, and with success, to give each element a new force and a new significance. Berlioz, I dare say, knew more about the orchestra than Wagner; he surely went further than Wagner in reaching out for new orchestral effects. But nothing he ever wrote has a fourth of the stability and value of "Die Meistersinger." He was so intrigued by his tone-colors that he forgot his music.

4
Tempo di Valse

Those Puritans who snort against the current dances are quite right when they argue that the tango and the shimmie are violently aphrodisiacal, but what they overlook is the fact that the abolition of such provocative wriggles would probably revive something worse, to wit, the Viennese waltz. The waltz never quite goes out of fashion; it is always just around the corner; every now and then it comes back with a bang. And to the sore harassment and corruption, I suspect, of chemical purity, the ideal of all right-thinkers. The shimmie and the tango are too gross to be very dangerous to civilized human beings; they suggest drinking beer out of buckets; the most elemental good taste is proof enough against them. But the waltz! Ah, the waltz, indeed! It is sneaking, insidious, disarming, lovely. It does its work, not like a college-yell or an explosion in a munitions plant, but like the rustle of the trees, the murmur of the illimitable sea, the sweet gurgle of a pretty girl. The jazz-band fetches only vulgarians, barbarians, idiots, pigs. But there is a mystical something in "Weiner Blut" or "Künstler Leben" that fetches even philosophers.

The waltz, in fact, is magnificently improper—the art of tone turned bawdy. I venture to say that the compositions of one man alone, Johann Strauss II, have lured more fair young creatures to lamentable complaisance than all the hyperdermic syringes of all the white slave scouts since the fall of the Western Empire. There is something about a waltz that is simply irresistible. Try it on the fattest and sedatest or even upon the thinnest and most acidulous of women, and she will be ready, in ten minutes, for a stealthy kiss behind the door—nay, she will forthwith impart the embarrassing news that her husband misunderstands her, and drinks too much, and cannot appreciate Maeterlinck, and is going to Cleveland, O., on business to-morrow. . . .

I often wonder that the Comstocks have not undertaken a crusade against the waltz. If they suppress "The 'Genius'" and "Jurgen," then why do they overlook "Rosen aus dem Süden"? If they are so hot against "Madame Bovary" and the Decameron, then why the immunity of "Wein, Weib und Gesang"?

. . . I throw out the suggestion and pass on. Nearly all the great waltzes of the world, incidently, were written by Germans—or Austrians. A waltz-pogrom would thus enlist the American Legion and the Daughters of the Revolution. Moreover, there is the Public Health Service: it is already engaged upon a campaign to enforce virginity in both sexes by statute and artillery. Imagine such an enterprise with every band free to play "Wiener Mad'l"!

5
The Puritan as Artist

The saddest thing that I have ever heard in the concert hall is Herbert K. Hadley's overture, "In Bohemia." The title is a magnificent piece of profound, if unconscious irony. One looks, at least, for a leg flung in the air, a girl kissed, a cork popped, a flash of drawer-ruffles. What one encounters is a meeting of the Lake Mohonk Conference. Such prosy correctness and hollowness, in music, is almost inconceivable. It is as if the most voluptuous of the arts were suddenly converted into an abstract and austere science, like comparative grammar or astro-physics. "Who's Who in America" says that Hadley was born in Somerville, Mass., and "studied violin and other branches in Vienna." A prodigy thus unfolds itself: here is a man who lived in Vienna, and yet never heard a Strauss waltz! This, indeed, is an even greater feat than being born an artist in Somerville.

6
The Human Face

Probably the best portrait that I have ever seen in America is one of Theodore Dreiser by Bror Nordfeldt. Who this Bror Nordfeldt may be I haven't the slightest notion—a Scandinavian, perhaps. Maybe I have got his name wrong; I can't find any Nordfeldt in "Who's Who in America." But whatever his name, he has painted Dreiser in a capital manner. The portrait not only shows the outward shell of the man; it also conveys something of his inner spirit—his simple-minded wonder at the mystery of existence, his constant effort to argue himself out of a despairing pessimism, his genuine amazement before life as a spectacle. The thing is worth a hundred Sargents, with their slick lying, their childish facility, their general hollowness and tackiness. Sargent should have been a designer of candy-box tops. The notion that he is a great artist is one of the astounding delusions of Anglo-Saxondom. What keeps it going is the patent fact that he is a very dexterous craftsman—one who understands thoroughly how to paint, just as a good plumber knows how to plumb. But of genuine æsthetic feeling the man is almost as destitute as the plumber. His portrait of the four Johns Hopkins professors is probably the worst botch ever palmed off on a helpless committee of intellectual hay and feed dealers. But Nordfeldt, in his view of Dreiser, somehow gets the right effect. It is rough painting, but real painting. There is a knock-kneed vase in the foreground, and a bunch of flowers apparently painted with a shaving-brush—but Dreiser himself is genuine. More, he is made interesting. One sees at once that he is no common man.

The artist himself seems to hold the portrait in low esteem. Having finished it, he reversed the canvas and used the back for painting a vapid snow scene—a thing almost bad enough to go into a Fifth Avenue show-window. Then he abandoned both pictures. I discovered the portrait by accidentally knocking the snow scene off a wall. It has never been framed. Drieser himself has probably forgotten it. . . . No, I do *not* predict that it will be sold to some Pittsburgh nail manufacturer, in 1950, for $100,000. If it lasts two or three more years, unframed and disesteemed, it will be running in luck. When Dreiser is hanged, I suppose, relic-hunters will make a search for it. But by that time it will have died as a doormat.

7
The Cerebral Mime

Of all actors, the most offensive to the higher cerebral centers is the one who pretends to intellectuality. His alleged intelligence, of course, is always purely imaginary: no man of genuinely superior intelligence has ever been an actor. Even supposing a young man of appreciable mental powers to be lured upon the stage, as philosophers are occasionally lured into bordellos, his mind would be inevitably and almost immediately destroyed by the gaudy nonsense issuing from his mouth every night. That nonsense enters into the very fiber of the actor. He becomes a grotesque boiling down of all the preposterous characters that he has ever impersonated. Their characteristics are seen in his manner, in his reactions to stimuli, in his point of view. He becomes a walking artificiality, a strutting dummy, a thematic catalogue of imbecilities.

There are, of course, plays that are not wholly nonsense, and now and then one encounters an actor who aspires to appear in them. This aspiration almost always overtakes the so-called actor-manager—that is to say, the actor who has got rich and is thus ambitious to appear as a gentleman. Such aspirants commonly tackle Shakespeare, and if not Shakespeare, then Shaw, or Hauptmann, or Rostand, or some other apparently intellectual dramatist. But this is seldom more than a passing madness. The actor-manager may do that sort of thing once in a while; but in the main he sticks to his garbage. Consider, for example, the late Henry Irving. He posed as an intellectual and was forever gabbling about his high services to the stage, and yet he appeared constantly in such puerile things as "The Bells," beside which the average newspaper editorial or college yell was literature. So with the late Mansfield. His pretension, deftly circulated by press-agents, was that he was a man of brilliant and polished mind. Nevertheless, he spent two-thirds of his life in the theater playing such abominable drivel as "A Parisian Romance" and "Dr. Jekyll and Mr. Hyde."

It is commonly urged in defense of certain actors that they are forced to appear in that sort of stuff by the public demand for it—that appearing in it painfully violates their secret pruderies. This defense is unsound and dishonest. An actor never disdains anything that gets him applause and money; he is almost completely devoid of that æsthetic conscience which is the chief mark of the genuine artist. If there were a large public willing to pay handsomely to hear him recite limericks, or to blow a cornet, or to strip off his underwear and dance a polonaise stark naked, he would do it without hesitation—and then convince himself that such buffooning constituted a difficult and elevated art, fully comparable to Wagner's or Dante's. In brief, the one essential, in his sight, is the chance to shine, the fat part, the applause. Who ever heard of an actor declining a fat part on the ground that it invaded his intellectual integrity? The thing is simply unimaginable.

VIII.
The Cult of Hope

O F all the sentimental errors which reign and rage in this incomparable republic, the worst, I often suspect, is that which confuses the function of criticism, whether æsthetic, political or social, with the function of reform. Almost invariably it takes the form of a protest: "The fellow condemns without offering anything better. Why tear down without building up?" So coo and snivel the sweet ones: so wags the national tongue. The messianic delusion becomes a sort of universal murrain. It is impossible to get an audience for an idea that is not "constructive"—*i.e.*, that is not glib, and uplifting, and full of hope, and hence capable of tickling the emotions by leaping the intermediate barrier of the intelligence.

In this protest and demand, of course, there is nothing but a hollow sound of words—the empty babbling of men who constantly mistake their mere feelings for thoughts. The truth is that criticism, if it were thus confined to the proposing of alternative schemes, would quickly cease to have any force or utility at all, for in the overwhelming majority of instances no alternative scheme of any intelligibility is imaginable, and the whole object of the critical process is to demonstrate it. The poet, if the victim is a poet, is simply one as bare of gifts as a herring is of fur: no conceivable suggestion will ever make him write actual poetry. The cancer cure, if one turns to popular swindles, is wholly and absolutely without merit—and the fact that medicine offers us no better cure does not dilute its bogusness in the slightest. And the plan of reform, in politics, sociology or what not, is simply beyond the pale of reason; no change in it or improvement of it will ever make it achieve the downright impossible. Here, precisely, is what is the matter with most of the notions that go floating about the country, particularly in the field of governmental reform. The trouble with them is not only that they won't and don't work; the trouble with them, more importantly, is that the thing they propose to accomplish is intrinsically, or at all events most probably, beyond accomplishment. That is to say, the problem they are ostensibly designed to solve is a problem that is insoluble. To tackle them with a proof of that insolubility, or even with a colorable argument of it, is sound criticism; to tackle them with another solution that is quite as bad, or even worse, is to pick the pocket of one knocked down by an automobile.

Unluckily, it is difficult for a certain type of mind to grasp the concept of insolubility. Thousands of poor dolts keep on trying to square the circle; other thousands keep pegging away at perpetual motion. The number of persons so afflicted is far greater than the records of the Patent Office show, for beyond the circle of frankly insane enterprise there lie circles of more and more plausible enterprise, and finally we come to a circle which embraces the great majority of human beings. These are the optimists and chronic hopers of the world, the believers in men, ideas and things. These are the advocates of leagues of nations, wars to make the world safe for democracy, political mountebanks, "clean-up" campaigns, laws, raids, Men and Religion Forward Movements, eugenics, sex hygiene, education, newspapers. It is the settled habit of such credulous folk to give ear to whatever is comforting; it is their settled faith that whatever is desirable will come to pass. A caressing confidence —but one, unfortunately, that is not borne out by human experience. The fact is that some of the things that men and women have desired most ardently for thousands of years are not nearer realization to-day than they were in the time of Rameses, and that there is not the slightest reason for believing that they will lose their coyness on any near to-morrow. Plans for hurrying them on have been tried since the beginning; plans for forcing them overnight are in copious and antagonistic operation to-day; and yet they continue to hold off and elude us, and the chances are that they will keep on holding off and eluding us until the angels get tired of the show, and the whole earth is set off like a gigantic bomb, or drowned, like a sick cat, between two buckets.

But let us avoid the grand and chronic dreams of the race and get down to some of the concrete problems of life under the Christian enlightenment. Let us take a look, say, at the so-called drink problem, a small sub-division of the larger problem of saving men from their inherent and incurable hoggishness. What is the salient feature of the discussion of the drink problem, as one observes it going on eternally in These States? The salient feature of it is that very few honest and intelligent men ever take a hand in the business—that the best men of the nation, distinguished for their sound sense in other fields, seldom show any interest in it. On the one hand it is labored by a horde of obvious jackasses, each confident that he can dispose of it overnight. And on the other hand it is sophisticated and obscured by a crowd of oblique fellows, hired by interested parties, whose secret desire is that it be kept unsolved. To one side, the professional gladiators of Prohibition; to the other side, the agents of the brewers and distillers. But why do all neutral and clear-headed men avoid it? Why does one hear so little about it from those who have no personal stake in it, and can thus view it fairly and accurately? Is it because they are afraid? Is it because they are not intrigued by it? I doubt that it would be just to accuse them in either way. The real reason why they steer clear of the gabble is simpler and more creditable. It is this: that none of them—that no genuinely thoughtful and prudent man—can imagine any solution which meets the tests of his own criticism—that no genuinely intelligent man believes the thing is soluble at all.

Here, of course, I generalize a bit heavily. Honest and intelligent men, though surely not many of them, occasionally come forward with suggestions. In the midst of so much debate it is inevitable that even a man of critical mind should sometimes lean to one side or the other—that some salient imbecility should make him react toward its rough opposite. But the fact still remains that not a single complete and comprehensive scheme has ever come from such a man, that no such man has ever said, in so many words, that he thought the problem could be solved, simply and effectively. All such schemes come from idiots or from sharpers disguised as idiots to win the public confidence. The whole discussion is based upon assumptions that even the most casual reflection must reject as empty balderdash.

And as with the drink problem, so with most of the other great questions that harass and dismay the helpless human race. Turn, for example, to the sex problem. There is no half-baked ecclesiastic, bawling in his galvanized-iron temple on a suburban lot, who doesn't know precisely how it ought to be dealt with. There is no fantoddish old suffragette, sworn to get her revenge on man, who hasn't a sovereign remedy for it. There is not a shyster of a district attorney, ambitious for higher office, who doesn't offer to dispose of it in a few weeks, given only enough help from the city editors. And yet, by the same token, there is not a man who has honestly studied it and pondered it, bringing sound information to the business, and understanding of its inner difficulties and a clean and analytical mind, who doesn't believe and hasn't stated publicly that it is intrinsically and eternally insoluble. I can't think of an exception, nor does a fresh glance through the literature suggest one. The latest expert to tell the disconcerting truth is Dr. Maurice Parmelee, the criminologist. His book, "Personality and Conduct," is largely devoted to demonstrating that the popular solutions, for all the support they get from vice crusaders, complaisant legislators and sensational newspapers, are unanimously imbecile and pernicious—that their only effect in practice is to make what was bad a good deal worse. His remedy is—what? An alternative solution? Not at all. His remedy, in brief, is to abandon all attempts at a solution, to let the whole thing go, to cork up all the reformers and try to forget it.

And in this proposal he merely echoes Havelock Ellis, undoubtedly the most diligent and scientific student of the sex problem that the world has yet seen—in fact, the one man who, above all others, has made a decorous and intelligent examination of it possible. Ellis' remedy is simply a denial of all remedies. He admits that the disease is bad, but he shows that the medicine is infinitely worse, and so he proposes going back to the plain disease, and advocates bearing it with philosophy, as we bear colds in the head, marriage, the noises of the city, bad cooking and the certainty of death. Man is inherently vile —but he is never so vile as when he is trying to disguise and deny his vileness. No prostitute was ever so costly to a community as a prowling and obscene vice crusader, or as the dubious legislator or prosecuting officer who jumps as he pipes.

Ellis, in all this, falls under the excommunication of the sentimentalists. He demolishes one scheme without offering an alternative scheme. He tears down without making any effort to build up. This explains, no doubt, his general unpopularity;

into mouths agape for peruna, he projects only paralyzing streams of ice-water. And it explains, too, the curious fact that his books, the most competent and illuminating upon the subject that they discuss, are under the ban of the Comstocks in both England and America, whereas the hollow treatises of ignorant clerics and smutty old maids are merchanted with impunity, and even commended from the sacred desk. The trouble with Ellis is that he tells the truth, which is the unsafest of all things to tell. His crime is that he is a man who prefers facts to illusions, and knows what he is talking about. Such men are never popular. The public taste is for merchandise of a precisely opposite character. The way to please is to proclaim in a confident manner, not what is true, but what is merely comforting. This is what is called building up. This is constructive criticism.

IX.
The Dry Millennium

The Holy War

THE fact that the enforcement of Prohibition entails a host of oppressions and injustices—that it puts a premium upon the lowest sort of spying, affords an easy livelihood to hordes of professional scoundrels, subjects thousands of decent men to the worst sort of blackmail, violates the theoretical sanctity of domicile, and makes for bitter and relentless enmities,—this fact is now adduced by its ever-hopeful foes as an argument for the abandonment of the whole disgusting crusade. By it they expect to convert even a large minority of the drys, apparently on the theory that the latter got converted emotionally and hastily, and that an appeal to their sense of justice and fair-dealing will debamboozle them.

No hope could be more vain. What all the current optimists overlook is that the illogical and indefensible persecutions certain to occur in increasing number under the Prohibition Amendment constitute the chief cause of its popularity among the sort of men who are in favor of it. The typical Prohibitionist, in other words, is a man full of religious excitement, with the usual sadistic overtones. He delights in persecution for its own sake. He likes to see the other fellow jump and to hear him yell. This thirst is horribly visible in all the salient mad mullahs of the land—that is, in all the genuine leaders of American culture. Such skillful boob-bumpers as the Rev. Dr. Billy Sunday know what that culture is; they know what the crowd wants. Thus they convert the preaching of the alleged Word of God into a rough-and-tumble pursuit of definite sinners— saloon-keepers, prostitutes, Sabbath-breakers, believers in the Darwinian hypothesis, German exegetes, hand-books, poker-players, adulterers, cigarette-smokers, users of profanity. It is the chase that heats up the great mob of Methodists, not the

Word. And the fact that the chase is unjust only tickles them the more, for to do injustice with impunity is a sign of power, and power is the thing that the inferior man always craves most violently.

Every time the papers print another account of a Prohibitionist agent murdering a man who resists him, or searching some woman's underwear, or raiding a Vanderbilt yacht, or blackmailing a Legislature, or committing some other such inordinate and anti-social act, they simply make a thousand more votes for Prohibition. It is precisely that sort of entertainment that makes Prohibition popular with the boobery. It is precisely because it is unjust, imbecile, arbitrary and tyrannical that they are so hot for it. The incidental violation of even the inferior man's liberty is not sufficient to empty him of delight in the chase. The victims reported in the newspapers are commonly his superiors; he thus gets the immemorial democratic satisfaction out of their discomfiture. Besides, he has no great rage for liberty himself. He is always willing to surrender it at demand. The most popular man under a democracy is not the most democratic man, but the most despotic man. The common folk delight in the exactions of such a man. They like him to boss them. Their natural gait is the goose-step.

It was predicted by romantics that the arrival of Prohibition would see the American workingman in revolt against its tyranny, with mills idle and industry paralyzed. Certain boozy labor leaders even went so far as to threaten a general strike. No such strike, of course, materialized. Not a single American workingman uttered a sound. The only protests heard of came from a few barbarous foreigners, and these malcontents were quickly beaten into submission by the *Polizei*. In a week or two all the reserve stocks of beer were exhausted, and every jug of authentic hard liquor was emptied. Since then, save for the ghastly messes that he has brewed behind locked doors, the American workingman has been dry. Worse, he has also been silent. Not a sound has come out of him. . . . But his liver is full of bile? He nourishes an intolerable grievance? He will get his revenge, soon or late, at the polls? All moonshine! He will do nothing of the sort. He will actually do what he always does —that is, he will make a virtue of his necessity, and straightway begin believing that he *likes* Prohibition, that it is doing him a lot of good, that he wouldn't be without it if he could. This is the habitual process of thought of inferior men, at all times and everywhere. This is the sturdy common sense of the plain people.

2

The Lure of Babylon

One of the ultimate by-products of Prohibition and the allied Puritanical barbarities will probably be an appreciable slackening in the present movement of yokels toward the large cities. The thing that attracted the peasant youth to our gaudy Sodoms and Ninevehs, in the past, was not, as sociologists have always assumed, the prospect of less work and more money. The country boy, in point of fact—that is, the average country boy, the normal country boy—had to work quite as hard in the city as he ever worked in the country, and his wages were anything but princely. Unequipped with a city trade, un-protected by a union, and so forced into competition with the lowest types of foreign labor, he had to be content with monotonous, uninspiring and badly-paid jobs. He did not become a stock-broker, or even a plumber; until the war gave him a temporary chance at its gigantic swag, he became a car conductor, a porter or a wagon-driver. And it took him many years to escape from that sordid fate, for the city boy, with a better education and better connections, was always a lap or two ahead of him. The notion that yokels always succeed in the cities is a great delusion. The overwhelming majority of our rich men are city-born and city-bred. And the overwhelming majority of our elderly motormen, forlorn corner grocerymen, neighborhood carpenters and other such blank cartridges are country-bred.

No, it was not money that lured the adolescent husbandman to the cities, but the gay life. What he dreamed of was a more spacious and stimulating existence than the farm could offer— an existence crowded with intriguing and usually unlawful recreations. A few old farmers may have come in now and then to buy gold bricks or to hear the current Henry Ward Beechers, but these oldsters were mere trippers—they never thought of settling down—the very notion of it would have appalled them. The actual settlers were all young, and what brought them on was less an economic impulse than an æsthetic one. They wanted to live magnificently, to taste the sweets that drummers talked of, to sample the refined divertisements described in such works as "The Confessions of an Actress," "Night Life in Chicago" and "What Every Young Husband Should Know." Specifically, they yearned for a semester or two in the theaters, the saloons and the bordellos—particularly, the saloons and bordellos. It was this gorgeous bait that dragged them out of their barn-yards. It was this bait that landed a select few in Wall street and the United States Senate—and millions on the front seats of trolley-cars, delivery-wagons and ash-carts.

But now Puritanism eats the bait. In all our great cities the public stews are closed, and the lamentable irregularities they catered to are thrown upon an individual initiative that is quite beyond the talents and enterprise of a plow-hand. Now the saloons are closed too, and the blind-pigs begin to charge such prices that no peasant can hope to pay them. Only the theater remains—and already the theater loses its old lavish devilishness. True enough, it still deals in pornography, but that pornography becomes exclusive and even esoteric: a yokel could not understand the higher farce, nor could he afford to pay for a seat at a modern leg-show. The cheap burlesque house of other days is now incurably moral; I saw a burlesque show lately which was almost a dramatization of a wall-card by Dr. Frank Crane. There remains the movie, but the peasant needn't come to the city to see movies—there is one in every village. What remains, then, of the old lure? What sane youth, comfortably housed on a farm, with Theda Bara performing at the nearest cross-roads, wheat at $2.25 a bushel and milkers getting $75 a month and board—what jejune rustic, not downright imbecile, itches for the city to-day?

3
Cupid and Well-Water

In the department of amour, I daresay, the first effect of Prohibition will be to raise up impediments to marriage. It was alcohol, in the past, that was the primary cause of perhaps a majority of alliances among civilized folk. The man, priming himself with cocktails to achieve boldness, found himself suddenly bogged in sentimentality, and so yielded to the ancient tricks of the lady. Absolutely sober men will be harder to snare. Coffee will never mellow them sufficiently. Thus I look for a fall in the marriage rate.

But only temporarily. In the long run, Prohibition will make marriage more popular, at least among the upper classes, than it has ever been in the past, and for the plain reason that, once it is in full effect, the life of a civilized bachelor will become intolerable. In the past he went to his club. But a club without a bar is as hideously unattractive as a beautiful girl without hair or teeth. No sane man will go into it. In two years, in fact, nine out of ten clubs will be closed. The only survivors will be a few bleak rookeries for senile widowers. The bachelor of less years, unable to put up with the society of such infernos, will inevitably decide that if he must keep sober he might just as well have a charming girl to ease his agonies, and so he will expose himself in society, and some fair one or other will nab him.

At the moment, observing only the first effect of Prohibition, the great majority of intelligent women are opposed to it. But when the secondary effect begins to appear they will become in favor of it. They now have the vote. I see no hope.

4
The Triumph of Idealism

Another effect of Prohibition will be that it will gradually empty the United States of its present small minority of civilized men. Almost every man that one respects is now casting longing eyes across the ocean. Some of them talk frankly of emigrating, once Europe pulls itself together. Others merely propose to go abroad every year and to stay there as long as possible, visiting the United States only at intervals, as a Russian nobleman, say, used to visit his estates in the Ukraine. Worse, Prohibition will scare off all the better sort of immigrants from the other side. The lower order of laborers may continue to come in small numbers—each planning to get all the money he can and then escape, as the Italians are even now escaping. But no first-rate man will ever come—no Stephen Girard, or William Osler, or Carl Schurz, or Theodore

Thomas, or Louis Agassiz, or Edwin Klebs, or Albert Gallatin, or Alexander Hamilton. It is not Prohibition *per se* that will keep them away; it is the whole complex of social and political attitudes underlying Prohibition—the whole clinical picture of Puritanism rampant. The United States will become a sort of huge Holland—fat and contented, but essentially undistinguished. Its superior men will leave it automatically, as nine-tenths of all superior Hollanders leave Holland.

But all this, from the standpoint of Prohibitionists, is no argument against Prohibition. On the contrary, it is an argument in favor of Prohibition. For the men the Prohibitionist—*i.e.*, the inferior sort of Puritan—distrusts and dislikes most intensely is precisely what the rest of humanity regards as the superior man. You will go wrong if you imagine that the honest yeomen of, say, Mississippi deplore the fact that in the whole state there is not a single distinguished man. They actually delight in it. It is a source of genuine pride to them that no such irreligious scoundrel as Balzac lives there, and no such scandalous adulterer as Wagner, and no scoundrelly atheist as Huxley, and no such rambunctious piano-thumper as Beethoven, and no such German spy as Nietzsche. Such men, settling there, would be visited by a Vigilance Committee and sharply questioned. The Puritan Commonwealth, now as always, has no traffic with heretics.

X.

Appendix on a Tender Theme

The Nature of Love

Whatever the origin (in the soul, the ductless glands or the convolutions of the cerebrum) of the thing called romantic love, its mere phenomenal nature may be very simply described. It is, in brief, a wholesale diminishing of disgusts, primarily based on observation, but often, in its later stages, taking on an hallucinatory and pathological character. Friendship has precisely the same constitution, but the pathological factor is usually absent. When we are attracted to a person and find his or her proximity agreeable, it means that he or she disgusts us less than the average human being disgusts us—which, if we have delicate sensibilities, is a good deal more than is comfortable. The elemental man is not much oppressed by this capacity for disgust; in consequence, he is capable of falling in love with almost any woman who seems sexually normal. But the man of a higher type is vastly more sniffish, and so the majority of women whom he meets are quite unable to interest him, and when he succumbs at last it is always to a woman of special character, and often she is also one of uncommon shrewdness and enterprise.

Because human contacts are chiefly superficial, most of the disgusts that we are conscious of are physical. We are never honestly friendly with a man who is dirtier than we are ourselves, or who has table manners that are cruder than our own (or merely noticeably different), or who laughs in a way that strikes us as gross, or who radiates some odor that we do not like. We never conceive a romantic passion for a woman who employs a toothpick in public, or who suffers from acne, or who offers the subtle but often quite unescapable suggestion that she has on soiled underwear. But there are also psychical disgusts. Our friends, in the main, must be persons who think substantially as we do, at least about all things that actively concern us, and who have the same general tastes. It is impossible to imagine a Brahmsianer being honestly fond of a man who enjoys jazz, or a man who admires Joseph Conrad falling in love with a woman who reads Rex Beach. By the same token, it is impossible to imagine a woman of genuine refinement falling in love with a Knight of Pythias, a Methodist or even a chauffeur; either the chauffeur is a Harvard aviator in disguise or the lady herself is a charwoman in disguise. Here, however, the force of aversion may be greatly diminished by contrary physical attractions; the body, as usual, is enormously more potent than the so-called mind. In the midst of the bitterest wars, with every man of the enemy held to be a fiend in human form, women constantly fall in love with enemy soldiers who are of pleasant person and wear attractive uniforms. And many a fair agnostic, as every one knows, is on good terms with a handsome priest. . . .

Imagine a young man in good health and easy circumstances, entirely ripe for love. The prompting to mate and beget arises within his interstitial depths, traverses his lymphatic system, lifts his blood pressure, and goes whooping through his *meatus auditorium externus* like a fanfare of slide trombones. The impulse is very powerful. It staggers and dismays him. He trembles like a stag at bay. Why, then, doesn't he fall head over heels in love with the first eligible woman that he meets? For the plain reason that the majority of women that he meets offend him, repel him, disgust him. Often it is in some small, inconspicuous and, at first glance, unanalyzable way. She is, in general, a very pretty girl—but her ears stand out too much. Or her hair reminds him of oakum. Or her mouth looks like his aunt's. Or she has beer-keg ankles. Here very impalpable things, such as bodily odors, play a capital part; their importance is always much underestimated. Many a girl has lost a husband by using the wrong perfume, or by neglecting to have her hair washed. Many another has come to grief by powdering her nose too much or too little, or by shrinking from the paltry pain of having some of her eyebrows pulled, or by employing a lip-salve with too much purple in it, or by patronizing a bad dentist, or by speaking incautiously of chilblains. . . .

But eventually the youth finds his love—soon or late the angel foreordained comes along. Who is this prodigy? Simply the *first* girl to sneak over what may be called the threshold of his disgusts—simply the *first* to disgust him so little, at first glance, that the loud, insistent promptings of the Divine Schadchen have a chance to be heard. If he muffs this first, another will come along, maybe soon, maybe late. For every normal man there are hundreds of thousands in Christendom, thousands in his own town, scores within his own circle of acquaintance. This normal man is not too delicate. His fixed foci of disgust are neither very numerous nor very sensitive. For the rest, he is swayed by fashion, by suggestion, by transient moods. Anon a mood of cynicism is upon him and he is hard to please, but anon he succumbs to sentimentality and is blind to everything save the grossest offendings. It is only the man of extraordinary sensitiveness, the man of hypertrophied delicacy, who must search the world for his elective affinity.

Once the threshold is crossed emotion comes to the aid of perception. That is to say, the blind, almost irresistible mating impulse, now fortuitously relieved from the contrary pressure of active disgusts, fortifies itself by manufacturing illusions. The lover sees with an eye that is both opaque and out of focus. Thus he begins the familiar process of editing and improving his girl. Features and characteristics that, observed in cold blood, might have quickly aroused his most active disgust are now seen through a rose-tinted fog, like drabs in a musical comedy. The lover ends by being almost anæsthetic to disgust. While the spell lasts his lady could shave her head or take to rubbing snuff, or scratch her leg at a communion service, or smear her hair with bear's grease, and yet not disgust him. Here the paralysis of the faculties is again chiefly physical—a matter of obscure secretions, of shifting pressure, of metabolism. Nature is at her tricks. The fever of love is upon its victim. His guard down, he is little more than a pathetic automaton. The shrewd observer of gaucheries, the sensitive sniffer, the erstwhile cynic, has become a mere potential papa.

This spell, of course, doesn't last forever. Marriage cools the fever and lowers the threshold of disgust. The husband begins to observe what the lover was blind to, and often his discoveries affect him as unpleasantly as the treason of a trusted friend. And not only is the fever cooled: the opportunities for exact observation are enormously increased. It is a commonplace of juridical science that the great majority of divorces have their origin in the connubial chamber. Here intimacy is so extreme that it is fatal to illusion. Both parties, thrown into the closest human contact that either has suffered since their unconscious days *in utero*, find their old capacity for disgust reviving, and then suddenly flaming. The girl who was perfect in her wedding gown becomes a ghastly caricature in her *robe de nuit*; the man who was a Chevalier Bayard as a wooer becomes a snuffling, shambling, driveling nuisance as a husband—a fellow offensive to eyes, ears, nose, touch and immortal soul. A learned judge of my acquaintance, constantly hearing divorce actions and as constantly striving to reconcile the parties, always tries to induce plaintiff and defendant to live apart for a while, or, failing that, to occupy separate rooms, or, failing that, to at least dress in separate rooms. According to this jurist, a husband who shaves in his wife's presence is either an idiot or a scoundrel. The spectacle, he argues, is intrinsically disgusting, and to force it upon a refined woman is either to subject her to the most exquisite torture or to degrade her gradually to the insensate level of an *Abortfrau*.

The day is saved, as every one knows, by the powerful effects of habit. The acquisition of habit is the process whereby disgust is overcome in daily life—the process whereby one may cease to be disgusted by a persistent noise or odor. One suffers horribly at first, but after a bit one suffers less, and in the course of time one scarcely suffers at all. Thus a man, when his marriage enters upon the stage of regularity and safety, gets used to his wife as he might get used to a tannery next door, and *vice versa*. I think that women, in this direction, have the harder row to hoe, for they are more observant than men, and vastly more sensitive in small ways. But even women succumb to habit with humane rapidity, else every marriage would end in divorce. Disgusts pale into mere dislikes, disrelishes, distastes. They cease to gag and torture. But though they thus shrink into the shadow, they are by no means disposed of. Deep down in the subconscious they continue to lurk, and some accident may cause them to flare up at any time, and so work havoc. This flaring up accounts for a familiar and yet usually very mystifying phenomenon—the sudden collapse of a marriage, a friendship or a business association after years of apparent prosperity.

2
The Incomparable Buzzsaw

The chief (and perhaps the only genuine) charm of women is seldom mentioned by the orthodox professors of the sex. I refer to the charm that lies in the dangers they present. The allurement that they hold out to men is precisely the allurement that Cape Hatteras holds out to sailors: they are enormously dangerous and hence enormously fascinating. To the average man, doomed to some banal and sordid drudgery all his life long, they offer the only grand hazard that he ever encounters. Take them away and his existence would be as flat and secure as that of a milch-cow. Even to the unusual man, the adventurous man, the imaginative and romantic man, they offer the adventure of adventures. Civilization tends to dilute and cheapen all other hazards. War itself, once an enterprise stupendously thrilling, has been reduced to mere caution and calculation; already, indeed, it employs as many press-agents, letter-openers, and chautauqua orators as soldiers. On some not distant tomorrow its salient personality may be Potash, and if not Potash, then Perlmutter. But the duel of sex continues to be fought in the Berserker manner. Whoso approaches women still faces the immemorial dangers. Civilization has not made them a bit more safe than they were in Solomon's time; they are still inordinately barbarous and menacing, and hence inordinately provocative, and hence inordinately charming and romantic. . . .

The most disgusting cad in the world is the man who, on grounds of decorum and morality, avoids the game of love. He is one who puts his own ease and security above the most laudable of philanthropies. Women have a hard time of it in this world. They are oppressed by man-made laws, man-made social customs, masculine egoism, the delusion of masculine superiority. Their one comfort is the assurance that, even though it may be impossible to prevail against man, it is always possible to enslave and torture a man. This feeling is fostered when one makes love to them. One need not be a great beau, a seductive catch, to do it effectively. Any man is better than none. No woman is ever offended by admiration. The wife of a millionaire notes the reverent glance of a head-waiter. To withhold that devotion, to shrink poltroonishly from giving so much happiness at such small expense, to evade the business on the ground that it has hazards—this is the act of a puling and tacky fellow.

3

Women as Spectacles

Women, when it comes to snaring men, through the eye, bait a great many hooks that fail to fluster the fish. Nine-tenths of their primping and decorating of their persons not only doesn't please men; it actually repels men. I often pass two days running without encountering a single woman who is charmingly dressed. Nearly all of them run to painful color schemes, absurd designs and excessive over-ornamentation. One seldom observes a man who looks an absolute guy, whereas such women are very numerous; in the average theater audience they constitute a majority of at least nine-tenths. The reason is not far to seek. The clothes of men are plain in design and neutral in hue. The only touch of genuine color is in the florid blob of the face, the center of interest—exactly where it ought to be. If there is any other color at all, it is a faint suggestion in the cravat—adjacent to the face, and so leading the eye toward it. It is color that kills the clothes of the average woman. She runs to bright spots that take the eye away from her face and hair. She ceases to be woman clothed and becomes a mere piece of clothing womaned.

Even at the basic feminine art of pigmenting their faces very few women excel. The average woman seems to think that she is most lovely when her sophistication of her complexion is most adroitly concealed—when the *poudre de riz* is rubbed in so hard that it is almost invisible, and the penciling of eyes and lips is perfectly realistic. This is a false notion. Most men of appreciative eye have no objection to artificiality *per se*, so long as it is intrinsically sightly. The marks made by a lip-stick may be very beautiful; there are many lovely shades of scarlet, crimson and vermilion. A man with eyes in his head admires them for themselves; he doesn't have to be first convinced that they are non-existent, that what he sees is not the mark of a lip-stick at all, but an authentic lip. So with the eyes. Nothing could be more charming than an eye properly reënforced; the naked organ is not to be compared to it; nature is an idiot when it comes to shadows. But it must be admired as a work of art, not as a miraculous and incredible eye. . . . Women, in this important and venerable art, stick too closely to crude representation. They forget that men do not admire the technique, but the result. What they should do is to forget realism for a while, and concentrate their attention upon composition, chiaroscuro and color.

4
Woman and the Artist

Much gabble is to be found in the literature of the world upon the function of woman as inspiration, stimulant and *agente provocateuse* to the creative artist. The subject is a favorite one with sentimentalists, most of whom are quite beyond anything properly describable as inspiration, either with or without feminine aid. I incline to think, as I hint, that there is little if any basis of fact beneath the theory. Women not only do not inspire creative artists to high endeavor; they actually stand firmly against every high endeavor that a creative artist initiates spontaneously. What a man's women folks almost invariable ask of him is that he be respectable—that he do something generally approved—that he avoid yielding to his aberrant fancies—in brief, that he sedulously eschew showing any sign of genuine genius. Their interest is not primarily in the self-expression of the individual, but in the well-being of the family organization, which means the safety of themselves. No sane woman would want to be the wife of such a man, say, as Nietzsche or Chopin. His mistress perhaps, yes—for a mistress can always move on when the weather gets too warm. But not a wife. I here speak by the book. Both Nietzsche and Chopin had plenty of mistresses, but neither was ever able to get a wife.

Shakespeare and Ann Hathaway, Wagner and Minna Planer,

Molière and Armande Béjart—one might multiply instances almost endlessly. Minna, at least in theory, knew something of music; she was thus what romance regards as an ideal wife for Wagner. But instead of helping him to manufacture his incomparable masterpieces, she was for twenty-five years the chief impediment to their manufacture. "Lohengrin" gave her the horrors; she begged Richard to give up his lunacies and return to the composition of respectable cornet music. In the end he had to get rid of her in sheer self-defense. Once free, with nothing worse on his hands than the illicit affection of Cosima Liszt von Bülow, he produced music drama after music drama in rapid succession. Then, married to Cosima, he descended to the anticlimax of "Parsifal," a truly tragic mixture of the stupendous and the banal, of work of genius and *sinfonia domestica*—a great man dying by inches, smothered by the smoke of French fried potatoes, deafened by the wailing of children, murdered in his own house by the holiest of passions.

Sentimentalists always bring up the case of Schumann and his Clara in rebuttal. But does it actually rebut? I doubt it. Clara, too, perpetrated her *attentat* against art. Her fair white arms, lifting from the keyboard to encircle Robert's neck, squeezed more out of him than mere fatuous smirks. He had the best head on him that music had seen since Beethoven's day; he was, on the cerebral side, a colossus; he might have written music of the very first order. Well, what he *did* write was piano music—some of it imperfectly arranged for orchestra. The sad eyes of Clara were always upon him. He kept within the limits of her intelligence, her prejudices, her wifely love. No grand experiments with the orchestra. No superb leapings and cavortings. No rubbing of sandpaper over critical ears. Robert lived and died a respectable musical *Hausvater*. He was a man of genuine genius—but he didn't leave ten lines that might not have been passed by old Prof. Jadassohn.

The truth is that, no matter how great the domestic concord and how lavish the sacrifices a man makes for his women-folk, they almost always regard him secretly as a silly and selfish fellow, and cherish the theory that it would be easily possible to improve him. This is because the essential interests of men and women are eternally antithetical. A man may yield over and over again, but in the long run he must occasionally look out for himself—and it is these occasions that his women-folk remember. The typical domestic situation shows a woman trying to induce a man to do something that he doesn't want to do, or to refrain from something that he does want to do. This is true in his bachelor days, when his mother or his sister is his antagonist. It is pre-eminently true just before his marriage, when the girl who has marked him down is hard at the colossal job of overcoming his reluctance. And after marriage it is so true that there is hardly need to state it. One of the things every man discovers to his disquiet is that his wife, after the first play-acting is over, regards him essentially as his mother used to regard him—that is, as a self-worshiper who needs to be policed and an idiot who needs to be protected. The notion that women *admire* their men-folks is pure moonshine. The most they ever achieve in that direction is to pity them. When a woman genuinely loves a man it is a sign that she regards him much as a healthy man regards a one-armed and epileptic soldier.

5
Martyrs

Nearly the whole case of the birth-controllers who now roar in Christendom is grounded upon the doctrine that it is an intolerable outrage for a woman to have to submit to motherhood when her private fancies may rather incline to automobiling, shopping or going to the movies. For this curse the husband is blamed; the whole crime is laid to his swinish lasciviousness. With the highest respect, nonsense! My private suspicion, supported by long observation, copious prayer and the most laborious cogitation, is that no woman delights in motherhood so vastly as this woman who theoretically abhors it. She experiences, in fact, a double delight. On the one hand, there is the caressing of her vanity—a thing enjoyed by every woman when she achieves the banality of viable offspring. And on the other hand, there is the fine chance it gives her to play the martyr—a chance that every woman seeks as diligently as a man seeks ease. All these so-called unwilling mothers wallow in their martyrdom. They revel in the opportunity to be pitied, made much over and envied by other women.

6
The Burnt Child

The fundamental trouble with marriage is that it shakes a man's confidence in himself, and so greatly diminishes his general competence and effectiveness. His habit of mind becomes that of a commander who has lost a decisive and calamitous battle. He never quite trusts himself thereafter.

7
The Supreme Comedy

Marriage, at best, is full of a sour and inescapable comedy, but it never reaches the highest peaks of the ludicrous save when efforts are made to escape its terms—that is, when efforts are made to loosen its bonds, and so ameliorate and denaturize it. All projects to reform it by converting it into a free union of free individuals are inherently absurd. The thing is, at bottom, the most rigid of existing conventionalities, and the only way to conceal the fact and so make it bearable is to submit to it docilely. The effect of every revolt is merely to make the bonds galling, and, what is worse, poignantly obvious. Who are happy in marriage? Those with so little imagination that they cannot picture a better state, and those so shrewd that they prefer quiet slavery to hopeless rebellion.

8
A Hidden Cause

Many a woman, in order to bring the man of her choice to the altar of God, has to fight him with such relentless vigilance and ferocity that she comes to hate him. This, perhaps, explains the unhappiness of many marriages. In particular, it explains the unhappiness of many marriages based upon what is called "love."

9
Bad Workmanship

The essential slackness and incompetence of women, their congenital incapacity for small expertness, already descanted upon at length in my psychological work, "In Defense of Women," is never more plainly revealed than in their manhandling of the primary business of their sex. If the average woman were as competent at her trade of getting a husband as the average car conductor is at his trade of robbing the farebox, then a bachelor beyond the age of twenty-five would be so rare in the world that yokels would pay ten cents to gape at him. But women, in this fundamental industry, pursue a faulty technique and permit themselves to be led astray by unsound principles. The axioms into which they have precipitated their wisdom are nearly all untrue. For example, the axiom that the way to capture a man is through his stomach—which is to say, by feeding him lavishly. Nothing could be more absurd. The average man, at least in England and America, has such rudimentary tastes in victualry that he doesn't know good food from bad. He will eat anything set before him by a cook that he likes. The true way to fetch him is with drinks. A single bottle of drinkable wine will fill more men with the passion of love than ten sides of beef or a ton of potatoes. Even a *Seidel* of beer, deftly applied, is enough to mellow the hardest bachelor. If women really knew their business, they would have abandoned cooking centuries ago, and devoted themselves to brewing, distilling and bartending. It is a rare man who will walk five blocks for a first-rate meal. But it is equally a rare man who, even in the old days of freedom, would *not* walk five blocks for a first-rate cocktail. To-day he would walk five miles.

Another unsound feminine axiom is the one to the effect that the way to capture a man is to be distant—to throw all the burden of the courtship upon him. This is precisely the way to lose him. A man face to face with a girl who seems reserved and unapproachable is not inspired thereby to drag her off in the manner of a caveman; on the contrary, he is inspired to thank God that here, at last, is a girl with whom it is possible to have friendly doings without getting into trouble—that here is one not likely to grow mushy and make a mess. The average man does not marry because some marble fair one challenges his enterprise. He marries because chance throws into his way a fair one who repels him less actively than most, and because his delight in what he thus calls her charm is reënforced by a growing suspicion that she has fallen in love with him. In brief, it is chivalry that undoes him. The girl who infallibly gets a husband—in fact, *any* husband that she wants— is the one who tracks him boldly, fastens him with sad eyes, and then, when his conscience has begun to torture him, throws her arms around his neck, bursts into maidenly tears on his shoulder, and tells him that she fears her forwardness will destroy his respect for her. It is only a colossus who can resist such strategy. But it takes only a man of the intellectual grade of a Y.M.C.A. secretary to elude the girl who is afraid to take the offensive.

A third bogus axiom I have already discussed, to wit, the axiom that a man is repelled by palpable cosmetics—that the wise girl is the one who effectively conceals her sophistication of her complexion. What could be more untrue? The fact is that very few men are competent to distinguish between a layer of talc and the authentic epidermis, and that the few who have the gift are quite free from any notion that the latter is superior to the former. What a man seeks when he enters the society of women is something pleasing to the eye. That is all he asks. He does not waste any time upon a chemical or spectroscopic examination of the object observed; he simply determines whether it is beautiful or not beautiful. Has it so long escaped women that their husbands, when led astray, are usually led astray by women so vastly besmeared with cosmetics that they resemble barber-poles more than human beings? Are they yet blind to the superior pull of a French maid, a chorus girl, a stenographer begauded like a painter's palette? . . . And still they go on rubbing off their varnish, brushing the lampblack from their eyelashes, seeking eternally the lip-stick that is so depressingly purple that it will deceive! Alas, what a folly!

PREJUDICES:
THIRD SERIES

I.

On Being an American

APPARENTLY there are those who begin to find it disagreeable
—nay, impossible. Their anguish fills the Liberal weeklies
and every ship that puts out from New York carries a groaning
cargo of them, bound for Paris, London, Munich, Rome and
way points—anywhere to escape the great curses and atrocities that make life intolerable for them at home. Let me say at
once that I find little to cavil at in their basic complaints. In
more than one direction, indeed, I probably go a great deal
further than even the Young Intellectuals. It is, for example,
one of my firmest and most sacred beliefs, reached after an inquiry extending over a score of years and supported by incessant prayer and meditation, that the government of the United
States, in both its legislative arm and its executive arm, is ignorant, incompetent, corrupt, and disgusting—and from this judgment I except no more than twenty living lawmakers and no
more than twenty executioners of their laws. It is a belief no
less piously cherished that the administration of justice in the
Republic is stupid, dishonest, and against all reason and equity
—and from this judgment I except no more than thirty judges,
including two upon the bench of the Supreme Court of
the United States. It is another that the foreign policy of the
United States—its habitual manner of dealing with other nations, whether friend or foe—is hypocritical, disingenuous,
knavish, and dishonorable—and from this judgment I consent
to no exceptions whatever, either recent or long past. And it is
my fourth (and, to avoid too depressing a bill, final) conviction
that the American people, taking one with another, constitute
the most timorous, sniveling, poltroonish, ignominious mob
of serfs and goose-steppers ever gathered under one flag in
Christendom since the end of the Middle Ages, and that they

grow more timorous, more sniveling, more poltroonish, more ignominious every day.

So far I go with the fugitive Young Intellectuals—and into the Bad Lands beyond. Such, in brief, are the cardinal articles of my political faith, held passionately since my admission to citizenship and now growing stronger and stronger as I gradually disintegrate into my component carbon, oxygen, hydrogen, phosphorus, calcium, sodium, nitrogen and iron. This is what I believe and preach, *in nomine Domini*, Amen. Yet I remain on the dock, wrapped in the flag, when the Young Intellectuals set sail. Yet here I stand, unshaken and undespairing, a loyal and devoted Americano, even a chauvinist, paying taxes without complaint, obeying all laws that are physiologically obeyable, accepting all the searching duties and responsibilities of citizenship unprotestingly, investing the sparse usufructs of my miserable toil in the obligations of the nation, avoiding all commerce with men sworn to overthrow the government, contributing my mite toward the glory of the national arts and sciences, enriching and embellishing the native language, spurning all lures (and even all invitations) to get out and stay out—here am I, a bachelor of easy means, forty-two years old, unhampered by debts or issue, able to go wherever I please and to stay as long as I please—here am I, contentedly and even smugly basking beneath the Stars and Stripes, a better citizen, I daresay, and certainly a less murmurous and exigent one, than thousands who put the Hon. Warren Gamaliel Harding beside Friedrich Barbarossa and Charlemagne, and hold the Supreme Court to be directly inspired by the Holy Spirit, and belong ardently to every Rotary Club, Ku Klux Klan, and Anti-Saloon League, and choke with emotion when the band plays "The Star-Spangled Banner," and believe with the faith of little children that one of Our Boys, taken at random, could dispose in a fair fight of ten Englishmen, twenty Germans, thirty Frogs, forty Wops, fifty Japs, or a hundred Bolsheviki.

Well, then, why am I still here? Why am I so complacent (perhaps even to the point of offensiveness), so free from bile, so little fretting and indignant, so curiously happy? Why did I answer only with a few academic "Hear, Hears" when Henry James, Ezra Pound, Harold Stearns and the *emigrés* of Greenwich Village issued their successive calls to the corn-fed *intelligentsia* to flee the shambles, escape to fairer lands, throw off the curse forever? The answer, of course, is to be sought in the nature of happiness which tempts to metaphysics. But let me keep upon the ground. To me, at least (and I can only follow my own nose) happiness presents itself in an aspect that is tripartite. To be happy (reducing the thing to its elementals) I must be:

a. Well-fed, unhounded by sordid cares, at ease in Zion.
b. Full of a comfortable feeling of superiority to the masses of my fellow-men.
c. Delicately and unceasingly amused according to my taste.

It is my contention that, if this definition be accepted, there is no country on the face of the earth wherein a man roughly constituted as I am—a man of my general weaknesses, vanities, appetites, prejudices, and aversions—can be so happy, or even one-half so happy, as he can be in these free and independent states. Going further, I lay down the proposition that it is a sheer physical impossibility for such a man to live in These States and *not* be happy—that it is as impossible to him as it would be to a schoolboy to weep over the burning down of his school-house. If he says that he isn't happy here, then he either lies or is insane. Here the business of getting a living, particularly since the war brought the loot of all Europe to the national strong-box, is enormously easier than it is in any other Christian land—so easy, in fact, that an educated and forehanded man who fails at it must actually make deliberate efforts to that end. Here the general average of intelligence, of knowledge, of competence, of integrity, of self-respect, of honor is so low that any man who knows his trade, does not fear ghosts, has read fifty good books, and practices the common decencies stands out as brilliantly as a wart on a bald head, and is thrown willy-nilly into a meager and exclusive aristocracy. And here, more than anywhere else that I know of or have heard of, the daily panorama of human existence, of private and communal folly—the unending procession of governmental extortions and chicaneries, of commercial brigandages and throat-slittings, of theological buffooneries, of æsthetic ribaldries, of legal swindles and harlotries, of miscellaneous rogueries, villainies, imbecilities, grotesqueries, and extravagances—is so inordinately gross and preposterous, so perfectly brought up to the highest conceivable amperage, so steadily enriched with an almost fabulous daring and originality, that only the man who was born with a petrified diaphragm can fail to laugh himself to sleep every night, and to awake every morning with all the eager, unflagging expectation of a Sunday-school superintendent touring the Paris peep-shows.

A certain sough of rhetoric may be here. Perhaps I yield to words as a chautauqua lecturer yields to them, belaboring and fermenting the hinds with his Message from the New Jerusalem. But fundamentally I am quite as sincere as he is. For example, in the matter of attaining to ease in Zion, of getting a fair share of the national swag, now piled so mountainously high. It seems to me, sunk in my Egyptian night, that the man who fails to do this in the United States to-day is a man who is somehow stupid—maybe not on the surface, but certainly deep down. Either he is one who cripples himself unduly, say by setting up a family before he can care for it, or by making a bad bargain for the sale of his wares, or by concerning himself too much about the affairs of other men; or he is one who endeavors fatuously to sell something that no normal American wants. Whenever I hear a professor of philosophy complain that his wife has eloped with some moving-picture actor or bootlegger who can at least feed and clothe her, my natural sympathy for the man is greatly corrupted by contempt for his lack of sense. Would it be regarded as sane and laudable for a man to travel the Soudan trying to sell fountain-pens, or Greenland offering to teach double-entry bookkeeping or counterpoint? Coming closer, would the judicious pity or laugh at a man who opened a shop for the sale of incunabula in Little Rock, Ark., or who demanded a living in McKeesport, Pa., on the ground that he could read Sumerian? In precisely the same way it seems to me to be nonsensical for a man to offer generally some commodity that only a few rare and dubious Americans want, and then weep and beat his breast because he is not patronized. One seeking to make a living in a country must pay due regard to the needs and tastes of that country. Here in the United States we have no jobs for grand dukes, and none for *Wirkliche Geheimräte*, and none for palace eunuchs, and none for masters of the buckhounds, and none (any more) for brewery *Todsaufer*—and very few for oboe-players, metaphysicians, astrophysicists, assyriologists, watercolorists, stylites and epic poets. There was a time when the *Todsaufer* served a public need and got an adequate reward, but it is no more. There may come a time when the composer of string quartettes is paid as much as a railway conductor, but it is not yet. Then why practice such trades—that is, as trades? The man of independent means may venture into them prudently; when he does so, he is seldom molested; it may even be argued that he performs a public service by adopting them. But the man who has a living to make is simply silly if he goes into them; he is like a soldier going over the top with a coffin strapped to his back. Let him abandon such puerile vanities, and take to the uplift instead, as, indeed, thousands of other victims of the industrial system have already done. Let him bear in mind that, whatever its neglect of the humanities and their monks, the Republic has never got half enough bond salesmen, quack doctors, ward leaders, phrenologists, Methodist evangelists, circus clowns, magicians, soldiers, farmers, popular song writers, moonshine distillers, forgers of gin labels, mine guards, detectives, spies, snoopers, and *agents provocateurs*. The rules are set by Omnipotence; the discreet man observes them. Observing them, he is safe beneath the starry bed-tick, in fair weather or foul. The *boobus Americanus* is a bird that knows no closed season—and if he won't come down to Texas oil stock, or one-night cancer cures, or building lots in Swampshurst, he will always come down to Inspiration and Optimism, whether political, theological, pedagogical, literary, or economic.

The doctrine that it is *infra dignitatem* for an educated man to take a hand in the snaring of this goose is one in which I see nothing convincing. It is a doctrine chiefly voiced, I believe, by those who have tried the business and failed. They take refuge behind the childish notion that there is something honorable about poverty *per se*—the Greenwich Village complex. This is nonsense. Poverty may be an unescapable misfortune, but that no more makes it honorable than a cocked eye is made honorable by the same cause. Do I advocate, then, the ceaseless, senseless hogging of money? I do not. All I advocate—and praise as virtuous—is the hogging of enough to provide security and ease. Despite all the romantic superstitions to the contrary, the artist cannot do his best work when he is oppressed by unsatisfied wants. Nor can the philosopher. Nor can the man of science. The best and clearest thinking of the world is done and the finest art is produced, not by men who are hungry, ragged and harassed, but by men who are well-fed, warm and easy in mind. It is the artist's first duty to his art to achieve that tranquility for himself. Shakespeare tried to achieve it; so did Beethoven, Wagner, Brahms, Ibsen and Balzac. Goethe, Schopenhauer, Schumann and Mendelssohn were born to it. Joseph Conrad, Richard Strauss and Anatole France have got it for themselves in our own day. In the older countries, where competence is far more general and competition is thus more sharp, the thing is often cruelly difficult, and sometimes almost impossible. But in the United States it is absurdly easy, given ordinary luck. Any man with a superior air, the intelligence of a stockbroker, and the resolution of a hat-check girl—in brief, any man who believes in himself enough, and with sufficient cause, to be called a journeyman—can cadge enough money, in this glorious commonwealth of morons, to make life soft for him.

And if a lining for the purse is thus facilely obtainable, given a reasonable prudence and resourcefulness, then balm for the ego is just as unlaboriously got, given ordinary dignity and decency. Simply to exist, indeed, on the plane of a civilized man is to attain, in the Republic, to a distinction that should be enough for all save the most vain; it is even likely to be too much, as the frequent challenges of the Ku Klux Klan, the American Legion, the Anti-Saloon League, and other such vigilance committees of the majority testify. Here is a country in which all political thought and activity are concentrated upon the scramble for jobs—in which the normal politician, whether he be a President or a village road supervisor, is willing to renounce any principle, however precious to him, and to adopt any lunacy, however offensive to him, in order to keep his place at the trough. Go into politics, then, without seeking or wanting office, and at once you are as conspicuous as a red-haired blackamoor—in fact, a great deal more conspicuous, for red-haired blackamoors have been seen, but who has ever seen or heard of an American politician, Democrat or

Republican, Socialist or Liberal, Whig or Tory, who did not
itch for a job? Again, here is a country in which it is an axiom
that a business man shall be a member of a Chamber of Commerce, an admirer of Charles M. Schwab, a reader of the *Saturday Evening Post*, a golfer—in brief, a vegetable. Spend your
hours of escape from *Geschäft* reading Remy de Gourmont
or practicing the violoncello, and the local Sunday newspaper
will infallibly find you out and hymn the marvel—nay, your
banker will summon you to discuss your notes, and your rivals
will spread the report (probably truthful) that you were pro-
German during the war. Yet again, here is a land in which
women rule and men are slaves. Train your women to get your
slippers for you, and your ill fame will match Galileo's or Darwin's. Once more, here is the Paradise of back-slappers, of democrats, of mixers, of go-getters. Maintain ordinary reserve,
and you will arrest instant attention—and have your hand
kissed by multitudes who, despite democracy, have all the inferior man's unquenchable desire to grovel and admire.

Nowhere else in the world is superiority more easily attained
or more eagerly admitted. The chief business of the nation, as
a nation, is the setting up of heroes, mainly bogus. It admired
the literary style of the late Woodrow; it respects the theological passion of Bryan; it venerates J. Pierpont Morgan; it takes
Congress seriously; it would be unutterably shocked by the
proposition (with proof) that a majority of its judges are ig-
noramuses, and that a respectable minority of them are
scoundrels. The manufacture of artificial *Durchlauchten, k.k.
Hoheiten* and even gods goes on feverishly and incessantly; the
will to worship never flags. Ten iron-molders meet in the back-
room of a near-beer saloon, organize a lodge of the Noble and
Mystic Order of American Rosicrucians, and elect a wheel-
wright Supreme Worthy Whimwham; a month later they send
a notice to the local newspaper that they have been greatly
honored by an official visit from that Whimwham, and that
they plan to give him a jeweled fob for his watch-chain. The
chief national heroes—Lincoln, Lee, and so on—cannot remain mere men. The mysticism of the mediæval peasantry gets
into the communal view of them, and they begin to sprout
haloes and wings. As I say, no intrinsic merit—at least, none
commensurate with the mob estimate—is needed to come to

such august dignities. Everything American is a bit amateurish and childish, even the national gods. The most conspicuous and respected American in nearly every field of endeavor, saving only the purely commercial (I exclude even the financial) is a man who would attract little attention in any other country. The leading American critic of literature, after twenty years of diligent exposition of his ideas, has yet to make it clear what he is in favor of, and why. The queen of the *haut monde*, in almost every American city, is a woman who regards Lord Reading as an aristocrat and her superior, and whose grandfather slept in his underclothes. The leading American musical director, if he went to Leipzig, would be put to polishing trombones and copying drum parts. The chief living American military man— the national heir to Frederick, Marlborough, Wellington, Washington and Prince Eugene—is a member of the Elks, and proud of it. The leading American philosopher (now dead, with no successor known to the average pedagogue) spent a lifetime erecting an epistemological defense for the national æsthetic maxim: "I don't know nothing about music, but I know what I like." The most eminent statesman the United States has produced since Lincoln was fooled by Arthur James Balfour, and miscalculated his public support by more than 5,000,000 votes. And the current Chief Magistrate of the nation—its defiant substitute for czar and kaiser—is a small-town printer who, when he wishes to enjoy himself in the Executive Mansion, invites in a homeopathic doctor, a Seventh Day Adventist evangelist, and a couple of moving-picture actresses.

2

All of which may be boiled down to this: that the United States is essentially a commonwealth of third-rate men—that distinction is easy here because the general level of culture, of information, of taste and judgment, of ordinary competence is so low. No sane man, employing an American plumber to repair a leaky drain, would expect him to do it at the first trial, and in precisely the same way no sane man, observing an American Secretary of State in negotiation with Englishmen and Japs, would expect him to come off better than second best. Third-rate men, of course, exist in all countries, but it is only here that they are in full control of the state, and with it of all the national standards. The land was peopled, not by the hardy adventurers of legend, but simply by incompetents who could not get on at home, and the lavishness of nature that they found here, the vast ease with which they could get livings, confirmed and augmented their native incompetence. No American colonist, even in the worst days of the Indian wars, ever had to face such hardships as ground down the peasants of Central Europe during the Hundred Years War, nor even such hardships as oppressed the English lower classes during the century before the Reform Bill of 1832. In most of the colonies, indeed, he seldom saw any Indians at all: the one thing that made life difficult for him was his congenital dunderheadedness. The winning of the West, so rhetorically celebrated in American romance, cost the lives of fewer men than the single battle of Tannenberg, and the victory was much easier and surer. The immigrants who have come in since those early days have been, if anything, of even lower grade than their forerunners. The old notion that the United States is peopled by the offspring of brave, idealistic and liberty loving minorities, who revolted against injustice, bigotry and mediævalism at home—this notion is fast succumbing to the alarmed study that has been given of late to the immigration of recent years. The truth is that the majority of non-Anglo-Saxon immigrants since the Revolution, like the majority of Anglo-Saxon immigrants before the Revolution, have been, not the superior men of their native lands, but the botched and unfit: Irishmen starving to death in Ireland, Germans unable to weather the *Sturm und Drang* of the post-Napoleonic reorganization, Italians weed-grown on exhausted soil, Scandinavians run to all bone and no brain, Jews too incompetent to swindle even the barbarous peasants of Russia, Poland and Roumania. Here and there among the immigrants, of course, there may be a bravo, or even a superman—*e.g.*, the ancestors of Volstead, Ponzi, Jack Dempsey, Schwab, Daugherty, Debs, Pershing—but the average newcomer is, and always has been simply a poor fish.

Nor is there much soundness in the common assumption, so beloved of professional idealists and wind-machines, that the people of America constitute "the youngest of the great peoples." The phrase turns up endlessly; the average newspaper editorial writer would be hamstrung if the Postoffice suddenly interdicted it, as it interdicted "the right to rebel" during the war. What gives it a certain specious plausibility is the fact that the American Republic, compared to a few other existing governments, is relatively young. But the American Republic is not necessarily identical with the American people; they might overturn it to-morrow and set up a monarchy, and still remain the same people. The truth is that, as a distinct nation, they go back fully three hundred years, and that even their government is older than that of most other nations, *e.g.*, France, Italy, Germany, Russia. Moreover, it is absurd to say that there is anything properly describable as youthfulness in the American outlook. It is not that of young men, but that of old men. All the characteristics of senescence are in it: a great distrust of ideas, an habitual timorousness, a harsh fidelity to a few fixed beliefs, a touch of mysticism. The average American is a prude and a Methodist under his skin, and the fact is never more evident than when he is trying to disprove it. His vices are not those of a healthy boy, but those of an ancient paralytic escaped from the *Greisenheim*. If you would penetrate to the causes thereof, simply go down to Ellis Island and look at the next shipload of immigrants. You will not find the spring of youth in their step; you will find the shuffling of exhausted men. From such exhausted men the American stock has sprung. It was easier for them to survive here than it was where they came from, but that ease, though it made them feel stronger, did not actually strengthen them. It left them what they were when they came: weary peasants, eager only for the comfortable security of a pig in a sty. Out of that eagerness has issued many of the noblest manifestations of American *Kultur*: the national hatred of war, the pervasive suspicion of the aims and intents of all other nations, the short way with heretics and disturbers of the peace, the unshakable belief in devils, the implacable hostility to every novel idea and point of view.

All these ways of thinking are the marks of the peasant—more, of the peasant long ground into the mud of his wallow, and determined at last to stay there—the peasant who has definitely renounced any lewd desire he may have ever had to gape at the stars. The habits of mind of this dull, sempiternal *fellah*—the oldest man in Christendom—are, with a few modifications, the habits of mind of the American people. The peasant has a great practical cunning, but he is unable to see any further than the next farm. He likes money and knows how to amass property, but his cultural development is but little above that of the domestic animals. He is intensely and cocksurely moral, but his morality and his self-interest are crudely identical. He is emotional and easy to scare, but his imagination cannot grasp an abstraction. He is a violent nationalist and patriot, but he admires rogues in office and always beats the tax-collector if he can. He has immovable opinions about all the great affairs of state, but nine-tenths of them are sheer imbecilities. He is violently jealous of what he conceives to be his rights, but brutally disregardful of the other fellow's. He is religious, but his religion is wholly devoid of beauty and dignity. This man, whether city or country bred, is the normal Americano—the 100 per cent. Methodist, Odd Fellow, Ku Kluxer, and Know Nothing. He exists in all countries, but here alone he rules—here alone his anthropoid fears and rages are accepted gravely as logical ideas, and dissent from them is punished as a sort of public offense. Around every one of his principal delusions—of the sacredness of democracy, of the feasibility of sumptuary law, of the incurable sinfulness of all other peoples, of the menace of ideas, of the corruption lying in all the arts—there is thrown a barrier of taboos, and woe to the anarchist who seeks to break it down!

The multiplication of such taboos is obviously not characteristic of a culture that is moving from a lower plane to a higher—that is, of a culture still in the full glow of its youth. It is a sign, rather, of a culture that is slipping downhill—one that is reverting to the most primitive standards and ways of thought. The taboo, indeed, is the trade-mark of the savage, and wherever it exists it is a relentless and effective enemy of civilized enlightenment. The savage is the most meticulously moral of men; there is scarcely an act of his daily life that is not conditioned by unyielding prohibitions and obligations, most of them logically unintelligible. The mob-man, a savage set amid civilization, cherishes a code of the same draconian kind. He believes firmly that right and wrong are immovable things—

that they have an actual and unchangeable existence, and that any challenge of them, by word or act, is a crime against society. And with the concept of wrongness, of course, he always confuses the concept of mere differentness—to him the two are indistinguishable. Anything strange is to be combatted; it is of the Devil. The mob-man cannot grasp ideas in their native nakedness. They must be dramatized and personalized for him, and provided with either white wings or forked tails. All discussion of them, to interest him, must take the form of a pursuit and scotching of demons. He cannot think of a heresy without thinking of a heretic to be caught, condemned, and burned.

The Fathers of the Republic, I am convinced, had a great deal more prevision than even their most romantic worshipers give them credit for. They not only sought to create a governmental machine that would be safe from attack without; they also sought to create one that would be safe from attack within. They invented very ingenious devices for holding the mob in check, for protecting the national polity against its transient and illogical rages, for securing the determination of all the larger matters of state to a concealed but none the less real aristocracy. Nothing could have been further from the intent of Washington, Hamilton and even Jefferson than that the official doctrines of the nation, in the year 1922, should be identical with the nonsense heard in the chautauqua, from the evangelical pulpit, and on the stump. But Jackson and his merry men broke through the barbed wires thus so carefully strung, and ever since 1825 *vox populi* has been the true voice of the nation. To-day there is no longer any question of statesmanship, in any real sense, in our politics. The only way to success in American public life lies in flattering and kowtowing to the mob. A candidate for office, even the highest, must either adopt its current manias *en bloc*, or convince it hypocritically that he has done so, while cherishing reservations *in petto*. The result is that only two sorts of men stand any chance whatever of getting into actual control of affairs—first, glorified mob-men who genuinely believe what the mob believes, and secondly, shrewd fellows who are willing to make any sacrifice of conviction and self-respect in order to hold their jobs. One finds perfect examples of the first class in Jackson and Bryan.

One finds hundreds of specimens of the second among the politicians who got themselves so affectingly converted to Prohibition, and who voted and blubbered for it with flasks in their pockets. Even on the highest planes our politics seems to be incurably mountebankish. The same Senators who raised such raucous alarms against the League of Nations voted for the Disarmament Treaty—a far more obvious surrender to English hegemony. And the same Senators who pleaded for the League on the ground that its failure would break the heart of the world were eloquently against the treaty. The few men who maintained a consistent course in both cases, voting either for or against both League and treaty, were denounced by the newspapers as deliberate marplots, and found their constituents rising against them. To such an extent had the public become accustomed to buncombe that simple honesty was incomprehensible to it, and hence abhorrent!

As I have pointed out in a previous work, this dominance of mob ways of thinking, this pollution of the whole intellectual life of the country by the prejudices and emotions of the rabble, goes unchallenged because the old landed aristocracy of the colonial era has been engulfed and almost obliterated by the rise of the industrial system, and no new aristocracy has arisen to take its place, and discharge its highly necessary functions. An upper class, of course, exists, and of late it has tended to increase in power, but it is culturally almost indistinguishable from the mob: it lacks absolutely anything even remotely resembling an aristocratic point of view. One searches in vain for any sign of the true *Junker* spirit in the Vanderbilts, Astors, Morgans, Garys, and other such earls and dukes of the plutocracy; their culture, like their aspiration, remains that of the pawnshop. One searches in vain too, for the aloof air of the don in the official *intelligentsia* of the American universities; they are timorous and orthodox, and constitute a reptile Congregatio de Propaganda Fide to match Bismarck's *Reptilienpresse*. Everywhere else on earth, despite the rise of democracy, an organized minority of aristocrats survives from a more spacious day, and if its personnel has degenerated and its legal powers have decayed it has at least maintained some vestige of its old independence of spirit, and jealously guarded its old right to be heard without risk of penalty. Even in England, where the

peerage has been debauched to the level of a political bap-
tismal fount for Jewish money-lenders and Wesleyan soap-
boilers, there is sanctuary for the old order in the two ancient
universities, and a lingering respect for it in the peasantry. But
in the United States it was paralyzed by Jackson and got its
death blow from Grant, and since then no successor to it has
been evolved. Thus there is no organized force to oppose the
irrational vagaries of the mob. The legislative and executive
arms of the government yield to them without resistance; the
judicial arm has begun to yield almost as supinely, particularly
when they take the form of witch-hunts; outside the official
circle there is no opposition that is even dependably articulate.
The worst excesses go almost without challenge. Discussion,
when it is heard at all, is feeble and superficial, and girt about
by the taboos that I have mentioned. The clatter about the so-
called Ku Klux Klan, two or three years ago, was typical. The
astounding program of this organization was discussed in the
newspapers for months on end, and a committee of Congress
sat in solemn state to investigate it, and yet not a single newspaper or Congressman, so far as I am aware, so much as mentioned the most patent and important fact about it, to wit, that
the Ku Klux was, to all intents and purposes, simply the secular arm of the Methodist Church, and that its methods were
no more than physical projections of the familiar extravagances of the Anti-Saloon League. The intimate relations
between church and Klan, amounting almost to identity, must
have been plain to every intelligent American, and yet the
taboo upon the realistic consideration of ecclesiastical matters
was sufficient to make every public soothsayer disregard it
completely.

I often wonder, indeed, if there would be any intellectual
life at all in the United States if it were not for the steady im-
portation in bulk of ideas from abroad, and particularly, in late
years, from England. What would become of the average
American scholar if he could not borrow wholesale from English scholars? How could an inquisitive youth get beneath the
surface of our politics if it were not for such anatomists as
Bryce? Who would show our statesmen the dotted lines for
their signatures if there were no Balfours and Lloyd-Georges?
How could our young professors formulate æsthetic judgments,

especially in the field of letters, if it were not for such gifted English mentors as Robertson Nicoll, Squire and Clutton-Brock? By what process, finally, would the true style of a visiting card be determined, and the *höflich* manner of eating artichokes, if there were no reports from Mayfair? On certain levels this naïve subservience must needs irritate every self-respecting American, and even dismay him. When he recalls the amazing feats of the English war propagandists between 1914 and 1917—and their even more amazing confessions of method since—he is apt to ask himself quite gravely if he belongs to a free nation or to a crown colony. The thing was done openly, shamelessly, contemptuously, cynically, and yet it was a gigantic success. The office of the American Secretary of State, from the end of Bryan's grotesque incumbency to the end of the Wilson administration, was little more than an antechamber of the British Foreign Office. Dr. Wilson himself, in the conduct of his policy, differed only legally from such colonial premiers as Hughes and Smuts. Even after the United States got into the war it was more swagger for a Young American blood to wear the British uniform than the American uniform. No American ever seriously questions an Englishman or Englishwoman of official or even merely fashionable position at home. Lord Birkenhead was accepted as a gentleman everywhere in the United States; Mrs. Asquith's almost unbelievable imbecilities were heard with hushed fascination; even Lady Astor, an American married to an expatriate German-American turned English viscount, was greeted with solemn effusiveness. During the latter part of 1917, when New York swarmed with British military missions, I observed in *Town Topics* a polite protest against a very significant habit of certain of their gallant members: that of going to dances wearing spurs, and so macerating the frocks and heels of the fawning fair. The protest, it appears, was not voiced by the hosts and hostesses of these singular officers: they would have welcomed their guests in trench boots. It was left to a dubious weekly, and it was made very gingerly.

The spectacle, as I say, has a way of irking the American touched by nationalistic weakness. Ever since the day of Lowell —even since the day of Cooper and Irving—there have been denunciations of it. But however unpleasant it may be, there is no denying that a chain of logical causes lies behind it, and that they are not to be disposed of by objecting to them. The average American of the Anglo-Saxon majority, in truth, is simply a second-rate Englishman, and so it is no wonder that he is spontaneously servile, despite all his democratic denial of superiorities, to what he conceives to be first-rate Englishmen. He corresponds, roughly, to an English Nonconformist of the better-fed variety, and he shows all the familiar characters of the breed. He is truculent and cocksure, and yet he knows how to take off his hat when a bishop of the Establishment passes. He is hot against the dukes, and yet the notice of a concrete duke is a singing in his heart. It seems to me that this inferior Anglo-Saxon is losing his old dominance in the United States—that is, biologically. But he will keep his cultural primacy for a long, long while, in spite of the overwhelming inrush of men of other races, if only because those newcomers are even more clearly inferior than he is. Nine-tenths of the Italians, for example, who have come to these shores in late years have brought no more of the essential culture of Italy with them than so many horned cattle would have brought. If they become civilized at all, settling here, it is the civilization of the Anglo-Saxon majority that they acquire, which is to say, the civilization of the English second table. So with the Germans, the Scandinavians, and even the Jews and Irish. The Germans, taking one with another, are on the cultural level of green-grocers. I have come into contact with a great many of them since 1914, some of them of considerable wealth and even of fashionable pretensions. In the whole lot I can think of but a score or two who could name offhand the principal works of Thomas Mann, Otto Julius Bierbaum, Ludwig Thoma or Hugo von Hofmannsthal. They know much more about Mutt and Jeff than they know about Goethe. The Scandinavians are even worse. The majority of them are mere clods, and they are sucked into the Knights of Pythias, the chautauqua and the Methodist Church almost as soon as they land; it is by no means a mere accident that the national Prohibition Enforcement Act bears the name of a man theoretically of the blood of Gustavus Vasa, Svend of the Forked Beard, and Eric the Red. The Irish in the United States are scarcely touched by the revival of Irish culture, despite their melodramatic concern with

Irish politics. During the war they supplied diligent and dependable agents to the Anglo-Saxon White Terror, and at all times they are very susceptible to political and social bribery. As for the Jews, they change their names to Burton, Thompson and Cecil in order to qualify as true Americans, and when they are accepted and rewarded in the national coin they renounce Moses altogether and get themselves baptized in St. Bartholomew's Church.

Whenever ideas enter the United States from without they come by way of England. What the London *Times* says to-day, about Ukranian politics, the revolt in India, a change of ministry in Italy, the character of the King of Norway, the oil situation in Mesopotamia, will be said week after next by the *Times* of New York, and a month or two later by all the other American newspapers. The extent of this control of American opinion by English news mongers is but little appreciated in the United States, even by professional journalists. Fully four-fifths of all the foreign news that comes to the American newspapers comes through London, and most of the rest is supplied either by Englishmen or by Jews (often American-born) who maintain close relations with the English. During the years 1914–1917 so many English agents got into Germany in the guise of American correspondents—sometimes with the full knowledge of their Anglomaniac American employers—that the Germans, just before the United States entered the war, were considering barring American correspondents from their country altogether. I was in Copenhagen and Basel in 1917, and found both towns—each an important source of war news—full of Jews representing American journals as a side-line to more delicate and confidential work for the English department of press propaganda. Even to-day a very considerable proportion of the American correspondents in Europe are strongly under English influences, and in the Far East the proportion is probably still larger. But these men seldom handle really important news. All that is handled from London, and by trustworthy Britons. Such of it as is not cabled directly to the American newspapers and press associations is later clipped from English newspapers, and printed as bogus letters or cablegrams.

The American papers accept such very dubious stuff, not

chiefly because they are hopelessly stupid or Anglomaniac, but because they find it impossible to engage competent American correspondents. If the native journalists who discuss our domestic politics avoid the fundamentals timorously, then those who venture to discuss foreign politics are scarcely aware of the fundamentals at all. We have simply developed no class of experts in such matters. No man comparable, say to Dr. Dillon, Wickham Steed, Count zu Reventlow or Wilfrid Scawen Blunt exists in the United States. When, in the Summer of 1920, the editors of the Baltimore *Sun* undertook plans to cover the approaching Disarmament Conference at Washington in a comprehensive and intelligent manner, they were forced, willy-nilly, into employing Englishmen to do the work. Such men as Brailsford and Bywater, writing from London, three thousand miles away, were actually better able to interpret the work of the conference than American correspondents on the spot, few of whom were capable of anything beyond the most trivial gossip. During the whole period of the conference not a professional Washington correspondent—the flower of American political journalism—wrote a single article upon the proceedings that got further than their surface aspects. Before the end of the sessions this enforced dependence upon English opinion had an unexpected and significant result. Facing the English and the Japs in an unyielding alliance, the French turned to the American delegation for assistance. The issue specifically before the conference was one on which American self-interest was obviously identical with French self-interest. Nevertheless, the English had such firm grip upon the machinery of news distribution that they were able, in less than a week, to turn American public opinion against the French, and even to set up an active Francophobia. No American, not even any of the American delegates, was able to cope with their propaganda. They not only dominated the conference and pushed through a set of treaties that were extravagantly favorable to England; they even established the doctrine that all opposition to those treaties was immoral!

When Continental ideas, whether in politics, in metaphysics or in the fine arts, penetrate to the United States they nearly always travel by way of England. Emerson did not read Goethe; he read Carlyle. The American people, from the end of 1914 to the end of 1918, did not read first-handed statements of the German case; they read English interpretations of those statements. In London is the clearing house and transformer station. There the latest notions from the mainland are sifted out, carefully diluted with English water, and put into neat packages for the Yankee trade. The English not only get a chance to ameliorate or embellish; they also determine very largely what ideas Americans are to hear of at all. Whatever fails to interest them, or is in any way obnoxious to them, is not likely to cross the ocean. This explains why it is that most literate Americans are so densely ignorant of many Continentals who have been celebrated at home for years, for example, Huysmans, Hartleben, Vaihinger, Merezhkovsky, Keyserling, Snoilsky, Mauthner, Altenberg, Heidenstam, Alfred Kerr. It also explains why they so grossly overestimate various third-raters, laughed at at home, for example, Brieux. These fellows simply happen to interest the English *intelligentsia*, and are thus palmed off upon the gaping colonists of Yankeedom. In the case of Brieux the hocus-pocus was achieved by one man, George Bernard Shaw, a Scotch blue-nose disguised as an Irish patriot and English soothsayer. Shaw, at bottom, has the ideas of a Presbyterian elder, and so the moral frenzy of Brieux enchanted him. Whereupon he retired to his chamber, wrote a flaming Brieuxiad for the American trade, and founded the late vogue of the French Dr. Sylvanus Stall on this side of the ocean.

This wholesale import and export business in Continental fancies is of no little benefit, of course, to the generality of Americans. If it did not exist they would probably never hear of many of the salient Continentals at all, for the obvious incompetence of most of the native and resident introducers of intellectual ambassadors makes them suspicious even of those who, like Boyd and Nathan, are thoroughly competent. To this day there is no American translation of the plays of Ibsen; we use the William Archer Scotch-English translations, most of them atrociously bad, but still better than nothing. So with the works of Nietzsche, Anatole France, Georg Brandes, Turgeniev, Dostoyevsky, Tolstoi, and other moderns after their kind. I can think of but one important exception: the work of Gerhart Hauptmann, done into English by and under the supervision of Ludwig Lewisohn. But even here Lewisohn used a number of English translations of single plays: the English were still ahead of him, though they stopped half way. He is, in any case, a very extraordinary American, and the Department of Justice kept an eye on him during the war. The average American professor is far too dull a fellow to undertake so difficult an enterprise. Even when he sports a German Ph.D. one usually finds on examination that all he knows about modern German literature is that a *Mass* of Hofbräu in Munich used to cost 27 *Pfennig* downstairs and 32 *Pfennig* upstairs. The German universities were formerly very tolerant of foreigners. Many an American, in preparation for professing at Harvard, spent a couple of years roaming from one to the other of them without picking up enough German to read the *Berliner Tageblatt*. Such frauds swarm in all our lesser universities, and many of them, during the war, became eminent authorities upon the crimes of Nietzsche and the errors of Treitschke.

3

In rainy weather, when my old wounds ache and the four humors do battle in my spleen, I often find myself speculating sourly as to the future of the Republic. Native opinion, of course, is to the effect that it will be secure and glorious; the superstition that progress must always be upward and onward will not down; in virulence and popularity it matches the superstition that money can accomplish anything. But this view is not shared by most reflective foreigners, as any one may find out by looking into such a book as Ferdinand Kürnberger's "Der Amerikamüde," Sholom Asch's "America," Ernest von Wolzogen's "Ein Dichter in Dollarica," W. L. George's "Hail, Columbia!", Annalise Schmidt's "Der Amerikanische Mensch" or Sienkiewicz's "After Bread," or by hearkening unto the confidences, if obtainable, of such returned immigrants as Georges Clemenceau, Knut Hamsun, George Santayana, Clemens von Pirquet, John Masefield and Maxim Gorky, and, via the ouija board, Antonin Dvořák, Frank Wedekind and Edwin Klebs. The American Republic, as nations go, has led a safe and easy life, with no serious enemies to menace it, either within or without, and no grim struggle with want. Getting a living here has always been easier than anywhere else in Christendom; getting a secure foothold has been possible to whole classes of men who would have remained submerged in Europe, as the character of our plutocracy, and no less of our *intelligentsia* so brilliantly shows. The American people have never had to face such titanic assults as those suffered by the people of Holland, Poland and half a dozen other little countries; they have not lived with a ring of powerful and unconscionable enemies about them, as the Germans have lived since the Middle Ages; they have not been torn by class wars, as the French, the Spaniards and the Russians have been torn; they have not thrown their strength into far-flung and exhausting colonial enterprises, like the English. All their foreign wars have been fought with foes either too weak to resist them or too heavily engaged elsewhere to make more than a half-hearted attempt. The combats with Mexico and Spain were not wars; they were simply lynchings. Even the Civil War, compared to the larger European conflicts since the invention of gunpowder, was trivial in its character and transient in its effects. The population of the United States, when it began, was about 31,500,000—say 10 per cent. under the population of France in 1914. But after four years of struggle, the number of men killed in action or dead of wounds, in the two armies, came but 200,000—probably little more than a sixth of the total losses of France between 1914 and 1918. Nor was there any very extensive destruction of property. In all save a small area in the North there was none at all, and even in the South only a few towns of any importance were destroyed. The average Northerner passed through the four years scarcely aware, save by report, that a war was going on. In the South the breath of Mars blew more hotly, but even there large numbers of men escaped service, and the general hardship everywhere fell a great deal short of the hardships suffered by the Belgians, the French of the North, the Germans of East Prussia, and the Serbians and Rumanians in the World War. The agonies of the South have been much exaggerated in popular romance; they were probably more severe during Reconstruction, when they were chiefly psychical, than they were during the actual war. Certainly General Robert E. Lee was in a favorable position to estimate the military achievement of the Confederacy. Well, Lee was of the opinion that his army was very badly supported by the civil population, and that its final disaster was largely due to that ineffective support.

Coming down to the time of the World War, one finds precious few signs that the American people, facing an antagonist of equal strength and with both hands free, could be relied upon to give a creditable account of themselves. The American share in that great straggle, in fact, was marked by poltroonery almost as conspicuously as it was marked by knavery. Let us consider briefly what the nation did. For a few months it viewed the struggle idly and unintelligently, as a yokel might stare at a sword-swallower at a county fair. Then, seeing a chance to profit, it undertook with sudden alacrity the ghoulish office of *Kriegslieferant*. One of the contestants being debarred, by the chances of war, from buying, it devoted its whole energies, for two years, to purveying to the other. Meanwhile, it made every effort to aid its customer by lending him the cloak of its neutrality—that is, by demanding all the privileges of a neutral and yet carrying on a stupendous whole-sale effort to promote the war. On the official side, this neutrality was fraudulent from the start, as the revelations of Mr. Tumulty have since demonstrated; popularly it became more and more fraudulent as the debts of the customer contestant piled up, and it became more and more apparent—a fact diligently made known by his partisans—that they would be worthless if he failed to win. Then, in the end, covert aid was transformed into overt aid. And under what gallant conditions! In brief, there stood a nation of 65,000,000 people, which, without effective allies, had just closed two and a half years of homeric conflict by completely defeating an enemy state of 135,000,000 and two lesser ones of more than 10,000,000 together, and now stood at bay before a combination of at least 140,000,000. Upon this battle-scarred and war-weary foe the Republic of 100,000,000 freemen now flung itself, so lifting the odds to 4 to 1. And after a year and a half more of struggle it emerged triumphant—a knightly victor surely!

There is no need to rehearse the astounding and unprecedented swinishness that accompanied this glorious business—

the colossal waste of public money, the savage persecution of all opponents and critics of the war, the open bribery of labor, the half-insane reviling of the enemy, the manufacture of false news, the knavish robbery of enemy civilians, the incessant spy hunts, the floating of public loans by a process of blackmail, the degradation of the Red Cross to partisan uses, the complete abandonment of all decency, decorum and self-respect. The facts must be remembered with shame by every civilized American; lest they be forgotten by the generations of the future I am even now engaged with collaborators upon an exhaustive record of them, in twenty volumes folio. More important to the present purpose are two things that are apt to be overlooked, the first of which is the capital fact that the war was "sold" to the American people, as the phrase has it, not by appealing to their courage, but by appealing to their cowardice —in brief, by adopting the assumption that they were not warlike at all, and certainly not gallant and chivalrous, but merely craven and fearful. The first selling point of the proponents of American participation was the contention that the Germans, with gigantic wars still raging on both fronts, were preparing to invade the United States, burn down all the towns, murder all the men, and carry off all the women—that their victory would bring staggering and irresistible reprisals for the American violation of the duties of a neutral. The second selling point was that the entrance of the United States would end the war almost instantly—that the Germans would be so overwhelmingly outnumbered, in men and guns, that it would be impossible for them to make any effective defense— above all, that it would be impossible for them to inflict any serious damage upon their new foes. Neither argument, it must be plain, showed the slightest belief in the warlike skill and courage of the American people. Both were grounded upon the frank theory that the only way to make the mob fight was to scare it half to death, and then show it a way to fight without risk, to stab a helpless antagonist in the back. And both were mellowed and reënforced by the hint that such a noble assault, beside being safe, would also be extremely profitable— that it would convert very dubious debts into very good debts, and dispose forever of a diligent and dangerous competitor for trade, especially in Latin America. All the idealist nonsense emitted by Dr. Wilson and company was simply icing on the cake. Most of it was abandoned as soon as the bullets began to fly, and the rest consisted simply of meaningless words—the idiotic babbling of a Presbyterian evangelist turned prophet and seer.

The other thing that needs to be remembered is the permanent effect of so dishonest and cowardly business upon the national character, already far too much inclined toward easy ventures and long odds. Somewhere in his diaries Wilfrid Scawen Blunt speaks of the marked debasement that showed itself in the English spirit after the brutal robbery and assassination of the South African Republics. The heroes that the mob followed after Mafeking Day were far inferior to the heroes that it had followed in the days before the war. The English gentleman began to disappear from public life, and in his place appeared a rabble-rousing bounder obviously almost identical with the American professional politician—the Lloyd-George, Chamberlain, F. E. Smith, Isaacs-Reading, Churchill, Bottomley, Northcliffe type. Worse, old ideals went with old heroes. Personal freedom and strict legality, says Blunt, vanished from the English tables of the law, and there was a shift of the social and political center of gravity to a lower plane. Precisely the same effect is now visible in the United States. The overwhelming majority of conscripts went into the army unwillingly, and once there they were debauched by the twin forces of the official propaganda that I have mentioned and a harsh, unintelligent discipline. The first made them almost incapable of soldierly thought and conduct; the second converted them into cringing goose-steppers. The consequences display themselves in the amazing activities of the American Legion, and in the rise of such correlative organizations as the Ku Klux Klan. It is impossible to fit any reasonable concept of the soldierly into the familiar proceedings of the Legion. Its members conduct themselves like a gang of Methodist vice-crusaders on the loose, or a Southern lynching party. They are forever discovering preposterous burglars under the national bed, and they advance to the attack, not gallantly and at fair odds, but cravenly and in overwhelming force. Some of their enterprises, to be set forth at length in the record I have mentioned, have been of almost unbelievable baseness—the mobbing of harmless Socialists, the prohibition of concerts by musicians of enemy nationality, the mutilation of cows designed for shipment abroad to feed starving children, the roughing of women, service as strike-breakers, the persecution of helpless foreigners, regardless of nationality.

During the last few months of the war, when stories of the tyrannical ill-usage of conscripts began to filter back to the United States, it was predicted that they would demand the punishment of the guilty when they got home, and that if it was not promptly forthcoming they would take it into their own hands. It was predicted, too, that they would array themselves against the excesses of Palmer, Burleson and company, and insist upon a restoration of that democratic freedom for which they had theoretically fought. But they actually did none of these things. So far as I know, not a single martinet of a lieutenant or captain has been manhandled by his late victims; the most they have done has been to appeal to Congress for revenge and damages. Nor have they thrown their influence against the mediæval despotism which grew up at home during the war; on the contrary, they have supported it actively, and if it has lessened since 1919 the change has been wrought without their aid and in spite of their opposition. In sum, they show all the stigmata of inferior men whose natural inferiority has been made worse by oppression. Their chief organization is dominated by shrewd ex-officers who operate it to their own ends—politicians in search of jobs, Chamber of Commerce witch-hunters, and other such vermin. It seems to be wholly devoid of patriotism, courage, or sense. Nothing quite resembling it existed in the country before the war, not even in the South. There is nothing like it anywhere else on earth. It is a typical product of two years of heroic effort to arouse and capitalize the worst instincts of the mob, and it symbolizes very dramatically the ill effects of that effort upon the general American character.

Would men so degraded in gallantry and honor, so completely purged of all the military virtues, so submerged in baseness of spirit—would such pitiful caricatures of soldiers offer the necessary resistance to a public enemy who was equal, or perhaps superior in men and resources, and who came on with confidence, daring and resolution—say England supported by

Germany as *Kriegslieferant* and with her inevitable swarms of Continental allies, or Japan with the Asiatic hordes behind her? Against the best opinion of the chatauquas, of Congress and of the patriotic press I presume to doubt it. It seems to me quite certain, indeed, that an American army fairly representing the American people, if it ever meets another army of anything remotely resembling like strength, will be defeated, and that defeat will be indistinguishable from rout. I believe that, at any odds less than two to one, even the exhausted German army of 1918 would have defeated it, and in this view, I think, I am joined by many men whose military judgment is far better than mine—particularly by many French officers. The changes in the American character since the Civil War, due partly to the wearing out of the old Anglo-Saxon stock, inferior to begin with, and partly to the infusion of the worst elements of other stocks, have surely not made for the fostering of the military virtues. The old cool head is gone, and the old dogged way with difficulties. The typical American of to-day has lost all the love of liberty that his forefathers had, and all their distrust of emotion, and pride in self-reliance. He is led no longer by Davy Crocketts; he is led by cheer leaders, press agents, word-mongers, uplifters. I do not believe that such a faint-hearted and inflammatory fellow, shoved into a war demanding every resource of courage, ingenuity and pertinacity, would give a good account of himself. He is fit for lynching-bees and heretic-hunts, but he is not fit for tight corners and desperate odds.

Nevertheless, his docility and pusillanimity may be overestimated, and sometimes I think that they *are* overestimated by his present masters. They assume that there is absolutely no limit to his capacity for being put on and knocked about—that he will submit to any invasion of his freedom and dignity, however outrageous, so long as it is depicted in melodious terms. He permitted the late war to be "sold" to him by the methods of the grind-shop auctioneer. He submitted to conscription without any of the resistance shown by his brother democrats of Canada and Australia. He got no further than academic protests against the brutal usage he had to face in the army. He came home and found Prohibition foisted on him, and contented himself with a few feeble objurgations. He is a pliant slave of capitalism, and ever ready to help it put down fellow-slaves who venture to revolt. But this very weakness, this very credulity and poverty of spirit, on some easily conceivable to-morrow, may convert him into a rebel of a peculiarly insane kind, and so beset the Republic from within with difficulties quite as formidable as those which threaten to afflict it from without. What Mr. James N. Wood calls the corsair of democracy —that is, the professional mob-master, the merchant of delusions, the pumper-up of popular fears and rages—is still content to work for capitalism, and capitalism knows how to reward him to his taste. He is the eloquent statesman, the patriotic editor, the fount of inspiration, the prancing milch-cow of optimism. He becomes public leader, Governor, Senator, President. He is Billy Sunday, Cyrus K. Curtis, Dr. Frank Crane, Charles E. Hughes, Taft, Wilson, Cal Coolidge, General Wood, Harding. His, perhaps, is the best of trades under democracy—but it has its temptations! Let us try to picture a master corsair, thoroughly adept at pulling the mob nose, who suddenly bethought himself of that Pepin the Short who found himself mayor of the palace and made himself King of the Franks. There were lightnings along that horizon in the days of Roosevelt; there were thunder growls when Bryan emerged from the Nebraska steppes. On some great day of fate, as yet unrevealed by the gods, such a professor of the central democratic science may throw off his employers and set up a business for himself. When that day comes there will be plenty of excuse for black type on the front pages of the newspapers.

I incline to think that military disaster will give him his inspiration and his opportunity—that he will take the form, so dear to democracies, of a man on horseback. The chances are bad to-day simply because the mob is relatively comfortable—because capitalism has been able to give it relative ease and plenty of food in return for its docility. Genuine poverty is very rare in the United States, and actual hardship is almost unknown. There are times when the proletariat is short of phonograph records, silk shirts and movie tickets, but there are very few times when it is short of nourishment. Even during the most severe business depression, with hundreds of thousands out of work, most of these apparent sufferers, if they are willing, are able to get livings outside their trades. The cities may be choked with idle men, but the country is nearly always short of labor. And if all other resources fail, there are always public agencies to feed the hungry: capitalism is careful to keep them from despair. No American knows what it means to live as millions of Europeans lived during the war and have lived, in some places, since: with the loaves of the baker reduced to half size and no meat at all in the meatshop. But the time may come and it may not be far off. A national military disaster would disorganize all industry in the United States, already sufficiently wasteful and chaotic, and introduce the American people, for the first time in their history, to genuine want—and capital would be unable to relieve them. The day of such disaster will bring the savior foreordained. The slaves will follow him, their eyes fixed ecstatically upon the newest New Jerusalem. Men bred to respond automatically to shibboleths will respond to this worst and most insane one. Bolshevism, said General Foch, is a disease of defeated nations.

But do not misunderstand me: I predict no revolution in the grand manner, no melodramatic collapse of capitalism, no repetition of what has gone on in Russia. The American proletarian is not brave and romantic enough for that; to do him simple justice, he is not silly enough. Capitalism, in the long run, will win in the United States, if only for the reason that every American hopes to be a capitalist before he dies. Its roots go down to the deepest, darkest levels of the national soil; in all its characters, and particularly in its antipathy to the dreams of man, it is thoroughly American. To-day it seems to be immovably secure, given continued peace and plenty, and not all the demagogues in the land, consecrating themselves desperately to the one holy purpose, could shake it. Only a cataclysm will ever do that. But is a cataclysm conceivable? Isn't the United States the richest nation ever heard of in history, and isn't it a fact that modern wars are won by money? It is not a fact. Wars are won to-day, as in Napoleon's day, by the largest battalions, and the largest battalions, in the next great struggle, may not be on the side of the Republic. The usurious profits it wrung from the last war are as tempting as negotiable securities hung on the wash-line, as pre-Prohibition Scotch stored in open cellars. Its knavish ways with friends and foes alike have left it only foes. It is plunging ill-equipped into a competition for a living in the world that will be to the death. And the late Disarmament Conference left it almost hamstrung. Before the conference it had the Pacific in its grip, and with the Pacific in its grip it might have parleyed for a fair half of the Atlantic. But when the Japs and the English had finished their operations upon the Feather Duster, Popinjay Lodge, Master-Mind Root, Vacuum Underwood, young Teddy Roosevelt and the rest of their so-willing dupes there was apparent a baleful change. The Republic is extremely insecure to-day on both fronts, and it will be more insecure to-morrow. And it has no friends.

However, as I say, I do not fear for capitalism. It will weather the storm, and no doubt it will be the stronger for it afterward. The inferior man hates it, but there is too much envy mixed with his hatred, in the land of the theoretically free, for him to want to destroy it utterly, or even to wound it incurably. He struggles against it now, but always wistfully, always with a sneaking respect. On the day of Armageddon he may attempt a more violent onslaught. But in the long run he will be beaten. In the long run the corsairs will sell him out, and hand him over to his enemy. Perhaps—who knows?—the combat may raise that enemy to genuine strength and dignity. Out of it may come the superman.

4

All the while I have been forgetting the third of my reasons for remaining so faithful a citizen of the Federation, despite all the lascivious inducements from expatriates to follow them beyond the seas, and all the surly suggestions from patriots that I succumb. It is the reason which grows out of my mediæval but unashamed taste for the bizarre and indelicate, my congenital weakness for comedy of the grosser varieties. The United States, to my eye, is incomparably the greatest show on earth. It is a show which avoids diligently all the kinds of clowning which tire me most quickly—for example, royal ceremonials, the tedious hocus-pocus of *haut politique*, the taking of politics seriously—and lays chief stress upon the kinds which delight me unceasingly—for example, the ribald combats of demagogues, the exquisitely ingenious operations of master rogues, the pursuit of witches and heretics, the desperate struggles of inferior men to claw their way into Heaven. We have clowns in constant practice among us who are as far above the clowns of any other great state as a Jack Dempsey is above a paralytic—and not a few dozen or score of them, but whole droves and herds. Human enterprises which, in all other Christian countries, are resigned despairingly to an incurable dullness—things that seem devoid of exhilarating amusement by their very nature—are here lifted to such vast heights of buffoonery that contemplating them strains the midriff almost to breaking. I cite an example: the worship of God. Everywhere else on earth it is carried on in a solemn and dispiriting manner; in England, of course, the bishops are obscene, but the average man seldom gets a fair chance to laugh at them and enjoy them. Now come home. Here we not only have bishops who are enormously more obscene than even the most gifted of the English bishops; we have also a huge force of lesser specialists in ecclesiastical mountebankery—tin-horn Loyolas, Savonarolas and Xaviers of a hundred fantastic rites, each performing untiringly and each full of a grotesque and illimitable whimsicality. Every American town, however small, has one of its own: a holy clerk with so fine a talent for introducing the arts of jazz into the salvation of the damned that his performance takes on all the gaudiness of a four-ring circus, and the bald announcement that he will raid Hell on such and such a night is enough to empty all the town blind-pigs and bordellos and pack his sanctuary to the doors. And to aid him and inspire him there are traveling experts to whom he stands in the relation of a wart to the Matterhorn—stupendous masters of theological imbecility, contrivers of doctrines utterly preposterous, heirs to the Joseph Smith, Mother Eddy and John Alexander Dowie tradition—Bryan, Sunday, and their like. These are the eminences of the American Sacred College. I delight in them. Their proceedings make me a happier American.

Turn, now, to politics. Consider, for example, a campaign for the Presidency. Would it be possible to imagine anything more uproariously idiotic—a deafening, nerve-wracking battle to the death between Tweedledum and Tweedledee, Harlequin and Sganarelle, Gobbo and Dr. Cook—the unspeakable, with fearful snorts, gradually swallowing the inconceivable? I defy any one to match it elsewhere on this earth. In other lands, at worst, there are at least intelligible issues, coherent ideas, salient personalities. Somebody says something, and somebody replies. But what did Harding say in 1920, and what did Cox reply? Who was Harding, anyhow, and who was Cox? Here, having perfected democracy, we lift the whole combat to symbolism, to transcendentalism, to metaphysics. Here we load a pair of palpably tin cannon with blank cartridges charged with talcum powder, and so let fly. Here one may howl over the show without any uneasy reminder that it is serious, and that some one may be hurt. I hold that this elevation of politics to the plane of undiluted comedy is peculiarly American, that nowhere else on this disreputable ball has the art of the sham-battle been developed to such fineness. Two experiences are in point. During the Harding-Cox combat of bladders an article of mine, dealing with some of its more melodramatic phases, was translated into German and reprinted by a Berlin paper. At the head of it the editor was careful to insert a preface explaining to his readers, but recently delivered to democracy, that such contests were not taken seriously by intelligent Americans, and warning them solemnly against getting into sweats over politics. At about the same time I had dinner with an Englishman. From cocktails to bromo seltzer he bewailed the political lassitude of the English populace—its growing indifference to the whole partisan harlequinade. Here were two typical foreign attitudes: the Germans were in danger of making politics too harsh and implacable, and the English were in danger of forgetting politics altogether. Both attitudes, it must be plain, make for bad shows. Observing a German campaign, one is uncomfortably harassed and stirred up; observing an English campaign (at least in times of peace), one falls asleep. In the United States the thing is done better. Here politics is purged of all menace, all sinister quality, all genuine significance, and stuffed with such gorgeous humors, such inordinate farce that one comes to the end of a campaign with one's ribs loose, and ready for "King Lear," or a hanging, or a course of medical journals.

But feeling better for the laugh. *Ridi si sapis*, said Martial. Mirth is necessary to wisdom, to comfort, above all, to happiness. Well, here is the land of mirth, as Germany is the land of metaphysics and France is the land of fornication. Here the buffoonery never stops. What could be more delightful than the endless struggle of the Puritan to make the joy of the minority unlawful and impossible? The effort is itself a greater joy to one standing on the side-lines than any or all of the carnal joys that it combats. Always, when I contemplate an uplifter at his hopeless business, I recall a scene in an old-time burlesque show, witnessed for hire in my days as a dramatic critic. A chorus girl executed a fall upon the stage, and Rudolph Krausemeyer, the Swiss comedian, rushed to her aid. As he stooped painfully to succor her, Irving Rabinovitz, the Zionist comedian, fetched him a fearful clout across the cofferdam with a slap-stick. So the uplifter, the soul-saver, the Americanizer, striving to make the Republic fit for Y.M.C.A. secretaries. He is the eternal American, ever moved by the best of intentions, ever running *à la* Krausemeyer to the rescue of virtue, and ever getting his pantaloons fanned by the Devil. I am naturally sinful, and such spectacles caress me. If the slap-stick were a sash-weight the show would be cruel, and I'd probably complain to the *Polizei*. As it is, I know that the uplifter is not really hurt, but simply shocked. The blow, in fact, does him good, for it helps to get him into Heaven, as exegetes prove from Matthew v, 11: *Heureux serez-vous, lorsqu'on vous outragera, qu'on vous persécutera*, and so on. As for me, it makes me a more contented man, and hence a better citizen. One man prefers the Republic because it pays better wages than Bulgaria. Another because it has laws to keep him sober and his daughter chaste. Another because the Woolworth Building is higher than the cathedral at Chartres. Another because, living here, he can read the New York *Evening Journal*. Another because there is a warrant out for him somewhere else. Me, I like it because it amuses me to my taste. I never get tired of the show. It is worth every cent it costs.

That cost, it seems to me is very moderate. Taxes in the United States are not actually high. I figure, for example, that my private share of the expense of maintaining the Hon. Mr. Harding in the White House this year will work out to less than 80 cents. Try to think of better sport for the money: in New York it has been estimated that it costs $8 to get comfortably tight, and $17.50, on an average, to pinch a girl's arm.

The United States Senate will cost me perhaps $11 for the year, but against that expense set the subscription price of the *Congressional Record*, about $15, which, as a journalist, I receive for nothing. For $4 less than nothing I am thus entertained as Solomon never was by his hooch dancers. Col. George Brinton McClellan Harvey costs me but 25 cents a year; I get Nicholas Murray Butler free. Finally, there is young Teddy Roosevelt, the naval expert. Teddy costs me, as I work it out, about 11 cents a year, or less than a cent a month. More, he entertains me doubly for the money, first as naval expert, and secondly as a walking *attentat* upon democracy, a devastating proof that there is nothing, after all, in that superstition. We Americans subscribe to the doctrine of human equality—and the Rooseveltii reduce it to an absurdity as brilliantly as the sons of Veit Bach. Where is your equal opportunity now? Here in this Eden of clowns, with the highest rewards of clowning theoretically open to every poor boy—here in the very citadel of democracy we found and cherish a clown *dynasty*!

II.

Huneker: A Memory

THERE was a stimulating aliveness about him always, an air of living eagerly and a bit recklessly, a sort of defiant resiliency. In his very frame and form something provocative showed itself—an insolent singularity, obvious to even the most careless glance. That Caligulan profile of his was more than simply unusual in a free republic, consecrated to good works; to a respectable American, encountering it in the lobby of the Metropolitan or in the smoke-room of a *Doppelschrauben-schnellpostdampfer*, it must have suggested inevitably the dark enterprises and illicit metaphysics of a Heliogabalus. More, there was always something rakish and defiant about his hat—it was too white, or it curled in the wrong way, or a feather peeped from the band—, and a hint of antinomianism in his cravat. Yet more, he ran to exotic tastes in eating and drinking, preferring occult goulashes and risi-bisi to honest American steaks, and great floods of Pilsner to the harsh beverages of God-fearing men. Finally, there was his talk, that cataract of sublime trivialities: gossip lifted to the plane of the gods, the unmentionable bedizened with an astounding importance, and even profundity.

In his early days, when he performed the tonal and carnal prodigies that he liked to talk of afterward, I was at nurse, and too young to have any traffic with him. When I encountered him at last he was in the high flush of the middle years, and had already become a tradition in the little world that critics inhabit. We sat down to luncheon at one o'clock; I think it must have been at Lüchow's, his favorite refuge and rostrum to the end. At six, when I had to go, the waiter was hauling in his tenth (or was it twentieth?) *Seidel* of Pilsner, and he was bringing to a close *prestissimo* the most amazing monologue that these ears (up to that time) had ever funnelled into this consciousness. What a stew, indeed! Berlioz and the question of the clang-tint of the viola, the psychopathological causes of the suicide of Tschaikowsky, why Nietzsche had to leave Sils

Maria between days in 1887, the echoes of Flaubert in Joseph
Conrad (then but newly dawned), the precise topography of
the warts of Liszt, George Bernard Shaw's heroic but vain
struggles to throw off Presbyterianism, how Frau Cosima saved
Wagner from the libidinous Swedish baroness, what to drink
when playing Chopin, what Cézanne thought of his disciples,
the defects in the structure of "Sister Carrie," Anton Seidl and
the musical union, the complex love affairs of Gounod, the early
days of David Belasco, the varying talents and idiosyncrasies of
Lillian Russell's earlier husbands, whether a girl educated at
Vassar could ever really learn to love, the exact composition of
chicken paprika, the correct tempo of the Vienna waltz, the
style of William Dean Howells, what George Moore said
about German bathrooms, the true inwardness of the affair
between D'Annunzio and Duse, the origin of the theory that
all oboe players are crazy, why Löwenbräu survived exporta-
tion better than Hofbräu, Ibsen's loathing of Norwegians, the
best remedy for Rhine wine *Katzenjammer*, how to play
Brahms, the degeneration of the Bal Bullier, the sheer physical
impossibility of getting Dvořák drunk, the genuine last words
of Walt Whitman. . . .

I left in a sort of fever, and it was a couple of days later
before I began to sort out my impressions, and formulate a
coherent image. Was the man allusive in his books—so allusive that popular report credited him with the actual manufacture of authorities? Then he was ten times as allusive in his
discourse—a veritable geyser of unfamiliar names, shocking
epigrams in strange tongues, unearthly philosophies out of the
backwaters of Scandinavia, Transylvania, Bulgaria, the Basque
country, the Ukraine. And did he, in his criticism, pass facilely
from the author to the man, and from the man to his wife, and
to the wives of his friends? Then at the *Biertisch* he began long
beyond the point where the last honest wife gives up the
ghost, and so, full tilt, ran into such complexities of adultery
that a plain sinner could scarcely follow him. I try to give you,
ineptly and grotesquely, some notion of the talk of the man,
but I must fail inevitably. It was, in brief, chaos, and chaos cannot be described. But it was chaos made to gleam and corrus-
cate with every device of the seven arts—chaos drenched in all
the colors imaginable, chaos scored for an orchestra which

made the great band of Berlioz seem like a fife and drum corps. One night a few months before the war, I sat in the Paris Opera House listening to the first performance of Richard Strauss's "Josef's Legend," with Strauss himself conducting. On the stage there was a riot of hues that swung the eyes 'round and 'round in a crazy mazurka; in the orchestra there were such volleys and explosions of tone that the ears (I fall into a Hunekeran trope) began to go pale and clammy with surgical shock. Suddenly, above all the uproar, a piccolo launched into a new and saucy tune—in an unrelated key! . . . Instantly and quite naturally, I thought of the incomparable James. When he gave a show at Lüchow's he never forgot that anarchistic passage for the piccolo.

I observe a tendency since his death to estimate him in terms of the content of his books. Even Frank Harris, who certainly should know better, goes there for the facts about him. Nothing could do him worse injustice. In those books, of course, there is a great deal of perfectly sound stuff; the wonder is, in truth, that so much of it holds up so well to-day—for example, the essays on Strauss, on Brahms and on Nietzsche, and the whole volume on Chopin. But the real Huneker never got himself formally between covers, if one forgets "Old Fogy" and parts of "Painted Veils." The volumes of his regular canon are made up, in the main, of articles written for the more intellectual magazines and newspapers of their era, and they are full of a conscious striving to qualify for respectable company. Huneker, always curiously modest, never got over the notion that it was a singular honor for a man such as he— a mere diurnal scribbler, innocent of academic robes—to be published by so austere a publisher as Scribner. More than once, anchored at the beer-table, we discussed the matter at length, I always arguing that all the honor was enjoyed by Scribner. But Huneker, I believe in all sincerity, would not have it so, any more than he would have it that he was a better music critic than his two colleagues, the pedantic Krehbiel and the nonsensical Finck. This illogical modesty, of course, had its limits; it made him cautious about expressing himself, but it seldom led him into downright assumptions of false personality. Nowhere in all his books will you find him doing the things that every right-thinking Anglo-Saxon critic is supposed to do—the Middleton Murry, Paul Elmer More, Clutton-Brock sort of puerility—solemn essays on Coleridge and Addison, abysmal discussions of the relative merits of Schumann and Mendelssohn, horrible treatises upon the relations of Goethe to the Romantic Movement, dull scratchings in a hundred such exhausted and sterile fields. Such enterprises were not for Hunker; he kept himself out of that black coat. But I am convinced that he always had his own raiment pressed carefully before he left Lüchow's for the temple of Athene—and maybe changed cravats, and put on a boiled shirt, and took the feather out of his hat. The simon-pure Huneker, the Huneker who was the true essence and prime motor of the more courtly Huneker—remained behind. This real Huneker survives in conversations that still haunt the rafters of the beer-halls of two continents, and in a vast mass of newspaper impromptus, thrown off too hastily to be reduced to complete decorum, and in two books that stand outside the official canon, and yet contain the man himself as not even "Iconoclasts" or the Chopin book contains him, to wit, the "Old Fogy" aforesaid and the "Painted Veils" of his last year. Both were published, so to speak, out of the back door—the former by a music publisher in Philadelphia and the latter in a small and expensive edition for the admittedly damned. There is a chapter in "Painted Veils" that is Huneker to every last hitch of the shoulders and twinkle of the eye—the chapter in which the hero soliloquizes on art, life, immortality, and women—especially women. And there are half a dozen chapters in "Old Fogy"—superficially buffoonery, but how penetrating! how gorgeously flavored! how learned!—that come completely up to the same high specification. If I had to choose one Huneker book and give up all the others, I'd choose "Old Fogy" instantly. In it Huneker is utterly himself. In it the last trace of the pedagogue vanishes. Art is no longer, even by implication, a device for improving the mind. It is wholly a magnificent adventure.

That notion of it is what Huneker brought into American criticism, and it is for that bringing that he will be remembered. No other critic of his generation had a tenth of his influence. Almost single-handed he overthrew the æsthetic theory that had flourished in the United States since the death of Poe, and set up an utterly contrary æsthetic theory in its place. If the younger men of to-day have emancipated themselves from the Puritan æsthetic, if the schoolmaster is now palpably on the defensive, and no longer the unchallenged assassin of the fine arts that he once was, if he has already begun to compromise somewhat absurdly with new and sounder ideas, and even to lift his voice in artificial hosannahs, then Huneker certainly deserves all the credit for the change. What he brought back from Paris was precisely the thing that was most suspected in the America of those days: the capacity for gusto. Huneker had that capacity in a degree unmatched by any other critic. When his soul went adventuring among masterpieces it did not go in Sunday broadcloth; it went with vine leaves in its hair. The rest of the appraisers and criers-up— even Howells, with all his humor—could never quite rid themselves of the professorial manner. When they praised it was always with some hint of ethical, or, at all events, of cultural purpose; when they condemned that purpose was even plainer. The arts, to them, constituted a sort of school for the psyche; their aim was to discipline and mellow the spirit. But to Huneker their one aim was always to make the spirit glad—to set it, in Nietzsche's phrase, to dancing with arms and legs. He had absolutely no feeling for extra-æsthetic valuations. If a work of art that stood before him was honest, if it was original, if it was beautiful and thoroughly alive, then he was for it to his last corpuscle. What if it violated all the accepted canons? Then let the accepted canons go hang! What if it lacked all purpose to improve and lift up? Then so much the better! What if it shocked all right-feeling men, and made them blush and tremble? Then damn all men of right feeling forevermore.

With this ethical atheism, so strange in the United States and so abhorrent to most Americans, there went something that was probably also part of the loot of Paris: an insatiable curiosity about the artist as man. This curiosity was responsible for two of Huneker's salient characters: his habit of mixing even the most serious criticism with cynical and often scandalous gossip, and his pervasive foreignness. I believe that it is almost literally true to say that he could never quite make up his mind about a new symphony until he had seen the composer's mistress, or at all events a good photograph of her. He

thought of Wagner, not alone in terms of melody and harmony, but also in terms of the Tribschen idyl and the Bayreuth
tragi-comedy. Go through his books and you will see how
often he was fascinated by mere eccentricity of personality. I
doubt that even Huysmans, had he been a respectable French
Huguenot, would have interested him; certainly his enthusiasm for Verlaine, Villiers de l'Isle Adam and other such fantastic fish was centered upon the men quite as much as upon the
artists. His foreignness, so often urged against him by defenders
of the national tradition, was grounded largely on the fact that
such eccentric personalities were rare in the Republic—rare,
and well watched by the *Polizei*. When one bobbed up, he was
alert at once—even though the newcomer was only a Roosevelt. The rest of the American people he dismissed as a horde
of slaves, goose-steppers, cads, Methodists; he could not imagine one of them be coming a first-rate artist, save by a miracle.
Even the American executant was under his suspicion, for he
knew very well that playing the fiddle was a great deal more
than scraping four strings of copper and catgut with a switch
from a horse's tail. What he asked himself was how a man
could play Bach decently, and then, after playing, go from the
hall to a soda-fountain, or a political meeting, or a lecture at
the Harvard Club. Overseas there was a better air for artists,
and overseas Huneker looked for them.

These fundamental theories of his, of course, had their defects. They were a bit too simple, and often very much too
hospitable. Huneker, clinging to them, certainly did his share
of whooping for the sort of revolutionist who is here to-day
and gone tomorrow; he was fugleman, in his time, for more
than one cause that was lost almost as soon as it was stated.
More, his prejudices made him somewhat anæsthetic, at times,
to the new men who were not brilliant in color but respectably
drab, and who tried to do their work within the law. Particularly in his later years, when the old gusto began to die out and
all that remained of it was habit, he was apt to go chasing after
strange birds and so miss seeing the elephants go by. I could put
together a very pretty list of frauds that he praised. I could
concoct another list of genuine *arrivés* that he overlooked.
But all that is merely saying that there were human limits to
him; the professors, on their side, have sinned far worse, and in

both directions. Looking back over the whole of his work, one must needs be amazed by the general soundness of his judgments. He discerned, in the main, what was good and he described it in terms that were seldom bettered afterward. His successive heroes, always under fire when he first championed them, almost invariably moved to secure ground and became solid men, challenged by no one save fools—Ibsen, Nietzsche, Brahms, Strauss, Cézanne, Stirner, Synge, the Russian composers, the Russian novelists. He did for this Western world what Georg Brandes was doing for Continental Europe—sorting out the new comers with sharp eyes, and giving mighty lifts to those who deserved it. Brandes did it in terms of the old academic bombast; he was never more the professor than when he was arguing for some hobgoblin of the professors. But Huneker did it with verve and grace; he made it, not schoolmastering, but a glorious deliverance from schoolmastering. As I say, his influence was enormous. The fine arts, at his touch, shed all their Anglo-American lugubriousness, and became provocative and joyous. The spirit of senility got out of them and the spirit of youth got into them. His criticism, for all its French basis, was thoroughly American—vastly more American, in fact, than the New England ponderosity that it displaced. Though he was an Easterner and a cockney of the cockneys, he picked up some of the Western spaciousness that showed itself in Mark Twain. And all the young men followed him.

A good many of them, I daresay, followed him so ardently that they got a good distance ahead of him, and often, perhaps, embarrassed him by taking his name in vain. For all his enterprise and iconoclasm, indeed, there was not much of the Berserker in him, and his floutings of the national æsthetic tradition seldom took the form of forthright challenges. Here the strange modesty that I have mentioned always stayed him as a like weakness stayed Mark Twain. He could never quite rid himself of the feeling that he was no more than an amateur among the gaudy doctors who roared in the reviews, and that it would be unseemly for him to forget their authority. I have a notion that this feeling was born in the days when he stood almost alone, with the whole faculty grouped in a pained circle around him. He was then too miserable a worm to be noticed at all. Later on, gaining importance, he was lectured somewhat severely for his violation of decorum; in England even Max Beerbohm made an idiotic assault upon him. It was the Germans and the French, in fact, who first praised him intelligently —and these friends were too far away to help a timorous man in a row at home. This sensation of isolation and littleness, I suppose, explains his fidelity to the newspapers, and the otherwise inexplicable joy that he always took in his forgotten work for the *Musical Courier*, in his day a very dubious journal. In such waters he felt at ease. There he could disport without thought of the dignity of publishers and the eagle eyes of campus reviewers. Some of the connections that he formed were full of an ironical inappropriateness. His discomforts in his *Puck* days showed themselves in the feebleness of his work; when he served the *Times* he was as well placed as a Cabell at a colored ball. Perhaps the *Sun*, in the years before it was munseyized, offered him the best berth that he ever had, save it were his old one on *Mlle. New York*. But whatever the flag, he served it loyally, and got a lot of fun out of the business. He liked the pressure of newspaper work; he liked the associations that it involved, the gabble in the press-room of the Opera House, the exchanges of news and gossip; above all, he liked the relative ease of the intellectual harness. In a newspaper article he could say whatever happened to pop into his mind, and if it looked thin the next day, then there was, after all, no harm done. But when he sat down to write a book—or rather to compile it, for all of his volumes were reworked magazine (and sometimes newspaper) articles—he became self-conscious, and so knew uneasiness. The tightness of his style, its one salient defect, was probably the result of this weakness. The corrected clippings that constituted most of his manuscripts are so beladen with revisions and rerevisions that they are almost indecipherable.

Thus the growth of Huneker's celebrity in his later years filled him with wonder, and never quite convinced him. He was certainly wholly free from any desire to gather disciples about him and found a school. There was, of course, some pride of authorship in him, and he liked to know that his books were read and admired; in particular, he was pleased by their translation into German and Czech. But it seemed to me that he shrank from the bellicosity that so often got into praise of them—that he disliked being set up as the opponent and superior of the professors whom he always vaguely respected and the rival newspaper critics whose friendship he esteemed far above their professional admiration, or even respect. I could never draw him into a discussion of these rivals, save perhaps a discussion of their historic feats at beer-guzzling. He wrote vastly better than any of them and knew far more about the arts than most of them, and he was undoubtedly aware of it in his heart, but it embarrassed him to hear this superiority put into plain terms. His intense gregariousness probably accounted for part of this reluctance to pit himself against them; he could not imagine a world without a great deal of easy comradeship in it, and much casual slapping of backs. But under it all was the chronic underestimation of himself that I have discussed—his fear that he had spread himself over too many arts, and that his equipment was thus defective in every one of them. "Steeplejack" is full of this apologetic timidity. In its very title, as he explains it, there is a confession of inferiority that is almost maudlin: "Life has been the Barmecide's feast to me," and so on. In the book itself he constantly takes refuge in triviality from the harsh challenges of critical parties, and as constantly avoids facts that would shock the Philistines. One might reasonably assume, reading it from end to end, that his early days in Paris were spent in the fashion of a Y.M.C.A. secretary. A few drinking bouts, of course, and a love affair in the manner of Dubuque, Iowa—but where are the wenches?

More than once, indeed, the book sinks to downright equivocation—for example, in the Roosevelt episodes. Certainly no one who knew Huneker in life will ever argue seriously that he was deceived by the Roosevelt buncombe, or that his view of life was at all comparable to that of the great demagogue. He stood, in fact, at the opposite pole. He saw the world, not as a moral show, but as a sort of glorified Follies. He was absolutely devoid of that obsession with the problem of conduct which was Roosevelt's main virtue in the eyes of a stupid and superstitious people. More, he was wholly against Roosevelt on many concrete issues—the race suicide banality, the Panama swindle, the war. He was far too much the realist to believe in the American case, either before or after 1917, and the manner in which it was urged, by Roosevelt and others, violated his notions of truth, honor and decency. I assume nothing here; I simply record what he told me himself. Nevertheless, the sheer notoriety of the Rough Rider—his picturesque personality and talent as a mountebank—had its effect on Huneker, and so he was a bit flattered when he was summoned to Oyster Bay, and there accepted gravely the nonsense that was poured into his ear, and even repeated some of it without a cackle in his book. To say that he actually believed in it would be to libel him. It was precisely such hollow tosh that he stood against in his rôle of critic of art and life; it was by exposing its hollowness that he lifted himself above the general. The same weakness induced him to accept membership in the National Institute of Arts and Letters. The offer of it to a man of his age and attainments, after he had been passed over year after year in favor of all sorts of cheapjack novelists and tenth-rate compilers of college textbooks, was intrinsically insulting; it was almost as if the Musical Union had offered to admit a Brahms. But with the insult went a certain gage of respectability, a certain formal forgiveness for old frivolities, a certain abatement of old doubts and self-questionings and so Huneker accepted. Later on, reviewing the episode in his own mind, he found it the spring of doubts that were even more uncomfortable. His last letter to me was devoted to the matter. He was by then eager to maintain that he had got in by a process only partly under his control, and that, being in, he could discover no decorous way of getting out.

But perhaps I devote too much space to the elements in the man that worked against his own free development. They were, after all, grounded upon qualities that are certainly not to be deprecated—modesty, good-will to his fellow-men, a fine sense of team-work, a distaste for acrimonious and useless strife. These qualities gave him great charm. He was not only humorous; he was also good-humored; even when the crushing discomforts of his last illness were upon him his amiability never faltered. And in addition to humor there was wit, a far rarer thing. His most casual talk was full of this wit, and it bathed everything that he discussed in a new and brilliant light. I have never encountered a man who was further removed from dullness; it seemed a literal impossibility for him to open his mouth without discharging some word or phrase that arrested the attention and stuck in the memory. And under it all, giving an extraordinary quality to the verbal fireworks, there was a solid and apparently illimitable learning. The man knew as much as forty average men, and his knowledge was well-ordered and instantly available. He had read everything and had seen everything and heard everything, and nothing that he had ever read or seen or heard quite passed out of his mind.

Here, in three words, was the main virtue of his criticism—its gigantic richness. It had the dazzling charm of an ornate and intricate design, a blazing fabric of fine silks. It was no mere pontifical statement of one man's reactions to a set of ideas; it was a sort of essence of the reactions of many men—of all the men, in fact, worth hearing. Huneker discarded their scaffolding, their ifs and whereases, and presented only what was important and arresting in their conclusions. It was never a mere *pastiche*; the selection was made delicately, discreetly, with almost unerring taste and judgment. And in the summing up there was always the clearest possible statement of the whole matter. What finally emerged was a body of doctrine that came, I believe, very close to the truth. Into an assembly of national critics who had long wallowed in dogmatic puerilities, Huneker entered with a taste infinitely surer and more civilized, a learning infinitely greater, and an address infinitely more engaging. No man was less the reformer by inclination, and yet he became a reformer beyond compare. He emancipated criticism in America from its old slavery to stupidity, and with it he emancipated all the arts themselves.

III.

Footnote on Criticism

NEARLY all the discussions of criticism that I am acquainted with start off with a false assumption, to wit, that the primary motive of the critic, the impulse which makes a critic of him instead of, say, a politician, or a stockbroker, is pedagogical—that he writes because he is possessed by a passion to advance the enlightenment, to put down error and wrong, to disseminate some specific doctrine: psychological, epistemological, historical, or æsthetic. This is true, it seems to me, only of bad critics, and its degree of truth increases in direct ratio to their badness. The motive of the critic who is really worth reading—the only critic of whom, indeed, it may be said truthfully that it is at all possible to read him, save as an act of mental discipline—is something quite different. That motive is not the motive of the pedagogue, but the motive of the artist. It is no more and no less than the simple desire to function freely and beautifully, to give outward and objective form to ideas that bubble inwardly and have a fascinating lure in them, to get rid of them dramatically and make an articulate noise in the world. It was for this reason that Plato wrote the "Republic," and for this reason that Beethoven wrote the Ninth Symphony, and it is for this reason, to drop a million miles, that I am writing the present essay. Everything else is afterthought, mock-modesty, messianic delusion—in brief, affectation and folly. Is the contrary conception of criticism widely cherished? Is it almost universally held that the thing is a brother to jurisprudence, advertising, laparotomy, chautauqua lecturing and the art of the schoolmarm? Then certainly the fact that it is so held should be sufficient to set up an overwhelming probability of its lack of truth and sense. If I speak with some heat, it is as one who has suffered. When, years ago, I devoted myself diligently to critical pieces upon the writings of Theodore Dreiser, I found that practically every one who took any notice of my proceedings at all fell into either one of two assumptions about my underlying purpose: (*a*) that I had a fanatical devotion for Mr. Dreiser's ideas and desired to propagate them, or (*b*) that I was an ardent patriot, and yearned to lift up American literature. Both assumptions were false. I had then, and I have now, very little interest in many of Mr. Dreiser's main ideas; when we meet, in fact, we usually quarrel about them. And I am wholly devoid of public spirit, and haven't the least lust to improve American literature; if it ever came to what I regard as perfection my job would be gone. What, then, was my motive in writing about Mr. Dreiser so copiously? My motive, well known to Mr. Dreiser himself and to every one else who knew me as intimately as he did, was simply and solely to sort out and give coherence to the ideas of Mr. Mencken, and to put them into suave and ingratiating terms, and to discharge them with a flourish, and maybe with a phrase of pretty song, into the dense fog that blanketed the Republic.

The critic's choice of criticism rather than of what is called creative writing is chiefly a matter of temperament—perhaps, more accurately of hormones—with accidents of education and environment to help. The feelings that happen to be dominant in him at the moment the scribbling frenzy seizes him are feelings inspired, not directly by life itself, but by books, pictures, music, sculpture, architecture, religion, philosophy— in brief, by some other man's feelings about life. They are thus, in a sense, secondhand, and it is no wonder that creative artists so easily fall into the theory that they are also second-rate. Perhaps they usually are. If, indeed, the critic continues on this plane—if he lacks the intellectual agility and enterprise needed to make the leap from the work of art to the vast and mysterious complex of phenomena behind it—then they *always* are, and he remains no more than a fugleman or policeman to his betters. But if a genuine artist is concealed within him—if his feelings are in any sense profound and original, and his capacity for self-expression is above the average of educated men —then he moves inevitably from the work of art to life itself, and begins to take on a dignity that he formerly lacked. It is impossible to think of a man of any actual force and originality, universally recognized as having those qualities, who spent his whole life appraising and describing the work of other men. Did Goethe, or Carlyle, or Matthew Arnold, or Sainte-Beuve, or Macaulay, or even, to come down a few pegs, Lewes, or

Lowell, or Hazlitt? Certainly not. The thing that becomes most obvious about the writings of all such men, once they are examined carefully, is that the critic is always being swallowed up by the creative artist—that what starts out as the review of a book, or a play, or other work of art, usually develops very quickly into an independent essay upon the theme of that work of art, or upon some theme that it suggests—in a word, that it becomes a fresh work of art, and only indirectly related to the one that suggested it. This fact, indeed, is so plain that it scarcely needs statement. What the pedagogues always object to in, for example, the *Quarterly* reviewers is that they forgot the books they were supposed to review, and wrote long papers —often, in fact, small books—expounding ideas suggested (or not suggested) by the books under review. Every critic who is worth reading falls inevitably into the same habit. He cannot stick to his task: what is before him is always infinitely less interesting to him than what is within him. If he is genuinely first-rate—if what is within him stands the test of type, and wins an audience, and produces the reactions that every artist craves—then he usually ends by abandoning the criticism of specific works of art altogether, and setting up shop as a general merchant in general ideas, *i.e.*, as an artist working in the materials of life itself.

Mere reviewing, however conscientiously and competently it is done, is plainly a much inferior business. Like writing poetry, it is chiefly a function of intellectual immaturity. The young literatus just out of the university, having as yet no capacity for grappling with the fundamental mysteries of existence, is put to writing reviews of books, or plays, or music, or painting. Very often he does it extremely well; it is, in fact, not hard to do well, for even decayed pedagogues often do it, as such graves of the intellect as the New York *Times* bear witness. But if he continues to do it, whether well or ill, it is a sign to all the world that his growth ceased when they made him *Artium Baccalaureus.* Gradually he becomes, whether in or out of the academic grove, a professor, which is to say, a man devoted to diluting and retailing the ideas of his superiors— not an artist, not even a bad artist, but almost the antithesis of an artist. He is learned, he is sober, he is painstaking and accurate—but he is as hollow as a jug. Nothing is in him save the ghostly echoes of other men's thoughts and feelings. If he were a genuine artist he would have thoughts and feelings of his own, and the impulse to give them objective form would be irresistible. An artist can no more withstand that impulse than a politician can withstand the temptations of a job. There are no mute, inglorious Miltons, save in the hallucinations of poets. The one sound test of a Milton is that he functions as a Milton. His difference from other men lies precisely in the superior vigor of his impulse to self-expression, not in the superior beauty and loftiness of his ideas. Other men, in point of fact, often have the same ideas, or perhaps even loftier ones, but they are able to suppress them, usually on grounds of decorum, and so they escape being artists, and are respected by right-thinking persons, and die with money in the bank, and are forgotten in two weeks.

Obviously, the critic whose performance we are commonly called upon to investigate is a man standing somewhere along the path leading from the beginning that I have described to the goal. He has got beyond being a mere cataloguer and valuer of other men's ideas, but he has not yet become an autonomous artist—he is not yet ready to challenge attention with his own ideas alone. But it is plain that his motion, in so far as he is moving at all, must be in the direction of that autonomy—that is, unless one imagines him sliding backward into senile infantilism: a spectacle not unknown to literary pathology, but too pathetic to be discussed here. Bear this motion in mind, and the true nature of his aims and purposes becomes clear; more, the incurable falsity of the aims and purposes usually credited to him becomes equally clear. He is not actually trying to perform an impossible act of arctic justice upon the artist whose work gives him a text. He is not trying with mathematical passion to find out exactly what was in that artist's mind at the moment of creation, and to display it precisely and in an ecstasy of appreciation. He is not trying to bring the work discussed into accord with some transient theory of æsthetics, or ethics, or truth, or to determine its degree of departure from that theory. He is not trying to lift up the fine arts, or to defend democracy against sense, or to promote happiness at the domestic hearth, or to convert sophomores into right-thinkers, or to serve God. He is not trying to fit a group of novel phenomena into the orderly process of history. He is not even trying to discharge the catalytic office that I myself, in a romantic moment, once sought to force upon him. He is, first and last, simply trying to express himself. He is trying to arrest and challenge a sufficient body of readers, to make them pay attention to him, to impress them with the charm and novelty of his ideas, to provoke them into an agreeable (or shocked) awareness of him, and he is trying to achieve thereby for his own inner ego the grateful feeling of a function performed, a tension relieved, a *katharsis* attained which Wagner achieved when he wrote "Die Walküre," and a hen achieves every time she lays an egg.

Joseph Conrad is moved by that necessity to write romances; Bach was moved to write music; poets are moved to write poetry; critics are moved to write criticism. The form is nothing; the only important thing is the motive power, and it is the same in all cases. It is the pressing yearning of every man who has ideas in him to empty them upon the world, to hammer them into plausible and ingratiating shapes, to compel the attention and respect of his equals, to lord it over his inferiors. So seen, the critic becomes a far more transparent and agreeable fellow than ever he was in the discourses of the psychologists who sought to make him a mere appraiser in an intellectual customs house, a gauger in a distillery of the spirit, a just and infallible judge upon the cosmic bench. Such offices, in point of fact, never fit him. He always bulges over their confines. So labelled and estimated, it inevitably turns out that the specific critic under examination is a very bad one, or no critic at all. But when he is thought of, not as pedagogue, but as artist, then he begins to take on reality, and, what is more, dignity. Carlyle was surely no just and infallible judge; on the contrary, he was full of prejudices, biles, naïvetés, humors. Yet he is read, consulted, attended to. Macaulay was unfair, inaccurate, fanciful, lyrical—yet his essays live. Arnold had his faults too, and so did Sainte-Beauve, and so did Goethe, and so did many another of that line—and yet they are remembered to-day, and all the learned and conscientious critics of their time, laboriously concerned with the precise intent of the artists under review, and passionately determined to set it forth with god-like care and to relate it exactly to this or that great stream of ideas—all these pedants are forgotten. What saved Carlyle, Macaulay and company is as plain as day. They were first-rate artists. They could make the thing charming, and that is always a million times more important than making it true.

Truth, indeed, is something that is believed in completely only by persons who have never tried personally to pursue it to its fastnesses and grab it by the tail. It is the adoration of second-rate men—men who always receive it at second-hand. Pedagogues believe in immutable truths and spend their lives trying to determine them and propagate them; the intellectual progress of man consists largely of a concerted effort to block and destroy their enterprise. Nine times out of ten, in the arts as in life, there is actually no truth to be discovered; there is only error to be exposed. In whole departments of human inquiry it seems to me quite unlikely that the truth ever *will* be discovered. Nevertheless, the rubber-stamp thinking of the world always makes the assumption that the exposure of an error is identical with the discovery of the truth—that error and truth are simple opposites. They are nothing of the sort. What the world turns to, when it has been cured of one error, is usually simply another error, and maybe one worse than the first one. This is the whole history of the intellect in brief. The average man of to-day does not believe in precisely the same imbecilities that the Greek of the fourth century before Christ believed in, but the things that he *does* believe in are often quite as idiotic. Perhaps this statement is a bit too sweeping. There is, year by year, a gradual accumulation of what may be called, provisionally, truths—there is a slow accretion of ideas that somehow manage to meet all practicable human tests, and so survive. But even so, it is risky to call them absolute truths. All that one may safely say of them is that no one, as yet, has demonstrated that they are errors. Soon or late, if experience teaches us anything, they are likely to succumb too. The profoundest truths of the Middle Ages are now laughed at by schoolboys. The profoundest truths of democracy will be laughed at, a few centuries hence, even by school-teachers.

In the department of æsthetics, wherein critics mainly disport themselves, it is almost impossible to think of a so-called truth that shows any sign of being permanently true. The most profound of principles begins to fade and quiver almost as soon as it is stated. But the work of art, as opposed to the theory behind it, has a longer life, particularly if that theory be obscure and questionable, and so cannot be determined accurately. "Hamlet," the Mona Lisa, "Faust," "Dixie," "Parsifal," "Mother Goose," "Annabel Lee," "Huckleberry Finn"—these things, so baffling to pedagogy, so contumacious to the categories, so mysterious in purpose and utility—these things live. And why? Because there is in them the flavor of salient, novel and attractive personality, because the quality that shines from them is not that of correct demeanor but that of creative passion, because they pulse and breathe and speak, because they are genuine works of art. So with criticism. Let us forget all the heavy effort to make a science of it; it is a fine art, or nothing. If the critic, retiring to his cell to concoct his treatise upon a book or play or what-not, produces a piece of writing that shows sound structure, and brilliant color, and the flash of new and persuasive ideas, and civilized manners, and the charm of an uncommon personality in free function, then he has given something to the world that is worth having, and sufficiently justified his existence. Is Carlyle's "Frederick" true? Who cares? As well ask if the Parthenon is true, or the C Minor Symphony, or "Wiener Blut." Let the critic who is an artist leave such necropsies to professors of æsthetics, who can no more determine the truth than he can, and will infallibly make it unpleasant and a bore.

It is, of course, not easy to practice this abstention. Two forces, one within and one without, tend to bring even a Hazlitt or a Huneker under the campus pump. One is the almost universal human susceptibility to messianic delusions—the irresistible tendency of practically every man, once he finds a crowd in front of him, to strut and roll his eyes. The other is the public demand, born of such long familiarity with pedagogical criticism that no other kind is readily conceivable, that the critic teach something as well as say something—in the popular phrase, that he be constructive. Both operate powerfully against his free functioning, and especially the former. He finds it hard to resist the flattery of his customers, however little he may actually esteem it. If he knows anything at all, he knows that his following, like that of every other artist in ideas, is chiefly made up of the congenitally subaltern type of man

and woman—natural converts, lodge joiners, me-toos, strag-
glers after circus parades. It is precious seldom that he ever gets
a positive idea out of them; what he usually gets is mere unintelligent ratification. But this troop, despite its obvious failings,
corrupts him in various ways. For one thing, it enormously
reënforces his belief in his own ideas, and so tends to make
him stiff and dogmatic—in brief, precisely everything that he
ought not to be. And for another thing, it tends to make him
(by a curious contradiction) a bit pliant and politic: he begins
to estimate new ideas, not in proportion as they are amusing
or beautiful, but in proportion as they are likely to please. So
beset, front and rear, he sometimes sinks supinely to the level
of a professor, and his subsequent proceedings are interesting
no more. The true aim of a critic is certainly not to make converts. He must know that very few of the persons who are susceptible to conversion are worth converting. Their minds are
intrinsically flabby and parasitical, and it is certainly not sound
sport to agitate minds of that sort. Moreover, the critic must
always harbor a grave doubt about most of the ideas that they
lap up so greedily—it must occur to him not infrequently, in
the silent watches of the night, that much that he writes is sheer
buncombe. As I have said, I can't imagine any idea—that is, in
the domain of æsthetics—that is palpably and incontrovertibly
sound. All that I am familiar with, and in particular all that I
announce most vociferously, seem to me to contain a core of
quite obvious nonsense. I thus try to avoid cherishing them
too lovingly, and it always gives me a shiver to see any one else
gobble them at one gulp. Criticism, at bottom, is indistinguishable from skepticism. Both launch themselves, the one by
æsthetic presentations and the other by logical presentations,
at the common human tendency to accept whatever is approved, to take in ideas ready-made, to be responsive to mere
rhetoric and gesticulation. A critic who believes in anything
absolutely is bound to that something quite as helplessly as a
Christian is bound to the Freudian garbage in the Book of Revelation. To that extent, at all events, he is unfree and unintelligent, and hence a bad critic.

The demand for "constructive" criticism is based upon the
same false assumption that immutable truths exist in the arts,

and that the artist will be improved by being made aware of them. This notion, whatever the form it takes, is always absurd —as much so, indeed, as its brother delusion that the critic, to be competent, must be a practitioner of the specific art he ventures to deal with, *i.e.*, that a doctor, to cure a belly-ache, must have a belly-ache. As practically encountered, it is disingenuous as well as absurd, for it comes chiefly from bad artists who tire of serving as performing monkeys, and crave the greater ease and safety of sophomores in class. They demand to be taught in order to avoid being knocked about. In their demand is the theory that instruction, if they could get it, would profit them—that they are capable of doing better work than they do. As a practical matter, I doubt that this is ever true. Bad poets never actually grow any better; they invariably grow worse and worse. In all history there has never been, to my knowledge, a single practitioner of any art who, as a result of "constructive" criticism, improved his work. The curse of all the arts, indeed, is the fact that they are constantly invaded by persons who are not artists at all—persons whose yearning to express their ideas and feelings is unaccompanied by the slightest capacity for charming expression—in brief, persons with absolutely nothing to say. This is particularly true of the art of letters, which interposes very few technical obstacles to the vanity and garrulity of such invaders. Any effort to teach them to write better is an effort wasted, as every editor discovers for himself; they are as incapable of it as they are of jumping over the moon. The only sort of criticism that can deal with them to any profit is the sort that employs them frankly as laboratory animals. It cannot cure them, but it can at least make an amusing and perhaps edifying show of them. It is idle to argue that the good in them is thus destroyed with the bad. The simple answer is that there *is* no good in them. Suppose Poe had wasted his time trying to dredge good work out of Rufus Dawes, author of "Geraldine." He would have failed miserably —and spoiled a capital essay, still diverting after three-quarters of a century. Suppose Beethoven, dealing with Gottfried Weber, had tried laboriously to make an intelligent music critic of him. How much more apt, useful and durable the simple note: "Arch-ass! Double-barrelled ass!" Here was absolutely sound

criticism. Here was a judgment wholly beyond challenge.
Moreover, here was a small but perfect work of art.

Upon the low practical value of so-called constructive criticism I can offer testimony out of my own experience. My
books are commonly reviewed at great length, and many critics devote themselves to pointing out what they conceive to be
my errors, both of fact and of taste. Well, I cannot recall a case
in which any suggestion offered by a constructive critic has
helped me in the slightest, or even actively interested me.
Every such wet-nurse of letters has sought fatuously to make
me write in a way differing from that in which the Lord God
Almighty, in His infinite wisdom, impels me to write—that is,
to make me write stuff which, coming from me, would be as
false as an appearance of decency in a Congressman. All the
benefits I have ever got from the critics of my work have come
from the destructive variety. A hearty slating always does me
good, particularly if it be well written. It begins by enlisting
my professional respect; it ends by making me examine my
ideas coldly in the privacy of my chamber. Not, of course, that
I usually revise them, but I at least examine them. If I decide
to hold fast to them, they are all the dearer to me thereafter,
and I expound them with a new passion and plausibility. If, on
the contrary, I discern holes in them, I shelve them in a *pianissimo* manner, and set about hatching new ones to take their
place. But constructive criticism irritates me. I do not object to
being denounced, but I can't abide being school-mastered, especially by men I regard as imbeciles.

I find, as a practicing critic, that very few men who write
books are even as tolerant as I am—that most of them, soon or
late, show signs of extreme discomfort under criticism, however polite its terms. Perhaps this is why enduring friendships
between authors and critics are so rare. All artists, of course,
dislike one another more or less, but that dislike seldom rises
to implacable enmity, save between opera singer and opera
singer, and creative author and critic. Even when the latter-
two keep up an outward show of good-will, there is always-
bitter antagonism under the surface. Part of it, I daresay, arises
out of the impossible demands of the critic, particularly if he
be tinged with the constructive madness. Having favored an
author with his good opinion, he expects the poor fellow to

live up to that good opinion without the slightest compromise or faltering, and this is commonly beyond human power. He feels that any let-down compromises *him*—that his hero is stabbing him in the back, and making him ridiculous—and this feeling rasps his vanity. The most bitter of all literary quarrels are those between critics and creative artists, and most of them arise in just this way. As for the creative artist, he on his part naturally resents the critic's air of pedagogical superiority and he resents it especially when he has an uneasy feeling that he has fallen short of his best work, and that the discontent of the critic is thus justified. Injustice is relatively easy to bear; what stings is justice. Under it all, of course, lurks the fact that I began with: the fact that the critic is himself an artist, and that his creative impulse, soon or late, is bound to make him neglect the punctilio. When he sits down to compose his criticism, his artist ceases to be a friend, and becomes mere raw material for his work of art. It is my experience that artists invariably resent this cavalier use of them. They are pleased so long as the critic confines himself to the modest business of interpreting them—preferably in terms of their own estimate of themselves—but the moment he proceeds to adorn their theme with variations of his own, the moment he brings new ideas to the enterprise and begins contrasting them with their ideas, that moment they grow restive. It is precisely at this point, of course, that criticism becomes genuine criticism; before that it was mere reviewing. When a critic passes it he loses his friends. By becoming an artist, he becomes the foe of all other artists.

But the transformation, I believe, has good effects upon him: it makes him a better critic. Too much *Gemütlichkeit* is as fatal to criticism as it would be to surgery or politics. When it rages unimpeded it leads inevitably either to a dull professorial sticking on of meaningless labels or to log-rolling, and often it leads to both. One of the most hopeful symptoms of the new *Aufklärung* in the Republic is the revival of acrimony in criticism—the renaissance of the doctrine that æsthetic matters are important, and that it is worth the while of a healthy male to take them seriously, as he takes business, sport and amour. In the days when American literature was showing its first vigorous growth, the native criticism was extraordinarily violent and even vicious; in the days when American literature swooned upon the tomb of the Puritan *Kultur* it became flaccid and childish. The typical critic of the first era was Poe, as the typical critic of the second was Howells. Poe carried on his critical jehads with such ferocity that he often got into law-suits, and sometimes ran no little risk of having his head cracked. He regarded literary questions as exigent and momentous. The lofty aloofness of the don was simply not in him. When he encountered a book that seemed to him to be bad, he attacked it almost as sharply as a Chamber of Commerce would attack a fanatic preaching free speech, or the corporation of Trinity Church would attack Christ. His opponents replied in the same Berserker manner. Much of Poe's surviving ill-fame, as a drunkard and dead-beat, is due to their inordinate denunciations of him. They were not content to refute him; they constantly tried to dispose of him altogether. The very ferocity of that ancient row shows that the native literature, in those days, was in a healthy state. Books of genuine value were produced. Literature always thrives best, in fact, in an atmosphere of hearty strife. Poe, surrounded by admiring professors, never challenged, never aroused to the emotions of revolt, would probably have written poetry indistinguishable from the hollow stuff of, say, Prof. Dr. George E. Woodberry. It took the persistent (and often grossly unfair and dishonorable) opposition of Griswold *et al* to stimulate him to his highest endeavors. He needed friends, true enough, but he also needed enemies.

To-day, for the first time in years, there is strife in American criticism, and the Paul Elmer Mores and Hamilton Wright Mabies are no longer able to purr in peace. The instant they fall into stiff professorial attitudes they are challenged, and often with anything but urbanity. The *ex cathedra* manner thus passes out, and free discussion comes in. Heretics lay on boldly, and the professors are forced to make some defense. Often, going further, they attempt counterattacks. Ears are bitten off. Noses are bloodied. There are wallops both above and below the belt. I am, I need not say, no believer in any magical merit in debate, no matter how free it may be. It certainly does not necessarily establish the truth; both sides, in fact, may be wrong, and they often are. But it at least accomplishes two important effects. On the one hand, it exposes all the cruder fallacies to hostile examination, and so disposes of many of them. And on the other hand, it melodramatizes the business of the critic, and so convinces thousands of bystanders, otherwise quite inert, that criticism is an amusing and instructive art, and that the problems it deals with are important. What men will fight for seems to be worth looking into.

IV.
Das Kapital

AFTER a hearty dinner of *potage créole*, planked Chesapeake shad, Guinea hen *en casserole* and some respectable salad, with two or three cocktails made of two-thirds gin, one-third Martini-Rossi vermouth and a dash of absinthe as *Vorspiel* and a bottle of Ruhländer 1903 to wash it down, the following thought often bubbles up from my subconscious: that many of the acknowledged evils of capitalism, now so horribly visible in the world, are not due primarily to capitalism itself but rather to democracy, that universal murrain of Christendom.

What I mean, in brief, is that capitalism, under democracy, is constantly under hostile pressure and often has its back to the wall, and that its barbaric manners and morals, at least in large part, are due to that fact—that they are, in essence, precisely the same manners and morals that are displayed by any other creature or institution so beset. Necessity is not only the mother of invention; it is also the mother of every imaginable excess and infamy. A woman defending her child is notoriously willing to go to lengths that even a Turk or an agent of the Department of Justice would regard as inordinate, and so is a Presbyterian defending his hell, or a soldier defending his fatherland, or a banker defending his gold. It is only when there is no danger that the average human being is honorable, just as it is only when there *is* danger that he is virtuous. He would commit adultery every day if it were safe, and he would commit murder every day if it were necessary.

The essential thing about democracy, as every one must know, is that it is a device for strengthening and heartening the have-nots in their eternal war upon the haves. That war, as every one knows again, has its psychological springs in envy pure and simple—envy of the more fortunate man's greater wealth, the superior pulchritude of his wife or wives, his larger mobility and freedom, his more protean capacity for and command of happiness—in brief, his better chance to lead a bearable life in this worst of possible worlds. It follows that under democracy, which gives a false power and importance to the have-nots by counting every one of them as the legal equal of George Washington or Beethoven, the process of government consists largely, and sometimes almost exclusively, of efforts to spoil that advantage artificially. Trust-busting, free silver, direct elections, Prohibition, government ownership and all the other varieties of American political quackery are but symptoms of the same general rage. It is the rage of the have-not against the have, of the farmer who must drink hard cider and forty-rod against the city man who may drink Burgundy and Scotch, of the poor fellow who must stay at home looking at a wife who regards the lip-stick as lewd and lascivious against the lucky fellow who may go to Atlantic City or Palm Beach and ride up and down in a wheelchair with a girl who knows how to make up and has put away the fear of God.

The ignobler sort of men, of course, are too stupid to understand various rare and exhilarating sorts of superiority, and so they do not envy the happiness that goes with them. If they could enter into the mind of a Wagner or a Brahms and begin to comprehend the stupendous joy that such a man gets out of the practice of his art, they would pass laws against it and make a criminal of him, as they have already made criminals, in the United States, of the man with a civilized taste for wines, the man so attractive to women that he can get all the wives he wants without having to marry them, and the man who can make pictures like Félicien Rops, or books like Flaubert, Zola, Dreiser, Cabell or Rabelais. Wagner and Brahms escape, and their arts with them, because the great masses of men cannot understand the sort of thing they try to do, and hence do not envy the man who does it well, and gets joy out of it. It is much different with, say, Rops. Every American Congressman, as a small boy, covered the fence of the Sunday-School yard with pictures in the manner of Rops. What he now remembers of the business is that the pictures were denounced by the superintendent, and that he was cowhided for making them; what he hears about Rops, when he hears at all, is that the fellow is vastly esteemed, and hence probably full of a smug æsthetic satisfaction. In consequence, it is unlawful in the United States to transmit the principal pictures of Rops by mail, or, indeed, "to have and possess" them. The man who owns them must conceal them from the *okhrána* of the Department of Justice just as carefully as he conceals the wines and whiskeys in his cellar, or the poor working girl he transports from the heat and noise of New York to the salubrious calm of the Jersey coast, or his hand-tooled library set of the "Contes Drôlatiques," or his precious first edition of "Jurgen."

But, as I say, the democratic pressure in such directions is relatively feeble, for there are whole categories of more or less æsthetic superiority and happiness that the democrat cannot understand at all, and is in consequence virtually unaware of. It is far different with the varieties of superiority and happiness that are the functions of mere money. Here the democrat is extraordinarily alert and appreciative. He can not only imagine hundreds of ways of getting happiness out of money; he devotes almost the whole of his intellectual activity, such as it is, to imagining them, and he seldom if ever imagines anything else. Even his sexual fancies translate themselves instantly into concepts of dollars and cents; the thing that confines him so miserably to one wife, and to one, alas, so unappetizing and depressing, is simply his lack of money; if he only had the wealth of Diamond Jim Brady he too would be the glittering Don Giovanni that Jim was. All the known species of democratic political theory are grounded firmly upon this doctrine that money, and money only, makes the mare go—that all the conceivable varieties of happiness are possible to the man who has it. Even the Socialists, who profess to scorn money, really worship it. Socialism, indeed, is simply the degenerate capitalism of bankrupt capitalists. Its one genuine object is to get more money for its professors; all its other grandiloquent objects are afterthoughts, and most of them are bogus. The democrats of other schools pursue the same single aim—and adorn it with false pretenses even more transparent. In the United States the average democrat, I suppose, would say that the establishment and safeguarding of liberty was the chief purpose of democracy. The theory is mere wind. The average American democrat really cares nothing whatever for liberty, and is always willing to sell it for money. What he actually wants, and strives to get by his politics, is more money. His fundamental political ideas nearly all contemplate restraints and raids upon capital, even when they appear superficially to be quite free from economic flavor, and most of the political banshees and bugaboos that alternately freeze and boil his blood have dollar marks written all over them. There is no need to marshal a long catalogue of examples from English and American political history: I simply defy any critic of my doctrine to find a single issue of genuine appeal to the populace, at any time during the past century, that did not involve a more or less obvious scheme for looting a minority—the slave-owners, Wall Street, the railroads, the dukes, or some other group representing capital. Even the most affecting idealism of the plain people has a thrifty basis. In the United States, during the early part of the late war, they were very cynical about the Allied cause; it was not until the war orders of the Allies raised their wages that they began to believe in the noble righteousness of Lloyd-George and company. And after Dr. Wilson had jockeyed the United States itself into the war, and the cost of living began to increase faster than wages, he faced a hostile country until he restored altruism by his wholesale bribery of labor.

It is my contention that the constant exposure of capitalism to such primitive lusts and forays is what makes it so lamentably extortionate and unconscionable in democratic countries, and particularly in the United States. The capitalist, warned by experience, collars all he can while the getting is good, regardless of the commonest honesty and decorum, because he is haunted by an uneasy feeling that his season will not be long. His dominating passion is to pile up the largest amount of capital possible, by fair means or foul, so that he will have ample reserves when the next raid comes, and he has to use part of it to bribe one part of the proletariat against the other. In the long run, of course, he always wins, for this bribery is invariably feasible; in the United States, indeed, every fresh struggle leaves capital more secure than it was before. But though the capitalist thus has no reason to fear actual defeat and disaster, he is well aware that victory is always expensive, and his natural prudence causes him to discount the cost in advance, even when he has planned to shift it to other shoulders. I point, in example, to the manner in which capital dealt with the discharged American soldiers after the war. Its first effort was to cajole them into its service, as they had been cajoled by the politicians after the Civil War. To this end, it borrowed the machine erected by Dr. Wilson and his agents for debauching the booboisie during the actual war, and by the skillful use of that machine it quickly organized the late conscripts into the American Legion, alarmed them with lies about a Bolshevist scheme to make slaves of them (*i.e.*, to cut off forever their hope of getting money), and put them to clubbing and butchering their fellow proletarians. The business done, the conscripts found themselves out of jobs: their gallant war upon Bolshevism had brought down wages, and paralysed organized labor. They now demanded pay for their work, and capital had to meet the demand. It did so by promising them a bonus—*i.e.*, loot—out of the public treasury, and by straightway inventing a scheme whereby the ultimate cost would fall chiefly upon poor folk.

Throughout the war, indeed, capital exhibited an inordinately extortionate spirit, and thereby revealed its underlying dread. First it robbed the Allies in the manner of bootleggers looting a country distillery, then it swindled the plain people at home by first bribing them with huge wages and then taking away all their profits and therewith all their savings, and then it seized and made away with the impounded property of enemy nationals—property theoretically held in trust for them, and the booty, if it was booty at all, of the whole American people. This triple burglary was excessive, to be sure, but who will say that it was not prudent? The capitalists of the Republic are efficient, and have foresight. They saw some lean and hazardous years ahead, with all sorts of raids threatening. They took measures to fortify their position. To-day their prevision is their salvation. They are losing some of their accumulation, of course, but they still have enough left to finance an effective defense of the remainder. There was never any time in the history of any country, indeed, when capital was so securely intrenched as it is to-day in the United States. It has divided the proletariat into two bitterly hostile halves, it has battered and crippled unionism almost beyond recognition, it has a firm grip upon all three arms of the government, and it controls practically every agency for the influencing of public opinion, from the press to the church. Had it been less prudent when times were good, and put its trust in God alone, the I.W.W. would have rushed it at the end of the war.

As I say, I often entertain the thought that it would be better, in the long run, to make terms with a power so hard to resist, and thereby purge it of its present compulsory criminality. I doubt that capitalists, as a class, are naturally vicious; certainly they are no more vicious than, say, lawyers and politicians—upon whom the plain people commonly rely, in their innocence, to save them. I have known a good many men of great wealth in my time, and most of them have been men showing all the customary decencies. They deplore the harsh necessities of their profession quite as honestly as a judge deplores the harsh necessities of his. You will never convince me that the average American banker, during the war, got anything properly describable as professional satisfaction out of selling Liberty bonds at 100 to poor stenographers, and then buying them back at 83. He knew that he'd need his usurious profit against the blue day when the boys came home, and so he took it, but it would have given him ten times as much pleasure if it had come from the reluctant gizzard of some other banker. In brief, there is a pride of workmanship in capitalists, just as there is in all other men above the general. They get the same spiritual lift out of their sordid swindles that Swinburne got out of composing his boozy dithyrambs, and I often incline to think that it is quite as worthy of respect. In a democratic society, with the arts adjourned and the sciences mere concubines of money, it is chiefly the capitalists, in fact, who keep pride of workmanship alive. In their principal enemies, the trades-unionists, it is almost extinct. Unionism seldom, if ever, uses such power as it has to insure better work; almost always it devotes a large part of that power to safeguarding bad work. A union man who, moved by professional pride, put any extra effort into his job would probably be punished by his union as a sort of scab. But a capitalist is still able to cherish some of the old spirit of the guildsman. If he invents a new device for corralling the money of those who have earned it, or operates an old device in some new and brilliant way, he is honored and envied by his colleagues. The late J. Pierpont Morgan was thus honored and envied, not because he made more actual money than any other capitalist of his time—in point of fact, he made a good deal less than some, and his own son, a much inferior man, has made more since his death than he did during his whole life—but because his operations showed originality, daring, coolness, and imagination—in brief, because he was a great virtuoso in the art he practiced.

What I contend is that the democratic system of government would be saner and more effective in its dealings with capital if it ceased to regard all capitalists as criminals *ipso facto,* and thereby ceased to make their armed pursuit the chief end of practical politics—if it gave over this vain effort to put them down by force, and tried to bring them to decency by giving greater play and confidence to the pride of workmanship that I have described. They would be less ferocious and immoderate, I think, if they were treated with less hostility, and put more upon their conscience and honor. No doubt the average democrat, brought up upon the prevailing superstitions and prejudices of his faith, will deny at once that they are actually capable of conscience or honor, or that they have any recognizable pride of workmanship. Well, let him deny it. He will make precisely the same denial with respect to kings. Nevertheless, it must be plain to every one who has read history attentively that the majority of the kings of the past, even when no criticism could reach them, showed a very great pride of workmanship—that they tried to be good kings even when it was easier to be bad ones. The same thing is true of the majority of capitalists—the kings of to-day. They are criminals by our democratic law, but their criminality is chiefly artificial and theoretical, like that of a bootlegger. If it were abolished by repealing the laws which create it—if it became legally just as virtuous to organize and operate a great industrial corporation, or to combine and rehabilitate railroads, or to finance any other such transactions as it is to organize a trades-union, a *Bauverein,* or a lodge of Odd Fellows—then I believe that capitalists would forthwith abandon a great deal of the scoundrelism which now marks their proceedings, that they could be trusted to police their order at least as vigilantly as physicians or lawyers police theirs, and that the activities of those members of it who showed no pride of workmanship at all would be effectively curbed.

The legal war upon them under democracy is grounded upon the false assumption that it would be possible, given laws enough, to get rid of them altogether. The *Ur*-Americanos, who set the tone of our legislation and provided examples for the legislation of every other democratic country, were chiefly what would be called Bolsheviki to-day. They dreamed of a republic wholly purged of capitalism—and taxes. They were have-nots of the most romantic and ambitious variety, and saw Utopia before them. Every man of their time who thought capitalistically—that is, who believed that things consumed had to be paid for—was a target for their revilings: for example, Alexander Hamilton. But they were wrong, and their modern heirs and assigns are wrong just as surely. That wrongness of theirs, in truth, has grown enormously since it was launched, for the early Americans were a pastoral people, and could get along with very little capital, whereas the Americans of to-day lead a very complex life, and need the aid of capitalism at almost every breath they draw. Most of their primary necessities—the railroad, the steamship lines, the trolley car, the telephone, refrigerated meats, machine-made clothes, phonograph records, moving-picture shows, and so on—are wholly unthinkable save as the products of capital in large aggregations. No man of to-day can imagine doing without them, or getting them without the aid of such aggregations. The most even the wildest Socialist can think of is to take the capital away from the capitalists who now have it and hand it over to the state—in other words, to politicians. A century ago there were still plenty of men who, like Thoreau, proposed to abolish it altogether. But now even the radicals of the extreme left assume as a matter of course that capital is indispensible, and that abolishing it or dispersing it would cause a collapse of civilization.

What ails democracy, in the economic department, is that it proceeds upon the assumption that the contrary is true—that it seeks to bring capitalism to a state of innocuous virtue by grossly exaggerating its viciousness—that it penalizes ignorantly what is, at bottom, a perfectly natural and legitimate aspiration, and one necessary to society. Such penalizings, I need not argue, never destroy the impulse itself; surely the American experience with Prohibition should make even a democrat aware of that. What they do is simply to make it evasive, intemperate, and relentless. If it were legally as hazardous in the United States to play a string quartette as it is to build up a great bank or industrial enterprise—if the performers, struggling with their parts, had to watch the windows in constant fear that a Bryan, a Roosevelt, a Lloyd-George or some other such predatory mountebank would break in, armed with a club and followed by a rabble—then string quartette players would become as devious and anti-social in their ways as the average American capitalist is today, and when, by a process of setting one part of the mob against the rest, they managed to get a chance to play quartettes in temporary peace, despite the general mob hatred of them, they would forget the lovely music of Haydn and Mozart altogether, and devote their whole time to a *fortissimo* playing of the worst musical felonies of Schönberg, Ravel and Strawinsky.

V.

Ad Imaginem Dei Creavit Illum

T HE old anthropomorphic notion that the life of the whole universe centers in the life of man—that human existence is the supreme expression of the cosmic process—this notion seems to be on its way toward the Sheol of exploded delusions. The fact is that the life of man, as it is more and more studied in the light of general biology, appears to be more and more empty of significance. Once apparently the chief concern and masterpiece of the gods, the human race now begins to bear the aspect of an accidental by-product of their vast, inscrutable and probably nonsensical operations. A blacksmith making a horse-shoe produces something almost as brilliant and mysterious— the shower of sparks. But his eye and thought, as we know, are not on the sparks, but on the horse-shoe. The sparks, indeed, constitute a sort of disease of the horse-shoe; their existence depends upon a wasting of its tissue. In the same way, perhaps, man is a local disease of the cosmos—a kind of pestiferous eczema or urethritis. There are, of course, different grades of eczema, and so are there different grades of men. No doubt a cosmos afflicted with nothing worse than an infection of Bee-thovens would not think it worth while to send for the doctor. But a cosmos infested by prohibitionists, Socialists, Scotsmen and stockbrokers must suffer damnably. No wonder the sun is so hot and the moon is so diabetically green!

2

The Anthropomorphic Delusion

As I say, the anthropomorphic theory of the world is made absurd by modern biology—but that is not saying, of course, that it will ever be abandoned by the generality of men. To the contrary, they will cherish it in proportion as it becomes more and more dubious. To-day, indeed, it is cherished as it was never cherished in the Ages of Faith, when the doctrine that man was god-like was at least ameliorated by the doctrine that woman was vile. What else is behind charity, philanthropy, pacifism, Socialism, the uplift, all the rest of the current sentimentalities? One and all, these sentimentalities are based upon the notion that man is a glorious and ineffable animal, and that his continued existence in the world ought to be facilitated and insured. But this notion is obviously full of fatuity. As animals go, even in so limited a space as our world, man is botched and ridiculous. Few other brutes are so stupid or so cowardly. The commonest yellow dog has far sharper senses and is infinitely more courageous, not to say more honest and dependable. The ants and the bees are, in many ways, far more intelligent and ingenious; they manage their government with vastly less quarreling, wastefulness and imbecility. The lion is more beautiful, more dignified, more majestic. The antelope is swifter and more graceful. The ordinary house-cat is cleaner. The horse, foamed by labor, has a better smell. The gorilla is kinder to his children and more faithful to his wife. The ox and the ass are more industrious and serene. But most of all, man is deficient in courage, perhaps the noblest quality of them all. He is not only mortally afraid of all other animals of his own weight or half his weight—save a few that he has debased by artificial inbreeding—; he is even mortally afraid of his own kind—and not only of their fists and hooves, but even of their sniggers.

No other animal is so defectively adapted to its environment. The human infant, as it comes into the world, is so puny that if it were neglected for two days running it would infallibly perish, and this congenital infirmity, though more or less concealed later on, persists until death. Man is ill far more than any other animal, both in his savage state and under civilization. He has more different diseases and he suffers from them oftener. He is easier exhausted and injured. He dies more horribly and usually sooner. Practically all the other higher vertebrates, at least in their wild state, live longer and retain their faculties to a greater age. Here even the anthropoid apes are far beyond their human cousins. An orang-outang marries at the age of seven or eight, raises a family of seventy or eighty children, and is still as hale and hearty at eighty as a European at forty-five.

All the errors and incompetencies of the Creator reach their climax in man. As a piece of mechanism he is the worst of them all; put beside him, even a salmon or a staphylococcus is a sound and efficient machine. He has the worst kidneys known to comparative zoölogy, and the worst lungs, and the worst heart. His eye, considering the work it is called upon to do, is less efficient than the eye of an earthworm; an optical instrument maker who made an instrument so clumsy would be mobbed by his customers. Alone of all animals, terrestrial, celestial or marine, man is unfit by nature to go abroad in the world he inhabits. He must clothe himself, protect himself, swathe himself, armor himself. He is eternally in the position of a turtle born without a shell, a dog without hair, a fish without fins. Lacking his heavy and cumbersome trappings, he is defenseless even against flies. As God made him he hasn't even a tail to switch them off.

I now come to man's one point of unquestionable natural superiority: he has a soul. This is what sets him off from all other animals, and makes him, in a way, their master. The exact nature of that soul has been in dispute for thousands of years, but regarding its function it is possible to speak with some authority. That function is to bring man into direct contact with God, to make him aware of God, above all, to make him resemble God. Well, consider the colossal failure of the device! If we assume that man actually does resemble God, then we are forced into the impossible theory that God is a coward, an idiot and a bounder. And if we assume that man, after all these years, does *not* resemble God, then it appears at once that the human soul is as inefficient a machine as the human liver or tonsil, and that man would probably be better off, as the chimpanzee undoubtedly *is* better off, without it.

Such, indeed, is the case. The only practical effect of having a soul is that it fills man with anthropomorphic and anthropocentric vanities—in brief with cocky and preposterous superstitions. He struts and plumes himself because he has this soul—and overlooks the fact that it doesn't work. Thus he is the supreme clown of creation, the *reductio ad absurdum* of animated nature. He is like a cow who believed that she could jump over the moon, and ordered her whole life upon that theory. He is like a bullfrog boasting eternally of fighting lions, of flying over the Matterhorn, and of swimming the Helle-spont. And yet this is the poor brute we are asked to venerate as a gem in the forehead of the cosmos! This is the worm we are asked to defend as God's favorite on earth, with all its mil-lions of braver, nobler, decenter quadrupeds— its superb lions, its lithe and gallant leopards, its imperial elephants, its honest dogs, its courageous rats! This is the insect we are besought, at infinite trouble, labor and expense, to reproduce!

3
Meditation on Meditation

Man's capacity for abstract thought, which most other mammals seem to lack, has undoubtedly given him his present mastery of the land surface of the earth—a mastery disputed only by several hundred species of microscopic organisms. It is responsible for his feeling of superiority, and under that feeling there is undoubtedly a certain measure of reality, at least within narrow limits. But what is too often overlooked is that the capacity to perform an act is by no means synonymous with its salubrious exercise. The simple fact is that most of man's thinking is stupid, pointless, and injurious to him. Of all animals, indeed, he seems the least capable of arriving at accu-rate judgments in the matters that most desperately affect his welfare. Try to imagine a rat, in the realm of rat ideas, arriving at a notion as violently in contempt of plausibility as the no-tion, say, of Swedenborgianism, or that of homeopathy, or that of infant damnation, or that of mental telepathy. Try to think of a congregation of educated rats gravely listening to such disgusting intellectual rubbish as was in the public bulls of Dr. Woodrow Wilson. Man's natural instinct, in fact, is never toward what is sound and true; it is toward what is specious and false. Let any great notion of modern times be confronted by two conflicting propositions, the one grounded upon the utmost probability and reasonableness and the other upon the most glaring error, and it will almost invariably embrace the latter. It is so in politics, which consists wholly of a succession of unintelligent crazes, many of them so idiotic that they exist only as battle-cries and shibboleths and are not reducible to logical statement at all. It is so in religion, which, like poetry, is simply a concerted effort to deny the most obvious realities. It is so in nearly every field of thought. The ideas that conquer the race most rapidly and arouse the wildest enthusiasm and are held most tenaciously are precisely the ideas that are most insane. This has been true since the first "advanced" gorilla put on underwear, cultivated a frown and began his first lecture tour in the first chautauqua, and it will be so until the high gods, tired of the farce at last, obliterate the race with one great, final blast of fire, mustard gas and streptococci.

No doubt the imagination of man is to blame for this singular weakness. That imagination, I daresay, is what gave him his first lift above his fellow primates. It enabled him to visualize a condition of existence better than that he was experiencing, and bit by bit he was able to give the picture a certain crude reality. Even to-day he keeps on going ahead in the same manner. That is, he thinks of something that he would like to be or to get, something appreciably better than what he is or has, and then, by the laborious, costly method of trial and error, he gradually moves toward it. In the process he is often severely punished for his discontent with God's ordinances. He mashes his thumb, he skins his shin; he stumbles and falls; the prize he reaches out for blows up in his hands. But bit by bit he moves on, or, at all events, his heirs and assigns move on. Bit by bit he smooths the path beneath his remaining leg, and achieves pretty toys for his remaining hand to play with, and accumulates delights for his remaining ear and eye.

Alas, he is not content with this slow and sanguinary progress! Always he looks further and further ahead. Always he imagines things just over the sky-line. This body of imaginings constitutes his stock of sweet beliefs, his corpus of high faiths and confidences—in brief, his burden of errors. And that burden of errors is what distinguishes man, even above his capacity for tears, his talents as a liar, his excessive hypocrisy and poltroonery, from all the other orders of mammalia. Man is the yokel *par excellence*, the booby unmatchable, the king dupe of the cosmos. He is chronically and unescapably deceived, not only by the other animals and by the delusive face of nature herself, but also and more particularly by himself—by his in-comparable talent for searching out and embracing what is false, and for overlooking and denying what is true.

The capacity for discerning the essential truth, in fact, is as rare among men as it is common among crows, bullfrogs and mackerel. The man who shows it is a man of quite extraordi-nary quality—perhaps even a man downright diseased. Exhibit a new truth of any natural plausibilty before the great masses of men, and not one in ten thousand will suspect its existence, and not one in a hundred thousand will embrace it without a ferocious resistance. All the durable truths that have come into the world within historic times have been opposed as bitterly as if they were so many waves of smallpox, and every individual who has welcomed and advocated them, absolutely without exception, has been denounced and punished as an enemy of the race. Perhaps "absolutely without exception" goes too far. I substitute "with five or six exceptions." But who were the five or six exceptions? I leave you to think of them; myself, I can't. . . . But I think at once of Charles Darwin and his as-sociates, and of how they were reviled in their time. This revil-ing, of course, is less vociferous than it used to be, chiefly because later victims are in the arena, but the underlying hos-tility remains. Within the past two years the principal Great Thinker of Britain, George Bernard Shaw, has denounced the hypothesis of natural selection to great applause, and a three-times candidate for the American Presidency, William Jennings Bryan, has publicly advocated prohibiting the teaching of it by law. The great majority of Christian ecclesiastics in both English-speaking countries, and with them the great majority of their catachumens, are still committed to the doctrine that Darwin was a scoundrel, and Herbert Spencer another, and Huxley a third—and that Nietzsche is to the three of them what Beelzebub himself is to a trio of bad boys. This is the re-action of the main body of respectable folk in two puissant and idealistic Christian nations to the men who will live in history as the intellectual leaders of the Nineteenth Century. This is the immemorial attitude of men in the mass, and of their cho-sen prophets, to whatever is honest, and important, and most probably true.

But if truth thus has hard sledding, error is given a loving welcome. The man who invents a new imbecility is hailed gladly, and bidden to make himself at home; he is, to the great masses of men, the *beau ideal* of mankind. Go back through the history of the past thousand years and you will find that nine-tenths of the popular idols of the world—not the heroes of small sects, but the heroes of mankind in the mass—have been merchants of palpable nonsense. It has been so in politics, it has been so in religion, and it has been so in every other department of human thought. Every such hawker of the not-true has been opposed, in his time, by critics who denounced and refuted him; his contention has been disposed of immediately it was uttered. But on the side of every one there has been the titanic force of human credulity, and it has sufficed in every case to destroy his foes and establish his immortality.

4
Man and His Soul

Of all the unsound ideas thus preached by great heroes and accepted by hundreds of millions of their eager dupes, probably the most patently unsound is the one that is most widely held, to wit, the idea that man has an immortal soul—that there is a part of him too ethereal and too exquisite to die. Absolutely the only evidence supporting this astounding notion lies in the hope that it is true—which is precisely the evidence underlying the late theory that the Great War would put an end to war, and bring in an era of democracy, freedom, and peace. But even archbishops, of course, are too intelligent to be satisfied permanently by evidence so unescapably dubious; in consequence, there have been efforts in all ages to give it logical and evidential support. Well, all I ask is that you give some of that corroboration your careful scrutiny. Examine, for example, the proofs amassed by five typical witnesses in five widely separated ages: St. John, St. Augustine, Martin Luther, Emanuel Swedenborg and Sir Oliver Lodge. Approach these proofs prayerfully, and study them well. Weigh them in the light of the probabilities, the ordinary intellectual decencies. And then ask yourself if you could imagine a mud-turtle accepting them gravely.

5
Coda

To sum up:

  1. The cosmos is a gigantic fly-wheel making 10,000 revolutions a minute.

  2. Man is a sick fly taking a dizzy ride on it.

  3. Religion is the theory that the wheel was designed and set spinning to give him the ride.

VI.
Star-Spangled Men

I open the memoirs of General Grant, Volume II, at the place where he is describing the surrender of General Lee, and find the following:

> I was without a sword, as I usually was when on horseback on (*sic*) the field, and wore a soldier's blouse for a coat, with the shoulder straps of my rank to indicate to the army who I was.

Anno 1865. I look out of my window and observe an officer of the United States Army passing down the street. Anno 1922. Like General Grant, he is without a sword. Like General Grant, he wears a sort of soldier's blouse for a coat. Like General Grant, he employs shoulder straps to indicate to the army who he is. But there is something more. On the left breast of this officer, apparently a major, there blazes so brilliant a mass of color that, as the sun strikes it and the flash bangs my eyes, I wink, catch my breath and sneeze. There are two long strips, each starting at the sternum and disappearing into the shadows of the axillia—every hue in the rainbow, the spectroscope, the kaleidoscope—imperial purples, *sforzando* reds, wild Irish greens, romantic blues, loud yellows and oranges, rich maroons, sentimental pinks, all the half-tones from ultra-violet to infra-red, all the vibrations from the impalpable to the unendurable. A gallant *Soldat*, indeed! How he would shame a circus ticketwagon if he wore all the medals and badges, the stars and crosses, the pendants and lavallières, that go with those ribbons! . . . I glance at his sleeves. A simple golden stripe on the one—six months beyond the raging main. None on the other—the Kaiser's cannon missed him.

Just what all these ribbons signify I am sure I don't know; probably they belong to campaign medals and tell the tale of butcheries in foreign and domestic parts—mountains of dead Filipinos, Mexicans, Haitians, Dominicans, West Virginia miners, perhaps even Prussians. But in addition to campaign medals and the Distinguished Service Medal there are now

certainly enough foreign orders in the United States to give a
distinct brilliance to the national scene, viewed, say, from
Mars. The Frederician tradition, borrowed by the ragged Continentals and embodied in Article I, Section 9, of the Constitution, lasted until 1918, and then suddenly blew up; to
mention it to-day is a sort of indecorum, and to-morrow, no
doubt, will be a species of treason. Down with Frederick; up
with John Philip Sousa! Imagine what General Pershing would
look like at a state banquet of his favorite American order, the
Benevolent and Protective one of Elks, in all the Byzantine
splendor of his casket of ribbons, badges, stars, garters, sun-
bursts and cockades—the lordly Bath of the grateful motherland, with its somewhat disconcerting "Ich dien"; the gorgeous
tricolor baldrics, sashes and festoons of the Légion d'Honneur;
the grand cross of SS. Maurizio e Lazzaro of Italy; the sinister
Danilo of Montenegro, with its cabalistic monogram of Danilo
I and its sinister hieroglyphics; the breastplate of the Paulownia of Japan, with its rising sun of thirty-two white rays, its
blood-red heart, its background of green leaves and its white
ribbon edged with red; the mystical St. Saviour of Greece,
with its Greek motto and its brilliantly enameled figure of
Christ; above all, the Croix de Guerre of Czecho-Slovakia, a
new one and hence not listed in the books, but surely no
shrinking violet! Alas, Pershing was on the wrong side—that
is, for one with a fancy for gauds of that sort. The most blinding of all known orders is the Medijie of Turkey, which not
only entitles the holder to four wives, but also absolutely requires him to wear a red fez and a frozen star covering his
whole façade. I was offered this order by Turkish spies during
the war, and it wabbled me a good deal. The Alexander of Bulgaria is almost as seductive. The badge consists of an eight-
pointed white cross, with crossed swords between the arms
and a red Bulgarian lion over the swords. The motto is "Za
Chrabrost!" Then there are the Prussian orders—the Red and
Black Eagles, the Pour le Mérite, the Prussian Crown, the Hohenzollern and the rest. And the Golden Fleece of Austria—
the noblest of them all. Think of the Golden Fleece on a man
born in Linn County, Missouri! . . . I begin to doubt that
the General would have got it, even supposing him to have
taken the other side. The Japs, I note, gave him only the grand

cordon of the Paulownia, and the Belgians and Montenegrins were similarly cautious. There are higher classes. The highest of the Paulownia is only for princes, which is to say, only for non-Missourians.

Pershing is the champion, with General March a bad second. March is a K.C.M.G., and entitled to wear a large cross of white enamel bearing a lithograph of the Archangel Michael and the motto, "Auspicium Melioris Aevi," but he is not a K.C.B. Admirals Benson and Sims are also grand crosses of Michael and George, and like most other respectable Americans, members of the Legion of Honor, but they seem to have been forgotten by the Greeks, the Montenegrins, the Italians and the Belgians. The British-born and extremely Anglomaniacal Sims refused the Distinguished Service Medal of his adopted country, but is careful to mention in "Who's Who in America" that his grand cross of Michael and George was conferred upon him, not by some servile gold-stick, but by "King George of England"; Benson omits mention of His Majesty, as do Pershing and March. It would be hard to think of any other American officer, real or bogus, who would refuse the D.S.M., or, failing it, the grand decoration of chivalry of the Independent Order of Odd Fellows. I once saw the latter hung, with ceremonies of the utmost magnificence, upon a bald-headed tinner who had served the fraternity long and faithfully; as he marched down the hall toward the throne of the Supreme Exalted Pishposh a score of little girls, the issue of other tinners, strewed his pathway with roses, and around the stem of each rose was a piece of glittering tinfoil. The band meanwhile played "The Rosary," and, at the conclusion of the spectacle, as fried oysters were served, "Wien Bleibt Wien."

It was, I suspect, by way of the Odd Fellows and other such gaudy heirs to the Deutsche Ritter and Rosicrucians that the lust to gleam and jingle got into the arteries of the American people. For years the austere tradition of Washington's day served to keep the military bosom bare of spangles, but all the while a weakness for them was growing in the civil population. Rank by rank, they became Knights of Pythias, Odd Fellows, Red Men, Nobles of the Mystic Shrine, Knights Templar, Patriarchs Militant, Elks, Moose, Woodmen of the World, Foresters, Hoo-Hoos, Ku Kluxers—and in every new order there were thirty-two degrees, and for every degree there was a badge, and for every badge there was a yard of ribbon. The Nobles of the Mystic Shrine, chiefly paunchy wholesalers of the Rotary Club species, are not content with swords, baldrics, stars, garters and jewels; they also wear red fezes. The Elks run to rubies. The Red Men array themselves like Sitting Bull. The patriotic ice-wagon drivers and Methodist deacons of the Ku Klux Klan carry crosses set with incandescent lights. An American who is forced by his profession to belong to many such orders—say a life insurance solicitor, a bootlegger or a dealer in Oklahoma oil stock—accumulates a trunk full of decorations, many of them weighing a pound. There is an undertaker in Hagerstown, Md., who has been initiated eighteen times. When he robes himself to plant a fellow joiner he weighs three hundred pounds and sparkles and flashes like the mouth of hell itself. He is entitled to bear seven swords, all jeweled, and to hang his watch chain with the golden busts of nine wild animals, all with precious stones for eyes. Put beside this lowly washer of the dead, Pershing newly polished would seem almost like a Trappist.

But even so the civil arm is robbed of its just dues in the department of gauds and radioactivity, no doubt by the direct operation of military vanity and jealousy. Despite a million proofs (and perhaps a billion eloquent arguments) to the contrary, it is still the theory at the official ribbon counter that the only man who serves in a war is the man who serves in uniform. This is soft for the Bevo officer, who at least has his service stripes and the spurs that gnawed into his desk, but it is hard upon his brother Irving, the dollar-a-year man, who worked twenty hours a day for fourteen months buying soap-powder, canned asparagus and raincoats for the army of God. Irving not only labored with inconceivable diligence; he also faced hazards of no mean order, for on the one hand was his natural prejudice in favor of a very liberal rewarding of commercial enterprise, and on the other hand were his patriotism and his fear of Atlanta Penitentiary. I daresay that many and many a time, after working his twenty hours, he found it difficult to sleep the remaining four hours. I know, in fact, survivors of that obscure service who are far worse wrecks to-day than Pershing is. Their reward is—what? Winks, sniffs, innuendos.

If they would indulge themselves in the now almost universal American yearning to go adorned, they must join the Knights of Pythias. Even the American Legion fails them, for though it certainly does not bar non-combatants, it insists that they shall have done their non-combatting in uniform.

What I propose is a variety of the Distinguished Service Medal for civilians,—perhaps, better still, a distinct order for civilians, closed to the military and with badges of different colors and areas, to mark off varying services to democracy. Let it run, like the Japanese Paulownia, from high to low—the lowest class for the patriot who sacrificed only time, money and a few nights' sleep; the highest for the great martyr who hung his country's altar with his dignity, his decency and his sacred honor. For Irving and his nervous insomnia, a simple rosette, with an iron badge bearing the national motto, "Safety First"; for the university president who prohibited the teaching of the enemy language in his learned grove, heaved the works of Goethe out of the university library, cashiered every professor unwilling to support Woodrow for the first vacancy in the Trinity, took to the stump for the National Security League, and made two hundred speeches in moving picture theaters—for this giant of loyal endeavor let no 100 per cent. American speak of anything less than the grand cross of the order, with a gold badge in polychrome enamel and stained glass, a baldric of the national colors, a violet plug hat with a sunburst on the side, the privilege of the floor of Congress, and a pension of $10,000 a year. After all, the cost would not be excessive; there are not many of them. Such prodigies of patriotism are possible only to rare and gifted men. For the grand cordons of the order, *e.g.*, college professors who spied upon and reported the seditions of their associates, state presidents of the American Protective League, alien property custodians, judges whose sentences of conscientious objectors mounted to more than 50,000 years, members of Dr. Creel's herd of 2,000 American historians, the authors of the Sisson documents, etc.—pensions of $10 a day would be enough, with silver badges and no plug hats. For the lower ranks, bronze badges and the legal right to the title of "the Hon.," already every true American's by courtesy.

Not, of course, that I am insensitive to the services of the gentlemen of those lower ranks, but in such matters one must go by rarity rather than by intrinsic value. If the grand cordon or even the nickel plated eagle of the third class were given to every patriot who bored a hole through the floor of his flat to get evidence against his neighbors, the Krausmeyers, and to every one who visited the Hofbräuhaus nightly, denounced the Kaiser in searing terms, and demanded assent from Emil and Otto, the waiters, and to every one who notified the catchpolls of the Department of Justice when the wireless plant was open in the garret of the Arion Liedertafel, and to all who took a brave and forward part in slacker raids, and to all who lent their stenographers funds at 6 per cent. to buy Liberty bonds at 4¼ per cent., and to all who sold out at 99 and then bought in again at 83.56 and to all who served as jurors or perjurers in cases against members and ex-members of the I.W.W., and to the German-American members of the League for German Democracy, and to all the Irish who snitched upon the Irish—if decorations were thrown about with any such lavishness, then there would be no nickel left for our bathrooms. On the civilian side as on the military side the great rewards of war go, not to mere dogged industry and fidelity, but to originality—to the unprecedented, the arresting, the bizarre. The New York *Tribune* liar who invented the story about the German plant for converting the corpses of the slain into soap did more for democracy and the Wilsonian idealism, and hence deserves a more brilliant recognition, than a thousand uninspired hawkers of atrocity stories supplied by Viscount Bryce and his associates. For that great servant of righteousness the grand cordon, with two silver badges and the chair of history at Columbia, would be scarcely enough; for the ordinary hawkers any precious metal would be too much.

Whether or not the Y.M.C.A. has decorated its chocolate pedlars and soul-snatchers I do not know; since the chief Y.M.C.A. lamassary in my town of Baltimore became the scene of a homo-sexual scandal I have ceased to frequent evangelical society. If not, then there should be some governmental recognition of those highly characteristic heroes of the war for democracy. The veterans of the line, true enough, dislike them excessively, and have a habit of denouncing them obscenely when the corn-juice flows. They charged too much for ciga-

rettes; they tried to discourage the amiability of the ladies of
France; they had a habit of being absent when the shells burst
in air. Well, some say this and some say that. A few, at least, of
the pale and oleaginous brethren must have gone into the
Master's work because they thirsted to save souls, and not simply because they desired to escape the trenches. And a few, I
am told, were anything but unpleasantly righteous, as a round
of Wassermanns would show. If, as may be plausibly argued,
these Soldiers of the Double Cross deserve to live at all, then
they surely deserve to be hung with white enameled stars
of the third class, with gilt dollar marks superimposed. Motto:
"Glory, glory, hallelujah!"

But what of the vaudeville actors, the cheer leaders, the
doughnut fryers, the camp librarians, the press agents? I am
not forgetting them. Let them be distributed among all the
classes from the seventh to the eighth, according to their sufferings for the holy cause. And the agitators against Beethoven, Bach, Brahms, Wagner, Richard Strauss, all the rest of
the cacophonous Huns? And the specialists in the crimes of
the German professors? And the collectors for the Belgians,
with their generous renunciation of all commissions above 80
per cent.? And the pathologists who denounced Johannes
Müller as a fraud, Karl Ludwig as an imbecile, and Ehrlich as a
thief? And the patriotic chemists who discovered arsenic in dill
pickles, ground glass in pumpernickel, bichloride tablets in
Bismarck herring, pathogenic organisms in aniline dyes? And
the inspired editorial writers of the New York *Times* and *Tribune*, the Boston *Transcript*, the Philadelphia *Ledger*, the Mo-
bile *Register*, the Jones Corners *Eagle*? And the headline writers?
And the Columbia, Yale and Princeton professors? And the authors of books describing how the Kaiser told them the whole
plot in 1913, while they were pulling his teeth or shining his
shoes? And the ex-ambassadors? And the *Nietzschefresser*? And
the chautauqua orators? And the four-minute men? And the
Methodist pulpit pornographers who switched so facilely from
vice-crusading to German atrocities? And Dr. Newell Dwight
Hillis? And Dr. Henry Van Dyke? And the master minds of the
New Republic? And Tumulty? And the Vigilantes? Let no grateful heart forget them!

Palmer and Burleson I leave for special legislation. If mere university presidents, such as Nicholas Murray Butler, are to have the grand cross, then Palmer deserves to be rolled in malleable gold from head to foot, and polished until he blinds the cosmos—then Burleson must be hung with diamonds like Mrs. Warren and bathed in spotlights like Gaby Deslys. . . . Finally, I reserve a special decoration, to be conferred in camera and worn only in secret chapter, for husbands who took chances and refused to read anonymous letters from Paris: the somber badge of the Ordre de la Cuculus Canorus, first and only class.

VII.

The Poet and His Art

I

"A GOOD prose style," says Prof. Dr. Otto Jerpersen in his great work, "Growth and Structure of the English Language," "is everywhere a late acquirement, and the work of whole generations of good authors is needed to bring about the easy flow of written prose." The learned *Sprachwissenschaftler* is here speaking of Old English, or, as it used to be called when you and I were at the breast of enlightenment, Anglo-Saxon. An inch or so lower down the page he points out that what he says of prose is by no means true of verse—that poetry of very respectable quality is often written by peoples and individuals whose prose is quite as crude and graceless as that, say of the Hon. Warren Gamaliel Harding—that even the so-called Anglo-Saxons of Beowulf's time, a race as barbarous as the modern Jugo-Slavs or Mississippians, were yet capable, on occasion, of writing dithyrambs of an indubitable sweet gaudiness.

The point needs no laboring. A glance at the history of any literature will prove its soundness. Moreover, it is supported by what we see around us every day—that is, if we look in literary directions. Some of the best verse in the modern movement, at home and abroad, has been written by intellectual adolescents who could no more write a first-rate paragraph in prose then they could leap the Matterhorn—girls just out of Vassar and Newnham, young army officers, chautauqua orators, New England old maids, obscure lawyers and doctors, newspaper reporters, all sorts of hollow dilettanti, male and female. Nine-tenths of the best poetry of the world has been written by poets less than thirty years old; a great deal more than half of it has been written by poets under twenty-five. One always associates poetry with youth, for it deals chiefly with the ideas that are peculiar to youth, and its terminology is quite as youthful as its content. When one hears of a poet past thirty-five, he seems somehow unnatural and even a trifle obscene; it is as if one encountered a graying man who still played the Chopin waltzes and believed in elective affinities. But prose, obviously, is a sterner and more elderly matter. All the great masters of prose (and especially of English prose, for its very resilience and brilliance make it extraordinarily hard to write) have had to labor for years before attaining to their mastery of it. The early prose of Abraham Lincoln was remarkable only for its badness; it was rhetorical and bombastic, and full of supernumerary words; in brief, it was a kind of poetry. It took years and years of hard striving for Abe to develop the simple and exquisite prose of his last half-decade. So with Thomas Henry Huxley, perhaps the greatest virtuoso of plain English who has ever lived. His first writings were competent but undistinguished; he was almost a grandfather before he perfected his superb style. And so with Anatole France, and Addison, and T. B. Macaulay, and George Moore, and James Branch Cabell, and Æ., and Lord Dunsany, and Nietzsche, and to go back to antiquity, Marcus Tullius Cicero. I have been told that the average age of the men who made the Authorized Version of the Bible was beyond sixty years. Had they been under thirty they would have made it lyrical; as it was, they made it colossal.

The reason for all this is not far to seek. Prose, however powerful its appeal to the emotions, is always based primarily upon logic, and is thus scientific; poetry, whatever its so-called intellectual content is always based upon mere sensation and emotion, and is thus loose and disorderly. A man must have acquired discipline over his feelings before he can write sound prose; he must have learned how to subordinate his transient ideas to more general and permanent ideas; above all, he must have acquired a good head for words, which is to say, a capacity for resisting their mere lascivious lure. But to write acceptable poetry, or even good poetry, he needs none of these things. If his hand runs away with his head it is actually a merit. If he writes what every one knows to be untrue, in terms that no sane adult would ever venture to use in real life, it is proof of his divine afflation. If he slops over and heaves around in a manner never hitherto observed on land or sea, the fact proves his originality. The so-called forms of verse and the rules of rhyme and rhythm do not offer him difficulties; they offer him refuges. Their purpose is not to keep him in order, but simply to give him countenance by providing him with a formal orderliness when he is most out of order. Using them is like swimming with bladders. The first literary composition of a quick-minded child is always some sort of jingle. It starts out with an inane idea—half an idea. Sticking to prose, it could go no further. But to its primary imbecility it now adds a meaningless phrase which, while logically unrelated, provides an agreeable concord in mere sound—and the result is the primordial tadpole of a sonnet. All the sonnets of the world, save a few of miraculous (and perhaps accidental) quality, partake of this fundamental nonsensicality. In all of them there are ideas that would sound idiotic in prose, and phrases that would sound clumsy and uncouth in prose. But the rhyme scheme conceals this nonsensicality. As a substitute for the missing logical plausibility it provides a sensuous harmony. Reading the thing, one gets a vague effect of agreeable sound, and so the logical feebleness is overlooked. It is, in a sense, like observing a pretty girl, competently dressed and made up, across the footlights. But translating the poem into prose is like meeting and marrying her.

II

Much of the current discussion of poetry—and what, save Prohibition, is more discussed in America?—is corrupted by a fundamental error. That error consists in regarding the thing itself as a simple entity, to be described conveniently in a picturesque phrase. "Poetry," says one critic, "is the statement of overwhelming emotional values." "Poetry," says another, "is an attempt to purge language of everything except its music and its pictures." "Poetry," says a third, "is the entering of delicately imaginative plateaus." "Poetry," says a fourth, "is truth carried alive into the heart by a passion." "Poetry," says a fifth, "is compacted of what seems, not of what is." "Poetry," says a sixth, "is the expression of thought in musical language." "Poetry," says a seventh, "is the language of a state of crisis." And so on, and so on. *Quod est poetica?* They all answer, and yet they all fail to answer. Poetry, in fact, is two quite distinct things. It may be either or both. One is a series of words that are intrinsically musical, in clang-tint and rhythm, as the single word *cellar-door* is musical. The other is a series of ideas, false in themselves, that offer a means of emotional and imaginative escape from the harsh realities of everyday. In brief, (I succumb, like all the rest, to phrase-making), poetry is a comforting piece of fiction set to more or less lascivious music—a slap on the back in waltz time—a grand release of longings and repressions to the tune of flutes, harps, sackbuts, psalteries and the usual strings.

As I say, poetry may be either the one thing or the other—caressing music or caressing assurance. It need not necessarily be both. Consider a familiar example from "Othello":

> Not poppy, nor mandragora,
> Nor all the drowsy syrups of the world
> Shall ever medicine thee to that sweet sleep
> Which thou owed'st yesterday.

Here the sense, at best, is surely very vague. Probably not one auditor in a hundred, hearing an actor recite those glorious lines, attaches any intelligible meaning to the archaic word *owed'st*, the cornerstone of the whole sentence. Nevertheless, the effect is stupendous. The passage assaults and benumbs the faculties like Schubert's "Ständchen" or the slow movement of Schumann's Rhenish symphony; hearing it is a sensuous debauch; the man anæsthetic to it could stand unmoved before Rheims cathedral or the Hofbräuhaus at Munich. One easily recalls many other such bursts of pure music, almost meaningless but infinitely delightful—in Poe, in Swinburne, in Marlowe, even in Joaquin Miller. Two-thirds of the charm of reading Chaucer (setting aside the Rabelaisian comedy) comes out of the mere burble of the words; the meaning, to a modern, is often extremely obscure, and sometimes downright undecipherable. The whole fame of Poe, as a poet, is based upon five short poems. Of them, three are almost pure music. Their intellectual content is of the vaguest. No one would venture to reduce them to plain English. Even Poe himself always thought of them, not as statements of poetic ideas, but as simple utterances of poetic (*i.e.,* musical) sounds.

It was Sidney Lanier, himself a competent poet, who first showed the dependence of poetry upon music. He had little to say, unfortunately, about the clang-tint of words; what concerned him almost exclusively was rhythm. In "The Science of English Verse," he showed that the charm of this rhythm could be explained in the technical terms of music—that all the old gabble about dactyls and spondees was no more than a dog Latin invented by men who were fundamentally ignorant of the thing they discussed. Lanier's book was the first intelligent work ever published upon the nature and structure of the sensuous content of English poetry. He struck out into such new and far paths that the professors of prosody still lag behind him after forty years, quite unable to understand a poet who was also a shrewd critic and a first-rate musician. But if, so deeply concerned with rhythm, he marred his treatise by forgetting clang-tint, he marred it still more by forgetting content. Poetry that is all music is obviously relatively rare, for only a poet who is also a natural musician can write it, and natural musicians are much rarer in the world than poets. Ordinary poetry, average poetry, thus depends in part upon its ideational material, and perhaps even chiefly. It is the *idea* expressed in a poem, and not the mellifluousness of the words used to express it, that arrests and enchants the average connoisseur. Often, indeed, he disdains this mellifluousness, and argues that the idea ought to be set forth without the customary pretty jingling, or, at most, with only the scant jingling that lies in rhythm—in brief, he wants his ideas in the altogether, and so advocates *vers libre*.

It was another American, this time Prof. Dr. F. C. Prescott, of Cornell University, who first gave scientific attention to the intellectual content of poetry. His book is called "Poetry and Dreams." Its virtue lies in the fact that it rejects all the customary mystical and romantic definitions of poetry, and seeks to account for the thing in straightforward psychological terms. Poetry, says Prescott, is simply the verbal materialization of a day-dream, the statement of a Freudian wish, an attempt to satisfy a subconscious longing by saying that it is satisfied. In brief, poetry represents imagination's bold effort to escape from the cold and clammy facts that hedge us in—to soothe the wrinkled and fevered brow with beautiful balderdash. On the precise nature of this beautiful balderdash you can get all the information you need by opening at random the nearest book of verse. The ideas you will find in it may be divided into two main divisions. The first consists of denials of objective facts; the second of denials of subjective facts. Specimen of the first sort:

> God's in His heaven,
> All's well with the world.

Specimen of the second:

> I am the master of my fate;
> I am the captain of my soul.

It is my contention that all poetry (forgetting, for the moment, its possible merit as mere sound) may be resolved into either the one or the other of these frightful imbecilities—that its essential character lies in its bold flouting of what every reflective adult knows to be the truth. The poet, imagining him to be sincere, is simply one who disposes of all the horrors of life on this earth, and of all the difficulties presented by his own inner weaknesses no less, by the childish device of denying them. Is it a well-known fact that love is an emotion that is almost as perishable as eggs—that it is biologically impossible for a given male to yearn for a given female more than a few brief years? Then the poet disposes of it by assuring his girl that he will nevertheless love her forever—more, by pledging his word of honor that he believes that *she* will love *him* forever. Is it equally notorious that there is no such thing as justice in the world—that the good are tortured insanely and the evil go free and prosper? Then the poet composes a piece crediting God with a mysterious and unintelligible theory of jurisprudence, whereby the torture of the good is a sort of favor conferred upon them for their goodness. Is it of almost equally widespread report that no healthy man likes to contemplate his own inevitable death—that even in time of war, with a vast pumping up of emotion to conceal the fact, every soldier hopes and believes that he, personally, will escape? Then the poet, first carefully introducing himself into a bomb-proof, achieves strophes declaring that he is free from all such weakness—that he will deliberately seek a rendezvous with death, and laugh ha-ha when the bullet finds him.

The precise nature of the imbecility thus solemnly set forth depends, very largely, of course, upon the private prejudices and yearnings of the poet, and the reception that is given it depends, by the same token, upon the private prejudices and yearnings of the reader. That is why it is often so difficult to get any agreement upon the merits of a definite poem, *i.e.*, to get any agreement upon its capacity to soothe. There is the man who craves only the animal delights of a sort of Moslem-Methodist paradise: to him "The Frost is on the Pumpkin" is a noble poem. There is the man who yearns to get out of the visible universe altogether and tread the fields of asphodel: for him there is delight only in the mystical stuff of Crashaw, Thompson, Yeats and company. There is the man who revolts against the sordid Christian notion of immortality—an eternity to be spent flapping wings with pious greengrocers and oleaginous Anglican bishops; he finds *his* escape in the gorgeous blasphemies of Swinburne. There is, to make an end of examples, the man who, with an inferiority complex eating out his heart, is moved by a great desire to stalk the world in heroic guise: he may go to the sonorous swanking of Kipling, or he may go to something more subtle, to some poem in which the boasting is more artfully concealed, say Christina Rossetti's "When I am Dead." Many men, many complexes, many secret yearnings! They collect, of course, in groups; if the group happens to be large enough the poet it is devoted to becomes famous. Kipling's great fame is thus easily explained. He appeals to the commonest of all types of men, next to the sentimental type—which is to say, he appeals to the bully and braggart type, the chest-slapping type, the patriot type. Less harshly described, to the boy type. All of us have been Kipling-omaniacs at some time or other. I was myself a very ardent one at 17, and wrote many grandiloquent sets of verse in the manner of "Tommy Atkins" and "Fuzzy-Wuzzy." But if the gifts of observation and reflection have been given to us, we get over it. There comes a time when we no longer yearn to be heroes, but seek only peace—maybe even hope for quick extinction. Then we turn to Swinburne and "The Garden of Proserpine"—more false assurances, more mellifluous play-acting, another tinkling make-believe—but how sweet on blue days!

III

One of the things to remember here (too often it is forgotten, and Dr. Prescott deserves favorable mention for stressing it) is that a man's conscious desires are not always identical with his subconscious longings; in fact, the two are often directly antithetical. No doubt the real man lies in the depths of the subconscious, like a carp lurking in mud. His conscious personality is largely a product of his environment—the reaction of his subconscious to the prevailing notions of what is meet and seemly. Here, of course, I wander into platitude, for the news that all men are frauds was already stale in the days of Hammurabi. The ingenious Freud simply translated the fact into pathological terms, added a bedroom scene, and so laid the foundations for his psychoanalysis. Incidentally, it has always seemed to me that Freud made a curious mistake when he brought sex into the foreground of his new magic. He was, of course, quite right when he set up the doctrine that, in civilized societies, sex impulses were more apt to be suppressed than any other natural impulses, and that the subconscious thus tended to be crowded with their ghosts. But in considering sex impulses, he forgot sex imaginings. Digging out, by painful cross-examination in a darkened room, some startling tale of carnality in his patient's past, he committed the incredible folly of assuming it to be literally true. More often than not, I believe, it was a mere piece of boasting, a materialization of desire—in brief, a poem. It is astonishing that this possibility never occurred to the venerable professor; it is more astonishing that it has never occurred to any of his disciples. He should have psychoanalyzed a few poets instead of wasting all his time upon psychopathic women with sclerotic husbands. He would have dredged amazing things out of their subconsciouses, heroic as well as amorous. Imagine the billions of Boers, Germans, Irishmen and Hindus that Kipling would have confessed to killing!

But here I get into morbid anatomy, and had better haul up. What I started out to say was that a man's preferences in poetry constitute an excellent means of estimating his inner cravings and credulities. The music disarms his critical sense, and he confesses to chershing ideas that he would repudiate with indignation if they were put into plain words. I say he cherishes those ideas. Maybe he simply tolerates them unwillingly; maybe they are no more than inescapable heritages from his barbarous ancestors, like his vermiform appendix. Think of the poems you like, and you will come upon many such intellectual fossils—ideas that you by no means subscribe to openly, but that nevertheless give you a strange joy. I put myself on the block as Exhibit A. There is my delight in Lizette Woodworth Reese's sonnet, "Tears." Nothing could do more violence to my conscious beliefs. Put into prose, the doctrine in the poem would exasperate and even enrage me. There is no man in Christendom who is less a Christian than I am. But here the dead hand grabs me by the ear. My ancestors were converted to Christianity in the year 1535, and remained of that faith until near the middle of the eighteenth century. Observe, now, the load I carry; more than two hundred years of Christianity, and perhaps a thousand years (maybe even two, or three thousand years) of worship of heathen gods before that—at least twelve hundred years of uninterrupted belief in the immortality of the soul. Is it any wonder that, betrayed by the incomparable music of Miss Reese's Anglo-Saxon monosyllables, my conscious faith is lulled to sleep, thus giving my subconscious a chance to wallow in its immemorial superstition?

Even so, my vulnerability to such superstitions is very low, and it tends to grow less as I increase in years and sorrows. As I have said, I once throbbed to the drum-beat of Kipling; later on, I was responsive to the mellow romanticism of Tennyson; now it takes one of the genuinely fundamental delusions of the human race to move me. But progress is not continuous; it has interludes. There are days when every one of us experiences a sort of ontogenetic back-firing, and returns to an earlier stage of development. It is on such days that grown men break down and cry like children; it is then that they play games, or cheer the flag, or fall in love. And it is then that they are in the mood for poetry, and get comfort out of its asseverations of the obviously not true. A truly civilized man, when he is wholly himself, derives no pleasure from hearing a poet state, as Browning stated, that this world is perfect. Such tosh not only does not please him; it definitely offends him, as he is offended by an idiotic article in a newspaper; it roils him to encounter so much stupidity in Christendom. But he may like it when he is drunk, or suffering from some low toxemia, or staggering beneath some great disaster. Then, as I say, the ontogenetic process reverses itself, and he slides back into infancy. Then he goes to poets, just as he goes to women, "glad" books, and dogmatic theology. The very highest orders of men, perhaps, never suffer from such malaises of the spirit, or, if they suffer from them, never succumb to them. These are men who are so thoroughly civilized that even the most severe attack upon the emotions is not sufficient to dethrone their reason. Charles Darwin was such a man. There was never a moment in his life when he sought religious consolation, and there was never a moment when he turned to poetry; in fact, he regarded all poetry as silly. Other first-rate men, more sensitive to the possible music in it, regard it with less positive aversion, but I have never heard of a truly first-rate man who got any permanent satisfaction out of its content. The Browning Societies of the latter part of the nineteenth century (and I choose the Browning Societies because Browning's poetry was often more or less logical in content, and thus above the ordinary intellectually) were not composed of such men as Huxley, Spencer, Lecky, Buckle and Trevelyan, but of third-rate schoolmasters, moony old maids, candidates for theosophy, literary vicars, collectors of Rogers groups, and other such Philistines. The chief propagandist for Browning in the United States was not Henry Adams, or William Summer, or Daniel C. Gilman, but an obscure professor of English who was also an ardent spook-chaser. And what is thus true ontogenetically is also true phylogenetically. That is to say, poetry is chiefly produced and esteemed by peoples that have not yet come to maturity. The Romans had a dozen poets of the first talent before they had a single prose writer of any skill whatsoever. So did the English. So did the Germans. In our own day we see the negroes of the South producing religious and secular verse of such quality that it is taken over by the whites, and yet the number of negroes who show a decent prose style is still very small, and there is no sign of it increasing. Similarly, the white authors of America, during the past ten or fifteen years, have produced a great mass of very creditable poetry, and yet the quality of our prose remains very low, and the Americans with prose styles of any distinction could be counted on the fingers of two hands.

IV

So far I have spoken chiefly of the content of poetry. In its character as a sort of music it is plainly a good deal more respectable, and makes an appeal to a far higher variety of reader, or, at all events, to a reader in a state of greater mental clarity. A capacity for music—by which I mean melody, harmony and clang-tint—comes late in the history of every race. The savage can apprehend rhythm, but he is quite incapable of carrying a tune in any intelligible scale. The negro roustabouts of our own South, who are commonly regarded as very musical, are actually only rhythmical; they never invent melodies, but only rhythms. And the whites to whom their barbarous dance-tunes chiefly appeal are in their own stage of culture. When one observes a room full of well-dressed men and women swaying and wriggling to the tune of some villainous mazurka from the Mississippi levees, one may assume very soundly that they are all the sort of folk who play golf and bridge, and prefer "The Sheik" to "Heart of Darkness" and believe in the League of Nations. A great deal of superficial culture is compatible with that pathetic barbarism, and even a high degree of æsthetic sophistication in other directions. The Greeks who built the Parthenon knew no more about music than a hog knows of predestination; they were almost as ignorant in that department as the modern Iowans or New Yorkers. It was not, indeed, until the Renaissance that music as we know it appeared in the world, and it was not until less than two centuries ago that it reached a high development. In Shakespeare's day music was just getting upon its legs in England; in Goethe's day it was just coming to full flower in Germany; in France and America it is still in the savage state. It is thus the youngest of the arts, and the most difficult, and hence the noblest. Any sane young man of twenty-two can write an acceptable sonnet, or design a habitable house or draw a horse that will not be mistaken for an automobile, but before he may write even a bad string quartet he must go through a long and arduous

training, just as he must strive for years before he may write
prose that is instantly recognizable as prose, and not as a string
of mere words.

The virtue of such great poets as Shakespeare does not lie in
the content of their poetry, but in its music. The content of
the Shakespearean plays, in fact, is often puerile, and sometimes quite incomprehensible. No scornful essays by George
Bernard Shaw and Frank Harris were needed to demonstrate
the fact; it lies plainly in the text. One snickers sourly over the
spectacle of generations of pedants debating the question of
Hamlet's mental processes; the simple fact is that Shakespeare
gave him no more mental processes than a Fifth avenue rector
has, but merely employed him as a convenient spout for some
of the finest music ever got into words. Assume that he has all
the hellish sagacity of a Nietzsche, and that music remains unchanged; assume that he is as idiotic as a Grand Worthy Flub-
dub of the Freemasons, and it still remains unchanged. As it is
intoned on the stage by actors, the poetry of Shakespeare commonly loses content altogether. One cannot make out what
the *cabotin* is saying; one can only observe that it is beautiful.
There are whole speeches in the Shakespearean plays whose
meaning is unknown even to scholars—and yet they remain
favorites, and well deserve to. Who knows, again, what the
sonnets are about? Is the bard talking about the inn-keeper's
wife at Oxford, or about a love affair of a pathological,
Y.M.C.A. character? Some say one thing, and some say the
other. But all who have ears must agree that the sonnets are
extremely beautiful stuff—that the English language reaches in
them the topmost heights of conceivable beauty. Shakespeare
thus ought to be ranked among the musicians, along with
Beethoven. As a philosopher he was a ninth-rater—but so was
old Ludwig. I wonder what he would have done with prose? I
can't make up my mind about it. One day I believe that he
would have written prose as good as Dryden's, and the next
day I begin to fear that he would have produced something as
bad as Swinburne's. He had the ear, but he lacked the logical
sense. Poetry has done enough when it charms, but prose
must also convince.

I do not forget, of course, that there is a borderland in
which it is hard to say, of this or that composition, whether it

is prose or poetry. Lincoln's Gettysburg speech is commonly
reckoned as prose, and yet I am convinced that it is quite as
much poetry as the Queen Mab speech or Marlowe's mighty
elegy on Helen of Troy. More, it is so read and admired by the
great masses of the American people. It is an almost perfect
specimen of a comforting but unsound asseveration put into
rippling and hypnotizing words; done into plain English, the
statements of fact in it would make even a writer of school history-books laugh. So with parts of the Declaration of Independence. No one believes seriously that they are true, but
nearly everyone agrees that it would be a nice thing if they
were true—and meanwhile Jefferson's eighteenth century rhetoric, by Johnson out of John Lyly's "Euphues," completes the
enchantment. In the main, the test is to be found in the audience rather than in the poet. If it is naturally intelligent and in
a sober and critical mood, demanding sense and proofs, then
nearly all poetry becomes prose; if, on the contrary, it is congenitally maudlin, or has a few drinks aboard, or is in love, or
is otherwise in a soft and believing mood, then even the worst
of prose, if it has a touch of soothing sing-song in it, becomes
moving poetry—for example, the diplomatic and political
gospel-hymns of the late Dr. Wilson, a man constitutionally
unable to reason clearly or honestly, but nevertheless one full
of the burbling that caresses the ears of simple men. Most of
his speeches, during the days of his divine appointment, translated into intelligible English, would have sounded as idiotic as
a prose version of "The Blessed Damozel." Read by his opponents, they sounded so without the translation.

But at the extremes, of course, there are indubitable poetry
and incurable prose, and the difference is not hard to distinguish. Prose is simply a form on writing in which the author
intends that his statements shall be accepted as conceivably
true, even when they are about imaginary persons and events;
its appeal is to the fully conscious and alertly reasoning man.
Poetry is a form of writing in which the author attempts to dis-
arm reason and evoke emotion partly by presenting images
that awaken a powerful response in the subconscious and
partly by the mere sough and blubber of words. Poetry is not
distinguished from prose, as Prof. Dr. Lowes says in his "Convention and Revolt in Poetry," by an exclusive phraseology,

but by a peculiar attitude of mind—an attitude of self-delusion, of fact-denying, of saying what isn't true. It is essentially an effort to elude the bitter facts of life, whereas prose is essentially a means of unearthing and exhibiting them. The gap is bridged by sentimental prose, which is half prose and half poetry—Lincoln's Gettysburg speech, the average sermon, the prose of an erotic novelette. Immediately the thing acquires a literal meaning it ceases to be poetry; immediately it becomes capable of convincing an adult and perfectly sober man during the hours between breakfast and luncheon it is indisputably prose.

This quality of untruthfulness pervades all poetry, good and bad. You will find it in the very best poetry that the world has so far produced, to wit, in the sonorous poems of the Jewish Scriptures. The ancient Jews were stupendous poets. Moreover, they were shrewd psychologists, and so knew the capacity of poetry, given the believing mind, to convince and enchant—in other words, its capacity to drug the auditor in such a manner that he accepts it literally, as he might accept the baldest prose. This danger in poetry, given auditors impressionable enough, is too little estimated and understood. It is largely responsible for the persistence of sentimentality in a world apparently designed for the one purpose of manufacturing cynics. It is probably chiefly responsible for the survival of Christianity, despite the hard competition that it has met with from other religions. The theology of Christianity—*i.e.*, its prose—is certainly no more convincing than that of half a dozen other religions that might be named; it is, in fact, a great deal less convincing than the theology of, say, Buddhism. But the poetry of Christianity is infinitely more lush and beautiful than that of any other religion ever heard of. There is more lovely poetry in one of the Psalms than in all of the Non-Christian scriptures of the world taken together. More, this poetry is in both Testaments, the New as well as the Old. Who could imagine a more charming poem than that of the Child in the manger? It has enchanted the world for nearly two thousand years. It is simple, exquisite and overwhelming. Its power to arouse emotion is so great that even in our age it is at the bottom of fully a half of the kindliness, romanticism and humane sentimentality that survive in Christendom. It is worth a million syllogisms.

Once, after plowing through sixty or seventy volumes of bad verse, I described myself as a poetry-hater. The epithet was and is absurd. The truth is that I enjoy poetry as much as the next man—when the mood is on me. But what mood? The mood, in a few words, of intellectual and spiritual fatigue, the mood of revolt against the insoluble riddle of existence, the mood of disgust and despair. Poetry, then, is a capital medicine. First its sweet music lulls, and then its artful presentation of the beautifully improbable soothes and gives surcease. It is an escape from life, like religion, like enthusiasm, like glimpsing a pretty girl. And to the mere sensuous joy in it, to the mere low delight in getting away from the world for a bit, there is added, if the poetry be good, something vastly better, something reaching out into the realm of the intelligent, to wit, appreciation of good workmanship. A sound sonnet is almost as pleasing an object as a well-written fugue. A pretty lyric, deftly done, has all the technical charm of a fine carving. I think it is craftsmanship that I admire most in the world. Brahms enchants me because he knew his trade perfectly. I like Richard Strauss because he is full of technical ingenuities, because he is a master-workman. Well, who ever heard of a finer craftsman than William Shakespeare? His music was magnificent, he played superbly upon all the common emotions—and he did it magnificently, he did it with an air. No, I am no poetry-hater. But even Shakespeare I most enjoy, not on brisk mornings when I feel fit for any deviltry, but on dreary evenings when my old wounds are troubling me, and some fickle one has just sent back the autographed set of my first editions, and bills are piled up on my desk, and I am too sad to work. Then I mix a stiff dram—and read poetry.

VIII.
Five Men at Random

I
Abraham Lincoln

THE backwardness of the art of biography in These States is made shiningly visible by the fact that we have yet to see a first-rate life of either Lincoln or Whitman. Of Lincolniana, of course, there is no end, nor is there any end to the hospitality of those who collect it. Some time ago a publisher told me that there are four kinds of books that never, under any circumstances, lose money in the United States—first, detective stories; secondly, novels in which the heroine is forcibly debauched by the hero; thirdly, volumes on spiritualism, occultism and other such claptrap, and fourthly, books on Lincoln. But despite all the vast mass of Lincolniana and the constant discussion of old Abe in other ways, even so elemental a problem as that of his religious faith—surely an important, matter in any competent biography—is yet but half solved. Here, for example, is the Rev. William E. Barton, grappling with it for more than four hundred large pages in "The Soul of Abraham Lincoln." It is a lengthy inquiry—the rev. pastor, in truth, shows a good deal of the habitual garrulity of his order—but it is never tedious. On the contrary, it is curious and amusing, and I have read it with steady interest, including even the appendices. Unluckily, the author, like his predecessors, fails to finish the business before him. Was Lincoln a Christian? Did he believe in the Divinity of Christ? I am left in doubt. He was very polite about it, and very cautious, as befitted a politician in need of Christian votes, but how much genuine conviction was in that politeness? And if his occasional references to Christ were thus open to question, what of his rather vague avowals of belief in a personal God and in the immortality of the soul? Herndon and some of his other close friends always maintained that he was an atheist, but Dr. Barton argues that this atheism was simply disbelief in the idiotic Methodist and Baptist dogmas of his time—that nine Christian churches out of ten, if he were alive

to-day, would admit him to their high privileges and prerogatives without anything worse than a few warning coughs. As
for me, I still wonder.

The growth of the Lincoln legend is truly amazing. He
becomes the American solar myth, the chief butt of American
credulity and sentimentality. Washington, of late years, has
been perceptibly humanized; every schoolboy now knows that
he used to swear a good deal, and was a sharp trader, and had
a quick eye for a pretty ankle. But meanwhile the varnishers
and veneerers have been busily converting Abe into a plaster
saint, thus making him fit for adoration in the chautauquas
and Y.M.C.A.'s. All the popular pictures of him show him in
his robes of state, and wearing an expression fit for a man
about to be hanged. There is, so far as I know, not a single
portrait of him showing him smiling—and yet he must have
cackled a good deal, first and last: who ever heard of a story-
teller who didn't? Worse, there is an obvious effort to pump all
his human weaknesses out of him, and so leave him a mere
moral apparition, a sort of amalgam of John Wesley and the
Holy Ghost. What could be more absurd? Lincoln, in point of
fact, was a practical politician of long experience and high talents, and by no means cursed with inconvenient ideals. On the
contrary, his career in the Illinois Legislature was that of a
good organization man, and he was more than once denounced by reformers. Even his handling of the slavery question was that of a politician, not that of a fanatic. Nothing
alarmed him more than the suspicion that he was an Abolitionist. Barton tells of an occasion when he actually fled town
to avoid meeting the issue squarely. A genuine Abolitionist
would have published the Emancipation Proclamation the day
after the first battle of Bull Run. But Lincoln waited until the
time was more favorable—until Lee had been hurled out of
Pennsylvania, and, more important still, until the political currents were safely running his way. Always he was a wary fellow,
both in his dealings with measures and in his dealings with
men. He knew how to keep his mouth shut.

Nevertheless, it was his eloquence that probably brought
him to his great estate. Like William Jennings Bryan, he was a
dark horse made suddenly formidable by fortunate rhetoric.
The Douglas debate launched him, and the Cooper Union

speech got him the presidency. This talent for emotional utterance, this gift for making phrases that enchanted the plain
people, was an accomplishment of late growth. His early
speeches were mere empty fireworks—the childish rhodomon-
tades of the era. But in middle life he purged his style of ornament and it became almost baldly simple—and it is for that
simplicity that he is remembered to-day. The Gettysburg
speech is at once the shortest and the most famous oration in
American history. Put beside it, all the whoopings of the Web-
sters, Sumners and Everetts seem gaudy and silly. It is eloquence brought to a pellucid and almost child-like perfection
—the highest emotion reduced to one graceful and irresistible
gesture. Nothing else precisely like it is to be found in the
whole range of oratory. Lincoln himself never even remotely
approached it. It is genuinely stupendous.

But let us not forget that it is oratory, not logic; beauty, not
sense. Think of the argument in it! Put it into the cold words
of everyday! The doctrine is simply this: that the Union soldiers who died at Gettysburg sacrificed their lives to the cause
of self-determination—"that government of the people, by the
people, for the people," should not perish from the earth. It is
difficult to imagine anything more untrue. The Union soldiers
in that battle actually fought against self-determination; it was
the Confederates who fought for the right of their people to
govern themselves. What was the practical effect of the battle
of Gettysburg? What else than the destruction of the old sovereignty of the States, *i.e.*, of the people of the States? The
Confederates went into battle an absolutely free people; they
came out with their freedom subject to the supervision and
vote of the rest of the country—and for nearly twenty years
that vote was so effective that they enjoyed scarcely any freedom at all. Am I the first American to note the fundamental
nonsensicality of the Gettysburg address? If so, I plead my æsthetic joy in it in amelioration of the sacrilege.

2
Paul Elmer More

Nothing new is to be found in the latest volume of Paul
Elmer More's Shelburne Essays. The learned author, undis-

mayed by the winds of anarchic doctrine that blow down his
Princeton stovepipe, continues to hold fast to the notions of
his earliest devotion. He is still the gallant champion sent
against the Romantic Movement by the forces of discipline
and decorum. He is still the eloquent fugleman of the Puritan
ethic and æsthetic. In so massive a certainty, so resolute an im-
movability there is something almost magnificent. These are
somewhat sad days for the exponents of that ancient correctness. The Goths and the Huns are at the gate, and as they bat-
ter wildly they throw dead cats, perfumed lingerie, tracts
against predestination, and the bound files of the *Nation*, the
Freeman and the *New Republic* over the fence. But the din
does not flabbergast Dr. More. High above the blood-bathed
battlements there is a tower, of ivory within and solid ferro-
concrete without, and in its austere upper chamber he sits
undaunted, solemnly composing an elegy upon Jonathan Edwards, "the greatest theologian and philosopher yet produced
in this country."

Magnificent, indeed—and somehow charming. On days
when I have no nobler business I sometimes join the barbarians and help them to launch their abominable bombs against
the embattled blue-noses. It is, in the main, fighting that is too
easy, too Anglo-Saxon to be amusing. Think of the decayed
professors assembled by Dr. Franklin for the *Profiteers' Review*;
who could get any genuine thrill out of dropping *them*? They
come out on crutches, and are as much afraid of what is
behind them as they are of what is in front of them. Facing all
the horrible artillery of Nineveh and Tyre, they arm themselves with nothing worse than the pedagogical birch. The
janissaries of Adolph Ochs, the Anglo-Saxon supreme archon,
are even easier. One has but to blow a *shofar*, and down they
go. Even Prof. Dr. Stuart P. Sherman is no antagonist to delight a hard-boiled heretic. Sherman is at least honestly American, of course, but the trouble with him is that he is *too*
American. The Iowa hayseed remains in his hair; he can't get
rid of the smell of the chautauqua; one inevitably sees in him a
sort of *reductio ad absurdum* of his fundamental theory—to
wit, the theory that the test of an artist is whether he hated the
Kaiser in 1917, and plays his honorable part in Christian Endeavor, and prefers Coca-Cola to Scharlachberger 1911, and has

taken to heart the great lessons of sex hygiene. Sherman is game, but he doesn't offer sport in the grand manner. Moreover, he has been showing sad signs of late of a despairing heart: he tries to be ingratiating, and begins to hug in the clinches.

The really tempting quarry is More. To rout him out of his armored tower, to get him out upon the glacis for a duel before both armies, to bring him finally to the wager of battle —this would be an enterprise to bemuse the most audacious and give pause to the most talented. More has a solid stock of learning in his lockers; he is armed and outfitted as none of the pollyannas who trail after him is armed and outfitted; he is, perhaps, the nearest approach to a genuine scholar that we have in America, God save us all! But there is simply no truculence in him, no flair for debate, no lust to do execution upon his foes. His method is wholly *ex parte*. Year after year he simply iterates and reiterates his misty protests, seldom changing so much as a word. Between his first volume and his last there is not the difference between Gog and Magog. Steadily, ploddingly, vaguely, he continues to preach the gloomy gospel of tightness and restraint. He was against "the electric thrill of freer feeling" when he began, and he will be against it on that last gray day—I hope it long post-dates my own hanging— when the ultimate embalmer sneaks upon him with velvet tread, and they haul down the flag to half-staff at Princeton, and the readers of the New York *Evening Journal* note that an obscure somebody named Paul E. More is dead.

3

Madison Cawein

A vast and hefty tome celebrates this dead poet, solemnly issued by his mourning friends in Louisville. The editor is Otto A. Rothert, who confesses that he knew Cawein but a year or two, and never read his poetry until after his death. The contributors include such local *literati* as Reuben Post Halleck, Leigh Gordon Giltner, Anna Blanche McGill and Elvira S. Miller Slaughter. Most of the ladies gush over the departed in the manner of high-school teachers paying tribute to Plato, Montaigne or Dante Alighieri. His young son, seventeen years old, contributes by far the most vivid and intelligent account of him; it is, indeed, very well written, as, in a different way, is the contribution of Charles Hamilton Musgrove, an old newspaper friend. The ladies, as I hint, simply swoon and grow lyrical. But it is a fascinating volume, all the same, and well worth the room it takes on the shelf. Mr. Rothert starts off with what he calls a "picturography" of Cawein—the poet's father and mother in the raiment of 1865, the coat-of-arms of his mother's great-grandfather's uncle, the house which now stands on the site of the house in which he was born, the rock spring from which he used to drink as a boy, a group showing him with his three brothers, another showing him with one brother and their cousin Fred, Cawein himself with sideboards, the houses he lived in, the place where he worked, the walks he liked around Louisville, his wife and baby, the hideous bust of him in the Louisville Public Library, the church from which he was buried, his modest grave in Cave Hill Cemetery—in brief, all the photographs that collect about a man as he staggers through life, and entertain his ribald grandchildren after he is gone. Then comes a treatise on the ancestry and youth of the poet, then a collection of newspaper clippings about him, then a gruesomely particular account of his death, then a fragment of autobiography, then a selection from his singularly dull letters, then some prose pieces from his pen, then the aforesaid tributes of his neighbors, and finally a bibliography of his works, and an index to them.

As I say, a volume of fearful bulk and beam, but nevertheless full of curious and interesting things. Cawein, of course, was not a poet of the first rank, nor is it certain that he has any secure place in the second rank, but in the midst of a great deal of obvious and feeble stuff he undoubtedly wrote some nature lyrics of excellent quality. The woods and the fields were his delight. He loved to roam through them, observing the flowers, the birds, the tall trees, the shining sky overhead, the green of Spring, the reds and browns of Autumn, the still whites of Winter. There were times when he got his ecstasy into words —when he wrote poems that were sound and beautiful. These poems will not be forgotten; there will be no history of American literature written for a hundred years that does not mention Madison Cawein. But what will the literary historians make of the man himself: How will they explain his possession, however fitfully, of the divine gift—his genuine kinship with Wordsworth and Shelley? Certainly no more unlikely candidate for the bays ever shinned up Parnassus. His father was a quack doctor; his mother was a professional spiritualist; he himself, for years and years, made a living as cashier in a gambling-house! Could anything be more grotesque? Is it possible to imagine a more improbable setting for a poet? Yet the facts are the facts, and Mr. Rothert makes no attempt whatever to conceal them. Add a final touch of the bizarre: Cawein fell over one morning while shaving in his bathroom, and cracked his head on the bathtub, and after his death there was a row over his life insurance. Mr. Rothert presents all of the documents. The autopsy is described; the death certificate is quoted. . . . A strange, strange tale, indeed!

4
Frank Harris

Though, so far as I know, this Harris is a perfectly reputable man, fearing God and obeying the laws, it is not to be gainsaid that a certain flavor of the sinister hangs about his aspect. The first time I ever enjoyed the honor of witnessing him, there bobbed up in my mind (instantly put away as unworthy and unseemly) a memory of the handsome dogs who used to chain shrieking virgins to railway tracks in the innocent, pre-Ibsenish dramas of my youth, the while a couple of stage hands imitated the rumble of the Empire State Express in the wings. There was the same elegance of turn-out, the same black mustachios, the same erect figure and lordly air, the same agate glitter in the eyes, the same aloof and superior smile. A sightly fellow, by all the gods, and one who obviously knew how to sneer. That afternoon, in fact, we had a sneering match, and before it was over most of the great names in the letters and politics of the time, *circa* 1914, had been reduced to faint hisses and ha-has. . . . Well, a sneerer has his good days and his bad days. There are times when his gift gives him such comfort that it can be matched only by God's grace, and there are times when it launches upon him such showers of darts that he is bound to feel a few stings. Harris got the darts first, for the year that he came back to his native land, after a generation of exile, was the year in which Anglomania rose to the dignity of a national religion—and what he had to say about the English, among whom he had lived since the early 80's, was chiefly of a very waspish and disconcerting character. Worse, he not only said it, twirling his mustache defiantly; he also wrote it down, and published it in a book. This book was full of shocks for the rapt worshippers of the Motherland, and particularly for the literary *Kanonendelicatessen* who followed the pious leadership of Woodrow and Ochs, Putnam and Roosevelt, Wister and Cyrus Curtis, young Reid and Mrs. Jay. So they called a special meeting of the American Academy of Arts and Letters, sang "God Save the King," kissed the Union Jack, and put Harris into Coventry. And there he remained for five or six long years. The literary reviews never mentioned him. His books were expunged from the minutes. When he was heard of at all, it was only in whispers, and the general burden of those whispers was that he was in the pay of the Kaiser, and plotting to garrot the Rev. Dr. William T. Manning. . . .

So down to 1921. Then the English, with characteristic lack of delicacy, played a ghastly trick upon all those dutiful and well-meaning colonists. That is to say, they suddenly forgave Harris his criminal refusal to take their war buncombe seriously, exhumed him from his long solitude among the Anglo-Ashkenazim, and began praising him in rich, hearty terms as a literary gentleman of the first water, and even as the chief adornment of American letters! The English notices of his "Contemporary Portraits: Second Series" were really quite amazing. The London *Times* gave him two solid columns, and where the *Times* led, all the other great organs of English literary opinion followed. The book itself was described as something extraordinary, a piece of criticism full of shrewdness and originality, and the author was treated with the utmost politeness. . . . One imagines the painful sensation in the New York *Times* office, the dismayed groups around far-flung campus pumps, the special meetings of the Princeton, N.J., and Urbana, Ill., American Legions, the secret conference between the National Institute of Arts and Letters and the Ku Klux Klan. But though there was tall talk by hot heads, nothing could be done. Say "Wo!" and the dutiful jackass turns to the right; say "Gee!" and he turns to the left. It is too much, of course, to ask him to cheer as well as turn—but he nevertheless turns. Since 1921 I have heard no more whispers against Harris from professors and Vigilantes. But on two or three occasions, the subject coming up, I have heard him sneer his master sneer, and each time my blood has run cold.

Well, what is in him? My belief, frequently expressed, is that there is a great deal. His "Oscar Wilde" is, by long odds, the best literary biography ever written by an American—an astonishingly frank, searching and vivid reconstruction of character —a piece of criticism that makes all ordinary criticism seem professorial and lifeless. The Comstocks, I need not say, tried to suppress it; a brilliant light is thrown upon Harris by the fact that they failed ignominiously. All the odds were in favor of the Comstocks; they had patriotism on their side and the help of all the swine who flourished in those days; nevertheless, Harris gave them a severe beating, and scared them half to death. In brief, a man of the most extreme bellicosity, enterprise and courage—a fellow whose ideas are expressed absolutely regardless of tender feelings, whether genuine or bogus. In "The Man Shakespeare" and "The Women of Shakespeare" he tackled the whole body of academic English critics *en masse*—and routed them *en masse*. The two books, marred perhaps by a too bombastic spirit, yet contain some of the soundest, shrewdest and most convincing criticism of Shakespeare that has ever been written. All the old hocus-pocus is thrown overboard. There is an entirely new examination of the materials, and to the business is brought a knowledge of the plays so ready and so vast that that of even the most learned don begins to seem a mere smattering. The same great grasp of facts and evidences is visible in the sketches which make up the three volumes of "Contemporary Portraits." What one always gets out of them is a feeling that the man knows the men he is writing about—that he not only knows what he sets down, but a great deal more. There is here nothing of the cold correctness of the usual literary "estimate." Warts are not forgotten, whether of the nose or of the immortal soul. The subject, beginning as a political shibboleth or a row of books, gradually takes on all the colors of life, and then begins to move, naturally and freely. I know of no more

· brilliant evocations of personality in any literature—and most of them are personalities of sharp flavor, for Harris, in his day, seems to have known almost everybody worth knowing, and whoever he knew went into his laboratory for vivisection.

The man is thus a first rate critic of his time, and what he has written about his contemporaries is certain to condition the view of them held in the future. What gives him his value in this difficult field is, first of all and perhaps most important of all, his cynical detachment—his capacity for viewing men and ideas objectively. In his life, of course, there have been friendships and some of them have been strong and long-continued, but when he writes it is with a sort of surgical remoteness, as if the business in hand were vastly more important than the man. He was lately protesting violently that he was and is quite devoid of malice. Granted. But so is a surgeon. To write of George Moore as he has written may be writing devoid of malice, but nevertheless the effect is precisely that which would follow if some malicious enemy were to drag poor George out of his celibate couch in the dead of night, and chase him naked down Shaftsbury avenue. The thing is appallingly revelatory—and I believe that it is true. The Moore that he depicts may not be absolutely the real Moore, but he is unquestionably far nearer to the real Moore than the Moore of the Moore books. The method, of course, has its defects. Harris is far more interested, fundamentally, in men than in their ideas: the catholic sweep of his "Contemporary Portraits" proves it. In consequence his judgments of books are often colored by his opinions of their authors. He dislikes Mark Twain as his own antithesis: a trimmer and poltroon. *Ergo*, "A Connecticut Yankee" is drivel, which leads us, as Euclid hath it, to absurdity. He once had a row with Dreiser. *Ergo*, "The Titan" is nonsense, which is itself nonsense. But I know of no critic who is wholly free from that quite human weakness. In the academic bunkophagi it is everything; they are willing to swallow anything so long as the author is sound upon the League of Nations. It seems to me that such aberrations are rarer in Harris than in most. He may have violent prejudices, but it is seldom that they play upon a man who is honest.

I judge from his frequent discussions of himself—he is happily free from the vanity of modesty—that the pets of his secret heart are his ventures into fiction, and especially, "The Bomb" and "Montes the Matador." The latter has been greatly praised by Arnold Bennett, who has also praised Leonard Merrick. I have read it four or five times, and always with enjoyment. It is a powerful and adept tale; well constructed and beautifully written; it recalls some of the best of the shorter stories of Thomas Hardy. Alongside it one might range half a dozen other Harris stories—all of them carefully put together, every one the work of a very skillful journeyman. But despite Harris, the authentic Harris is not the story-writer: he has talents, of course, but it would be absurd to put "Montes the Matador" beside "Heart of Darkness." In "Love in Youth" he descends to unmistakable fluff and feebleness. The real Harris is the author of the Wilde volumes, of the two books about Shakespeare, of the three volumes of "Contemporary Portraits." Here there is stuff that lifts itself clearly and brilliantly above the general—criticism that has a terrific vividness and plausibility, and all the gusto that the professors can never pump up. Harris makes his opinions not only interesting, but important. What he has to say always seems novel, ingenious, and true. Here is the chief lifework of an American who, when all values are reckoned up, will be found to have been a sound artist and an extremely intelligent, courageous and original man—and infinitely the superior of the poor dolts who once tried so childishly to dispose of him.

5

Havelock Ellis

If the test of the personal culture of a man be the degree of his freedom from the banal ideas and childish emotions which move the great masses of men, then Havelock Ellis is undoubtedly the most civilized Englishman of his generation. He is a man of the soundest and widest learning, but it is not his positive learning that gives him distinction; it is his profound and implacable skepticism, his penetrating eye for the transient, the disingenuous, and the shoddy. So unconditioned a skepticism, it must be plain, is not an English habit. The average Englishman of science, though he may challenge the Continentals within his speciality, is only too apt to sink to the level

of a politician, a green grocer, or a suburban clergyman outside it. The examples of Wallace, Crookes, and Lodge are anything but isolated. Scratch an English naturalist and you are
likely to discover a spiritualist; take an English metaphysician
to where the band is playing, and if he begins to snuffle patri-
otically you need not be surprised. The late war uncovered this
weakness in a wholesale manner. The English *Gelehrten*, as a
class, not only stood by their country; they also stood by the
Hon. David Lloyd George, the *Daily Mail*, and the mob in
Trafalgar Square. Unluckily, the asinine manifestations ensuing
—for instance, the "proofs" of the eminent Oxford philologist
that the Germans had never contributed anything to philology—are not to be described with good grace by an American,
for they were far surpassed on this side of the water. England at
least had Ellis, with Bertrand Russell, Wilfrid Scawen Blunt,
and a few others in the background. We had, on that plane, no
one.

Ellis, it seems to me, stood above all the rest, and precisely
because his dissent from the prevailing imbecilities was quite
devoid of emotion and had nothing in it of brummagen moral
purpose. Too many of the heretics of the time were simply orthodox witch-hunters off on an unaccustomed tangent. In
their disorderly indignation they matched the regular professors; it was only in the objects of their ranting that they differed. But Ellis kept his head throughout. An Englishman of
the oldest native stock, an unapologetic lover of English scenes
and English ways, an unshaken believer in the essential soundness and high historical destiny of his people, he simply stood
aside from the current clown-show and waited in patience for
sense and decency to be restored. His "Impressions and Comments," the record of his war-time reflections, is not without
its note of melancholy; it was hard to look on without depression. But for the man of genuine culture there were at least
some resources remaining within himself, and what gives this
volume its chief value is its picture of how such a man made
use of them. Ellis, facing the mob unleashed, turned to concerns and ideas beyond its comprehension—to the humanism
that stands above all such sordid conflicts. There is something
almost of Renaissance dignity in his chronicle of his speculations. The man that emerges is not a mere scholar immured in

a cell, but a man of the world superior to his race and his time—a philosopher viewing the childish passion of lesser men disdainfully and yet not too remote to understand it, and even to see in it a certain cosmic use. A fine air blows through the book. It takes the reader into the company of one whose mind is a rich library and whose manner is that of a gentleman. He is the complete anti-Kipling. In him the Huxleian tradition comes to full flower.

His discourse ranges from Beethoven to Comstockery and from Spanish architecture to the charm of the English village. The extent of the man's knowledge is really quite appalling. His primary work in the world has been that of a psychologist, and in particular he has brought a great erudition and an extraordinarily sound judgment to the vexatious problems of the psychology of sex, but that professional concern, extending over so many years, has not prevented him from entering a dozen other domains of speculation, nor has it dulled his sensitiveness to beauty nor his capacity to evoke it. His writing was never better than in this volume. His style, especially towards the end, takes on a sort of glowing clarity. It is English that is as transparent as a crystal, and yet it is English that is full of fine colors and cadences. There could be no better investiture for the questionings and conclusions of so original, so curious, so learned, and, above all, so sound and hearty a man.

IX.

The Nature of Liberty

EVERY time an officer of the constabulary, in the execution of his just and awful powers under American law, produces a compound fracture of the occiput of some citizen in his custody, with hemorrhage, shock, coma and death, there comes a feeble, falsetto protest from specialists in human liberty. Is it a fact without significance that this protest is never supported by the great body of American freemen, setting aside the actual heirs and creditors of the victim? I think not. Here, as usual, public opinion is very realistic. It does not rise against the policeman for the plain and simple reason that it does not question his right to do what he has done. Policemen are not given night-sticks for ornament. They are given them for the purpose of cracking the skulls of the recalcitrant plain people, Democrats and Republicans alike. When they execute that high duty they are palpably within their rights.

The specialists aforesaid are the same fanatics who shake the air with sobs every time the Postmaster-General of the United States bars a periodical from the mails because its ideas do not please him, and every time some poor Russian is deported for reading Karl Marx, and every time a Prohibition enforcement officer murders a bootlegger who resists his levies, and every time agents of the Department of Justice throw an Italian out of the window, and every time the Ku Klux Klan or the American Legion tars and feathers a Socialist evangelist. In brief, they are Radicals, and to scratch one with a pitchfork is to expose a Bolshevik. They are men standing in contempt of American institutions and in enmity to American idealism. And their evil principles are no less offensive to right-thinking and red-blooded Americans when they are United States Senators or editors of wealthy newspapers than when they are degraded I.W.W.'s throwing dead cats and infernal machines into meetings of the Rotary Club.

What ails them primarily is the ignorant and uncritical monomania that afflicts every sort of fanatic, at all times and everywhere. Having mastered with their limited faculties the theoretical principles set forth in the Bill of Rights, they work themselves into a passionate conviction that those principles are identical with the rules of law and justice, and ought to be enforced literally, and without the slightest regard for circumstance and expediency. It is precisely as if a High Church rector, accidentally looking into the Book of Chronicles, and especially Chapter II, should suddenly issue a mandate from his pulpit ordering his parishioners, on penalty of excommunication and the fires of hell, to follow exactly the example set forth, to wit: "And Jesse begat his first born Eliab, and Abinadab the second, and Shimma the third, Netheneel the fourth, Raddai the fifth, Ozen the sixth, David the seventh," and so on. It might be very sound theoretical theology, but it would surely be out of harmony with modern ideas, and the rev. gentleman would be extremely lucky if the bishop did not give him 10 days in the diocesan hoosegow.

So with the Bill of Rights. As adopted by the Fathers of the Republic, it was gross, crude, inelastic, a bit fanciful and transcendental. It specified the rights of a citizen, but it said nothing whatever about his duties. Since then, by the orderly processes of legislative science and by the even more subtle and beautiful devices of juridic art, it has been kneaded and mellowed into a far greater pliability and reasonableness. On the one hand, the citizen still retains the great privilege of membership in the most superb free nation ever witnessed on this earth. On the other hand, as a result of countless shrewd enactments and sagacious decisions, his natural lusts and appetites are held in laudable check, and he is thus kept in order and decorum. No artificial impediment stands in the way of his highest aspiration. He may become anything, including even a policeman. But once a policeman, he is protected by the legislative and judicial arms in the peculiar rights and prerogatives that go with his high office, including especially the right to jug the laity at his will, to sweat and mug them, to subject them to the third degree, and to subdue their resistance by beating out their brains. Those who are unaware of this are simply ignorant of the basic principles of American jurisprudence, as they have been exposed times without number by the courts of first instance and ratified in lofty terms by the

Supreme Court of the United States. The one aim of the controlling decisions, magnificently attained, is to safeguard public order and the public security, and to substitute a judicial process for the inchoate and dangerous interaction of discordant egos.

Let us imagine an example. You are, say, a peaceable citizen on your way home from your place of employment. A police sergeant, detecting you in the crowd, approaches you, lays his hand on your collar, and informs you that you are under arrest for killing a trolley conductor in Altoona, Pa., in 1917. Amazed by the accusation, you decide hastily that the officer has lost his wits, and take to your heels. He pursues you. You continue to run. He draws his revolver and fires at you. He misses you. He fires again and fetches you in the leg. You fall and he is upon you. You prepare to resist his apparently maniacal assault. He beats you into insensibility with his espantoon, and drags you to the patrol box.

Arrived at the watch house you are locked in a room with five detectives, and for six hours they question you with subtle art. You grow angry—perhaps robbed of your customary politeness by the throbbing in your head and leg—and answer tartly. They knock you down. Having failed to wring a confession from you, they lock you in a cell, and leave you there all night. The next day you are taken to police headquarters, your photograph is made for the Rogues' Gallery, and a print is duly deposited in the section labeled "Murderers." You are then carted to jail and locked up again. There you remain until the trolley conductor's wife comes down from Altoona to identify you. She astonishes the police by saying that you are not the man. The actual murderer, it appears, was an Italian. After holding you a day or two longer, to search your house for stills, audit your income tax returns, and investigate the premarital chastity of your wife, they let you go.

You are naturally somewhat irritated by your experience and perhaps your wife urges you to seek redress. Well, what are your remedies? If you are a firebrand, you reach out absurdly for those of a preposterous nature: the instant jailing of the sergeant, the dismissal of the Police Commissioner, the release of Mooney, a fair trial for Sacco and Vanzetti, free trade with Russia, One Big Union. But if you are a 100 per cent. American and respect the laws and institutions of your country, you send for your solicitor—and at once he shows you just how far your rights go, and where they end. You cannot cause the arrest of the sergeant, for you resisted him when he attempted to arrest you, and when you resisted him he acquired an instant right to take you by force. You cannot proceed against him for accusing you falsely, for he has a right to make summary arrests for felony, and the courts have many times decided that a public officer, so long as he cannot be charged with corruption or malice, is not liable for errors of judgment made in the execution of his sworn duty. You cannot get the detectives on the mat, for when they questioned you you were a prisoner accused of murder, and it was their duty and their right to do so. You cannot sue the turnkey at the watch house or the warden at the jail for locking you up, for they received your body, as the law says, in a lawful and regular manner, and would have been liable to penalty if they had turned you loose.

But have you no redress whatever, no rights at all? Certainly you have a right, and the courts have jealously guarded it. You have a clear right, guaranteed to you under the Constitution, to go into a court of equity and apply for a mandamus requiring the *Polizei* to cease forthwith to expose your portrait in the Rogues' Gallery among the murderers. This is your inalienable right, and no man or men on earth can take it away from you. You cannot prevent them cherishing your portrait in their secret files, but you can get an order commanding them to refrain forever from exposing it to the gaze of idle visitors, and if you can introduce yourself unseen into their studio and prove that they disregard that order, you can have them haled into court for contempt and fined by the learned judge.

Thus the law, statute, common and case, protects the free American against injustice. It is ignorance of that subtle and perfect process and not any special love of liberty *per se* that causes radicals of anti-American kidney to rage every time an officer of the *gendarmerie*, in the simple execution of his duty, knocks a citizen in the head. The *gendarme* plainly has an inherent and inalienable right to knock him in the head: it is an essential part of his general prerogative as a sworn officer of the public peace and a representative of the sovereign power of the state. He may, true enough, exercise that prerogative in a manner liable to challenge on the ground that it is imprudent and lacking in sound judgment. On such questions reasonable men may differ. But it must be obvious that the sane and decorous way to settle differences of opinion of that sort is not by public outcry and florid appeals to sentimentality, not by ill-disguised playing to class consciousness and antisocial prejudice, but by an orderly resort to the checks and remedies superimposed upon the Bill of Rights by the calm deliberation and austere logic of the courts of equity.

The law protects the citizen. But to get its protection he must show due respect for its wise and delicate processes.

X.
The Novel

AN unmistakable flavor of effeminacy hangs about the novel, however heroic its content. Even in the gaudy tales of a Rex Beach, with their bold projections of the Freudian dreams of go-getters, ice-wagon drivers, Ku Kluxers, Rotary Club presidents and other such carnivora, there is a subtle something that suggests water-color painting, lip-sticks and bon-bons. Well, why not? When the novel, in the form that we know to-day, arose in Spain toward the end of the sixteenth century, it was aimed very frankly at the emerging women of the Castilian seraglios—women who were gradually emancipating themselves from the *Küche-Kinder-Kirche* darkness of the later Middle Ages, but had not yet come to anything even remotely approaching the worldly experience and intellectual curiosity of men. They could now read and they liked to practice the art, but the grand literature of the time was too profound for them, and too somber. So literary confectioners undertook stuff that would be more to their taste, and the modern novel was born. A single plot served most of these confectioners; it became and remains one of the conventions of the form. Man and maid meet, love, and proceed to kiss—but the rest must wait. The buss remains chaste through long and harrowing chapters; not until the very last scene do fate and Holy Church license anything more. This plot, as I say, still serves, and Arnold Bennett is authority for the doctrine that it is the safest known. Its appeal is patently to the feminine fancy, not to the masculine. Women like to be wooed endlessly before they loose their girdles and are wooed no more. But a man, when he finds a damsel to his taste, is eager to get through the preliminary hocus-pocus as soon as possible.

That women are still the chief readers of novels is known to every book clerk: Joseph Hergesheimer, a little while back, was bemoaning the fact as a curse to his craft. What is less often noted is that women themselves, as they have gradually become fully literate, have forced their way to the front as makers of the stuff they feed on, and that they show signs of ousting the men, soon or late, from the business. Save in the department of lyrical verse, which demands no organization of ideas but only fluency of feeling, they have nowhere else done serious work in literature. There is no epic poem of any solid value by a woman, dead or alive; and no drama, whether comedy or tragedy; and no work of metaphysical speculation; and no history; and no basic document in any other realm of thought. In criticism, whether of works of art or of the ideas underlying them, few women have ever got beyond the *Schwärmerei* of Madame de Staël's "L'Allemagne." In the essay, the most competent woman barely surpasses the average Fleet Street *causerie* hack or Harvard professor. But in the novel the ladies have stood on a level with even the most accomplished men since the day of Jane Austen, and not only in Anglo-Saxondom, but also everywhere else—save perhaps in Russia. To-day it would be difficult to think of a contemporary German novelist of sounder dignity than Clara Viebig, Helene Böhlau or Ricarda Huch, or a Scandinavian novelist clearly above Selma Lagerlöf, or an Italian above Mathilda Serao, or, for that matter, more than two or three living Englishmen above May Sinclair, or more than two Americans equal to Willa Cather. Not only are women writing novels quite as good as those written by men—setting aside, of course, a few miraculous pieces by such fellows as Joseph Conrad: most of them not really novels at all, but metaphysical sonatas disguised as romances—; they are actually surpassing men in their experimental development of the novel form. I do not believe that either Evelyn Scott's "The Narrow House" or May Sinclair's "Life and Death of Harriet Frean" has the depth and beam of, say, Dreiser's "Jennie Gerhardt" or Arnold Bennett's "Old Wives' Tale," but it is certainly to be argued plausibly that both books show a far greater venturesomeness and a far finer virtuosity in the novel form—that both seek to free that form from artificialities which Dreiser and Bennett seem to be almost unaware of. When men exhibit any discontent with those artificialities it usually takes the shape of a vain and uncouth revolt against the whole inner spirit of the novel—that is, against the characteristics which make it what it is. Their lusher imagination tempts them to try to convert it into something that it isn't—for example, an epic,

a political document, or a philosophical work. This fact ex-
plains, in one direction, such dialectical parables as Dreiser's
"The 'Genius,'" H. G. Wells' "Joan and Peter" and Upton
Sinclair's "King Coal," and, in a quite different direction, such
rhapsodies as Cabell's "Jurgen," Meredith's "The Shaving of
Shagpat" and Jacob Wassermann's "The World's Illusion."
These things are novels only in the very limited sense that
Beethoven's "Vittoria" and Goldmark's "Landliche Hochzeit"
are symphonies. Their chief purpose is not that of prose fiction; it is either that of argumentation or that of poetry. The
women novelists, with very few exceptions, are far more careful to remain within the legitimate bounds of the form; they
do not often abandon representation to exhort or exult. Miss
Cather's "My Ántonia" shows a great deal of originality in its
method; the story it tells is certainly not a conventional one,
nor is it told in a conventional way. But it remains a novel none
the less, and as clearly so, in fact, as "The Ordeal of Richard
Feverel" or "Robinson Crusoe."

Much exertion of the laryngeal and respiratory muscles is
wasted upon a discussion of the differences between realistic
novels and romantic novels. As a matter of fact, every authentic novel is realistic in its method, however fantastic it may be
in its fable. The primary aim of the novel, at all times and
everywhere, is the representation of human beings at their follies and villainies, and no other art form clings to that aim so
faithfully. It sets forth, not what might be true, or what ought
to be true, but what actually *is* true. This is obviously not the
case with poetry. Poetry is the product of an effort to invent a
world appreciably better than the one we live in; its essence is
not the representation of the facts, but the deliberate conceal-
ment and denial of the facts. As for the drama, it vacillates, and
if it touches the novel on one side it also touches the epic on
the other. But the novel is concerned solely with human nature as it is practically revealed and with human experience as
men actually know it. If it departs from that representational
fidelity ever so slightly, it becomes to that extent a bad novel; if
it departs violently it ceases to be a novel at all. Cabell, who
shows all the critical deficiencies of a sound artist, is one who
has spent a good deal of time questioning the uses of realism.
Yet it is a plain fact that his own stature as an artist depends

almost wholly upon his capacity for accurate observation and realistic representation. The stories in "The Line of Love," though they may appear superficially to be excessively romantic, really owe all of their charm to their pungent realism. The pleasure they give is the pleasure of recognition; one somehow delights in seeing a mediæval baron acting precisely like a New York stockbroker. As for "Jurgen," it is as realistic in manner as Zola's "La Terre," despite its grotesque fable and its burden of political, theological and epistemological ideas. No one not an idiot would mistake the dialogue between Jurgen and Queen Guinevere's father for romantic, in the sense that Kipling's "Mandalay" is romantic; it is actually as mordantly realistic as the dialogue between Nora and Helmer in the last act of "A Doll's House."

It is my contention that women succeed in the novel—and that they will succeed even more strikingly as they gradually throw off the inhibitions that have hitherto cobwebbed their minds—simply because they are better fitted for this realistic representation than men—because they see the facts of life more sharply, and are less distracted by mooney dreams. Women seldom have the pathological faculty vaguely called imagination. One doesn't often hear of them groaning over colossal bones in their sleep, as dogs do, or constructing heavenly hierarchies or political utopias, as men do. Their concern is always with things of more objective substance—roofs, meals, rent, clothes, the birth and upbringing of children. They are, I believe, generally happier than men, if only because the demands they make of life are more moderate and less romantic. The chief pain that a man normally suffers in his progress through this vale is that of disillusionment; the chief pain that a woman suffers is that of parturition. There is enormous significance in the difference. The first is artificial and self-inflicted the second is natural and unescapable. The psychological history of the differentiation I need not go into here: its springs lie obviously in the greater physical strength of man and his freedom from child-bearing, and in the larger mobility and capacity for adventure that go therewith. A man dreams of utopias simply because he feels himself free to construct them; a woman must keep house. In late years, to be sure, she has toyed with the idea of escaping that necessity, but I shall not bore you with arguments showing that she never will. So long as children are brought into the world and made ready for the trenches, the sweatshops and the gallows by the laborious method ordained of God she will never be quite as free to roam and dream as man is. It is only a small minority of her sex who cherish a contrary expectation, and this minority, though anatomically female, is spiritually male. Show me a woman who has visions comparable, say, to those of Swedenborg, Woodrow Wilson, Strindberg or Dr. Ghandi, and I'll show you a woman who is a very powerful anaphrodisiac.

Thus women, by their enforced preoccupation with the harsh facts of life, are extremely well fitted to write novels, which must deal with the facts or nothing. What they need for the practical business, in addition, falls under two heads. First, they need enough sense of social security to make them free to set down what they see. Secondly, they need the modest technical skill, the formal mastery of words and ideas, necessary to do it. The latter, I believe, they have had ever since they learned to read and write, say three hundred years ago; it comes to them more readily than to men, and is exercised with greater ease. The former they are fast acquiring. In the days of Aphra Behn and Ann Radcliffe it was almost as scandalous for a woman to put her observations and notions into print as it was for her to show her legs; even in the days of Jane Austen and Charlotte Brontë the thing was regarded as decidedly un-ladylike. But now, within certain limits, she is free to print whatever she pleases, and before long even those surviving limits will be obliterated. If I live to the year 1950 I expect to see a novel by a women that will describe a typical marriage under Christianity, from the woman's standpoint, as realistically as it is treated from the man's standpoint in Upton Sinclair's "Love's Pilgrimage." That novel, I venture to predict, will be a cuckoo. At one stroke it will demolish superstitions that have prevailed in the Western World since the fall of the Roman Empire. It will seem harsh, but it will be true. And, being true, it will be a good novel. There can be no good one that is not true.

What ailed the women novelists, until very recently, was a lingering ladyism—a childish prudery inherited from their mothers. I believe that it is being rapidly thrown off; indeed, one often sees a concrete woman novelist shedding it. I give you two obvious examples: Zona Gale and Willa Cather. Miss Gale started out by trying to put into novels the conventional prettiness that is esteemed along the Main Streets of her native Wisconsin. She had skill and did it well, and so she won a good deal of popular success. But her work was intrinsically as worthless as a treatise on international politics by the Hon. Warren Gamaliel Harding or a tract on the duties of a soldier and a gentleman by a state president of the American Legion. Then, of a sudden, for some reason quite unknown to the deponent, she threw off all that flabby artificiality, and began describing the people about her as they really were. The result was a second success even more pronounced than her first, and on a palpably higher level. The career of Miss Cather has covered less ground, for she began far above Main Street. What she tried to do at the start was to imitate the superficial sophistication of Edith Wharton and Henry James—a deceptive thing, apparently realistic in essence, but actually as conventional as table manners or the professional buffooneries of a fashionable rector. Miss Cather had extraordinary skill as a writer, and so her imitation was scarcely to be distinguished from the original, but in the course of time she began to be aware of its hollowness. Then she turned to first-hand representation—to pictures of the people she actually knew. There ensued a series of novels that rose step by step to the very distinguished quality of "My Ántonia." That fine piece is a great deal more than simply a good novel. It is a document in the history of American literature. It proves, once and for all time, that accurate representation is not, as the campus critics of Dreiser seem to think, inimical to beauty. It proves, on the contrary, that the most careful and penetrating representation is itself the source of a rare and wonderful beauty. No romantic novel ever written in America, by man or woman, is one-half so beautiful as "My Ántonia."

As I have said, the novel, in the United States as elsewhere, still radiates an aroma of effeminacy, in the conventional sense. Specifically, it deals too monotonously with the varieties of human transactions which chiefly interest the unintelligent women who are its chief patrons and the scarcely less intelligent women who, until recently, were among its chief commercial manufacturers, to wit, the transactions that re-volve around the ensnarement of men by women—the puerile tricks and conflicts of what is absurdly called romantic love. But I believe that the women novelists, as they emerge into the fullness of skill, will throw overboard all that old baggage, and leave its toting to such male artisans as Chambers, Beach, Coningsby Dawson and Emerson Hough, as they have already left the whole flag-waving and "red-blooded" buncombe. True enough, the snaring of men will remain the principal business of women in this world for many generations, but it would be absurd to say that intelligent women, even to-day, view it ro-mantically—that is, as it is viewed by bad novelists. They see it realistically, and they see it, not as an end in itself, but as a means to other ends. It is, speaking generally, after she has got her man that a woman begins to live. The novel of the future, I believe, will show her thus living. It will depict the intricate complex of forces that conditions her life and generates her ideas, and it will show, against a background of actuality, her conduct in the eternal struggle between her aspiration and her destiny. Women, as I have argued, are not normally ha-rassed by the grandiose and otiose visions that inflame the giz-zards of men, but they too discover inevitably that life is a conflict, and that it is the harsh fate of *Homo sapiens* to get the worst of it. I should like to read a "Main Street" by an articu-late Carol Kennicott, or a "Titan" by one of Cowperwood's mistresses, or a "Cytherea" by a Fanny Randon—or a Savina Grove! It would be sweet stuff, indeed. . . . And it will come.

XI.

The Forward-Looker

WHEN the history of the late years in America is written, I suspect that their grandest, gaudiest gifts to *Kultur* will be found in the incomparable twins: the right-thinker, and the forward-looker. No other nation can match them, at any weight. The right-thinker is privy to all God's wishes, and even whims; the forward-looker is the heir to all His promises to the righteous. The former is never wrong; the latter is never despairing. Sometimes the two are amalgamated into one man, and we have a Bryan, a Wilson, a Dr. Frank Crane. But more often there is a division: the forward-looker thinks wrong, and the right-thinker looks backward. I give you Upton Sinclair and Nicholas Murray Butler as examples. Butler is an absolute masterpiece of correct thought; in his whole life, so far as human records show, he has not cherished a single fancy that might not have been voiced by a Fifth Avenue rector or spread upon the editorial page of the New York *Times*. But he has no vision, alas, alas! All the revolutionary inventions for lifting up humanity leave him cold. He is against them all, from the initiative and referendum to birth control, and from Fletcherism to osteopathy. Now turn to Sinclair. He believes in every one of them, however daring and fantoddish; he grasps and gobbles all the new ones the instant they are announced. But the man simply cannot think right. He is wrong on politics, on economics, and on theology. He glories in and is intensely vain of his wrongness. Let but a new article of correct American thought get itself stated by the constituted ecclesiastical and secular authorities—by Bishop Manning, or Judge Gary, or Butler, or Adolph Ochs, or Dr. Fabian Franklin, or Otto Kahn, or Dr. Stephen S. Wise, or Roger W. Babson, or any other such inspired omphalist—and he is against it almost before it is stated.

On the whole, as a neutral in such matters, I prefer the forward-looker to the right-thinker, if only because he shows more courage and originality. It takes nothing save lack of humor to believe what Butler, or Ochs, or Bishop Manning believes, but it takes long practice and a considerable natural gift to get down the beliefs of Sinclair. I remember with great joy the magazine that he used to issue during the war. In the very first issue he advocated Socialism, the single tax, birth control, communism, the League of Nations, the conscription of wealth, government ownership of coal mines, sex hygiene and free trade. In the next issue he added the recall of judges, Fletcherism, the Gary system, the Montessori method, paper-bag cookery, war gardens and the budget system. In the third he came out for sex hygiene, one big union, the initiative and referendum, the city manager plan, chiropractic and Esperanto. In the fourth he went to the direct primary, fasting, the Third International, a federal divorce law, free motherhood, hot lunches for school children, Prohibition, the vice crusade, *Expressionismus*, the government control of newspapers, deep breathing, international courts, the Fourteen Points, freedom for the Armenians, the limitation of campaign expenditures, the merit system, the abolition of the New York Stock Exchange, psychoanalysis, crystal-gazing, the Little Theater movement, the recognition of Mexico, *vers libre*, old age pensions, unemployment insurance, coöperative stores, the endowment of motherhood, the Americanization of the immigrant, mental telepathy, the abolition of grade crossings, federal labor exchanges, profit-sharing in industry, a prohibitive tax on Poms, the clean-up-paint-up campaign, relief for the Jews, osteopathy, mental mastery, and the twilight sleep. And so on, and so on. Once I had got into the swing of the Sinclair monthly I found that I could dispense with at least twenty other journals of the uplift. When he abandoned it I had to subscribe for them anew, and the gravel has stuck in my craw ever since.

In the first volume of his personal philosophy, "The Book of Life: Mind and Body," he is estopped from displaying whole categories of his ideas, for his subject is not man the political and economic machine, but man and mammal. Nevertheless, his characteristic hospitality to new revelations is abundantly visible. What does the mind suggest? The mind suggests its dark and fascinating functions and powers, some of them very recent. There is, for example, psychoanalysis. There is mental telepathy. There is crystal-gazing. There is double personality. Out of each springs a scheme for the uplift of the race—in each there is something for a forward-looker to get his teeth into. And if mind, then why not also spirit? Here even a forward-looker may hesitate; here, in fact, Sinclair himself hesitates. The whole field of spiritism is barred to him by his theological heterodoxy; if he admits that man has an immortal soul, he may also have to admit that the soul can suffer in hell. Thus even forward-looking may turn upon and devour itself. But if the meadow wherein spooks and poltergeists disport is closed, it is at least possible to peep over the fence. Sinclair sees materializations in dark rooms, under red, satanic lights. He is, perhaps, not yet convinced, but he is looking pretty hard. Let a ghostly hand reach out and grab him, and he will be over the fence! The body is easier. The new inventions for dealing with it are innumerable and irresistible; no forward-looker can fail to succumb to at least some of them. Sinclair teeters dizzily. On the one hand he stoutly defends surgery—that is, provided the patient is allowed to make his own diagnosis!—on the other hand he is hot for fasting, teetotalism, and the avoidance of drugs, coffee and tobacco, and he begins to flirt with osteopathy and chiropractic. More, he has discovered a new revelation in San Francisco—a system of diagnosis and therapeutics, still hooted at by the Medical Trust, whereby the exact location of a cancer may be determined by examining a few drops of the patient's blood, and syphilis may be cured by vibrations, and whereby, most curious of all, it can be established that odd numbers, written on a sheet of paper, are full of negative electricity, and even numbers are full of positive electricity.

The book is written with great confidence and address, and has a good deal of shrewdness mixed with its credulities; few licensed medical practitioners could give you better advice. But it is less interesting than its author, or, indeed, than forward-lookers in general. Of all the known orders of men they fascinate me the most. I spend whole days reading their pronunciamentos, and am an expert in the ebb and flow of their singularly bizarre ideas. As I have said, I have never encountered one who believed in but one sure cure for all the sorrows of the world, and let it go at that. Nay, even the most timorous of them gives his full faith and credit to at least two. Turn, for example, to the official list of eminent single taxers issued by the Joseph Fels Fund. I defy you to find one solitary man on it who stops with the single tax. There is David Starr Jordan: he is also one of the great whales of pacifism. There is B. O. Flower: he is the emperor of anti-vaccinationists. There is Carrie Chapman Catt: she is hot for every peruna that the suffragettes brew. There is W. S. U'Ren: he is in general practise as a messiah. There is Hamlin Garland: he also chases spooks. There is Jane Addams: vice crusader, pacifist, suffragist, settlement worker. There is Prof. Dr. Scott Nearing: Socialist and martyr. There is Newt Baker: heir of the Wilsonian idealism. There is Gifford Pinchot: conservationist, Prohibitionist, Bull Moose, and professional Good Citizen. There is Judge Ben B. Lindsey: forward-looking's Jack Horner, forever sticking his thumb into new pies. I could run the list to columns, but no need. You know the type as well as I do. Give the forward-looker the direct primary, and he demands the short ballot. Give him the initiative and referendum, and he bawls for the recall of judges. Give him Christian Science, and he proceeds to the swamis and yogis. Give him the Mann Act, and he wants laws providing for the castration of fornicators. Give him Prohibition, and he launches a new crusade against cigarettes, coffee, jazz, and custard pies.

I have a wide acquaintance among such sad, mad, glad folks, and know some of them very well. It is my belief that the majority of them are absolutely honest—that they believe as fully in their baroque gospels as I believe in the dishonesty of politicians—that their myriad and amazing faiths sit upon them as heavily as the fear of hell sits upon a Methodist deacon who has degraded the vestry-room to carnal uses. All that may be justly said against them is that they are chronically full of hope, and hence chronically uneasy and indignant—that they belong to the less sinful and comfortable of the two grand divisions of the human race. Call them the tender-minded, as the late William James used to do, and you have pretty well described them. They are, on the one hand, pathologically sensitive to the sorrows of the world, and, on the other hand, pathologically susceptible to the eloquence of quacks. What seems to lie in all of them is the doctrine that evils so vast as those they see about them *must* and *will* be laid—that it would be an insult to a just God to think of them as permanent and irremediable. This notion, I believe, is at the bottom of much of the current pathetic faith in Prohibition. The thing itself is obviously a colossal failure—that is, when viewed calmly and realistically. It has not only not cured the rum evil in the United States; it has plainly made that evil five times as bad as it ever was before. But to confess that bald fact would be to break the forward-looking heart: it simply refuses to harbor the concept of the incurable. And so, being debarred by the legal machinery that supports Prohibition from going back to any more feasible scheme of relief, it cherishes the sorry faith that somehow, in some vague and incomprehensible way, Prohibition will yet work. When the truth becomes so horribly evident that even forward-lookers are daunted, then some new quack will arise to fool them again, with some new and worse scheme of super-Prohibition. It is their destiny to wobble thus endlessly between quack and quack. One pulls them by the right arm and one by the left arm. A third is at their coat-tail pockets, and a fourth beckons them over the hill.

The rest of us are less tender-minded, and, in consequence, much happier. We observe quite clearly that the world, as it stands, is anything but perfect—that injustice exists, and turmoil, and tragedy, and bitter suffering of ten thousand kinds—that human life, at its best, is anything but a grand, sweet song. But instead of ranting absurdly against the fact, or weeping over it maudlinly, or trying to remedy it with inadequate means, we simply put the thought of it out of our minds, just as a wise man puts away the thought that alcohol is probably bad for his liver, or that his wife is a shade too fat. Instead of mulling over it and suffering from it, we seek contentment by pursuing the delights that are so strangely mixed with the horrors—by seeking out the soft spots and endeavoring to avoid the hard spots. Such is the intelligent habit of practical and sinful men, and under it lies a sound philosophy. After all, the world is not our handiwork, and we are not responsible for what goes on in it, save within very narrow limits. Going outside them with our protests and advice tends to become contumacy to the celestial hierarchy. Do the poor suffer in the midst of plenty? Then let us thank God politely that we are not that poor. Are rogues in offices? Well, go call a policeman, thus setting rogue upon rogue. Are taxes onerous, wasteful, unjust? Then let us dodge as large a part of them as we can. Are whole regiments and army corps of our fellow creatures doomed to hell? Then let them complain to the archangels, and, if the archangels are too busy to hear them, to the nearest archbishop.

Unluckily for the man of tender mind, he is quite incapable of any such easy dismissal of the great plagues and conundrums of existence. It is of the essence of his character that he is too sensitive and sentimental to put them ruthlessly out of his mind: he cannot view even the crunching of a cockroach without feeling the snapping of his own ribs. And it is of the essence of his character that he is unable to escape the delusion of duty—that he can't rid himself of the notion that, whenever he observes anything in the world that might conceivably be improved, he is commanded by God to make every effort to improve it. In brief, he is a public-spirited man, and the ideal citizen of democratic states. But Nature, it must be obvious, is opposed to democracy—and whoso goes counter to nature must expect to pay the penalty. The tender-minded man pays it by hanging forever upon the cruel hooks of hope, and by fermenting inwardly in incessant indignation. All this, perhaps, explains the notorious ill-humor of uplifters—the wowser touch that is in even the best of them. They dwell so much upon the imperfections of the universe and the weaknesses of man that they end by believing that the universe is altogether out of joint and that every man is a scoundrel and every woman a vampire. Years ago I had a combat with certain eminent reformers of the sex hygiene and vice crusading species, and got out of it a memorable illumination of their private minds. The reform these strange creatures were then advocating was directed against sins of the seventh category, and they proposed to put them down by forcing through legislation of a very harsh and fantastic kind—statutes forbidding any woman, however forbidding, to entertain a man in her apartment without the presence of a third party, statutes providing for the garish lighting of all dark places in the public parks, and so on. In the course of my debates with them I gradually jockeyed them into abandoning all of the arguments they started with, and so brought them down to their fundamental doctrine, to wit, that no woman, without the aid of the police, could be trusted to protect her virtue. I pass as a cynic in Christian circles, but this notion certainly gave me pause. And it was voiced by men who were the fathers of grown and unmarried daughters!

It is no wonder that men who cherish such ideas are so ready to accept any remedy for the underlying evils, no matter how grotesque. A man suffering from hay-fever, as every one knows, will take any medicine that is offered to him, even though he knows the compounder to be a quack; the infinitesimal chance that the quack may have the impossible cure gives him a certain hope, and so makes the disease itself more bearable. In precisely the same way a man suffering from the conviction that the whole universe is hell-bent for destruction—that the government he lives under is intolerably evil, that the rich are growing richer and the poor poorer, that no man's word can be trusted and no woman's chastity, that another and worse war is hatching, that the very regulation of the weather has fallen into the hands of rogues—such a man will grab at anything, even birth control, osteopathy or the Fourteen Points, rather than let the foul villainy go on. The apparent necessity of finding a remedy without delay transforms itself, by an easy psychological process, into a belief that the remedy has been found; it is almost impossible for most men, and particularly for tender-minded men, to take in the concept of the insoluble. Every problem that remains unsolved, including even the problem of evil, is in that state simply because men of strict virtue and passionate altruism have not combined to solve it—because the business has been neglected by human laziness and rascality. All that is needed to dispatch it is the united effort of enough pure hearts: the accursed nature of things will yield inevitably to a sufficiently desperate battle; mind (usually written Mind) will triumph over matter (usually written Matter—or maybe Money Power, or Land Monopoly, or Beef Trust, or Conspiracy of Silence, or Commercialized Vice, or Wall Street, or the Dukes, or the Kaiser), and the Kingdom of God will be at hand. So, with the will to believe in full function, the rest is easy. The eager forward-looker is exactly like the man with hay-fever, or arthritis, or nervous dyspepsia, or diabetes. It takes time to try each successive remedy—to search it out, to take it, to observe its effects, to hope, to doubt, to shelve it. Before the process is completed another is offered; new ones are always waiting before their predecessors have been discarded. Here, perhaps, we get a glimpse of the causes behind the protean appetite of the true forward-looker—his virtuosity in credulity. He is in all stages simultaneously—just getting over the initiative and referendum, beginning to have doubts about the short ballot, making ready for a horse doctor's dose of the single tax, and contemplating an experimental draught of Socialism tomorrow.

What is to be done for him? How is he to be cured of his great thirst for sure-cures that do not cure, and converted into a contented and careless backward-looker, peacefully snoozing beneath his fig tree while the oppressed bawl for succor in forty abandoned lands, and injustice stalks the world, and taxes mount higher and higher, and poor working-girls are sold into white slavery, and Prohibition fails to prohibit, and cocaine is hawked openly, and jazz drags millions down the primrose way, and the trusts own the legislatures of all Christendom, and judges go to dinner with millionaires, and Europe prepares for another war, and children of four and five years work as stevedores and locomotive firemen, and guinea pigs and dogs are vivisected, and Polish immigrant women have more children every year, and divorces multiply, and materialism rages, and the devil runs the cosmos? What is to be done to save the forward-looker from his torturing indignation, and set him in paths of happy dalliance? Answer: nothing. He was born that way, as men are born with hare lips or bad livers, and he will remain that way until the angels summon him to eternal rest. Destiny has laid upon him the burden of seeing unescapably what had better not be looked at, of believing what isn't so. There is no way to help him. He must suffer vicariously for the carnal ease of the rest of us. He must die daily that we may live in peace, corrupt and contented.

As I have said, I believe fully that this child of sorrow is honest —that his twinges and malaises are just as real to him as those that rack the man with arthritis, and that his trusting faith in quacks is just as natural. But this, of course, is not saying that the quacks themselves are honest. On the contrary, their utter dishonesty must be quite as obvious as the simplicity of their dupes. Trade is good for them in the United States, where hope is a sort of national vice, and so they flourish here more luxuriously than anywhere else on earth. Some one told me lately that there are now no less than 25,000 national organizations in the United States for the uplift of the plain people and the snaring and shaking down of forward-lookers—societies for the Americanization of immigrants, for protecting poor working-girls against Jews and Italians, for putting Bibles into the bedrooms of week-end hotels, for teaching Polish women how to wash their babies, for instructing school-children in ring-around-a-rosy, for crusading against the cigarette, for preventing accidents in rolling-mills, for making street-car conductors more polite, for testing the mentality of Czecho-Slovaks, for teaching folk-songs, for restoring the United States to Great Britain, for building day-nurseries in the devastated regions of France, for training deaconesses, for fighting the house-fly, for preventing cruelty to mules and Tom-cats, for forcing householders to clean their backyards, for planting trees, for saving the Indian, for sending colored boys to Harvard, for opposing Sunday movies, for censoring magazines, for God knows what else. In every large American city such organizations swarm, and every one of them has an executive secretary who tries incessantly to cadge space in the newspapers. Their agents penetrate to the remotest hamlets in the land, and their circulars, pamphlets and other fulminations swamp the mails. In Washington and at every state capital they have their lobbyists, and every American legislator is driven half frantic by their innumerable and preposterous demands. Each of them wants a law passed to make its crusade official and compulsory; each is forever hunting for forward-lookers with money.

One of the latest of these uplifting vereins to score a ten-strike is the one that sponsored the so-called Maternity Bill. That measure is now a law, and the over-burdened American taxpayer, at a cost of $3,000,000 a year, is supporting yet one more posse of perambulating gabblers and snouters. The influences behind the bill were exposed in the Senate by Senator Reed, of Missouri, but to no effect: a majority of the other Senators, in order to get rid of the propagandists in charge of it, had already promised to vote for it. Its one intelligible aim, as Senator Reed showed, is to give government jobs at good salaries to a gang of nosey old maids. These virgins now traverse the country teaching married women how to have babies in a ship-shape and graceful manner, and how to keep them alive after having them. Only one member of the corps has ever been married herself; nevertheless, the old gals are authorized to go out among the Italian and Yiddish women, each with ten or twelve head of kids to her credit, and tell them all about it. According to Senator Reed, the ultimate aim of the forward-lookers who sponsored the scheme is to provide for the official registration of expectant mothers, that they may be warned what to eat, what movies to see, and what midwives to send for when the time comes. Imagine a young bride going down to the County Clerk's office to report herself! And imagine an elderly and anthropopagous spinster coming around next day to advise her! Or a boozy political doctor!

All these crazes, of course, are primarily artificial. They are set going, not by the plain people spontaneously, nor even by the forward-lookers who eventually support them, but by professionals. The Anti-Saloon League is their archetype. It is owned and operated by gentlemen who make excellent livings stirring up the tender-minded; if their salaries were cut off to-morrow, all their moral passion would ooze out, and Prohibition would be dead in two weeks. So with the rest of the uplifting camorras. Their present enormous prosperity, I believe, is due in large part to a fact that is never thought of, to wit, the fact that the women's colleges of the country, for a dozen years past, have been turning out far more graduates than could be utilized as teachers. These supernumerary lady Ph.D's almost unanimously turn to the uplift—and the uplift saves them. In the early days of higher education for women in the United States, practically all the graduates thrown upon the world got jobs as teachers, but now a good many are left over. Moreover, it has been discovered that the uplift is easier than teaching, and that it pays a great deal better. It is a rare woman professor who gets more than $5,000 a year, but there are plenty of uplifting jobs at $8,000 and $10,000 a year, and in the future there will be some prizes at twice as much. No wonder the learned girls fall upon them so eagerly!

The annual production of male Ph.D's is also far beyond the

legitimate needs of the nation, but here the congestion is re-lieved by the greater and more varied demand for masculine labor. If a young man emerging from Columbia or Ohio Wes-leyan as *Philosophiæ Doctor* finds it impossible to get a job teaching he can always go on the road as a salesman of dental supplies, or enlist in the marines, or study law, or enter the ministry, or go to work in a coal-mine, or a slaughter-house, or a bucket-shop, or begin selling Oklahoma mine-stock to wid-ows and retired clergymen. The woman graduate faces far fewer opportunities. She is commonly too old and too worn by meditation to go upon the stage in anything above the grade of a patent-medicine show, she has been so poisoned by instruction in sex hygiene that she shies at marriage, and most of the standard professions and grafts of the world are closed to her. The invention of the uplift came as a godsend to her. Had not some mute, inglorious Edison devised it at the right time, humanity would be disgraced to-day by the spectacle of hordes of Lady Ph.D's going to work in steam-laundries, hooch shows and chewing-gum factories. As it is, they are all taken care of by the innumerable societies for making the whole world virtuous and happy. One may laugh at the aims and methods of many such societies—for example, at the ab-surd vereins for Americanizing immigrants, *i.e.*, degrading them to the level of the native peasantry. But one thing, at least, they accomplish: they provide comfortable and perma-nent jobs for hundreds and thousands of deserving women, most of whom are far more profitably employed trying to make Methodists out of Sicilians than they would be if they were trying to make husbands out of bachelors. It is for this high purpose also that the forward-looker suffers.

XII.

Memorial Service

WHERE is the grave-yard of dead gods? What lingering mourner waters their mounds? There was a day when Jupiter was the king of the gods, and any man who doubted his puissance was *ipso facto* a barbarian and an ignoramus. But where in all the world is there a man who worships Jupiter to-day? And what of Huitzilopochtli? In one year—and it is no more than five hundred years ago—50,000 youths and maidens were slain in sacrifice to him. To-day, if he is remembered at all, it is only by some vagrant savage in the depths of the Mexican forest. Huitzilopochtli, like many other gods, had no human father; his mother was a virtuous widow; he was born of an apparently innocent flirtation that she carried on with the sun. When he frowned, his father, the sun, stood still. When he roared with rage, earthquakes engulfed whole cities. When he thirsted he was watered with 10,000 gallons of human blood. But to-day Huitzilopochtli is as magnificently forgotten as Allen G. Thurman. Once the peer of Allah, Buddha and Wotan, he is now the peer of General Coxey, Richmond P. Hobson, Nan Patterson, Alton B. Parker, Adelina Patti, General Weyler and Tom Sharkey.

Speaking of Huitzilopochtli recalls his brother, Tezcatilpoca. Tezcatilpoca was almost as powerful: he consumed 25,000 virgins a year. Lead me to his tomb: I would weep, and hang a *couronne des perles*. But who knows where it is? Or where the grave of Quitzalcoatl is? Or Tialoc? Or Chalchihuitlicue? Or Xiehtecutli? Or Centeotl, that sweet one? Or Tlazolteotl, the goddess of love? Or Mictlan? Or Ixtlilton? Or Omacatl? Or Yacatecutli? Or Mixcoatl? Or Xipe? Or all the host of Tzitzimitles? Where are their bones? Where is the willow on which they hung their harps? In what forlorn and unheard-of hell do they await the resurrection morn? Who enjoys their residuary estates? Or that of Dis, whom Cæser found to be the chief god of the Celts? Or that of Tarves, the bull? Or that of Moccos, the pig? Or that of Epona, the mare? Or that of Mullo, the celestial jack-ass? There was a time when the Irish revered all these gods as violently as they now hate the English. But to-day even the drunkest Irishman laughs at them.

But they have company in oblivion: the hell of dead gods is as crowded as the Presbyterian hell for babies. Damona is there, and Esus, and Drunemeton, and Silvana, and Dervones, and Adsalluta, and Deva, and Belisama, and Axona, and Vintios, and Taranuous, and Sulis, and Cocidius, and Adsmerius, and Dumiatis, and Caletos, and Moccus, and Ollovidius, and Albiorix, and Leucitius, and Vitucadrus, and Ogmios, and Uxellimus, and Borvo, and Grannos, and Mogons. All mighty gods in their day, worshiped by millions, full of demands and impositions, able to bind and loose—all gods of the first class, not dilettanti. Men labored for generations to build vast temples to them—temples with stones as large as hay-wagons. The business of interpreting their whims occupied thousands of priests, wizards, archdeacons, evangelists, haruspices, bishops, archbishops. To doubt them was to die, usually at the stake. Armies took to the field to defend them against infidels: villages were burned, women and children were butchered, cattle were driven off. Yet in the end they all withered and died, and to-day there is none so poor to do them reverence. Worse, the very tombs in which they lie are lost, and so even a respectful stranger is debarred from paying them the slightest and politest homage.

What has become of Sutekh, once the high god of the whole Nile Valley? What has become of:

Resheph	Baal
Anath	Astarte
Ashtoreth	Hadad
El	Addu
Nergal	Shalem
Nebo	Dagon
Ninib	Sharrab
Melek	Yau
Abijah	Amon-Re
Isis	Osiris
Ptah	Sebek
Anubis	Molech?

All these were once gods of the highest eminence. Many of them are mentioned with fear and trembling in the Old Testament. They ranked, five or six thousand years ago, with Jahveh himself; the worst of them stood far higher than Thor. Yet they have all gone down the chute, and with them the following:

Bilé	Gwydion
Lêr	Manawyddan
Arianrod	Nuada Argetlam
Morrigu	Tagd
Govannon	Goibniu
Gunfled	Odin
Sokk-mimi	Llaw Gyffes
Memetona	Lleu
Dagda	Ogma
Kerridwen	Mider
Pwyll	Rigantona
Ogyrvan	Marzin
Dea Dia	Mars
Ceros	Jupiter
Vaticanus	Cunina
Edulia	Potina
Adeona	Statilinus
Iuno Lucina	Diana of Ephesus
Saturn	Robigus
Furrina	Pluto
Vediovis	Ops
Consus	Meditrina
Cronos	Vesta
Enki	Tilmun
Engurra	Zer-panitu
Belus	Merodach
Dimmer	U-ki
Mu-ul-lil	Dauke
Ubargisi	Gasan-abzu
Ubilulu	Elum
Gasan-lil	U-Tin-dir ki
U-dimmer-an-kia	Marduk
Enurestu	Nin-lil-la
U-sab-sib	Nin

U-Mersi	Persephone
Tammuz	Istar
Venus	Lagas
Bau	U-urugal
Mulu-hursang	Sirtumu
Anu	Ea
Beltis	Nirig
Nusku	Nebo
Ni-zu	Samas
Sahi	Ma-banba-anna
Aa	En-Mersi
Allatu	Amurru
Sin	Assur
Abil Addu	Aku
Apsu	Beltu
Dagan	Dumu-zi-abzu
Elali	Kuski-banda
Isum	Kaawanu
Mami	Nin-azu
Nin-man	Lugal-Amarada
Zaraqu	Qarradu
Suqamunu	Ura-gala
Zagaga	Ueras

You may think I spoof. That I invent the names. I do not. Ask the rector to lend you any good treatise on comparative religion: you will find them all listed. They were gods of the highest standing and dignity—gods of civilized peoples— worshipped and believed in by millions. All were theoretically omnipotent, omniscient and immortal. And all are dead.

XIII.

Education

I

NEXT to the clerk in holy orders, the fellow with the worst job in the world is the schoolmaster. Both are underpaid, both fall steadily in authority and dignity, and both wear out their hearts trying to perform the impossible. How much the world asks of them, and how little they can actually deliver! The clergyman's business is to save the human race from hell: if he saves one-eighth of one per cent., even within the limits of his narrow flock, he does magnificently. The schoolmaster's is to spread the enlightenment, to make the great masses of the plain people intelligent—and intelligence is precisely the thing that the great masses of the plain people are congenitally and eternally incapable of.

Is it any wonder that the poor birchman, facing this labor that would have staggered Sisyphus Æolusohn, seeks refuge from its essential impossibility in a Chinese maze of empty technic? The ghost of Pestalozzi, once bearing a torch and beckoning toward the heights, now leads down stairways into black and forbidding dungeons. Especially in America, where all that is bombastic and mystical is most esteemed, the art of pedagogics becomes a sort of puerile magic, a thing of preposterous secrets, a grotesque compound of false premises and illogical conclusions. Every year sees a craze for some new solution of the teaching enigma, at once simple and infallible—manual training, playground work, song and doggerel lessons, the Montessori method, the Gary system—an endless series of flamboyant arcanums. The worst extravagances of *privatdozent* experimental psychology are gravely seized upon; the uplift pours in its ineffable principles and discoveries; mathematical formulæ are worked out for every emergency; there is no sure-cure so idiotic that some superintendent of schools will not swallow it.

A couple of days spent examining the literature of the New Thought in pedagogy are enough to make the judicious weep.

Its aim seems to be to reduce the whole teaching process to a sort of automatic reaction, to discover some master formula that will not only take the place of competence and resourcefulness in the teacher but that will also create an artificial receptivity in the child. The merciless application of this formula (which changes every four days) now seems to be the chief end and aim of pedagogy. Teaching becomes a thing in itself, separable from and superior to the thing taught. Its mastery is a special business, a transcendental art and mystery, to be acquired in the laboratory. A teacher well grounded in this mystery, and hence privy to every detail of the new technic (which changes, of course, with the formula), can teach anything to any child, just as a sound dentist can pull any tooth out of any jaw.

All this, I need not point out, is in sharp contrast to the old theory of teaching. By that theory mere technic was simplified and subordinated. All that it demanded of the teacher told off to teach, say, geography, was that he master the facts in the geography book and provide himself with a stout rattan. Thus equipped, he was ready for a test of his natural pedagogical genius. First he exposed the facts in the book, then he gilded them with whatever appearance of interest and importance he could conjure up, and then he tested the extent of their transference to the minds of his pupils. Those pupils who had ingested them got apples; those who had failed got fanned with the rattan. Followed the second round, and the same test again, with a second noting of results. And then the third, and fourth, and the fifth, and so on until the last and least pupil had been stuffed to his subnormal and perhaps moronic brim.

I was myself grounded in the underlying delusions of what is called knowledge by this austere process, and despite the eloquence of those who support newer ideas, I lean heavily in favor of it, and regret to hear that it is no more. It was crude, it was rough, and it was often not a little cruel, but it at least had two capital advantages over all the systems that have succeeded it. In the first place, its machinery was simple; even the stupidest child could understand it; it hooked up cause and effect with the utmost clarity. And in the second place, it tested the teacher as and how he ought to be tested—that is, for his actual capacity to teach, not for his mere technical virtuosity.

There was, in fact, no technic for him to master, and hence none for him to hide behind. He could not conceal a hopeless inability to impart knowledge beneath a correct professional method.

That ability to impart knowledge, it seems to me, has very little to do with technical method. It may operate at full function without any technical method at all, and contrariwise, the most elaborate of technical methods, whether out of Switzerland, Italy or Gary, Ind., cannot make it operate when it is not actually present. And what does it consist of? It consists, first, of a natural talent for dealing with children, for getting into their minds, for putting things in a way that they can comprehend. And it consists, secondly, of a deep belief in the interest and importance of the thing taught, a concern about it amounting to a sort of passion. A man who knows a subject thoroughly, a man so soaked in it that he eats it, sleeps it and dreams it—this man can always teach it with success, no matter how little he knows of technical pedagogy. That is because there is enthusiasm in him, and because enthusiasm is almost as contagious as fear or the barber's itch. An enthusiast is willing to go to any trouble to impart the glad news bubbling within him. He thinks that it is important and valuable for to know; given the slightest glow of interest in a pupil to start with, he will fan that glow to a flame. No hollow formalism cripples him and slows him down. He drags his best pupils along as fast as they can go, and he is so full of the thing that he never tires of expounding its elements to the dullest.

This passion, so unordered and yet so potent, explains the capacity for teaching that one frequently observes in scientific men of high attainments in their specialties—for example, Huxley, Ostwald, Karl Ludwig, Virchow, Billroth, Jowett, William G. Sumner, Halsted and Osler—men who knew nothing whatever about the so-called science of pedagogy, and would have derided its alleged principles if they had heard them stated. It explains, too, the failure of the general run of high-school and college teachers—men who are undoubtedly competent, by the professional standards of pedagogy, but who nevertheless contrive only to make intolerable bores of the things they presume to teach. No intelligent student ever learns much from the average drover of undergraduates; what he actually carries away has come out of his textbooks, or is the fruit of his own reading and inquiry. But when he passes to the graduate school, and comes among men who really understand the subjects they teach, and, what is more, who really love them, his store of knowledge increases rapidly, and in a very short while, if he has any intelligence at all, he learns to think in terms of the thing he is studying.

So far, so good. But an objection still remains, the which may be couched in the following terms: that in the average college or high school, and especially in the elementary school, most of the subjects taught are so bald and uninspiring that it is difficult to imagine them arousing the passion I have been describing—in brief that only an ass could be enthusiastic about them. In witness, think of the four elementals: reading, penmanship, arithmetic and spelling. This objection, at first blush, seems salient and dismaying, but only a brief inspection is needed to show that it is really of very small validity. It is made up of a false assumption and a false inference. The false inference is that there is any sound reason for prohibiting teaching by asses, if only the asses know how to do it, and do it well. The false assumption is that there are no asses in our schools and colleges to-day. The facts stand in almost complete antithesis to these notions. The truth is that the average schoolmaster, on all the lower levels, is and always must be essentially an ass, for how can one imagine an intelligent man engaging in so puerile an avocation? And, the truth is that it is precisely his inherent asininity, and not his technical equipment as a pedagogue, that is responsible for whatever modest success he now shows.

I here attempt no heavy jocosity, but mean exactly what I say. Consider, for example, penmanship. A decent handwriting, it must be obvious, is useful to all men, and particularly to the lower orders of men. It is one of the few things capable of acquirement in school that actually helps them to make a living. Well, how is it taught to-day? It is taught, in the main, by schoolmarms so enmeshed in a complex and unintelligible technic that, even supposing them able to write clearly themselves, they find it quite impossible to teach their pupils. Every few years sees a radical overhauling of the whole business. First the vertical hand is to make it easy; then certain curves are the

favorite magic; then there is a return to slants and shadings.
No department of pedagogy sees a more hideous cavorting of
quacks. In none is the natural talent and enthusiasm of the
teacher more depressingly crippled. And the result? The result
is that our American school children write abominably—that a
clerk or stenographer with a simple, legible hand becomes
almost as scarce as one with Greek.

Go back, now, to the old days. Penmanship was then taught,
not mechanically and ineffectively, by unsound and shifting
formulæ, but by passionate penmen with curly patent-leather
hair and far-away eyes—in brief, by the unforgettable professors of our youth, with their flourishes, their heavy down-
strokes and their lovely birds-with-letters-in-their-bills. You
remember them, of course. Asses all! Preposterous popinjays
and numskulls! Pathetic idiots! But they loved penmanship,
they believed in the glory and beauty of penmanship, they
were fanatics, devotees, almost martyrs of penmanship—and so
they got some touch of that passion into their pupils. Not
enough, perhaps, to make more flourishers and bird-blazoners,
but enough to make sound penmen. Look at your old writing
book; observe the excellent legibility, the clear strokes of your
"Time is money." Then look at your child's.

Such idiots, despite the rise of "scientific" pedagogy, have
not died out in the world. I believe that our schools are full of
them, both in pantaloons and in skirts. There are fanatics who
love and venerate spelling as a tom-cat loves and venerates cat-
nip. There are grammatomaniacs; schoolmarms who would
rather parse than eat; specialists in an objective case that doesn't
exist in English; strange beings, otherwise sane and even intelligent and comely, who suffer under a split infinitive as you or
I would suffer under gastro-enteritis. There are geography
cranks, able to bound Mesopotamia and Beluchistan. There
are zealots for long division, experts in the multiplication
table, lunatic worshipers of the binomial theorem. But the system has them in its grip. It combats their natural enthusiasm
diligently and mercilessly. It tries to convert them into mere
technicians, clumsy machines. It orders them to teach, not by
the process of emotional osmosis which worked in the days
gone by, but by formulæ that are as baffling to the pupil as they
are paralyzing to the teacher. Imagine what would happen to

one of them who stepped to the blackboard, seized a piece of chalk, and engrossed a bird that held the class spell-bound—a bird with a thousand flowing feathers, wings bursting with parabolas and epicycloids, and long ribbons streaming from its bill! Imagine the fate of one who began "Honesty is the best policy" with an H as florid and—to a child—as beautiful as the initial of a mediæval manuscript! Such a teacher would be cashiered and handed over to the secular arm; the very enchantment of the assembled infantry would be held as damning proof against him. And yet it is just such teachers that we should try to discover and develop. Pedagogy needs their enthusiasm, their naïve belief in their own grotesque talents, their capacity for communicating their childish passion to the childish.

But this would mean exposing the children of the Republic to contact with monomaniacs, half-wits, defectives? Well, what of it? The vast majority of them are already exposed to contact with half-wits in their own homes; they are taught the word of God by half-wits on Sundays; they will grow up into Knights of Pythias, Odd Fellows, Red Men and other such half-wits in the days to come. Moreover, as I have hinted, they are already face to face with half-wits in the actual schools, at least in three cases out of four. The problem before us is not to dispose of this fact, but to utilize it. We cannot hope to fill the schools with persons of high intelligence, for persons of high intelligence simply refuse to spend their lives teaching such banal things as spelling and arithmetic. Among the teachers male we may safely assume that 95 per cent. are of low mentality, else they would depart for more appetizing pastures. And even among the teachers female the best are inevitably weeded out by marriage, and only the worst (with a few romantic exceptions) survive. The task before us, as I say, is not to make a vain denial of this cerebral inferiority of the pedagogue, nor to try to combat and disguise it by concocting a mass of technical hocus-pocus, but to search out and put to use the value lying concealed in it. For even stupidity, it must be plain, has its uses in the world, and some of them are uses that intelligence cannot meet. One would not tell off a Galileo or a Pasteur to drive an ash-cart or an Ignatius Loyola to be a stockbroker, or a Brahms to lead the orchestra in a Broadway cabaret. By the same token, one would not ask a Herbert Spencer or a Duns Scotus to instruct sucklings. Such men would not only be wasted at the job; they would also be incompetent. The business of dealing with children, in fact, demands a certain childishness of mind. The best teacher, until one comes to adult pupils, is not the one who knows most, but the one who is most capable of reducing knowledge to that simple compound of the obvious and the wonderful which slips easiest into the infantile comprehension. A man of high intelligence, perhaps, may accomplish the thing by a conscious intellectual feat. But it is vastly easier to the man (or woman) whose habits of mind are naturally on the plane of a child's. The best teacher of children, in brief, is one who is essentially childlike.

I go so far with this notion that I view the movement to introduce female bachelors of arts into the primary schools with the utmost alarm. A knowledge of Bergsonism, the Greek aorist, sex hygiene and the dramas of Percy MacKaye is not only no help to the teaching of spelling, it is a positive handicap to the teaching of spelling, for it corrupts and blows up that naïve belief in the glory and portentousness of spelling which is at the bottom of all successful teaching of it. If I had my way, indeed, I should expose all candidates for berths in the infant grades to the Binet-Simon test, and reject all those who revealed the mentality of more than fifteen years. Plenty would still pass. Moreover, they would be secure against contamination by the new technic of pedagogy. Its vast wave of pseudo-psychology would curl and break against the hard barrier of their innocent and passionate intellects—as it probably does, in fact, even now. They would know nothing of cognition, perception, attention, the sub-conscious and all the other half-fabulous fowl of the pedagogic aviary. But they would see in reading, writing and arithmetic the gaudy charms of profound and esoteric knowledge, and they would teach these ancient branches, now so abominably in decay, with passionate gusto, and irresistible effectiveness, and a gigantic success.

II

Two great follies corrupt the present pedagogy, once it gets beyond the elementals. One is the folly of overestimating the receptivity of the pupil; the other is the folly of overestimating the possible efficiency of the teacher. Both rest upon that tendency to put too high a value upon mere schooling which characterizes democratic and upstart societies—a tendency born of the theory that a young man who has been "educated," who has "gone through college," is in some subtle way more capable of making money than one who hasn't. The nature of the schooling on tap in colleges is but defectively grasped by the adherents of the theory. They view it, I believe, as a sort of extension of the schooling offered in elementary schools—that is, as an indefinite multiplication of training in such obviously valuable and necessary arts as reading, writing and arithmetic. It is, of course, nothing of the sort. If the pupil, as he climbs the educational ladder, is fortunate enough to come into contact with a few Huxleys or Ludwigs, he may acquire a great deal of extremely sound knowledge, and even learn how to think for himself. But in the great majority of cases he is debarred by two things: the limitations of his congenital capacity and the limitations of the teachers he actually encounters. The latter is usually even more brilliantly patent than the former. Very few professional teachers, it seems to me, really know anything worth knowing, even about the subjects they essay to teach. If you doubt it, simply examine their contributions to existing knowledge. Several years ago, while engaged upon my book, "The American Language," I had a good chance to test the matter in one typical department, that of philology. I found a truly appalling condition of affairs. I found that in the whole United States there were not two dozen teachers of English philology—in which class I also include the innumerable teachers of plain grammar—who had ever written ten lines upon the subject worth reading. It was not that they were indolent or illiterate: in truth, they turned out to be enormously diligent. But as I plowed through pyramid after pyramid of their doctrines and speculations, day after day and week after week, I discovered little save a vast laboring of the obvious, with now and then a bold flight into the nonsensical. A few genuinely original philologians revealed themselves —pedagogues capable of observing accurately and reasoning clearly. The rest simply wasted time and paper. Whole sections of the field were unexplored, and some of them appeared to be even unsuspected. The entire life-work of many an industrious professor, boiled down, scarcely made a footnote in my book, itself a very modest work.

This tendency to treat the superior pedagogue too seriously —to view him as, *ipso facto*, a learned man, and one thus capable of conveying learning to others—is supported by the circumstance that he so views himself, and is, in fact, very pretentious and even bombastic. Nearly all discussions of the educational problem, at least in the United States, are carried on by schoolmasters or ex-schoolmasters—for example, college presidents, deans, and other such magnificoes—and so they assume it to be axiomatic that such fellows are genuine bearers of the enlightenment, and hence capable of transmitting it to others. This is true sometimes, as I have said, but certainly not usually. The average high-school or college pedagogue is not one who has been selected because of his uncommon knowledge; he is simply one who has been stuffed with formal ideas and taught to do a few conventional intellectual tricks. Contact with him, far from being inspiring to any youth of alert mentality, is really quite depressing; his point of view is commonplace and timorous; his best thought is no better than that of any other fourth-rate professional man, say a dentist or an advertisement writer. Thus it is idle to talk of him as if he were a Socrates, an Aristotle, or even a Leschetizky. He is actually much more nearly related to a barber or a lieutenant of marines. A worthy man, industrious and respectable—but don't expect too much of him. To ask him to struggle out of his puddle of safe platitudes and plunge into the whirlpool of surmise and speculation that carries on the fragile shallop of human progress—to do this is as absurd as to ask a neighborhood doctor to undertake major surgery.

In the United States his low intellectual status is kept low, not only by the meager rewards of his trade in a country where money is greatly sought and esteemed, but also by the democratic theory of education—that is, by the theory that mere education can convert a peasant into an intellectual aristocrat, with all of the peculiar superiorities of an aristocrat—in brief, that it is possible to make purses out of sow's ears. The intellectual collapse of the American *Gelehrten* during the late war —a collapse so nearly unanimous that those who did not share it attained to a sort of immortality overnight—was perhaps largely due to this error. Who were these bawling professors, so pathetically poltroonish and idiotic? In an enormous number of cases they were simply peasants in frock coats—oafs from the farms and villages of Iowa, Kansas, Vermont, Alabama, the Dakotas and other such backward states, horribly stuffed with standardized learning in some freshwater university, and then set to teaching. To look for a civilized attitude of mind in such Strassburg geese is to look for honor in a valet; to confuse them with scholars is to confuse the Knights of Pythias with the Knights Hospitaller. In brief, the trouble with them was that they had no sound tradition behind them, that they had not learned to think clearly and decently, that they were not gentlemen. The youth with a better background behind him, passing through an American university, seldom acquires any yearning to linger as a teacher. The air is too thick for him; the rewards are too trivial; the intrigues are too old-maidish and degrading. Thus the chairs, even in the larger universities, tend to be filled more and more by yokels who have got themselves what is called an education only by dint of herculean effort. Exhausted by the cruel process, they are old men at 26 or 28, and so, hugging their Ph.D's, they sink into convenient instructorships, and end at 60 as *ordentliche Professoren*. The social status of the American pedagogue helps along the process. Unlike in Europe, where he has a secure and honorable position, he ranks, in the United States, somewhere between a Methodist preacher and a prosperous brickyard owner—certainly clearly below the latter. Thus the youth of civilized upbringings feels that it would be stooping a bit to take up the rattan. But the plow-hand obviously makes a step upward, and is hence eager for the black gown. Thereby a vicious circle is formed. The plow-hand, by entering the ancient guild, drags it down still further, and so makes it increasingly difficult to snare apprentices from superior castes.

A glance at "Who's Who in America" offers a good deal of support for all this theorizing. There was a time when the typical American professor came from a small area in New England—for generations the seat of a high literacy, and even of a certain austere civilization. But to-day he comes from the region of silos, revivals, and saleratus. Behind him there is absolutely no tradition of aristocratic aloofness and urbanity, or even of mere civilized decency. He is a hind by birth, and he carries the smell of the dunghill into the academic grove—and not only the smell, but also some of the dung itself. What one looks for in such men is dullness, superficiality, a great credulity, an incapacity for learning anything save a few fly-blown rudiments, a passionate yielding to all popular crazes, a malignant distrust of genuine superiority, a huge megalomania. These are precisely the things that one finds in the typical American pedagogue of the new dispensation. He is not only a numskull; he is also a boor. In the university president he reaches his heights. Here we have a so-called learned man who spends his time making speeches before chautauquas, chambers of commerce and Rotary Clubs, and flattering trustees who run both universities and street-railways, and cadging money from such men as Rockefeller and Carnegie.

III

The same educational fallacy which fills the groves of learning with such dunces causes a huge waste of energy and money on lower levels—those, to wit, of the secondary schools. The theory behind the lavish multiplication of such schools is that they outfit the children of the mob with the materials of reasoning, and inculcate in them a habit of indulging in it. I have never been able to discover any evidence in support of that theory. The common people of America—at least the white portion of them—are rather above the world's average in literacy, but there is no sign that they have acquired thereby any capacity for weighing facts or comparing ideas. The school statistics show that the average member of the American Legion can read and write after a fashion, and is able to multiply eight by seven after four trials, but they tell us nothing about his actual intelligence. The returns of the Army itself, indeed, indicate that he is stupid almost beyond belief—that there is at least an even chance that he is a moron. Is such a fellow appreciably superior to the villein of the Middle Ages? Sometimes I am tempted to doubt it. I suspect, for example, that the belief in witchcraft is still almost as widespread among the plain people of the United States, at least outside the large cities, as it was in Europe in the year 1500. In my own state of Maryland all of the negroes and mulattoes believe absolutely in witches, and so do most of the whites. The belief in ghosts penetrates to quite high levels. I know very few native-born Americans, indeed, who reject it without reservation. One constantly comes upon grave defenses of spiritism in some form or other by men theoretically of learning; in the two houses of Congress it would be difficult to muster fifty men willing to denounce the thing publicly. It would not only be politically dangerous for them to do so; it would also go against their consciences.

What is always forgotten is that the capacity for knowledge of the great masses of human blanks is very low—that, no matter how adroitly pedagogy tackles them with its technical sorceries, it remains a practical impossibility to teach them anything beyond reading and writing, and the most elementary arithmetic. Worse, it is impossible to make any appreciable improvement in their congenitally ignoble tastes, and so they devote even the paltry learning that they acquire to degrading uses. If the average American read only the newspapers, as is frequently alleged, it would be bad enough, but the truth is that he reads only the most imbecile *parts* of the newspapers. Nine-tenths of the matter in a daily paper of the better sort is almost as unintelligible to him as the theory of least squares. The words lie outside his vocabulary; the ideas are beyond the farthest leap of his intellect. It is, indeed, a sober fact that even an editorial in the New York *Times* is probably incomprehensible to all Americans save a small minority—and not, remember, on the ground that it is too nonsensical but on the ground that it is too subtle. The same sort of mind that regards Rubinstein's Melody in F as too "classical" to be agreeable is also stumped by the most transparent English.

Like most other professional writers I get a good many letters from my customers. Complaints, naturally, are more numerous than compliments; it is only indignation that can induce the average man to brave the ardors of pen and ink. Well, the complaint that I hear most often is that my English is unintelligible —that it is too full of "hard" words. I can imagine nothing more astounding. My English is actually almost as bald and simple as the English of a college yell. My sentences are short and plainly constructed: I resolutely cultivate the most direct manner of statement; my vocabulary is deliberately composed of the words of everyday. Nevertheless, a great many of my readers in my own country find reading me an uncomfortably severe burden upon their linguistic and intellectual resources. These readers are certainly not below the American average in intelligence; on the contrary, they must be a good deal above the average, for they have at least got to the point where they are willing to put out of the safe harbor of the obvious and respectable, and to brave the seas where more or less novel ideas rage and roar. Think of what the ordinary newspaper reader would make of my compositions! There is, in fact, no need to think; I have tried them on him. His customary response, when, by mountebankish devices, I forced him to read—or, at all events, to try to read—, was to demand resolutely that the guilty newspaper cease printing me, and to threaten to bring the matter to the attention of the *Polizei*. I do not exaggerate in the slightest; I tell the literal truth.

It is such idiots that the little red schoolhouse operates upon, in the hope of unearthing an occasional first-rate man. Is that hope ever fulfilled? Despite much testimony to the effect that it is, I am convinced that it really isn't. First-rate men are never begotten by Knights of Pythias; the notion that they sometimes are is due to an optical delusion. When they appear in obscure and ignoble circles it is no more than a proof that only an extremely wise sire knows his own son. Adultery, in brief, is one of nature's devices for keeping the lowest orders of men from sinking to the level of downright simians: sometimes for a few brief years in youth, their wives and daughters are comely—and now and then the baron drinks more than he ought to. But it is foolish to argue that the gigantic machine of popular education is needed to rescue such hybrids from their environment. The truth is that all the education rammed into the average pupil in the average American public school could be acquired by the larva of any reasonably intelligent man in no more than six weeks of ordinary application, and that where schools are unknown it actually *is* so acquired. A bright child, in fact, can learn to read and write without any save the most casual aid a great deal faster than it can learn to read and write in a classroom, where the difficulties of the stupid retard it enormously and it is further burdened by the crazy formulæ, invented by pedagogues. And once it can read and write, it is just as well equipped to acquire further knowledge as nine-tenths of the teachers it will subsequently encounter in school or college.

IV

I know a good many men of great learning—that is, men born with an extraordinary eagerness and capacity to acquire knowledge. One and all, they tell me that they can't recall learning anything of any value in school. All that school-masters managed to accomplish with them was to test and de-termine the amount of knowledge that they had already acquired independently—and not infrequently the determina-tion was made clumsily and inaccurately. In my own nonage I had a great desire to acquire knowledge in certain limited di-rections, to wit, those of the physical sciences. Before I was ever permitted, by the regulations of the secondary seminary I was penned in, to open a chemistry book I had learned a great deal of chemistry by the simple process of reading the texts and then going through the processes described. When, at last, I was introduced to chemistry officially, I found the teaching of it appalling. The one aim of that teaching, in fact, seemed to be to first purge me of what I already knew and then refill me with the same stuff in a formal, doltish, unintelligible form. My experience with physics was even worse. I knew nothing about it when I undertook its study in class, for that was before the days when physics swallowed chemistry. Well, it was taught so abominably that it immediately became incompre-hensible to me, and hence extremely distasteful, and to this day I know nothing about it. Worse, it remains unpleasant to me, and so I am shut off from the interesting and useful knowledge that I might otherwise acquire by reading.

One extraordinary teacher I remember who taught me something: a teacher of mathematics. I had a dislike for that science, and knew little about it. Finally, my neglect of it brought me to bay: in transferring from one school to another I found that I was hopelessly short in algebra. What was needed, of course, was not an actual knowledge of algebra, but simply the superficial smattering needed to pass an examination. The teacher that I mention, observing my distress, generously offered to fill me with that smattering after school hours. He got the whole year's course into me in exactly six lessons of half an hour each. And how? More accurately, why? Simply because he was an algebra fanatic—because he believed that algebra was not only a science of the utmost importance, but also one of the greatest fascination. He was the penmanship professor of years ago, lifted to a higher level. A likable and plausible man, he convinced me in twenty minutes that ignorance of algebra was as calamitous, socially and intellectually, as ignorance of table manners—that acquiring its elements was as necessary as washing behind the ears. So I fell upon the book and gulped it voraciously, greatly to the astonishment of my father, whose earlier mathematical teaching had failed to set me off because it was too pressing—because it bombarded me, not when I was penned in a school and so inclined to make the best of it, but when I had got through a day's schooling, and felt inclined to play. To this day I comprehend the binomial theorem, a very rare accomplishment in an author. For many years, indeed, I was probably the only American newspaper editor who knew what it was.

Two other teachers of that school I remember pleasantly as fellows whose pedagogy profitted me—both, it happens, were drunken and disreputable men. One taught me to chew tobacco, an art that has done more to give me an evil name, perhaps, than even my Socinianism. The other introduced me to Shakespeare, Congreve, Wycherly, Marlowe and Sheridan, and so filled me with that taste for coarseness which now offends so many of my customers, lay and clerical. Neither ever came to a dignified position in academic circles. One abandoned pedagogy for the law, became involved in causes of a dubious nature, and finally disappeared into the shades which engulf third-rate attorneys. The other went upon a fearful drunk one Christmastide, got himself shanghaied on the water-front and is supposed to have fallen overboard from a British tramp, bound east for Cardiff. At all events, he has never been heard from since. Two evil fellows, and yet I hold their memories in affection, and believe that they were the best teachers I ever had. For in both there was something a good deal more valuable than mere pedagogical skill and diligence, and even more valuable than correct demeanor, and that was a passionate love of sound literature. This love, given reasonably receptive soil, they knew how to communicate, as a man can nearly always communicate whatever moves him profoundly. Neither ever made the slightest effort to "teach" literature, as the business is carried on by the usual idiot schoolmaster. Both had a vast contempt for the text-books that were official in their school, and used to entertain the boys by pointing out the nonsense in them. Both were full of derisory objections to the principal heroes of such books in those days: Scott, Irving, Pope, Jane Austen, Dickens, Trollope, Tennyson. But both, discoursing in their disorderly way upon heroes of their own, were magnificently eloquent and persuasive. The boy who could listen to one of them intoning Whitman and stand unmoved was a dull fellow indeed. The boy who could resist the other's enthusiasm for the old essayists was intellectually deaf, dumb and blind.

I often wonder if their expoundings of their passions and prejudices would have been half so charming if they had been wholly respectable men, like their colleagues of the school faculty. It is not likely. A healthy boy is in constant revolt against the sort of men who surround him at school. Their puerile pedantries, their Christian Endeavor respectability, their sedentary pallor, their curious preference for the dull and uninteresting, their general air of so many Y.M.C.A. secretaries—these things infallibly repel the youth who is above milksoppery. In every boys' school the favorite teacher is one who occasionally swears like a cavalryman, or is reputed to keep a jug in his room, or is known to receive a scented note every morning. Boys are good judges of men, as girls are good judges of women. It is not by accident that most of them, at some time or other, long to be cowboys or ice-wagon drivers, and that none of them, not obviously diseased in mind, ever longs to be a Sunday-school superintendent. Put that judgment to a simple test. What would become of a nation in which all of the men were, at heart, Sunday-school superintendents—or Y.M.C.A. secretaries, or pedagogues? Imagine it in conflict with a nation of cowboys and ice-wagon drivers. Which would be the stronger, and which would be the more intelligent, resourceful, enterprising and courageous?

XIV.
Types of Men

1
The Romantic

THERE is a variety of man whose eye inevitably exaggerates, whose ear inevitably hears more than the band plays, whose imagination inevitably doubles and triples the news brought in by his five senses. He is the enthusiast, the believer, the romantic. He is the sort of fellow who, if he were a bacteriologist, would report the streptoccocus pyogenes to be as large as a St. Bernard dog, as intelligent as Socrates, as beautiful as Beauvais Cathedral and as respectable as a Yale professor.

2
The Skeptic

No man ever quite believes in any other man. One may believe in an idea absolutely, but not in a man. In the highest confidence there is always a flavor of doubt—a feeling, half instinctive and half logical, that, after all, the scoundrel *may* have something up his sleeve. This doubt, it must be obvious, is always more than justified, for no man is worthy of unlimited reliance—his treason, at best, only waits for sufficient temptation. The trouble with the world is not that men are too suspicious in this direction, but that they tend to be too confiding—that they still trust themselves too far to other men, even after bitter experience. Women, I believe, are measurably less sentimental, in this as in other things. No married woman ever trusts her husband absolutely, nor does she ever act as if she *did* trust him. Her utmost confidence is as wary as an American pickpocket's confidence that the policeman on the beat will stay bought.

3
The Believer

Faith may be defined briefly as an illogical belief in the occurrence of the improbable. Or, psychoanalytically, as a wish neurose. There is thus a flavor of the pathological in it; it goes beyond the normal intellectual process and passes into the murky domain of transcendental metaphysics. A man full of faith is simply one who has lost (or never had) the capacity for clear and realistic thought. He is not a mere ass: he is actually ill. Worse, he is incurable, for disappointment, being essentially an objective phenomenon, cannot permanently affect his subjective infirmity. His faith takes on the virulence of a chronic infection. What he usually says, in substance, is this: "Let us trust in God, *who has always fooled us in the past.*"

4
The Worker

All democratic theories, whether Socialistic or bourgeois, necessarily take in some concept of the dignity of labor. If the have-not were deprived of this delusion that his sufferings in the sweat-shop are somehow laudable and agreeable to God, there would be little left in his ego save a belly-ache. Nevertheless, a delusion is a delusion, and this is one of the worst. It arises out of confusing the pride of workmanship of the artist with the dogged, painful docility of the machine. The difference is important and enormous. If he got no reward whatever, the artist would go on working just the same; his actual reward, in fact, is often so little that he almost starves. But suppose a garment-worker got nothing for his labor: would he go on working just the same? Can one imagine him submitting voluntarily to hardship and sore want that he might express his soul in 200 more pairs of pantaloons?

5
The Physician

Hygiene is the corruption of medicine by morality. It is impossible to find a hygienist who does not debase his theory of the healthful with a theory of the virtuous. The whole hygienic art, indeed, resolves itself into an ethical exhortation, and, in the sub-department of sex, into a puerile and belated advocacy of asceticism. This brings it, at the end, into diametrical conflict with medicine proper. The aim of medicine is surely not to make men virtuous; it is to safeguard and rescue them from the consequences of their vices. The true physician does not preach repentance; he offers absolution.

6

The Scientist

The value the world sets upon motives is often grossly unjust and inaccurate. Consider, for example, two of them: mere insatiable curiosity and the desire to do good. The latter is put high above the former, and yet it is the former that moves some of the greatest men the human race has yet produced: the scientific investigators. What animates a great pathologist? Is it the desire to cure disease, to save life? Surely not, save perhaps as an afterthought. He is too intelligent, deep down in his soul, to see anything praiseworthy in such a desire. He knows by life-long observation that his discoveries will do quite as much harm as good, that a thousand scoundrels will profit to every honest man, that the folks who most deserve to be saved will probably be the last to be saved. No man of self-respect could devote himself to pathology on such terms. What actually moves him is his unquenchable curiosity—his boundless, almost pathological thirst to penetrate the unknown, to uncover the secret, to find out what has not been found out before. His prototype is not the liberator releasing slaves, the good Samaritan lifting up the fallen, but the dog sniffing tremendously at an infinite series of rat-holes. And yet he is one of the greatest and noblest of men. And yet he stands in the very front rank of the race.

7

The Business Man

It is, after all, a sound instinct which puts business below the professions, and burdens the business man with a social inferiority that he can never quite shake off, even in America. The business man, in fact, acquiesces in this assumption of his inferiority, even when he protests against it. He is the only man who is forever apologizing for his occupation. He is the only one who always seeks to make it appear, when he attains the object of his labors, *i.e.*, the making of a great deal of money, that it was not the object of his labors.

8

The King

Perhaps the most valuable asset that any man can have in this world is a naturally superior air, a talent for sniffishness and reserve. The generality of men are always greatly impressed by it, and accept it freely as a proof of genuine merit. One need but disdain them to gain their respect. Their congenital stupidity and timorousness make them turn to any leader who offers, and the sign of leadership that they recognize most readily is that which shows itself in external manner. This is the true explanation of the survival of monarchism, which invariably lives through its perennial deaths. It is the popular theory, at least in America, that monarchism is a curse fastened upon the common people from above—that the monarch saddles it upon them without their consent and against their will. The theory is without support in the facts. Kings are created, not by kings, but by the people. They visualize one of the ineradicable needs of all third-rate men, which means of nine men out of ten, and that is the need of something to venerate, to bow down to, to follow and obey.

The king business begins to grow precarious, not when kings reach out for greater powers, but when they begin to resign and renounce their powers. The czars of Russia were quite secure upon the throne so long as they ran Russia like a reformatory, but the moment they began to yield to liberal ideas, *i.e.*, by emancipating the serfs and setting up constitutionalism, their doom was sounded. The people saw this yielding as a sign of weakness; they began to suspect that the czars, after all, were not actually superior to other men. And so they turned to other and antagonistic leaders, all as cock-sure as the czars had once been, and in the course of time they were stimulated to rebellion. These leaders, or, at all events, the two or three most resolute and daring of them, then undertook to run the country in the precise way that it had been run in the palmy days of the monarchy. That is to say, they seized and exerted irresistible power and laid claim to infallible wisdom. History will date their downfall from the day they began to ease their pretensions. Once they confessed, even by implication, that they were merely human, the common people began to turn against them.

9

The Average Man

It is often urged against the so-called scientific Socialists, with their materialistic conception of history, that they overlook certain spiritual qualities that are independent of wage scales and metabolism. These qualities, it is argued, color the aspirations and activities of civilized man quite as much as they are colored by his material condition, and so make it impossible to consider him simply as an economic machine. As examples, the anti-Marxians cite patriotism, pity, the æsthetic sense and the yearning to know God. Unluckily, the examples are ill-chosen. Millions of men are quite devoid of patriotism, pity and the æsthetic sense, and have no very active desire to know God. Why don't the anti-Marxians cite a spiritual quality that is genuinely universal? There is one readily to hand. I allude to cowardice. It is, in one form or other, visible in every human being; it almost serves to mark off the human race from all the other higher animals. Cowardice, I believe, is at the bottom of the whole caste system, the foundation of every organized society, including the most democratic. In order to escape going to war himself, the peasant was willing to give the warrior certain privileges—and out of those privileges has grown the whole structure of civilization. Go back still further. Property arose out of the fact that a few relatively courageous men were able to accumulate more possessions than whole hordes of cowardly men, and, what is more, to retain them after accumulating them.

10
The Truth-Seeker

The man who boasts that he habitually tells the truth is simply a man with no respect for it. It is not a thing to be thrown about loosely, like small change; it is something to be cherished and hoarded, and disbursed only when absolutely necessary. The smallest atom of truth represents some man's bitter toil and agony; for every ponderable chunk of it there is a brave truth-seeker's grave upon some lonely ash-dump and a soul roasting in hell.

11
The Pacifist

Nietzsche, in altering Schopenhauer's will-to-live to will-to-power, probably fell into a capital error. The truth is that the thing the average man seeks in life is not primarily power, but peace; all his struggle is toward a state of tranquillity and equilibrium; what he always dreams of is a state in which he will have to do battle no longer. This dream plainly enters into his conception of Heaven; he thinks of himself, *post mortem*, browsing about the celestial meadows like a cow in a safe pasture. A few extraordinary men enjoy combat at all times, and all men are inclined toward it at orgiastic moments, but the race as a race craves peace, and man belongs among the more timorous, docile and unimaginative animals, along with the deer, the horse and the sheep. This craving for peace is vividly displayed in the ages-long conflict of the sexes. Every normal woman wants to be married, for the plain reason that marriage offers her security. And every normal man avoids marriage as long as possible, for the equally plain reason that marriage invades and threatens *his* security.

12
The Relative

The normal man's antipathy to his relatives, particularly of the second degree, is explained by psychologists in various tortured and improbable ways. The true explanation, I venture, is a good deal simpler. It lies in the plain fact that every man sees in his relatives, and especially in his cousins, a series of grotesque caricatures of himself. They exhibit his qualities in disconcerting augmentation or diminution; they fill him with a disquieting feeling that this, perhaps, is the way he appears to the world and so they wound his *amour propre* and give him intense discomfort. To admire his relatives whole-heartedly a man must be lacking in the finer sort of self-respect.

13
The Friend

One of the most mawkish of human delusions is the notion that friendship should be eternal, or, at all events, life-long, and that any act which puts a term to it is somehow discreditable. The fact is that a man of active and resilient mind outwears his friendships just as certainly as he outwears his love affairs, his politics and his epistemology. They become threadbare, shabby, pumped-up, irritating, depressing. They convert themselves from living realities into moribund artificialities, and stand in sinister opposition to freedom, self-respect and truth. It is as corrupting to preserve them after they have grown fly-blown and hollow as it is to keep up the forms of passion after passion itself is a corpse. Every act and attitude that they involve thus become an act of hypocrisy, an attitude of dishonesty. . . . A prudent man, remembering that life is short, gives an hour or two, now and then, to a critical examination of his friendships. He weighs them, edits them, tests the metal of them. A few he retains, perhaps with radical changes in their terms. But the majority he expunges from his minutes and tries to forget, as he tries to forget the cold and clammy loves of year before last.

XV.

The Dismal Science

EVERY man, as the Psalmist says, to his own poison, or poisons, as the case may be. One of mine, following hard after theology, is political economy. What! Political economy, that dismal science? Well, why not? Its dismalness is largely a delusion, due to the fact that its chief ornaments, at least in our own day, are university professors. The professor must be an obscurantist or he is nothing; he has a special and unmatchable talent for dullness; his central aim is not to expose the truth clearly, but to exhibit his profundity, his esotericity—in brief, to stagger sophomores and other professors. The notion that German is a gnarled and unintelligible language arises out of the circumstance that it is so much written by professors. It took a rebel member of the clan, swinging to the antipodes in his unearthly treason, to prove its explicitness, its resiliency, its downright beauty. But Nietzsches are few, and so German remains soggy, and political economy continues to be swathed in dullness. As I say, however, that dullness is only superficial. There is no more engrossing book in the English language than Adam Smith's "The Wealth of Nations"; surely the eighteenth century produced nothing that can be read with greater ease to-day. Nor is there any inherent reason why even the most technical divisions of its subject should have gathered cobwebs with the passing of the years. Taxation, for example, is eternally lively; it concerns nine-tenths of us more directly than either smallpox or golf, and has just as much drama in it; moreover, it has been mellowed and made gay by as many gaudy, preposterous theories. As for foreign exchange, it is almost as romantic as young love, and quite as resistent to formulæ. Do the professors make an autopsy of it? Then read the occasional treatises of some professor of it who is not a professor, say, Garet Garrett or John Moody.

Unluckily, Garretts and Moodys are almost as rare as Nietzsches, and so the amateur of such things must be content to wrestle with the professors, seeking the violet of human interest beneath the avalanche of their graceless parts of speech. A hard business, I daresay, to one not practiced, and to its hardness there is added the disquiet of a doubt. That doubt does not concern itself with the doctrine preached, at least not directly. There may be in it nothing intrinsically dubious; on the contrary, it may appear as sound as the binomial theorem, as well supported as the dogma of infant damnation. But all the time a troubling question keeps afloat in the air, and that is briefly this: What would happen to the learned professors if they took the other side? In other words, to what extent is political economy, as professors expound and practice it, a free science, in the sense that mathematics and physiology are free sciences? At what place, if any, is speculation pulled up by a rule that beyond lies treason, anarchy and disaster? These questions, I hope I need not add, are not inspired by any heterodoxy in my own black heart. I am, in many fields, a flouter of the accepted revelation and hence immoral, but the field of economics is not one of them. Here, indeed, I know of no man who is more orthodox than I am. I believe that the present organization of society, as bad as it is, is better than any other that has ever been proposed. I reject all the sure cures in current agitation, from government ownership to the single tax. I am in favor of free competition in all human enterprises, and to the utmost limit. I admire successful scoundrels, and shrink from Socialists as I shrink from Methodists. But all the same, the aforesaid doubt pursues me when I plow through the solemn disproofs and expositions of the learned professors of economics, and that doubt will not down. It is not logical or evidential, but purely psychological. And what it is grounded on is an unshakable belief that no man's opinion is worth a hoot, however well supported and maintained, so long as he is not absolutely free, if the spirit moves him, to support and maintain the exactly contrary opinion. In brief, human reason is a weak and paltry thing so long as it is not wholly free reason. The fact lies in its very nature, and is revealed by its entire history. A man may be perfectly honest in a contention, and he may be astute and persuasive in maintaining it, but the moment the slightest compulsion to maintain it is laid upon him, the moment the slightest external reward goes with his partisanship or the slightest penalty with its abandonment, then there appears a defect in his ratiocination that is more deep-seated than any error in fact and more destructive than any conscious and deliberate bias. He may seek the truth and the truth only, and bring up his highest talents and diligence to the business, but always there is a specter behind his chair, a warning in his ear. Always it is safer and more hygienic for him to think one way than to think another way, and in that bald fact there is excuse enough to hold his whole chain of syllogisms in suspicion. He may be earnest, he may be honest, but he is not free, and if he is not free, he is not anything.

Well, are the reverend professors of economics free? With the highest respect, I presume to question it. Their colleagues of archeology may be reasonably called free, and their colleagues of bacteriology, and those of Latin grammar and sidereal astronomy, and those of many another science and mystery, but when one comes to the faculty of political economy one finds that freedom as plainly conditioned, though perhaps not as openly, as in the faculty of theology. And for a plain reason. Political economy, so to speak, hits the employers of the professors where they live. It deals, not with ideas that affect those employers only occasionally or only indirectly or only as ideas, but with ideas that have an imminent and continuous influence upon their personal welfare and security, and that affect profoundly the very foundations of that social and economic structure upon which their whole existence is based. It is, in brief, the science of the ways and means whereby they have come to such estate, and maintain themselves in such estate, that they are able to hire and boss professors. It is the boat in which they sail down perilous waters—and they must needs yell, or be more or less than human, when it is rocked. Now and then that yell duly resounds in the groves of learning. One remembers, for example, the trial, condemnation and execution of Prof. Dr. Scott Nearing at the University of Pennsylvania, a seminary that is highly typical, both in its staff and in its control. Nearing, I have no doubt, was wrong in his notions —honestly, perhaps, but still wrong. In so far as I heard them stated at the time, they seemed to me to be hollow and of no validity. He has since discharged them from the chautauquan stump, and at the usual hinds. They have been chiefly accepted and celebrated by men I regard as asses. But Nearing was not

thrown out of the University of Pennsylvania, angrily and ignominiously, because he was honestly wrong, or because his
errors made him incompetent to prepare sophomores for their
examinations; he was thrown out because his efforts to get at
the truth disturbed the security and equanimity of the rich ig-
noranti who happened to control the university, and because
the academic slaves and satellites of these shopmen were
restive under his competition for the attention of the student-
body. In three words, he was thrown out because he was not
safe and sane and orthodox. Had his aberration gone in the
other direction, had he defended child labor as ardently as he
denounced it and denounced the minimum wage as ardently
as he defended it, then he would have been quite as secure in
his post, for all his cavorting in the newspapers, as Chancellor
Day was at Syracuse.

Now consider the case of the professors of economics, near
and far, who have *not* been thrown out. Who will say that the
lesson of the Nearing *débâcle* has been lost upon them? Who
will say that the potency of the wealthy men who command
our universities—or most of them—has not stuck in their minds?
And who will say that, with this sticking remembered, their arguments against Nearing's so-called ideas are as worthy of
confidence and respect as they would be if they were quite free
to go over to Nearing's side without damage? Who, indeed,
will give them full credit, even when they are right, so long as
they are hamstrung, nose-ringed and tied up in gilded pens? It
seems to me that these considerations are enough to cast a
glow of suspicion over the whole of American political economy, at least in so far as it comes from college economists.
And, in the main, it has that source, for, barring a few brilliant
journalists, all our economists of any repute are professors.
Many of them are able men, and most of them are undoubtedly honest men, as honesty goes in the world, but over practically every one of them there stands a board of trustees with
its legs in the stock-market and its eyes on the established
order, and that board is ever alert for heresy in the science of
its being, and has ready means of punishing it, and a hearty enthusiasm for the business. Not every professor, perhaps, may
be sent straight to the block, as Nearing was, but there are

plenty of pillories and guardhouses on the way, and every last pedagogue must be well aware of it.

Political economy, in so far as it is a science at all, was not pumped up and embellished by any such academic clients and ticket-of-leave men. It was put on its legs by inquirers who were not only safe from all dousing in the campus pump, but who were also free from the mental timorousness and conformity which go inevitably with school-teaching—in brief, by men of the world, accustomed to its free air, its hospitality to originality and plain speaking. Adam Smith, true enough, was once a professor, but he threw up his chair to go to Paris, and there he met, not more professors, but all the current enemies of professors—the Nearings and Henry Georges and Karl Marxes of the time. And the book that he wrote was not orthodox, but revolutionary. Consider the others of that bulk and beam: Bentham, Ricardo, Mill and their like. Bentham held no post at the mercy of bankers and tripesellers; he was a man of independent means, a lawyer and politician, and a heretic in general practice. It is impossible to imagine such a man occupying a chair at Harvard or Princeton. He had a hand in too many pies: he was too rebellious and contumacious: he had too little respect for authority, either academic or worldly. Moreover, his mind was too wide for a professor; he could never remain safely in a groove; the whole field of social organization invited his inquiries and experiments. Ricardo? Another man of easy means and great worldly experience—by academic standards, not even educated. To-day, I daresay, such meager diplomas as he could show would not suffice to get him an instructor's berth in a freshwater seminary in Iowa. As for Mill, he was so well grounded by his father that he knew more, at eighteen, than any of the universities could teach him, and his life thereafter was the exact antithesis of that of a cloistered pedagogue. Moreover, he was a heretic in religion and probably violated the Mann act of those days—an offense almost as heinous, in a college professor of economics, as giving three cheers for Prince Kropotkin.

I might lengthen the list, but humanely refrain. The point is that these early English economists were all perfectly free men, with complete liberty to tell the truth as they saw it, regardless of its orthodoxy or lack of orthodoxy. I do not say that the typical American economist of to-day is not as honest, nor even that he is not as diligent and competent, but I do say that he is not as free—that penalties would come upon him for stating ideas that Smith or Ricardo or Bentham or Mill, had he so desired, would have been free to state without damage. And in that menace there is an ineradicable criticism of the ideas that he does state, and it lingers even when they are plausible and are accepted. In France and Germany, where the universities and colleges are controlled by the state, the practical effect of such pressure has been frequently demonstrated. In the former country the violent debate over social and economic problems during the quarter century before the war produced a long list of professors cashiered for heterodoxy, headed by the names of Jean Jaures and Gustave Herve. In Germany it needed no Nietzsche to point out the deadening produced by this state control. Germany, in fact, got out of it an entirely new species of economist—the state Socialist who flirted with radicalism with one eye and kept the other upon his chair, his salary and his pension.

The Nearing case and the rebellions of various pedagogues elsewhere show that we in America stand within the shadow of a somewhat similar danger. In economics, as in the other sciences, we are probably producing men who are as good as those on view in any other country. They are not to be surpassed for learning and originality, and there is no reason to believe that they lack honesty and courage. But honesty and courage, as men go in the world, are after all merely relative values. There comes a point at which even the most honest man considers consequences, and even the most courageous looks before he leaps. The difficulty lies in establishing the position of that point. So long as it is in doubt, there will remain, too, the other doubt that I have described. I rise in meeting, I repeat, not as a radical, but as one of the most hunkerous of the orthodox. I can imagine nothing more dubious in fact and wobbly in logic than some of the doctrines that amateur economists, chiefly Socialists, have set afloat in this country during the past dozen years. I have even gone to the trouble of writing a book against them; my convictions and instincts are all on the other side. But I should be a great deal more comfortable in those convictions and instincts if I were convinced that the learned professors were really in full and absolute possession of academic freedom—if I could imagine them taking the other tack now and then without damnation to their jobs, their lecture dates, their book sales and their hides.

XVI.
Matters of State

I
Le Contrat Social

ALL government, in its essence, is a conspiracy against the superior man: its one permanent object is to police him and cripple him. If it be aristocratic in organization, then it seeks to protect the man who is superior only in law against the man who is superior in fact; if it be democratic, then it seeks to protect the man who is inferior in every way against both. Thus one of its primary functions is to regiment men by force, to make them as much alike as possible and as dependent upon one another as possible, to search out and combat originality among them. All it can see in an original idea is potential change, and hence an invasion of its prerogatives. The most dangerous man, to any government, is the man who is able to think things out for himself, without regard to the prevailing superstitions and taboos. Almost inevitably he comes to the conclusion that the government he lives under is dishonest, insane and intolerable, and so, if he is romantic, he tries to change it. And even if he is not romantic personally he is very apt to spread discontent among those who are. Ludwig van Beethoven was certainly no politician. Nor was he a patriot. Nor had he any democratic illusions in him: he held the Viennese in even more contempt than he held the Hapsburgs. Nevertheless, I am convinced that the sharp criticism of the Hapsburg government that he used to loose in the cafés of Vienna had its effects—that some of his ideas of 1818, after a century of germination, got themselves translated into acts in 1918. Beethoven, like all other first-rate men, greatly disliked the government he lived under. I add the names of Goethe, Heine, Wagner and Nietzsche, to keep among Germans. That of Bismarck might follow: he admired the Hohenzollern idea, as Carlyle did, not the German people or the German administration. In his "Errinerungen," whenever he discusses the government that he was a part of, he has difficulty keeping his contempt within the bounds of decorum.

Nine times out of ten, it seems to me, the man who proposes a change in the government he lives under, no matter how defective it may be, is romantic to the verge of sentimentality. There is seldom, if ever, any evidence that the kind of government he is unlawfully inclined to would be any better than the government he proposes to supplant. Political revolutions, in truth, do not often accomplish anything of genuine value; their one undoubted effect is simply to throw out one gang of thieves and put in another. After a revolution, of course, the successful revolutionists always try to convince doubters that they have achieved great things, and usually they hang any man who denies it. But that surely doesn't prove their case. In Russia, for many years, the plain people were taught that getting rid of the Czar would make them all rich and happy, but now that they have got rid of him they are poorer and unhappier than ever before. The Germans, with the Kaiser in exile, have discovered that a shoemaker turned statesman is ten times as bad as a Hohenzollern. The Alsatians, having become Frenchmen again after 48 years' anxious wait, have responded to the boon by becoming extravagant Germanomaniacs. The Tyrolese, though they hated the Austrians, now hate the Italians enormously more. The Irish, having rid themselves of the English after 700 years of struggle, instantly discovered that government by Englishmen, compared to government by Irishmen, was almost paradisiacal. Even the American colonies gained little by their revolt in 1776. For twenty-five years after the Revolution they were in far worse condition as free states than they would have been as colonies. Their government was more expensive, more inefficient, more dishonest, and more tyrannical. It was only the gradual material progress of the country that saved them from starvation and collapse, and that material progress was due, not to the virtues of their new government, but to the lavishness of nature. Under the British hoof they would have got on just as well, and probably a great deal better.

The ideal government of all reflective men, from Aristotle to Herbert Spencer, is one which lets the individual alone—one which barely escapes being no government at all. This ideal, I believe, will be realized in the world twenty or thirty centuries after I have passed from these scenes and taken up my home in Hell.

2

On Minorities

It is a commonplace of historical science that the forgotten worthies who framed the Constitution of the United States had no belief in democracy. Prof. Dr. Beard, in a slim, sad book, has laboriously proved that most obvious of obviousities. Two prime objects are visible in the Constitution, beautifully enshrouded in disarming words: to protect property and to safeguard minorities—in brief, to hold the superior few harmless against the inferior many. The first object is still carried out, despite the effort of democratic law to make capital an outlaw. The second, alas, has been defeated completely. What is worse, it has been defeated in the very holy of holies of those who sought to attain it, which is to say, in the funeral chamber of the Supreme Court of the United States. Bit by bit this great bench of master minds has gradually established the doctrine that a minority in the Republic has no rights whatever. If they still exist theoretically, as fossils surviving from better days, there is certainly no machinery left for protecting and enforcing them. The current majority, if it so desired tomorrow, could add an amendment to the Constitution prohibiting the ancient Confederate vice of chewing the compressed leaves of the tobacco plant (*Nicotiana tabacum*); the Supreme Court, which has long since forgotten the Bill of Rights, would promptly issue a writ of *nihil obstat*, with a series of moral reflections as *lagniappe*. More, the Supreme Court would as promptly uphold a law prohibiting the chewing of gum (*Achras sapota*)—on the ground that any unnecessary chewing, however harmless in itself, might tempt great hordes of morons to chew tobacco. This is not a mere torturing of sardonic theory: the thing has been actually done in the case of Prohibition. The Eighteenth Amendment prohibits the sale of intoxicating beverages; the Supreme Court has decided plainly that, in order to enforce it, Congress also has the right to prohibit the sale of beverages that are admittedly *not* intoxicating. It could, indeed, specifically prohibit near-beer tomorrow, or any drink containing malt or hops, however low in alcohol; the more extreme Prohibitionists actually demand that it do so forthwith.

Worse, a minority not only has no more inalienable rights in the United States; it is not even lawfully entitled to be heard. This was well established by the case of the Socialists elected to the New York Assembly. What the voters who elected these Socialists asked for was simply the privilege of choosing spokesmen to voice their doctrines in a perfectly lawful and peaceable manner,—nothing more. This privilege was denied them. In precisely the same way, the present national House of Representatives, which happens to be Republican in complexion, might expel all of its Democratic members. The voters who elected them would have no redress. If the same men were elected again, or other men of the same views, they might be expelled again. More, it would apparently be perfectly constitutional for the majority in Congress to pass a statute denying the use of the mails to the minority—that is, for the Republicans to bar all Democratic papers from the mails. I do not toy with mere theories. The thing has actually been done in the case of the Socialists. Under the present law, indeed—upheld by the Supreme Court—the Postmaster-General, without any further authority from Congress, might deny the mails to all Democrats. Or to all Catholics. Or to all single-taxers. Or to all violoncellists.

Yet more, a citizen who happens to belong to a minority is not even safe in his person: he may be put into prison, and for very long periods, for the simple offense of differing from the majority. This happened, it will be recalled, in the case of Debs. Debs by no means advised citizens subject to military duty, in time of war, to evade that duty, as the newspapers of the time alleged. On the contrary, he advised them to meet and discharge that duty. All he did was to say that, even in time of war, he was against war—that he regarded it as a barbarous method of settling disputes between nations. For thus differing from the majority on a question of mere theory he was sentenced to ten years in prison. The case of the three young Russians arrested in New York was even more curious. These

poor idiots were jailed for the almost incredible crime of circu-
lating purely academic protests against making war upon a
country with which the United States was legally at peace, to
wit, Russia. For this preposterous offense two of them were
sent to prison for fifteen years, and one, a girl, for ten years,
and the Supreme Court upheld their convictions. Here was a
plain case of proscription and punishment for a mere opinion.
There was absolutely no contention that the protest of the
three prisoners could have any practical result—that it might,
for example, destroy the *morale* of American soldiers 6,000
miles away, and cut off from all communication with the
United States. The three victims were ordered to be punished
in that appalling manner simply because they ventured to crit-
icise an executive usurpation which happened, at the moment,
to have the support of public opinion, and particularly of the
then President of the United States and of the holders of Russian government securities.

It must be obvious, viewing such leading cases critically—
and hundreds like them might be cited—that the old rights of
the free American, so carefully laid down by the Bill of Rights,
are now worth nothing. Bit by bit, Congress and the State
Legislatures have invaded and nullified them, and today they
are so flimsy that no lawyer not insane would attempt to defend his client by bringing them up. Imagine trying to defend
a man denied the use of the mails by the Postmaster-General,
without hearing or even formal notice, on the ground that the
Constitution guarantees the right of free speech! The very
catchpolls in the courtroom would snicker. I say that the legislative arm is primarily responsible for this gradual enslave-
ment of the Americano; the truth is, of course, that the
executive and judicial arms are responsible to a scarcely less degree. Our law has not kept pace with the development of our
bureaucracy; there is no machinery provided for curbing its excesses. In Prussia, in the old days, there were special courts for
the purpose, and a citizen oppressed by the police or by any
other public official could get relief and redress. The guilty
functionary could be fined, mulcted in damages, demoted,
cashiered, or even jailed. But in the United States to-day there
are no such tribunals. A citizen attacked by the Postmaster-
General simply has no redress whatever; the courts have re-

fused, over and over again, to interfere save in cases of obvious fraud. Nor is there, it would seem, any remedy for the unconstitutional acts of Prohibition agents. Some time ago, when Senator Stanley, of Kentucky, tried to have a law passed forbidding them to break into a citizen's house in violation of the Bill of Rights, the Prohibitionists mustered up their serfs in the Senate against him, and he was voted down.

The Supreme Court, had it been so disposed, might have put a stop to all this sinister buffoonery long ago. There was a time, indeed, when it was alert to do so. That was during the Civil War. But since then the court has gradually succumbed to the prevailing doctrine that the minority has no rights that the majority is bound to respect. As it is at present constituted, it shows little disposition to go to the rescue of the harassed freeman. When property is menaced it displays a laudable diligence, but when it comes to the mere rights of the citizen it seems hopelessly inclined to give the prosecution the benefit of every doubt. Two justices commonly dissent—two out of nine. They hold the last switch-trench of the old constitutional line. When they depart to realms of bliss the Bill of Rights will be buried with them.

XVII.

Reflections on the Drama

T HE drama is the most democratic of the art forms, and
perhaps the only one that may legitimately bear the label.
Painting, sculpture, music and literature, so far as they show
any genuine æsthetic or intellectual content at all, are not for
crowds, but for selected individuals, mostly with bad kidneys
and worse morals, and three of the four are almost always enjoyed in actual solitude. Even architecture and religious ritual,
though they are publicly displayed, make their chief appeal to
man as individual, not to man as mass animal. One goes into a
church as part of a crowd, true enough, but if it be a church
that has risen above mere theological disputation to the beauty
of ceremonial, one is, even in theory, alone with the Lord God
Jehovah. And if, passing up Fifth Avenue in the 5 o'clock
throng, one pauses before St. Thomas's to drink in the beauty
of that archaic facade, one's drinking is almost sure to be done
a cappella; of the other passers-by, not one in a thousand so
much as glances at it.

But the drama, as representation, is inconceivable save as a
show for the mob, and so it has to take on protective coloration to survive. It must make its appeal, not to individuals as
such, nor even to individuals as units in the mob, but to the
mob as mob—a quite different thing, as Gustav Le Bon long
ago demonstrated in his "Psychologie des Foules." Thus its intellectual content, like its æsthetic form, must be within the
mental grasp of the mob, and what is more important, within
the scope of its prejudices. *Per corollary*, anything even remotely approaching an original idea, or an unpopular idea, is
foreign to it, and if it would make any impression at all, abhorrent to it. The best a dramatist can hope to do is to give
poignant and arresting expression to an idea so simple that the
average man will grasp it at once, and so banal that he will approve it in the next instant. The phrase "drama of ideas" thus
becomes a mere phrase. What is actually meant by it is "drama
of platitudes."

So much for the theory. An appeal to the facts quickly sub-stantiates it. The more one looks into the so-called drama of ideas of the last age—that is, into the acting drama—the more one is astounded by the vacuity of its content. The younger Dumas' "La Dame aux Camélias," the first of all the propa-ganda plays (it raised a stupendous pother in 1852, the echoes of which yet roll), is based upon the sophomoric thesis that a prostitute is a human being like you and me, and suffers the slings and arrows of the same sorrows, and may be potentially quite as worthy of heaven. Augier's "La Mariage d'Olympe" (1854), another sensation-making pioneer, is even hollower; its four acts are devoted to rubbing in the revolutionary discovery that it is unwise for a young man of good family to marry an elderly cocotte. Proceed now to Ibsen. Here one finds the same tasteless platitudes—that it is unpleasant for a wife to be treated as a doll; that professional patriots and town boomers are frauds; that success in business is often grounded upon a mere willingness to do what a man of honor is incapable of; that a woman who continues to live with a debauched hus-band may expect to have unhealthy children; that a joint sor-row tends to bring husband and wife together; that a neurotic woman is apt to prefer death to maternity; that a man of 55 is an ass to fall in love with a flapper of 17. Do I burlesque? If you think so, turn to Ibsen's "Nachgelassene Schriften" and read his own statements of the ideas in his social dramas—read his own succinct summaries of their theses. You will imagine your-self, on more than one page, in the latest volume of mush by Orison Swett Marden. Such "ideas" are what one finds in news-paper editorials, speeches before Congress, sermons by evan-gelical divines—in brief, in the literature expressly addressed to those persons whose distinguishing mark is that ideas never enter their heads.

Ibsen himself, an excellent poet and a reflective man, was under no delusions about his "dramas of ideas." It astounded him greatly when the sentimental German middle-classes hailed "Ein Puppenheim" as a revolutionary document; he protested often and bitterly against being mistaken for a prophet of feminism. His own interest in this play and in those that followed it was chiefly technical; he was trying to displace the well-made play of Scribe and company with something simpler, more elastic and more hospitable to character. He wrote "Ghosts" to raise a laugh against the fools who had seen something novel and horrible in the idea of "A Doll's House"; he wanted to prove to them that that idea was no more than a platitude. Soon afterward he became thoroughly disgusted with the whole "drama of ideas." In "The Wild Duck" he cruelly burlesqued it, and made a low-comedy Ibsenist his chief butt. In "Hedda Gabler" he played a joke on the Ibsen fanatics by fashioning a first-rate drama out of the oldest, shoddiest materials of Sardou, Feuillet, and even Meilhac and Halévy. And beginning with "Little Eyolf" he threw the "drama of ideas" overboard forever, and took to mysticism. What could be more comical than the efforts of critical talmudists to read a thesis into "When We Dead Awaken"? I have put in many a gay hour perusing their commentaries. Ibsen, had he lived, would have roared over them—as he roared over the effort to inject portentous meanings into "The Master Builder," at bottom no more than a sentimental epitaph to a love affair that he himself had suffered at 60.

Gerhart Hauptmann, another dramatist of the first rank, has gone much the same road. As a very young man he succumbed to the "drama of ideas" gabble, and his first plays showed an effort to preach this or that in awful tones. But he soon discovered that the only ideas that would go down, so to speak, on the stage were ideas of such an austere platitudinousness that it was beneath his artistic dignity to merchant them, and so he gave over propaganda altogether. In other words, his genius burst through the narrow bounds of mob ratiocination, and he began appealing to the universal emotions—pity, religious sentiment, patriotism, amorousness. Even in his first play, "Vor Sonnenaufgang," his instinct got the better of his mistaken purpose, and reading it to-day one finds that the sheer horror of it is of vastly more effect than its nebulous and unimportant ideas. It really says nothing; it merely makes us dislike some very unpleasant people.

Turn now to Shaw. At once one finds that the only plays from his pen which contain actual ideas have failed dismally on the stage. These are the so-called "discussions"—e.g., "Getting Married." The successful plays contain no ideas; they contain only platitudes, balderdash, buncombe that even a suffragette might think of. Of such sort are "Man and Superman," "Arms and the Man," "Candida," "Androcles and the Lion," and their like. Shaw has given all of these pieces a specious air of profundity by publishing them hooked to long and garrulous prefaces and by filling them with stage directions which describe and discuss the characters at great length. But as stage plays they are almost as empty as "Hedda Gabler." One searches them vainly for even the slightest novel contribution to the current theories of life, joy and crime. Shaw's prefaces, of course, have vastly more ideational force and respectability than his plays. If he fails to get any ideas of genuine savor into them it is not because the preface form bars them out but because he hasn't any to get in. By attaching them to his plays he converts the latter into colorable imitations of novels, and so opens the way for that superior reflectiveness which lifts the novel above the play, and makes it, as Arnold Bennett has convincingly shown, much harder to write. A stage play in the modern realistic manner—that is, without soliloquies and asides —can seldom rise above the mere representation of some infinitesimal episode, whereas even the worst novel may be, in some sense, an interpretation as well. Obviously, such episodes as may be exposed in 20,000 words—the extreme limit of the average play—are seldom significant, and not often clearly intelligible. The author has a hard enough job making his characters recognizable as human beings; he hasn't time to go behind their acts to their motives, or to deduce any conclusions worth hearing from their doings. One often leaves a "social drama," indeed, wondering what the deuce it is all about; the discussion of its meaning offers endless opportunities for theorists and fanatics. The Ibsen symbolists come to mind again. They read meanings into such plays as "Rosmersholm" and "The Wild Duck" that aroused Ibsen, a peaceful man, to positive fury. In the same way the suffragettes collared "A Doll's House." Even "Peer Gynt" did not escape. There is actually an edition of it edited by a theosophist, in the preface to which it is hymned as a theosophical document. Luckily for Ibsen, he died before this edition was printed. But one may well imagine how it would have made him swear.

The notion that there are ideas in the "drama of ideas," in truth, is confined to a special class of illuminati, whose chief visible character is their capacity for ingesting nonsense—Maeterlinckians, uplifters, women's clubbers, believers in all the sure cures for all the sorrows of the world. To-day the Drama League carries on the tradition. It is composed of the eternally young—unsuccessful dramatists who yet live in hope, young college professors, psychopathic old maids, middle-aged ladies of an incurable jejuneness, the innumerable caravan of the ingenuous and sentimental. Out of the same intellectual *Landsturm* comes the following of Bergson, the parlor metaphysician; and of the third-rate novelists praised by the newspapers; and of such composers as Wolf-Ferrari and Massenet. These are the fair ones, male and female, who were ecstatically shocked by the platitudes of "Damaged Goods," and who regard Augustus Thomas as a great dramatist, and what is more, as a great thinker. Their hero, during a season or two, was the Swedish John the Baptist, August Strindberg—a lunatic with a gift for turning the preposterous into the shocking. A glance at Strindberg's innumerable volumes of autobiography reveals the true horse-power of his so-called ideas. He believed in everything that was idiotic, from transcendentalism to witchcraft. He believed that his enemies were seeking to destroy him by magic; he spent a whole winter trying to find the philosopher's stone. Even among the clergy, it would be difficult to find a more astounding ass than Strindberg. But he had, for all his folly, a considerable native skill at devising effective stage-plays—a talent that some men seem to be born with—and under cover of it he acquired his reputation as a thinker. Here he was met half-way by the defective powers of observation and reflection of his followers, the half-wits aforesaid; they mistook their enjoyment of his adept technical trickery for an appreciation of ideas. Turn to the best of his plays, "The Father." Here the idea—that domestic nagging can cause insanity—is an almost perfect platitude, for on the one hand it is universally admitted and on the other hand it is not true. But as a stage play pure and simple, the piece is superb—a simple and yet enormously effective mechanism. So with "Countess Julie." The idea here is so vague and incomprehensible that no two commentators agree in stating it, and yet the play is so cleverly written, and appeals with such a sure touch to the universal human weakness for the obscene, that it never fails to enchant an audience. The. case of "Hedda Gabler" is parallel. If the actresses playing Hedda in this country made up for the part in the scandalous way their sisters do in Germany (that is, by wearing bustles in front), it would be as great a success here as it is over there. Its general failure among us is due to the fact that it is not made indelicate enough. This also explains the comparative failure of the rest of the Ibsen plays. The crowd has been subtly made to believe that they are magnificently indecent—and is always dashed and displeased when it finds nothing to lift the diaphragm. I well remember the first production of "Ghosts" in America—a business in which I had a hand. So eager was the audience for the promised indecencies that it actually read them into the play, and there were protests against it on the ground that Mrs. Alving was represented as trying to seduce her own son! Here comstockery often helps the "drama of ideas." If no other idea is visible, it can always conjure up, out of its native swinishness, some idea that is offensively sexual, and hence pleasing to the mob.

That mob rules in the theater, and so the theater remains infantile and trivial—a scene, not of the exposure of ideas, nor even of the exhibition of beauty, but one merely of the parading of mental and physical prettiness and vulgarity. It is at its worst when its dramatists seek to corrupt this function by adding a moral or intellectual purpose. It is at its best when it confines itself to the unrealities that are its essence, and swings amiably from the romance that never was on land or sea to the buffoonery that is at the bottom of all we actually know of human life. Shakespeare was its greatest craftsman: he wasted no tortured ratiocination upon his plays. Instead, he filled them with the gaudy heroes that all of us see ourselves becoming on some bright tomorrow, and the lowly frauds and clowns we are to-day. No psychopathic problems engaged him; he took love and ambition and revenge and braggadocio as he found them. He held no clinics in dingy Norwegian apartment-houses: his field was Bohemia, glorious Rome, the Egypt of the scene-painter, Arcady. . . . But even Shakespeare, for all the vast potency of his incomparable, his stupefying poetry, could not long hold the talmudists out in front from their search for invisible significances. Think of all the tomes that have been written upon the profound and revolutionary "ideas" in the moony musings of the diabetic sophomore, Hamlet von Dänemark!

XVIII.
Advice to Young Men

I
To Him That Hath

THE most valuable of all human possessions, next to a superior and disdainful air, is the reputation of being well to do. Nothing else so neatly eases one's way through life, especially in democratic countries. There is in ninety-nine per cent. of all democrats an irresistible impulse to crook the knee to wealth, to defer humbly to the power that goes with it, to see all sorts of high merits in the man who has it, or is said to have it. True enough, envy goes with the pliant neck, but it is envy somehow purged of all menace: the inferior man is afraid to do evil to the man with money in eight banks; he is even afraid to *think* evil of him—that is, in any patent and offensive way. Against capital as an abstraction he rants incessantly, and all of the laws that he favors treat it as if it were criminal. But in the presence of the concrete capitalist he is singularly fawning. What makes him so is easy to discern. He yearns with a great yearning for a chance to tap the capitalist's purse, and he knows very well, deep down in his heart, that he is too craven and stupid to do it by force of arms. So he turns to politeness, and tries to cajole. Give out the news that one has just made a killing in the stock market, or robbed some confiding widow of her dower, or swindled the government in some patriotic enterprise, and at once one will discover that one's shabbiness is a charming eccentricity, and one's judgment of wines worth hearing, and one's politics worthy of attention and respect. The man who is thought to be poor never gets a fair chance. No one wants to listen to him. No one gives a damn what he thinks or knows or feels. No one has any active desire for his good opinion.

I discovered this principle early in life, and have put it to use ever since. I have got a great deal more out of men (and women) by having the name of being a well-heeled fellow than I have ever got by being decent to them, or by dazzling them with my sagacity, or by hard industry, or by a personal beauty that is singular and ineffable.

2
The Venerable Examined

The older I grow the more I distrust the familiar doctrine that age brings wisdom. It is my honest belief that I am no wiser to-day than I was five or ten years ago; in fact, I often suspect that I am appreciably *less* wise. Women can prevail over me to-day by devices that would have made me hoof them out of my studio when I was thirty-five. I am also an easier mark for male swindlers than I used to be; at fifty I'll probably be joining clubs and buying Mexican mine stock. The truth is that every man goes up-hill in sagacity to a certain point, and then begins sliding down again. Nearly all the old fellows that I know are more or less balmy. Theoretically, they should be much wiser than younger men, if only because of their greater experience, but actually they seem to take on folly faster than they take on wisdom. A man of thirty-five or thirty-eight is almost woman-proof. For a woman to marry him is a herculean feat. But by the time he is fifty he is quite as easy as a Yale sophomore. On other planes the same decay of the intelligence is visible. Certainly it would be difficult to imagine any committee of relatively young men, of thirty or thirty-five, showing the unbroken childishness, ignorance and lack of humor of the Supreme Court of the United States. The average age of the learned justices must be well beyond sixty, and all of them are supposed to be of finished and mellowed sagacity. Yet their knowledge of the most ordinary principles of justice often turns out to be extremely meager, and when they spread themselves grandly upon a great case their reasoning powers are usually found to be precisely equal to those of a respectable Pullman conductor.

3
Duty

Some of the loosest thinking in ethics has duty for its theme. Practically all writers on the subject agree that the individual owes certain unescapable duties to the race—for example, the duty of engaging in productive labor, and that of marrying and begetting offspring. In support of this position it is almost always argued that if *all* men neglected such duties the race would perish. The logic is hollow enough to be worthy of the college professors who are guilty of it. It simply confuses the conventionality, the pusillanimity, the lack of imagination of the majority of men with the duty of *all* men. There is not the slightest ground for assuming, even as a matter of mere argumentation, that *all* men will ever neglect these alleged duties. There will always remain a safe majority that is willing to do whatever is ordained—that accepts docilely the government it is born under, obeys its laws, and supports its theory. But that majority does not comprise the men who render the highest and most intelligent services to the race; it comprises those who render nothing save their obedience.

For the man who differs from this inert and well-regimented mass, however slightly, there are no duties *per se*. What he is spontaneously inclined to do is of vastly more value to all of us than what the majority is willing to do. There is, indeed, no such thing as duty-in-itself; it is a mere chimera of ethical theorists. Human progress is furthered, not by conformity, but by aberration. The very concept of duty is thus a function of inferiority; it belongs naturally only to timorous and incompetent men. Even on such levels it remains largely a self-delusion, a soothing apparition, a euphemism for necessity. When a man succumbs to duty he merely succumbs to the habit and inclination of other men. Their collective interests invariably pull against his individual interests. Some of us can resist a pretty strong pull—the pull, perhaps, of thousands. But it is only the miraculous man who can withstand the pull of a whole nation.

4
Martyrs

"History," says Henry Ford, "is bunk." I inscribe myself among those who dissent from this doctrine; nevertheless, I am often hauled up, in reading history, by a feeling that I am among unrealities. In particular, that feeling comes over me when I read about the religious wars of the past—wars in which thousands of men, women and children were butchered on account of puerile and unintelligible disputes over transubstantiation, the atonement, and other such metaphysical banshees. It does not surprise me that the majority murdered the minority; the majority, even to-day, does it whenever it is possible. What I can't understand is that the minority went voluntarily to the slaughter. Even in the worst persecutions known to history—say, for example, those of the Jews of Spain—it was always possible for a given member of the minority to save his hide by giving public assent to the religious notions of the majority. A Jew who was willing to be baptized, in the reign of Ferdinand and Isabella, was practically unmolested; his descendants today are 100% Spaniards. Well, then, why did so many Jews refuse? Why did so many prefer to be robbed, exiled, and sometimes murdered?

The answer given by philosophical historians is that they were a noble people, and preferred death to heresy. But this merely begs the question. Is it actually noble to cling to a religious idea so tenaciously? Certainly it doesn't seem so to me. After all, no human being really *knows* anything about the exalted matters with which all religions deal. The most he can do is to match his private guess against the guesses of his fellow-men. For any man to say absolutely, in such a field, that this or that is wholly and irrefragably true and this or that is utterly false is simply to talk nonsense. Personally, I have never encountered a religious idea—and I do not except even the idea of the existence of God—that was instantly and unchallengeably convincing, as, say, the Copernican astronomy is instantly and unchallengeably convincing. But neither have I ever encountered a religious idea that could be dismissed offhand as palpably and indubitably false. In even the worst nonsense of such theological mountebanks as the Rev. Dr. Billy Sunday, Brigham Young and Mrs. Eddy there is always enough lingering plausibility, or, at all events, possibility, to give the judicious pause. Whatever the weight of the probabilities against it, it nevertheless *may* be true that man, on his decease, turns into a gaseous vertebrate, and that this vertebrate, if its human larva has engaged in embezzlement, bootlegging, profanity or adultery on this earth, will be boiled for a million years in a cauldron of pitch. My private inclination, due to my defective upbringing, is to doubt it, and to set down any one who believes it as an ass, but it must be plain that I have no means of disproving it.

In view of this uncertainty it seems to me sheer vanity for any man to hold his religious views too firmly, or to submit to any inconvenience on account of them. It is far better, if they happen to offend, to conceal them discreetly, or to change them amiably as the delusions of the majority change. My own views in this department, being wholly skeptical and tolerant, are obnoxious to the subscribers to practically all other views; even atheists sometimes denounce me. At the moment, by an accident of American political history, these dissenters from my theology are forbidden to punish me for not agreeing with them. But at any succeeding moment some group or other among them may seize such power and proceed against me in the immemorial manner. If it ever happens, I give notice here and now that I shall get converted to their nonsense instantly, and so retire to safety with my right thumb laid against my nose and my fingers waving like wheat in the wind. I'd do it even to-day, if there were any practical advantage in it. Offer me a case of Rauenthaler 1903, and I engage to submit to baptism by any rite ever heard of, provided it does not expose my gothic nakedness. Make it ten cases, and I'll agree to be both baptized and confirmed. In such matters I am broad-minded. What, after all, is one more lie?

5
The Disabled Veteran

The science of psychological pathology is still in its infancy. In all its literature in three languages, I can't find a line about the permanent ill effects of acute emotional diseases—say, for example, love affairs. The common assumption of the world is that when a love affair is over it is over—that nothing remains behind. This is probably grossly untrue. It is my belief that every such experience leaves scars upon my psyche, and that they are quite as plain and quite as dangerous as the scars left on the neck by a carbuncle. A man who has passed through a love affair, even though he may eventually forget the lady's very name, is never quite the same thereafter. His scars may be small, but they are permanent. The sentimentalist, exposed incessantly, ends as a psychic cripple; he is as badly off as the man who has come home from the wars with shell-shock. The precise nature of the scars remains to be determined. My own notion is that they take the form of large yellow patches upon the self-esteem. Whenever a man thinks of one of his dead love affairs, and in particular whenever he allows his memory to dredge up an image of the woman he loved, he shivers like one taken in some unmanly and discreditable act. Such shivers, repeated often enough, must inevitably shake his inner integrity off its base. No man can love, and yet remain truly proud. It is a disarming and humiliating experience.

6
Patriotism

Patriotism is conceivable to a civilized man in times of stress and storm, when his country is wobbling and sore beset. His country then appeals to him as any victim of misfortune appeals to him—say, a street-walker pursued by the police. But when it is safe, happy and prosperous it can only excite his loathing. The things that make countries safe, happy and prosperous—a secure peace, an active trade, political serenity at home—are all intrinsically corrupting and disgusting. It is as impossible for a civilized man to love his country in good times as it would be for him to respect a politician.

XIX.

Suite Américaine

I

Aspiration

POLICE sergeants praying humbly to God that Jews will start poker-rooms on their posts, and so enable them to educate their eldest sons for holy orders. . . . Newspaper reporters resolving firmly to work hard, keep sober and be polite to the city editor, and so be rewarded with jobs as copy-readers. . . . College professors in one-building universities on the prairie, still hoping, at the age of sixty, to get their whimsical essays into the *Atlantic Monthly*. . . . Car-conductors on lonely suburban lines, trying desperately to save up $500 and start a Ford garage. . . . Pastors of one-horse little churches in decadent villages, who, whenever they drink two cups of coffee at supper, dream all night that they have been elected bishops. . . . Movie actors who hope against hope that the next fan letter will be from Bar Harbor. . . . Delicatessen dealers who spend their whole lives searching for a cheap substitute for the embalmed veal used in chicken-salad. . . . Italians who wish that they were Irish. . . . Mulatto girls in Georgia and Alabama who send away greasy dollar bills for bottles of Mme. Celestine's Infallible Hair-Straightener. . . . Ash-men who pull wires to be appointed superintendents of city dumps. . . . Mothers who dream that the babies in their cradles will reach, in the mysterious after years, the highest chairs in the Red Men and the Maccabees. . . . Farmers who figure that, with good luck, they will be able to pay off their mortgages by 1943. . . . Contestants for the standing broad-jump championship of the Altoona, Pa., Y.M.C.A. . . . Editorial writers who essay to prove mathematically that a war between England and the United States is unthinkable. . . .

2
Virtue

Pale druggists in remote towns of the Epworth League and flannel nightgown belts, endlessly wrapping up bottles of Peruna. . . . Women hidden away in the damp kitchens of unpainted houses along the railroad tracks, frying tough beefsteaks. . . . Lime and cement dealers being initiated into the Knights of Pythias, the Red Men or the Woodmen of the World. . . . Watchmen at lonely railroad crossings in Iowa, hoping that they'll be able to get off to hear the United Brethren evangelist preach. . . . Ticket-choppers in the subway, breathing sweat in its gaseous form. . . . Family doctors in poor neighborhoods, faithfully relying upon the therapeutics taught in their Eclectic Medical College in 1884. . . . Farmers plowing sterile fields behind sad meditative horses, both suffering from the bites of insects. . . . Greeks tending all-night coffee-joints in the suburban wildernesses where the trolley-cars stop. . . . Grocery-clerks stealing prunes and ginger-snaps, and trying to make assignations with soapy servant-girls. . . . Women confined for the ninth or tenth time, wondering helplessly what it is all about. . . . Methodist preachers retired after forty years of service in the trenches of God, upon pensions of $600 a year. . . . Wives and daughters of Middle Western country bankers, marooned in Los Angeles, going tremblingly to swami séances in dark, smelly rooms. . . . Chauffeurs in huge fur coats waiting outside theaters filled with folks applauding Robert Edeson and Jane Cowl. . . . Decayed and hopeless men writing editorials at midnight for leading papers in Mississippi, Arkansas and Alabama. . . . Owners of the principal candy-stores in Green River, Neb., and Tyrone, Pa. . . . Presidents of one-building universities in the rural fastnesses of Kentucky and Tennessee. . . . Women with babies in their arms weeping over moving-pictures in the Elks' Hall at Schmidtsville, Mo. . . . Babies just born to the wives of milk-wagon drivers. . . . Judges on the benches of petty county courts in Virginia, Vermont and Idaho. . . . Conductors of accommodation trains running between Kokomo, Ind., and Logansport. . . .

3
Eminence

The leading Methodist layman of Pottawattamie county, Iowa. . . . The man who won the limerick contest conducted by the Toomsboro, Ga., *Banner*. . . . The secretary of the Little Rock, Ark., Kiwanis Club. . . . The president of the Johann Sebastian Bach *Bauverein* of Highlandtown, Md. . . . The girl who sold the most Liberty Bonds in Duquesne, Pa. . . . The captain of the champion basket-ball team at the Gary, Ind., Y.M.C.A. . . . The man who owns the best bull in Coosa county, Ala. . . . The tallest man in Covington, Ky. . . . The oldest subscriber to the Raleigh, N.C., *News and Observer*. . . . The most fashionable milliner in Bucyrus, O. . . . The business agent of the Plasterers' Union of Somerville, Mass. . . . The author of the ode read at the unveiling of the monument to General Robert E. Lee at Valdosta, Ga. . . . The original Henry Cabot Lodge man. . . . The owner of the champion Airedale of Buffalo, N.Y. . . . The first child named after the Hon. Warren Gamaliel Harding. . . . The old lady in Wahoo, Neb., who has read the Bible 38 times. . . . The boss who controls the Italian, Czecho-Slovak and Polish votes in Youngstown, O. . . . The professor of chemistry, Greek, rhetoric and piano at the Texas Christian University, Fort Worth, Tex. . . . The boy who sells 225 copies of the *Saturday Evening Post* every week in Cheyenne, Wyo. . . . The youngest murderer awaiting hanging in Chicago. . . . The leading dramatic critic of Pittsburgh. . . . The night watchman in Penn Yan, N.Y., who once shook hands with Chester A. Arthur. . . . The Lithuanian woman in Bluefield, W. Va., who has had five sets of triplets. . . . The actor who has played in "Lightning" 1,600 times. . . . The best horsedoctor in Oklahoma. . . . The highest-paid church-choir soprano in Knoxville, Tenn. . . . The most eligible bachelor in Cheyenne, Wyo. . . . The engineer of the locomotive which pulled the train which carried the Hon. A. Mitchell Palmer to the San Francisco Convention. . . . The girl who got the most votes in the popularity contest at Egg Harbor, N.J. . . .

APPENDIX

from

MY LIFE
AS AUTHOR AND EDITOR

My Life as Author and Editor

My second large enterprise of 1919 was the launching of my "Prejudices" series, the first volume of which came out in September. The idea of this series was rather obvious, for my periodical writings, and especially my *Smart Set* reviews, were getting more and more notice, but rather strangely it did not occur to either Knopf or me. Knopf, indeed, was against it when he first heard it proposed. Its originator was a bookseller in Cleveland named Richard Laukhuff, and in a letter of April 23, 1943 he told me the story, which Knopf corroborated. Thus:

> During the days of the *Smart Set* I collected your book reviews and placed them in folders for easy reference by people coming to the shop. I found them much to the point, and thought others might, so I kept them lying around. People did pick them up and read them, and most lively discussions were started and people discovered books. One day Mr. Knopf, who in those days was his own salesman, came to the store. He invited suggestions. Among other ideas, I suggested publication of some of your reviews.
> Mr. Knopf: Nobody would buy them.
> Laukhuff: Many people will buy them.
> The next Knopf catalog had the announcement of "Prejudices."

I was myself rather dubious about the project, for it was common publishing experience that reprinted reviews did not sell. Moreover, I was full of plans in those days for editing a history of the American share in World War I—not the military history, but the record of the spy-hunting, profiteering and patrioteering at home—and was eager to get to work on it. I had conceived it on a large scale, and figured that it would run to 25 or 30 volumes, and perhaps more—one, for example, to be devoted to the record of the American clergy in the war, another to the wholesale stealing of German property, a third to the war-mongering in the colleges, a fourth to the Liberty loan campaigns, a fifth to the part played by the newspapers and so on and so on. Such an enterprise, of course, was beyond the capacity of one man, so I counted on getting together a committee of like-minded persons, raising a fund to finance the writing and printing, and perhaps setting a mob of nascent Ph.D.'s to work at the amassing of materials. This amassing would involve an examination of all the principal American newspapers from 1914 to date, and of many minor ones, and it would also take a great deal of traveling. Unhappily, I soon found that executing the scheme on anything approaching an adequate scale would cost at least $1,000,000, and inasmuch as I could find no one willing to put up so much money I had to abandon it. But while I cherished it it entertained me pleasantly, and I accumulated myself a great mass of newspaper clippings and other documents. They nearly filled the loft of the little pony-stable in Hollins street, and there they remained until I returned to the old house in 1936, when I called in a colored trash man and presented the whole lot to him as waste-paper. The history of the American share in World War I has not been written to this day, and I doubt that it ever will be. The academic historians adopted the official view of it, and only a few of them—for example, Sidney B. Fay of Harvard*—have ever made any effort, however slight, to unearth and print the extremely discreditable facts. The same thing is now happening (1945) in the case of World War II, and I suppose the American people will continue to be fed balderdash until the end of the chapter. It is always possible, however, that some foreigner—say an Englishman—will attempt some day to tell the truth, but I should add at once that it is not likely. I often wonder whether the history of the remoter past is any more reliable. It has been investigated at enormous length by earnest and diligent men, and some of the delusions that once prevailed have been exploded, but in the main what we believe about it is probably quite as dubious as what Americans believe about World War I.

Following Laukhuff's plan, "Prejudices: First Series" was mainly made up of things that had been printed in the *Smart Set*, but I did some painstaking rewriting, and also added material from my articles in other magazines and in newspapers, and some stuff written especially for the book. On September 6, 1919 I wrote to Fielding H. Garrison: "It is full of rough stuff, perhaps too cruel—but, after all, it is foolish to be polite

*His Origins of the World War was published in 1928.

to frauds". And on September 28: "It is light stuff, chiefly rewritten from the *Smart Set*, but with now and then a blast from the lower woodwind. It will outrage the umbilicari, if that is the way to spell it. Such books are mere stinkpots, heaved occasionally to keep the animals perturbed. The real artillery fire will begin a bit later".* How many copies of the first edition Knopf printed I do not recall, but he had sold 1678 by December 31—a very pleasant surprise to both of us. The second printing was already on the press, and it came out in January, 1920. A third followed in April, 1920, and a fourth in March, 1921. There was a fifth in December, and a sixth in March, 1923, and in February of the latter year Knopf issued a reprint in his Borzoi Pocket Books. Reprints in this series and in the regular edition followed in 1924, 1926 and 1929, and the book remained in print until 1933, when the plates were at last melted. Jonathan Cape took 500 sheets for England, but had sold only 296 copies by November, 1921. In the United States it did much better. Though it was overtaken by "Prejudices: Second Series" in October, 1920, it sold 1052 copies in that year. It kept on selling steadily until 1931, eleven years after its first publication, when there was a drop, and Knopf and I began to discuss letting it go out of print. When the plates were melted in 1933 about 300 copies remained in stock. They were finally disposed of by 1942, and "Prejudices: First Series" perished from this earth. The total sales by that time, if I calculate correctly, were 15,712, and counting in the small fees paid by Cape for the English rights and the sums received from reprint rights, my receipts from it amounted altogether to $3222.33. This was certainly good pay for a book that I had compounded out of clippings in no more than a few weeks of intermittent labor. Requests for reprint rights still occasionally come in.† After the first edition was published Knopf told me that he thought he should adopt a standard format for all of my books, and we decided upon dark blue cloth with gilt stamping, and my coat-of-arms in blind stamping on the front

---

*This is a reference, of course, to my projected history of the war.

†The copy from which Prejudices I was set up is in a volume entitled Prejudices: First Series—Original Typescript—1919, in the Mencken collection at the Pratt Library, Baltimore.

cover. This was first used for the second printing, and was retained for my books thereafter, though not invariably.*

My description of "Prejudices: First Series" as a stinkpot designed "to keep the animals perturbed" was not altogether inept, for if that was not the fundamental purpose of the book, then it was certainly its effect. Most of the contents were not new, for they had been printed before in the *Smart Set*, but their impact, coming out in small instalments, had been much less than their impact in one blast. I made a deliberate effort to lay as many quacks as possible, and chose my targets, not only from the great names of the past, but also from the current company of favorites. Thus butcheries of some of the elder demigods were accompanied by onslaughts upon some of the reigning favorites of 1919, ranging from H. G. Wells, William Dean Howells and George Bernard Shaw down to Henry Van Dyke, William Allen White, Irvin Cobb, Henry Sydnor Harrison, Hamlin Garland, Amy Lowell, Ernest Poole, Thorstein Veblen, Will Levington Comfort and Joyce Kilmer. Some of these attacks drew blood, and their victims never recovered afterward, notably Veblen, Poole, Garland, Comfort, Harrison and Cobb.† Nor did I spare, in my laying about, men with whom I was on good terms personally, and in whom I saw, mixed with fustian, some sound merit—for example, Edgar Lee Masters, Vachel Lindsay, Ezra Pound and Robert Frost. My book, of course, was not all abuse, for I had friendly words in it for all these men, and also for Arnold Bennett, Jack London, George Ade, Elsie Clews Parsons, Hermann Sudermann,

*It was still used for my Supplement I to The American Language, 1945.
†After Veblen's death in 1929 a biography of him appeared, and I was somewhat upset to learn from it that my *reductio ad absurdum* of his pompous pseudo-philosophy had greatly disconcerted him, and in fact thrown him into despair. Before I tackled him he had been the favorite sage of all the advanced thinkers of the time, and the *New Republic* whooped him up in terms fit for Aristotle, but a little while afterward he was abandoned for an even worse quack, John Dewey. I regretted his sufferings, but I still believe that my denunciation of him was deserved. Garland attempted to strike back at me in one of his volumes of autobiography, published in his later years, but this riposte was too transparent to be effective, and he was by that time pretty well frayed. He died in 1940. Comfort, Harrison, Cobb and Poole were never taken seriously after 1919. Comfort died in 1932, Harrison in 1930 and Cobb in 1944. Poole is still living (1945), but all his books since those I excoriated have fallen flat.

George Jean Nathan* and many others. Also, I gave over several chapters to less personal themes—for example, the uproar over sex, then in full blast; the psychology of Puritanism, and the general state of civilization in the United States. On the latter theme, though the Treaty of Versailles was but three months old, I had this to say:

A mongrel and inferior people, incapable of any spiritual aspiration above that of second-rate English colonials, we seek refuge inevitably in the one sort of superiority that the lower castes of men can authentically boast, to wit, superiority in docility, in credulity, in resignation, in morals. We are the most moral race in the world; there is not another that we do not look down upon in that department; our confessed aim and destiny as a nation is to inoculate them all with our incomparable rectitude. In the last analysis, all ideas are judged among us by moral standards; moral values are our only permanent tests of worth, whether in the arts, in politics, in philosophy or in life itself. Even the instincts of man, so intrinsically immoral, so innocent, are fitted with moral false-faces. That bedevilment by sex ideas which punishes continence, so abhorrent to nature, is converted into a moral frenzy, pathological in the end. The impulse to cavort and kick up one's legs, so healthy, so universal, is hedged in by incomprehensible taboos; it becomes stealthy, dirty, degrading. The desire to create and linger over beauty, the sign and touchstone of man's rise above the brute, is held down by doubts and hesitations; when it breaks through it must do so by orgy and explosion, half ludicrous and half pathetic. Our function, we choose to believe, is to teach and inspire the world. We are wrong. Our function is to amuse the world.

This sort of thing naturally alarmed many of the book reviewers, so they dealt with "Prejudices: First Series" in a rather gingery fashion, avoiding too particular an account of its contents and tempering their approval with caution. This was true, for example, of Philip Littell, who gave it a generally favorable notice in the *New Republic* for January 21, 1920, but

*Some of the reviewers professed to be surprised and amused by my notion that Nathan was a better dramatic critic than any of the others then practising in New York, for example, Clayton Hamilton, whom I derided as a jackass, but it must be manifest today (1945) that I was right. I did not believe then, and do not believe now, that writing notices of current theatrical exhibitions is a very lofty branch of the literary art, but such as it is Nathan carried it on with wit, sound information and plenty of acumen. No other New York dramatic critic of his day, or of any other day, has been better.

saved himself with many prudent whereases and howevers. It
was true, likewise, of many newspaper reviews, for example,
those of the Indianapolis *News*, the Detroit *News* (D. Kenneth
Laub),* the Binghampton (N.Y.) *Sun*, the San Francisco *Bulletin* (who led off with "Everybody is reading Mencken"), the
Pittsburgh *Press*, the New York *World*, the Brooklyn *Eagle*,
the Newark *News*, the Toledo *Blade* and the New York *Sun*. The
book puzzled and disquieted these poor dolts. They saw that it
was far more than a collection of book reviews, and were inclined to treat it seriously, but they shied at its fundamental
doctrine, not only as aesthetes of the current model but also as
patriotic Americans. A common way out for them was to al-
lege that I was not in earnest—that the whole thing was only a
buffoonish play to the galleries, full of exaggerations and conscious falsifications. But just what galleries I was playing to
they did not explain. This warning note was struck by the reviewers of the Hartford *Courant*, the New York *Evening Sun*,
the Boston *Herald*, the Springfield *Republican*, the Springfield
Union,† the Baltimore *Sun*,‡ and the New York *Tribune*. But
the author of the last-named, signing himself W.H.C., admitted some merit in the book, despite its obnoxious Nietzschean
flavor. It was, he said, "a tremendously successful experiment
in the revaluation of American critical values" (a Nietzschean
phrase, borrowed in spite of himself), and the author was "one
of the few men who redeem American criticism from the
charge of hopeless mediocrity". The downright excoriations
were rather more amusing. The most violent of them was Stuart Pratt Sherman's, printed in the New York *Times* for December 7, 1919 under the title of "Mr. Mencken and the Jeune
Fille".§ I had used Sherman harshly in the first chapter of my

---

*Laub was one of the innumerable young literati of the time who showed
some promise, but never came to anything.

†The author of the *Union* review was A.L.S. Wood, a frustrated Taine who
is dealt with on p. 501 of this chronicle.

‡The *Sun's* review, printed Nov. 1, 1919, was signed Malcolm Meiklejohn, a
pseudonym. The identity of the author I do not know. No one in the *Sun*
office today (1945) remembers him. He spoke sadly of my "alcohol-saturated
stomach," my "uncivilized moral standards," and my "Nietzschean obsession," and described me as having "no sympathy with the ignoble feelings of
pity, compassion, tenderness and sacrifice."

§This was reprinted in Sherman's book, American; New York, 1922, with book, and on sundry other occasions, and he came back, characteristically, with the hint that I was somehow connected with the German spy system. Another appeal to the prevailing fears was made by the reviewer of the Los Angeles *Times* (shades of Willard Wright!)* on November 30. He spoke of me as *Herr* Mencken, and declared that I had "a complete *Kultur*, but no culture whatever".

But there were also some friendly reviews, notably those in the San Francisco *Bulletin*, the New York *American*, the San Francisco *Argonaut*, the *Dial* (by Winthrop Parkhurst), the Richmond *Times-Dispatch* and the Albany *Knickerbocker-Press* (by Belford Forrest). The Chicago *News* printed a review by the Montana pythoness, Mary Maclane, who was dealt with in the book under the title of the Butte Bashkirtseff—Chapter X.† The Boston *Transcript* reviewed the book no less than three times. The first notice, published October 8, 1919, appeared anonymously in the department headed "The Librarian," and was full of patriotic tremors. It began "Mr. H. L. Mencken is fully ninety per cent Prussian in all his utterances, and proud of it. His most malignant and persistent sneers are reserved for any American who was active in enmity to Germany and Austria". But even this anonymous granted that there are some true hits in the book—for example, in the chapters on Thorstein Veblen and the sex hygiene racket—and toward the end of his diatribe he mellowed considerably. There must have been some sharp dissent from his general position in the *Transcript* office, for the two reviews that followed were both predominantly friendly. On November 1, 1919, over the initials H.T.S., I was dealt with as follows:

Considered altogether, Mr. Mencken has about the sanest views on literature of any well known critic in the country. He has a way of brushing aside all cobwebby traditions and dogmas and pointing

---

the title expanded to Mr. Mencken, the Jeune Fille, and the New Spirit in Letters.

*See p. 382 of this chronicle.

†See my Thirty-five Years of Newspaper Work, 1906–41, pp. 266–67. See also a note on La Maclane by Miriam deFord in *American Notes and Queries*, Jan., 1945, p. 155. Her letters to me, not many, are in my letter-file, to go to the New York Public Library at my death.

unerringly to the truth of whatever matter he decides to discuss, and he doesn't care whom he offends when he is about it. He has no reverence and no fear. His style is little short of fascinating, smacking a little of Shaw, for whom he appears to entertain a mingled admiration and contempt. "Prejudices" is a book full of sound, hard sense.

The third *Transcript* review was printed on December 27 and signed D.L.M. It was altogether favorable, though somewhat pedantic and even spinsterish. The English notices, save that of the Manchester *Guardian*, which has always sneered at my books, were friendly. The *Guardian's* reviewer, who signed himself B.S., apparently unaware of the American significance of the letters, objected strongly to my way of writing, and had this to say of it:

He has absorbed a sham-comedy, swashbuckling style in some backwater of provincial journalism, and he has never reflected that ears of the shape and size a critic must catch hold of before they will attend to him are by nature impervious to critical distinctions. Slang and slapdash will not do for the work of the literary critic, and readers who want that kind of thing must be left to find it where it belongs. And there is another consideration: the manner is bad in itself, and also it has no general currency. English is understood in the four quarters of the globe, but Mr. Mencken's comic cuts are merely doleful for people whose patois is not the same as his.

The London *Times*, dissenting from all this, credited me with "a fine style" and called "Prejudices" "a lively book to dip into". The London *Athenaeum* printed three notices, the first of which described the book as "refreshing" and "delightful," but added: "Mr. Mencken writes brightly, perhaps too brightly: the brilliance of his style suggests the flash of the best American dentistry". The second notice, signed A.L.H.,* ran in part as follows:

Mr. Mencken turns a pair of civilized eyes on the extraordinary and fantastic spectacle which is contemporary American life. It passes before him, a circus parade—vast ponderous elephants, lions, shy gazelles, apes, performing horses—and he comments upon it, laughingly, in that brilliant, masterfully vulgar style of which he knows the strange secret. All the animals interest him, graceful and ugly alike, noble and repulsive; but by preference he lingers, fascinated no doubt

---

*This was Aldous Huxley, as will appear a bit later on.

by the fabulous grotesqueness of their swollen shapes, among the
solemn mammoths of stupidity, mountain-bodied and mouse-brained,
slow-moving, prehistoric. They exist everywhere, these monsters, but
it is surely in America that they reach their greatest growth. Puritanism there swells into Comstockism; our harmless little European
uplift becomes a sinister, rapacious philanthropic beast; religions pul-
lulate, strange and improbable as the saurians of the Mesozoic age.
Mr. Mencken contemplates them with a civilized man's astonishment
and horror, then sets his pen in rest and charges upon them. His pen
is sharp, his aim unerring, and the punctured monsters collapse with a
dolorous whistling of escaping gas. It is a wonderful display. Admiring his skill, one thinks of what Dryden said of himself in his Essay on
Satire: "There is still a vast difference between the slovenly butchering of a man and the fineness of a stroke that separates the head from
the body and leaves it standing in its place. A man may be capable, as
Jack Ketch's wife said of his servant, of a plain piece of work, a bare
hanging; but to make a malefactor die sweetly was only belonging to
her husband". Mr. Mencken is a worthy apprentice of this great Jack
Ketch of literature. . . . We should welcome his appearance among
us here, for we have sore need of critics who hate humbug, who are
not afraid of putting out their tongues at pretentiousness, however
noble an aspect it may wear, who do not mind being vulgar at need,
and who, finally, know not only how to make us think, but how to
make us laugh as well.

This notice, which appeared on January 2, 1920, undoubtedly colored some of the later discussions of the earlier "Prejudices" books, for American criticism is always extremely
responsive to English leading. It was supported by reviews in
the London *New Statesman*, the London *New Witness* (by
Vincent O'Sullivan) and other English journals and by high
praise in a number of British colonial publications, for example, the *Triad* of Sydney, Australia, the Sydney *Sunday Times*
and the Toronto *Saturday Night*. Also, it was supported by a
blast in the *Mercure de France*, printed before the appearance
of "Prejudices: First Series," in which "A Book of Prefaces" was
described as "the best and most free criticism of literature that
has appeared in the United States since Poe". This *Mercure*
judgment was quoted in a number of the American notices of
"Prejudices," and it obviously had some influence upon them.
Nor was there any encouragement to the aroused and alarmed
patriots when Hugh Walpole, the English novelist, landed in

New York late in 1919, and announced that the four American
authors who interested him most were Willa Cather, Hergesheimer, Cabell and myself. Of me he said in an interview:

Mencken is an extraordinarily keen and effective critic. He puts
things with amazing honesty and force. Such a change, you know,
from the stupid blurb and indiscriminate praise that so generally
passes for criticism over here. I should think that Mencken will do a
lot of good for your literature.*

The discussion of "Prejudices: First Series" went far beyond
the reviews. It continued, in fact, for months after the book
came out, and was participated in by columnists, editorial

---

*Philadelphia *Press* (magazine section), Nov. 2, 1919, p. 3. Walpole came to
Baltimore to see me, and we had a pleasant session on Nov. 20. The next day I
wrote to Blanche Knopf: "At the end of it Janvier, the local Pirie MacDonald,
made a couple of pictures of us sitting together on an old sofa, gazing into
each other's eyes. I doubt that the pictures will be fit to show. I had a bleary
eye and Walpole snickered. The result will probably be a Portrait of Two
Souses. I'll send you a clipping of the halftone from the *Police Gazette*". A
print of this photograph is in a book entitled Photographs and Other Portraits
—H. L. Mencken—1881–1936, to go to the Pratt Library, Baltimore, at my
death. In 1922 I paid Walpole a return visit in London, and had lunch with him
in his luxurious house at 24 York Terrace, Regent's Park, served by a butler
out of an English society play. The place was very charming, with a garden
behind it and all the rooms within crowded with books and manuscripts, including some of Sir Walter Scott. In 1925, in response to my frequent charge
that the English reviewers neglected American novels and devoted too much
time to log-rolling for their fellow-nationals, he wrote me an open letter that
was published in the *Bookman*, then edited by John Farrar. I replied soon
afterward, and my reply was printed as a pamphlet by the George H. Doran
Company, under the title of My dear Walpole. I never saw him after 1922, and
our correspondence soon dropped off. In 1923 or thereabout Joseph
Hergesheimer told me that Walpole was a homosexual, and had actually made
an attempt upon him (Hergesheimer) when on a visit to West Chester. He
gave no evidence of this when I met him myself, but maybe that was because
homosexuals always avoid me. Reports to the same effect reached me from
other sources during the years following. Walpole was knighted in 1937 and
died in 1944. I reviewed his The Gods and Mr. Perrin very favorably in the
Smart Set for Feb., 1912, but after that I began to have doubts about him, and
in Dec., 1914 I described The Duchess of Wrexe as a bore, which it undoubtedly was. Of his later novels, which were numerous, I reviewed only The
Green Mirror (March, 1918), The Thirteenth Traveler (Jan., 1922) and The
Cathedral (March, 1923). I treated The Cathedral politely, but dismissed the
other two without ceremony.

writers and a miscellany of other sages.* Indeed, it launched that debate over my ideas—and, by an easy transition, my objects and motives—which roared on for years afterward, and produced so vast a crop of invective that in 1928 I was moved to gather some of its pearls in "Menckeniana: A Schimpflexikon". All of the discussion of me printed before the end of 1917 found room in little more than a single volume of the 300-odd-page scrapbooks that I set up in that year, but 1918 needed more than 150 pages and 1919 more than 200, and after that there were many years that filled two or three whole volumes. I am now (August, 1945) in Volume 89, and the flood still continues.†

It had been my plan to bring out a volume of "Prejudices" every two years, for they were to be made up largely of selections from my magazine stuff, and I wanted as wide a range of choice as possible, but the pother raised by Series I suggested to Knopf that we had better schedule Series II for 1920 instead of 1921. "I have discovered something," he said to me one day. "It is that H. L. Mencken has become a good property". "Prejudices: Second Series" was accordingly published in October, 1920, and had already sold 1853 copies by the end of the year. The first printing was 3000 copies, and Knopf was reprinting in June. There were other reprintings in February, 1922; February‡ and December, 1923; and October and December, 1924, making seven in all. By 1927 the sales as a single volume began

*I also received a great many letters from readers, most of them friendly. On September 29, 1919 Fielding H. Garrison wrote to me: "It certainly is a rip-snorter—a cyclone of vigorous thinking and common sense, expressed in language that is *strepitoso e veloce*. I know nothing of many of the people you excoriate and from what you say of them I am glad I don't. But the chapters on the Dean, Veblen, Ade, Shaw, London et al are stone-fences and corpse-reviewers".

†The incoming clippings are entered by Mrs. C. F. Lappin of Minneapolis, once my secretary. When she married and left Baltimore she said she would like to go on handling them, and she has been doing it ever since. There are, of course, many gaps in the collection, for clipping bureaus are far from infallible. Moreover, large numbers of clippings have been diverted from these books to my collecteana on the American language, and enough to fill a pushcart went into The "Hatrack" Case 1926–27, now in the Pratt Library, Baltimore.

‡In this reprinting I made many corrections in the book.

to bog down, but it continued to sell as a part of three different sets of "Prejudices," one of the first four series, one of the first five, and the other of all six. It went out of print finally in 1933, by which time, disregarding these sets, it had sold a little short of 8000 copies, and earned me about $2400. Like "Prejudices: First Series," it was published by Jonathan Cape in London, bound in staring yellow cloth that made the gaudiest effort of Knopf seem pale. In 1925 some extracts from it were printed in various fonts of small type by Dr. E. F. Darling, a New York oculist, and used by him for testing the eyes of his patients.* The book had "Prejudices: First Series" but thirteen months ahead of it, and thus faced stiff competition in its own house. The sets of "Prejudices" that I have mentioned were issued in boxes for gift purposes, and the first of them, embracing the first four volumes, did pretty well, for it sold 768 sets and brought me in $1152. The second with five volumes sold 261 sets and earned me nearly $500. The third, including all six volumes, sold only 25 copies, and earned me but $156.25. "Selected Prejudices," brought out in 1927, was made up of chapters from the first five volumes. It sold 2246 copies and brought me $872.04. It was not Knopf's idea, but Cape's. Cape, who was an enterprising and resourceful publisher and very friendly to me, had found it impossible to work up a satisfactory sale for the successive volumes of "Prejudices" in England, despite the extensive newspaper notice they got there, so he suggested that it might be worth while to try a volume of selections, made up of the stuff most likely to interest Englishmen. I fell in with the plan willingly, selected things that seemed to meet that specification, and undertook to translate them from American into English. The result was "Selected Prejudices," a little volume of 256 pages, published by Cape in his charming Traveller's Library in 1926. It was an immediate success, and a year later it was followed by a second volume. These two books of selections remained in print for years; indeed, I receive occasional small royalties on them from Cape to this day (1945). In 1929 Régis Michaud made a French trans-

---

*His little pamphlet consisted of twelve pages, 2 ⅞ by 4 ⅛ inches, and was bound in gray paper.

lation on the same plan, and it was published by Furne, Boivin & Cie in Paris. It came out in two forms, one of them an edition of 25 copies on vellum.

"Prejudices: Second Series" followed the plan of the first series closely. It opened with a 93–page blast entitled "The National Letters," mainly made up of reworkings of my *Smart Set* reviews and my contributions to "Répétition Générale," but it also included some surplus material left out of the 1922 revision of "In Defense of Women," under way in 1921, and some revisions of newspaper articles, for example, "The Sahara of the Bozart," from the New York *Evening Mail* of November 13, 1917 and "The Divine Afflatus" from the same paper of November 16. "Exeunt Omnes" came from the *Smart Set* for December, 1919, and "Roosevelt: an Autopsy" was mainly lifted from my book article in the issue for March, 1920.* "The National Letters" was based upon an article called "The National Literature" which I contributed to the *Yale Review* for June, 1920, but there was material in it from "Observations Upon the National Letters" in the *Smart Set* for July of the

---

*I wrote to Fielding H. Garrison on Nov. 4: "The formula of the 'Prejudices' books is simple: a fundamental structure of serious argument, with enough personal abuse to engage the general, and one or two Rabelaisian touches. The Roosevelt chapter will get more attention than any other. The Roosevelt family, having tasted the preliminary blast in the *Smart Set*, is furious. In particular, the doctrine that Theodore was not an aristocrat is offensive to his heirs and assigns". Theodore, Jr., denounced me violently in his book of reminiscences, All in the Family, published in 1929, but cooled off afterward, and on Sept. 7, 1934 he wrote me a cordial letter about an article I had written for *Liberty* discussing crime and punishment. We presently became friends, and he visited me more than once in Baltimore. I had met his sister Alice in 1928. See my Thirty-five Years of Newspaper Work, 1906–41, p. 521. Both Alice and young Teddy were bitterly opposed to Franklin D. Roosevelt's efforts to horn into World War II, and so delighted in my articles on the subject in the Baltimore *Sun* down to Jan., 1941. One day Teddy said to me: "Franklin will make the war, but it is our branch of the family that will fight in it". As a reserve officer he was called up for service before Pearl Harbor, and was soon promoted to brigadier-general. He died of pneumonia in France. He was a considerable boozer, and when tight loved to recite poetry. His memory was amazing, and he specialized in dramatic recitations of the longer Kipling poems. He bought stock in the publishing firm of Doubleday, Doran & Co. in 1935 and was active in its management. My last letter from him was dated Aug. 28, 1941. He was then in camp at Fort Devens, Mass., in command of the 26th Infantry. He often invited me to visit him at Oyster Bay, but I never did so.

same year, "Notes and Queries" in the issue for September, and various other book articles. From this time forward I kept the "Prejudices" books in mind in all my magazine and newspaper work, and not infrequently an idea that was first tried out in the Baltimore *Evening Sun* was later expanded and embellished in the *Smart Set* or some other magazine, and then finally polished for book form. This preparedness made the putting together of the successive "Prejudices" relatively easy. I did, of course, a good deal of rewriting but I also did a lot of mere pasting in, and my scissors and pot were worked almost as hard as my typewriter.* From the first volume onward I provided each of the "Prejudices" books with an adequate index. Making it was tedious work, but I believed that that work was well expended.

The reviews of "Prejudices: Second Series" paid relatively little attention to the contents of the book, but were devoted mainly to discussions of the author. I had suddenly become, by the end of 1920, a sort of symbol of all the disillusionment following World War I, and was credited with a leadership in dissent that I did not want, and tried constantly to avoid. The messianic passion was simply not in me, then or afterward; indeed, it is probable that no articulate American ever lived who had less taste for the shroud of the evangelist. It was thus somewhat disconcerting for me to discover that I was becoming the text of all sorts of manifestos and homilies by propagandists of a score of warring sects, and the frequent theme of editorials by the dull idiots who write such things, and a favorite subject of debate in the colleges and women's clubs.†

---

*Nevertheless, constant interruptions sometimes greatly incommoded the business. On April 3, 1920 I wrote to a correspondent in New York: "The second volume of Prejudices is giving me hell, and I am in a fearful humor. The bloody thing has to be delivered June 1, and I haven't two chapters written. Worse, editorial nuisances are driving me crazy. My next address will be Matteawan". On May 13 I wrote to Fielding H. Garrison: "Still at work on Prejudices II and still cursing the Lord God Jehovah".

†So far as I can make out by a somewhat sketchy examination of my early clipping-books, the first women's club to wrestle with me was that of Helena, Mont., on May 19, 1919. The programme of the meeting, published in the year-book of the club for 1918–19 (Clippings—H. L. Mencken—Vol. III, p. 329), shows that two members were appointed to expound me to the others. The first was a Mrs. Le Lano, whose theme was "His View-point in Criticism,"

The pedagogues of the land of course, were against me almost to a man, and tried their best to stem the rising tide of interest in me among the youth they afflicted. I responded by picking out one of them anon and anon, and subjected him to a third degree worse than any ever staged by a police lieutenant. For example, a poor ass named T. E. Rankin, Kansas born and educated at Princeton, who professed rhetoric at the University of Michigan. When he printed the first edition of a work called "American Authorship of the Present Day" in 1918 I missed it, but when a second edition followed in 1920 I fell upon it with all arms in the *Smart Set* for May, 1921.* The book was an almost incredible exhibition of academic imbecility, for in it the author whooped up Ernest Poole, F. Marion Crawford, Cale Young Rice and other such quacks, cried down Huneker, Dreiser and Carl Sandburg and passed over altogether Cabell, Miss Cather, Sherwood Anderson, Eugene O'Neill and George Ade. I gave a long summary of his curiously idiotic judgments, and then went on:

What interests me is the effect upon the poor yokels who strive heroically for a "liberal" education at such universities as Michigan, and are then belabored and stupified with such balderdash. Can you imagine the thirst for enlightenment that must be in some of those candidates for the arts degree, and the vast sacrifices that must stand behind their candidacy—remote farmers sweating like slaves for year after year that their sons and daughters may be "educated," farmwives wearing out their lives in miserable drudgery and loneliness, pennies saved one by one, thousands of little deprivations, hopes

---

and the other was a Miss Mosher, who undertook a review of "A Book of Prefaces". The ensuing discussion was led by a Mrs. Plum. My name was spelled Menken on the programme, and there was a quotation from Mrs. Wiggs of the Cabbage Patch, to the effect that "the way to get cheerful is to smile when you feel bad, to think about somebody else's headache when your own is most bustin', to keep on believin' the sun is shinin' when the clouds are thick enough to cut". The spy who sent me the programme reported that La Mosher was "big of bust and short of waist and brains," and that she bucked at the last minute and her job fell to another member, unnamed.

*Born in 1872, Rankin at first dallied with divinity, but in 1901 took to the rattan. Michigan fired him in 1929 and he went to Carleton College, a one-horse seminary maintained by the Congregationalists at Northfield, Minn. There it still survives. He has a Phi Beta Kappa key and is a member of the Authors' Club of London, a famous boob-trap for American suckers.

cherished through whole generations? And then the result—a bath of bosh. If a professor writes a text-book, I assume that it is for his students: who else would want to read it? Well, imagine a young man or woman outfitted with such a notion of literature of the country as one finds in the tome of Prof. Rankin! Think of raising chickens and milking cows for twenty years to pay for such an education! I am surely not one to laugh at the spectacle. To me it seems to be tragic.

The aim here, of course, was to brush off the yokel students as well as the yokel professor, but unhappily it failed. The campus newspaper, the *Michigan Daily*, printed a dutiful denunciation of my review on April 24, 1921, but it was so feeble that it opened the way for a vigorous riposte by a student signing himself Menckenite, three days later.* Indeed, after reading the two I began to suspect that the former may have been only a plant for the latter.† Thus I found myself a champion of the students against their professors, and this unwilling rôle afflicted me for fifteen years afterward. I became, on the one hand, a constant point of reference in the campus revolts that then went on throughout the American colleges, and on the other hand I was besought with great frequency to come to this or that campus and harangue the rebels on the issues of the hour. Having, as I have said, no taste for saving humanity, and being, moreover, averse to making speeches, I refused all these invitations. In all my life, in fact, I talked to college boys but once, and that violation of my rules was forced on me in 1926, when the Harvard students staged a demonstration in my support when I tackled the Boston wowsers on Boston Common.‡ But the invitations came on pouring in, and sometimes they were underwritten by the sassier faction of young tutors. Unhappily, I preserved none of these invitations, for I have always made a practise to destroy mail of no permanent interest. But there have been times since when I have doubted that such letters were as little interesting as I thought they

*He was, I heard afterward, one Bob Sage.

†The controversy raged for a month, in the *Michigan Chimes* as well as in the *Daily*. The former, in its May issue, took my side flatfootedly, and heaped scorn upon the *Daily*.

‡This was at the time of the attempt to suppress the *American Mercury* because of its publication of Hatrack. The episode will be described in its proper chronological place.

were when they came in. If I had them today they would throw an illuminating light upon the play of opinion on American campuses in the 1920's.

Of the things that went into "Prejudices: Second Series," as opposed to my current *Smart Set* stuff, the one that made the greatest uproar was my revision and expansion of "The Sahara of the Bozart". When it appeared originally in the New York *Evening Mail*, which had only a small circulation outside New York City, it seems to have been missed by the sub-Potomac editorial writers, but now they all became suddenly and painfully aware of it, and many of them had at me with great ferocity. The Nashville *Tennessean* led off on November 28, 1920, with the now familiar hints that I was the American front for Nietzsche and the other German enemies of the true, the good and the beautiful, and the usual loud boast that the Southern whites were the purest Anglo-Saxons in the Western world, and hence models of patriotism, piety and intelligence. My criticism of the post-Confederate *Kultur*, it argued hotly, was marked by ignorance and wickedness, and all I knew of the subject had been "gained by making a ten-day Cook's tour of the Potomac river". From Tennessee the conflagration spread to other States, and soon it was roaring fiercest in Arkansas. Here the principal defenders of the outraged South were the *Daily News* and *Arkansas Democrat* of Little Rock, but they got gallant support from the Little Rock *Trade Record*, the organ of the State Babbitts, and the *Arkansas Writer*, a strange monthly operated by one Clio Harper, a member of the *Smart Set* Rejection-Slip Association. The stuff these heroes printed was so amusing that I decided to throw some gasoline upon their flames, and in the *Smart Set* for August, 1921, I printed "The South Begins to Mutter". In this article, under cover of praising three Southern magazines that showed some impatience with the circumambient imbecility—*All's Well*, published by Charles J. Finger at Fayetteville, Ark.; the *Double-Dealer*, published at New Orleans by a small group of young intellectuals, nearly all of them Jews; and the *Reviewer*, set up at Richmond, Va., in February, 1921, by a rebellious young woman named Emily Clark, with the imprimatur of James Branch Cabell*—,

*The first issue appeared on Feb. 15, 1921. In it Miss Clark's a chief associate,

I piled insult on insult. Save for a few walled towns, I declared, the South was so far steeped in savagry that civilized men not only refused to live in it, but even avoided visiting it. "I know New Yorkers," I said, "who have been in Cochin China, Kafristan, Paraguay, Somaliland and West Virginia, but not one who has ever penetrated the miasmatic jungles of Arkansas".

This device worked very effectively, and the second wave of denunciation was ten times as violent as the first. Harper had at me with especial violence in the *Arkansas Writer*, describing me as "an imported scion of German *Schrecklichkeit*," a "self-appointed emissary of the Wilhelmstrasse," and "an insufferable excrescence on the body of American literature". "Even Sing Sing and Matteawan," he went on, "would be contaminated by such as he," and he concluded by calling upon "every prominent newspaper and civic organization throughout the South . . . to see if there is not some recourse in law to banish him as a pestilent nuisance from the country he has so contumaciously insulted, and whose soil his presence contaminates". This call was answered by the Hon. Virgil C. Pettie, president of the Arkansas Advancement Association, who petitioned "the Arkansas members of Congress to call all other Southern Congressmen into conference to see what action can be taken against H. L. Mencken," and went about the State recruiting support from the Rotarians, Kiwanians, Lions and other such idealists, and also from chambers of commerce and women's clubs. Unhappily, this campaign came to nothing, for some of the statesmen consulted must have discovered that I was a native American and the son of native Americans, and let fall a warning that the main postulate of the Harper-Pettie holy war was libellous, legally speaking. On August 26, 1921, after printing all of the current denunciations of *Herr* Mencken at length, the *Arkansas Democrat* prudently sought cover in a news article headed

---

Hunter T. Stagg, had a cautious but generally favorable review of Prejudices: Second Series. He quoted from The Sahara of the Bozart, and after protesting that some of it was "unjust, some merely unsound," admitted that "the main outline of the argument, the outstanding deductions, are so true that it were petty to cavil at the weaknesses". It was The Sahara of the Bozart, in fact, that inspired the setting up of the *Reviewer*. There is more about it and Miss Clark later on.

MENCKEN IS NATIVE
OF BALTIMORE, MD.
Editor of *Smart Set*, Who
Attacked South, Not
a Native of Germany

The *Democrat* put all the blame on the Arkansas Advance Association, and made a somewhat painful effort, probably inspired by its lawyer, to clear its skirts.* Thus I lost the pleasant experience of being investigated by a committee of Southern congressmen, and though the uproar continued for months longer it soon lost its steam, for the German spy note had to be avoided. Meanwhile, a number of the more intelligent Southern newspapers—for example, the New Orleans *Picayune*, the Miami *Herald*, and the Greensboro (N. C.) *Record*— took to discussing my allegations with some rationality and tolerance, and even with mild approval. This heretical party gradually gained recruits, and in the course of time the theory began to be heard that "The Sahara of the Bozart" had really done the South a valuable service, and was responsible for the resuscitation of its literature. I have since read many an article, written by a Southerner and printed in the South, which credited me formally with having set off such Southern authors of the new generation as Erskine Caldwell, William Faulkner, Frances Newman,† and even Thomas Wolfe. Thus I became once more a prophet in spite of myself.

*I kept banging away at Arkansas until 1931, when I had a bout in the grand manner with one of its former Governors, Charles H. Brough. But this went on in the Baltimore *Evening Sun*. See my Thirty-five Years of Newspaper Work, 1906–41, p. 638. I received more one threat that if I ever showed myself in Arkansas I'd be lynched, but this did not incommode me, for I was barred by similar threats from other areas, including the lower Eastern Shore of my native Maryland. As a matter of fact, I visited the Ozark region of Arkansas in the Summer of 1928, on my way by automobile from the Republican National Convention in Kansas City to the Democratic Convention in Houston, and no one offered me any affront.

†Frances Newman was a member of one of the first families of Atlanta, and joined the staff of the Carnegie Library there in 1912. She wrote a weekly column of literary news for one of the Atlanta papers, and reviewed Prejudices: Second Series in it. Her review was very cautious. Soon afterward she came to New York and I met her. She was an extraordinarily homely woman, but very

In the North the reviews of "Prejudices: Second Series" were evenly divided between praise and denunciation, and most of them were discussions of me rather than of the book. A good many of the reviewers tried to account for and dispose of me by labelling me, and I was likened variously to George Bernard Shaw, Nietzsche, Brann the iconoclast and Elbert Hubbard! A few papers—for example, the Chicago *Tribune*—came out for me without qualification, but the majority were more cautious, and not a few expressed the opinion, plainly born of a hope, that Stuart P. Sherman had finished me, once and for all time. The debate over my ideas throughout the country had curious repercussions in Baltimore, where the notion that a local newspaper man could become a national figure caused astonishment, and even a kind of resentment. In the Baltimore *Evening Sun* for November 27, 1920, Samuel C. Chew* thus described the situation:

---

amusing. In 1924 she published her first book, The Short Story's Mutations. It showed an immense range of reading, but was chaotic and overwritten. Two years later she came to me with a novel, and I found a good deal of merit in it. Unhappily, she proposed to call it, absurdly, The Hard-Boiled Virgin, and her publisher, Horace Liveright, supported her. I argued against so gratuitously sensational a title, but she persisted, and her book was denounced by many reviewers who never read it. Her highly respectable family was grossly outraged. In May, 1924 she contributed a short story to the *American Mercury*, Rachel and Her Children, which was adjudged the best story of the year by the judges in the annual O. Henry contest. Frances's extreme lack of pulchritude was a sore affliction to her, for her sisters were all beautiful women. She became more and more depressed, and on Oct. 22, 1928 she committed suicide at the Algonquin Hotel by swallowing veronal. She had some talent, but was unbridled and without judgment. If she had lived ten years longer, and settled down a bit, she might have come to something.

*Chew was a Baltimorean himself, and the son of a once famous medical consultant of the same given names, called at the time of my father's last illness in 1899. After taking his Ph.D. at the Johns Hopkins young Chew became a schoolmaster, and in 1914 joined the faculty of Bryn Mawr College, where he is now professor of English (1945). He has published the usual definitive editions of a diligent pedagogue, but his original writings are of small importance. He was in the 1920 era, a friend of Harry C. Black, and was recruited by Black to write for the *Sunpapers*. In 1918 he fell in love from his academic pulpit with one of the students, Lucy Evans, and presently married her. She was a very pretty girl. I have not seen or heard from him for years.

There must be enlightened souls here who realize the worth and significance of Mr. Mencken. . . . but most prominent Baltimoreans. . . . imagine that they have disposed of this extraordinary person when they have said: "Oh, it's only Mencken," or, "It's just Mencken," or, more laconically, "Mencken". They are totally unconscious of the fact that saving always his Eminence,* the author of "Prejudices" is the most truly prominent citizen the town possesses. When he dies it will take ten years to raise funds for a tombstone, and even then the memorial will be cheap and hideous, like Poe's. He must content himself meanwhile with the applause of the *Athenaeum*, the *New Statesman* and the *Mercure de France*. New York doesn't say "It's just Mencken" when he drops into town. There he is "the Baltimore critic," "the Baltimore philosopher," "the Sage of Baltimore".

On July 13, 1921 the Cincinnati *Times-Star* printed a dispatch from its London correspondent headed "Mencken's Fame Growing Apace" and saying:

The remarkable growth in England and continental Europe of the fame of Henry L. Mencken, the Baltimore author, is one of the curious literary phenomena of the time. A series of articles in the London *Times* on current American literature is largely devoted to his work, and nearly all his estimates of contemporary American authors are accepted. J. C. Squire and other English critics have been writing about him meanwhile in other English journals. He has been the subject of several extensive articles in German reviews, and many of his essays have been translated and published. In France, too, his work is being translated, particularly his political writings. In Australia he is constantly discussed, and even in South America he has a number of eager disciples.

The reception given to the first two series of "Prejudices," when Cape brought them out in England, was generally favorable, but there were some sharp dissents and many of the reviewers attempted straddles in the manner of their American colleagues. But the reviews were at least numerous, and many of them were long, so that they covered altogether, counting only those that reached me, more than twelve feet of column space. Several papers printed more than one notice. The London *Times*, having given the American edition of "Prejudices: First Series," a very cordial welcome, now began to develop

---

i.e., James, Cardinal Gibbons (1834–1921), archbishop of Baltimore from 1877 until his death.

doubts, and its two reviews, on June 16 and July 14, showed an increasing coldness, but it gave space in May and June to five long articles by C. E. Bechhofer (just mentioned in the Cincinnati *Times-Star* dispatch) in which I was treated politely indeed.* Contrariwise, the Manchester *Guardian* became more friendly, and its two reviews, on July 24 and December 21, showed more amiability than it was ever to exhibit in noticing my books thereafter. Thomas Moult went to the bat for me in two reviews, one in *John o' London's Weekly* and the other in the Christmas *Bookman*, and John C. Squire had his say, which was far from enthusiastic, in the *Observer*.† The London *Morning Post*, the *Saturday Review*, the *Publishers' Circular*, the *Tatler*, the *Daily Graphic* and even the Edinburgh *Scotsman* were friendly, but the Liverpool *Post*, the *New Statesman*, the London *Telegraph* (Arthur Waugh), *Eve*, the *Daily Herald* (Alan Porter), the *Illustrated London News*, the *Athenaeum* (by now absorbed by the *Nation*), the *Westminster Gazette*, the *Daily News* (R. Ellis Roberts), *Country Life*, the Glasgow *Herald*, the *Daily Express* (S. P. Mais) and the *Spectator* were cool,‡ and the *Pall Mall Gazette*, the Liverpool *Daily Post* and the *Sunday Times* (H. C. Minchin) were hostile.

*These articles were printed on May 26, and June 9, 16, 23 and 30. Bechhofer reprinted them in 1923, considerably expanded, as The Literary Renaissance in America. He was a London Jew who had spent some time in youth in the United States. I met him in London in 1922, and we had a couple of boozy evenings together. He hung about the fringes of English letters for many years, but never got very far. He also held various minor political jobs and tried his hand as a newspaper correspondent in Russia. In 1936 he brought out an extraordinarily vituperative biography of Stanley Baldwin. Some time after World War I he attached his mother's surname to his own, and became C. E. Bechhofer-Roberts. Later on he dropped the hyphen and became Carl Eric Bechhofer Roberts.

†My only encounter with Squire was in London in 1922. He was then editor of the London *Mercury*. His position in the London literary world was curious. There was little in his numerous books in prose and verse that was of any moment, but he was, by a sort of general consent, the spokesman for literature on public occasions, much as Howells had been in the United States, and in that capacity was a frequent speaker at public dinners. In 1933 he was knighted for this heroic service. Squire was a heavy boozer, and in the later 1930's began to fade out.

‡But the *Spectator*, on June 18, 1931, listed Prejudices: First Series among seven contemporary Books Worth Reading, along with volumes by Benedetto Croce, Bertrand Russell and Sir T. Clifford Allbutt.

Meanwhile, articles on the two "Prejudices" appeared in various languages other than English—for example, in *Das literarische Echo* of Berlin, *El Porvenit* (the future) of Cartagena, Colombia, the *Frankfurter Zeitung*, *Die Neue Zeit* (Berlin), and *El Universal* (Caracas, Venezuela)*—and news came from Paris, where Charles Cestre had just been appointed professor of American literature and civilization at the Sorbonne, that he was putting my books in a collection being gathered to instruct his students. At home extensive articles on me were published by Frank Harris in *Pearson's Magazine* for May, 1921,[†] S. K. Ratcliffe (an Englishman) in the *New Republic* for April 13, F. Scott Fitzgerald in the *Bookman*, William McFee in the same for December, 1921, Edmund Wilson, Jr., in the *New Republic* for June 1, and Ernest A. Boyd in the *Freeman* for February 2. Cape, in London, brought out a pamphlet entitled "The New American Literary Movement," in which he whooped up Edgar Lee Masters, Dorothy Canfield, Sherwood Anderson, Henry G. Aikman[‡] and myself, all recent recruits to his list, and Knopf, in New York, issued on March 22, 1921 a press sheet quoting encomiums on my work from papers in four foreign countries. On December 4, 1920 the Baltimore *Evening Sun* reported that "Prejudices: Second Series" was a best-seller in Baltimore, and on July 30, 1921 the London correspondent of the *Publishers' Weekly* reported that it was a best-seller there, along with Shaw's "Back to Methuselah". In

---

*All this notice naturally led to the publication of translations from my books and articles. So far as my records show, the first was of a group of epigrams, done by Herman George Scheffauer (1878–1927), and published in *Jugend*, Nov. 28, 1920 under the title of Amerikanisches. My first appearance in Spanish seems to have been in *La Revista Mexicana* in 1921. I got into French the same year, into Italian the year following, into Russian in 1928, and into Swedish in 1930. There will be more about Scheffauer hereafter.

†Reprinted in his Contemporary Portraits: Fourth Series, 1923.

‡Aikman was one of the many promising authors of the period who quickly blew up. His first novel, The Groper, was published by Liveright in 1919 and I reviewed it favorably in the *Smart Set* for October of that year. In 1920 he wrote a second called Zell and brought the MS. to me. I liked it so well that I induced Knopf to take him over. The book got very good notices, including mine in the *Smart Set* for March, 1921, and Cape liked it so much that he added Aikman to his list. But it was the last thing of any significance to come from its author. He kept on writing for some years, but never did anything else worth reading.

1920 I saw books of mine listed, for the first time, in an antiquarian bookseller's catalogue. The bookseller was Meredith Janvier of Baltimore,* and he asked $6 for "Pistols For Two" and $20 for an autographed first edition of "The American Language," then only a year old. I was so delighted that I gave him the typescripts of two chapters, "Roosevelt: an Autopsy" and "The Sahara of the Bozart," in "Prejudices: Second Series". Soon afterward he was offering the first for $25 and the second for $15.† In September, 1921, the booksellers' trade-journal, *Biblio*, reported that, during the three months ending August 30, my books ranked eighth among the American first editions advertised for. In October they went up to third place, and that place they also held in November. On June 11, 1921 the New York *Evening Mail* listed Nathan and me among persons who need "no press-agents," along with Margot Asquith, Lloyd-George, William J. Bryan, Andrew Volstead and Babe Ruth.

*A strange fellow who started out as a lawyer, became famous as a strong man, took to professional photography, and ended as a dealer in old books and prints. See my Thirty-five Years of Newspaper Work, 1906–41, p. 821; also p. 777 of the present record.

†At the sale of the Charles Romm collection in New York, early in 1921, four of my books and a copy of Pistols For Two sold for $25. At the same sale forty-eight books by Brander Matthews also fetched $25. In both cases all of the items were autographed. See Book Prices Current (editorial), Chicago *Post*, May 27, 1921.

CHRONOLOGY

NOTE ON THE TEXTS

NOTES

INDEX

Chronology

1880   Born Henry Louis Mencken on September 12, at what was then 380 West Lexington Street, Baltimore, Maryland, now 811 West Lexington Street; eldest child of August Mencken and Anna Abhau Mencken. (Grandfather Burkhardt Ludwig Mencken, born 1828 in Laas, Germany, landed in Baltimore, November 1848; was naturalized October 1852, and set up a tobacco business. Father, born June 16, 1854, established August Mencken & Bro. between 1873–75, managing it with his brother Henry, and building it into one of the most successful cigar manufacturers along the South Atlantic coast. An agnostic and a high-tariff Republican, August was a loyal member of the Masonic order, also part owner of the National Baseball Club of Washington, D.C. Mother, Anna Abhau, born June 11, 1858, was the daughter of Carl Heinrich Abhau from Hesse, Germany. August and Anna were married on November 11, 1879.)

1882   Brother, Charles Edward, born May 16.

1883   Family moves to 1524 Hollins Street, in a prosperous German-American neighborhood in West Baltimore, facing Union Square.

1886   Mencken enrolls at F. Knapp's Institute, a private school, in September. Sister Anna Gertrude born November 17.

1888   Begins piano lessons. Receives a self-inking printing press for Christmas.

1889   Brother, August, born February 18. Reads Mark Twain's *Huckleberry Finn*, which makes a huge impact on him. Family begins spending summers in Ellicott City, Howard County, west of Baltimore (1889–1892), and Mt. Washington (1892–1899), then a northwestern suburb.

1892   Mencken enters Baltimore Polytechnic Institute, a public high school, on September 5.

1893   Mencken keenly interested in chemistry, photography, journalism and literature. Visits the Enoch Pratt Free Library, reads four or five books a week, mostly English literature (including Dickens, Chaucer, Shakespeare, Herrick,

Pepys, Addison, Steele, Pope, Swift, Johnson, Boswell, Fielding, Smollett, Sterne, Arnold, Macaulay, George Eliot, Tennyson, Swinburne, Thackeray, Kipling). Mencken will later call the library "my school"; his brother August will recall that Mencken "read like an athlete." Fire engulfs August Mencken & Bro. Cigar factory, causing $25,000 worth of damage, December 2.

1895   Reads Stephen Crane's *The Red Badge of Courage.*

1896   Graduates at age 15 from the Baltimore Polytechnic Insti-
        tute, with highest grade point average yet recorded, June
        23. Publishes a poem ("Ode to the Pennant on the Cen-
        terfield Pole") anonymously in the Baltimore *American*,
        summer. Tells his father that he plans to become a news-
        paper reporter, but is strongly dissuaded. Starts full-time
        work as clerk and salesman at August Mencken & Bro.

1898   Subscribes to *The Criterion* (New York) and is influenced
        by the work of James Gibbons Huneker, Percival Pollard,
        Ambrose Bierce, Oscar Wilde, George Bernard Shaw, and
        Friedrich Nietzsche. Becomes an admirer of the prose
        style and ideas of Thomas Henry Huxley. Studies books
        on journalism; enrolls in a correspondence school, the As-
        sociated Newspaper Bureau School of Journalism in New
        York, and states his career goal is "to begin as a reporter
        & after that trust to hard work and luck for something
        better." Resolves to quit working at August Mencken
        & Bro.; his father asks him to postpone the decision for
        at least another year. In a moment of despair, Mencken
        contemplates suicide. August Mencken, Sr., collapses un-
        conscious with acute kidney infection, December 31.
        (Mencken writes later: "I remember well how . . . I
        kept saying to myself that if my father died I'd be free at
        last . . . I had got along with him very well, but I de-
        tested business and was frantic to get into newspaper
        work.")

1899   Father dies on January 13 and is buried at Loudon Park
        Cemetery. Two weeks later Mencken visits the offices of
        the Baltimore *Herald* and asks for a job. First story pub-
        lished February 24. Hired at $7 a week, the youngest
        (and first) cub reporter on the *Herald* to get paid a salary,
        July 2. A poem addressed to Rudyard Kipling appears in
        December 1899 issue of *Bookman* magazine. Quits work-
        ing part-time for his Uncle Henry at August Mencken &
        Bro. to devote himself to journalism, which he later calls

"the maddest, gladdest, damnedest existence ever enjoyed by mortal youth."

1900   Reads Edward Kingsbury's editorials in the New York *Sun*, George Ade's *Fables in Slang*, the work of Émile Zola. Discovers Theodore Dreiser's *Sister Carrie*. Works twelve hours a day, seven days a week reporting for the *Herald*, writing short stories, poetry, and articles for out-of-town newspapers. Suffers from chronic bronchitis. Travels to Jamaica to recover, June. Gets third raise in salary, to $14 a week, August. Assigned to cover presidential election between William Jennings Bryan and William McKinley, November.

1901   Salary increased to $18 a week, February 1. Covers fire that devastated Jacksonville, Florida, in May. Becomes drama critic of the *Herald*, September, and editor of *Sunday Herald*, October (holds both positions until October 1903). Becomes an advocate of the work of playwrights Shaw and Ibsen.

1903   Becomes city editor of the *Morning Herald* in October 1903. Publication of *Ventures Into Verse*, a book of poetry modeled on Kipling. Begins subscribing to a service that provides clippings mentioning him or his books. (The clippings will fill more than 100 volumes during his lifetime.)

1904   Fire destroys more than 140 acres and 1,500 buildings in downtown Baltimore, February 7–8. The *Herald* is printed in Washington and Philadelphia and does not miss a single issue. Mencken attends the Republican National Convention in Chicago, June 19–24, and the Democratic National Convention in St. Louis, July 5–11. Made city editor of the Baltimore *Evening Herald*, August 25. Saturday Night Club established, a group of musicians who meet regularly, with Mencken at the piano.

1905   Promoted to managing editor of the *Herald*. Publication of *George Bernard Shaw: His Plays*, first book-length study of Shaw.

1906   The *Herald* ceases publication, June 17. Becomes editor of the Baltimore *Sunday Sun*, July 25. Makes sweeping changes in typography and content, introduces poetry, music criticism by John Philip Sousa; runs a twenty-four part report on the city's health concerns and serializes work by popular authors (such as George Ade's revised history of slang). Circulation climbs steadily.

1908   Publication of *The Philosophy of Friedrich Nietzsche*, first book in English on the philosopher. Meets Theodore Dreiser. First trip to Europe, March; he visits England and Germany. Meets George Jean Nathan, theater critic, in New York in May. Assumes additional duties as editorial writer for the *Sun* papers. Begins monthly book reviews for *The Smart Set*, November (to be continued until December 1923), and praises the work of James Branch Cabell, Twain, Joseph Conrad, and Dreiser among others.

1909   Works (in collaboration with Holger A. Koppel, Danish consul in Baltimore) on notes and introductions to a new edition of Ibsen's *A Doll's House* and *Little Eyolf*, to be published as part of *The Player's Ibsen*. The volumes are a commercial failure, and the series is discontinued.

1910   Baltimore *Evening Sun* established, April 18, with Mencken as an editor. Ghostwrites *What You Ought to Know About Your Baby* with Leonard Hirshberg. Publication of *The Gist of Nietzsche* and of *Men Versus the Man* (written with Robert Rives La Monte).

1911   Becomes close friends with Percival Pollard, American writer who widens Mencken's understanding of German culture. Begins "The Free Lance," a satirical daily column in the Baltimore *Evening Sun*, May 8, addressing issues of local public health, the plight of the city's African Americans, the women's movement, the American language, the pretensions of moralists, as well as several humorous pieces including the kernel of what would become his fictitious history of the bathtub. "Before it had gone on a year," he later notes, "I knew precisely where I was heading."

1912   Travels to Europe in April, visiting England, France, Switzerland, and Germany. Covers the Democratic National Convention in Baltimore, June 28. Publication of *The Artist: A Drama Without Words.*

1913   Meets publisher Alfred A. Knopf. Covers suffragist parade in Washington, D.C., March 3.

1914   Meets and becomes close friends with James Gibbons Huneker, influential American critic. Sails to Europe with George Jean Nathan and Willard Huntington Wright, April. Publication of *Europe After 8:15* with Nathan and Wright. First World War begins, July 28–August 4. Mencken and Nathan become co-editors of *The Smart*

Set, September. Publishes material from writers including F. Scott Fitzgerald, Edgar Lee Masters, Sherwood Anderson, Willa Cather, Ben Hecht, Eugene O'Neill, and Ezra Pound, as well as British and European writers such as Alexei Tolstoy, Anatole France, D. H. Lawrence, and James Joyce. The book reviews by Mencken, as well as the theater criticism by Nathan, attract wide attention.

1915   German sinking of the British liner *Lusitania* on May 7 increases anti-German sentiment in the United States. First issue of *Parisienne* magazine, edited anonymously with Nathan, is launched (last issue under their editorship will be October 1916). Mencken's pro-German stance become dominant in his increasingly controversial "Free Lance" column, as he scrutinizes the role of the press and examines stories of deliberate propaganda. "The Free Lance" ends abruptly, without explanation, on October 23.

1916   Dreiser's novel *The "Genius"* is suppressed when passages are deemed obscene by the New York Society for the Prevention of Vice. Mencken solicits the support of the Author's League of America for a petition in defense of the book (the novel remains out of circulation until 1922). Launches *Saucy Stories*, which (from August to October) he edits anonymously with Nathan. Publication of *A Book of Burlesques* and *A Little Book in C Major*. Resigns editorship at the *Sun*. Sails to England, December 28; travels to Germany to report on World War I.

1917   Germany commences unrestricted submarine warfare against neutral shipping on February 1. Mencken departs Germany to cover the Liberal revolt in Cuba against the U.S.-supported government of President García Menocal. Arrives in Havana, March 5, and returns to the U.S. on March 14. Stops writing for the *Sun* with publication of last dispatch, March 29. The United States declares war on Germany, April 6. Espionage Act goes into effect June 15. Writes for the New York *Evening Mail* from June 18 to July 8, 1918. Mencken meets James Weldon Johnson, begins to focus attention on African-American and cultural issues. "The Sahara of the Bozart," an indictment of Southern culture, published in the New York *Evening Mail*, November 13. "A Neglected Anniversary," Mencken's comic history of the bathtub, published in the New York *Evening Mail*, December 28. Publication of *A Book of Prefaces*, and of *Pistols for Two*, written with Nathan under the joint pseudonym "Owen Hatteras."

1918   The editor of the New York *Evening Mail*, Edward Rum-
            ley, is arrested July 8 over allegations that the paper re-
            ceived secret German government funding; control then
            passes to pro-war individuals and Mencken stops writing
            for it. (Mencken later reflects, "I stopped writing and
            believed I was done with newspaper work forever.") Ger-
            man language eliminated from Baltimore City Schools,
            July; anti-German feeling rampant. The Bureau of Inves-
            tigation (later the FBI) opens a case file on Mencken; his
            mail is opened and he is watched by agents. Mencken's
            Damn! A Book of Calumny is published by his close
            friend, Broadway producer Philip Goodman, who also
            publishes *In Defense of Women* (later editions published
            by Knopf beginning in 1919). Germany signs armistice,
            November 11.

1919   Publication of *The American Language* (first edition
            quickly sells out) and *Prejudices: First Series*, which also
            proves successful. With *Sun* publishers Paul Patterson and
            Harry Black, Mencken helps develop plan for expanded
            national coverage and an independent approach. Attorney
            General Mitchell Palmer orders mass arrests of radicals
            and foreigners. Mencken becomes increasingly frustrated
            by his work at *The Smart Set*, telling a friend: "We live,
            not in a literary age, but in a fiercely political age."

1920   Begins series of regular Monday columns in the Baltimore
            Evening Sun (they continue until January 31, 1938), regu-
            larly denouncing interference with free speech and calling
            for civil rights for all Americans. Reads manuscript of
            Main Street by Sinclair Lewis and encourages its publi-
            cation. With Nathan, launches *Black Mask*, a mystery mag-
            azine, April. Publication of *Prejudices: Second Series*.
            Publication of *Heliogabalus* and *The American Credo*,
            both written with Nathan. Publication of *The Anti-Christ*
            by Nietzsche, translated with an introduction by Mencken.

1921   Becomes contributing editor of *The Nation*, May (until
            December 1932). Covers the naval disarmament confer-
            ence in Washington, D.C. November-December. Publica-
            tion of the second edition of *The American Language*.

1922   Travels to England and Germany, August-October. Pub-
            lication of *Prejudices: Third Series*.

1923   On May 8, while lecturing at Baltimore's Goucher Col-
            lege, he meets Sara Powell Haardt (born March 1, 1898, in

Montgomery, Alabama), a fiction writer and member of the English faculty. Mencken solicits manuscripts from American writers for a new magazine focusing exclusively on American cultural and political themes, summer. Mencken and Nathan resign as co-editors of *The Smart Set*, December. Publication of the third edition of *The American Language*.

1924   First issue of *The American Mercury* is published in January with Mencken and Nathan as co-editors. Contributors will include Countee Cullen, James Weldon Johnson, W.E.B. Du Bois, Dorothy Parker, Sherwood Anderson, George Schuyler, as well as bricklayers, hoboes, bishops, senators, lawyers, American Indians, prisoners. Its layout, typeface, buoyant tone, and sections "Americana" (items culled from newspapers and magazines across the country) and "Profiles" (portraits written by well-known writers about well-known subjects) are widely imitated. Covers Republican National Convention in Cleveland, June 9–13, and Democratic National Convention in New York City, June 23–29. Writes columns for the Chicago *Tribune* (until January 29, 1928). Publication of *Prejudices: Fourth Series*.

1925   Tension between Nathan and Mencken increases, with Mencken insisting on more social and political commentary in *The American Mercury* and Nathan favoring an equal emphasis on literature. Nathan withdraws as co-editor of *The American Mercury* in July. Mencken travels to Dayton, Tennessee, in July to cover trial of John Scopes, high school teacher arrested for teaching theory of evolution in contravention of newly passed state law. Mother, Anna Abhau Mencken, dies 6 P.M. December 13 and is buried at Loudon Park Cemetery. Publication of *Americana 1925*. The first two books about Mencken are published (*H. L. Mencken* by Ernest Boyd and *The Man Mencken: A Biographical and Critical Survey* by Isaac Goldberg). Breaks friendship with Dreiser, because of a series of misunderstandings, among them Dreiser's seeming lack of sympathy concerning the death of Mencken's mother and Dreiser's callous treatment of women.

1926   Walter Lippmann calls Mencken "the most powerful personal influence on this whole generation of educated people." Through the influence of the New England Watch and Ward Society, the April issue of *The American Mercury* is banned in Boston because of Herbert

Asbury's short story, "Hatrack"; Mencken courts arrest by personally selling a copy to the Society's secretary; a judge declares the story not obscene and dismisses the complaint. Mencken tours the American South and arrives in California, October. Father's cigar factory, August Mencken & Bro., managed by uncle Henry, goes bankrupt. Publication of *Notes on Democracy, Prejudices: Fifth Series*, and *Americana, 1926*.

1927   Publication of *Prejudices: Sixth Series* and *Selected Prejudices*.

1928   Travels to Havana, Cuba, to cover Pan American Conference, January. Covers Republican National Convention, Kansas City, June 11–16, and Democratic National Convention, Houston, June 23–39. Travels with Al Smith on campaign tour, October 12–30. Publication of *Menckeniana: A Schimpflexicon*, a humorous collection of anti-Mencken invective that had appeared in newspapers and magazines across the country. Circulation of *The American Mercury* reaches its height of 84,000. Begins courting Sara Powell Haardt on a steadier basis.

1929   Sara Powell Haardt undergoes surgery for the removal of a tubercular kidney, July 6.

1930   Covers London Naval Conference, January–February. Announces secret engagement to Sara Powell Haardt to family members, April. Marries Sara Powell Haardt August 27 at St. Stephen the Martyr Church, Baltimore; they travel to Canada on their honeymoon. Moves to new residence, 704 Cathedral Street, Baltimore. Publication of *Treatise on the Gods*. Book sells well, but stirs controversy because of passage in which Mencken describes Jews as "plausibly the most unpleasant race ever heard of." (Passage is deleted in later editions.) In newspaper interview he denies he is an anti-Semite: "I don't like religious Jews. I don't like religious Catholics and Protestants." Begins writing a diary.

1931   Writes a series of controversial columns against lynching of Matthew Williams in Salisbury, Maryland, on December 4, causing a boycott of Baltimore businesses and the *Sun* papers by residents of the Eastern Shore. The *Nation* recognizes Mencken for "distinguished journalism in the face of personal danger," December.

1932   Mencken sails to the West Indies with Sara, January 9. Covers Republican National Convention in Chicago,

June 13–18, and Democratic National Convention in Chicago, June 26–July 2. Franklin D. Roosevelt elected President, November. Publication of *Making a President*. Continues suggesting authors and ideas for books to his publisher, Alfred Knopf; elected board member of Knopf, Inc.

1933   Mencken becomes increasingly critical of the New Deal, directing most of his criticism against the "quacks" of the Brain Trust rather than the President himself. Writes controversial columns against lynching of George Arnwood in Princess Anne on Maryland's Eastern Shore, October 18 (last lynching in Maryland). With Mencken's popularity at a low ebb, circulation of *The American Mercury* sinks to 28,329; Mencken resigns as editor with the December issue.

1934   Travels on a two-month cruise to the Mediterranean with Sara, January–March, and is fascinated by his visit to Jewish colonists in Palestine; his writing on the subject for the *Evening Sun* is privately printed in a book entitled *Eretz Israel*. Writes series of articles on American English for the New York *American*, July 9–May 20, 1935. Joins Board of Directors of the A. S. Abell Company, October 15. Resumes friendship with Theodore Dreiser. Speaks before the Gridiron Club in Washington, D.C., December 8; his address is mildly critical of the New Deal, but when it is Roosevelt's turn to speak, he turns Mencken's commentary on journalists against him by quoting a passage from *Prejudices: Sixth Series*. Publication of *Treatise on the Right and Wrong*. Last article for *The Nation*, December 12.

1935   Testifies in favor of the Costigan-Wagner Anti-Lynching Bill at Senate hearing, February 14. (Bill is later blocked by Senate filibuster.) Wife Sara Haardt Mencken dies of tubercular meningitis, May 31. Edits a compilation of her work, *Southern Album*; travels to England with his brother August, June 15.

1936   Returns to his family home at 1524 Hollins Street, which he calls "as much a part of me as my two hands." Publishes "Three Years of Dr. Roosevelt," a scathing attack on the President whom he compares to "a snake-oil vendor at a village carnival," in *The American Mercury*, March. *The New Yorker* publishes autobiographical essays, April. Covers Republican National Convention, Cleveland, June 8–13, and Democratic National Convention,

Philadelphia, June 22–28, as well as convention in support
of the Townsend Plan (Cleveland, July 14–20) and Union
Party convention organized by Father Charles Coughlin
(Cleveland, August 13–18). Travels with Republican nominee Alf Landon on his campaign tour, August-October.
Publication of the fourth edition of *The American Language*.

1937   Vacations in Daytona Beach, Florida, with his brother August, January. Publication of *The Sunpapers of Baltimore*,
written with Frank R. Kent, Gerald W. Johnson, and
Hamilton Owens. Publication of *The Charlatanry of the
Learned*, edited by Mencken and translated from the
Latin by Francis Litz; the book is a satirical attack on academic pretension, written by Mencken's ancestor, Leipzig
scholar Johann Burkhard Mencke (1674–1732).

1938   Alarmed by what he sees as the Roosevelt administration's
mastery at setting the agenda with the press, Mencken
writes publisher Paul Patterson that "we confront a high
development of government propaganda," and at Patterson's request becomes temporary editor of the Baltimore
Evening Sun, January 24–May 9. Writes "Sunday Articles" for the Baltimore *Sun*, May 16–February 2, 1941.
Appointed Chairman of the *Sunpapers*' committee to ne-
gotiate with the Newspaper Guild, summer. Travels to
Germany, June–July; refrains from reporting on any of
his observations. Writes column, "Help for the Jews,"
proposing the United States open its doors to German
Jewish refugees fleeing Nazi persecution, November 27,
1938.

1939   Convinced that America's security would depend on
America's abstention from European conflict, Mencken
becomes increasingly isolationist. In a speech given before
the American Society of Newspaper Editors, on April 20,
Mencken reminds his audience of government censorship
in 1917 and warns that war will once again pose a threat to
freedom of the press. Suffers a minor stroke, "generalized
arteriosclerosis," July 31. Hitler invades Poland, September 1. England declares war on Germany, September 3.

1940   Covers Republican National Convention in Philadelphia,
June 22–29 and Democratic National Convention in
Chicago, July 13–19. Travels with Wendell Wilkie on his
campaign tour, August 16–November 3. Publication of
Happy Days: 1880–1892, first of a series of memoirs. Death

of best friend, Raymond Pearl, biometrician at the Johns Hopkins University School of Medicine.

1941   Resigns from the *Sun* papers, January 16, because of publishers' unease with his anti-Roosevelt and anti-war views. Begins writing memoir on his journalism career, "Thirty-Five Years of Newspaper Work" (published in 1994). Publication of *Newspaper Days: 1899–1906*. Travels to Havana, April. Helps several Jewish refugees find asylum in the United States; pleads their case in person to the United States State Department, August 26. Japanese attack on Pearl Harbor brings the United States into war, December 7.

1942   Begins writing memoir that focuses on his literary career, "My Life as Author and Editor"; works on it periodically until 1948 (published 1993). Publication of *A New Dictionary of Quotations*.

1943   Testifies in October on behalf of *Esquire* magazine, which had lost its mailing privileges on charges of obscenity. Publication of *Heathen Days: 1889–1906*.

1945   Publication of *The American Language: Supplement I*. The end of World War II officially declared September 2. In the aftermath of Allied bombing, which had appalled him, Mencken sends packages of food, shoes and other necessities to friends in Berlin, copies of his books to correspondents in Japan. Theodore Dreiser dies, December 28.

1946   Publication of *Christmas Story*, a satirical account of a holiday feast among the homeless of Baltimore, and how the organizers impose their Puritanical morality among the crowd.

1947   Buoyed by news of Truman's plans to help the economic recovery of Europe, March; argues for immediate economic rehabilitation of Germany. In August suffers a minor stroke but recovers after a few days. The autobiographical trilogy is published in one volume as *The Days of H. L. Mencken*. Interviewed by Edgar Kemler and William Manchester, who are separately writing biographies of Mencken.

1948   Vacations in Florida with brother August, February. Rejoins *Sun* staff to cover Republican Party Convention, June 19–22; covers Democratic National Convention, July 10–15, and Progressive Party Convention, July 23–26, all held in Philadelphia. Revival of interest in Mencken's life and work demonstrated by cover story in *Newsweek* magazine, April 5. Records an interview for the Library of Congress, June 30. Publication of *The American Language, Supplement II.* Last public appearance speaking before the American Philosophical Society, November 4. Writes series of articles for the *Sun*, August 1–November 9. Publication of last column, arguing against segregation, November 9. Suffers a massive stroke that prevents any further reading or writing for the remainder of his life, November 23. (In his remaining years he is cared for largely by his younger brother August.)

1949   Publication of *A Mencken Chrestomathy*, Mencken's selection from his writings. Spends remaining years helping his secretary organize his papers for posterity, well over 100,000 letters, as well as original manuscripts, memoirs, and books, dedicating the bulk of the collection to the Enoch Pratt Free Library, as well as to the New York Public Library and Dartmouth.

1950   Suffers heart attack, October 12. Members of the Saturday Night Club agree in December to disband permanently. Spends five months in hospital, before he is discharged in March, 1951.

1955   *Inherit the Wind*, play about the Scopes Trial by Jerome Lawrence and Robert E. Lee, featuring a character based on Mencken, opens in April. On Mencken's 75th birthday, Alistair Cooke's edition of *The Vintage Mencken* is published, selling out in two days. Secretary Rosalind Lohrfinck comes across an unpublished manuscript written by Mencken before his 1948 stroke (published posthumously the following year as *Minority Report: H. L. Mencken's Notebooks*).

1956   Dies in his sleep from a coronary occlusion, between 4 and 5 A.M. on January 29, leaving an estate valued at $300,000. Three-fourths of his estate is willed to the Enoch Pratt Free Library. He is cremated, and his ashes are interred at Loudon Park Cemetery, in West Baltimore, January 31.

Note on the Texts

This volume contains the complete texts of H. L. Mencken's *Prejudices: First Series* (1919), *Prejudices: Second Series* (1920), and *Prejudices: Third Series* (1922), along with an excerpt from Mencken's unfinished autobiography, *My Life as Author and Editor* (written 1942–48), in which he discusses the composition and reception of the first two series of *Prejudices*. A Library of America companion volume, *Prejudices: Fourth, Fifth, and Sixth Series*, presents the complete contents of the three subsequent *Prejudices*, published in 1924, 1926, and 1927. The texts of the *Prejudices* have been taken from the corrected second printings of the first editions of each collection, all published in New York by Alfred A. Knopf. The text of *My Life as Author and Editor* has been taken from Mencken's hand-corrected typescript, now in the Mencken Collection at the Enoch Pratt Free Library in Baltimore.

By Mencken's account, the initial suggestion that he gather his periodical writings in book form came from Richard Laukhuff, a Cleveland bookseller, who proposed such a collection to Mencken's publisher. *Prejudices: First Series* was assembled largely out of articles from the *Smart Set*, to which Mencken had been contributing since 1908; he also drew on his writing in newspapers, including the New York *Evening Mail* and the Baltimore *Evening Sun*.

Setting the pattern for all of his *Prejudices*, he revised these original articles extensively—rewriting, and adding new material—before he sent his finished work to Knopf. Mencken's subsequent *Prejudices* also began, though to a lesser extent, with contributions to the *Smart Set* and *The American Mercury*; for a more detailed account of the periodical publication history of individual pieces in the *Prejudices*, see S. T. Joshi, *H. L. Mencken: An Annotated Bibliography* (Lanham, Maryland: Scarecrow Press, 2009).

Mencken's relationship with Knopf was a congenial one, and he exercised an exceptional degree of control over the form in which his works appeared. He was also a careful proofreader of his own work, and encouraged Knopf (in a letter of March 24, 1921, noting some typographical errors in the first printing of *Prejudices: Second Series*) to "correct all such errors whenever the opportunity offers. Nothing looks worse than a dirty book. The English reviewers, in particular, are very waspish about typographical errors." In the case of all of his *Prejudices*, Mencken's final textual corrections were not incorporated in the first Knopf printings, where they are listed separately as errata (for *Prejudices: Second Series* through *Prejudices: Sixth Series*), or not noted (in *Prejudices: First Series*). No evidence has been found for Mencken's further correction or revision of his texts in subsequent printings and editions of the *Prejudices* in the United States or in England, though he did permit minor changes to be made, for the benefit of English readers, in two English editions: *Prejudices* (London: Jonathan Cape, 1925), and *Selected Prejudices: Second Series* (London: Jonathan Cape, 1927). The present volume prints the texts of the corrected second printings of the Knopf first editions, issued in January 1920 (*Prejudices: First Series*), June 1921 (*Prejudices: Second Series*), and November 1922 (*Prejudices: Third Series*).

Mencken began writing *My Life as Author and Editor* in November 1942 and continued—with interruptions to finish *The American Language: Supplement 1* (1945) and *The American Language: Supplement 2* (1948)—until November 1948, when a stroke left him permanently disabled. Afterwards, he donated his unfinished corrected typescript to the Enoch Pratt Free Library in Baltimore, with the instruction that it not be accessible until 1980 or thirty-five years after his death, whichever came later.

In 1992, Alfred A. Knopf published a substantial portion of Mencken's work (which runs to almost 2000 pages, including appendices, in the original typescript) as *My Life as Author and Editor* (Jonathan Yardley, ed.). The present volume includes an excerpt from the autobiography in which Mencken discusses his first and second series of *Prejudices*. The text printed here has been taken from Mencken's typescript.

This volume presents the texts of the printings and typescript chosen for inclusion, but it does not attempt to reproduce nontextual features of their typographic design. The texts are printed without change, except for the correction of typographical errors. Spelling, punctuation, and capitalization may be expressive features, and they are not altered, even when inconsistent or irregular. The following is a list of typographical errors corrected, cited by page and line number: 14.23, Liége.; 74.34, chair; 99.9, Bastile,; 147.4, Aristotolean; 163.38, letters!); 167.17, Sweet; 167.36, of forty; 175.13, Russion; 178. 35, Provençe,; 191.23, astouning; 195.2, on on; 210.3, Weil; 218.6, developement; 250.7, or gross; 256.2, one-hundred-and forty-fifth; 274.28, drival; 276.7, condems; 282.5, Prohibionist; 305.30, *digitatem*; 313.5, incurable; 313.31, too for; 316.14, biologically But; 332.5, that; 332.16, *a la*; 346.30, fugelman; 387.40, get all in the; 389.22, Rosetti's; 392.22, Travelyn; 394.22, ever; 404.3, Shelly; 418.8, Goldmarck's; 418.14, "My Antonía" (and *passim*); 427.24, life at; 430.34, contented,; 433.9, women; 438.29, *privat dozent*; 453.24, sedentery; 461.16, it downright; 469.21, years; 477.35, collared,; 482.8, appreciable; 482.32, [no "4"]; 493.20, "Prejudices"; 496.37, reposte; 497.18, fitter; 498.20, last-named signing; 498.24, phrases,; 502.37, Perrin"; 502.39, Wrex; 504.1, difference; 510.39, to setting; 512.35, jointed; 514.18, *Westminister.*

Notes

In the notes below, the reference numbers denote page and line of this volume (the line count includes headings). No note is made for material included in standard desk-reference books. Quotations from Shakespeare are keyed to *The Riverside Shakespeare*, ed. G. Blakemore Evans (Boston: Houghton Mifflin, 1974). Biographical information beyond that included in the Chronology may be found in Marion Elizabeth Rodgers, *Mencken: The American Iconoclast* (Oxford, New York: Oxford University Press, 2005); Marion Elizabeth Rodgers, editor, *Mencken and Sara: A Life in Letters* (New York: McGraw-Hill, 1987); Marion Elizabeth Rodgers, editor, *The Impossible H. L. Mencken: A Selection of His Best Newspaper Stories* (New York: Anchor/Doubleday, 1991); Guy J. Forgue, editor, *Letters of H. L. Mencken* (New York: Knopf, 1961); Carl Bode, editor, *The New Mencken Letters* (New York: Dial Press, 1977); Thomas P. Riggio, editor, *Dreiser-Mencken Letters: The Correspondence of Theodore Dreiser and H. L. Mencken* (Philadelphia: University of Pennsylvania Press, 1986); Edward A. Martin, editor, *In Defense of Marion: The Love Letters of Marion Bloom and H. L. Mencken* (Athens: University of Georgia Press, 1996); Carl Bode, *Mencken* (Carbondale: Southern Illinois University Press, 1969); Charles Scruggs, *The Sage in Harlem: H. L. Mencken and the Black Writers of the 1920s* (Baltimore: Johns Hopkins University Press, 1984); Vincent Fitzpatrick, *H. L. Mencken* (Macon: Mercer University Press, 2004); Fred Hobson, *Mencken: A Life* (New York: Random House, 1994); William Manchester, *Disturber of the Peace: The Life of H. L. Mencken* (Amherst: University of Massachusetts Press, 1986); Terry Teachout, *The Skeptic: A Life of H. L. Mencken* (New York: HarperCollins, 2002); Charles A. Fecher, *Mencken: A Study of His Thought* (New York: Alfred A. Knopf, 1978); Richard J. Schrader, *H. L. Mencken: A Descriptive Bibliography* (Pittsburgh: University of Pittsburgh Press, 1998); and S. T. Joshi, *H. L. Mencken: An Annotated Bibliography* (Lanham, Maryland: Scarecrow Press, 2009).

PREJUDICES: FIRST SERIES

3.33 Major J. E. Spingarn] Joel Elias Spingarn (1875–1939), professor of comparative literature at Columbia and literary critic. His books included *The New Criticism* (1911) and *Creative Criticism* (1917).

4.14–15   William Lyon Phelps]   Literary scholar (1865–1943) and professor of English at Yale, who became popular as lecturer and columnist. Author of *Essays on Modern Novelists* (1910), *The Advance of the English Novel* (1916), and other works.

4.17   W. C. Brownell]   William Crary Brownell (1851–1928), literary critic, author of *American Prose Masters* (1909), *Standards* (1917), *The Genius of Style* (1924), and other books.

4.19–20   Stuart P. Sherman]   Stuart Pratt Sherman (1881–1926), literary critic and professor at the University of Illinois (1907–24). In 1917 Sherman charged Mencken with being unpatriotic and a defender of licentious literature, using Theodore Dreiser as an example. Mencken ridiculed Sherman in his article, "The Dreiser Bugaboo," published in *Seven Arts* (August 1917), and Sherman responded with a negative review of *A Book of Prefaces* in *The Nation* (November 1917).

5.29   "What Is Man?"]   Essay (1906) by Mark Twain.

6.14   Espionage Act]   The Espionage Act, passed on June 15, 1917, included among its provisions severe penalties (up to $10,000 fine and twenty years' imprisonment) for persons found guilty of interfering with the draft or encouraging disloyalty to the United States. Some newspapers were barred from the mails, notably the *New York Call* and *Milwaukee Leader*. More than 1500 persons were arrested, among them labor leaders Eugene Debs and Victor Berger.

7.7   *Privatdozenten*]   German academic title corresponding roughly to associate professor.

7.15   Hamilton Wright Mabie's "White List of Books"]   Mabie (1846–1916), essayist, lecturer, and editor of the Christian magazine *The Outlook*; his books included *Books and Culture* (1896), *The Life of the Spirit* (1899), and *American Ideals, Character and Life* (1913). His "White List" itemized works suitable for Christian homes and the perusal of children.

7.28–29   Hermann Bahr]   Austrian playwright, novelist, and critic (1863–1934).

7.29   Georg Brandes]   Georg Morris Cohen Brandes (1872–1927), preeminent Danish critic and scholar of his time, a leading proponent of realism and a prolific commentator on literature, politics, religion, and philosophy. He was the author of many books including *Main Currents in the Literature of the Nineteenth Century* (1872–75) and monographs on Kierkegaard, Ibsen, Nietzsche, and Goethe, among others.

7.29   James Huneker]   James Gibbons Huneker (1857–1921), critic of literature, music, and art. He was founder of the magazine *M'lle New York* and musical editor of the New York *Sun*. His many books include *Chopin: The Man and His Music* (1900), *Iconoclasts, a Book of Dramatists* (1905), *Egoists:*

A Book of Supermen (1909), *Ivory Apes and Peacocks* (1915), the memoirs *Old Fogy* (1913) and *Steeplejack* (1920), and the novel *Painted Veils* (1920).

7.31   Paul Elmer More] Critic and philosopher (1864–1937) associated with the New Humanist movement. His *Shelburne Essays* were published in fourteen volumes (1904–36), and his other works included *Platonism* (1917), *The Religion of Plato* (1921), and *The Christ of the New Testament* (1924).

9.7–8   Rufus Griswold] Journalist and editor (1815–1857) of literary anthologies including *The Poets and Poetry of America* (1842) and *The Female Poets of America* (1849). He quarreled with Edgar Allan Poe and as Poe's literary executor published a defamatory biography that had lingering influence.

9.17   Mr. W. H.] Unidentified dedicatee of Shakespeare's sonnets ("the onlie begetter of these insuing sonnets"), subject of Oscar Wilde's speculative story "The Portrait of Mr. W. H." (1889).

11.2   Mr. Wells] H. G. Wells (1866–1946), English novelist whose later works, discussed by Mencken, included *Tono-Bungay* (1909), *Ann Veronica* (1909), *The History of Mr. Polly* (1910), *The New Machiavelli* (1911), *Marriage* (1912), *The Passionate Friends* (1913), *The Wife of Sir Isaac Harman* (1914), *Bealby: A Holiday* (1915), *Boon* (1915), *The Research Magnificent* (1916), *Mr. Britling Sees It Through* (1917), *The Soul of a Bishop* (1917), *Joan and Peter: The Story of an Education* (1918), and *The Undying Fire* (1919). *First and Last Things* (1908) was a book of essays intended, in Wells's words, "to put down what I believe."

11.4–5   Richard Remington] Protagonist of Wells's novel *The New Machiavelli* (1911).

11.16   Scribe] Eugène Scribe (1791–1861), French playwright, author of hundreds of plays alone or in collaboration, noted for his mastery of stagecraft and plot construction. His plays included *Le Mariage de raison* (1826), *Le Mariage d'argent* (1828), *Une Chaîne* (1841), and *Le Verre d'eau* (1842).

12.15   A Trip to Chinatown] Long-running musical comedy (1891), by Charles H. Hoyt (1859–1900).

12.15   Peck's Bad Boy] Series of books written by George Wilbur Peck (1840–1916), beginning with *Peck's Bad Boy and His Pa* (1883).

12.30–31   The Four Horsemen of the Apocalypse] Novel (1916) by Spanish novelist Vicente Blasco Ibáñez (1867–1928).

13.2   William Archer] Scottish dramatic critic (1886–1924) and translator of Henrik Ibsen's plays. (The Ibsen translations were published in eleven volumes, 1906–8.) *The Old Drama and the New*, a defense of modern playwriting, appeared in 1923.

14.15–16   *Privatdozenten*] See note 7.7.

16.23–24 Fabian Society] British socialist movement founded in 1884, and favoring incremental rather than revolutionary change. Among its early members were George Bernard Shaw, H. G. Wells, and Beatrice and Sidney Webb.

16.24 Lord Northcliffe] Alfred Charles William Harmsworth, 1st Viscount Northcliffe (1865–1922), British newspaper and publishing magnate, proprietor of the London *Times* and the *Daily Mail*; appointed Director of Propaganda during World War I.

17.27 Dr. Wilson] Woodrow Wilson (1856–1924), president of the United States (1913–1921).

17.27 British Socialists] British Socialist Party, Marxist political movement established in England in 1911, a predecessor to the Communist Party of Great Britain (founded 1920).

17.27–28 Romain Rolland] French man of letters (1866–1941), author of biographical and critical studies of Beethoven, Michelangelo, and Tolstoy, plays, political tracts, and novels including the ten-volume *Jean-Christophe*; winner of the Nobel Prize in Literature in 1915.

17.28 James M. Beck] James Montgomery Beck (1861–1936), lawyer, Solicitor General of the United States (1921–1925), and member of the U.S. House of Representatives (1927–1934).

18.15 Van Wyck Brooks] Critic and literary biographer (1886–1963), author of *America's Coming-of-Age* (1915), *The Ordeal of Mark Twain* (1920), *The Flowering of New England* (1936), and many other works. His study *The World of H. G. Wells* was published in 1915.

18.21 William Bayard Hale] American journalist (1869–1924). An Episcopal minister, he became editor of *Cosmopolitan* in 1900 and wrote the campaign biography *Woodrow Wilson: The Story of His Life* (1912). Wilson's 1913 volume *The New Freedom: A Call for the Emancipation of the Generous Energies of a People* was edited by Hale from the president's campaign speeches. Hale was subsequently a propaganda advisor to the German government before America's entry into the war, and in 1915 published *American Rights and British Pretension on the Seas*, an attack on Britain's blockade of German shipping. After the war he was an object of public denunciation and spent the remainder of his life in Europe.

21.32 W. L. George] Walter Lionel George (1882–1926), French-born English novelist best known for *A Bed of Roses* (1911), about the life of a prostitute.

21.37–38 Blind Alley] Novel (1919) by W. L. George.

21.38 The Pretty Lady] Novel (1918) by Arnold Bennett (1867–1931).

22.10 Bayards and Cids] Pierre LeVieux, seigneur de Bayard (1473–

1524), French soldier lauded in his lifetime as an emblem of chivalry, *le cheva-
lier sans peur et sans reproche*; Rodrigo Diaz de Bivar (1040?-1099), known as
El Cid, Castilian military leader commemorated in the twelfth-century poem
Cantar de Mio Cid.

22.28   The Roll-Call]   The fourth volume (1918) of Arnold Bennett's series of novels about the Clayhanger family.

24.20   Haeckel]   Ernst Heinrich Haeckel (1834–1919), German biologist
and philosopher who published many works helping to popularize evolution-
ary theory. His books include *The Riddle of the Universe* (1901), *Artforms of
Nature* (1904), and *The History of Creation* (1914). He was the author of the
subsequently contested formulation that "ontogeny recapitulates phylogeny."

24.20   Bradlaugh]   Charles Bradlaugh (1833–1891), English political activist and atheist, a founder of the National Secular Society in 1866. Elected
to Parliament in 1880, he was denied his seat because of his refusal to swear
the religious Oath of Allegiance, initiating a long controversy not resolved
until 1886. His books include *A Plea for Atheism* (1864) and *Humanity's
Gain from Unbelief* (1889).

25.7–8   Buried Alive . . . The Lion's Share]   Novels by Arnold Bennett,
published respectively in 1908 and 1918.

25.12   Dr. Orison Swett Marden]   American writer (1850–1924) associated
with the New Thought movement, and author of self-help books emphasizing the power of positive thinking in order to achieve success, including *The
Secret of Achievement* (1898), *Cheerfulness as a Life Power* (1899), and *The
Hour of Opportunity* (1900).

25.12   Dr. Frank Crane]   American Methodist clergyman (1861–1928)
whose syndicated inspirational newspaper column appeared across the country from 1909–1928. His writings were collected in ten volumes in *Four-
Minute Essays* (1919).

27.19   Whom God Hath Joined]   Novel (1906) by Arnold Bennett.

28.9   Paris Nights]   Novel (1914) by Arnold Bennett.

29.11–12   Joseph H. Choate]   Joseph Hodges Choate (1832–1917), lawyer
and diplomat. He played a major role in the prosecution of the Tweed Ring
in New York and represented the Standard Oil Company in antitrust cases,
and also served as U.S. Ambassador to Great Britain (1899–1905) and head of
the U.S. Delegation of the International Peace Conference at the Hague
(1907).

29.15   Alexander Harvey]   Editor and author (1868–1949), associated with
Literary Digest, *Current Opinion*, and *The Atlantic Monthly*. His study
William Dean Howells appeared in 1917.

30.12–14   The Minister's Charge . . . The Leatherwood God]   *The*

Minister's Charge (1887), *An Imperative Duty* (1893), *The Unexpected Guests* (1893), *Out of the Question* (1877), *No Love Lost* (1869), *The Leatherwood God* (1916), novels and plays by William Dean Howells.

31.24   Agnes Repplier] Philadelphia-born essayist (1855–1950) whose works were collected in many volumes including *Books and Men* (1888), *Points of View* (1891), *Essays in Idleness* (1893), and *The Fireside Sphinx* (1901).

31.25   New Leaf Mills] Memoir (1913) by William Dean Howells describing a childhood year spent living with his family in a Utopian commune at Eureka Mills, Ohio.

31.29–30   E. W. Howe's "The Story of a Country Town"] Novel (1883) by Edgar Watson Howe (1853–1937), a realistic treatment of life in a Midwestern town.

32.13   W. B. Trites] William Budd Trites, author of the novels *John Cave* (1909) and *Barbara Gwynne: Life* (1913).

32.13–14   Frank A. Munsey] Frank Andrew Munsey (1854–1925), publisher, owner of the New York *Evening Sun* and *Evening Telegram*, *Munsey's Magazine*, and *Argosy All-Story Weekly*.

32.15–16   Phillpses] Stephen Phillips (1864–1915), English poet and playwright, noted for his attempts to revive verse drama.

32.16   Pollards] Joseph Percival Pollard (1869–1911), German-born literary critic, a close friend of Mencken; he was educated in England and emigrated with his family to the United States in 1885. He was a frequent contributor to *The Criterion*. His books included *Their Day in Court* (1909) and *Masks and Minstrels of New Germany* (1911).

32.16   Meltzers] Charles Henry Meltzer (1853–1936), English music critic and translator, later resident in the United States.

32.33   Hannah More] English playwright (1745–1833), who in later life devoted herself to religious writing. She participated with William Wilberforce in the antislavery movement. The Religious Tract Society was founded to carry on her work.

34.7   Elihu Root] Lawyer and statesman (1845–1937), U.S. Secretary of War under Presidents McKinley and Roosevelt (1899–1904) and Secretary of State under President Roosevelt (1905–1909). He was a supporter of the League of Nations and founding chairman of the Council on Foreign Relations.

34.8   Otto Kahn] Otto Hermann Kahn (1867–1934), investment banker and financier, and patron of the arts.

34.10   Thorstein Veblen] Norwegian-American sociologist and economist (1857–1929), author of *The Theory of the Leisure Class* (1899), *The Theory of Business Enterprise* (1904), *The Instinct of Workmanship* (1914), *Imperial Germany and the Industrial Revolution* (1915), *The Higher Learning in America* (1918), *The Vested Interests and the State of the Industrial Arts* (1919), *An Inquiry into the Nature of Peace and the Terms of Its Perpetuation* (1919), and other works.

34.25 "Men Versus the Man"] *Men Versus the Man: A Correspondence Between Rives La Monte, Socialist, and H. L. Mencken, Individualist*, published in 1910.

34.26 Baxter's "Saint's Rest"] *The Saint's Everlasting Rest: or, Treatise on the Blessed State of the Saints and Their Enjoyment of God in Heaven* (1672) by English Puritan theologian Richard Baxter (1615–1691).

35.16 Judge Ben B. Lindsey] Benjamin Barr Lindsey (1869–1943), judge of the juvenile court of Colorado (1900–27), which became a model for the rest of the country. He was recognized as an authority on juvenile delinquency; his writings included *Problems of the Children* (1903) and *The Revolt of Modern Youth* (1925).

35.16 The late Major-General Roosevelt] President Theodore Roosevelt (1858–1924).

35.16–17 Tom Lawson] Thomas William Lawson (1857–1925), American stockbroker and author of *Frenzied Finance* (1902), about stock market operations in copper.

35.18 Hall Caine] English novelist (1853–1931), author of *The Shadow of a Crime* (1885), *The Deemster* (1887), and *The Manxman* (1894).

35.18 Brieux] Eugène Brieux (1858–1932), French playwright whose best-known works included *The Red Robe* (1900) and *Damaged Goods* (1901).

35.23 Jane Addams] American social reformer (1860–1935), founder in 1889 of Hull House in Chicago, the first settlement house in the United States. She was active as a pacifist during World War I and received the Nobel Peace Prize in 1931.

35.25 Bernstorff] Johann Heinrich von Bernstorff (1862–1939), German ambassador to the United States, 1908–17. After 1914 he was involved in secret efforts to promote sabotage of American industrial targets to aid the German war effort.

35.26 Eucken] Rudolph Christian Eucken (1846–1926), German philosopher, winner of the 1908 Nobel Prize in Literature. His books included *The Struggle for a Spiritual Content of Life* (1896), *The Truth of Religion* (1901), and *The Meaning and Value of Life* (1908).

35.26–27 Ludendorff] Erich Friedrich Wilhelm Ludendorff (1865–1937), German army officer who (with Paul von Hindenburg) directed the German army during World War I from August 1916 until his resignation in October

1918. Following the armistice he fled to Sweden and while in exile wrote books and articles propounding the idea that Germany had been defeated from within. He returned to Germany in 1920.

35.37 Sir Oliver Lodge] British physicist and inventor (1851–1940) who in later life devoted himself to the study of telepathy, mediums, and the afterlife.

36.26 Scott Nearing] American writer and radical political activist (1883–1983), who over the course of his long career advocated pacifism and a return to natural agrarian living. His many books include *Social Religion* (1910), *Poverty and Riches* (1916), *The Menace of Militarism* (1917), *The American Empire* (1921), *Must We Starve?* (1932), *The Revolution of Our Times* (1947), and *The Making of a Radical: A Political Autobiography* (1972).

38.16 Louis James] American actor (1842–1910), known for his touring Shakespearean company.

42.19 Robert W. Chambers] Artist and bestselling author (1865–1933), best remembered for *The King in Yellow* (1895).

42.20 Elinor Glyn] British novelist (1864–1943) who became famous for the scandalous bestseller *Three Weeks* (1907). Many of her works were filmed; the title story of *"It" and Other Stories* (1927) became a vehicle for Clara Bow.

45.26 Flexner] Abraham Flexner (1866–1955), educator, author of *The American College* (1908) and *Medical Education in the United States and Canada* (1910). He was associated with the cause of medical education reform and later was a founder of the Institute of Advanced Studies at Princeton.

45.26 Ehrlich] Eugen Ehrlich (1862–1922), Austrian legal scholar, author of *Fundamental Principles of the Sociology of Law* (1913).

45.26 Metchnikoff] Ilya Ilyich Mechnikov (1845–1916), Russian microbiologist who received the Nobel Prize in Medicine in 1908. He did pioneering research on the immune system.

45.27 Loeb] Jacques Loeb (1859–1924), German-American physiologist, known for his work on animal tropisms. His most famous experiment induced artificial parthenogenesis in sea urchins. He taught at Bryn Mawr and the Universities of Chicago and California before becoming a member of the Rockefeller Institute for Medical Research in 1910.

45.27 Carrel] Alexis Carrel (1873–1944), French biologist and proponent of eugenics. He received the Nobel Prize in 1912.

46.14 Ellen Key] Swedish feminist writer (1849–1926), author of *The Century of the Child* (1909), *Love and Marriage* (1911), and *The Woman Movement* (1912).

46.14   Signorina Montessori] Maria Montessori (1870–1952), Italian physician and educator, founder of the Montessori method of education for children.

48.8–9   Braithwaite] William Stanley Braithwhite (1878–1962), African American poet and anthologist, author of *Lyrics of Life and Love* (1904) and *Essayists and Critics of Today* (1920). From 1913 to 1929 he published the annual collection *Anthology of Magazine Verse*. He was a literary editor and columnist for the *Boston Evening Transcript*, 1906–31.

48.13   Alfred Kreymborg] American poet (1883–1966), editor of the magazine *Others* (1917–20). His poetry was collected in *Mushrooms* (1916), *Scarlet and Mellow* (1926), and other volumes. His autobiography *Troubador* appeared in 1925. He later edited numerous anthologies including *The American Caravan* (1927–36) and *Lyric America* (1930).

48.23   "Others" group] Poets published in Alfred Kreymborg's *Others* included William Carlos Williams, Wallace Stevens, Marianne Moore, T. S. Eliot, Mina Loy, and Carl Sandburg.

49.11–12   Knish-Morgan burlesque] *Spectra: A Book of Poetic Experiments* (1916), a collection of mock-modernist poems of the "Spectrist" school, written by Witter Bynner and Arthur Davison Ficke under the pseudonyms Emanuel Morgan and Anne Knish. The hoax was revealed in 1918.

49.12   Witter Bynner] American poet (1881–1968) whose many collections included *The Beloved Stranger* (1919), *A Canticle of Pan* (1920), and *Indian Earth* (1929).

49.12   Arthur Davison Ficke] American poet (1883–1945), author of many books including *The Breaking of Bonds* (1910), *The Man on the Hilltop* (1915), and *Selected Poems* (1926).

49.24   James Whitcomb Riley] American poet (1849–1916) whose humorous poems of Indiana life made him immensely popular. A six-volume edition of his complete works was published in 1913.

49.37   Stedman's anthology] Edmund Clarence Stedman (1833–1908), American poet and critic. He edited *An American Anthology, 1787–1899* (1900), an influential survey of American poetry. He also co-edited, with Ellen M. Hutchinson, the eleven-volume *Library of American Literature 1880–1890* (1889–90), and, with George Woodberry, a ten-volume edition of Poe's works.

49.37   McGuffey's Sixth Reader] The series of readers edited by William Holmes McGuffey (1800–1873) began appearing in 1836. The Sixth Reader, designed for the most advanced level, was edited by his brother Alexander McGuffey in the 1840s. The series was widely used and remains in print.

50.2   James Oppenheim] American poet and novelist (1882–1932). He was editor of the influential little magazine *The Seven Arts*. His poem "Bread and Roses" (1911) became a rallying point for labor activists.

50.10   Hermann Hagedorn] American author (1882–1964). His poetry was collected in *A Troop of the Guard* (1909), *Poems and Ballads* (1912), and other volumes. He was a close friend of Theodore Roosevelt, of whom he published a biography in 1918. He also published the novels *Faces in the Dawn* (1914) and *Barbara Picks a Husband* (1918).

50.10–11   Charles Hanson Towne] Poet (1877–1949), author of *The Quiet Singer* (1908), *Manhattan* (1909), and other volumes. He was an editor for *The Smart Set, McClure's Magazine, Harper's Bazaar*, and other publications, and later a columnist for the *New York American*.

50.28   Richard Aldington] English poet and novelist (1892–1962). He married the American poet H.D. (Hilda Doolittle) in 1911; the marriage broke up long before their divorce in 1938. He fought in World War I, an experience which provided the basis for some of his poetry and for the novel *Death of a Hero* (1929).

50.29   John Gould Fletcher] American poet (1886–1950) associated with the Imagist group; his collections included *Irradiations* (1915), *Sand and Spray* (1915), and *Goblins and Pagodas* (1916).

51.9   Tendencies in Modern Poetry] Critical study (1917) by Amy Lowell.

51.10–11   Louis Untermeyer] American poet, critic, and editor (1885–1977). His *The New Era in American Poetry* appeared in 1919. He was a prolific anthologist, responsible for the frequently revised *Modern American and British Poetry* (first published in 1919).

51.12   John Livingston Lowes] American scholar, critic, and educator (1867–1945), author of *Convention and Revolt in Poetry* (1919), *The Road to Xanadu* (first edition, 1927), and other works.

51.27   *Ubi sunt*] Literally "Where are"; a convention of medieval Latin poetry, imitated by François Villon (in his *Où sont les neiges d'antan?*— "Where are the snows of yesteryear?") and others.

52.2   Jubilee Songs] Spirituals, as collected in *Jubilee Songs as Sung by the Jubilee Singers of Fisk University* (1872).

52.11   Henry Bordeaux] French novelist (1870–1963). His *George Guynemer: Knight of the Air* (1918) was published with a preface by Theodore Roosevelt.

52.11   Pastor Wagner] Charles Wagner (1852–1916), French clergyman, author of *The Simple Life* (1904). He was admired by Theodore Roosevelt and invited to preach at the White House.

52.11   Francis Warrington Dawson] Novelist (1878–1962), author of *The*

Scourge (1908) and *The Scar* (1910). When working as a reporter for the United Press Dawson was invited by Theodore Roosevelt to accompany him on an African safari; he later published *Opportunity and Theodore Roosevelt* (1924).

52.12   Giovannitti] Arturo Giovannitti (1884–1959), poet and political activist. He was born in Italy and immigrated to the United States in 1902. He was a member of the IWW, and spent ten months in jail following his participation in the Lawrence, Massachusetts, textile strike of 1912.

52.17   fantee] Amok; gone native.

53.32   Benét] William Rose Benét (1886–1950), American poet, author of *Merchants from Cathay* (1913) and *The Great White Wall* (1916). He was a founder of the *Saturday Review of Literature* and won the Pulitzer Prize in 1942.

54.11   Walt Mason] Humorist and poet (1862–1939); his prose poems were syndicated in more than 200 newspapers and collected in *Uncle Walt: The Poet Philosopher* (1911). He was a colleague of William Allen White on the *Emporia Gazette*.

54.12   Ella Wheeler Wilcox] American poet (1850–1919); her poetry was collected in over twenty volumes including *Poems of Passion* (1883), *Poems of Pleasure* (1888), *Poems of Power* (1901), and *Poems of Sentiment* (1906). For some years she published a daily poem as a syndicated newspaper feature.

55.5   Richard Henry Stoddard] American critic and poet (1825–1903), author of *Poems* (1852) and *Songs of Summer* (1857).

55.19   Henry Van Dyke] American clergyman, educator, and author (1852–1933), a prolific poet.

55.40   Lizette Woodworth Reese] Poet (1856–1935), born in Maryland. She worked as a schoolteacher in the Baltimore area. Her poetry was collected in *A Branch of May* (1887), *A Handful of Lavender* (1891), *A Quiet Road* (1896), and other volumes. Her sonnet "Tears," published in 1899, became especially popular.

56.4   Neihardt] John G. Neihardt (1881–1973), American poet, specialized in themes of religion and the history of the American West. In 1913 he began publishing his long poetic sequence *A Cycle of the West* (collected in a single volume in 1949). He collaborated with the Sioux shaman Black Elk on *Black Elk Speaks* (1932).

56.5   John McClure] American lyric poet (1893–1956), author of *Airs and Ballads* (1918). His work appeared frequently in *The Smart Set*.

57.4   Irvin S. Cobb] Humorous writer (1876–1944), born in Kentucky and later a New York journalist. His books included *Cobb's Anatomy* (1912), *Cobb's Bill of Fare* (1913), and *Old Judge Priest* (1915).

58.2   Bill Nye]   Edgar Wilson Nye (1850–1896), American humorist and popular lecturer, known for his comic sketches about the Wyoming Territory.

58.6–7   Owen Johnson]   Novelist and short story writer (1878–1952), author of *The Varmint* (1910), *Stover at Yale* (1911), *The Salamander* (1913), and other works.

58.11   Wilson Mizner]   Playwright and screenwriter (1876–1933) who after an early career as confidence man and adventurer became widely known as entrepreneur and raconteur.

58.15–16   *Ayer's Almanac*]   Patent medicine catalogue published annually in the late nineteenth and early twentieth centuries by J. C. Ayer & Co. of Lowell, Massachusetts.

59.22   Petroleum V. Nasby]   Pseudonym of David Ross Locke (1833–1888), journalist and political satirist. His writings were collected in many volumes, beginning with *The Nasby Papers* (1864).

62.2   *Hermann Sudermann*]   German novelist and playwright (1857–1928). His novels included *Frau Sorge* (*Dame Care*, 1887), *Der Katzensteg* (*Cats' Bridge*, 1889), and *Das Hohe Lied* (*The Song of Songs*, 1908). He turned to the stage with *Die Ehre* (*Honor*, 1889) and followed it with *Sodoms Ende* (*Sodom's End*, 1890), *Heimat* (*Homeland*, 1893), and other plays.

62.9–10   Marguerite Gautier]   Tragic protagonist of *The Lady of the Camellias* (1848) by Alexandre Dumas fils.

62.12   The Princess Bonnie]   Operetta (1893) with words and music by Willard Spenser.

62.16   Arno Holz]   German poet, playwright, and critic (1863–1929), a leading proponent of Naturalism.

62.17   Johannes Schlaf]   German novelist and playwright (1862–1941). He collaborated in his youth with Arno Holz.

62.19   *Uberbrettl'*]   The Überbrettl, artistic cabaret established in Berlin in 1901; see also note 320.29–30.

62.23   Franz Adam Beyerlein]   German novelist and playwright (1871–1949). *Zapfenstreich* (1903) concerns military life.

62.23   Carl Bleibtreu]   German novelist and historian (1859–1928). His comedy *Die Edelsten der Nation* was published in 1901.

62.28   Hanneles Himmelfahrt]   *Hannele's Trip to Heaven*, play (1893) by Gerhart Hauptmann, which after a realistic opening scene veers into the world of dreams.

62.30   sardoodledum]   Style of internationally popular theater associated with Victorien Sardou (1831–1908), whose plays included *La Perle Noire* (1862), *Fédora* (1882), *La Tosca* (1887), and *Madame Sans-Gêne* (1893).

62.34–35   Augier's "Le Mariage d'Olympe"] *The Marriage of Olympia* (1855) by Emile Augier (1820–1889), play about a scheming courtesan.

63.13   Brieux's "Les Avariés"] Play (1901) on the social ravages of syphilis, by Eugène Brieux. It was translated into English as *Damaged Goods*.

63.40   Ludwig Thoma] Bavarian novelist, story writer, and playwright (1867–1921).

66.13   *scènes à faire*] Theatrically obligatory scenes, in the nineteenth-century tradition of the well-made play.

67.15–16   George William Curtis] Popular essayist and travel writer (1824–1892), editor of *Harper's Weekly* from 1863. His books included *Niles Notes of a Howadji* (1851), *Lotus-Eating* (1852), and *The Potiphar Papers* (1853).

67.18   Artemus Ward] Pseudonym of Charles Farrar Browne (1834–1867), Maine-born humorous writer who became internationally popular.

67.19   Petroleum V. Nasby] See note 59.22.

67.21   Frank R. Stockton] Novelist and humorist (1834–1902), best known for his short story "The Lady, or the Tiger?" published in *Century* magazine in 1882.

67.22   Richard Henry Stoddard] See note 55.5

67.22–23   Edmund Clarence Stedman] See note 49.37.

67.24   Donald G. Mitchell] Donald Grant Mitchell (1822–1908), American author popularly known as Ik Marvel, whose books included *Reveries of a Bachelor* (1850) and *Dream Life* (1851).

68.18   William Lyon Phelps] See note 4.14–15.

68.33   Robert W. Chambers] See note 42.19.

68.33   Henry Sydnor Harrison] American novelist (1880–1930), a frequent contributor to *The Atlantic Monthly*. His works included *Queed* (1911), *V. V.'s Eyes* (1913), and *Angela's Business* (1915).

68.34   Oliver Herford] English-born American humorist (1863–1935), whose works included *A Child's Primer of Natural History* (1899), *Rubaiyat of a Persian Kitten* (1904), and *A Little Book of Bores* (1906).

68.34   E. S. Martin] Edward Sandford Martin (1856–1939), editor and writer. He was a founder of *The Harvard Lampoon* (1876) and *Life* (1883), and contributed columns to *Scribner's Magazine* and *Harper's Weekly*.

68.34   E. W. Townsend] Edward Waterman Townsend (1855–1942), politician and journalist, served as a Congressman from New Jersey, 1911–15. His sketches of life on New York's Bowery were collected in *Chimmie Fadden, Major Max, and Other Stories* (1895) and *Chimmie Fadden Explains* (1895).

69.3   Fred Lewis Pattee] Literary scholar (1863–1950), professor at Pennsylvania State College. His *History of American Literature Since 1870* appeared in 1915, followed by *The New American Literature, 1890–1930* (1930) and *The Feminine Fifties* (1940).

69.5   Marion Harland] Pseudonym of Mary Virginia Hawes Terhune (1830–1922), prolific author of novels including *Alone* (1854), *The Hidden Path* (1855), and *Sunnybank* (1866), along with travel books, cookbooks, and books of household advice such as *Common Sense in the Household: A Manual of Practical Housewifery* (1871)

69.5   Amélie Rives] Novelist, poet, and playwright (1863–1945), author of *The Quick or the Dead?* (1888) and *Barbara Dering* (1892). She was the wife of Prince Pierre Troubetzkoy, Russian artist.

69.6   R. K. Munkittrick] Richard Kendall Munkittrick (1853–1911), humorist, editor of the comic magazine *Judge*, and author of *New Jersey Arabian Nights* (1893) and *The Acrobatic Muse* (1896).

67.2   George Ade] Indiana-born humorist and playwright (1866–1944), author of *Fables in Slang* (1899), *People You Know* (1903), *Hand-Made Fables* (1920), and many other books. His plays included *The College Widow* (1904) and *The Fair Co-ed* (1908).

69.7   Gelett Burgess] American humorist, illustrator, and poet (1866–1951). He edited the literary magazine *The Lark* (1895–97), in which he published the poem "The Purple Cow." His later books included *Goops and How To Be Them* (1900), *Are You a Bromide?* (1907), and *Burgess Unabridged: A New Dictionary of Words You Have Always Needed* (1914).

69.8   Carolyn Wells] Writer of fiction and light verse (1869–1942). She edited popular anthologies including *The Nonsense Anthology* (1902), *A Parody Anthology* (1904), and *A Satire Anthology* (1905). She wrote many detective novels and children's novels.

69.8   John Kendrick Bangs] Popular author (1862–1922), known especially for his humorous and fantastic fiction. He worked at various times as editor of *Life*, *Harper's Magazine*, *Munsey's Magazine*, and *Puck*.

69.13   Joseph Jefferson] American actor (1829–1905), known especially for his starring role in his adaptation of *Rip Van Winkle*, which he first played in 1858 and repeated countless times for the rest of his life.

70.9   Billy Sunday] Evangelist (1862–1935), who gave up a career as a major league baseball player to become one of the most influential preachers of the early twentieth century.

71.17   Blix] Novel (1899) by Frank Norris.

71.22   Sganarelle] Stock comic character in various plays by Molière.

72.2 "mute, inglorious Milton"] See Thomas Gray, "Elegy Written in a Country Churchyard," stanza 15.

72.2 "somewheres East of Suez"] See Rudyard Kipling, "Mandalay," stanza 6.

73.2 Bashkirtseff] Marie Bashkirtseff (1858–1884), diarist and artist. An abridged edition of her diary (begun at age 13) was published in English as *The Journal of Marie Bashkirtseff* (1890); a complete edition runs to sixteen volumes.

73.4 Mary MacLane] Canadian-born American writer (1881–1929), whose memoir, *The Story of Mary MacLane*, became a bestseller in 1902. It was followed by *I, Mary MacLane: A Diary of Human Days* (1917).

73.17 *Kartoffelsuppe*] Potato soup.

73.33 Mrs. Atherton] Gertrude Atherton (1857–1948), San Francisco-born novelist, author of *The Californians* (1898), *The Conqueror* (1902), *Rezánov* (1906), and *Black Oxen* (1923).

74.12 Bill Sykes] Bill Sikes, brutal criminal in Dickens' *Oliver Twist* (1838).

74.31–32 Francis X. Bushman] Movie actor (1883–1966), best known for his portrayal of Messala in *Ben-Hur* (1925). He appeared in some 200 films.

74.32 Vincent Astor] Businessman and philanthropist (1891–1959), who inherited a large fortune in 1912 when his father went down with the *Titanic*.

75.8 Krafft-Ebing] Richard von Krafft-Ebing (1840–1902), German psychiatrist, author of *Psychopathia Sexualis* (1886), a compendium of case histories of sexual perversion.

76.5 Percival Pollard] See note 32.16.

76.7 Criterion] *The Criterion* (not to be confused with the English magazine of the same name) originated in St. Louis as *Life* before changing its name and moving to New York in 1897. It published articles on George Bernard Shaw, Henrik Ibsen, George Moore, and other modern authors. It ceased publication in 1905.

76.8 Vance Thompson] Critic, novelist, and poet (1863–1925), co-editor with James Huneker of *M'lle New York* (1895–99) and author of *French Portraits: Being Appreciations of the Writers of Young France* (1900).

76.23 Town Topics] Scandalous gossip magazine founded by Colonel William Mann before the turn of the century. It ceased publication in 1932.

76.35 Stuart P. Sherman] See note 4.19–20.

77.1 Cabell] James Branch Cabell (1878–1958), novelist whose works often explored a world of medieval fantasy. His books included *The Cream of the Jest* (1917), *Jurgen* (1919), which became a bestseller when it was denounced for obscenity, *Figures of Earth* (1921), and *The High Place* (1923).

77.12   Otto Julius Bierbaum] German poet, novelist, and literary editor (1865–1910).

77.21   Winston Churchill] American novelist (1871–1947), author of historical novels including *Richard Carvel* (1899), *The Crisis* (1901), *The Crossing* (1904), and *Coniston* (1906).

77.21   David Graham Phillips] American novelist and muckraking journalist (1867–1911), author of *The Cost* (1904), *The Plum Tree* (1905), *The Fortune Hunter* (1906), and *The Second Generation* (1907). He was murdered by a music teacher convinced that his family had been defamed in Phillips's most recent novel.

79.5   *Chap-Book*] Small literary magazine (1894–98) that published work by Stephen Crane, Hamlin Garland, William Dean Howells, George Santayana, and others.

79.9–10   The King in Yellow] Collection of linked fantasy stories (1895) by Robert W. Chambers.

79.12   Ailsa Page] Novel *Alisa Paige* (1910) by Robert W. Chambers.

79.14   Hamlin Garland] Author (1860–1940) of fiction, memoirs, and poems, known for his realistic studies of farm life in Wisconsin. His early stories, collected in *Main-Travelled Roads* (1891) and *Boy Life on the Prairie* (1899), were followed by the autobiographies *A Son of the Middle Border* (1917) and *A Daughter of the Middle Border* (1921). Of other works cited by Mencken, *The Shadow World* appeared in 1908 and *The Forester's Daughter* in 1914.

79.26   The Single Tax] Economic theory propounded by Henry George (1839–1897) in *Progress and Poverty* (1879) and other works, advocating a tax on land. Hamlin Garland's novel *Jason Edwards: An Average Man* (1892) was written in support of the Single Tax.

80.23   saleratus belt] The American Midwest; Mencken sometimes also employed the phrases "silo and saleratus belt" and "saleratus and hog cholera belt."

80.24   perunas] Peruna was a patent medicine marketed as a panacea.

80.26–27   Plunderbund] Moneyed interests; the term was evidently coined by Arthur McEwen, chief editorial writer the *New York American*, during William Randolph Hearst's 1906 campaign for governor of New York.

80.28   Claude Kitchin] American politician (1869–1923), North Carolina congressman, 1900–20. He campaigned vigorously in favor of depriving

African Americans of voting rights, and resisted American entry into World War I.

80.28–29   Newell Dwight Hillis] Congregationalist clergyman (1858–1929), pastor of the Plymouth Congregational Church in Brooklyn, New York, from 1899 to 1924. He led a campaign against immorality in Broadway plays and subsequently wrote a number of books decrying alleged German atrocities in World War I.

81.23   Henry Sydnor Harrison] See note 68.33.

81.27–28   W. J. Locke] William John Locke (1863–1930), British novelist whose bestselling romantic novels included *The Beloved Vagabond* (1906) and *Stella Maris* (1913).

82.3   Laddie] *Laddie: A True Blue Story* (1913), novel by Gene Stratton-Porter; see also note 167.20–21.

82.3   Pollyanna] Novel (1913) by Eleanor H. Porter; see also note 167.20.

82.17   William Allen White] Journalist (1868–1944), owner and editor of the Emporia (Kansas) *Gazette*. His 1896 anti-Populist editorial "What's the Matter with Kansas?" made him famous. He published many books on politics and public affairs, and also wrote novels including *A Certain Rich Man* (1909) and *In the Heart of a Fool* (1918).

82.32   Clayton Hamilton] American critic, playwright and producer (1881–1946), who wrote theatrical criticism for various magazines including *Bookman* (1910–18), *Everybody's Magazine* (1911–13) and *Vogue* (1912–20).

83.1   Felicia Hemens] Felicia Hemans, English poet (1793–1835), whose many volumes of verse included *The Forest Sanctuary* (1825) and *Songs of the Affections* (1830). She is best remembered for the poem "Casabianca."

83.1   Samuel Smiles] Scottish biographer and essayist (1812–1904) whose immensely popular *Self-Help: With Illustrations of Character and Conduct* (1859) was followed by similar works on *Character* (1871), *Thrift* (1875), and *Duty* (1880).

83.3   "The Duchess"] Margaret Wolfe Hungerford (1855–1897), prolific Irish novelist whose works were published in the United States as by "The Duchess." Her novels included *Phyllis* (1877), *Molly Bawn* (1878), and *A Mental Struggle* (1886). The line "Beauty is in the eye of the beholder" comes from *Molly Bawn*.

83.17   Harold Bell Wright] Novelist (1872–1944) whose books included *The Shepherd of the Hills* (1907) and *The Winning of Barbara Worth* (1911).

83.34   Coxey's Army] Protest march of unemployed men, led by Populist politician Jacob Coxey (1854–1951), that headed to Washington D.C. during the economic depression of March 1894, to demand job creation. Coxey also led a later march in 1914.

84.31   Epworth League] Organization formed in 1889 by the Methodist Episcopal Church in Cleveland, Ohio, to encourage and train young people in churchmanship and religious life.

85.11   Vincent O'Sullivan] Poet, essayist, and fiction writer (1868–1940). He was born in New York but spent much of his life in Europe, and was a friend of Oscar Wilde and Aubrey Beardsley. His books included *Poems* (1896), *The Houses of Sin* (1897), *Human Affairs* (1907), and *Sentiment and Other Stories* (1913).

85.33   Upton Sinclair] Novelist (1878–1968) who became famous with the publication of *The Jungle*, an exposé of conditions in the Chicago stockyards, in 1906. (It was originally serialized in the Socialist newspaper *The Appeal to Reason*.) His many other books included *The Metropolis* (1908), *King Coal* (1917), *Oil!* (1927), and *The Wet Parade* (1931).

86.11   Ernest Poole] Novelist (1880–1950), author of *The Voice of the Street* (1906), *The Harbor* (1915), *The Family* (1917), *His Second Wife* (1918), and many other books. He was a war correspondent in Germany, France, and Russia during World War I.

86.31   I.W.W.] Industrial Workers of the World, popularly known as "Wobblies," international labor union founded in Chicago in 1905 and reaching its peak of influence in the 1920s.

88.21   Binét test] Intelligence test devised by Alfred Binet (1857–1911), French psychologist, along with Theodore Simon (1873–1961), to evaluate child development. The Simon-Binet scale became the standard intelligence test used in the United States during the 1920s, with their term "I.Q." ("intelligence quotient") entering the vocabulary.

89.4–5   Sir Oliver Lodge] See note 35.37.

89.13   Cagliostro] Count Alessandro di Cagliostro, pseudonym of Giuseppe Balsamo (1743–1795), Italian adventurer posing as a freemason, physician, and alchemist. He engaged in many intrigues and sold amulets and elixirs of youth throughout Europe before being arrested by the Inquisition in 1789. He died in prison.

90.27   Gustav le Bon] Gustave Le Bon, French sociologist (1841–1931), author of *La Psychologie des foules* (*The Crowd: A Study of the Popular Mind*, 1895).

91.15–16   Elsie Clews Parsons] Anthropologist and sociologist (1875–1941), whose studies of Native American cultures included *Hopi and Zuni Ceremonialism* (1933) and *Pueblo Indian Religion* (1939). Her earlier works included *The Family* (1906), *The Old-Fashioned Woman* (1913), *Fear and Conventionality* (1914), *Social Freedom* (1915), and *Social Rule* (1916).

92.19   Geheimrat] German court title equivalent to privy councillor.

98.15   Bleaseism]   Extreme populism and white supremacism of the sort identified with Coleman Livingston Blease (1868–1942), South Carolina governor (1910–14) and later senator.

98.23   The Mann Act]   The White-Slave Traffic Act of 1910 addressed human trafficking for prostitution and prohibited the transportation of females across state lines for "immoral purposes." It was named after its sponsor, James Robert Mann (1856–1922), Republican congressman from Illinois.

99.38   Alfred Adler]   Viennese psychologist (1870–1937), a member of Freud's circle who subsequently broke away to form his own school. His books include *The Theory and Practice of Individual Psychology* (1918).

101.28   Griswold]   See note 9.7–8.

102.12–13   Edmund Clarence Stedman]   See note 49.37.

102.13   Donald G. Mitchell]   See note 67.24.

102.14–15   William Winter]   Drama critic (1836–1917), reviewer for the *New York Tribune* from 1865 to 1909. His writings were collected in *Other Days* (1908), *Old Friends* (1909), *Shakespeare on the Stage* (1911–13), and *The Wallet of Time* (1913).

102.19–20   Baalam's ass]   See Numbers 22:1–35.

102.26   Charles Eliot Norton]   Author and educator (1827–1908), professor of art history at Harvard, 1873–97. He was a founder of *The Nation* (1865) and a frequent contributor to *The Atlantic Monthly* and other publications. He was a translator of Dante and wrote prolifically on art and literature.

102.29   Godkin]   Edwin Lawrence Godkin (1831–1902), founder and editor of *The Nation*.

102.34   *Godey's Lady's Book*]   American monthly magazine, 1830–98, influential on taste and fashion. It was edited from 1837 to 1877 by Sarah Josepha Hale.

103.18   *McClure's*]   Literary and political magazine founded in 1884 by muckraking journalist Samuel Sidney McClure (1857–1949) and John Sanborn Philips (1861–1949). Its contributors included Jack London, O. Henry, Lincoln Steffens, and Ida Tarbell. It ceased publication in 1929.

103.31–32   *Everybody's*]   Popular American magazine, 1899–1928.

103.34   *Munsey's*]   See note 32.13–14.

103.38–39   John Brisben Walker . . . *Cosmopolitan*]   Walker (1847–1931) purchased *Cosmopolitan* (originally a conservative family publication) in 1889 and began publishing work by well-known authors such as Mark Twain, Henry James, Rudyard Kipling, Willa Cather, and Theodore Dreiser. Walker sold the magazine in 1905 to William Randolph Hearst.

104.9   Argosy]   Frank Munsey founded *Argosy* in December 1882, and by 1894 had begun to transform it into what was later recognized as the first of the pulp magazines. In 1920 it merged with another Munsey publication to become *Argosy All-Story Weekly*.

104.27–28   Street & Smith]   New York publisher eventually specializing in pulp novels and magazines, founded in 1855.

105.3   Steffenses]   Lincoln Steffens (1866–1936), American journalist and editor at *McClure's* (1902–06), and both *American* and *Everybody's* (1906–11). He wrote *The Shame of the Cities* (1904), *The Struggle for Self-Government* (1906), and *The Autobiography of Lincoln Steffens* (1931).

105.3   Tarbells]   Ida Minerva Tarbell (1857–1944), journalist and editor who worked at *McClure's* (1894–1906) and *American* (1906–1915). She was best known for her exposé *The History of the Standard Oil Company* (1904).

105.3   Phillipses]   Magazine publisher John S. Phillips (1861–1949), co-founder with S. S. McClure of *McClure's* and with Ida Tarbell of *American*, which he edited from 1906 to 1915.

105.11   Aldrich]   Nelson Wilmarth Aldrich (1841–1915), financier and politician. He served as Republican senator from Rhode Island, 1881–1911, and exerted great influence on all matters of financial and monetary policy.

105.11   Boss Cox]   James Middleton Cox (1870–1957), newspaper publisher and politician. He served as Ohio congressman and governor of Ohio (1913–15, 1917–21); he was the Democratic presidential nominee in 1920, losing to Warren G. Harding. He published the *Dayton Daily News* and founded the newspaper company Cox Enterprises.

105.11   Gas Addicks]   John Edward Addicks (1841–1919), industrialist who became wealthy in the natural gas business. His struggle with Henry DuPont for political power in Delaware was marked by bribery and corruption.

105.14   Ben B. Lindsey]   See note 35.16.

105.14   Francis J. Heney]   Lawyer (1859–1937); as deputy district attorney of San Francisco, secured the conviction of the mayor for corruption in 1908.

105.14   Governor Folk]   Joseph Wingate Folk (1869–1923), lawyer and politician, nicknamed "Holy Joe" for his exposure of municipal corruption while serving as prosecutor in St. Louis, Missouri. He served as governor of Missouri, 1905–9.

107.33   Simon Magnus]   More usually Simon Magus, he appears as Simon in Acts 8:9–24, and was regarded in some early Christian sources as the founder of all heresies.

108.24   *scandalum magnatum*]   In early English law, defamation of high personages of the realm.

110.9–10   Ramsden Balmforth] English Unitarian minister active in South Africa; he was the author of *The New Reformation and Its Relation to Moral and Social Problems* (1893) and *The New Testament in the Light of the Higher Criticism* (1905).

112.4   General Booth] William Booth, known as General Booth (1829–1912), English religious leader and founder of the Salvation Army.

112.4   Mrs. Pankhurst] Emmeline Pankhurst (1858–1928), English suffragist, founder of the Women's Social and Political Union in 1898, which became notorious for its violent tactics.

114.40   Hermann Grimm] Scholar and critic (1828–1901), author of studies of Michelangelo and Goethe.

114.40   Tyndall] John Tyndall (1820–1893), British physicist.

115.6   the New Thought] Spiritual movement originating in the U.S. in the late nineteenth century, emphasizing positive thinking, healing, and personal power.

116.13   Havelock Ellises] Henry Havelock Ellis (1859–1939), English scientist and man of letters who studied the psychology and sociology of sex. His books included *The New Spirit* (1890), *Man and Woman* (1894), and the seven-volume *Studies in the Psychology of Sex* (1897–1928).

117.6   Margaret of Navarre] Queen of Navarre (1492–1549), a patron of Humanism in arts and letters, and author of the story collection *The Heptameron*, published in 1559.

117.6–7   Balzac's "Droll Tales"] *Contes drôlatiques* (1832–37), collection of ribald stories by Honore de Balzac, written in a pastiche of medieval French.

118.20–21   "The Repeal of Reticence"] Essay by Agnes Repplier, published in the *Atlantic Monthly*, March 1914; Repplier objected to "the obsession of sex."

118.26   Forel] Auguste Henri Forel (1848–1941), Swiss entomologist, neurologist, and psychiatrist; he contributed the early sexological studies *The Sexual Question* (1905) and *Sexual Ethics* (1906).

118.26   Sylvanus Stall] Lutheran minister (1847–1915), author of books on sex such as *What A Young Boy Ought to Know* and *What a Young Woman Ought to Know*.

118.26   Reginald Wright Kauffman] American journalist and author (1877–1959). His books included *The House of Bondage* (1910), *The Girl That Goes Wrong* (1911), and other works.

118.32   Press Cuttings] Play (1909) by George Bernard Shaw.

119.25   Brieux's "Les Avariés"]   See note 63.13.

119.27–28   Frank Wedekind's "Frühlings Erwachen"]   *Spring's Awakening* (1891) by Frank Wedekind (1864–1918), on the theme of youthful sexuality; see also note 320.36.

119.34–35   Le Mariage d'Olympe . . . Damaged Goods]   See notes 62.34–35 and 63.13.

124.2   George Jean Nathan]   Drama critic (1882–1958), co-editor with Mencken of *The Smart Set*, 1914–24, and in 1924 co-founder with Mencken of *The American Mercury*, of which he was co-editor until 1930. His many books included *Another Book on the Theater* (1915), *Mr. George Jean Nathan Presents* (1917), *Bottoms Up: An Application of the Slapstick to Satire* (1917), *The Popular Theatre* (1918), *The Critic and the Drama* (1922), *Art of the Night* (1928), *Testament of a Critic* (1931), and *Encyclopaedia of the Theatre* (1940).

124.7–8   Drama League of America]   Organization founded in Chicago in 1910 to stimulate interest in drama and support worthy plays. By 1926, thirty-seven local chapters existed across the country.

124.13   Captain of Köpenick]   Friedrich Wilhelm Voigt (1848-1922), German impostor who masqueraded as a Prussian officer in a 1906 incident which became internationally famous.

124.19   Gordon Craig]   Edward Henry Gordon Craig (1872–1966), English theater designer whose theories exerted great influence on the British and American stage. He was founder and editor of the journal *The Mask*, and author of *The Art of the Theater* (1905).

124.16   Archers]   See note 13.2.

124.16   Walkleys]   Arthur Bingham Walkley (1855–1926), English drama critic for the London *Times* and other publications. His books included *Playhouse Impressions* (1892) and *Dramatic Criticism* (1903).

124.18   Maeterlinck]   Maurice Maeterlinck (1862–1949), Belgian poet and playwright associated with the Symbolist movement. His plays included *The Intruder* (1890), *Pelléas and Mélisande* (1892), *Monna Vanna* (1902), and *The Blue Bird* (1909).

124.22   Florenz Ziegfeld]   American theatrical impresario (1867–1932) famous for his series of revues *The Ziegfeld Follies* (1907–31).

124.24   Belasco]   David Belasco (1853–1931), American playwright and theater producer involved in more than a hundred Broadway productions. As a producer he was notable for technical advances in lighting and stage design. His plays included *Madame Butterfly* (1900) and *The Girl of the Golden West* (1905).

124.24   Augustus Thomas] American playwright (1857–1934) known for his use of American backgrounds in such plays as *Alabama* (1891), *In Mizzoura* (1893), *The Witching Hour* (1907), and *The Copperhead* (1918).

124.24   Mrs. Fiske] Minnie Maddern Fiske (1865–1932), American actress who promoted realism and Ibsen's plays on the New York stage.

125.30   Alan Dale] Pseudonym of Alfred J. Cohen (1861–1928), English-born writer who became drama critic for the New York *Journal* and the New York *American*. He was known for his interviews with theatrical celebrities.

126.16   Benedetto Croce] Italian philosopher (1866–1952), author of *Aesthetics* (1912).

126.16   J. E. Spingarn] See note 3.33.

127.2   Avery Hopwood] Broadway playwright (1882–1928) whose works included *The Gold Diggers* (1919) and *Getting Gertie's Garter* (1921, with Wilson Collison).

127.3   Ludwig Thoma] See note 63.40.

127.3   Lord Dunsany] Edward John Moreton Drax Plunkett, known as Lord Dunsany (1878–1957), Irish poet, dramatist, and story writer. His plays included *The Glittering Gate* (1909), *The Gods of the Mountain* (1909), and *A Night at an Inn* (1916).

127.3   Sasha Guitry] Sacha Guitry (1885–1957), French actor and dramatist who later wrote and produced motion pictures.

127.3   Lothar Schmidt] German playwright best known for *Only a Dream* (1909), filmed twice by Ernst Lubitsch as *The Marriage Circle* (1924) and *One Hour with You* (1932).

127.4   Ferenz Molnar] Ferenc Molnar (1878–1952), Hungarian playwright and fiction writer. His plays included *Liliom* (1909), *The Guardsman* (1910), *The Swan* (1920), and *The Play's the Thing* (1926).

127.4   Roberto Bracco] Italian playwright and novelist (1862–1943), author of *The Hidden Spring* (1907).

127.4   Gerhart Hauptmann] German playwright (1862–1946), author of *The Weavers* (1892), *The Beaver Coat* (1893), *The Sunken Bell* (1896), and many other works. He won the Nobel Prize in Literature in 1912.

127.34   *Ambrosia artemisiaefolia*] Ragweed.

127.40   William Winter] See note 102.14–15.

129.5   Metcalfe] James S. Metcalfe, drama critic for *Life*. He brought a lawsuit against the Theatre Managers' Assocation in 1906, claiming he had been barred from their theaters.

130.4–5   Max Reinhardt]   Theatrical producer (1873–1943) who achieved fame in Berlin and Vienna for his elaborate anti-naturalistic style. His production of *The Miracle* played in New York in 1923, and he emigrated to the United States in 1937.

130.10–11   Eleanor Gates]   American writer (1875–1951), author of the play and novel *The Poor Little Rich Girl* (1913).

130.11   Clare Kummer]   American playwright and lyricist (1873–1943), author of *The Opera Ball* (1912), *A Successful Calamity* (1917), *The Rescuing Angel* (1917), and other comedies and musicals.

130.20   Dr. Frank Crane]   See note 25.12.

131.9   Granville Barker]   Harley Granville-Barker (1877–1946), English theater manager, actor, and playwright, author of *The Voysey Inheritance* (1904) and *The Madras House* (1910).

131.12   Richard Burtonism]   Richard Eugene Burton (1861–1940), poet and critic, author of *From the Book of Life* (1909) and *Masters of the British Novel* (1909).

134.15   Mitchell Kennerley]   American publisher (1878–1950).

134.20   One Man]   Novel by Robert Steele (pseudonym of R. A. Lindsay), based on the author's experiences as a convicted criminal, published in 1915.

135.14   Thackeray's Louis XIV]   See "Meditations at Versailles," *The Paris Sketch Book* (1840).

141.18   Science and Health]   *Science and Health with Key to the Scriptures* (1875) by Mary Baker Eddy.

141.36   E. Phillips Oppenheim]   English novelist (1866–1946), prolific author of thrillers and adventure stories such as *Enoch Strone* (1901), *The Malefactor* (1906), and *The Great Impersonation* (1920).

141.38–39   The Scarlet Plague . . . The Little Lady of the Big House]   Novels by Jack London, published in 1912 and 1916 respectively.

143.9   Peruna]   See note 80.24.

143.9   Mandrake Pills]   Nineteenth-century patent medicine for the alleviation of liver complaints and other conditions, introduced in 1836 by Dr. Joseph H. Schenck.

143.9   Fletcherism]   Named after Horace Fletcher (1849–1919), American nutritionist who touted the health benefits of the thorough mastication of food.

143.10   The Emmanuel Movement]   Practice of medical psychotherapy or religious healing introduced in 1906 by the Emmanuel Church in Boston, Massachusetts.

143.10   the New Thought]   See note 115.6.

143.11   Edwin Markham]   American poet (1852–1940), author of *The Man with the Hoe* (1899), *Lincoln and Other Poems* (1901), and *The Star of Araby* (1937). He was an adherent in the 1870s of Thomas Lake Harris's spiritualist movement, the Brotherhood of the New Life.

143.11–12   Ella Wheeler Wilcox]   See note 54.12.

143.12–13   Will Levington Comfort]   American novelist (1880–1932), author of adventure novels such as *Routledge Rides Alone* (1910); his theosophical speculations were expounded in *The Will Levington Comfort Letters* (1920–21).

145.32   Mother Tingley]   Katherine Augusta Tingley (1847–1929), spiritualist leader in New York City, later head of the Universal Brotherhood, a theosophical movement.

145.33   Edward Bok]   Dutch-born American writer and journalist (1863–1930), editor of *The Ladies' Home Journal*, 1889–1919. He won the Pulitzer Prize for his autobiography *The Americanization of Edward Bok* (1920).

145.33   the Archangel Eddy]   Mary Baker Eddy (1821–1910), founder of Christian Science.

148.37   Rufus W. Griswold]   See note 9.7–8.

149.5–6   James Harlan]   Politician (1820–1899), U.S. senator from Iowa and Secretary of the Interior, 1865–66.

PREJUDICES: SECOND SERIES

154.24   *Waldhorn*]   Hunting horn.

154.26   the elder Channing]   William Ellery Channing (1780–1842), Unitarian minister whose sermons and writing had wide intellectual influence. His *Remarks on American Literature* appeared in 1830.

154.27–28   Samuel Lorenzo Knapp]   American writer (1783–1838), author of *Lectures on American Literature, with Remarks on Some Passages in American History* (1829).

154.29   Mores]   See note 7.31.

154.29   Brownells]   See note 4.17.

154.29   Phelpses]   See note 4.14–15.

154.30   Mabies]   See note 7.15.

154.30   Brander Mathewses]   American scholar and playwright (1852–

1929), known for his studies of dramatic literature including *The Development of the Drama* (1904), *Shakspere as a Playwright* (1913), *A Book About the Theater* (1916), and *Principles of Playmaking* (1919).

155.13   Van Wyck Brooks]   Literary critic (1886–1963), author of *America's Coming-of-Age* (1916), *Letters and Leadership* (1918), *The Ordeal of Mark Twain* (1920), *The Pilgrimage of Henry James* (1925), and many other studies.

155.29   Adam Forepaugh]   American entrepreneur (1831–1890) who operated a circus from 1865 to 1890.

155.33–34   Barrett Wendell]   American scholar (1855–1921), professor at Harvard and author of *A Literary History of America* (1900).

155.34   *Aufklärung*]   Enlightenment.

156.10–11   J. G. Brainard]   John Gardiner Brainard (1795–1828), New England lawyer, editor and poet. Poe's essay, "A Few Words About Brainard," appeared in *Graham's Magazine* in 1842.

158.21   Richard Harding Davis]   Journalist and novelist (1864–1916). His novels included *Soldiers of Fortune* (1897). His war reporting was collected in many volumes including *Cuba in War Time* (1897), *The Cuban and Porto Rican Campaigns* (1898), *With Both Armies in South Africa* (1900), and *Notes of a War Correspondent* (1910).

158.22   Hamilton Wright Mabie's "white list"]   See note 7.15.

159.10   Judge Grant]   Robert Grant (1852–1940), jurist and author. His novels, often centered on social issues, included *An Average Man* (1883), *Unleavened Bread* (1900), *The Undercurrent* (1904), and *The High Priestess* (1915). He served in 1927 on the commission which ruled that the trial of Sacco and Vanzetti had been fairly conducted.

159.10   Alice Brown]   New Hampshire-born writer (1857–1948), author of *Fools of Nature* (1887), *The Rose of Hope* (1896), *The Mannerings* (1906), and many other books.

159.12   Woodberry]   George Edward Woodberry (1855–1930), Massachusetts-born poet and scholar, author of *The North Shore Watch* (1890) and other volumes of verse; his *Collected Poems* appeared in 1903. He was the author of numerous literary studies including *Makers of Literature* (1900) and *Nathaniel Hawthorne* (1902).

159.12   the elder Johnson]   Robert Underwood Johnson (1853–1937), American man of letters, author of *The Winter Hour* (1891) and *Poems of War and Peace* (1916). He served as U.S. Ambassador to Italy, 1920–21. His son Owen McMahon Johnson (1878–1952) wrote novels and short stories.

159.13   Crothers]   Samuel McChord Crothers (1857–1927), Unitarian Universalist minister whose essays were collected in numerous volumes, among them *The Understanding Heart* (1903), *By the Christmas Fire* (1908), and *Humanly Speaking* (1912).

159.13   Miss Repplier]   See note 31.24.

159.15   Babbitt]   Irving Babbitt (1865–1933), American scholar who, with Paul Elmer More, founded the New Humanism movement; he was the author of *The New Laokoön* (1910), *The Masters of Modern French Criticism* (1912), *Rousseau and Romanticism* (1919), and other works.

159.26   *Augenmusik*]   "Eye music": presentation of a musical score in symbolic fashion (i.e., a love song in which the staves are heart-shaped), seen only by the performer.

160.13   Henry Van Dyke]   See note 55.19.

160.26   Boynton]   Percy Holmes Boynton (1875–1946), professor of English at the University of Chicago, author of *American Poetry* (1918), *Some Contemporary Americans* (1924), *The Challenge of Modern Criticism* (1931), and other works.

160.26   Perry]   Bliss Perry (1860–1954), professor of English at Williams, Princeton, and Harvard, and editor of *The Atlantic Monthly*, 1899–1909. He published many literary studies including biographies of Whitman, Whittier, and Emerson.

161.20   the Becker case]   Charles Becker (1870–1915), a New York City police officer, was tried, convicted, and executed for ordering the murder of the gambler Herman Rosenthal. He was the first American police officer to receive the death penalty. Some later writers have suggested that he was wrongly convicted.

161.25–26   *ordentlichen Professoren*]   Full professors.

161.27   Shelburne Essays]   See note 7.31.

161.30   Donald G. Mitchell]   See note 67.24.

162.5   *Privat-Dozenten*]   See note 7.7.

162.19   Up in Mabel's Room]   Farce (1919) by Wilson Collison and Otto Harbach.

162.19   Ben-Hur]   Dramatization by William W. Young, first produced in 1899, of Lew Wallace's novel *Ben-Hur: A Tale of the Christ* (1880).

162.20   The Witching Hour]   Play (1907) by Augustus Thomas involving the themes of telepathy and hypnosis.

162.39   Lewes]   George Henry Lewes (1817–1878), English philosopher and literary and dramatic critic who founded and edited *The Fortnightly Review*. He was the author of *Physiology of Common Life* (1859), *The Problems of Life and Mind* (1874–79), and *Actors and Acting* (1875).

163.2 Saintsbury] George Saintsbury (1845–1933), English critic and journalist. His many books included *Short History of French Literature* (1882), *Essays in English Literature* (1890–95), *History of Nineteenth Century Literature* (1896), *History of English Prose Rhythm* (1912), and *The English Novel* (1913).

163.21 Zoë Akins] (1886–1958) American poet and playwright. Her plays included *Déclassée* (1919), *Papa* (1919), *Daddy's Gone A-Hunting* (1921), and *The Greeks Had a Word for It* (1930). She won the Pulitzer Prize for *The Old Maid* (1935), based on Edith Wharton's novella.

163.34 Sherman] See note 4.19–20.

164.2–3 Robert Underwood Johnson] See note 159.12.

164.3 Owen Wister] Novelist (1860–1938), author of *The Virginian* (1902).

164.3 James Lane Allen] Novelist (1849–1925), best known for his local color stories set in Kentucky, including *A Kentucky Cardinal* (1894) and *The Choir Invisible* (1897).

164.3–4 George E. Woodberry] See note 159.12.

164.4 William Roscoe Thayer] American author (1859–1923) of *Theodore Roosevelt: An Intimate Biography* (1919) and works on Italian history.

164.5 Margaret Deland] Novelist (1857–1945) whose work evoked life in a small Pennsylvania town; author of *The Awakening of Helena Richie* (1906), *The Iron Woman* (1911), and *The Rising Tide* (1916).

164.5–6 Mary Johnston] American author (1870–1936) of romantic fiction set against the backdrop of Virginia history; best known for *To Have and to Hold* (1900).

164.8 Brian Hooker] American academic and poet (1880–1946), noted for his 1923 translation of Edmond Rostand's *Cyrano de Bergerac*.

164.8 George Sterling] American poet (1869–1926), leader of an artistic and literary circle in Carmel, California; a close friend of Mencken. His books included *A Wine of Wizardry* (1909), *The House of Orchids* (1911), and *The Caged Eagle* (1916).

164.9–10 "Chimmie Fadden" Townsend] See note 68.34.

164.18 *héliogabalisme*] A favorite term of Mencken's. In *In Defense of Women* (1922) he defines it as "the fascination of what is strange, the charm of the unlike."

164.20 Palmerism of Torquemada] A. Mitchell Palmer (1872–1936), U.S. attorney general, 1919–21, initiated in November 1919 a series of raids directed against members of radical groups and others suspected of subversive activities; thousands were arrested, and ultimately 556 individuals were deported.

Tomás de Torquemada (1420–1498), a Dominican friar, was Inquisitor General of Spain, 1483–98.

164.40   Schnitzler] Arthur Schnitzler (1862–1931), Austrian dramatist and novelist, author of the plays *Anatol* (1893), *Liebelei* (1895), and *Reigen* (1900).

165.33   Miss Reese] See note 55.40.

165.33   Miss Teasdale] American poet (1884–1933), author of *Rivers to the Sea* (1915), *Love Songs* (1917), *Flame and Shadow* (1920), and *Dark of the Moon* (1926). Following her suicide her late poems were collected in *Strange Victory* (1933).

165.33   John McClure] See note 56.5.

165.35   Robert Loveman] American poet (1864–1923) whose poem "The Rain Song" ("It isn't raining rain to me, / It's raining daffodils") was widely anthologized.

165.37   Rita Wellman] Playwright (1890–1965), a member of the Provincetown Players. Her plays included *Barbarians* (1916), *The Rib-Person* (1917), and *The Gentile Wife* (1919).

165.39   Dr. Baker's *Ibsenfabrik*] George Pierce Baker (1866–1935) founded the Harvard Dramatic Club in 1908 and the 47 Workshop (his "Ibsen factory") dedicated to performing plays by his students. He moved to Yale in 1925, where he was instrumental in founding the Yale School of Drama. Baker's students included Eugene O'Neill, George Abbott, Thomas Wolfe, and Sidney Howard.

166.18   Agnes Repplier] See note 31.24.

167.9   Rex Beach] Novelist (1877–1949), author of adventure stories including *The Spoilers* (1906) and *The Iron Trail* (1913).

167.9   Emerson Hough] Novelist and journalist (1857–1923), author of *The Mississippi Bubble* (1902), *The Sagebrusher* (1919), and *The Covered Wagon* (1922). He wrote many articles on national parks and wildlife preservation.

167.11–12   Cyrus Townsend Brady] Novelist (1861–1920), author of many historical romances and popular histories including *Indian Fights and Fighters* (1904) and *Three Daughters of the Confederacy* (1905).

167.12   Mary Roberts Rinehart] American fiction writer and playwright (1876–1958), author of many mystery novels including *The Circular Staircase* (1908), *Where There's a Will* (1912), and *The Case of Jennie Brice* (1913). With Avery Hopwood she wrote the long-running mystery play *The Bat* (1920).

167.17   Dr. Frank Crane] See note 25.12.

167.17   Orison Swett Marden] See note 25.12.

167.17–18   Porter Emerson Browne] Playwright (1879–1934), author of *A Fool There Was* (1908) and *The Spendthrift* (1910).

167.18   Gerald Stanley Lee] Clergyman, lecturer, and writer (1862–1944), author of *The Lost Art of Reading* (1902), *Crowds: A Moving-Picture of Democracy* (1915), and *Seven Studies in Self-Command* (1921).

167.18   E. S. Martin] See note 68.34.

167.18–19   Ella Wheeler Wilcox] See note 54.12.

167.19   Newell Dwight Hillis] See note 80.28–29.

167.20   Harold Bell Wright] See note 83.17.

167.20   Eleanor H. Porter] Novelist (1868–1920), author of *Cross Currents* (1907), *Pollyanna* (1913), and *Pollyanna Grows Up* (1915).

167.20–21   Gene Stratton-Porter] Novelist and naturalist (1868–1924), author of such books as *The Song of the Cardinal* (1902), *Freckles* (1904), *A Girl of the Limberlost* (1909), and *Friends in Feathers* (1917).

167.30   Corra Harris] Corra White Harris (1869–1935), Georgia writer best known for her novel *A Circuit Rider's Wife* (1910).

167.30–31   Gouverneur Morris] Novelist and screenwriter (1876–1953), author of *The Pagan's Progress* (1904), *The Penalty* (1913), and other works.

167.31   Harold MacGrath] Novelist (1871–1932), author of popular romances such as *Arms and the Woman* (1899), *Hearts and Masks* (1905), and *Half a Rogue* (1906). He wrote the scenario of the silent serial *The Perils of Pauline*.

167.35   Zona Gale] Wisconsin writer (1874–1938) known for stories collected in *Friendship Village* (1908) and *Yellow Gentians and Blue* (1927), and for novels including *Birth* (1918) and *Miss Lulu Bett* (1920).

167.36   Montague Glass] English-born playwright and story writer (1877–1934), known for stories about Jewish businessmen dramatized as *Potash and Perlmutter* (1913), *Business Before Pleasure* (1917), and *His Honor Abe Potash* (1919).

168.3   Henry Milner Rideout] Maine-born novelist (1877–1927), author of *Admiral's Light* (1907), *Dragon's Blood* (1909), *The Twisted Foot* (1910), and other works.

168.4   Chester Bailey Fernald] Fiction writer (1869–1938), author of the story collections *The Cat and the Cherub* (1896) and *Chinatown Stories* (1899), both set in San Francisco's Chinatown.

168.4–5   Will Levington Comfort] See note 143.12–13.

168.5   Stephen French Whitman] Novelist (1880–1950), author of *Predes-*

tined: A Novel of New York Life (1910), *The Isle of Life* (1913), and other works.

168.5 James Hopper] Novelist and journalist (1876–1956) who settled in Carmel, California.

168.6 Harry Leon Wilson] Fiction writer (1867–1939) best known for *Ruggles of Red Gap* (1915) and *Merton of the Movies* (1922). He was editor of *Puck*, 1896–1902.

168.12 Louis Joseph Vance] Novelist (1879–1933), best known for *The Lone Wolf* (1914) and other novels of intrigue featuring the series character Michael Lanyard.

168.12 Rupert Hughes] Historian, novelist, playwright, and filmmaker (1872–1956), author of many novels including *Excuse Me!* (1911), *Souls for Sale* (1922), and *Destiny* (1925). He was the uncle of Howard Hughes.

168.13 George Bronson-Howard] Writer and journalist (1844–1922), reporter for the Baltimore *American* and other newspapers, author of novels including *Scars of the Southern Seas* (1907) and *Norroy, Diplomatic Agent* (1920), and plays including *The Only Law* (1909, with Wilson Mizner). He committed suicide in Los Angeles where he was working as a scenarist for Universal.

168.13–14 David Graham Phillips] See note 77.21.

168.14 Elbert Hubbard] Writer and publisher (1856–1915), founder of the Roycroft Press, an active figure in the Arts and Crafts movement, and editor of *The Philistine*, a monthly magazine in which he published humorous and philosophical musings. He died in the sinking of the *Lusitania* on May 7, 1915.

169.11 Marie Corelli] Pseudonym of Mary Mackay (1855–1924), immensely popular English writer, whose bestselling novels, sometimes on spiritualist themes, included *A Romance of Two Worlds* (1886), *The Soul of Lilith* (1892), *The Sorrows of Satan* (1895), and *The Master Christian* (1900).

169.11 Elinor Glyn] See note 42.20.

169.11–12 E. Phillips Oppenheim] See note 141.36.

169.12 William Le Quex] William Le Queux (1864–1927), Anglo-French journalist and author of thrillers and futuristic fantasies, including *The Great War in England in 1897* (1894) and *The Invasion of 1910* (1906).

169.12 Hall Caine] See note 35.18.

169.31 Selznicks, Goldfishes, Zukors] Movie moguls Lewis J. Selznick (1870–1933), Samuel Goldwyn (1882–1974), who was known until 1918 by his given name Samuel Goldfish, and Adolph Zukor (1873–1976).

170.15   Pearl White]   Silent movie actress (1889–1938) whose starring role in the cliffhanging serial *The Perils of Pauline* (1914) was followed by similar roles in *The Exploits of Elaine* (1915), *The Iron Claw* (1916), and *The Fatal Ring* (1917).

170.15   Theda Bara]   Silent movie actress (1855–1955), born Theodosia Burr Goodman, and known as The Vamp following her starring role in *A Fool There Was* (1915). Her other films included *Carmen* (1915), *Cleopatra* (1917), and *Madame Du Barry* (1918).

170.21   McCutcheons]   George Barr McCutcheon (1866–1928), American newspaper editor and writer of popular novels including *Brewster's Millions* (1902) and *A Fool and His Money* (1913).

170.29   George Moore]   Irish author (1852–1933), author of *A Mummer's Wife* (1885), *Confessions of a Young Man* (1886), *Esther Waters* (1896), and many other realist novels.

170.29   Hugh Walpole]   English novelist (1884–1941) whose many books included *Fortitude* (1913), *The Dark Forest* (1916), *The Cathedral* (1922), and *Rogue Herries* (1930).

170.30   E. F. Benson]   Edward Frederic Bensen (1867–1940), novelist and story writer, author of works variously satiric, melodramatic, and fantastic, including the series of comic novels featuring Miss Mapp and Lucia, beginning with *Queen Lucia* (1920).

170.37   saleratus]   See note 80.23.

173.33–34   Andrieff's "Silence"]   Novella by Leonid Andreyev (1871–1919), published in English translation in 1910.

173.34   Sudermann's "Das Sterbelied"]   "The Song of Death," short story by Hermann Sudermann (1857–1928).

174.12   Freneau]   Philip Freneau (1752–1832), American poet of French Huguenot descent, author of *A Poem on the Rising Glory of America* (1772), *American Liberty* (1775), and *The British Prison-Ship* (1781), a long poem based on his wartime imprisonment by the British. Many further collections followed, including *The Poems of Philip Freneau* (1786) and *A Collection of Poems on American Affairs* (1815).

174.14   H. R. Haweis]   Hugh Reginald Haweis (1838–1901), English clergyman and writer.

174.21   Bancroft]   George Bancroft (1800–1891), American historian, studied in Heidelburg, Göttingen, and Berlin, and later returned to Germany as U.S. ambassador, 1867–74. His multivolume *History of the United States* was published between 1834 and 1874.

174.40   John C. van Dyke]   John Charles van Dyke (1856–1932), American art historian, author of *Principles of Art* (1887), *How to Judge a Picture*

(1888), *Art for Art's Sake* (1893), *A History of Painting* (1894), and other works. *American Painting and Its Tradition* was publishing in 1919.

175.7 Frank Harris] British-born American author (1854–1931) whose books included *The Bomb* (1908), a novel; *The Man Shakespeare and His Tragic Love Story* (1909); *The Women of Shakespeare* (1911); *Contemporary Portraits* (1915–27); *Oscar Wilde, His Life and Confessions* (1916); and the long-banned autobiography *My Life and Loves* (1922–27).

175.7 Vincent O'Sullivan] See note 85.11.

175.7–8 Herman Scheffauer] Herman George Scheffauer (1878–1927), San Francisco-born poet and playwright, an associate of Ambrose Bierce and George Sterling. His poetry collection *Looms of Life* was published in 1908. He moved to Germany in 1910 and committed suicide in 1927 after murdering his female secretary.

175.8 Henry B. Fuller] Henry Blake Fuller (1857–1929), American novelist whose novels of Chicago included *The Cliff-Dwellers* (1893), *With the Procession* (1895), and *On the Stairs* (1918).

175.8 Stuart Merrill] American poet (1863–1915) educated and later resident in France; most of his work was written in French, including the collections *Les Fastes* (1891), *Une Voix dans la Foule* (1909), and *Poèmes 1887–1897*. He was associated with the literary circle of Stéphane Mallarmé.

175.14 *The Little Review*] Literary quarterly, 1914–29, founded by Margaret Anderson and edited by her with Jane Heap. It was among the most influential magazines of its time, publishing W. B. Yeats, Ernest Hemingway, T. S. Eliot, Djuna Barnes, and Hart Crane. Its serialization of James Joyce's *Ulysses*, 1918–21, led to the editors being fined for obscenity.

175.19 Ben Hecht] Writer and journalist (1894–1964), a reporter for the *Chicago Daily News* (1914–1923), and author of *Erik Dorn* (1921), 1001 *Afternoons in Chicago* (1923), and *Count Bruga* (1926). He wrote the play *The Front Page* (1928) with Charles MacArthur and had a long and successful career as a Hollywood screenwriter, his credits including *Scarface* (1932), *Nothing Sacred* (1937), *Wuthering Heights* (1939), and *Notorious* (1946).

175.19–20 Elsa von Freytag-Loringhoven] Poet and artist (1874–1927), born Elsa Hildegard Plötz in present-day Poland; she emigrated to the United States in 1910 and married the Baron von Freytag-Loringhoven in 1913. Her poems were published in *The Little Review* and other magazines; she became notorious for her outlandish appearance and extreme behavior. She returned to Europe in 1923 and died of asphyxiation in her Paris apartment three years later.

177.5 Flexner] See note 45.26.

177.5 Loeb] See note 45.27.

177.6   Carrel] See note 45.27.

177.14   D. C. Gilman] Daniel Coit Gilman (1831–1908), American educator and first president of Johns Hopkins, 1875–1901, and the Carnegie Institution in Washington D.C., 1901–4.

177.26   The 'Genius'] Novel (1915) by Dreiser; it was withdrawn from sale by the publisher after the New York Society for the Suppression of Vice declared it lewd and profane. A review of the book by Stuart P. Sherman in *The Nation* attributed its defects in part to Dreiser's German heritage.

179.5   Joyce Kilmer] American poet (1886–1918), author of *Trees and Other Poems* (1914); he enlisted to fight in World War I and was killed near Seringes, France.

179.16   Coxey] See note 87.34.

179.16   Dr. Mary Walker] Mary Edwards Walker (1832–1919), American physician and advocate of women's rights.

179.16–17   George Francis Train] Businessman and author (1829–1904), promoter of the Union Pacific Railroad who became embroiled in the Crédit Mobilier scandal of 1872. He referred to himself as "Citizen Train" and was noted for his eccentric behavior and espousal of a number of causes. His books included *Young America Abroad* (1857) and *Championship of Women* (1868).

179.28   Leon Kellner] Author (1859–1928), professor of English in Vienna. His history of American literature was published in German in 1913.

179.37   the Gorky scandal] In April 1906, during a trip to raise funds for revolutionary activities, the novelist and playwright Maxim Gorky was asked to leave the Manhattan hotel where he was staying when it was revealed in the press that his companion was not his wife, as stated in the hotel register, but his mistress.

179.40   the Dreiser Protest] Petition protesting the suppression of *The "Genius"*, organized by Mencken.

180.5   Treitschke] Heinrich von Treitschke (1834–1896), German historian and politician of strong nationalist and anti-Semitic views.

180.25   Charles G. Norris] Novelist (1881–1945), brother of Frank Norris. His books, often dealing with social problems, included *The Amateur* (1915), *Salt* (1917), and *Brass* (1921).

180.34   the Comstocks] Pro-censorship forces associated with Anthony Comstock (1844–1915), U.S. Postal Inspector who founded the New York Society for the Suppression of Vice. In 1873 Congress passed the Comstock Law, which made it illegal to mail, transport, or deliver "obscene, lewd, and/or lascivious" information.

180.17   A Good Girl]   Novel (1916) by Vincent O'Sullivan.

180.19   Kathleen Norris]   Novelist (1880–1966), wife of Charles G. Norris. Her many books included *Mother* (1911), *Saturday's Child* (1914), and *The Sea Gull* (1927).

180.21   Abraham Cahan]   Novelist and editor (1860–1951). He was the longtime editor of the *Jewish Daily Forward* and author of *Yekl, a Tale of the New York Ghetto* (1896) and *The Rise of David Levinsky* (1917).

181.39   Alfred Noyes]   English poet (1880–1958), best known for his ballad "The Highwayman."

182.9   Rufus W. Griswold]   See note 9.7–8.

182.18   Lyman Abbott]   Congregational clergyman (1835–1922) who joined Henry Ward Beecher in editorship of the weekly *Christian Union*, before succeeding him as editor; his many books included *The Evolution of Christianity* (1896), *Problems of Life* (1900), and *The Spirit of Democracy* (1910).

182.18   Frank Crane]   See note 25.12.

182.33   his son]   Julian Hawthorne (1846–1934), novelist and journalist, author of *Idolatry: A Romance* (1874), *Archibald Malmaison* (1879), and numerous other novels and works of popular history.

182.35   a grand-daughter]   Hildegarde Hawthorne (1871–1952), poet and journalist, author of *Old Seaport Towns of New England* (1916).

183.33   N. P. Willis]   Nathaniel Parker Willis (1806–1867), poet and journalist. Founded the *American Monthly* (1829–31) in Boston and later became a prolific reporter on social matters in the U.S. and abroad for the *New-York Mirror*. His journalism was collected in numerous volumes such as *Pencillings by the Way* (1835) and *Dashes at Life with a Free Pencil* (1845).

185.2   Maeterlinckism]   See note 124.18.

185.21   Arthur Ransome]   English author (1884–1967). His study of Poe appeared in 1910.

185.37   John Burroughs]   American naturalist (1837–1921), a close friend of Walt Whitman, John Muir, and Theodore Roosevelt. His many books included *Notes on Walt Whitman as Poet and Person* (1867), *Wake Robin* (1871), *Birds and Poets* (1877), *Ways of Nature* (1905), and *Camping and Tramping with Roosevelt* (1907).

186.22   Jurgen]   See note 77.1.

187.17   Lord Northcliffe]   See note 16.24.

187.17   Lord Iveagh]   Edward Cecil (1847–1927), 1st earl of Iveagh, chairman of the Guinness Brewery at Dublin, who contributed large sums to slum clearance and endowed the Lister Institute for bacteriological research.

187.17–18   Lord Reading] Rufus Daniel Isaacs (1860–1935), lst Marquis of Reading, first British attorney general to be a member of the cabinet; special envoy to the United States, 1918–19.

190.3   *Gelehrten*] Scholars.

190.17   Jakob Böhme] German mystic and theologian (1575–1624), author of *Aurora, oder die Morgenröte im Aufgang* (1612, published 1634), *Of the Earthly and of the Heavenly Mystery* (1620), *The Signature of All Things* (1621), *The Mysterium Magnum* (1623), and other treatises.

190.18   Allen G. Thurman] Democratic politician (1813–1895), congressman and senator from Ohio, and Grover Cleveland's running mate in his unsuccessful 1888 presidential run.

191.16   Carranzas] Venustiano Carranza (1859–1920), Mexican revolutionary leader, president of Mexico from 1917 until his assassination in May 1920.

191.16–17   Ludendorffs] See note 35.26–27.

192.16–17   David Ricardo] English economist (1772–1823), author of *Principles of Political Economy and Taxation* (1817).

192.18   John Bright] English orator and reformist statesman (1811–1889), with Richard Cobden a founder of the Anti-Corn Law League. He was an advocate of free trade and religious freedom.

192.18   Richard Cobden] English statesman and economist (1804–1865) known as "The Apostle of Free Trade," who succeeded in forcing repeal of corn laws, and was a promoter of peace and reduced armaments.

192.18   George Grote] English historian (1794–1871), author of *A History of Greece* (1846–56).

192.19   Walther von Rathenau] German industrialist and politician (1867–1922) who was appointed foreign minister of the Weimar Republic in 1922. In that capacity he insisted that Germany pay its war reparations while at the same time working toward a revision of the terms of the Versailles treaty; he also negotiated a treaty with the Soviet Union. As a prominent German-Jewish figure, he advocated assimilation and opposed Zionism, and despite his ardent German nationalism was a target for extremist right-wing groups. He was assassinated by a right-wing army faction.

196.27   *Juris utriusque Doctor*] Doctor of Canon and Civil Law.

198.4   Mr. Creel] George Creel (1876–1953), journalist and publicity director; chairman of the Committee of Public Information (1917–19), created by Woodrow Wilson as a propaganda organization to enlist support for American entry into World War I.

198.31   Sisson documents] Documents, now believed to have been mostly forged, obtained in 1918 by Edgar Sisson, the Petrograd representative for the U.S. Committee on Public Information, purporting to show that Trotsky, Lenin, and other Bolsheviks were paid agents of the German government during World War I.

201.5   Billroth] Theodor Billroth (1829–1894), German surgeon and pianist; a close friend of Brahms, he pioneered the application of scientific methods to musicology.

201.12   Dr. Brownell] See note 4.17.

201.14   Comstockery] See note 180.34.

203.6–7   Coningsby Dawson] English writer (1883–1959), author of *The Garden Without Walls* (1913) and *Living Bayonets* (1919). He served with the Canadian army in World War I and later lectured throughout the United States on the aftereffects of the war.

203.7   Ian Hay] Pseudonym of John Hay Beith (1876–1952), Scottish novelist and playwright. His experiences in World War I are recounted in *The First Hundred Thousand* (1915).

203.7–8   Zangwill] Israel Zangwill (1864–1926), English novelist and playwright whose works included the plays *The Melting Pot* (1908), *The War God* (1911), and *We Moderns* (1924), and the novels *Children of the Ghetto* (1892) and *The King of Schnorrers* (1894).

203.10   Sir Auckland Geddes] British diplomat (1879–1954) who served as ambassador to the United States during 1920–24.

203.13   Free Church Federation] Association of British Nonconformist churches founded in the late nineteenth century. The movement, dedicated to religious social work, broadened to become international in scope.

207.22   Harold Stearns] American writer (1891–1943), author of *America and the Young Intellectual* (1921) and *The Street I Know* (1935).

207.23   Waldo Frank] American novelist and critic (1889–1967), founder and editor of the short-lived but influential magazine *The Seven Arts* (1916–17). His critical and travel writings included *Our America* (1919), *Salvos* (1924), *Virgin Spain* (1926), and *South American Journey* (1943).

209.10–11   Chevalier Bayard] See note 22.10.

209.22   Morley's life of Gladstone] *The Life of William Ewart Gladstone* (1903) by John Morley, Viscount Morley of Blackburn (1838–1923).

209.22   Trevelyan's life of Macaulay] *The Life and Letters of Lord*

Macaulay (1876) by Sir George Otto Trevelyan (1838–1928), who was Macaulay's nephew.

209.23   Carlyle's Frederick] *History of Friedrich II of Prussia, Called Frederick the Great* (1858–65) by Thomas Carlyle.

209.23–24   Winston Churchill's life of his father] *Lord Randolph Churchill* (1906).

209.24–25   William Graham Sumner's study of Andrew Jackson] *Andrew Jackson as a Public Man* (1882).

209.28   Daniel Coit Gilman] See note 177.14.

209.35   The Nicolay-Hay work] *Abraham Lincoln: A History*, published in ten volumes in 1890.

210.3–4   those of Lamon . . . and Miss Tarbell] *Life of Abraham Lincoln from His Birth to His Inauguration as President* (1872) by Ward Hill Lamon; *Herndon's Lincoln: The True Story of a Great Life* (1889) by William Henry Herndon (1818–1891, with Jesse W. Weik); *Abraham Lincoln: The True Story of a Great Life* (1885) by William Osborn Stoddard; *Abraham Lincoln* (1893) by John T. Morse, Jr.; *The Life of Abraham Lincoln* (1920) by Ida M. Tarbell.

210.13   William E. Barton] Congregational clergyman (1861–1930), author of *The Soul of Abraham Lincoln* (1920), among other books about him.

211.15   Dr. Creel] See note 198.4.

211.18   H. P. Davison] American banker (1867–1922), chairman of the American Red Cross Council during World War I.

211.18   Admiral Sims] William Sims (1858–1936), commander of naval operations in European waters, 1917–19.

211.19   Nicholas Murray Butler] American educator and diplomat (1862–1947), president of Columbia University, 1902–45, and president for Carnegie Endowment for International Peace, 1925–45. He was active in various international peace conferences in the years preceding World War I.

211.20   Barney Baruch] Bernard Baruch (1870–1965), American businessman and statesman, appointed by President Wilson to Advisory Commission of the Council for National Defense (1916); he served as chairman of the War Industries Board (1918–19), and was a member of the American peace commission in 1919.

211.29–30   Lawrence Abbott's "Impressions of Theodore Roosevelt"] Published in 1919. Abbott (1859–1933) was Roosevelt's secretary during his 1909–10 tour of Europe and Africa and editor of his *African and European Addresses* (1910).

211.30–31   William Roscoe Thayer's "Theodore Roosevelt"] *Theodore Roosevelt: An Intimate Biography* (1919).

212.1   Murat Halstead] American journalist and author (1829–1908), editor of the Cincinnati *Gazette* and author of a biography of President McKinley.

212.14   Lansdowne] Henry Charles Keith Petty-Fitzmaurice, 5th Marquess of Lansdowne (1845–1927), who served as governor general of Canada, 1883–88; viceroy of India, 1888–94; secretary of state for war, 1895–1900; and secretary of state for foreign affairs, 1900–5. In a letter published in November 1917, he called for a negotiated settlement with Germany.

212.14–15   Loreburn] Robert Reid, 1st Earl of Loreburn (1846–1923).

212.15   Austin Harrison] British journalist (1873–1928), editor of *The English Review*, 1909–23. He favored lenient peace terms for Germany after World War I.

212.15   Morel] E. D. Morel (1873–1924), French-born British journalist who was a leader of the pacifist movement during World War I.

212.15   Keynes] John Maynard Keynes (1883–1946), English economist and representative at the Paris Peace Conference in 1919.

212.15   Haldane] Richard Burdon, Viscount Haldane (1856–1928), British statesman and philosopher. Prior to World War I he implemented a set of reforms aimed at preparing the British army for a war in Europe. In 1915 he was forced to resign as Lord Chancellor after being accused of pro-German sympathies.

212.15   Hirst] Francis W. Hirst (1873–1953), English economist and author of *Political Economy of War* (1915). He was editor of *The Economist*, 1907–15.

212.15–16   Balfour] Arthur James Balfour (1848–1930), British statesman who served as prime minister, 1902–5. He was the author of the Balfour Declaration of 1917, favoring the establishment of a Jewish homeland in Palestine.

212.16   Robert Cecil] 1st Viscount Cecil of Chelwood (1864–1958), British statesman and an architect of the League of Nations.

212.19   Horatio Bottomley] British financier and journalist (1860–1933), founded *The Financial Times* in 1888 and *John Bull* in 1906. After 1914 he called for the extermination of the German nation and the trial for treason of anti-war English politicians. In 1921 he was convicted of financial fraud and perjury and served five years in prison.

212.36   Treitschke] See note 180.5.

212.36   Delcassé] Théophile Delcassé (1852–1923), French statesman and minister of foreign affairs. He played a leading role in French colonial expansion and was strongly anti-German in his policy views.

213.5   chautauqual rhetoric]   Following the New York Chatauqua Assembly of 1874, the term *chatauqua* was widely used to denote adult summer camps bringing education and entertainment to rural areas.

213.22   Bullitt]   William Christian Bullitt (1891–1967), American diplomat who worked for Woodrow Wilson at the Paris Peace Conference of 1919.

213.23   Shantung]   At the Paris Peace Conference, special privileges that had been exercised by Germany in the Chinese province of Shantung were transferred to Japan, provoking Chinese nationalist sentiment.

214.24–25   Also sprach Zarathustra . . . Jenseits von Gut und Böse]   *Thus Spoke Zarathustra* (1883–85) and *Beyond Good and Evil* (1886).

214.29–30   The Strenuous Life]   Speech given by Theodore Roosevelt in Chicago, Illinois on April 10, 1899, in which he declared, "I wish to preach, not the doctrine of ignoble ease, but the doctrine of the strenuous life, the life of toil and effort, of labor and strife."

215.38   Blaine]   James G. Blaine (1830–1893), American politician who served as congressman, senator, and secretary of state, and was a dominant figure in the Republican Party in the period after the Civil War. He was defeated by Grover Cleveland in the 1884 presidential race.

217.40   Barbarossa]   Frederick I (1122–1190), Holy Roman Emperor.

218.32   Liberty Loan]   Series of five bond issues floated by the U.S. Treasury Department that helped finance World War I.

221.21   rice converts]   The term refers to persons converting nominally to Christianity in order to receive rice and other material benefits from missionaries.

223.22–23   Paterson anarchists]   In 1900 an Italian anarchist resident in Paterson, New Jersey, traveled to Italy and assassinated King Umberto. Following the assassination of President McKinley in 1901, Theodore Roosevelt called for strong action against international anarchists, stating: "Anarchy is a crime against the whole human race; and all mankind should band against the anarchist."

223.24   Charles J. Bonaparte]   Charles Joseph Bonaparte (1851–1921) served as Roosevelt's Secretary of the Navy (1905–1906) and U.S. Attorney General (1906–09), in which capacity he founded the Bureau of Investigation.

229.5   J. Gordon Coogler]   South Carolina-born poet (1865–1901), whose *Purely Original Verse* was published in five editions between 1891 and 1897.

230.27   Robert Loveman]   See note 165.35.

230.28   John McClure]   See note 56.5.

232.18   Leo Frank affair]   In 1913, Leo Frank (1884–1915), the Jewish manager of a pencil factory in Atlanta, Georgia, was accused of the rape and murder of Mary Phagan, a thirteen–year-old worker in his employ. Frank was
found guilty but in 1915 Georgia governor John Slaton, convinced of his innocence, commuted his sentence to life imprisonment. Frank was abducted
from prison by a group including a former governor and the son of a state
senator, and lynched on August 17, 1915.

234.17   John Temple Graves]   Journalist and lecturer (1856–1925), editor
of the *Atlanta Journal* and the *Atlanta Georgian*, a strident spokesman for
white supremacism and an open apologist for lynching.

234.18   Frank L. Stanton]   Georgia-born poet (1857–1927) whose poems
appeared regularly in the *Atlanta Constitution*.

235.22   Caradoc Evans]   Welsh fiction writer (1878–1945), author of *My
People* (1915), *My Neighbors* (1919), *Taffy* (1923), and other books.

235.32–33   Philip Alexander Bruce]   American historian (1856–1933), a specialist in the history of Virginia.

235.40   Fanny Kemble Butler]   Fanny Kemble (1809–95), English actress
who came to America in 1832 and left the stage two years later to marry
Pierce Butler, a Georgia plantation-owner. The marriage ended in 1846. Her
Journal of a Residence on a Georgian Plantation (1868), written 1838–39, was
a highly critical account of the culture of slavery.

238.11   Weber & Fields]   Joe Weber (1867–1942) and Lew Fields (1867–
1941), team of comedians known for their German and Yiddish dialect
routines; their many successful shows included *Helter Skelter* (1899) and
Whoop-dee-doo.

247.19   Hugo Wolf]   Austrian composer (1860–1903) of over two hundred *Lieder*.

248.10   the elder Beecham]   Thomas Beecham (1820–1907), creator of
Beecham's Pills, a laxative that he began selling around 1847.

248.11   the younger Beecham]   Sir Thomas Beecham (1879–1961), En-
glish conductor and impresario. He founded the London Philharmonic and
Royal Philharmonic orchestras, conducted the first English performances of
Richard Strauss's *Elektra* and *Salome*, and accompanied the Ballets Russes at
Covent Garden and elsewhere.

248.18–19   "La force et la foiblesse . . . des organes du corps"]   The
strength and weakness of the mind are misnamed; they are only, in effect, the
good or poor condition of the physical organs.

248.32   *spirochaete pallida*]   Causative agent of syphilis.

250.24   Dr. Jacques Loeb]   See note 45.27.

251.23 *Durchlaucht*] Serene Highness.

256.36 *couronnes des perles*] Crowns of pearls.

258.21 George W. Crile] American surgeon (1864–1943), author of studies including *Hemorrhage and Transfusion* (1909), *Origin and Nature of the Emotions* (1915), *A Mechanistic View of War and Peace* (1915), and *Man: An Adaptive Mechanism* (1916).

259.3–4 F. Parkes Weber] Physician and numismatist (1863–1962).

259.35 Sir William Osler] Canadian-born physician and medical administrator (1849–1919), first chief of staff of the Johns Hopkins Hospital. From 1905 he held the Regius Chair of Medicine at Oxford.

260.22 *Char-Freitag*] Good Friday.

261.20 Dr. Alexis Carrel] See note 45.27.

262.13 Edmund Gosse] British literary critic, poet and biographer (1849–1928), author of the autobiography *Father and Son* (1907).

262.15–16 William Archer] See note 13.2.

262.23 *Allgemeine-krankenhaus*] General hospital.

263.31 Ellen La Motte] American journalist (1873–1961) who served as a nurse in France during World War I. Her book *The Backwash of War: The Human Wreckage of the Battlefield as Witnessed by an American Hospital Nurse* (1916) was adapted from her journals.

266.22 The Duchess] See note 83.3.

268.14 Thaïs] Opera (1894) by Jules Massenet, based on the novel by Anatole France.

268.15 Gung'l] Josef Gung'l (1810–1889), Hungarian composer.

269.7 Carl Van Vechten] Novelist and critic (1880–1964). Early in his career he was music critic for the *New York Times*.

270.18–19 René Lenormand] French composer (1846–1932), author of *A Study of Modern Harmony* (1915).

271.20 Wiener Blut . . . Künstler Leben] "Vienna Blood" and "Artists' Life," waltzes by Johann Strauss II.

271.37–39 Rosen aus dem Süden . . . Wein, Weib und Gesang] "Roses from the South" and "Wine, Women, and Song," waltzes by Johann Strauss II.

272.8 Wiener Mad'l] "Vienna Girls," waltz by Carl Michael Ziehrer.

272.12 Herbert K. Hadley . . . In Bohemia] American composer (1871–1937). "In Bohemia" was his Concert Overture, Op. 28.

272.29   Bror Nordfeldt] Bror Julius Olsson Nordfeldt (1878–1955), artist who emigrated to the United States from Sweden in 1891 and first drew attention with solo exhibits in Chicago, 1911–12. He later settled in New Mexico.

274.21–24   Henry Irving . . . The Bells] English actor-manager (1838–1905) who dominated the London stage for many decades. His celebrated melodramatic vehicle *The Bells* was adapted by Leopold Lewis from Erckmann-Chatrian's *Le Juif Polonais*. The play opened in New York in 1883.

274.25–29   the late Mansfield . . . Dr. Jekyll and Mr. Hyde] Richard Mansfield (1854–1907), American actor, educated in England, who had his first major American success in the role of the brutal roué Baron Chevrial in A. M. Palmer's production *A Parisian Romance* (1883). Mansfield's production of *Dr. Jekyll and Mr. Hyde* opened in 1887.

279.13–14   Maurice Parmelee] American sociologist (1882–1969), author of *Personality and Conduct* (1918), *Criminology* (1918), *The Science of Human Behavior* (1924), and *The New Gymnosophy* (1927), a defense of nudism.

280.4   the Comstocks] See note 180.34.

284.25–26   Dr. Frank Crane] See note 25.12.

284.29   Theda Bara] See note 170.15.

285.37–38   Stephen Girard] French-born banker and philanthropist (1750–1831) who saved the U.S. government from financial collapse during the War of 1812 and helped found the Second Bank of the United States (1816). He left most of his fortune to charitable institutions in Philadelphia and New Orleans.

285.38–286.1   Theodore Thomas] German-born conductor (1835–1905) of the Chicago Symphony.

286.1   Edwin Klebs] German-Swiss pathologist (1834–1913) known for work on infectious diseases. He taught at Rush Medical College in Chicago, 1896–1900.

288.5   Rex Beach] See note 167.9.

288.22   *meatus auditorium externus*] Auditory canal.

290.22   *Abortfrau*] Cleaning woman.

293.38   Minna Planer] Christine Wilhelmine Planer (1809–1866), first wife of Richard Wagner. They were married in 1836 and separated in 1857.

294.1   Armande Béjart] French actress (1642–1700), wife of Molière from 1662 until his death in 1673.

294.10–11   Cosima Liszt von Bülow] Cosima Wagner (1837–1930), daughter of Franz Liszt. Her first marriage to Hans von Bülow ended in divorce in 1869; she married Richard Wagner in 1870.

PREJUDICES: THIRD SERIES

302.30   Anti-Saloon League] Organization, founded in Ohio in 1893, that played a major role in lobbying for Prohibition.

302.40   Harold Stearns] See note 207.22.

304.40   *Wirkliche Geheimräte*] Privy Councilors.

305.2   *Todsaufer*] In his memoir *Happy Days* (1940), Mencken writes: "A *Todsäufer* (literally, dead-drinker) was, and is, a sort of brewer's customers' man. He is commonly called a collector, but his duties go far beyond collecting the bills owed to breweries by saloonkeepers. He is supposed to stand a general treat in the bar whenever he calls, to go to all weddings, birthday parties and funerals in the families of saloonkeepers, and to cultivate their wives and children with frequent presents. . . . He is also one of the brewery's political agents, and must handle all the license difficulties of his clients."

307.4   Charles M. Schwab] Steel industry magnate (1862–1939), chief executive of Bethlehem Steel, known for his lavish spending.

307.6   *Geschäft*] Business.

307.6   Remy de Gourmont] French poet, novelist, and critic (1858–1915), author of *The Natural Philosophy of Love* (1904) and *A Night in the Luxembourg* (1906).

307.27–28   *Durchlauchten, k.k. Hoheiten*] German forms of royal address.

308.9   Lord Reading] See note 187.17–18.

308.15   Prince Eugene] Francois Eugène de Savoy-Carignan, Prince of Savoy (1633–1736), Austrian military commander.

308.21–22   Arthur James Balfour] See note 212.14–15.

309.12   Reform Bill of 1832] Act of Parliament that introduced major changes to the electoral system of the United Kingdom, increasing the size of the electorate by as much as 80 percent.

309.16   Volstead] Minnesota congressman Andrew John Volstead (1860–1947), sponsor of The National Prohibition Act of 1919, also known as the Volstead Act.

309.16   Ponzi] Charles Ponzi (1882–1949), financial swindler whose method of paying early investors with money from later investors originated the term "Ponzi scheme."

309.16   Jack Dempsey] Boxer (1895–1983), heavy-weight champion 1919–26.

309.16   Daugherty]   Harry M. Daugherty (1860–1914), Republican Party boss and U.S. Attorney General under President Harding.

309.16   Debs]   Eugene Victor Debs (1855–1926), American socialist leader and founder of the Social Democratic Party. Debs was arrested under the Espionage Act for an anti-war speech made in 1918.

310.11   *Greisenheim*]   Old People's Home.

313.29   Garys]   Elbert Henry Gary (1846–1927), president of U.S. Steel, 1901–27. Having served two terms as a county judge, 1884–92, he was commonly known as "Judge Gary."

313.33–34   Congregatio de Propaganda Fide]   Congregation for the Propagation of the Faith.

313.34   Bismarck's *Reptilienpresse*]   Newspapers bribed by Otto von Bismarck to publish articles favorable to the government; they were paid out of a secret "reptile fund," so-called because it was created to counter opponents Bismarck described as "reptiles."

314.37–38   Bryce]   James Bryce (1838–1922), English politician and historian, author of *The American Commonwealth* (1888).

315.2   Robertson Nicoll]   Sir William Roberston Nicoll (1851–1923), Scottish minister and journalist, founder of the literary monthly *The Bookman* in 1891. His *History of English Literature* appeared in 1906.

315.2   Squire]   Sir John Collings Squire (1884–1958), poet and critic. He was editor of the *London Mercury*, 1919–34. His books included *Books in General* (1918–21) and *Life and Letters* (1920).

315.2–3   Clutton-Brock]   Arthur Clutton-Brock (1868–1924), English essayist and critic, a frequent contributor to the *Times Literary Supplement*. His books included *Shelley: The Man and the Poet* (1909) and *Essays on Art* (1918).

315.23   Birkenhead]   Frederick Birkenhead (1872–1930), British attorney general (1915) and lord chancellor (1919–1922).

315.29   *Town Topics*]   See note 76.23.

316.30   Otto Julius Bierbaum]   German poet and critic (1865–1910).

316.30   Ludwig Thoma]   See note 63.40.

318.7–8   Dr. Dillon]   Emile Joseph Dillon (1854–1933), journalist and philologist.

318.8   Wickham Steed]   English journalist (1871–1956), foreign editor (1914–19) and editor (1920–22) of the London *Times*. His books included *The Hapsburg Monarchy* (1913) and *The Antecedents of Post-War Europe* (1932).

318.8   Count zu Reventlow]   Ernst zu Reventlow (1869–1943), German journalist who wrote on military and political matters; he founded the newspaper *Der Reichswart*, which he published until his death. He joined the Nazi party in 1927.

318.8   Wilfrid Scawen Blunt]   English poet and essayist (1840–1922). Aside from collections of verse, his books included *The Future of Islam* (1882), *India under Ripon* (1909), and *The Land War in Ireland* (1912).

318.11   Disarmament Conference]   Also called the Washington Naval Conference, held in Washington D.C. November 12, 1921–February 6, 1922. The primary aim of the conference was to restrain the expansion of the Japanese Navy.

318.14   Brailsford]   Henry Noel Brailsford (1873–1958), British journalist.

318.14   Bywater]   Hector Charles Bywater (1884–1940), British journalist and writer on military and naval subjects, author of *Sea Power in the Pacific: A Study of the American-Japanese Naval Problem* (1921).

318.25–26   The issue . . . before the conference]   Mencken refers to the question of allowed capital ship tonnage for each signatory to the treaty.

319.13   Huysmans]   Joris Karl Huysmans (1848–1907), French novelist, author of *The Vatard Sisters* (1879), *Against the Grain* (1884), and *Down There* (1891).

319.13   Hartleben]   Otto Erich Hartleben (1864–1905), German writer of poetry, fiction, and plays.

319.13   Vaihinger]   Hans Vaihinger (1852–1933), German philosopher, author of *The Philosophy of As If* (1911). He was a leading scholar of the work of Kant.

319.13   Merezhkovsky]   Dmitri Sergeyevich Merezhkovski (1865–1941), Russian novelist and poet, a leader of the Russian Symbolist movement. His fictional trilogy *Christ and Antichrist* was comprised of *The Death of the Gods* (1896), *The Romance of Leonardo da Vinci* (1902), and *Peter and Alexis* (1905).

319.13   Keyserling]   Count Hermann Alexander Keyserling (1880–1946), German social philosopher from an aristocratic Estonian family. Following World War I he founded the Society for Free Philosophy at Darmstadt. His book *The Travel Diary of a Philosopher* (1919), recounting his 1911 world tour, was an international bestseller.

319.14   Snoilsky]   Count Carl Snoilsky (1841–1903), Swedish lyric poet.

319.14   Mauthner]   Fritz Mauthner (1849–1923), German novelist and philosopher.

319.14   Altenberg]   Peter Altenberg (1859–1919), author of essays and sketches.

319.14   Heidenstam]   Verner von Heidenstam (1859–1940), Swedish poet, awarded the Nobel Prize in Literature in 1916.

319.14   Alfred Kerr]   German drama critic (1867–1948), an advocate of Naturalism. He emigrated to London in 1933.

319.16   Brieux]   See note 35.18.

319.25   Dr. Sylvanus Stall]   See note 118.26.

319.35   Boyd]   Ernest Augustus Boyd (1887–1946), Irish-born critic, essayist, and translator from French and German. He settled permanently in the United States in 1920. His books included *Contemporary Drama of Ireland* (1917) and *Appreciations and Depreciations* (1918). He published a study of Mencken in 1925.

319.35   Nathan]   See note 124.2.

319.37   William Archer]   See note 13.2.

319.37   Georg Brandes]   See note 7.29.

319.40   Gerhart Hauptmann]   See note 127.4.

320.1   Ludwig Lewisohn]   German-born American writer (1882–1955). His books included the autobiographies *Upstream* (1922) and *Mid-Channel* (1929), and many novels including *The Case of Mr. Crump* (1926) and *The Island Within* (1928).

320.29   Der Amerikamüde]   Novel (1855) by the Austrian writer Ferdinand Kürnberger (1829–1879).

320.29   America]   Novel (1911) by Sholem Asch (1880–1957), Polish-born American dramatist and novelist.

320.29–30   Ernst von Wolzogen]   German author of satirical plays and fiction (1855–1934), founder of the Berlin cabaret Das Überbrettl.

320.30–31   Hail Columbia!]   "Hail, Columbia! Random Impressions of a Conservative Radical" (1921); for W. L. George, see note 21.32.

320.31   Annalise Schmidt's "Der Amerikanische Mensch"]   Study of "the American individual" published in 1920.

320.32   Sienkiewicz's "After Bread"]   Novel (1880) by Polish writer Henryk Sienkiewicz (1846–1916), published in America in 1897 as *After Bread: A Story of Polish Emigrant Life to America*. Sienkiewicz's other novels included *With Fire and Sword* (1884) and *Quo Vadis* (1896).

320.35   Clemens von Pirquet]   Austrian scientist and pediatrician (1874–1929) who did major work in immunological research. He declined an invitation to teach at Johns Hopkins University in 1909.

320.35   John Masefield]   English poet (1878–1967), author of *Salt Water*

Poems and Ballads (1916), which included the poem "Sea-Fever." Named Poet Laureate in 1930, he lived briefly in New York in his youth.

320.36   Frank Wedekind] German playwright (1864–1918), author of *Spring's Awakening* (1891), *Earth Spirit* (1895), and *Pandora's Box* (1904).

320.36–37   Edwin Klebs] See note 286.1.

322.15   *Kriegslieferant*] War supplier.

324.18   Chamberlain] Joseph Chamberlain (1836–1914), British statesman.

324.18   F. E. Smith] Frederick Edwin Smith, 1st Earl of Birkenhead (1872–1930), English lawyer and statesman; Lord Chancellor, 1919–22.

324.18   Isaacs-Reading] See note 187.17–18.

324.19   Bottomley] See note 212.18.

324.19   Northcliffe] See note 16.24.

325.12   Palmer] See note 164.20.

325.12   Burleson] Albert S. Burleson (1863–1937) served as U.S. post-master general from 1913–21. During World War I he vigorously enforced the Espionage Act by attempting to bar radical and anti-war materials from the mails.

327.7   James M. Wood] Author of *Democracy and the Will to Power* (1921). The book contained an introduction by Mencken.

327.14   Billy Sunday] See note 70.9.

327.14   Cyrus K. Curtis] Cyrus Hermann Kotzschmar Curtis (1850–1933), American publisher, founder of the Curtis Publishing Co., publisher of *Ladies' Home Journal*, *The Country Gentleman*, and *The Saturday Evening Post*.

327.14   Dr. Frank Crane] See note 25.12.

327.15   Charles E. Hughes] Charles Evans Hughes (1862–1948), governor of New York, 1907–10; associate justice of the U.S. Supreme Court, 1910–16; Republican nominee for president (1916). He served as secretary of state, 1921–25, and as chief justice of the U.S. Supreme Court from 1930 until his retirement in 1941.

327.15   General Wood] Leonard Wood (1860–1927), physician and army officer. He helped Theodore Roosevelt in raising and organizing the Rough Riders, and later became chief of staff of the U.S. Army, 1910–14.

329.6   the Feather Duster] Charles Evans Hughes; see note 327.15.

329.6   Popinjay Lodge] Henry Cabot Lodge (1850–1924), legislator and author; member of the U.S. House of Representatives, 1887–93, and U.S.

Senate, 1893–1924. He led opposition to the Peace Treaty of 1919 and the Covenant of the League of Nations.

329.7   Master-Mind Root] Elihu Root (1845–1937), lawyer and statesman, secretary of war under McKinley and Theodore Roosevelt; he was appointed secretary of state following the death of John Hay. He received the Nobel Peace Prize in 1912. He later served as senator from New York, 1909–14, and as president of the Carnegie Endowment for International Peace, 1910–25.

329.7   Vacuum Underwood] Oscar Wilder Underwood (1862–1929), lawyer and politician; represented Alabama in the U.S. House of Representatives, 1896–1915, and U.S. Senate, 1915–27.

330.31   Mother Eddy] See note 145.33.

330.32   John Alexander Dowie] Scottish-born evangelist and faith healer (1847–1907) who in 1896 founded the Christian Catholic Apostolic Church in Zion. In 1900 he established the city of Zion, Illinois, forty-two miles from Chicago.

331.5   Cox] James Middleton Cox (1856–1919), newspaper publisher and politician. He served as governor of Ohio (1913–15, 1917–21) and was Democratic nominee for president in 1920.

331.38   *Ridi si sapis*] Laugh if you are wise.

332.23–24   Matthew v, 11] "Blessed are ye, when men revile you, and persecute you, and say all manner of evil against you falsely, for my sake."

334.2   Huneker] See note 7.29.

334.10–11   *Doppelschraubenschnellpostdampfer*] Fast ocean liner.

334.36–335.1   Sils Maria] Nietzsche spent many summers in Sils Maria, near St. Moritz in Switzerland.

335.4   Frau Cosima] See note 294.10–11.

335.7   Anton Seidel] Anton Seidl (1850–1898), Hungarian conductor who led the New York Philharmonic from 1891 to 1898.

335.9   David Belasco] See note 124.24.

335.10   Lillian Russell] The American singer and actress (1861–1922) was married four times.

335.13   George Moore] See note 170.29.

335.15   D'Annunzio and Duse] Gabriele D'Annunzio (1863–1938), Italian poet and playwright; Eleanora Duse (1859–1924), Italian actress.

335.19   Bal Bullier] Celebrated Paris dance hall.

336.4   Josef's Legend] *Josephslegende*, Opus 63, ballet music composed in 1914.

336.15   Frank Harris] See note 175.7.

336.20–21   essays on Strauss . . . Chopin] See "The Music of the Future," "Richard Strauss and Nietzsche," and "The Greater Chopin" in *Mezzotints in Modern Music* (1899); "Richard Strauss" and "Nietzsche the Rhapsodist" in *Over Tones* (1904); "Phases of Nietzsche" in *Egoists: A Book of Supermen* (1909); "Richard Strauss at Stuttgart" in *Ivory Apes and Peacocks* (1915); "Brahmsody" and "The Classic Chopin" in *Unicorns* (12917); "Phases of the Greater Chopin" in *Variations* (1922); and *Chopin: The Man and His Music* (1900). See also *Essays by James Huneker* (1929), edited by Mencken.

336.35   Krehbiel] Henry Edward Krehbiel (1854–1923), American music critic, music editor of the *New York Tribune*. His books included *Studies in the Wagnerian Drama* (1891), *How to Listen to Music* (1897), and *Afro-American Folksongs: A Study in Racial and National Music* (1914).

336.36   Finck] Henry Theophilus Finck (1854–1926), American musical critic, musical editor of the *New York Evening Post* and writer for *The Nation*. He published, among other books, *Wagner and His Works* (1891), *Anton Seidl* (1899), and *Edward Grieg* (1905).

337.1   Middleton Murry] John Middleton Murry (1889–1957), English critic, author of *The Evolution of an Intellectual* (1920), *The Problem of Style* (1922), *D. H. Lawrence* (1930), and many other books.

337.1   Paul Elmer More] See note 7.31.

337.1–2   Clutton-Brock] See note 315.2–3.

340.10   Georg Brandes] See note 7.29.

341.2–3   Max Beerbohm] English essayist and caricaturist (1872–1956), a frequent contributor to *The Yellow Book* (1894–97) and *The Saturday Review*, where he succeeded George Bernard Shaw as dramatic critic. His books included *The Happy Hypocrite* (1897), *Zuleika Dobson* (1911), and *Seven Men* (1919).

341.16–18   *Sun . . . Mlle. New York*] Under the editorship (1868–97) of Charles H. Dana, the New York *Sun* (1833–1950) was known for its lively criticism. *M'lle New York*, founded by Vance Thompson in 1895, helped introduce French symbolist poetry, Nietzsche, and other modern European intellectual and artistic trends to American readers.

351.20   Carlyle's "Frederick"] See note 209.23.

353.33–34   Rufus Dawes] Massachusetts-born poet and dramatist (1803–1859). His *Geraldine, Athenia of Damascus, and Miscellaneous Poems* was published in 1839.

353.36–37   Gottfried Weber] German writer on music (1779–1839), editor of the influential periodical *Cäcilia*, 1824–39, and author of *Theory of Musical Composition* (1817–21).

355.35   *Aufklärung*] Enlightenment.

356.23   George E. Woodberry] See note 159.12.

356.29–30   Hamilton Wright Mabie] See note 7.15.

358.6   *Vorspiel*] Prelude.

359.26   Félicien Rops] Belgian artist (1833–1898) associated with writers including Baudelaire, Gautier, and Mallarmé; noted for the erotic and supposedly blasphemous elements of his work.

360.21   Diamond Jim Brady] James Buchanan Brady (1856–1917), American financier famous for his vast appetite and lavish lifestyle.

364.34   *Bauverein*] Building Society.

367.2   *Ad Imaginem Dei Creavit Illum*] Genesis 1:27 in the Latin Vulgate version: "In the Divine image he created him."

373.33   Sir Oliver Lodge] See note 35.37.

379.32   American Protective League] Private organization active during World War I, whose aim was to work with federal agencies to combat radicals, anti-war activists, and left-wing political groups.

379.34   Dr Creel] See note 198.4.

380.10   Arion Liedertafel] German singing group.

381.22–23   Johannes Müller] German physiologist (1801–1858).

381.23   Karl Ludwig] German astronomer (1765–1834).

381.23   Ehrlich] German scientist (1854–1915) who won the Nobel Prize in Medicine in 1908. He developed the cure for syphilis.

381.36–37   Newell Dwight Hillis] See note 80.28–29.

381.37   Henry Van Dyke] See note 55.19.

381.40   Palmer and Burleson] See notes 164.20 and 325.12.

382.5   Gaby Deslys] French dancer and actress (1881–1920).

383.4   Otto Jespersen] Danish linguist (1860–1943), founder of the International Phonetic Association. *Growth and Structure of the English Language* appeared in 1905.

384.17   Æ] Pseudonym of George William Russell (1867–1935), Irish poet.

384.17   Lord Dunsany] See note 127.3.

386.13–16   Not poppy . . . thou owed'st yesterday.]   *Othello* III.iii.330–333.

386.28   Joaquin Miller]   Pseudonym of Cincinnatus Heine Miller (1837–1913), American poet and essayist, author of *Song of the Sierras* (1871).

386.38   Sidney Lanier]   Georgia-born poet (1842–1881), whose prosodical study *The Science of English Verse* appeared in 1880.

387.27   F. C. Prescott]   Prescott (1871–1957) published *Poetry and Dreams* in 1912.

388.5–6   God's in . . . with the world.]   cf. Robert Browning, song from *Pippa Passes* (1841): "God's in his Heaven — / All's right with the world!"

388.8–9   I am the . . . captain of my soul.]   William Ernest Henley, "Invictus," lines 15–16.

389.8   "The Frost is on the Pumpkin"]   "When the Frost is on the Punkin," poem by James Whitcomb Riley (1849–1916).

389.11   Crashaw]   Richard Crashaw (1613–1649), English metaphysical poet.

389.12   Thompson]   Francis Thompson (1889–1907), English poet best known for the religious allegory "The Hound of Heaven" (1893).

389.32   "Tommy Atkins" and "Fuzzy-Wuzzy"]   Poems from Kipling's collection *Barrack-Room Ballads* (1892).

391.8–9   Lizette Woodworth Reese]   See note 55.40.

392.22   Lecky]   William Hartpole Lecky (1838–1903), Irish historian, author of *History of Rationalism in Europe* (1865) and *History of European Morals from Augustus to Charlemagne* (1869).

392.22   Buckle]   Henry Thomas Buckle (1821–1862), English historian, author of the unfinished *History of Civilization in England*.

392.24   Rogers groups]   Clay and plaster statue groups created by the English sculptor John Rogers (1829–1904) that were widely collected in late nineteenth-century America.

392.26   William Sumner]   William Graham Sumner (1840–1910), American economist, sociologist and educator, author of *Folkways* (1907).

392.26   Daniel C. Gilman]   See note 177.14.

393.19–20   The Sheik]   Novel (1919) by Edith Maude Hull, filmed in 1921 with Rudolph Valentino in the title role.

394.20   *cabotin*]   Ham.

395.27   "The Blessed Damozel"]   Poem (1850) by Dante Gabriel Rossetti.

395.39–40   John Livingston Lowes]   See note 51.12.

398.19   Barton]   See note 210.13.

400.36   *Paul Elmer More*]   See note 7.31.

401.24   Dr. Franklin . . . *Profiteers' Review*]   Dr. Fabian Franklin, Hungarian-born journalist (1853–1939), associate editor of *The New York Evening Post* and founder in 1919 of *The Review*.

401.32   Stuart P. Sherman]   See note 4.19–20.

402.29   *Madison Cawein*]   Kentucky-born poet (1865–1914), author of many volumes of verse including *Lyrics and Idyls* (1890), *The Garden of Dreams* (1896), *Weeds by the Wall* (1901), and *Minions of the Moon* (1913).

403.3   Charles Hamilton Musgrove]   Kentucky-born poet, author of *The Dream Beautiful* (1898) and *Pan and Æolus* (1913).

404.17   *Frank Harris*]   See note 175.7.

408.3   Leonard Merrick]   English novelist (1864–1939), author of *The Man Who Was Good* (1892), *Conrad in Quest of His Youth* (1903), and other works.

408.27   Havelock Ellis]   See note 116.13.

409.2   Wallace]   Alfred Russel Wallace (1823–1913), English scientist and naturalist who developed an independent theory of evolution by natural selection. He later became involved in political activism and spiritualism.

409.2   Crookes]   Sir William Crookes (1832–1919), English physicist and chemist, pioneer of vacuum tubes. He later became interested in spiritualism and joined the Society for Psychic Research.

409.2   Lodge]   See note 35.37.

409.15   Wilfrid Scawen Blunt]   See note 318.8.

413.39   Mooney]   Thomas Mooney (1882–1942), American labor leader tried and convicted for the bombing that killed nine and wounded forty during a Preparedness Parade in San Francisco on July 22, 1916. His death sentence was commuted to life imprisonment in 1918, and became the object of a worldwide campaign to free him. He was pardoned in 1938.

413.40   One Big Union]   Slogan of the IWW.

416.5   Rex Beach]   See note 167.9.

416.13   *Küche-Kinder-Kirche*]   Children, kitchen, church: German slogan defining the traditional role of women.

416.33   Joseph Hergesheimer]   American novelist (1880–1954) whose many books, widely popular and in their time often critically acclaimed, included *The Three Black Pennys* (1917) and *Java Head* (1919).

417.10   *Schwärmerei*]   Excessive enthusiasm.

417.11   L'Allemagne]   *De l'Allemagne* (1810–13) by the French writer Anne Louise Germaine Necker, Madame de Staël (1766–1817), a study of German culture that became a crucial work for the Romantic movement.

417.18   Clara Viebig]   German naturalistic novelist (1860–1952), author of *Our Daily Bread* (1902), *The Watch on the Rhine* (1902), and other works.

417.18   Helene Böhlau]   German writer of naturalistic novels and stories (1859–1940), author of *Ratsmädelgeschichten* (1888), *Der Rangierbahnhof* (1895), and other works.

417.18–19   Ricarda Huch]   German author (1864–1947) of poetry, plays, novels and literary criticism, whose works included *The Last Summer* (1910) and *The Deruda Trial* (1917).

417.19   Selma Lagerlöf]   Swedish novelist and poet (1858–1940), recipient of 1909 Nobel Prize in Literature.

417.20   Mathilda Serao]   Matilda Serao (1856–1927), Italian novelist and journalist. She was founder and editor of *Il Mattino* and *Il Giorno*.

417.21   May Sinclair]   English novelist (1866–1952), author of *Divine Fire* (1904), *Mary Oliver* (1919), *The Life and Death of Harriet Frean* (1922), and other works.

417.28–29   Evelyn Scott's "The Narrow House"]   Scott (1893–1963) published *The Narrow House* in 1921. It was followed by *Narcissus* (1922), *The Golden Door* (1923), *Escapade* (1923), *The Wave* (1929), and other books.

418.5–6   Meredith's "The Shaving of Shagpat"]   *The Shaving of Shagpat: An Arabian Entertainment* (1856) by George Meredith (1828–1909).

418.6   Jacob Wasserman's "The World Illusion"]   *Christian Wannschaffe* (1919), internationally popular novel by Jakob Wasserman (1873–1934).

418.8   Beethoven's "Vittoria"]   Orchestral fantasia "Wellington's Victory, or The Battle of Vittoria," Opus 91 (1813).

418.8   Goldmarck's "Landliche Hochzeit"]   "Rustic Wedding Symphony," Opus 26 (1876), by Hungarian composer Karl Goldmark (1830–1915).

418.18   The Ordeal of Richard Feverel]   Novel (1859) by George Meredith.

419.2   The Line of Love]   A series of linked stories (1905) by James Branch Cabell. It was reissued in 1921 with a preface by Mencken.

419.8   Zola's "La Terre"]   *The Earth* (1887), the fifteenth novel in Emile Zola's *Rougon-Macquart* series.

420.22 Aphra Behn] Playwright and novelist (1640–1689), considered the first English professional woman writer. Her works included the play *The Rover* (1681) and the novel *Oroonoko* (1688).

420.32 Love Pilgrimage] Novel (1911) by Upton Sinclair.

421.2 Zona Gale] See note 167.35.

422.6 Chambers] See note 42.19.

422.7 Coningsby Dawson] See note 203.6–7.

422.7 Emerson Hough] See note 167.9.

423.29 Bishop Manning] William Thomas Manning (1866–1949), Episcopal bishop of New York, 1921–46.

423.29 Judge Gary] See note 313.29.

423.30 Dr. Fabian Franklin] See note 401.24.

423.31 Dr. Stephen S. Wise] American Reform rabbi and Zionist leader (1874–1949).

423.31 Roger W. Babson] Entrepreneur and author of books on business theory (1875–1967); founder of Babson College.

424.9 the Gary system] Innovative educational approach fostered by the public school system of Gary, Indiana, in the 1920s.

424.27 twilight sleep] Drug-induced state advocated as a means of painless childbirth, developed in Germany and popular in the United States following the publication of Hanna Rion's *The Truth About Twilight Sleep* (1915).

426.3 David Starr Jordan] Eugenicist and peace activist (1851–1931).

426.4–5 B. O. Flower] Benjamin Orange Flower (1858–1918), journalist, editor of *The Arena* (1889–1909).

426.7 W. S. U'Ren] William Simon U'Ren (1859–1949), progressive Oregon politician, an advocate of Henry George's single tax.

426.9 Jane Addams] See note 35.23.

426.10 Dr. Scott Nearing] See note 36.26.

426.11 Newt Baker] Newton Baker (1871–1937), American politician who served as secretary of war, 1916–21.

426.12 Gifford Pinchot] American statesman (1865–1946), who was first chief of the United States Forest Service (1905–10).

426.13–14 Judge Ben B. Lindsey] See note 35.16.

431.32 vereins] Associations.

434.19   Allen G. Thurman]   See note 190.18.

434.20   General Coxey]   See note 87.34.

434.20–21   Richmond P. Hobson]   Rear admiral and U.S. congressman from Alabama (1870–1937).

434.21   Nan Patterson]   Showgirl, a member of the Florodora Girls, who at nineteen stood trial in 1905 for the murder of her lover Caesar Young, a bookmaker, who was killed by gunshot while the two were riding together in a hansom cab. Patterson claimed that Young had committed suicide; she was released after two mistrials.

434.21   Alton B. Parker]   Lawyer and judge (1852–1926), Democratic presidential nominee in 1904.

434.21–22   General Weyler]   Spanish army officer (1838–1930) who served in Cuba and the Philippines.

434.22   Tom Sharkey]   Boxer (1873–1953) whose career ran from 1893 to 1904.

444.17   Percy MacKaye]   Poet and playwright (1875–1956) who attempted to revive verse drama.

446.24   Leschetizky]   Theodor Leschetizky (1830–1915), Polish pianist and composer.

461.33   Garet Garrett or John Moody]   Garrett (1878–1954), American journalist, author of *The Driver* (1922); *Moody* (1868–1958), financial analyst.

465.36   Prince Kropotkin]   Prince Pyotr Alekseyevich Kropotkin (1842–1921), Russian social philosopher, a leading advocate of anarchism.

466.15   Gustave Herve]   Gustave Hervé (1871–1944), French politician who was imprisoned in 1910 for pacifist activities and upon his release changed his position to one of ultranationalism, forming the protofascist Parti Socialiste Nationale.

470.9   Dr. Beard]   Charles A. Beard (1874–1948), historian, author of *An Economic Interpretation of the Constitution* (1911).

474.24   Gustav le Bon]   See note 90.27.

475.5   La Dame aux Camélias]   *The Lady of the Camellias*, play adapted by Alexandre Dumas fils from his 1848 novel; it became the basis for Verdi's *La Traviata*.

475.10   Le Mariage d'Olympe]   See note 62.34–35.

475.24   Nachgelassene Schriften]   Unpublished writings.

475.36   Ein Puppenheim]   *A Doll's House.*

476.10   Meilhac and Halévy] Henri Meilhac (1831–1897) and Ludovic Halévy (1834–1908), popular team of French playwrights and opera librettists, whose plays were collected in twelve volumes, 1900–2.

476.20   Gerhart Hauptmann] See note 127.4.

478.4   Maeterlinckians] See note 124.18.

478.13   Wolf-Ferrari] Ermanno Wolf-Ferrari (1876–1948), Italian composer of comic operas such as *Il Segreto di Susanna* (1909).

478.13   Massenet] Jules Emile Frederic Massenet (1842–1912), French composer whose operas included *Manon* (1884), *Werther* (1892), and *Thaïs* (1894).

478.15   Damaged Goods] See note 35.18.

478.16   Augustus Thomas] See note 124.24.

484.32   Reverend Billy Sunday] See note 70.9.

484.33   Mrs. Eddy] See note 145.33.

from MY LIFE AS AUTHOR AND EDITOR

493.8   Knopf] Alfred A. Knopf (1892–1984), publisher.

494.18   Sidney B. Fay] American historian (1876–1967).

494.37   Fielding H. Garrison] Medical historian and bibliographer (1870–1935), a close friend of Mencken.

497.32   Philip Littell] Literary critic (1868–1943), author of *Books and Things* (1919).

498.35   p. 501] The reference is to an earlier page of Mencken's manuscript.

501.16   Jack Ketch] Public executioner during the reign of Charles II.

502.14   Pirie MacDonald] Portrait photographer (1867–1942).

507.13   Ernest Poole] See note 86.11.

507.13   F. Marion Crawford] American fiction writer (1854–1909), author of *Dr. Claudius* (1883), *A Roman Singer* (1884), *Zoroaster* (1885), and many other novels.

507.14   Cale Young Rice] Kentucky-born poet and playwright (1872–1943), author of *Nirvana Days* (1908) and *The Immortal Lure* (1911).

510.10   *Schrecklichkeit*] "Frightfulness," German military doctrine of harsh measures designed to suppress civilian resistance in Belgium and elsewhere during World War I.

511.24   Frances Newman] Novelist (1883–1928), author of *The Gold-Fish Bowl* (1921), *The Hard-Boiled Virgin* (1926) and *Dead Lovers Are Faithful Lovers* (1928). At the time of her death Newman was suffering from severe and painful vision problems.

512.6   Brann the iconoclast] William Cowper Brann (1855–1898), owner and editor of *The Iconoclast*, published in Waco, Texas. He was shot to death by a reader angry over a published attack on Baylor University; Brann mortally wounded his attacker.

512.6   Elbert Hubbard] See note 168.14.

514.9   Thomas Moult] English poet and journalist (1893–1974).

515.18   Dorothy Canfield] Novelist and social activist (1879–1958) who later published as Dorothy Canfield Fisher.

515.19   Henry G. Aikman] Novelist and short story writer (1884–1979).

Index

THE LIBRARY OF AMERICA SERIES

The Library of America fosters appreciation and pride in America's literary heritage by publishing, and keeping permanently in print, authoritative editions of America's best and most significant writing. An independent nonprofit organization, it was founded in 1979 with seed money from the National Endowment for the Humanities and the Ford Foundation.

To subscribe to the series or to order individual copies,
please visit www.loa.org or call (800) 964.5778.

*This book is set in 10 point Linotron Galliard,
a face designed for photocomposition by Matthew Carter
and based on the sixteenth-century face Granjon. The paper
is acid-free lightweight opaque and meets the requirements
for permanence of the American National Standards Institute.
The binding material is Brillianta, a woven rayon cloth made
by Van Heek-Scholco Textielfabrieken, Holland. Composition by Dedicated Business Services. Printing by
Malloy Incorporated. Binding by Dekker Book-
binding. Designed by Bruce Campbell.*

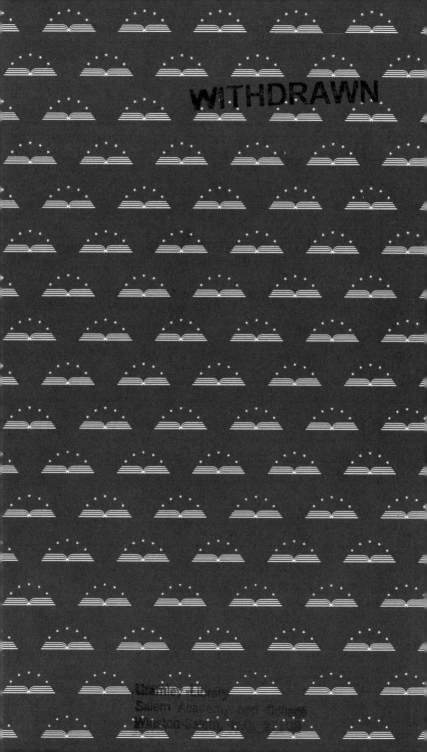

WITHDRAWN

Gramley Library
Salem Academy and College
Winston-Salem, N.C. 27108